OFFICIAL
(ISC)² GUIDE TO THE
CISSP®-ISSEP® CBK®

AUERBACH PUBLICATIONS

OTHER INFORMATION SECURITY BOOKS FROM AUERBACH

Asset Protection and Security Management Handbook
POA Publishing
ISBN: 0-8493-1603-0

Building a Global Information Assurance Program
Raymond J. Curts and Douglas E. Campbell
ISBN: 0-8493-1368-6

Building an Information Security Awareness Program
Mark B. Desman
ISBN: 0-8493-0116-5

Critical Incident Management
Alan B. Sterneckert
ISBN: 0-8493-0010-X

Cyber Crime Investigator's Field Guide, Second Edition
Bruce Middleton
ISBN: 0-8493-2768-7

Cyber Forensics: A Field Manual for Collecting, Examining, and Preserving Evidence of Computer Crimes
Albert J. Marcella, Jr. and Robert S. Greenfield
ISBN: 0-8493-0955-7

The Ethical Hack: A Framework for Business Value Penetration Testing
James S. Tiller
ISBN: 0-8493-1609-X

The Hacker's Handbook: The Strategy Behind Breaking into and Defending Networks
Susan Young and Dave Aitel
ISBN: 0-8493-0888-7

Information Security Architecture: An Integrated Approach to Security in the Organization
Jan Killmeyer Tudor
ISBN: 0-8493-9988-2

Information Security Fundamentals
Thomas R. Peltier
ISBN: 0-8493-1957-9

Information Security Management Handbook, 5th Edition
Harold F. Tipton and Micki Krause
ISBN: 0-8493-1997-8

Information Security Policies, Procedures, and Standards: Guidelines for Effective Information Security Management
Thomas R. Peltier
ISBN: 0-8493-1137-3

Information Security Risk Analysis
Thomas R. Peltier
ISBN: 0-8493-0880-1

Information Technology Control and Audit, Second Edition
Fredrick Gallegos, Daniel Manson, Sandra Allen-Senft, and Carol Gonzales
ISBN: 0-8493-2032-1

Investigator's Guide to Steganography
Gregory Kipper
0-8493-2433-5

Managing a Network Vulnerability Assessment
Thomas Peltier, Justin Peltier, and John A. Blackley
ISBN: 0-8493-1270-1

Network Perimeter Security: Building Defense In-Depth
Cliff Riggs
ISBN: 0-8493-1628-6

The Practical Guide to HIPAA Privacy and Security Compliance
Kevin Beaver and Rebecca Herold
ISBN: 0-8493-1953-6

A Practical Guide to Security Engineering and Information Assurance
Debra S. Herrmann
ISBN: 0-8493-1163-2

The Privacy Papers: Managing Technology, Consumer, Employee and Legislative Actions
Rebecca Herold
ISBN: 0-8493-1248-5

Public Key Infrastructure: Building Trusted Applications and Web Services
John R. Vacca
ISBN: 0-8493-0822-4

Securing and Controlling Cisco Routers
Peter T. Davis
ISBN: 0-8493-1290-6

Strategic Information Security
John Wylder
ISBN: 0-8493-2041-0

Surviving Security: How to Integrate People, Process, and Technology, Second Edition
Amanda Andress
ISBN: 0-8493-2042-9

A Technical Guide to IPSec Virtual Private Networks
James S. Tiller
ISBN: 0-8493-0876-3

Using the Common Criteria for IT Security Evaluation
Debra S. Herrmann
ISBN: 0-8493-1404-6

AUERBACH PUBLICATIONS

www.auerbach-publications.com
To Order Call: 1-800-272-7737 • Fax: 1-800-374-3401
E-mail: orders@crcpress.com

OFFICIAL
(ISC)² GUIDE TO THE
CISSP®-ISSEP® CBK®

Susan Hansche, CISSP-ISSEP

SECURITY TRANSCENDS TECHNOLOGY®

Auerbach Publications
Taylor & Francis Group
Boca Raton   New York

Published in 2006 by
Auerbach Publications
Taylor & Francis Group
6000 Broken Sound Parkway NW, Suite 300
Boca Raton, FL 33487-2742

International Standard Book Number-10: 0-8493-2341-X (Hardcover)
International Standard Book Number-13: 978-0-8493-2341-6 (Hardcover)
Library of Congress Card Number 2005041144

Library of Congress Cataloging-in-Publication Data

Hansche, Susan.
Official (ISC)2 guide to the CISSP-ISSEP CBK / Susan Hansche.
p. cm.
Includes bibliographical references and index.
ISBN 0-8493-2341-X (alk. paper)
1. Electronic data processing personnel--Certification. 2. Computer security--Examinations--Study guides. I. Title: Official ISC squared guide. II. Title.

QA76.3.H364 2005
005.8--dc22   2005041144

Taylor & Francis Group
is the Academic Division of T&F Informa plc.

Visit the Taylor & Francis Web site at
http://www.taylorandfrancis.com

and the Auerbach Publications Web site at
http://www.auerbach-publications.com

This book is dedicated to my late father, Sam Hansche, who encouraged me to do my best and gave me confidence to believe in myself, and my mother, Sandra Montgomery, who showers me with love and support.

Table of Contents

ISSEP Domain 4: Introduction to United States Government Information Assurance Regulations

11 Information Assurance Organizations, Public Laws, and Public Policies..537

Preface

When I started to write this book, my goal was to provide one reference source for information system security practitioners that would be preparing to take the Information Systems Security Engineering Professional® (ISSEP) exam. As the book began to take shape, I realized it was developing into more than just a study book for the ISSEP exam. It had become an encompassing overview of information systems security for the federal government sector, which has been the focus of my career as an information systems security professional.

By the time I took the Certified Information Systems Security Professional (CISSP®) exam in September 2000, I had already been working for several years as a government contractor performing information systems security work for the U.S. government (USG). An important part of my job is to read, understand, and interpret federal laws, regulations, and guidance. In addition to staying current on this wide array of information, I must also adequately provide guidance on how to make it apply and fit within a government agency. Since 1998, I have been working as a contractor for the U.S. Department of State at the Diplomatic Security Training Center. The primary focus of my professional work is on training and mentoring employees who have responsibility for adequately protecting information systems. The recently created ISSEP concentration exam has similar aims in that it tests the knowledge and skills of security professionals in the federal sector. My practical experience in designing and conducting training courses requires that I am well versed in the federal requirements for information systems security, thus the ISSEP exam provided me an opportunity to integrate my experience, practical knowledge, and the documented research in this field into a new publication.

Information Systems Security Engineering (ISSE) is considered a generic process that is applied throughout the system life cycle and provides mechanisms for identifying and evolving security products and processes. An ISSEP follows and practices the ISSE model to ensure that security is included in the life cycle of systems. Regardless of where in its life cycle the system is, the ISSEP provides security expertise to analyze the protection needs, define the security requirements, and identify the security controls (i.e., products, policies, etc.) in order to meet the security requirements. Security professionals also ensure security controls have been implemented, as well as verifying and validating that the controls have met the necessary security requirements. Thus, the core responsibility of performing the role of an ISSEP is using the ISSE model and then verifying that security has been implemented and is operational (certification and accreditation).

One of the most important and most daunting challenges for an ISSEP lies in having a basic familiarity with various sets of USG regulations. Because of this, you will find that more than one-half of this book is devoted to providing an in-depth overview of some USG policies and procedures. About half way through my research for this book, I began to tire of reading policy and regulations and, no doubt, you will too. This book is written to provide candidates for the ISSEP exam and those professionals who are already performing ISSEP duties a synopsis of the regulations defined in the ISSEP Common Body of Knowledge and also those that I think are the most important. Note that the ISSEP Common Body of Knowledge was defined as a collaboration between (ISC)²® and the National Security Agency. If you are performing ISSEP or other information systems security work for the USG, you should take the time to read the entire policies in more detail. Remember you are responsible for the implementation of information security policies. If your organization requires you to follow a specific policy or guideline, it is absolutely necessary that you take the time to read the entire requirement. A note of caution: the information in this book provides a general and often detailed overview; however it is not so specific that it explains the implementation of every policy or procedure.

Systems engineers will find the ISSE model and concepts similar to systems engineering processes. However, there is one important difference. The ISSE model adds a security element into each phase of the system life cycle. Regardless of your specific background, the principles described throughout the book will be beneficial in all aspects of performing the role of an information systems security professional. One does not need to be a systems engineer to understand the ISSE framework, nor does one need to be a systems engineer to find the ISSE framework useful. Although my background is not systems engineering, for the past eight years I have worked alongside and learned from senior security engineers who are responsible for providing technical security implementations worldwide and also securing the enterprise information systems. Through this experience I have seen the growth and innovation of designing and implementation security through various phases of the system life cycle. For security professionals, the change in having security as a focus seems slow and arduous. However, like me, I hope you too can see that the focus is changing and security is becoming an important attribute of information systems.

With its focus on the federal sector, the ISSEP certification is one of three concentrations of the CISSP certification. However, even if you are not a CISSP nor plan to take the CISSP or ISSEP certification, the material covered in this book will assist you with understanding security requirements for the USG. Moreover, the principles covered in this text can be beneficial to any project or organization, regardless of whether it is for the private or public sector.

If you are reading this book it means you have become passionate about information systems security. Hopefully, you have also accepted another mission: to speak assertively in meetings about the importance of security matters, to ask the tough questions, and also to provide solutions that will change the way that information is protected. Be assured that your efforts will have an immediate and long-term impact on security issues. It is my sincerest hope that this book will help you make a difference in your organization and in your career, and also, that it will play a role in protecting the nation's information and information systems.

Susan Hansche
September 2005

About the Author

Susan Hansche, CISSP-ISSEP, is the training director for information assurance at Nortel PEC Solutions in Fairfax, Virginia. She is the lead author of *The Official (ISC)²® Guide to the CISSP Exam*, which is a reference for professionals in the information systems security field who are studying for the Certified Information Systems Security Professional (CISSP) exam. *The Official (ISC)²® Guide to CISSP®–ISSEP® CBK®* is her second book. She has over 15 years of experience in the design and development of training and, since 1998, Ms. Hansche has been instrumental in establishing a full-scale, role-based Information Assurance (IA) training program for the U.S. Department of State. This includes the design, development, and instruction of role-based IA courses to over 1,000 employees per year. In addition, she has taught many IA courses, seminars, and workshops for both the public and private sectors. Since 1992, she has been an adjunct faculty member in the Communication Department at George Mason University in Fairfax, Virginia. Ms. Hansche has written numerous articles on information systems security and training and is a regular speaker at conferences and seminars.

Errata and Comments

Please send errata and other comments to the e-mail address: issep-book@cox.net. A list of current errata can be obtained by sending an e-mail request to this same address.

ISSE Domain 1

INFORMATION SYSTEMS SECURITY ENGINEERING (ISSE)

Overview

This domain is based on information from the Information Assurance Technical Framework (IATF) version 3.1 (September 2002). The IATF defines a process for designing and developing systems that includes information protection needs and security requirements. Essentially, the IATF outlines the requirements and activities necessary to provide Information Assurance (IA) to the system life-cycle phases.

The IATF is supported by the Information Assurance Technical Framework Forum (IATFF). The IATFF is a National Security Agency (NSA) sponsored outreach activity created to foster dialog among U.S. government agencies, U.S. industry, and U.S. academia that provide their customers with solutions for information assurance problems. According to the IATFF, "The ultimate objective of the IATFF is to agree on a framework for information assurance solutions that meet customers' needs and foster the development and use of solutions that are compatible with the framework" (IATFF Introduction, p. 1).

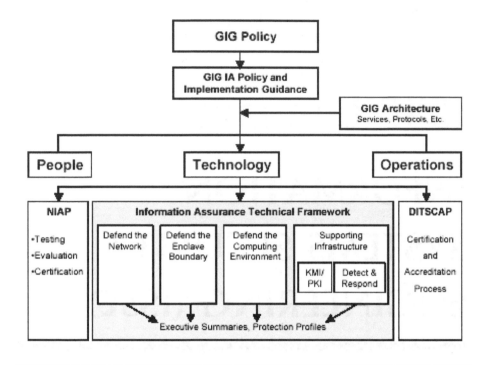

Figure D1.1   IATF relationship to GIG policy. (*Source:* From IATF, Introduction, p. 2.)

The principles outlined in the IATF provide protection based on the concept of layers called "defense-in-depth." Because this concept is important to IA and the ISSE process, more information on defense-in-depth is provided in Chapter 1. Another important concept of the IATF is using a risk-based approach to making decisions, which is discussed in various chapters.

Figure D1.1 shows the relationship of the Department of Defense (DoD) Global Information Grid (GIG) to the IATF and provides an overview of the intended use of the IATF. It is the combination of people, technology, and operations that provides adequate protections. Federal agencies could follow a similar relationship format. According to its designers, the IATF is "a leading source of information on security solutions implemented through the application of technology" (IATF, Introduction, p. 2).

The IATF has four main sections. Figure D1.2 is a graphical view of the IATF sections. In the first four chapters, general IA guidance is provided so that information system users, security architects, software architects,

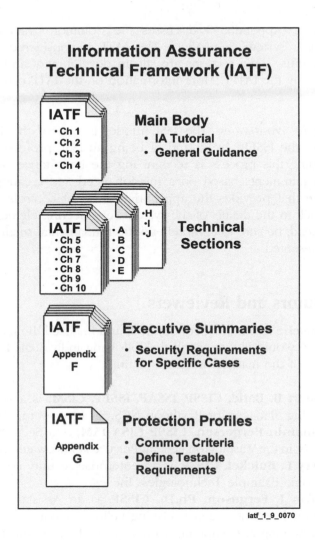

Figure D1.2 IATF composition. (*Source:* From IATF, p. 1-16.)

system architects, security engineers, software engineers, systems engineers, and others can gain a better understanding of the IA issues involved in protecting today's interconnected information systems.

The chapters in this domain are based primarily on IATF Chapter 3, "The Information Systems Security Engineering Process." IATF Chapters 5 through 10 and Appendices A through E, H, and J provide specific requirements and solutions for each of the defense-in-depth areas. The Executive Summaries provide outlines of the threats, requirements, and recommended solutions for a variety of specific protection needs in specific environments. Appendix G discusses the Common Criteria Protection Profiles for a system or product. The IATF is considered an evolving document; thus, some sections are still in development and continue to be updated by the IATFF. More information on the IATF can be found at www.iatf.net.

Note to ISSEP candidates: The ISSE model is one of the fundamental elements of the ISSEP® exam and of being an ISSE professional. Key to understanding this process is recognizing the importance of identifying security requirements based on a mission need and creating a security architecture that provides the appropriate level of controls needed. Do not get stuck in the details of the systems engineering elements for each phase; instead, be sure to comprehend the fundamental security elements that are presented.

Contributors and Reviewers

Susan Hansche researched, contributed, and finalized the material in this domain. She would like to thank the following individuals for reviewing some or all of the material in this domain:

> **Robert B. Batie, CISSP, ISSAP, ISSEP, CISM,** is a Security Engineering Manager for Raytheon NCS, St. Petersburg, Florida.
> **Benjamin Bergersen, CISSP CISA IAM,** is a Security & Privacy Senior in the Washington Federal Practice at PricewaterhouseCoopers.
> **Larry L. Buickel, CISSP,** is an enterprise security consultant with Graphic Example Technologies, Inc.
> **Aaron J. Ferguson, Ph.D., CISSP,** is an Assistant Professor & National Security Agency Visiting Fellow, Department of Electrical Engineering & Computer Science, United States Military Academy at West Point, New York.
> **Richard K. McAllister** is a developer and instructor of the Protection Needs Elicitation Course and other ISSE courses for the NSA/National Cryptologic School, as well as a practitioner in ISSE as a senior scientist at SPARTA Inc.
> **Cheryl Resch** works in the Information Operations Group at Johns Hopkins University Applied Physics Lab, Columbia, Maryland.
> **Steven Rodrigo, CISSP,** is a senior systems security analyst at Tenacity Solutions, Herndon, Virginia.

Blair Semple, CISSP, is the Director of Business Development and a Technology Officer for Kasten Chase in Sterling, Virginia.
Carl H. Stucke, Ph.D., is Security SIG Coordinator in the Department of Computer Information System at Robinson College of Business, Georgia State University.

1

ISSE Introduction

Introduction

Information systems are increasingly connected and shared among many U.S. government (USG) entities, such as the Department of Defense, federal agencies, private-sector entities, and, in some cases, international entities. The expansion of inter-networked computer systems has evolved into a globally integrated distributed network with worldwide users. The availability of information to users continues to grow so that at any time, users have access to the information they need. The only mechanisms to control which users have access to what information are the security controls that are implemented.

Of critical importance and necessity is the USG's ability to adequately protect its information and information systems. Along with this is the fact that networks and systems processing get more complex every day. It is this vital need and increasing complexity that requires a new way of thinking — one that combines information systems security with traditional security disciplines, such as physical security and personnel security.

In response to the emerging demands for greater USG information systems security capabilities, the National Security Agency's Information Systems Security Organization (NSA ISSO) instituted a Systems Security Engineering Process Action Team (SSE PAT) in mid-1993. The mission of the SSE PAT was to synthesize previous and new information systems security initiatives into a consistent, customer-focused model for Information Systems Security Engineering (ISSE), which is intended as a discipline of Systems Engineering. Although the ISSE process can be tailored to any organization, the design is intended for and focuses on following USG standards and directives for systems acquisition, system life cycle, system components, system certification and accreditation, etc. (IATF Introduction).

To help understand the field of ISSE, this chapter (Figure 1.1) begins with definitions of several key terms related to ISSE and Systems Engineering. The second section defines the six phases of the ISSE model. The remaining sections discuss several concepts important to the role of an Information Systems Security Engineering Professional (ISSEP®). The sections are:

- SE and ISSE Overview
- ISSE Model
- Life Cycle and ISSE
- Risk Management
- Defense in Depth

SE and ISSE Overview

Because it is fundamental to this domain, we begin with some definitions — the first is answering the question, "What is a **system**?"

> *A system can be defined as a combination of **elements** or parts that are designed to function as a unitary whole to achieve an objective.*

In 1998, the Institute of Electrical and Electronics Engineers (IEEE) released the "IEEE 1220 Standard for Application and Management of the Systems Engineering Process." This standard defines systems "as related elements (subsystems and components) and their interfaces" (p. 2). These elements include the hardware, software, and people required to develop, produce, test, distribute, operate, support, or dispose of the element's products, or to train those people to accomplish their role within the system. The system may also be an element of a larger system, where it is then necessary to understand and define the boundaries of the system and the interfaces between this system and other systems.

To fully appreciate the definition, it is important to look at some key words. For it to be a system, the **elements** must have been designed with the purpose of achieving a goal. Having a specific purpose is a fundamental characteristic of a system. The system can have one or multiple functions to achieve its purpose or objective.

Not every combination of components is a system — it is the combination of components specifically designed to meet a goal that makes a *system*. Not only must the components be designed together, but they

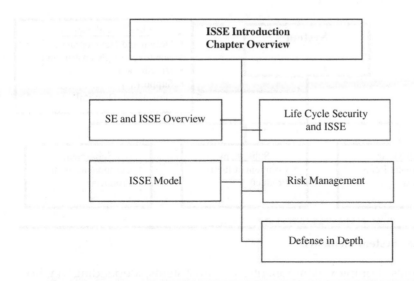

Figure 1.1   Chapter overview.

also need to be designed in such a manner that they function together — they perform certain actions in specific ways. Thus, they are not merely a collection of things, but rather components assembled to function as a whole. This whole must then, as a system, achieve an objective. For example, an air conditioning system contains a compressor, air handler, vents, and thermostat controller — these components, when combined, function for a purpose: cooling air. Therefore, a system must have at least one defined function that is designed to achieve a specific goal.

A system can also be viewed as an element of a larger system. The challenge is to understand the boundary of the system and the relationships between this system and other systems.

The basic building blocks of a system are shown in Figure 1.2. Of importance to this definition is the inclusion of several life-cycle phases such as design and development, manufacturing and construction, test, distribution, operation, support, training, and disposal. IEEE 1220 defines the elements as the:

- System itself
- System's-related product(s) and subsystems
- Life-cycle processes required to support the products and sub-systems that make up the product(s)

Typically, a system combines products developed by the organization or outside vendors. Each vendor considers its product as part of its system. Products purchased by vendors are typically referred to as subcomponents,

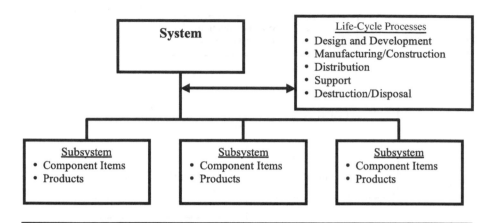

Figure 1.2   System elements.

components, complex components, or subsystems, depending on how the element contributes to the system's performance, functionality, and costs. An important consideration in the design and life-cycle processes of the product is the human element of the system, such as operators, maintainers, manufacturing personnel, and training personnel. These human elements ensure that the system products are producible, maintainable, and usable, and that the system processes are effectively established to ensure production quality levels and reduce overall ownership cost.

Before discussing the **engineering** of a system, it can be helpful to define the concept of systems approach. Grady (2000) defines a *systems approach* as "incorporating careful planning, definition of the problem as a prerequisite to solution, active integration across cross-organizational interfaces, an energetic search for potential problems (risks) followed by active reduction in their potential for occurrence and degree of damage to the program, and clear proof of requirements compliance as a way to develop better systems" (p. 269). Essentially, it is the opposite of an ad-hoc approach in which there is not a concrete plan for the design and development of systems.

Harris (2002) states that a systems approach occurs when the following conditions exist:

- A holistic viewpoint is used.
- The system objectives can be defined at the beginning of the program.
- The owners or stakeholders share the objectives and believe a solution is achievable.
- The process can be summarized as something that can be moved from an initial state to a different end state.
- The environment, such as the technology, organization, and policies, is relatively stable.

To achieve a true system — that is, an entity that functions as a whole and is designed to achieve an objective — some process should be followed. This process can be defined as the **systems engineering approach**. The Systems Engineering (SE) discipline was synthesized from best industry practices in the engineering, manufacturing, and quality areas.

Note to the ISSEP candidate: The next several pages provide common SE definitions. The definitions are included to provide a historical and definitive perspective on the SE approach. To understand ISSE it is necessary to also understand SE. Even if you are familiar with SE, it is helpful to make the connections between IEEE 1220 documentation and the ISSE model.

One SE perspective is from Sage and Armstrong (1999), who state that SE must address structure, function, and purpose to be complete. These concepts are defined as:

> "**Structure** — SE is managing technology to assist clients through the formulation, analysis, and interpretation of the impacts of proposed policies, controls, or complete systems upon the need perspectives, institutional perspectives, and value perspectives of stakeholders to issues under consideration.
>
> **Function** — The function is to use an appropriate combination of SE methods and tools (made possible through use of a suitable methodology and systems management procedures) in a useful process oriented setting that is appropriate for the resolution of real-world needs, often of large scale and scope.
>
> **Purpose** — The purpose of SE is information and knowledge organization that will assist clients who desire to define, develop, and deploy total systems to achieve a high standard of overall quality, integrity, and integration as related to performance, trustworthiness, reliability, availability, and maintainability of the resulting system" (p. 10).

The SE term has also been defined and mandated in Department of Defense (DoD) documents, including Directives, Instructions, Regulations, and Military Standards. The first DoD SE reference was in MIL-STD-499B (which was never officially released). It referred to SE as an interdisciplinary approach to evolve and verify an integrated and life-cycle balanced set of system product and process solutions that satisfy the customer's needs.

The MIL-STD-499B draft defined SE as "...the application of scientific and engineering efforts to:

■ Transform an operational need into a description of system performance parameters and a system configuration through the use of an iterative process of definition, synthesis, analysis, design, test, and evaluation;

■ Integrate related technical parameters and ensure compatibility of all physical, functional, and program interfaces in a manner that optimizes the total system definition and design;

■ Integrate reliability, maintainability, safety, survivability, human engineering and other factors into the total engineering effort to meet cost, schedule, supportability, and technical performance objectives." (MIL-STD-499B, Forward Section)

MIL-STD-499B stated the benefits of SE as a process that:

■ "Encompasses the scientific and engineering efforts related to the development, manufacturing, verification, deployment, operations, support, and disposal of system products and processes;

■ Develops needed user training equipment, procedures, and data;

■ Establishes and maintains configuration management of the system;

■ Develops work breakdown structures and statements of work, and provides information for management decision-making." (MIL-STD-499B, Definitions)

The Electronic Industries Alliance (EIA) Systems Engineering Committee issued an Interim Standard (IS) EIA 632 in December 1994, which was based partly on MIL-STD-499B. The EIA SE Committee converted MIL-STD-499B to EIA/IS 632 in 1994. The EIAIS 632 is a demilitarized version of the SE standard and was meant to be applicable for both the military and commercial environments. The EIA/IS 632 (1994) defines SE as:

> "...an interdisciplinary approach encompassing the entire technical effort to evolve and verify an integrated and life-cycle balanced set of systems, people, product, and process solutions that satisfy customer needs. Systems engineering encompasses (a) the technical efforts related to the development, manufacturing, verification, deployment, operations, support, disposal of, and user training for system products and processes; (b) the definition and management of the system configuration; (c) the translation of the system definition into work breakdown structures; and (d) development of information for management decision making." (p. 43)

IEEE 1220 contains minor variations of the EIA standard and was first released in 1994 and revised in 1998. The original intent was to merge

EIA/IS 632 with IEEE 1220 and establish a unified model for SE practices that would be applicable to the developmental efforts of both commercial and government systems. However, in June 1995, the EIA SE Working Group decided to keep IEEE 1220 as a separate standard. Thus, EIA/IS 632 would be a higher-level abstraction of the SE practices under which domain-specific standards such as IEEE 1220 would reside.

IEEE 1220 defines the objective for SE as:

> "...to provide high-quality products and services, with the correct people and performance features, at an affordable price, and on time. This involves developing, producing, testing, and supporting an integrated set of products (hardware, software, people, data, facilities, and material) and processes (services and techniques) that is acceptable to customers, satisfies enterprise and external constraints, and considers and defines the processes for developing, producing, testing, handling, operating, and supporting the products and life cycle processes." (p. iii)

The next step in our definition of ISSE is to tie the concept of SE to the information systems security field. To begin, an *information system* can be defined as any telecommunications or computer-related equipment or interconnected system or subsystem of equipment that is used in the acquisition, storage, manipulation, management, movement, control, display, switching, interchange, transmission, or reception of voice or data, and includes people, software, firmware, and hardware.

A newer term in the field, **information infrastructure**, attempts to cover the far-reaching expansion and interconnectedness of information systems. The information infrastructure "comprises communications networks, computers, databases, management, applications, and consumer electronics and can exist at a global, national, or local level." (IATF, p. 12) When considering security for information infrastructures, it is important to understand the concept of boundaries. Information assets exist in physical and logical locations, and boundaries exist between these locations. It can exist at the global, national, or local level.

A global information infrastructure is not necessarily controlled or owned by a single organization. For example, "ownership" can be distributed among individuals and corporate, academic, and government entities. The Internet is an example of a global information infrastructure. A national information infrastructure can be defined as a collection of information infrastructures used by a nation to conduct its business, whether government or commercial. An example of this is a critical infrastructure (i.e., telecommunications, banking and finance, transportation, power, water, and emergency systems) defined in the 1998 Presidential Decision Directive 63. Local information infrastructures are comprised of the dedicated assets that an organization operates in order to conduct its business such as commercial information systems, network technologies, and applications (IATF S.1-3-1).

Information systems security (InfoSec) is defined as the "protection of an information system against unauthorized access to or modification of information, whether in storage, processing, or transit, and against the denial of service to authorized users or the provision of service to unauthorized users, including those measures necessary to detect, document and counter such threats" (NSTISSI No. 4009, p. 33). InfoSec, as a term, has been replaced with Information Assurance (IA). IA as a term provides a more comprehensive view. Thus, you will probably not see InfoSec used, except in legacy documents.

Information Assurance (IA) is defined as the "measures that protect and defend information and information systems by ensuring their availability, integrity, authentication, confidentiality, and non-repudiation. These measures include providing for restoration of information systems by incorporating protection, detection, and reaction capabilities" (NSTISSI No. 4009, p. 32).

The blending of information assurance with SE is termed **Information Systems Security Engineering (ISSE)**. ISSE is seen as an emerging discipline of systems engineering. It seeks to provide integrated processes and solutions during all phases of a system's life cycle in order to meet the system's information assurance needs. The focus of the process is to first identify the information protection needs and then to use a process-oriented approach to identify security risks and subsequently to minimize or contain those risks.

In today's ISSE environment, the Information Systems Security Engineering Professional (ISSEP) is faced with a range of tools and techniques that can be utilized for any given design problem. Under the guidance of subject matter experts, the Information Assurance Technical Framework (IATF) was developed to standardize an information systems security process model that would follow the design of SE principles, but would also emphasize the role of security in designing and developing information systems.

Essentially, ISSE is the functional application of processes for the **secure** design, development, and operation of efficient and economical networks for the communication of information and knowledge. To meet the security requirement, the process must review and decide what controls are needed to provide the three primary security services — confidentiality, integrity, and availability — and the newest additions — authentication and non-repudiation.

An important element of the ISSE model is to first understand the security needs of the organization in relationship to the security services.

As important as it is to comprehend the security needs of the organization, it is also important to understand the security objectives of the system based upon the organization. Thus, the business mission for the organization must also be considered. An additional element of the ISSE methodology is to design and develop a system in such a manner that it can safely resist the forces to which it may be subjected. Thus, an encompassing definition could be stated as:

> ISSE is the art and science of discovering the users' security needs and the overall security needs of the organization; designing and developing with economy, sophistication, and diligence an information system that ensures an appropriate level of availability, integrity, confidentiality, authentication, and non-repudiation based upon valid risk management decisions; and ensuring that the system can safely resist the forces to which it may be subjected.

IEEE 1220 Overview

The IEEE 1220 standard is important for ISSE because it defines the non-security phases and activities of the SE process for components and systems. The fundamental SE phases are seen in the ISSE model, except that security is integrated into each of the ISSE phases. Because the standard is important for the ISSE, a brief introduction to the IEEE 1220 SE model is provided in this chapter and, when appropriate, included in the SE approach of the remaining Domain 1 chapters.

A key component of IEEE 1220 is its interdisciplinary approach to developing systems. The standard defines the tasks that are required throughout a system's life cycle to transform customer needs, requirements, and constraints into a system solution. The core concepts — needs, requirements, and constraints — will be seen again in the ISSE model, except that they appear as **security** needs, **security** requirements, and constraints that affect those security needs and requirements.

The IEEE 1220 is intended to guide the development of systems, including computers and software, for commercial, government, military, and space applications. It applies to an enterprise within an organization that is responsible for developing a product design and establishing the life-cycle infrastructure needed throughout the product's life cycle.

It is centered on the Systems Engineering Process (SEP), which is a generic problem-solving process that is outlined in the Systems Engineering Management Plan (SEMP). Throughout the product life cycle, the SEP provides the mechanisms for identifying and evolving the product and process definitions of the system.

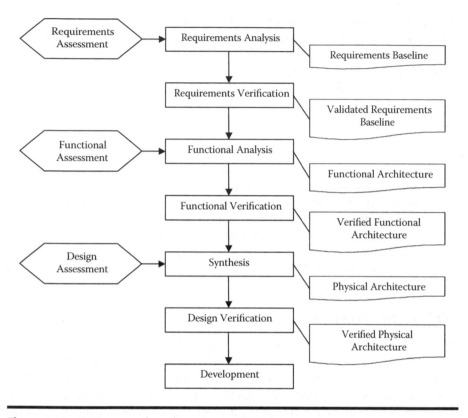

Figure 1.3 Systems engineering process (SEP).

As shown in Figure 1.3, the basic phases of the SEP are Requirements Analysis and Verification, Functional Analysis and Verification, Synthesis (design), and Design Verification.

The first step in the SEP is the analysis stage, which is represented in IEEE 1220 as the requirements analysis and the functional analysis. During the synthesis stage, the functional architecture is translated into a design architecture that defines the system elements, their composition, interfaces, and design constraints. The final stage of the SEP is evaluation. The IEEE 1220 notes that evaluation should occur throughout the entire process, such as conducting baseline validations, functional verifications, and physical verifications.

Because this domain is divided into various chapters, each of these process phases will be discussed in more detail within the chapters. For example, the IEEE 1220 engineering plan plays a central role in technical planning and management, which includes a master schedule, a detailed schedule, and various technical plans, such as risk management, technical reviews, configuration management, maintenance, training, and human systems engineering. More information on these topics is provided in the technical management domain.

The next section provides an overview of the ISSE model and serves as an introduction to the six phases. The specific activities and tasks of each phase are explained in Chapters 2 through 7.

The ISSE Model

The IATF defines a generic SE model with six activities that also form the basis for describing the ISSE model. Figure 1.4 depicts this model, showing that the Assess Effectiveness activity is not only a final element, but is actually an important consideration of each phase. The six activities are:

1. Discover Needs
2. Define System Requirements
3. Design System Architecture
4. Develop Detailed Design
5. Implement System
6. Assess Effectiveness

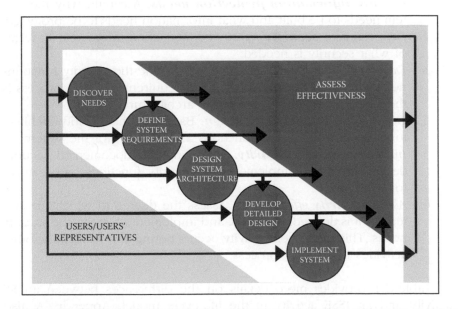

Figure 1.4   ISSE model.

It may be helpful to consider the following incorrect methodology of designing systems:

1. *Design it.* One begins by designing the system.
2. *Define requirements.* In this step, the requirements are written to match the system that has already been designed or even built.
3. *Evaluate it.* The evaluation of the system is based on the tailored requirements.
4. *Declare success.* Because the evaluation was based on the requirements written specifically for the system, the evaluation was successful.
5. *Add Security.* Better late than never, it's now time to add some security functions.

Such a design process rarely leads to a successful system that meets the needs of the mission it was intended to support. Although you may have seen this type of system design before (or even done it), following the ISSE process avoids this incorrect methodology.

When the ISSE model incorporates the fundamental SE activities, security is included in each of the steps. The activities in the ISSE model are:

1. *Discover **information protection needs**.* Ascertain why the system needs to be built and what information needs to be protected.
2. *Define system **security** requirements.* Define the system in terms of what security is needed.
3. *Define system **security** architecture.* Define the security functions needed to meet the specific security requirements. This process is the core of designing the security architecture.
4. *Develop detailed **security** design.* Based on the security architecture, design the security functions and features for the system.
5. *Implement system **security**.* Following the documented security design, build and implement the security functions and features for the system.
6. *Assess **security** effectiveness.* Assess the degree to which the system, as it is defined, designed, and implemented, meets the security needs. This assessment activity occurs during and with all the other activities in the ISSE process.

Table 1.1 provides more details on the differences between an SE activity and an ISSE activity in the life-cycle model. Appendix A also contains two mappings of the ISSE activities: the first compares DoD 5000.2-R with the ISSE phases and the second compares IEEE 1220 with the ISSE phases. In some life-cycle models, each element is considered a

Table 1.1   Corresponding SE and ISSE Activities

SE Activities	ISSE Activities
Discover Needs	**Discover Information Protection Needs**
The systems engineer helps the customer understand and document the information management needs that support the business or mission. Statements about information needs may be captured in an Information Management Model (IMM).	The information systems security engineer helps the customer understand the information protection needs that support the mission or business. Statements about information protection needs may be captured in an Information Protection Policy (IPP).
Define System Requirements	**Define System Security Requirements**
The systems engineer allocates identified needs to systems. A system context is developed to identify the system environment and to show the allocation of system functions to that environment. A preliminary system Concept of Operations (CONOPS) is written to describe operational aspects of the candidate system (or systems). Baseline requirements are established.	The information systems security engineer allocates information protection needs to systems. A system security context, a preliminary system security CONOPS, and baseline security requirements are developed.
Design System Architecture	**Design System Security Architecture**
The systems engineer performs functional analysis and allocation by analyzing candidate architectures, allocating requirements, and selecting mechanisms. The systems engineer identifies components or elements, allocates functions to those elements, and describes the relationships between the elements.	The information systems security engineer works with the systems engineer in the areas of functional analysis and allocation by analyzing candidate architectures, allocating security services, and selecting security mechanisms. The information systems security engineer identifies components or elements, allocates security functions to those elements, and describes the relationships between the elements.
Develop Detailed Design	**Develop Detailed Security Design**
The systems engineer analyzes design constraints, analyzes trade-offs, does detailed system design,	The information systems security engineer analyzes design constraints, analyzes trade-offs,

Table 1.1 (continued) Corresponding SE and ISSE Activities

SE Activities	ISSE Activities
and considers life-cycle support. The systems engineer traces all of the system requirements to the elements until all are addressed. The final detailed design results in component and interface specifications that provide sufficient information for acquisition when the system is implemented.	does detailed system and security design, and considers life-cycle support. The information systems security engineer traces all of the system security requirements to the elements until all are addressed. The final detailed security design results in component and interface specifications that provide sufficient information for acquisition when the system is implemented.
Implement System The systems engineer moves the system from specifications to the tangible. The main activities are acquisition, integration, configuration, testing, documentation, and training. Components are tested and evaluated to ensure that they meet the specifications. After successful testing, the individual components — hardware, software, and firmware — are integrated, properly configured, and tested as a system.	**Implement System Security** The information systems security engineer participates in a multidisciplinary examination of all system issues and provides inputs to C&A process activities, such as verification that the system as implemented protects against the threats identified in the original threat assessment; tracking of information protection assurance mechanisms related to system implementation and testing practices; and providing inputs to system life-cycle support plans, operational procedures, and maintenance training materials.
Assess Effectiveness The results of each activity are evaluated to ensure that the system will meet the users' needs by performing the required functions to the required quality standard in the intended environment. The systems engineer examines how well the system meets the needs of the mission.	**Assess Information Protection Effectiveness** The information systems security engineer focuses on the effectiveness of the information protection required for mission success — whether the system can provide the confidentiality, integrity, availability, authentication, and non-repudiation for the information it is processing.

Source: From IATF, p. 3-3 to 3-4.

step of the process. The ISSE model considers the elements as activities rather than steps. The use of the word "step" indicates some type of hierarchical movement from one place to another. The ISSE model views the activities as a holistic entity, not a timeline where one activity needs to be completed before the other. Rather, each activity is something that must be considered in relationship to another activity. To adequately discover the information protection needs, it is necessary to also understand the organization's system security requirements.

Whether a system is to be built or acquired, there are two primary threads to the process. The first is the identification of **what** functions the system must perform, and the second is the determination of **how** the system will perform these functions. Although the threads cross over the phases of the ISSE model at various points, one thread may dominate over the other. The "what" issues primarily occur during the Discover Needs, Define Requirements, and Define the Architecture phases — these are typically considered the **requirement functions**. The "how" issues are primarily covered in the Design System, Implement System, and Assess Effectiveness phases — these are considered the **implementation functions**. The critical connection between these two threads is made in the fourth phase, designing the system.

Basic SE and ISSE Principles

When using the SE approach, it is important to not only build the system right, but also to build the right system. The distinction is important to understand; most ISSEPs can remember projects where the organization spent time and money to design and develop a system that worked correctly. However, the system did not solve the problem and therefore the organization did not build the right system.

SE must be used for the total development effort necessary to establish a system (or component) design that can be tested, manufactured, supported, operated, distributed, and disposed of. It also includes the training for operation, support, distribution, and disposal. The process of engineering a system to satisfy the combination of either organizational or customer expectations, enterprise policies, legal constraints, and social or political restrictions requires a structured methodology. This method should allow for exploring options in system alternatives that will ensure that the design is cost-effective and practical. Part of this process is to understand the **problem space** and **solution space**, which is shown in Figure 1.5. The problem space should be explored before beginning to develop a system or component solution.

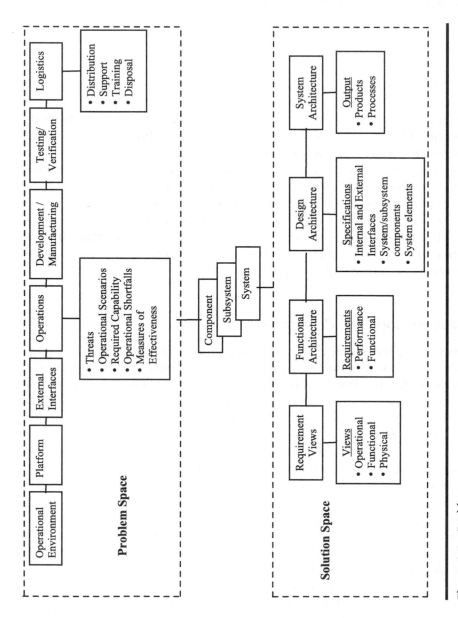

Figure 1.5 Problem space.

Note to the ISSEP candidate. It is necessary to understand the difference between the problem space and the solution space and its importance to the roles performed by the SE and ISSE.

The IATF model defines three important principles related to the problem and solution spaces that can help to build the right system:

1. Always keep the problem and solution spaces separate.
2. The problem space is defined by the customer's mission or business needs.
3. The systems engineer and information systems security engineer define the solution space, which is driven by the problem space.

Principle 1: Always keep the problem and the solution spaces separate.

The problem is defined as what the system is supposed to do. The solution is defined as how the system will do what it is supposed to do. If we begin by looking at the solution, we may lose sight of the problem, which can result in solving the wrong problem and thus building the wrong system. For example, if the client wants high-speed encryption, the client is defining the solution, which may not be the right solution for the problem. Common sense tells us that nothing is more inefficient than solving the wrong problem and building the wrong system.

Principle 2: The problem space is defined by the customer's mission or business needs.

The problem space is defined in terms of the customer's mission or business needs in combination with and taking into consideration the constraints of the organization, such as legal or regulatory restrictions.

The customer usually has a method and capability of doing business or accomplishing the mission. The focus of the ISSEP is to work with the customer to understand the underlying business needs and, based on those needs, the ISSEP determines the best solutions. Typically, customers will recognize the need to change their methods or capabilities needed to accomplish their missions. The customer then talks to system engineers in terms of technology and their notion of solutions to their problems, rather than in terms of the problem. Those individuals tasked with helping the customer, such as systems engineers and information systems security engineers, must set these solutions aside and discover the customer's underlying problem. For example, the customer may require more efficiency, or the mission of the organization may have changed. Thus, the engineering problem to be solved is to design and develop a system that gives the customer new or efficient capabilities to accomplish the mission.

If the customer declares, "I need this and I need that," how does a systems engineer know that the customer understands the problem? One method of determining whether the problem is defined adequately is to evaluate whether it is described in terms of the customer's mission or business.

Defining the problem space in terms of needs is not only important, it is critical; there are years of failed projects within the USG (and private industry) because the system requirements and problems were not correctly defined. Look at your own experiences; you can probably think of projects you were involved with or completed that did not solve the customers' requirements because the needs were not defined adequately in the beginning.

Understanding needs is important because it can provide a direction for the solution, an objective criterion to measure progress, and a method of determining whether the solution is good enough. Knowing what you want the system to do can provide a direction to your search for the solution. It can also help create boundaries for the scope of the problem.

> Have you heard the saying, if you don't know where you are going, then any road will do? The same can be said of systems — if you do not know what your mission or business need is, then any system to support it will do. Is the problem this easy? As you will see, the answer is, not quite.

By knowing what you want the system to do, you can define the goal you are trying to achieve through the SE process. When there is a well-defined goal, charting a systematic course is easier. Not having a goal is similar to not knowing the needs. In some instances, sub-goals may need to be defined as part of the overall mission's goals. Because systems are often defined, designed, and implemented in phases, it may be necessary to define incremental goals as well. These phases may be viewed as stages where the systems engineer needs to make design decisions, the sum of which may result in a system design that meets the mission goals.

There can be problems when the customer only views the system in terms of the constraints placed on it. These entities are called constraints and are part of the problem space. Constraints can have a significant impact on the methods you choose to meet the mission needs. They are limitations that affect the engineering process and ultimately the solutions formulated during that process. An example of a constraint is an interface that needs to remain compatible with a legacy system that does not have current capabilities. However, constraints do provide help in defining the environment in which the solution must exist and can provide one basis on which to make design decisions. Constraints can also be resources, such as financial budgets, time limitations, and personnel issues, including lack of personnel or lack of sufficiently trained personnel. If constraints are understood from the beginning, the design decisions can be made so as to avoid constraints and still meet the mission needs.

There can be problems when the customer only views the system in terms of the constraints placed on it. While determining the needs of the system, it is necessary to think beyond the constraints and truly identify what the system is supposed to do. Rather than looking at the environment in which the system will operate, focus on what you want the system to do. By limiting yourself to only identifying the constraints, it is difficult to chart the course of identifying the system needs and goals. "Constraint avoidance" is the term used when the systems engineer knows the constraints but cannot identify the mission goals. It may be easier to find solutions that circumvent the constraints, but the system will not be successful because it does not support the mission's needs.

Having clearly defined and well-documented goals allows the engineer to answer the questions, "How well are we doing?" "Are we there yet?" and "Is it good enough?" To answer these questions, one must know the endpoint or goals of the problem.

One note of caution associated with defining the problem (needs and constraints): do not define the problem in such a manner that will make it impossible to come up with a solution. For example, the customer may want to build a new global routing system that will connect 250 LANs worldwide, have the capability to automatically spot and correct errors by itself, and be deployed within six months. This type of system, while it may sound good, may be costly, take too much time to implement, and thus is impractical to construct. This is why the concept of trade-offs is important; in a situation similar to this, the customer, SEs, and ISSEPs would begin to look at features and functions in terms of costs, benefits, and realities.

Principle 3: The systems engineer and information systems security engineer define the solution space driven by the problem space.

The solution space is where the systems engineer addresses how to meet the needs within the confines of the constraints and the organization's mission. Thus, it is critical to have a complete picture of the problem space in order to formulate a good, thorough solution that will meet all the requirements.

Another aspect of this principle is that the customer must recognize the important role of the systems engineer. This principle can be stated another way, as "the solution is defined by the systems engineer and the problem is defined by the customer." The customer is the expert on the problem and the engineer is the expert on the solution. Thus, the systems engineer must be seen as the expert that is there to help the customer achieve a reasonable solution. If a customer insists on intervening in the design of the solution, the customer may actually place unnecessary constraints on the solution and limit the flexibility or capability of the systems engineer to develop a system that meets the user's requirements. This is not to say that the customer is not kept informed of the process and is not involved in the process. Simply put, systems engineers are there to support and provide expertise on the design of the solution, and in this role they must be leaders of the process.

At the same time, systems engineers must recognize that their task is to meet the customer's needs, not the engineer's. It is the systems engineer's responsibility to get clearly defined needs or requirements from the customer. The customer is the expert on the customer's mission and business needs, not the systems engineer. Thus, the systems engineer must have the skills to discover and capture the mission needs as defined by the customer. In some cases, the engineer will need to help the customer discover and define the mission needs and the system requirements. Helping the customer define the needs is discussed in more detail in Chapter 2.

These three principles are important to ISSE for the following reasons:

1. Many customers and information systems security engineers tend to look at solutions instead of needs. For example, a customer might think that the solution is Voice-over-Internet-Protocol (VoIP), but the need (i.e., the requirement) is to have reachback capability (reachback capabilities are those that support a DoD theater commander without having to deploy to forward locations, such as command and control functions, imagery and intelligence analysis, and supply depot processes). The customer's perceived solution, Voice over Internet Protocol (VoIP), is not necessarily the one that will provide the best answer to the need, which is reachback capability.

2. Focusing on the solution without discovering the underlying need usually misses the target need. Even if the customer has expressed the requirements in terms of solutions, the engineer must stop the process and discover the underlying needs and problems that need to be resolved.

3. Following the three principles will typically allow more flexibility in the solution. If the need and problem are clearly defined, the

engineer will have more flexibility in developing a solution. Instead of using the customer's solution, the engineer can work to find the best solution to resolve the problem (e.g., meeting the business needs and overcoming any constraints).

Here is an example: the *problem* may be that the customer cannot securely share Web pages with its allies. The *requirement* is that the customer needs a secure Web solution that will allow secure sharing of html files with its allies. The *constraints* may be cost or bandwidth. The *solution* after reviewing the requirements and constraints (i.e., the problem) may be a high-assurance software guard that protects the content of Web pages from unauthorized users.

The next sections discuss some important concepts to the ISSE model. First is the theory of life cycle and how it should be combined with the ISSE process, followed by an overview of risk management and defense in depth. Throughout the remaining chapters in this domain, these concepts will be discussed; thus, it is appropriate to include a brief overview in this introduction.

Life Cycle and ISSE

For the ISSEP exam, the candidate should have a basic understanding of what is meant by life cycle and its impact on the security design and development of information systems.

An important concept of SE and ISSE is that all systems are associated with life cycles. IEEE 1220 defines eight essential life-cycle phases as:

1. *Development.* The planning and execution of system and subsystem definition tasks required to evolve the system from customer needs to product solutions and their life-cycle processes.
2. *Manufacturing.* The tasks, actions, and activities for fabrication and assembly of engineering test models and brassboards, prototypes, and production of product solutions and their life-cycle process products.
3. *Test.*
   a. The tasks, actions, and activities for planning for evaluation and conducting evaluation of synthesis products against the functional architecture or requirements baseline, or the functional architecture against the requirements baseline.
   b. The tasks, actions, and activities for evaluating the product solutions and their life-cycle processes to measure specification conformance or customer satisfaction.

4. *Distribution.* The tasks, actions, and activities to initially transport, deliver, assemble, install, test, and check out products to effect proper transition to users, operators, or consumers.
5. *Operations.* The tasks, actions, and activities associated with the use of the product or a life-cycle process.
6. *Support.* The tasks, actions, and activities to provide supply, maintenance, and support material and facility management for sustaining operations.
7. *Training.* The measurable tasks, actions, and activities (including instruction and applied exercises) required to achieve and maintain the knowledge, skills, and abilities necessary to efficiently and effectively perform operations, support, and disposal throughout the system life cycle. Training is inclusive of the tools, devices, techniques, procedures, and materials developed and employed to provide training for all required tasks.
8. *Disposal.* The tasks, actions, and activities to ensure that disposal of or recycling destroyed or irreparable consumer and life-cycle processes and by-products comply with applicable environmental regulations and directives. (p. 7–8)

Some ISSEP candidates may be familiar with the nine life-cycle phases of the MIL-STD 499B Systems Engineering Phases and Events. These are: Preconcept Phase, Concept Phase, Requirements Phase, System Design Phase, Preliminary Design Phase, Detailed Design Phase, Implementation and Testing Phase, Configuration Audit Phase, and Operations and Support Phase.

Blanchard and Fabrycky (1998) define the life-cycle phases as: Definition of Need, Conceptual and Preliminary Design, Detail Design and Development, Production and/or Construction, Product Use, Phase-out, and Disposal. As another example, Sage and Armstrong (1999) define the life cycle in three essential phases: Definition, Development, and Deployment.

As can be seen by these three examples, there are many models of life-cycle phases. Another example can be seen in NIST SP 800-27, which also combines engineering principles with life-cycle activities.

NIST SP 800-27, Rev. A: Engineering Principles

NIST SP 800-27, Rev. A (June 2004) "Engineering Principles for Information Technology Security (A Baseline for Achieving Security), Revision A" provides 33 recommended system-level security principles that should be considered in the design, development, and operation of an information system. NIST SP 800-27 is an effort to combine the various security principles and practices into one document. These principles are based on a system-level engineering approach and are designed to provide a foundation upon which a more consistent and structured security approach can be used throughout the life cycle of every system. More information on NIST SP 800-27 and a complete list of all 33 principles are found in Chapter 14.

More information on how life cycles relate to the ISSE is contained within the chapters for each phase. Next we look at the concept of risk management and the ISSE model.

Risk Management

In the ISSE process, risk can be defined as a measure of the uncertainty of attaining a goal, objective, or requirement pertaining to technical performance, cost, and schedule. A risk level is categorized by the probability of occurrence and the consequences of occurrence.

Security risks are the measures of uncertainty of satisfying technical requirements for system security. Risk management is the process of identifying the likelihood of an attack and the related consequences, and, if necessary, applying appropriate resources so the risk is reduced to an acceptable level.

The sources of risk to projects can include:

- Technical issues (i.e., feasibility, operability, producibility, testability, and system effectiveness)
- Costs (i.e., initial estimates and actual expenditures)
- Schedule (i.e., availability of technology, meeting milestones and objectives, technical advances such as version changes occurring during the development)
- Programmatic (i.e., resources, contractual issues, and personnel changes)
- Adversaries trying to attack a system in progress and thus prevent an organization from reaching its technical goals

The reason why ISSEPs perform risk management during the ISSE process is to help customers accomplish their mission(s) by:

- Better securing the IT systems that store, process, or transmit organizational information
- Enabling the customer to make well-informed risk management decisions to justify the expenditures that are part of an IT budget
- Assisting the customer in authorizing (or accrediting) the IT systems on the basis of the supporting documentation resulting from the performance of risk management (NIST SP 800-30, p. 2)

NIST SP 800-30 (2002), "Risk Management Guide for Information Technology Systems," states that minimizing negative impact on an organization and a need for sound basis in decision making are the fundamental reasons organizations implement a risk management process for their IT systems. Accordingly, effective risk management must be integrated into all phases of the System Development Life Cycle (SDLC), which is defined in five phases: initiation, development or acquisition, implementation, operation or maintenance, and disposal. It can be performed regardless of the phase and should be an iterative process that is performed during each major phase of system development. Risk can be identified at any time during the ISSE process — during system security definition, requirements, architecture design, development, implementation, etc. Table 1.2 is modified from NIST SP 800-30 to not only include the SDLC and the role of risk management, but to also include the ISSE phases.

One benefit of the risk management process is using the information to develop new or review current security policies. According to Resch (2004), the results of risk assessments can be used to analyze and review both security policies and security requirements. For each identified risk, a policy statement is written that also includes the identified level of risk (i.e., low, medium, high). For example, the higher the risk, the stronger the policy statement should be written. Based on Resch's model for defining policy statements based on the identified risks, a matrix can be formed as shown in Table 1.3.

According to the ISSE Handbook (1994), the following elements should be considered and documented as part of a security risk management plan:

- How and when security risk assessments will be conducted
- Planning for security risk documentation outputs, such as risk assessment reports
- Planning for collection and distribution of security risk information
- Establishment of an authorized risk acceptance authority — someone needs to have the final approval authority for accepting risk (recently, federal agencies have assigned this to the Chief Information Officer)
- Review and approval procedures for the risk assessment reports and documentation
- List of team members supporting the risk assessments
- Estimate of total level of effort required during each phase to support the specified risk assessment activity
- Establishing how the risk assessment/management reports will support the C&A process

Table 1.2   Integration of Risk Management into the SDLC and ISSE

SDLC Phase	ISSE Phase	Phase Characteristics	Support from Risk Management Activities
Phase 1: Initiation	Discover information protection needs Define system security requirements	The need for an IT system is expressed and the purpose and scope of the IT system is documented	Identified risks are used to support the development of the system requirements, including security requirements and a security concept of operations (strategy)
Phase 2: Development or Acquisition	Design system security architecture Develop detailed security design	The IT system is designed, purchased, programmed, developed, or otherwise constructed	The risks identified during this phase can be used to support the security analyses of the IT system that may lead to architecture and design trade-offs during system development
Phase 3: Implementation	Implement system security	The system security features should be configured, enabled, tested, and verified	The risk management process supports the assessment of the system implementation against its requirements and within its modeled operational environment Decisions regarding risks identified must be made prior to system operation

Table 1.2 (continued) Integration of Risk Management into the SDLC and ISSE

SDLC Phase	ISSE Phase	Phase Characteristics	Support from Risk Management Activities
Phase 4: Operation or Maintenance	Assess security effectiveness	The system performs its functions Typically the system is being modified on an ongoing basis through the addition of hardware and software and by changes to organizational processes, policies, and procedures	Risk management activities are performed for periodic system reauthorization (or reaccreditation) or whenever major changes are made to an IT system in its operational, production environment (e.g., new system interfaces)
Phase 5: Disposal	Destroy obsolete information and systems	This phase may involve the disposition of information, hardware, and software Activities may include moving, archiving, discarding, or destroying information and sanitizing the hardware and software	Risk management activities are performed for system components that will be disposed of or replaced to ensure that the hardware and software are properly disposed of, that residual data is appropriately handled, and that system migration is conducted in a secure and systematic manner

The role of the ISSEP in security risk activities is to ensure that the focus is on the right aspects of the system — those that will be or are affected by vulnerabilities and threats. The ISSEP should also establish

Table 1.3 Sample Security Policy Statements Based on Identified Threat

Type of Information	Threat	Attack	Policy
Marketing	Careless employees	Malicious code	Marketing information requires confidentiality and integrity and must be protected by daily backups
Sales	Competitors, careless employees, disgruntled employees	Malicious code, modifying data in transit or in storage, and physical destruction	Sales information requires confidentiality and integrity and must be protected using encryption while in transit or storage

with the customer a benchmark by which security risks are assessed. This benchmark should be based on the security requirements for the system and also the overall business security objectives and goals.

The ISSEP should assist in documenting the outputs of the risk activities, such as identifying all possible scenarios, events, threats, or vulnerabilities that could result in the inability of the system to maintain compliance with stated security requirements. The results of the activities can then be ranked based on specific system consequences and the likelihood of the event or threat occurring.

Once the initial risk assessment has been conducted, additional controls (i.e., countermeasures) that could be used to mitigate the threats or events should be identified. An important element in documenting the controls is to also document how the controls might affect the operational stance of the system. For example, the control might state that anti-virus software must be updated at periodic scheduled intervals throughout a 24-hour time period. What happens if the updates cause network congestion and slow the transmission capabilities of the network? Should the control be changed? This type of information should be included in the risk assessment documentation. The risk management documentation should also include a recommended course of action.

Keep in mind that risk management is fundamental to the concepts of information systems security. The senior executives of an organization must be knowledgeable about their responsibility to accept the known level of risks to their information systems. Certification and Accreditation (C&A) is based on a series of processes that when completed can provide information (through various documents) about the risks that have been mitigated, those that have been reduced, or those not addressed. Senior management must make the decision to accept the remaining risk called the residual risk, and allow the system to operate. Therefore, it is a critical concept not only to information systems security in general, but also to following the ISSE model when designing new systems or revising legacy systems.

Typically, risk decision points closely precede major system milestones and should involve formal consensus-based risk analysis. At other technical milestones, less-structured risk analysis can be performed, such as a comparison and analysis of current risk information against the system description, threats, weaknesses, and assumptions that formed the bases of the most recent formal risk analysis. It should be understood, however, that risk decisions will vary, depending on where the project is in the life-cycle phase, whether it is in analysis, design, development, implementation, operation, or disposal.

To assist the ISSEP in understanding the role of risk management within the ISSE phases, a section on risk management is included in each chapter, where appropriate. Also, more information on risk management and NIST SP 800-30 is available in Chapter 14.

The final concept in this chapter is defense in depth. Defense in depth is a strategy for achieving IA in the current interdependent networks. It is considered a practical strategy because it relies on the intelligent application of all techniques and technologies currently in existence.

Defense in Depth

Simply put, defense in depth is a strategy based on creating layers of protection for a system in a specified environment. Although some may view the layered approach as too much solution to a problem, the complexities of today's IT security threats require a new protective approach — one that uses multiple methods and techniques to counter threats. The defense-in-depth strategy recommends a balance among protection capability, cost, performance, and operational considerations.

The IATF layered approach as shown in Figure 1.6 is a balanced focus on three primary elements: people, technology, and operations. Consider the following information system security scenario and determine how it relates to the three elements.

> To begin, an organization was proactive in writing its policy and broadcasting its policy via email to all users. The policy clearly states: when transferring documents from an outside source (i.e., through a floppy disk, CD-ROM, Zip drive, etc.), the employee must scan the document for viruses or malicious

Figure 1.6   Defense in depth.

code before opening or executing the document using the system. A new employee brings an infected disk from home, opens a document, and saves it on the local system, which causes the system to be infected with malicious code. The infected system is then immediately quarantined from the rest of the enterprise network to eliminate total network infection. After several days of checking every local machine for infection and eradicating any malicious code, the local system is determined to be virus-free and is reconnected to the enterprise network.

From a "people" perspective, what can be done to correct this type of problem and ensure that it does not repeat itself? From a technology perspective, what can be done? Finally, from an operational standpoint, what can be done?

People

The first element, people, begins with a commitment from senior-level executives to establish a culture that values Information Assurance (IA). It involves the establishment of effective IA policies and procedures, the assignment of roles and responsibilities, and a commitment of resources. Other factors include the training of critical personnel, especially those responsible for the technical management of the system. A final element is the enforcement of personal accountability.

Technology

There are many technologies available for providing IA services, including detecting malicious code. It is important for organizations to purchase and implement the right technologies. They should establish effective policies and processes for technology acquisition that includes security. The IATF states that policies and processes should include "security policy, IA principles, system-level IA architectures and standards, criteria for needed IA products, acquisition of products that have been validated by a reputable third party, configuration guidance, and processes for assessing the risk of the integrated systems" (p. 2-8).

Operations

The operations element of the defense-in-depth strategy concentrates on all the activities required to maintain an organization's security posture on a daily basis. This includes security policy, certification and accreditation, security management, key management, readiness assessment, and recovery plans.

Because of its direct importance to understanding the full concept of defense in depth, the following information is taken directly from IATF and reprinted here.

"In implementing an effective and enduring IA capability or in adopting a Defense in Depth strategy for IA, organizations should consider —

■ Taking into consideration the effectiveness of the information protection required, based on the value of the information to the organization and the potential impact that loss or compromise of the information would have on the organization's mission or business. IA decisions should be based on risk analysis and keyed to the organization's operational objectives.

■ Using a composite approach, based on balancing protection capability against cost, performance, operational impact, and changes to the operation itself considering both today's and tomorrow's operations and environments.

■ Drawing from all three facets of Defense in Depth — people, operations, and technology. Technical mitigations are of no value without trained people to use them and operational procedures to guide their application.

■ Establishing a comprehensive program of education, training, practical experience, and awareness. Professionalization and certification licensing provide a validated and recognized expert cadre of system administrators.

- Exploiting available commercial off-the-shelf (COTS) products and relying on in-house development for those items not otherwise available.
- Planning and following a continuous migration approach to take advantage of evolving information processing and network capabilities — both functional and security-related — and to ensure adaptability to changing organizational needs and operating environments.
- Assessing periodically the IA posture of the information infrastructure. Technology tools, such as automated scanners for networks, can assist in vulnerability assessments.
- Taking into account not only the actions of those with hostile intent, but also inadvertent or unwitting actions that may have ill effects and natural events that may affect the system.
- Adhering to the principles of commonality, standardization, and procedures, and interoperability and to policies.
- Judiciously using emerging technologies, balancing enhanced capability with increased risk.
- Employing multiple means of threat mitigation, overlapping protection approaches to counter anticipated events so that loss or failure of a single barrier does not compromise the overall information infrastructure.
- Implementing and holding to a robust IA posture — one that can cope with the unexpected.
- Ensuring that only trustworthy personnel have physical access to the system. Methods of providing such assurance include appropriate background investigations, security clearances, credentials, and badges.
- Monitoring vulnerability listings and implementing fixes, ensuring that security mechanisms are interoperable, keeping constant watch over the security situation and mechanisms, properly employing and upgrading tools and techniques, and dealing rapidly and effectively with issues.
- Using established procedures to report incident information provided by intrusion detection mechanisms to authorities and specialized analysis and response center" (IATF, Chapter 2, p. 2-8 to 2-11).

The key defense-in-depth principles taken from IATF, Chapter 2, that are important for the ISSEP to note include defense in multiple places, layered defenses, security robustness, deploying KMI/PKI, and deploying intrusion detection systems.

Defense in Multiple Places

Because attacks can come from both insiders and outsiders accessing multiple points, an organization must deploy protection mechanisms at multiple locations to reduce the number of locations at which an attack can take place.

The defense in multiple places strategy is organized into several focus areas:

- Defend the computing environment (IATF, p. 2-12/13):
  - Ensure that clients, servers, and applications are adequately defended against denial of service, unauthorized disclosure, and modification of data.
  - Ensure the confidentiality and integrity of data processed by the client, server, or application, both inside and outside the enclave.
  - Defend against the unauthorized use of a client, server, or application.
  - Ensure that clients and servers follow secure configuration guidelines and have all appropriate patches applied.
  - Maintain configuration management of all clients and servers to track patches and system configuration changes.
  - Ensure that a variety of applications can be readily integrated with no reduction in security.
  - Ensure adequate defenses against subversive acts by trusted persons and systems, both internal and external.
- Defend the enclave boundaries (IATF, p. 2-12):
  - Ensure that physical and logical enclaves are adequately protected.
  - Enable dynamic throttling of services in response to changing threats.
  - Ensure that systems and networks within protected enclaves maintain acceptable availability and are adequately defended against denial-of-service intrusions.
  - Ensure that data exchanged between enclaves or via remote access is protected from improper disclosure.
  - Provide boundary defenses for those systems within the enclave that cannot defend themselves due to technical or configuration problems.
  - Provide a risk-managed means of selectively allowing essential information to flow across the enclave boundary.
  - Provide protection against the undermining of systems and data within the protected enclave by external systems or forces.
  - Provide strong authentication, and thereby authenticated access control, of users sending or receiving information from outside their enclave.

- ▪ Defend the networks and infrastructure (IATF, p. 2-12):
  - – Protect local and wide area communications networks (e.g., from denial-of-service attacks).
  - – Provide confidentiality and integrity protection for data transmitted over these networks (e.g., use encryption and traffic flow security measures to resist passive monitoring).
  - – Ensure that all data exchanged over WAN is protected from disclosure to anyone not authorized to access the network.
  - – Ensure that WANs supporting mission-critical and mission-support data provide appropriate protection against denial-of-service attacks.
  - – Protect against the delay, misdelivery, or nondelivery of otherwise adequately protected information.
  - – Protect from traffic flow analysis:
    - ▪ User traffic
    - ▪ Network infrastructure control information
  - – Ensure that protection mechanisms do not interfere with otherwise seamless operation with other authorized backbone and enclave networks.
- ▪ Defend the supporting infrastructures (IATF, p. 2-11):
  - – Protect the key management infrastructure.
  - – Protect the public key infrastructure.
  - – Ensure the ability to detect and respond to intrusions is secure.

Layered Defenses

IA technologies and products have inherent weaknesses; thus, an attacker will, given enough time, find an exploitable vulnerability in almost any system. To counter this, an organization deploys "multiple layered" defense mechanisms so that if the adversary can break through the first countermeasure, another is already built into the system. An analogy of a layered defense can be seen in the physical security arena. The first layer is the front door that contains a locking mechanism. If that control is bypassed, the second layer would include a locking mechanism on inside doors or an elevator key. A third layer of control would include locking office suites, followed by locking individual offices.

Important to a layered defense is that each countermeasure mechanism presents a unique obstacle to the adversary. In addition, each layer should include both protection and detection measures. For example, in the physical security analogy, the second or third layer would also include an after-hours alarm system that would indicate movement in the area. Thus, a lock would protect the area, while a penetration alarm would

Table 1.4   Examples of Layered Defenses

Class of Attack	First Line of Defense	Second Line of Defense
Passive	Link and network layer and encryption and traffic flow security	Security-enabled applications
Active	Defend the enclave boundaries	Defend the computing environment
Insider	Physical and personnel security	Authenticated access controls, audit
Close-In	Physical and personnel security	Technical surveillance countermeasures
Distribution	Trusted software development and distribution	Runtime integrity controls

Source: From IATF, p. 2-13.

detect an intrusion if the lock failed. Table 1.4 provides other examples of layered defenses.

Security Robustness

Specify the security robustness of each IA component. "Robustness" is the strength and assurance of the mechanism related to the value of what it is protecting and the threat at the point of application.

Deploy KMI/PKI

Organizations should implement robust key management and public key infrastructures that will support all of the incorporated IA technologies and mechanisms and ensure they are highly resistant to attack. Important to this element is providing a cryptographic infrastructure that supports key, privilege, and certificate management. It should also enable positive identification of individuals using network services.

Deploy Intrusion Detection Systems

An infrastructure should be able to (1) detect intrusions, (2) analyze and correlate the results, and (3) react as needed. The core system infrastructures should help the staff answer questions such as, "Am I under attack?" "Who is the source?," "What is the target?," "Who else is under attack?," and

"What are my options?" (IATF, p. 2-13). This would include an infrastructure that provides intrusion detection, reporting, analysis, assessment, and response capabilities that enables rapid detection and response to intrusions and other anomalous events and provides operational situation awareness. The organizations should also plan for execution and reporting requirements for contingencies and reconstitution (IATF, p. 2-14).

One of the most important needs of a user community is to have immediate access to the information infrastructure and its information, which supports the operational objectives and needs of the organization. To provide this access, the organization must deploy robust information-processing technology and reliable connectivity. The use of IA and defense-in-depth strategies that use people, technology, and operations will provide organizations with the abilities to maintain adequate protection of their information and at the same time provide the necessary access to their users.

Summary

Through various concept definitions of systems, systems engineering, and information systems security engineering, the final definition for ISSE was identified as the art and science of discovering the user's security needs and the overall security needs of the organization; designing and developing, with economy and elegance, an information system that ensures an appropriate level of confidentiality, integrity, availability, authentication, and non-repudiation that is based upon valid risk management decisions; and ensuring the system can securely resist the forces to which it may be subjected.

From this definition, the phases and activities of both the systems-engineering model and the ISSE model were introduced. Each of these phases is discussed in further detail in the remaining chapters of this domain.

The importance of separating the problem space (the combination of the mission needs and constraints) from the solution space was defined with the key point that the security requirements should be a driving force of the solution. Discovering the customer's needs takes time and hard work from both the ISSEP and the customer. Sometimes it is easier to define the solutions without bothering to identify and document the requirements and constraints. However, the result will be a system that does not support the customer's mission.

The ISSEP must help the customer define and document the problem. Although the customer owns the system and any subsequent problems, the engineer has the expertise to help the customer discover the true problem. The engineer is expected to be the expert in developing solutions; thus, the engineer must not miss the real problem and develop the wrong solution.

References

Blanchard, Benjamin S. and Wolter J. Fabrycky (1998). *Systems Engineering and Analysis*, 3rd edition. Prentice Hall: Upper Saddle River, NJ.

DoD 5000.2-R (June 2001). Mandatory Procedures for Major Defense Acquisition Programs (MDAP) and Major Automated Information System (MAIS) Acquisition Programs. Available at http://acc.dau.mil.

EIA/IS 632 (1994). Systems Engineering. Electronic Industries Alliance, 2001 Pennsylvania Avenue NW, Washington, D.C., p. 43.

Grady, Jeffrey O. (2000). *Systems Engineering Deployment*. CRC Press: Boca Raton, FL.

Harris, Michael B. (2002). A Systems Approach to Open-Inquiry Evaluation of Engineering Programmes. This paper was published in the proceedings of the Australasian Evaluation Society's 19th International Conference, held in Canberra, Australia in 2001. The AES Web site is at: http://www.aes.asn.au/.

IAEC3186 (February 2002). Introduction to Information Systems Security Engineering, ISSE Training, student guide.

IEEE Std 1220-1998 (December 1998, © January 1999). IEEE Standard for Application and Management of the Systems Engineering Process. IEEE: New York, NY. (Revision of IEEE Std 1220-1994)

Information Assurance Technical Framework (IATF), Version 3.1 (September 2002). National Security Agency, Information Assurance Solutions, Technical Directors; Fort Meade, MD.

Information Assurance Technical Framework Forum (IATFF) (undated). Introduction to the Information Assurance Technical Framework Forum. Available at the IATF Web site: http://www.iatf.net/file_serve.cfm?chapter=introduction.pdf.

Information Systems Security Handbook, Release 1.0 (February 28, 1994). National Security Agency, Central Security Service. Only available for official USG use.

MIL-STD-499A and MIL-STD 499B, U.S. Department of Defense Systems Engineering Standards. May 1974 and May 1991.

NIST SP 800-14 (September 1996). Generally Accepted Principles and Practices for Securing Information Technology Systems. NIST Publications, Computer Security Division, NIST: Gaithersburg, MD. Available at the NIST Web site: http://www.nist.gov.

NIST SP 800-27, Rev. A (June 2004). Engineering Principles for Information Technology Security (A Baseline for Achieving Security), Revision A. NIST Publications, Computer Security Division, NIST: Gaithersburg, MD. Available at the NIST Web site: http://www.nist.gov.

NIST SP 800-30 (July 2002). Risk Management Guide for Information Technology Systems. NIST Publications, Computer Security Division, NIST: Gaithersburg, MD. Available at the NIST Web site: http://www.nist.gov.

NSTISSI No. 4009 (May 2003). National Information Assurance Glossary. CNSS: Ft. Meade, MD. Available from www.nstissc.gov.

PDD 63 (May 1998). Critical Infrastructur e Protection. Available from www.fas.org/irp/offdocs/pdd/pdd63.html.

Resch, Cheryl (2004). Designing an Information Security System. Published in the *Proceedings of the 2004 IEEE Workshop on Information Assurance*. USMA: West Point, NY.

Sage, Andrew P. and James E. Armstrong (1999). *Introduction to Systems Engineering: Methods and Technologies for the Engineering of Trustworthy Systems*. John Wiley & Sons, Custom Textbook.

2

ISSE Model Phase 1: Discover Information Protection Needs

Introduction

The phases in the Information Systems Security Engineering (ISSE) life-cycle model are:

1. **Discover Information Protection Needs. Ascertain why the system needs to be built and what information needs to be protected.**
2. Define System Security Requirements. Define the system in terms of what security is needed.
3. Define System Security Architecture. Define the security functions needed to meet the specific security requirements.
4. Develop Detailed Security Design. Based on the security architecture, design the security functions and features for the system.
5. Implement System Security. Following the documented security design, build and implement the security functions and features for the system.
6. Assess Security Effectiveness. Assess the degree to which the security of the system, as it is defined, designed, and implemented, meets the security needs.

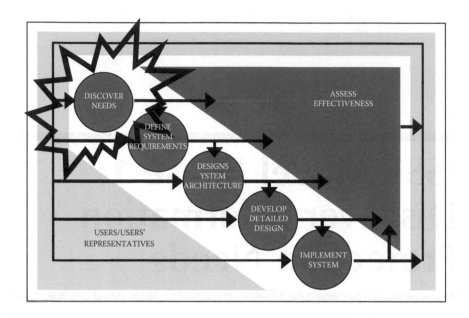

Figure 2.1   ISSE model: Discover protection needs. (*Source:* Adapted from IATF, p. 3-2.)

During Phase 1 of the ISSE model, the Information Systems Security Engineering Professional (ISSEP®) works closely with the customer to help understand the business or organization's mission and define the information protection needs that support it (Figure 2.1).

In the early 1990s, the Department of Defense (DoD) saw the need to create a program that would guide the "evolution of the DoD enterprise and capture benefits of the information revolution" (Taylor, 1996). This program, Corporate Information Management (CIM), was established to change the current business methods to use a new model — figure out what you want to do and how you want to do it before investing thousands or millions of dollars in new information technologies. Although the CIM program was plagued with difficulties, including lack of sufficient funding and management support, it did evolve into part of the Business Process Reengineering Program (BPRP). The BPRP is based on the concept that redesigning business processes can be used to optimize or improve the level of performance or service at a reduced cost.

This concept is similar to the essence of this chapter and of the ISSE model — rethink the systems engineering design processes to improve the performance of the system and, specifically, to rethink the process to include security needs. The goal of the first activity in the ISSE model is

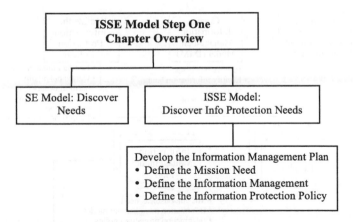

Figure 2.2   Chapter overview.

to discover the information protection needs of the system before beginning the design of the project. To do this, Phase 1 of the ISSE model defines a framework and various methodologies to assist the ISSEP in discovering the customer's protection needs. The ISSEP is responsible for helping the customer to define and document these needs *before* moving into the design and development activities.

ISSE Phase 1, Discover Information Protection Needs, is based on the Information Assurance Technical Framework (IATF) version 3.1 (September 2002), specifically Chapter 3. In addition, Appendix H of the IATF provides details on conducting a Protection Needs Elicitation (PNE), including the guidelines for discovering information protection needs from the customer.

The chapter begins by briefly explaining the Systems Engineering (SE) activity associated with discovering needs. As shown in Figure 2.2, the second section defines the ISSE activity, Discover Information Protection Needs and the associated tasks.

The **Information Management Plan (IMP)** includes three primary tasks. The first is to **define the mission need**. The second task is to identify how the organization manages its information. This type of analysis can be accomplished using an **Information Management Model (IMM)**. An IMM is a methodological analysis to obtain, model, and document the customer's information, processes, user access to information, and security policy for the information. The third task is to define the **Information Protection Policy (IPP)**. This includes discovering the information protection needs by defining the potential threats to the information system and what security services are needed to counteract or reduce those threats.

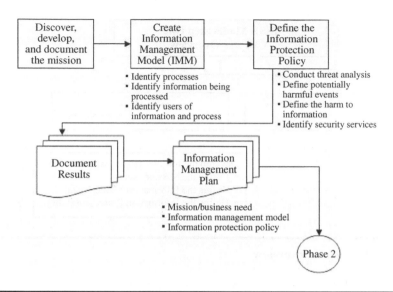

Figure 2.3   Information protection needs.

The final outcome of these tasks is an IMP. The three tasks combined into the IMP are used in Phase 2 of the ISSE model to define the system security requirements. A flowchart of Phase 1 activities is shown in Figure 2.3.

Systems Engineering Activity: Discover System Needs

Although there are several terms for this activity, such as "needs analysis" or "requirements analysis," the outcome is essentially the same — defining what the system shall be capable of accomplishing and how well the system shall perform in quantitative, measurable terms.

Discovering needs includes customers defining their expectations, their internal or external constraints, their management's point of view, and any legacy system requirements that will affect the design. These discovered and defined needs are captured in the needs or requirements document. This information guides the remaining systems engineering activities and represents the definition of the problem that should be solved and the expectation of the system to meet that need. Specific information on defining and documenting system requirements is given in Chapter 3, "Defining System Security Requirements."

ISSE Activity: Discover Information Protection Needs

This important first activity in the ISSE model defines the system and its security needs before a solution is selected. Because the system will manage information, it is important to understand the following:

- What information will be managed
- Who will manage the information and who will establish the manager's responsibilities
- The environment in which the system components will operate
- The system or human interfaces needed
- The physical characteristics of the design
- Any known constraints that will affect the design solution

Based on the information and system needs identified during this activity, an IPP is defined. The IPP is then applied within the context for a target system or systems to be developed or modified. The context also provides a framework for the allocation of security services to systems external to the target.

If the basic SE activity of conducting a needs baseline has not been performed or is incomplete, the ISSEP must begin the ISSE process by completing the following tasks:

1. *Define the mission need.* Discover and develop an understanding of the customer's mission or business.
2. *Define the information management.* Work with the customer to determine what information management is needed to support the mission or business. In concurrence with the customer, create an Information Management Model (IMM).
3. *Define the information protection policy.* In concurrence with the customer, conduct a threat analysis that is the basis for the creation of the IPP.

The results of these three tasks are documented in the Information Management Plan (IMP) and become the basis for defining an information system that meets the customer's specific mission/business needs. In some situations, prior specific written authorization and agreed upon "Rules of Engagement" from the customer may be needed, especially if the baselining includes anything other than paper-based exercises.

The remaining topics in this chapter are separated based on these tasks. First is a discussion of how an ISSEP conducts the activities in discovering and documenting the customer's business or mission needs.

Task 1: Define the Customer's Mission/Business Needs

A huge emphasis is placed on this initial step of the ISSE process — if the SEs or ISSEPs do not understand the mission of the organization and the mission of the system, they may design the wrong system for the customer — that is, a system that will not meet the customer's needs. There should be strong emphasis on understanding customers, their environment, their mission, and their needs. When time and patience are taken to discover the true needs of the customer, it can explain why a system is needed, which can ultimately result in designing the right system. Part of discovering the customer's needs is for the ISSEP to differentiate between what a customer **wants** and what a customer **needs**.

Can you distinguish the difference between wants and needs? How about these two statements:

I want a Mercedes Benz. I need a Mercedes Benz.

Some customers may have already defined what they want and will tell the ISSEP something like, "I *want* a secure connection between the classified and unclassified network so I can electronically transfer unclassified information stored on the classified network to the unclassified network." This may be what they want, but is it what they need?

It is the goal of the ISSEP to help customers translate their wants into mission/business needs. If necessary, the ISSEP may need to explain that particular customer wants may actually place constraints upon the system design. As part of the consultant role, the ISSEP should not demean the customer for what is wanted or diminish what the customer wants; instead, the focus should be on translating wants into some type of relation to mission needs. Thus, if the customer's wants do not clearly relate to a mission need, it may be appropriate and necessary for the ISSEP to document these wants as design constraints.

The important element is the ISSEP's ability to help the customer translate wants into mission/business needs. The ISSEP can view the experience as an educational opportunity, where the ISSEP educates or trains the customer on the *needs* of the system. This requires the ISSEP to have good interpersonal skills, such as verbal communication and problem-solving skills. Because the customer may not want to hear what the ISSEP is proposing, the ISSEP needs to gain respect from the customer by interfacing with the customer in a professional and effective manner.

To begin, the ISSEP performs initial research on the customer's organization to become aware of the mission. Available source material may include operational doctrine (i.e., a set of documents that describe how an organization conducts its mission), Web pages, annual reports, public audit reports, proprietary documentation, and colleagues' past experiences with the customer. The organization's mission may also be summarized in documents such as a mission needs statement or a high-level version of a Concept of Operations (CONOPS). Although these documents can be used for background research about the mission, the most important source of information is direct contact and interaction with the customer. The customer's mission can be obtained through various questions, including:

- Is there a system that is currently operational? If so, what type of system? If there is a current system, is it possible to diagram the system to show the type of connections, users, workstations, servers, operating systems, applications, etc.? The goal is to discover how the current system supports the organization's mission/business.
- What are the deficiencies of the current system?
- What new capability does the customer want added to the current system?
- What does the customer want a new system to do that the current system cannot do?
- What does the current system do that the customer wants it to do differently or better?
- What type of information or sensitivity level (classification) is processed and stored on the current system?
- What value is given to the current processed and stored information on the current system?
- Who needs access to information processed and stored on the current system?
- With what organizational or Federal regulations, policies, or procedures does the current or future system need to comply?

When asking these types of questions, it is important that the ISSEP does not allow the discussions to lead to how the system will be designed. The approach should focus on defining and documenting the mission/business information with no system considerations (not "as is" and "to be"). Customers often do not recognize all of the information management activities they do and need. Thus, in these initial discussions, the ISSEP is asking questions to help the customer review and think more thoroughly about their information and the system that is needed to support that information.

How the ISSEP approaches the customer can be an important factor in working with the customer to learn the organization and the mission. As noted in IATF, Appendix H, there are six activities involved in approaching the customer in a professional manner. They are:

1. *Make initial contact.* Although the initial contacts may be with the technical representatives of the organization, the ISSEP must also meet with the decision makers to build concurrence on the customer's needs and solutions.
2. *Learn the mission and business.* To gain respect and the confidence of the customer, the ISSEP should learn as much as possible about the customer before the initial meeting. This includes discovering the customer's internal organization, its objectives, mission statements, major functions, products, supporting or supported organizations, and any future plans. It also includes reviewing previous projects or public domain information about the customer.
3. *Develop contacts.* During initial meetings, the ISSEPs need to build trust and cooperation with their first employee contacts. From these employees, they should learn about others who may be helpful in the process and also the decision makers who will be involved in or make the final decisions of the project.
4. *Selling the value.* It may be necessary to sell the value of the ISSE model and especially the time and resources needed to define the need, including the creation of an IMM and IMP. It may be helpful to explain that defining and documenting the information protection needs have both non-security and security benefits for the customer.

- The non-security benefits of conducting this process include:
  - Providing a better understanding of how their information is managed
  - Documenting the requirements of the system in a thorough, thoughtful format
  - Using the IMM as a baseline for evaluating the operational performance of the solution
  - Defining needed personnel and administrative resources, such as defining the users, functions, processes, and information into a manageable format
- The security benefits of conducting this process include:
  - Identifying and documenting the threats to the information. The ISSEP, when conducting the threat analysis, will investigate the motivation of adversaries who might attack the information, the likelihood of the attack, and the effect of an attack.
  - Documenting the policies of the customer. The customer, when reviewing the potential harm and the value of information, can determine the priorities for information protection and security services.

- Prioritizing information protection. The ISSEP works with the customer to prioritize available resources in an efficient manner — so that the initial protection mechanisms implemented are in direct proportion to the most likely threats.

5. *Planning for the information protection needs analysis.* One of the first items is for the ISSEP to present a plan to the customer on how the information protection needs will be defined and documented. The analysis must be based on the context of the customer's program and should include a justification of how important the IMM and threat analysis is to meeting the customer's needs. The ISSEP explains the scope of the project, including the personnel effort by the ISSEP and customer teams, plus any costs and schedule considerations.

6. *Setting project roles and responsibilities.* The plan for the analysis should identify all ISSE team members and customer team members, and their expected contributions and commitment to the project. In addition to these two groups, other members might include decision makers, technical representatives, operations personnel, security administrators, and certifiers and accreditors.

Once the ISSEP and the customer, by working together, have discovered and defined the mission needs and any design constraints (i.e., wants), the ISSEP documents this information. Before moving to the next task, the ISSEP asks the customer to agree with the documented mission need for the information system. Once the customer sees this information in a formal document, he or she has an opportunity to read the need statements and completely digest the information. The customer and the ISSEP have then agreed on what is truly needed from the system to support the mission needs. The next step is to identify how the information is managed.

Task 2: Define the Information Management

From Mission Needs to Information Management Needs

The next important element for the ISSEP is to understand how the organization manages information. Underlying the customer's mission/business is the information management that supports operations. Thus, a subset of its overall mission needs is its information management needs. The ISSEP must not only review the products and services the operation provides, but must also assess other important support functions that create, process, and store information, such as command and control, logistics, human resources, finance, research and development, management, marketing, and manufacturing.

As noted in the IATF, a basic definition of information management is any method of:

- Creating information
- Acquiring information
- Processing information (processing indicates a broad set of manipulations of data that select, transform, reorganize, or otherwise process the many forms of data called information)
- Storing and retrieving information
- Transferring information
- Deleting information (p. 14–18)

Next we will discuss how to use an information management model as a technique for defining the information management. This topic is followed by a methodology for documenting how an organization manages information. Keep in mind that SEs and ISSEPs will use a variety of models and these are just a few examples.

Creating an Information Management Model (IMM)

As shown in Figure 2.4, to define the information management needs an IMM is used to:

1. Identify processes
2. Identify the information being processed
3. Identify the users of the information and the processes

The IMM, similar to other models, is used as a tool to reduce ambiguous concepts. Essentially, the IMM is a structured analysis tool that helps the ISSEP to break down user roles, processes, and information until ambiguity is reduced to a satisfactory degree.

Most likely, the ISSEP will be faced with three options for creating an IMM (IATF, p. H-19):

1. *Information management is already modeled.* In this option, discovering information management needs may be easier because the customer has already done much of the work. Note that even if the customer has used some other type of model to define or map information, the ISSEP still needs to develop an IMM.

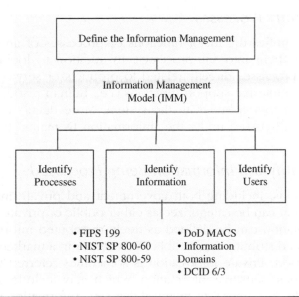

Figure 2.4 Define the information management.

2. *Model needs translation.* The customer has already performed some type of information management modeling, but the modeling is inadequate and requires additional information or restructuring. In this option, the ISSEP may need to make fundamental changes in the customer model.

3. *No information management modeling.* Obviously, with this option, the ISSEP must conduct the research and design an IMM.

If the ISSEP needs to create the IMM, the first step is to acquire the right information. The two methods that work best are conducting interviews and reviewing documents. The ISSEPs should keep in mind that when conducting interviews, they are asking the customer to spend time and other resources. In these situations, the ISSEPs must be sensitive to the effects on customer operations. Therefore, to minimize the effect on the customer's operations, the ISSEPs must be prepared, know what is wanted, and make clear, concise requests. In some cases, it may be necessary to develop a pre-interview questionnaire that the customer can complete.

The IMM is an analysis of three identified items: processes, information, and the users who utilize the processes to access the information. The following topics address each item individually.

Step 1: Identify Processes

The ISSEP identifies the major functions or processes of an organization and relegates them into sub-processes. In addition to looking at major functions or processes directly related to products or services, the ISSEP should include internal support functions (i.e., human resources, finance) that may be accomplished with the system. More details on identifying processes are discussed under the "Information Domains" topic.

Step 2: Identify the Information Being Processed

All organizations, including both government and private industry, have information that can be categorized as either public or private information. Public information can be defined as freely distributed information, such as information distributed on a public Web site, or in a marketing brochure or annual report. Private information is sometimes referred to as proprietary or business-sensitive information, which may include trade secrets, personnel data, customer lists, financial data, etc. Information in the United States Government (USG) typically uses the classifications: Unclassified, Sensitive but Unclassified (SBU), Confidential, Secret, Top Secret (TS), and Sensitive Compartmentalized Information (SCI). Although the Unclassified category may seem to indicate public information, this is not necessarily the case. Some unclassified information, such as For Official Use Only (FOUO) or No Foreigners (NOFORN), is considered proprietary or sensitive to the USG and is not freely distributed to the public. These categorizations of information can also be considered an information domain.

The activity of identifying information can be accomplished using various methods. The first is to review Federal and DoD recommendations and guidelines on how to categorize information systems. The second is to identify information domains. Specifically, we will look at the following methods of categorizing information:

- FIPS Publication 199
- NIST SP 800-60
- NIST SP 800-59
- DoDD 8500.1 Mission Assurance Categories
- Information Domains
- DCID 6/3

FIPS 199

One mandatory standard from the National Institute of Standards and Technology (NIST) is the Federal Information Processing Standards Publication

199 (FIPS 199) released in February 2004, "Standards for Security Categorization of Federal Information and Information Systems." Although FIPS 199 is discussed in Chapter 14 it is a required categorization for ISSEPs to use when identifying USG information, thus it is also discussed in this chapter.

FIPS 199 provides requirements on how Federal agencies must categorize information and information systems based on a range of risk levels. It begins by stating the importance of why security categorization is needed, "Security categorization standards for information and information systems provide a common framework and understanding for expressing security that, for the Federal government, promotes: (i) effective management and oversight of information security programs, including the coordination of information security efforts throughout the civilian, national security, emergency preparedness, homeland security, and law enforcement communities; and (ii) consistent reporting to the Office of Management and Budget (OMB) and Congress on the adequacy and effectiveness of information security policies, procedures, and practices" (p. 1).

FIPS 199 applies to "(i) all information within the Federal government other than that information that has been determined pursuant to Executive Order 12958 or any predecessor order, or by the Atomic Energy Act of 1954, as amended, to require protection against unauthorized disclosure and is marked to indicate its classified status, and (ii) all Federal information systems other than those information systems designated as national security systems as defined in 44 United States Code Section 3542(b)(2). Agency officials shall use the security categorizations described in this standard whenever there is a Federal requirement to provide such a categorization of information or information systems. Additional security designators may be developed and used at agency discretion" (p. 1).

FIPS 199 outlines three potential impact levels — low, moderate, and high — for each of the three security objectives — confidentiality, integrity, and availability (CIA). The impact levels consider both impact and threat, but are weighted toward impact. NIST chose to focus on impact because every Federal system faces some level of threat that changes daily. The impact is based on the potential magnitude of harm that the loss of CIA would have on agency operations, assets, or individuals and its ability to accomplish its assigned mission or maintain daily functions. Table 2.1 provides an overview of the three risk levels and three security objectives.

FIPS 199 establishes security categories for both information and information systems. An **information type** is defined as "a specific category of information (e.g., privacy, medical, proprietary, financial, investigative, contractor sensitive, security management) defined by an organization or, in some instances, by a specific law, Executive Order, directive, policy, or regulation" (p. 1). **Information systems** can contain information types

Table 2.1   Potential Impact Definitions for Security Objectives

Security Objective	Potential Impact		
	Low	Moderate	High
Confidentiality Preserving authorized restrictions on information access and disclosure, including means for protecting personal privacy and proprietary information. [44 U.S.C., SEC. 3542]	The unauthorized disclosure of information could be expected to have a **limited** adverse effect on organizational operations, organizational assets, or individuals.	The unauthorized disclosure of information could be expected to have a **serious** adverse effect on organizational operations, organizational assets, or individuals.	The unauthorized disclosure of information could be expected to have a **severe or catastrophic** adverse effect on organizational operations, organizational assets, or individuals.
Integrity Guarding against improper information modification or destruction, and includes ensuring information non-repudiation and authenticity. [44 U.S.C., SEC. 3542]	The unauthorized modification or destruction of information could be expected to have a **limited** adverse effect on organizational operations, organizational assets, or individuals.	The unauthorized modification or destruction of information could be expected to have a **serious** adverse effect on organizational operations, organizational assets, or individuals.	The unauthorized modification or destruction of information could be expected to have a **severe or catastrophic** adverse effect on organizational operations, organizational assets, or individuals.
Availability Ensuring timely and reliable access to and use of information. [44 U.S.C., SEC. 3542]	The disruption of access to or use of information or an information system could be expected to have a **limited** adverse	The disruption of access to or use of information or an information system could be expected to have a **serious** adverse	The disruption of access to or use of information or an information system could be expected to have a **severe or catastrophic**

Table 2.1 (continued)   Potential Impact Definitions for Security Objectives

Security Objective	Potential Impact		
	Low	*Moderate*	*High*
	effect on organizational operations, organizational assets, or individuals.	effect on organizational operations, organizational assets, or individuals.	adverse effect on organizational operations, organizational assets, or individuals.

Source: From FIPS 199, p. 6.

that, when combined on the same system, may dictate significant differences in security categorization.

The security category of an information type can be associated with both user information and system information, such as network routing tables and password files. It can be applicable to information in either electronic or non-electronic form. It can also be used as input in considering the appropriate security category of an information system. Establishing the appropriate security category of an information type essentially requires determining the *potential impact* for each security objective associated with the particular information type (FIPS 199, p. 3).

The generalized format for expressing the security category (SC) of an information type is:

> **SC** information type = {(**confidentiality**, *impact*), (**integrity**, *impact*), (**availability**, *impact*)}, where the acceptable values for potential impact are LOW, MODERATE, HIGH, or NOT APPLICABLE (FIPS 199, p. 3)

Two examples from FIPS 199 are:

> "EXAMPLE 1: An organization managing *public information* on its Web server determines that there is no potential impact from a loss of confidentiality (i.e., confidentiality requirements are not applicable), a moderate potential impact from a loss of integrity, and a moderate potential impact from a loss of availability. The resulting SC of this information type is expressed as:

> **SC** public information = {(**confidentiality**, NA), (**integrity**, MODERATE), (**availability**, MODERATE)}."

This information can also be expressed in table format as shown in Table 2.2.

Table 2.2   Example 1 of Security Category for Information Type

Information Type	Confidentiality	Integrity	Availability
Public information	N/A	Moderate	Moderate

"EXAMPLE 2: A law enforcement organization managing extremely sensitive *investigative information* determines that the potential impact from a loss of confidentiality is high, the potential impact from a loss of integrity is moderate, and the potential impact from a loss of availability is moderate. The resulting SC of this information type is expressed as:

SC investigative information = {(**confidentiality**, HIGH), (**integrity**, MODERATE), (**availability**, MODERATE)}" (p. 3).

This information can also be expressed in table format as shown in Table 2.3.

Table 2.3   Example 2 of Security Category for Information Type

Information Type	Confidentiality	Integrity	Availability
Investigate information	High	Moderate	Moderate

Determining the security category of an **information system** requires slightly more analysis and must consider the security categories of all information types resident on the information system. For an information system, the potential impact values assigned to the respective security objectives (confidentiality, integrity, availability) shall be the highest values (i.e., high water mark) from among those security categories that have been determined for each type of information resident on the information system (FIPS 199).

The generalized format for expressing the security category (SC) of an information system is:

SC information system = {(**confidentiality**, *impact*), (**integrity**, *impact*), (**availability**, *impact*)}, where the acceptable values for potential impact are LOW, MODERATE, or HIGH.

Note that the value of *not applicable* cannot be assigned to any security objective in the context of establishing a security category for an information system. This is in recognition that there is a low minimum potential impact (i.e., low water mark) on the loss of confidentiality, integrity, and availability for an information system due to the fundamental requirement to protect the system-level processing functions and information critical to the operation of the information system" (p. 4).

An example of categorizing an information system is:

"An information system used for large acquisitions in a contracting organization contains both sensitive, pre-solicitation phase contract information and routine administrative information. The management within the contracting organization determines that: (i) for the sensitive contract information, the potential impact from a loss of confidentiality is moderate, the potential impact from a loss of integrity is moderate, and the potential impact from a loss of availability is low; and (ii) for the routine administrative information (non-privacy-related information), the potential impact from a loss of confidentiality is low, the potential impact from a loss of integrity is low, and the potential impact from a loss of availability is low. The resulting SC of these information types are expressed as:

SC contract information = {(**confidentiality**, MODERATE), (**integrity**, MODERATE), (**availability**, LOW)},

and

SC administrative information = {(**confidentiality**, LOW), (**integrity**, LOW), (**availability**, LOW)}.

The resulting security category of the information system is expressed as:

SC acquisition system = {(**confidentiality**, MODERATE), (**integrity**, MODERATE), (**availability**, LOW)}, representing the high water mark or maximum potential impact values for each security objective from the information types resident on the acquisition system (FIPS 199, p. 4).

Table 2.4 expresses this data for the two types of information on the acquisition system. Table 2.5 shows the security category for the "Acquisition Information System" that contains the contract and administrative information.

Table 2.4   Example of Security Category for Information Type

Information Type	Confidentiality	Integrity	Availability
Contract information	Moderate	Moderate	Low
Administrative information	Low	Low	Low

Table 2.5   Example of Security Category for Information Type

Information System	Confidentiality	Integrity	Availability
Acquisition	Moderate	Moderate	Low

This initial categorization of information is not a true risk category for the information. To determine the risk to the information (or information system), it is necessary to also identify vulnerabilities, threats, current controls, likelihood of incidents or attacks, and the impact on the organization if the incident or attack occurred.

The next Federal policy of importance to defining information is NIST SP 800-60.

NIST SP 800-60

Note to ISSEP. At time of press, this policy was not listed as content for the ISSEP exam. However, it provides useful information in understanding how to categorize information based on security categories.

NIST SP 800-60, Version 2.0 (June 2004), "Guide for Mapping Types of Information and Information Systems to Security Categories, Volume 1 and 2," provides guidelines for mapping information types and information systems to the security categories defined in FIPS 199. It applies to all federal systems other than national security systems. The information types outlined in SP 800-60 are based on the OMB Federal Enterprise Architecture (FEA) Business Reference Model (BRM) 2.0 (June 2003). More information on the FEA can be found at www.whitehouse.gov/omb/egov/.

SP 800-60 states that "Generally, information systems process many types of information. Not all of these information types are likely to have the same impact levels. The compromise of some information types will jeopardize system functionality and agency mission more than the compromise of other information types. System impact levels must be assessed in the context of system mission and function as well as on the basis of the aggregate of the component information types" (Vol. 1, p. 5). This statement is an important justification of why it is necessary for the ISSEP to first document the mission and business needs.

It is noted in SP 800-60 that the first step in mapping types of federal information and information systems to security objectives and impact levels is the development of an information taxonomy, or creation of a catalog of information types. The FEA BRM describes 39 lines of government business distributed among four business areas. The business areas are high-level categories relating to the:

■ Purpose of government (*missions or services to citizens*)
■ Mechanisms the government uses to achieve its purpose (*modes of delivery*)
■ Support functions necessary to conduct government (*support delivery of services*)
■ Resource management functions that support all areas of the government's business (*management of resources*)" (Vol. 1, p. 27).

The information needed to support the services is further separated into two categories: those that "support delivery of services" and those related to "management of resources." The *support delivery of services* and *management of resource* business areas are common to most Federal government agencies, and the information associated with each of their sub-functions is identified in SP 800-60 as a *management and support* information type.

As in the case of mission-based information, the first step in mapping types of *management and support* information and information systems to security objectives and impact levels is to identify the information types stored in, processed by, or generated by the system. Using criteria identified in the context of the security objectives, the next step is to select the levels of impact and consequent security category for each applicable information type. System security categorization is based on the impact levels associated with each security objective for each type of information stored in, processed by, or generated by the system plus additional factors governing determination of system level impact (SP 800-60, Vol. 1, pp. 27–28). Figure 2.5 provides an outline of the types of information contained in each category.

Figure 2.6 is an example of how to assign a service or management type of information to the three security services of confidentiality, integrity, and availability. This example shows the ratings for the category *Support Delivery of Services, Internal Risk Management and Mitigation.*

Similar to FIPS 199, these initial impact assignments should be considered as provisional and as the first step in impact assignment and subsequent risk assessment processes. These provisional assignments are not intended to be used by organizations (or auditors) as a definitive checklist for information types and impact assignments.

Controls and Oversight
Corrective Action (Policy/Regulation)
Program Evaluation
Program Monitoring

Regulatory Development
Policy & Guidance Development
Public Comment Tracking
Regulatory Creation
Rule Publication

Planning & Resource Allocation
Budget Formulation
Capital Planning
Enterprise Architecture
Strategic Planning
Budget Execution
Workforce Planning
Management Improvement

Internal Risk Management/Mitigation
Contingency Planning
Continuity of Operations
Service Recovery

Public Affairs
Customer Services
Official Information Dissemination
Product Outreach
Public Relations

Revenue Collection
Debt Collection
User Fee Collection
Federal Asset Sales

Legislative Relations
Legislation Tracking
Legislation Testimony
Proposal Development
Congressional Liaison

General Government
Central Fiscal Operations
Legislative Functions
Executive Functions
Central Property Management
Central Personnel Management
Taxation Management
Central Records & Statistics Management
Income Information
Personal Identity and Authentication
Entitlement Event Information
Representative Payee Information

Government Resource Management Information

Human Resources Management
Benefits Management
Personnel Management
Payroll Mgt/Expense Reimbursement
Resource Training & Development
Security Clearance Management
Staff Recruitment & Employment

Administrative Management
Facilities/Fleet/Equipment Management
Help Desk Services
Security Management
Travel
Workplace Policy Development & Mgt

Information & Technology Mgt
System Development
Lifecycle/Change Management
System Maintenance
IT Infrastructure Maintenance
IT Security
Record Retention
Information Management

Financial Management
Accounting
Budget and Finance
Payments
Collections and Receivables
Asset and Liability Management
Reporting and Information

Supply Chain Management
Goods Acquisition
Inventory Control
Logistics Management
Services Acquisition

Figure 2.5   Management and support information types. (*Source:* From SP 800-60, Vol. 1, p. 28.)

	Confidentiality	Integrity	Availability
Internal Risk Management and Mitigation	Supports all activities relating to the processes of analyzing exposure to risk and determining appropriate countermeasures.		
Contingency Planning	Supports the actions required to plan for, respond to, and mitigate damaging events.	Moderate	Moderate	Moderate
Continuity of Operations	Supports the activities associated with the identification of critical systems and processes, and the planning and preparation required to ensure that these systems and processes will be available in the event of a catastrophic event.	Moderate	Moderate	Moderate
Service Recovery	Supports the internal actions necessary to develop a plan for resuming operations after a catastrophe occurs, such as a fire or earthquake.	Low	Low	Low

Figure 2.6 Support delivery of services example. (*Source:* From SP 800-60, Vol. 2, p. 14.)

ISSEPs should refer to the entire document for more details of how Federal information can be categorized and assigned a security impact level. NIST SP 800-60 can be downloaded from the NIST Web site. The next Federal policy of importance to information categorization is NIST SP 800-59, which provides information on categorizing information for national security systems in the Federal environment.

NIST SP 800-59

If the system is categorized as a national security system, the ISSEP should refer to NIST SP 800-59 for further information. SP 800-59 (August 2003), "Guideline for Identifying an Information System as a National Security System," provides procedures developed in conjunction with the DoD and NSA for identifying an information system as a national security system.

As background information, the definition of a national security system as defined by federal law is:

"(2)(A) The term 'national security system' means any information system (including any telecommunications system) used or operated by an agency or by a contractor of an agency, or other organization on behalf of an agency —

(i) the function, operation, or use of which —
–involves intelligence activities;
–involves cryptologic activities related to national security;
–involves command and control of military forces;
–involves equipment that is an integral part of a weapon or weapons system; or
–is critical to the direct fulfillment of military or intelligence missions (excluding a system that is to be used for routine administrative and business applications); or

(ii) is protected at all times by procedures established for information that have been specifically authorized under criteria established by an Executive order or an Act of Congress to be kept classified in the interest of national defense or foreign policy. Systems not meeting any of these criteria are not national security systems" [44 U.S.C. Sec. 3542(b) (2)].

SP 800-59 provides a National Security System Identification Checklist that can be used as one method for determining the type of system. Because national security systems are required to follow different regulations and standards, it is important to make this determination early in the life-cycle process. Note that each agency is responsible for identification of all national security systems under its ownership or control.

Before looking at the concept of information domains, a brief overview of one DoD information categorization is discussed. More information on DoD policies and regulations are in Domain 4, Chapter 12, "DoD IA Regulations."

DoD Mission Assurance Categories (MACs)

For those working with DoD customers, DoD Directive 8500.1 (2002) states that "All DoD information systems shall be assigned to one of three Mission Assurance Categories (MACs) that are directly associated with the importance of the information they contain relative to the achievement of DoD goals and objectives, particularly the war fighters' combat mission. Requirements for availability and integrity are associated with the mission assurance category, while requirements for confidentiality are associated with the information classification or sensitivity and need-to-know. Both sets of requirements are primarily expressed in the form of IA controls and shall be satisfied by employing the tenets of defense-in-depth for layering IA solutions within a given IT asset and among assets; and ensuring appropriate robustness of the solution, as determined by the relative strength of the mechanism and the confidence that it is implemented and will perform as intended. The IA solutions that provide availability, integrity, and confidentiality also provide authentication and non-repudiation" (Sec 4.7, p. 4).

The baseline MACs for availability and integrity are as follows.

- Mission Assurance Category I
  - Vital to mission effectiveness or operational readiness of deployed or contingency forces
  - Loss or degradation results in immediate and sustained loss of mission effectiveness
  - Must be highly accurate and highly available
  - Most stringent protection measures required
- Mission Assurance Category II
  - Important to support of deployed or contingency forces
  - Loss or degradation could delay services or commodities essential for operational readiness or mission effectiveness
  - Loss of integrity is unacceptable
  - Loss of availability difficult to manage; only tolerable in the short term
  - Additional safeguards beyond best practices required

■ Mission Assurance Category III
  – Needed for day-to-day business, but does not affect support to deployed or contingency forces in the short term
  – Loss can be tolerated or overcome without significant impact on mission effectiveness or operational readiness — can be reconstituted
  – Protective measures commensurate with commercial best practices

For example, a MAC I system would require both *high* integrity and availability; a MAC II system would need *high* integrity and *medium* availability; and a MAC III system would need *basic* integrity and availability.

More information on MACs and robustness is discussed in Chapter 12. Next we will look at another method of identifying information, which is to identify an information domain.

Information Domains

One aspect of identifying information and creating an IMM is to define the customer's **information domains**. An information domain is a collection of information objects that share the same security policy for privileges and access by its users. Information can be further partitioned based on access control needs and various levels of protections required for that information. For example, personnel data may be considered sensitive, but it would be contained in the unclassified information domain. However, only personnel officers are able to access the personnel data. Thus, within the unclassified information domain there is a sub-information domain for the personnel data that requires specific access controls and other protection levels. One of the challenges for organizations is to manage the flow of information between information domains.

As an example of the complexity involved in the sharing of information across information domains, think of the following initiative after the September 11 terrorist attack in the United States. To provide better security protection, the goal was to combine law enforcement databases from various agencies into one central database, allowing the various agencies to share information. To meet this goal, the ISSEPs and SEs would need to work with several different agencies to design a system that provides adequate security controls, including access permissions, such as who can access the database, how will data be entered, who can make changes, who can delete data, etc. One of the initial steps in this initiative would be to have all agencies required to share its information agree upon the sensitivity level of the information as well as methods to protect it. Although the agencies may have different policies and procedures that define the information and the requisite security protections, officials from all agencies would need to negotiate a mutually agreeable solution.

The DoD Goal Security Architecture (DGSA) [Volume 6 of the DoD Technical Architecture Framework for Information Management (TAFIM)] defines an information domain as "a set of users, their information objects, and a security policy. An information domain security policy is the statement of the criteria for membership in an information domain and the required protection of the information objects. Information domains are not hierarchically related, nor may they implicitly or explicitly infer sensitivity relative to multiple categories of sensitivity" (p. 3-7). Thus, an information domain can be viewed as a "triple" containing:

1. *Users:* the users or members of the information domain.
2. *Information objects:* the objects being managed, including processes.
3. *Security policy:* the rules, privileges, roles, and responsibilities that apply to the users in managing all the information. The model should include the requirements of any information management policies, regulations, and agreements that apply to the information being managed.

This triple is similar to the previous IMM triple of identifying user roles, processes, and information. In an information domain, a security policy is also identified and defined. An information domain has a different meaning than the term "domain," which can refer to the boundary of systems or networks. Systems or even networks of systems do not bind an information domain. Instead, an information domain is bounded by identifiable information objects and may be supported by any information system that can meet the protection requirements of the information domain security policy. In this concept, a specific mission security policy can define several information domains, each with its own distinct information domain security policy. The security mechanisms of any number of information systems can be evaluated for their ability to meet these information domain security policies. Through the process of accreditation, these security mechanisms may be usable for part or all of one or more missions (DGSA, 1996, p. 3-8).

The information domain is also different from the security domain. A security domain is based on the authority to control systems. Information domains are based on the authority to control or access information.

Each information domain is identified uniquely. The unique identification indicates (directly or indirectly) the sensitivity of all the information objects in an information domain. Any security-relevant attributes and attribute values of information objects in an information domain must be the same for all information objects in the information domain. That is, there must be no security-relevant distinction made among the information objects in an information domain.

In the concept of information domain, if a user has access to an object in an information domain, the user will also have access to all objects in that information domain. The users may have different privileges, such as read, write, or delete. Regardless of the privileges, it will apply to all information objects within the domain. For example, some members might have only read permission for information objects in an information domain, while other members might have read and write permissions. Again, because all information objects in an information domain have the same security-relevant attributes and attribute values, users who have read and write permissions in an information domain have those permissions for *every* information object in the information domain (DGSA, 1996).

Table 2.6 is an example of an information domain using a training database. In this example there are four information domains that correspond to the four types of processes: Data Entry, Accept Students, Distribute Materials, and Review Data. In the Data Entry domain, the data entry personnel enter the raw student data. In both the Accept Students and Distribute Materials domains, the course coordinator can analyze and move the raw data into acceptance and then release data for distribution to the students (such as the student receiving notification of acceptance into a class). The manager can read all data and print reports but cannot add new data into the system. A complete IMM would document each of these information domains.

Because information access is an IMM issue, an important element in defining the IMM is to apply the concept of "least privilege." Least privilege

Table 2.6   IMM Table

Information Domain	User	Rules/ Privileges	Process	Information
Data Entry	Data entry personnel	Read/write	Entry	Raw
Accept Students	Course coordinator/ manager	Read/write	Accept	Analyzed
Distribute Materials	Course coordinator	Read/write	Distribute	Releasable/ processed
Review Data	Manager	Read	Review/print reports	Processed

is when users are allowed access to only those processes and information required to do their jobs.

> Least Privilege Concept: 'Security protection is better when only those who need access to information are allowed access.' IATF, p. H-25

The modeling of information management should try to define only those people or jobs that are necessary to accomplish mission/business functions. In many instances, it may be necessary for the ISSEP to review with the customer the necessary access for users. Typically, the customer assigns privileges based on a Concept of Operation (CONOPS) that associates people (users) with their jobs (processes). If users need to perform a specific job duty, then those users need access to the processes that can access that information. An important element of least privilege is to provide the least privileges first and then, based on business needs or need to know, expand those privileges. A least privilege version of the IMM can help eliminate unnecessary access to information and, as we will see later, provide a better baseline for threat analysis.

DCID 6/3

Note to ISSEP candidate. As of the printing of this book this document is considered For Official Use Only; thus, it is not included on the ISSEP study guide requirements. However, if you are working in an environment where this manual is applicable you will need to identify the information and the IMM based on the DCID 6/3 guidance.

The May 2000 DCID 6/3 manual "Protecting Sensitive Compartmented Information within Information Systems" provides policy guidance and requirements for ensuring adequate protection of certain categories of information that is stored or processed on an information system. Similar to the categorization used in FIPS 199, information is rated for confidentiality, integrity, and availability.

Important to this IMM would be the following: the category, classification, and security identifiers for all information on the system; the need-to-know and clearance status of the users; the boundary and interfaces of the system; the environment of the system and interconnecting systems; and the defined security policies and procedures for the system and any interconnecting systems.

So far we have discussed how to identify the processes and the information. The next step is to relate the *users* to these identified processes and information.

Step 3: Identify the Users of the Information and the Process

Once the processes have been identified and the information has been defined, the next step is to add users to the equation. Keep in mind that the division of processes should continue until the sub-processes provide no new subsets of users and their information. The decision of how far down to define the sub-processes must be based on the judgment of the ISSEP and the customer. Providing too much detail may add too much complexity, while not enough detail could miss an important user or function. Later in the process, the ISSEP can consolidate the subsets for clarity and functionality; but in the beginning stages, the ISSEP needs to gain a full understanding of how the current system supports the management of information.

Figure 2.7A is one type of IMM Mapping. In the first set, all users use a specific process to process or store information. The line connections imply that the user employs the process to manage the information. In the figure, Users A use Process 1 to access Information C and may also use Process 2 to access Information C. An example is in the Human Resource (HR) office, where HR personnel use a personnel records application (Process 1) to access Information C and also use a security clearance application (Process 2) to access Information C. In this example, Users B would only have access to the security clearance application to review Information C and not the personnel records application (Process 1).

Another representation of an IMM is to create a table that includes users, rules, process, and information. As shown in Figure 2.7B, the employees can read and write their employee hours using the timekeeping process. The managers can read, write, and approve employee hours using the same timekeeping process.

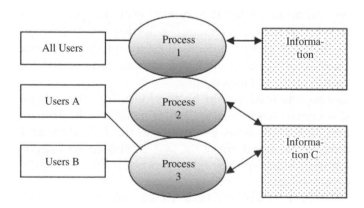

Figure 2.7A   IMM mapping.

Users	Rules	Process	Information
Managers	Read, Write, Approve	Timekeeping	Employee Hours
Employees	Read, Write		

Figure 2.7B   Example of an IMM (based on IATF, H-20).

Because the purpose of the initial draft of an IMM is to collect all information domains, it can be very detailed and extensive. However, when an IMM is completed, at least in initial draft form, the ISSE team and the customer can begin to analyze what is and is not necessary for the system, including the distinction between what is needed and what is wanted. (This is also viewed as the first stage in defining access control and privileges.) The finished product should define the information management to be accomplished by the solution using details such as (1) who are the users and the rules for those users, (2) what does the user intend to do (process), and (3) with what information.

When the customer agrees to the IMM, the ISSEP is ready to begin the next action conducting the threat analysis. In fact, the IMM can also be used as a baseline for threat analysis at the desired level of specificity, and for security services such as identification and authentication, access control, confidentiality, integrity, availability, and non-repudiation.

Task 3: Define the Information Protection Policy (IPP)

Conducting the Threat Analysis and Developing the Information Protection Policy

Although this may seem obvious, the ISSEP must understand and acknowledge in a quantifiable manner that there are threats to the customer's mission/business needs. These threats and their ability to take advantage of vulnerabilities drive the level of protection that is required. The threats may be to the information or information management functions and may have varying levels of damage. In this activity, the ISSEP identifies threats to the information domains and the likelihood of the threat occurring. Documenting this information is the initial step of creating the IPP, which will also contain the required security services (Step 2 of developing the IPP). The IPP becomes part of the Information Management Policy (IMP).

The importance of the IPP becomes clearer during the second phase of the ISSE model when the security requirements are defined. The security requirements are derived based on what is identified in the IPP. The security requirements then become the driving factor for defining the

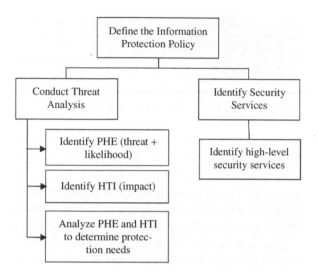

Figure 2.8 Define the information protection policy.

security architecture in Phase 3 of the ISSE model. The security design defined in Phase 4 is ultimately based on what is included in the IPP. Therefore, it is very important for the ISSEP to work with the customer to properly identify the threats, their likelihood, and impact, and document those needs in the IPP. It is the ISSEP's responsibility to help the customer discover the threats and document them in the IPP.

To begin it is necessary to define a process (as shown in Figure 2.8) that the ISSEP can use to identify the protection needs and security services for the IPP. The IATF recommends a three-step process for identifying the protection needs. The first step is to determine the **threat potential and likelihood of the threat to exercise**. Second, assess what **level of harm of impact** would occur if the information was disclosed, modified, or unavailable. Third, based on the likelihood and impact, **determine protection need levels**. Once the protection needs have been identified, the next activity is to assign security services to those needs.

1. *Identify Potentially Harmful Events (PHE)*. PHE identifies the likely potential of the attack occurring to the information. PHE considers the existence of malicious adversaries, their degree of motivation, and the potential for accidents and natural disasters.
2. *Identify Harm to Information (HTI)*. The term "Harm To Information" is shorthand for harm to the mission or business through attacks on the information. HTI considers the value of the information and the degree of harm to the mission if the information

was disclosed, modified, destroyed, or unavailable when needed (IATF, p. 3-7).

3. *Combining PHE and HTI to determine protection.* Analyzing and combining the HTI and PHE for each information domain into a metric to determine a protection level, based on none, low, medium, or high.

Once the PHE, HTI, and protection levels are determined, the second element of the IPP is to identify the security services needed for the identified threats.

A key point for the ISSEP to remember is that while the customer is usually the best source of knowledge for threats, the ISSEP is the best source of expertise on deciding whether the threats are realistic. The ISSEP is also well suited for helping the customer determine the effect of harm to the customer's mission/business.

Potential Harmful Events (PHEs)

To begin, the ISSEP works with the customer to determine the PHEs — that is, the existence of malicious adversaries, their degree of motivation, and the potential for accidents and natural disasters. Based on information management, the customer and the ISSEP begin to analyze what kind of events, either natural or caused by humans (as shown in Figure 2.9), could happen that would harm the information being managed or the processes that interface with that information.

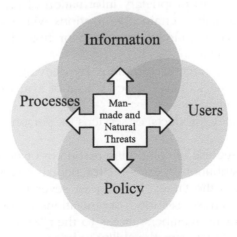

Figure 2.9 Information domains and threats.

Obviously, a harmful event is one that would result in harm to the mission/business. The potential of the event occurring is based on the existence of an adversary, the adversary's motivation, and the adversary's ability. This potential is assessed based on the three CIA security services. The ISSEP determines whether an adversary is capable of disclosing (confidentiality) information, modifying information (integrity), disrupting (availability) access to the information, or modifying authenticity (repudiation) of an electronic transaction. A PHE must also include the probability that natural disasters or accidents will expose, modify, or destroy information and thus cause harm to the mission/business.

To understand the potential of a threat, it is first necessary to be aware of those individuals or events that might threaten the information. Table 2.7 (IATF, p. 4-3) lists several potential adversaries. Adversaries are usually thought of as having malicious intent — that is, they want to harm the system in some manner — through denying confidentiality, integrity, or availability. When defining the PHE for information systems, it is also important to consider the nonmalicious intent, such as careless or untrained employees. The adversaries that apply to each customer depend on the organization and the customer's mission/business objective. For example, almost all USG agencies are targets for hackers. At the same time, only a few USG agencies may be targets for foreign agents.

When identifying an adversary, it is also necessary to evaluate the adversary's motive. Some common reasons why an adversary might want to attack are:

- To gain access to USG classified or sensitive information.
- To gain access to proprietary information of private industry.
- For financial gain. Certain organizations will pay for information, such as USG classified information or financial institution bank account information.
- To disrupt the target's operations by denying access. Some malicious code attacks have caused a loss of availability for extended periods of time.
- To steal money, products, or services for personal or organizational gain.
- To obtain free use of computing resources or networks. For example, the distribution of zombies for denial-of-service attacks.
- To embarrass the target. In the past several years, hackers have tried to embarrass "security" organizations by defacing their Web sites or denying members access to their Web sites.
- To prove that they have the ability to become a hacker. Distribution of malicious code (i.e., viruses) is usually done just to prove that it can be done and to confirm to the hacker underworld that they are true hackers.

Table 2.7   Potential Adversaries

Adversary	Description
Malicious	
Nation states	Well-organized and financed.
	Use foreign service agents to gather classified or critical information from countries viewed as hostile or as having economic, military, or political advantage.
Hackers	A group or individuals (e.g., hackers, phreakers, crackers, trashers, and pirates) who attack networks and systems seeking to exploit the vulnerabilities in operating systems or other flaws.
Terrorists/ cyberterrorists	Individuals or groups operating domestically or internationally who represent various terrorist or extremist groups that use violence or the threat of violence to incite fear with the intention of coercing or intimidating governments or societies into succumbing to their demands.
Organized crime	Coordinated criminal activities, including gambling, racketeering, narcotics trafficking, and many others.
	An organized and well-financed criminal organization.
Other criminal elements	Another facet of the criminal community, but one that is normally not very well organized or financed.
	Usually consists of very few individuals or of one individual acting alone.
International press	Organizations that gather and distribute news, at times illegally, selling their services to both print and entertainment media.
	Involved in gathering information on everything and anyone at any given time.
Industrial competitors	Foreign and domestic corporations operating in a competitive market and often engaged in the illegal gathering of information from competitors or foreign governments through corporate espionage.
Disgruntled employees	Angry, dissatisfied individuals who can inflict harm on the local network or system.
	Can represent an insider threat, depending on the current state of the individual's employment and access to the system.

Table 2.7 (continued)   Potential Adversaries

Adversary	Description
Nonmalicious	
Careless or poorly trained employees	Users, who, through lack of training, lack of concern, or lack of attentiveness, pose a threat to information and information systems.
	This is another example of an insider threat or adversary.

Source: From IATF, p. 4-3.

The IATF considers five classes of attacks: Passive, Active, Close-In, Insider, and Distribution. Tables 2.8 through 2.12 (IATF, pp. 1.12 and 4-6 to 4-10) provide a definition of these five types of attacks.

Table 2.8   Passive Attacks

Passive Attack	Description
	Passive attacks include traffic analysis, monitoring of unprotected communications, decrypting weakly encrypted traffic, and capturing authentication information (e.g., passwords).
	Passive intercept of network operations can give adversaries indications and warnings of impending actions.
	Passive attacks can result in the disclosure of information or data files to an attacker without the consent or knowledge of the user.
	Examples include the disclosure of personal information such as credit card numbers and medical files.
Monitoring plaintext	An attacker monitoring the network could capture user or enclave data that is not otherwise protected from disclosure.
Decrypting weakly encrypted traffic	Cryptanalytic capability is available in the public domain, as witnessed by the June 1997 collaborative breaking of the 56-bit-strength Data Encryption Standard. While the near-term potential for attack on large volumes of traffic is questionable given the number of machines and hours involved, breaking of DES does show the vulnerability of any single transaction.

Table 2.8 (continued)   Passive Attacks

Passive Attack	Description
Password sniffing	This type of attack involves use of protocol analyzers to capture passwords for unauthorized reuse.
Traffic analysis	Observation of external traffic patterns can give critical information to adversaries even without decryption of the underlying information. For example, extension of a network into a tactical theater of operations may indicate the imminence of offensive operations thereby removing the element of surprise.

Source: From IATF, p. 4-6.

Table 2.9   Active Attacks

Active Attack	Description
	Active attacks include attempts to circumvent or break protection features, introduce malicious code, or steal or modify information. These include attacks mounted against a network backbone, exploitation of information in transit, electronic penetrations into an enclave, or attacks on an authorized remote user when attempting to connect to an enclave. Active attacks can result in the disclosure or dissemination of data files, denial of service, or modification of data.
Modifying data in transit	In the financial community, it would be disastrous if electronic transactions could be modified to change the amount of the transaction or redirect the transaction to another account.
Replaying (insertion of data)	Reinsertion of previous messages could delay timely actions. Research shows how the ability to splice messages together can be used to change information in transit.
Session hijacking	This attack involves unauthorized use of an established communications session.
Masquerading as authorized user/server	This attack involves an attacker identifying himself or herself as someone else, thereby gaining unauthorized access to resources and information.

Table 2.9 (continued) Active Attacks

Active Attack	Description
	An attacker first gets user or administrator information by employing sniffers or other means, and then uses that information to log in as an authorized user.
	This class of attack also includes use of rogue servers to obtain sensitive information after establishing what is believed to be a trusted service relationship with the unsuspecting user.
Exploiting system-application and operating system software	An attacker exploits vulnerabilities in software that runs with system privileges.
	New vulnerabilities for various software and hardware platforms are discovered almost daily.
	Attacks, vulnerabilities, and patches are reported through the various computer emergency response alerts and bulletins.
Exploiting host or network trust	An attacker exploits transitive trust by manipulating files that facilitate the provision of services on virtual/remote machines.
	Well-known attacks involve UNIX commands, .rhosts and .rlogin, which facilitate workstations' sharing of files and services across an enterprise network.
Exploiting data execution	An attacker can get the user to execute malicious code by including the code in seemingly innocent software or e-mail for downloading.
	The malicious code might be used to destroy or modify files, especially files that contain privilege parameters or values.
	Well-known attacks have involved PostScript, Active-X, and MS Word macro viruses.
Inserting and exploiting malicious code (Trojan horse, trap door, virus, worm)	An attacker can gain execution access to a user's system commands through one of the vulnerabilities previously identified and use that access to accomplish his or her objectives.
	This could include implanting software to be executed based on the occurrence of some future event.
	Hacker tools are available on the Internet. These tools have turnkey capabilities, including an insertion script, root grabbing, Ethernet sniffing, and track hiding to mask the presence of a hacker.

Table 2.9 (continued) Active Attacks

Active Attack	Description
Exploiting protocols or infrastructure bugs	An attacker exploits weaknesses in protocols to spoof users or reroute traffic.
	Well-known attacks of this type include spoofing domain name servers to gain unauthorized remote login, and bombing using Internet Control Message Protocol (ICMP) to knock a machine off the air.
	Other well-known attacks are source routing to impersonate a trusted host source, Transmission Control Protocol (TCP) sequence guessing to gain access, and TCP splicing to hijack a legitimate connection.
	Malicious code can infiltrate information through a lower-level tunnel within a VPN.
	At least one published article points out potential security concerns revolving around use of IPSec default security mechanisms.
	In addition, the integrity functions of DES in Cipher Block Chaining mode can be circumvented, with the right applications, by splicing of packets.
Denial of service	An attacker has many alternatives in this category, including ICMP bombs to effectively get a router off the network, flooding the network with garbage packets, and flooding mail hubs with junk mail.

Source: IATF, p. 4-6, 4-7.

Table 2.10 Close-In Attacks

Close-In Attack	Description
	Close-in attack is where an unauthorized individual is in physical close proximity to networks, systems, or facilities for the purpose of modifying, gathering, or denying access to information.
	Close proximity is achieved through surreptitious entry, open access, or both.
Modification of data/ information gathering	This results from an individual gaining physical access to the local system and modifying or stealing information, such as, Internet Protocol addresses, log-in ID schemes, and passwords.

Table 2.10 (continued)   Close-In Attacks

Close-In Attack	Description
System tampering	This type of attack results from an individual in close proximity gaining access to and tampering with the system (e.g., bugging, degrading).
Physical destruction	This type of attack results from an individual in close proximity gaining physical access and causing the physical destruction of a local system.

Source: IATF, p. 4-8.

Table 2.11   Insider Attacks

Insider Attack	Description
	Insider attacks can be malicious or nonmalicious. Malicious insiders have the intent to eavesdrop, steal or damage information, use information in a fraudulent manner, or deny access to other authorized users. Nonmalicious attacks typically result from carelessness, lack of knowledge, or intentionally circumventing security for nonmalicious reasons such as to "get the job done."
Malicious	
Modification of data or security mechanisms	Insiders often have access to information due to commonality of shared networks. This access can allow manipulation or destruction of information without authorization.
Establishment of unauthorized network connections	This results when users with physical access to a classified network create an unauthorized connection to a lower classification level or lower sensitivity network. Typically, this connection is in direct violation of the classified network's security policy or user directives and procedures.
Covert channels	Covert channels are unauthorized communication paths used for transferring misappropriated information from the local enclave to a remote site.
Physical damage/ destruction	This is intentional damage to, or destruction of, a local system resulting from the physical access afforded the insider.

Table 2.11 (continued)   Insider Attacks

Insider Attack	Description
Nonmalicious	
Modification of data	This type of attack results when insiders, either through lack of training, lack of concern, or lack of attentiveness, modify or destroy information located on the system.
Physical damage/ destruction	This type of attack is also listed under malicious.
	As a nonmalicious attack, it can result from carelessness on the part of the insider; for example, failure to obey posted guidance and regulations, resulting in accidental damage to or destruction of a system.

Source: IATF, p. 4-9.

Table 2.12   Distribution Attacks

Distribution Attack	Description
	Distribution attacks focus on the malicious modification of hardware or software at the factory or during distribution.
	These attacks can introduce malicious code into a product such as a backdoor to gain unauthorized access to information or a system function at a later date.
Modification of software/ hardware at manufacturer's facility	These attacks can involve modifying of the configuration of software or hardware while it is cycling through the production process.
	Countermeasures for attacks during this phase include rigid integrity controls, including high-assurance configuration control and cryptographic signatures on tested software products.
Modification of software/ hardware during distribution	These attacks can involve modifying of the configuration of software or hardware during its distribution (e.g., embedding of listening devices during shipment).
	Countermeasures for attacks during this phase include use of tamper detection technologies during packaging, use of authorized couriers and approved carriers, and use of blind-buy techniques.

Source: IATF, p. 4-10.

During the threat analysis, the ISSEP works with the customer to understand adversaries and their motivations. Part of this process is to determine the likelihood of adversaries initiating an attack, the adversaries' motivation level, and finally assign a metric category of the threat occurring. The IATF metrics for the PHE are None, Low, Medium, and High. Table 2.13 is an example of how the PHE can be documented.

Table 2.13 Potentially Harmful Events (PHEs)

Information Domain	Disclosure (Confidentiality)	Loss/ Modification (Integrity)	Denial of Service (Availability)	Repudiation
Marketing	Low	Low	Low	None
Sales	Medium	Medium	Low	None

The next step is to determine the Harm to Information (HTI) — that is, the *impact* or degree of harm to the mission if the information was disclosed, modified, destroyed, or unavailable when needed.

Harm to Information (HTI)

When developing the HTI, the ISSEP helps the customer identify the most to least valuable information and the types of harm that would result if it were exploited. The questions to answer include the following: How do the customer and ISSEP determine the value of information? What gives value to information? Answers include the costs associated with replacing destroyed or corrupted data, the disadvantage of losing secrets, any lives that could be lost from disclosure of the information, and the impact of the loss on the organization's reputation. All of these can be considered harmful to the organization.

Figure 2.10 shows a simplified view of how to value information. The question to answer: What is the cost to the organization if the information was disclosed (loss of confidentiality), modified (loss of integrity), or not available (loss of access or service)? The ISSEP then asks the question: would the impact of disclosure to the information domain be none, mild, significant, or serious?

Although there are several metric formulae that can be used, the IATF provides the following metric formula for determining the HTI: None, Mild, Significant, and Serious. This metric would be applied to each information domain. Table 2.14 shows an example of how this metric can be documented. While the HTI identifies the degree or level of harm that

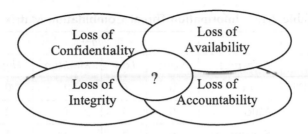

Figure 2.10   Determining information value.

Table 2.14   Harm to Information (HTI)

Information Domain	Disclosure (Confidentiality)	Loss/ Modification (Integrity)	Denial of Service (Availability)	Repudiation
Marketing	Significant	Mild	Mild	None
Sales	Significant	Significant	Significant	None

would occur if a threat was successful in attacking the information, the PHE identifies the likely success level of the attack occurring to the information.

At this point, the **PHE (likelihood of a threat executing)** has been determined as either None, Low, Medium, or High. In addition, the **HTI (impact)** has been determined as either None, Mild, Significant, or Serious.

Each information domain will then have an HTI and a PHE assigned for disclosure, loss/modification, denial of service, and repudiation. The final step is to combine the PHE and HTI to produce a single information protection need metric, such as 0, 1, 2, 3, with 0 representing no threat and 3 denoting the highest information threat. Again, the actual choice of metrics and the method of combining them can be varied. The important thing is that the metrics are understandable and acceptable to the customer. One recommendation for choosing and combining metrics is given in IATF, Appendix H.

Using the IATF approach of combining PHE and HTI to create a two-dimensional matrix as shown in Table 2.15. The row headings contain the HTI metrics (None, Mild, Significant, and Serious) and the column headings contain the PHE metrics (None, Low, Medium, and High). Combining the PHE and HTI produces the **protection needs** on the scale of 0 to 3, with 0 denoting the lowest information threat and 3 denoting the highest information threat.

Table 2.15   Information Threat Combination Matrix

		PHE			
	Measures	*None*	*Low*	*Medium*	*High*
HTI	None	0	0	0	0
	Mild	0	1	1	2
	Significant	0	1	2	3
	Serious	0	2	3	3

It may be helpful to write this out in a formula, such as:

Information Domain: [insert information type or system]
Confidentiality: HTI is _____ PHE is _____ = Protection Need _____
Integrity: HTI is _____ PHE is _____ = Protection Need _____
Availability: HTI is _____ PHE is _____ = Protection Need _____

Before continuing, take a look at the PHE and HTI examples from Tables 2.13 and 2.14 (marketing and sales). When analyzed, the information protection need matrix would look like Figure 2.11 (a combination of several previously defined tables).

For the marketing domain, the written combination is:

- *Disclosure:* HTI is Significant, PHE is Low, and therefore the protection need is 1 or low.
- *Loss/Modification:* HTI is Mild, PHE is Low, and therefore the protection need is 1 or low.
- *Denial of Service (Availability):* HTI is Mild, PHE is Low, and therefore the protection need is 1 or low.
- *Repudiation:* HTI is none, PHE is none, and therefore the protection need is 0 or none.

The information protection need table (Table 2.16) is populated by looking up the value at the intersection of the PHE and HTI. The results are recorded in an information protection need table.

Table 2.16   Information Protection Need (IPN) Table

Information Domain: Corporate (contains Marketing and Sales)			
Disclosure	*Loss/Modification*	*Denial of Service*	*Repudiation*
1 (Mild)	1 (Mild)	1 (Mild)	0 (None)

Harm to Information (HTI)				
Information Domain	Disclosure (Confidentiality)	Loss/Modification (Integrity)	Denial of Service (Availability)	Repudiation
Marketing	Significant	Mild	Mild	None
Sales	Significant	Significant	Significant	None

Potentially Harmful Events (PHE)				
Information Domain	Disclosure (Confidentiality)	Loss/Modification (Integrity)	Denial of Service (Availability)	Repudiation
Marketing	Low	Low	Low	None
Sales	Medium	Medium	Low	None

PHE

HTI	Measures	None	Low	Medium	High
	None	0	0	0	0
	Mild	0	1 | 1	1	2
	Significant	0	1	2	3
	Serious	0	2	3	3

Information Domain: Marketing			
Disclosure	Loss/Modification	Denial of Service	Repudiation
1	1	1	0

Information Domain: Sales			
Disclosure	Loss/Modification	Denial of Service	Repudiation
?	?	?	?

Figure 2.11   Information protection need analysis.

In our example, what would be the highest concerns? At first glance, the highest concerns are a loss of disclosure and modification to the sales information domain. An example of how this could be written in an IPP is:

Marketing

Threats: Marketing information wherein sales people promote products and services to customers and potential customers, assess markets, quote standard pricing, and acquire information about the competition has a low threat by the possibility of information being lost or damaged. The impact of such loss is considered mild, requiring an investment in the rebuilding of the information.

Sales

Threats: Sales information wherein non-standard pricing arrangements are afforded to specific customers, or planning for special sales or agreements is threatened has a medium disclosure threat and a medium threat to loss or damage. The impact of disclosure is significant and the impact of loss or damage is significant.

The ISSEP then documents this information protection needs into an easy-to-read categorization for the customer, especially the decision makers. It is also important for the ISSEP to record the rationale that supports the results and justifies the selected PHE and HTI values.

An important component of presenting the information protection needs to the customer is to make sure that the customer has an opportunity to accept or modify the results. During the presentation, the ISSEP should view the briefing as an opportunity to discover any changes in priorities and to achieve consensus by all parties.

When conducting this type of customer briefing, the ISSEP should keep the following suggestions in mind (IATF, p. H-34):

- Summarize the results when briefing.
- Illustrate unusual highs and lows.
- Explain any other anomalies.
- Present any unresolved issues.
- Receive the reactions and expressed priorities of the decision makers, who now begin to decide what is important.

When presenting the information, the ISSEP should present a coordinated result from the entire ISSE team and any input previously provided by the customer. The focus of the presentation should be on the highest level of concerns. If there were threat levels at the second or third levels, these should be discussed first. It is not to say that a level 1 threat is not important, but it should be discussed after the highest threat levels. Because most presentations will not show all the tables and metrics used to assess the threat levels, the ISSEP should have available the backup material of the specifics to offer to the customer. It may also be appropriate to present any issues that surfaced during the information threat process. The customer will, if appropriate, provide guidance on how to resolve the issues.

Following the ISSEP's presentation, the customer should respond by giving opinions and comments. The ISSEP then records customer reactions to each problem and notes whether the customer agreed or disagreed.

An important part of the presentation is for the ISSEP to manage the customer's reactions and set priorities.

First is managing the customer's reactions. Because the customer's feedback on the threat analysis is very important, the ISSEP must carefully manage the responses. To begin, the ISSEP should assure the customer that results will be amended to reflect their comments and decisions. The ISSEP should be prepared for disagreements. If the customer, especially the decision makers, disagree with the results, the ISSEP must remind the customer that the results reflect the findings of the customer's staff as well as those of the ISSE team. Although the ISSEP makes all efforts to "manage" the customer, if a disagreement cannot be resolved, the ISSEP must make a record of the difference in the final report.

Next is managing the setting of priorities. As the ISSEP is explaining the highest threat levels *and* receiving the feedback, the ISSEP also notes any specific priorities given by the customer. In fact, it may be necessary to ask the client if there are any priorities or to provide suggestions so that priorities can be ascertained.

The final step in presenting the protection needs to the customer is to obtain consensus from the customer. This may not be possible during the first presentation; thus, the ISSEP should be prepared to continue fine-tuning the analysis and circulate the amended results as many times as needed. If appropriate, the customer should formally agree to the information by signing their acceptance.

Once the IMM and the protection needs have been determined, documented, and accepted, the ISSEP completes the IPP by taking the results of the IMM with threats applied and identifying the security services required to counter those threats. Identifying the security services is the next activity necessary for the IPP. When the security services needed to counter the threats have been identified, the information is documented in the Information Protection Policy (IPP). The IPP is a form of a "security policy" that has sufficient detail to be useful when defining solutions. It is included in the IMP, which is the bridging document between the first ISSE activity, Define Information Protection Needs and the second ISSE activity, Define System Security Requirements.

Identifying Security Services for the Information Protection Policy

Following the completion of determining the protection needs, the next activity in completing the IPP is to identify the security services and also the strength needed for the security services. It may appear obvious but the ISSEP must ensure that the security services are based on the identified threats detected in the protection needs analysis. Because the information threats and their levels of concern have been identified, the ISSEP now focuses on the kinds of security services that can be implemented to reduce the vulnerabilities and thus counter the threats.

This section reviews how to identify security services that can counter the identified threats and how to document them in the IPP. The first topic defines security services and the second topic discusses a model for determining what level or strength of security service is needed.

Security Services

Security services are functions needed to protect information from threats. Security services should not be confused with security controls or counter-measures. Security services are high-level security needs, while security controls are the technologies or procedures implemented to meet the security services.

The security services functions are defined as the information protection needs used to set information protection priorities. The IATF guidance incorporates six primary security services areas:

1. Access control
2. Confidentiality
3. Integrity
4. Availability
5. Non-repudiation
6. Security management

In reality, these security services do not exist as separate entities; instead, each interacts with and depends on other services. Although most ISSEP candidates should be familiar with these security services, a brief description is provided for reference.

Access Control

In the realm of network security (we are not concerned with physical access controls in this discussion), access control means limiting access to network resources and data. Access controls are used to prevent unauthorized use of network resources and the unauthorized disclosure or modification of data. This can also include preventing the use of network resources, such as dial-in modems or limiting Internet access.

The elements of access control are (IATF, p. 4-11):

- *Identification and Authentication (I&A):* establishing the identities of entities with some level of assurance (an authenticated identity).
- *Authorization:* determining the access rights of an entity, also with some level of assurance.
- *Decision:* comparing the rights (authorization) of an authenticated identity with the characteristics of a requested action to determine whether the request should be granted.
- *Enforcement:* may involve a single decision to grant or deny, or may entail periodic or continuous enforcement functions (continuous authentication).

Confidentiality

Confidentiality is defined as preventing unauthorized disclosure of data. Confidentiality security services prevent disclosure of data in storage, being processed on a local machine, transiting a local network, or flowing over a public Internet. An aspect of confidentiality is "anonymity," a service that prevents disclosure of information that could lead to the identification of the end user.

The elements of confidentiality are (IATF, p. 4-19):

- *Data protection.* This is prevention of disclosure of the contents of data even if it is accessible (e.g., flowing over a network). This element invokes mechanisms that act directly on the data (or act in response to characteristics of the data) rather than acting in response to an entity's attempt to access data.
- *Data separation.* This traditionally refers to the concept of providing for separate paths (Red/Black or physical) or process separation (computer security [COMPUSEC] techniques, etc.).
- *Traffic flow protection.* Data characteristics include frequency, quantity, destination of traffic flow, etc. Traffic flow protection includes not only characteristics, but also inference information such as command structure and even the instance of communication (e.g., a network communication).

Integrity

Integrity security services are composed of the prevention of unauthorized modification of data, detection and notification of unauthorized modification of data, and recording of all changes to data. Modification includes items such as insertions, deletions, or duplications.

The elements of integrity are:

- *Single data integrity.* To provide integrity of a single data unit that is in transit, the sending entity calculates an additional data item that is bound to the originating data unit. The receiving entity that wishes to verify the integrity of this data unit must recalculate the corresponding quantity and compare it with the transferred value. If the original and receiving entities do not match, the data unit has been modified in transit. Methods for calculating this data item include checksums, cyclic redundancy check (CRC) values, and hashes (also known as message digests).
- *Multiple data integrity.* To provide integrity for a sequence of data units in transit, some type of ordering information must be provided within the communications protocol, such as sequence numbers and timestamps. Encrypting the sequence of data units can also provide integrity; specifically, if a chaining cryptographic algorithm is used in which encryption of each sequence depends on the encryption of all previous sequences.

Availability

Availability is the timely, reliable access to network resources, data, and information services for authorized users. Availability in a networked environment includes not only the user's ability to access network resources, such as hardware and software, but also the user's ability to obtain a desired network bandwidth with reasonable throughput (quality of service). To provide availability, network traffic must be able to traverse local area networks (LANs) and wide area networks (WANs) to reach its intended destination.

The elements of availability are (IATF, p. 4-23):

- *Protection from attack.* Some network-based attacks are designed to destroy, degrade, or "crash" network resources. The solution is to harden these resources against such attacks. Means of doing this include closing security holes in operating systems or network configurations, limiting access to resources to authorized entities, and limiting an adversary's ability to manipulate or view the data flowing through and to those resources (thus preventing insertion of harmful data, such as viruses, or disclosure of sensitive network data, such as routing tables).

- *Protection from unauthorized use.* Availability is also limited if a resource is in use, occupied, or overloaded. If unauthorized users are using limited resources (e.g., processing power, network bandwidth, or modem connections), the resources are not available for authorized users. Identifying and authenticating the users of these resources can provide access controls to limit unauthorized use. However, the process of requesting IA too frequently may be used to slow or stop network operations (i.e., nondelivery notice floods).
- *Resistance to routine failures.* Normal operational failures and acts of nature also contribute to loss of availability. Solutions include use of equipment designed for high reliability, redundancy in equipment, and network connectivity that provides multiple routes.

Non-Repudiation

Repudiation is when one of the entities involved in a communication denies that it participated in that communication — by either denying sending the communication or denying receiving the communication. The non-repudiation security service provides the ability to prove to a third party that either the sending or receiving entity did participate in the communication.

Because users are usually concerned with non-repudiation for application information, such as e-mails or file transfers, the non-repudiation service is primarily provided by application layer protocols. Digital signatures are one method of providing non-repudiation. Public key certificates, verified by a third-party entity, can also be used for non-repudiation.

Security Management

Security management is the pervasive security service needed to support and control the provisions of the other security services. It includes policy implementation and maintenance, security database management, security service management, security mechanism management, security context and association management, and interactions with security infrastructures, such as keys and certificates.

Although an ISSEP may find it necessary to add additional high-level security services to those mentioned, the IATF recognizes these six services as essential to documenting the IPP. Thus, the ISSEP should have a clear understanding of how these security services will be addressed within the context of the previously conducted threat analysis.

To get a complete view of security services, the ISSEP should be aware of NIST SP 800-35 (October 2003), "Guide to Information Technology

Security Services." This document provides assistance with the selection, implementation, and management of IT security services by guiding organizations through the various phases of the IT security services life cycle. The life cycle provides a framework for enabling IT security decision makers to organize their IT security efforts from initiation to closeout. SP 800-35 (NIST SP800-35, p. ii) points out that the systematic management of the IT security services process is of critical importance to organizations. Failure to consider the many issues involved and to manage the organizational risks can seriously impact the organization. IT security decision makers must think about the costs involved and the underlying security requirements, as well as the potential impact of their decisions on the organizational mission, operations, strategic functions, personnel, and service provider arrangements.

SP 800-35 focuses on how organizations should evaluate and select a variety of IT security services from either an internal IT group or an outside vendor to maintain their overall IT security program (i.e., policy development or patch management). You will again see a reference to security services in Chapters 5 and 6, which provide more information on selecting security services/controls. In this chapter, the concern focuses on identifying and documenting the security services needed, not in how to select the best method of implementing the security service. With that in mind, the inclusion of NIST SP 800-35 at this point is to show the NIST model for categorizing security services belonging to one of three categories (NIST SP 800-35, p. 3-1):

1. *Management services:* techniques and concerns normally addressed by management in the organization's computer security program. They focus on managing the computer security program and the risk within the organization.
2. *Operational services:* services focused on controls implemented and executed by people as opposed to systems. They often require technical or specialized expertise and rely on management activities and technical controls.
3. *Technical services:* services focused on the security controls a computer system executes. These services depend on the proper function of the system for effectiveness.

Note that ISSEPs working in the Federal arena are probably aware of these NIST categories. However, it is also important to know the six IATF security service categories. The ISSEP ensure that the IATF security services (i.e., access control, confidentiality, integrity, availability, non-repudiation, and security management) are met and which security controls must be implemented to provide the identified services.

Security Service Strength

Once the security services have been identified, the next question to answer is what level of strength is needed. The scale for strength of the security service is none, minimum, moderate, or strong. One method of determining strength is to first assign the security-service strength to each type of harm. This is shown in Table 2.17 (note that the target column is shown for reference only). For example, an information protection need of 1 would require the strength of the security service to be minimum. Another method is to combine data from the information protection need matrix with the strength matrix as shown in Table 2.18.

Table 2.17   Harm-Security Service-Target Matrix

Type of Harm	Security Service	Target
Unauthorized access	Access control	Any data or system component
Disclosure	Confidentiality	Any data or process
Modification/damage	Integrity	Any data, process, or component
Denial of service/use	Availability	Any data, process, or component
Spoofing/Denial	Non-repudiation	Proof of origin or delivery of data
Unauthorized control	Security management	Security management data

Source: From IATF, p. H-41.

Table 2.18   Map "Information Protection Need" to "Strength"

Information Threat	Strength of Security Service
0	None
1	Minimum
2	Moderate
3	Strong

Source: From IATF, p. H-41.

Table 2.19 Information Threat Data

Quantitative Data	Scale
Potentially Harmful Event (PHE) — a probability	None, Low, Medium, High
Harm To Information (HTI) — impact	None, Mild, Significant, Serious
Information Protection Need — combining PHE and HTI	0, 1, 2, 3 (3 denotes highest information threat)
Strength of Security Service	None, Minimum, Moderate, Strong

For each information domain and for each type of threat, map the information protection need to the security service strength. The scales for HTI, PHE, information protection need, and strength of security service are shown in Table 2.19. Two assumptions to keep in mind are (IATF, p. H-41):

1. Within an information domain, the strength of the security service needed to protect against a type of harm is proportional to the information threat for that type of harm.
2. The strength of Identification & Authentication (I&A) and security management security services must be commensurate with the strongest of the other security services in the information domain.

If we attach this matrix to our previous examples for the marketing and sales information domains, the matrix would look like Table 2.20.

Remember that all this information in its final form will appear in the IPP. An example of how it can be written in the IPP is:

■ Marketing
  – *Security Services.* Marketing information shall be protected for data confidentiality and integrity using a minimum level security service. Controls to ensure availability shall be at a minimum level. There is no current security service needed for non-repudiation.
■ Sales
  – *Security Services.* This sales information requires confidentiality and integrity using a moderate level security service. Availability controls must provide a minimum level of security service. There is no current security service needed for non-repudiation.

As of the date of publication, the IATF authors are working on a "security service robustness strategy" that will provide further guidance

Table 2.20   Data for Information Protection Requirements

Information Domain	Disclosure	Loss/ Modification	Denial of Service	Repudiation
Marketing				
Information protection need	1	1	1	0
Security service	Confidentiality	Integrity	Availability	Non-repudiation
Strength needed	Minimum	Minimum	Minimum	None
Sales				
Information protection need	2	2	1	0
Security service	Confidentiality	Integrity	Availability	Non-repudiation
Strength needed	Moderate	Moderate	Minimum	None

on how to rate the strength of security services. Robustness is defined as the level of security mechanism strength and assurances recommended for an information systems security solution. Although robustness is now included as part of the IATF, it is a relatively new term in the IA field. It is intended to be seen as a unifying successor to a variety of similar existing concepts, such as completeness, assurance, and accreditation.

The robustness strategy is intended to offer security engineering guidance to the developers, integrators, and managers engaged in risk management. "Users of the IATF can employ the robustness strategy to:

■ Help developers and integrators assess what strength of mechanisms, what levels of assurance (in development methodology, evaluation, and testing) and what criteria are recommended for a particular configuration meant to protect information of a particular value; with a specific intelligence life; in a specific, static threat environment.
■ Define product requirements for different customer scenarios (value of information, threat, configuration, etc.), for example, as described in the IATF.

- Provide feedback to security requirement developers, decision makers, customer representatives, customers, etc.
- Constitute developmental requirements when a security solution does not exist.
- Work with academe to foster research in the network security arena and to educate future engineers, architects, and users on network security technology.
- Perform subsequent risk assessments made necessary by reconfiguration of the system or network under review or by a change in threat or value of information" (IATF, p. 4-30).

Note to ISSEP: As of the date of this publication, the robust strategy is still in development, thus it is not included as part of the ISSEP examination. However, for the ISSEP, the IATF Chapter 4 document does provide some useful theories and examples for assessing the strength and assurance of security services and technologies.

Although system security plans will be mentioned throughout the ISSE model, in this first step, the security services selection and specification process are documented in the security plan. During the development process, the security plan may go through various stages; but in the final version, all of the security services and controls, either planned or later included, must be documented in the system plan. Thus, the documentation process for the security plan should be started during this initial ISSE phase. Also, the security plan should include any justification and rationale for the security services and controls selected and how they meet the organization's security requirements. Keep in mind that the security services and controls documented in the security plan provide the foundation for conducting the subsequent security control certification and accreditation.

Some organizations also document the association of specific security requirements to particular security controls. This can be accomplished by using what is referred to as a Requirements Traceability Matrix (RTM). RTMs are discussed in more detail in Chapter 4.

Creating the Information Protection Policy (IPP)

Based on all the previous work of identifying the threats and security services, the ISSEP now concentrates on writing the IPP. Have you ever read an Inspector General or other formal audit report? If so, have you seen the following statement? "There were several security matters that should be addressed.... The Department's information protection policies and procedures are not consolidated in one formal document." The IPP is the answer to that statement; it provides a formal documented plan that defines the protection policies for an organization's information. The IPP is a formal, authoritative document that serves as a commitment by the customer to the security functions that are required to protect the customer's information and meet the mission/business needs.

Once the security services have been associated with the results of the protection need analysis, the ISSEP begins to create (and thus document) the IPP. The IPP is the output that defines the information protection needs for the development and security life cycles of an information protection solution. The IPP reflects these items:

- Information management policy based on an information management model
- Threats to information and likelihood of threat occurring
- Impact to information and mission if the threat was executed
- Prioritized security services required to counter information management threats

Although the IATF calls the document "the IPP," the title or name of this document does not matter. What is important is whether the document contains the information necessary to help the ISSEPs, SEs, and architects satisfy the customer's protection needs.

Creating the IPP Document

A basic outline of the IPP includes an introduction, general policies, establishing roles and responsibilities, identifying the decision makers, defining Certification and Accreditation (C&A) team members and procedures, identifying information domains and information management, identifying security service requirements, and signatures.

Introduction

Security policies can have a wide range of definitions and purposes. Stating the purpose of the IPP in the document is a good way to distinguish it from other policies. As a reminder, policy should not define how something is to be accomplished; it should document only what is to be accomplished. For example, the purpose of the *information protection policy* is to document the security services required to counter the identified threats to the identified information domains.

General Policies

Identify existing policies, regulations, and procedures. Before writing the IPP, the ISSEP should have done background research to discover and understand the structure and content of existing policy. As applicable, transfer any current policies, regulations, or procedures as possible design constraints. When a mechanism, such as a password policy, is identified in the existing documentation, record the fact for later analysis.

Establish Roles and Responsibilities

Because most customers will already have existing roles and responsibilities defined, the ISSEP needs to discover who exists in the role and how responsibilities are performed. This is then documented in the IPP. For example, the role might be a security officer who is responsible for verifying security clearances for physical access to the building and may also have the responsibility for verifying security clearances for access to the system.

The IPP also identifies individuals who will serve as the security evaluators, certifiers, and accreditors and their responsibilities. A helpful item in this section is to suggest a security administration staff hierarchy, including specific staff responsibilities. The ISSEP can use the IPP to help the customer define a complete administrative staff for life-cycle support that is consistent with specific customer functions. A final role to define is who will be responsible for updates or changes to the IPP.

Identify Decision Makers

Identify decision makers and involve them and their staff members in the IPP process. The signatures on the IPP should be those of the authoritative decision makers; thus they should be identified in the policy. Examples of decision makers in a corporate environment may be the Chief Operating Officer, Chief Security Officer, or Chief Executive Officer; in the DoD environment, the Designated Approving Authority (DAA) is a decision maker; and in the Federal sector, the Chief Information Officer (usually the DAA as well) or the Chief Information Security Officer (CISO) is the decision maker.

Define Certification and Accreditation (C&A) Team Members and Procedures

If a major modification or a new system will be developed, it will need to go through the C&A process. The IPP can help the C&A process by defining the C&A team members, such as the accreditor, evaluator, and certifier. It may also be necessary to identify any specific C&A processes that the system will need to follow, such as the Defense Information Technology Security C&A Process (DITSCAP) or the National Information Assurance C&A Process (NIACAP) (both DITSCAP and NIACAP are discussed further in Chapter 8).

Identify Information Domains and Information Management

The information outlined in the IMM should be summarized and documented in the IPP. This provides a basic outline of the users, roles, processes, information management, and security policies needing the IPP. An example of a documented information domain might look like the following:

Information Domain: Marketing

Marketing personnel, sales personnel, and sales managers maintain product catalogs and price information available to the general public as potential customers. The accessibility of this information is both desirable (as advertising to potential customers) and threatening (malicious intent could occur). Care must be taken to provide adequate separation for the protection of other domains. The access rules indicate that unidentified users can view this information but any authenticated marketing personnel, sales personnel, or the sales managers can prepare it.

Information Domain: Sales

The sales personnel and sales manager maintain statistics on a per-customer basis that will indicate sales performance. This information is only available to authorized direct-hire personnel. The access rules indicate that sales personnel and the sales manager will have read and write access.

Identify Security Service Requirements

The information identified in the security services activity should be documented. This could include the six main security services: access control, confidentiality, integrity, availability, non-repudiation, and security management. An example of how this would be documented in the IPP is:

Marketing

Threats: Marketing information wherein sales people promote products and services to customers and potential customers, assess markets, quote standard pricing, and acquire information about the competition has a low threat by the possibility of information being lost or damaged. The impact of such loss is considered mild, requiring an investment in the rebuilding of the information.

Security Services: Marketing information shall be protected for data confidentiality and integrity using a minimum level security service. Controls to ensure availability shall be at a minimum level. There is no current security service needed for non-repudiation.

Sales

Threats: Sales information wherein nonstandard pricing arrangements are afforded to specific customers, or planning for special sales or agreements is threatened has a medium disclosure threat and a medium threat to loss or damage. The impact of disclosure is significant and of loss or damage is significant.

Security Services: This sales information requires confidentiality and integrity using a moderate level security service. Availability controls must provide a minimum level of security service. There is no current security service needed for non-repudiation.

Signatures

A "signature of authority page" should be included. The customer needs to understand that the IPP represents the rules according to the customer's mission/business needs. The ISSEP has simply worked with the customer to provide expertise and guidance on developing an IPP for the customer. Thus, the decision-makers' signatures are evidence of approval for the IPP.

An IPP should establish both broad general policies and the daily internal controls, procedures, and practices that the organization must implement to protect the information processing environment against the risks identified in the threat analysis. The most effective plans are documented in easy-to-understand language, are comprehensive, and cover all aspects of the information processing environment. Also, to be effective, the IPP must be reviewed and updated periodically.

The final activity is to put all of the previous activities and documents into the master document, the Information Management Plan (IMP).

The Information Management Plan (IMP)

The IMP is a comprehensive document describing how an organization manages data and information to support the mission. The identified mission need, IMM, and IPP are part of the final IMP.

This IMP should describe the organization's current approach and implementation of data and information management for a specific system. The IMP is intended to provide information for the implementation and maintenance of a system that serves the mission/business needs. This would include existing capabilities and upcoming design and development enhancements. It should contain a technical and project management approach that has been chosen to support this purpose and fulfill the organization's evolving information management needs. Topic items include:

- How the IMP will support program objectives
- How information is made available to users
- Requirements and priorities of data users
- Guidelines for the originators of information
- Functional and system requirements (defined in ISSE model, Step 2)
- System security requirements (defined in ISSE model, Step 2)
- Project management issues for ensuring the effectiveness of the system
- Activities needed for maintaining and enhancing the system over a specific time period

In summary, the IMP details the activities that the ISSEP will use to ensure that the information associated to the system (or components) is managed as a mission/business asset and is in accordance with existing legislation, regulations, policies, and procedures. It describes how customer information needs will be identified, and how information will be generated, processed, stored, or used in any manner related to the system or components. In addition, it describes how access to information, privacy, confidentiality, and security requirements, as well as other life-cycle management of information considerations, will be taken into account in the project life cycle.

Final Deliverable of Step 1

The final outcome or "deliverable" is the Information Management Plan (IMP), which contains the (1) Mission Need; (2) the Information Management, which used an Information Management Model (IMM) to define the users, roles, processes, information, and security policies; and, (3) the Information Protection Policy (IPP), which identified the threats and security services.

Summary

Throughout this chapter, the focus has been on defining the customer's true mission/business needs and the information needed to support that mission. The ISSEP is responsible for presenting the process to the customer. This includes defining the information management, identifying the threats and security services, and determining the threats' and security services' relative strengths and priorities.

The final outcome of this first ISSE activity — *discover information protection needs* — is to have a well-defined and documented Information Management Plan (IMP). The first assignment was to discover and develop an understanding of the customer's mission or business. Next was working with the customer to determine what information management is needed to support the mission or business needs. As part of this process, the ISSEP, in concurrence with the customer, used an Information Management Model (IMM) to help identify the users, processes, information, and security policies (i.e., the information domain).

Once the mission needs had been identified and the information needs for that mission had been defined and documented in the IMM, the next activity was to conduct a preliminary threat analysis to define the threats. The threat analysis is the basis for creating the Information Protection Policy (IPP). The IPP takes the information from the threat analysis and adds the security services necessary to protect the information.

The IPP provides customer's with their information management and protection needs — information that is the foundation for further ISSE development efforts. The IPP provides a detailed description of the first and perhaps the most important activity of the ISSE process. It provides an opportunity for the customer to become involved in discovering, defining, and documenting the protection needs of their own information.

The results of the IMM and the IPP are coordinated and documented into the IMP. The IMP becomes the basis for defining information systems that will meet the customer's specific mission/business needs. The various procedures, from approaching the customer to documenting the IMP, provide a solid foundation for the next ISSE activity, Defining System Security Requirements, where the system's security context, concept, and requirements are defined.

References

IAEC3186 (February 2002). "Introduction to Information Systems Security Engineering," ISSE Training, student guide.

Information Assurance Technical Framework (IATF), Version 3.1 (September 2002). National Security Agency, Information Assurance Solutions, Technical Directors; Fort Meade, MD.

Blanchard, Benjamin S. and Wolter J. Fabrycky (1998). *Systems Engineering and Analysis*, 3rd edition, Prentice Hall: Upper Saddle River, NJ.

DCID 6/3 (June 1999). Protecting Sensitive Compartmented Information Within Information Systems. *For Official Use Only.*

DoD Directive No. 8500.1 (October 2002). Information Assurance. (Certified Current as of November 21, 2003.) Available from www.dtic.mil/whs/directives.

DoD Directive No. 8500.2 (February 2003). Information Assurance Implementation. Available from www.dtic.mil/whs/directives.

DoD Technical Architecture Framework for Information Management, Volume 6: Department of Defense (DoD) Goal Security Architecture, Version 3.0 (30 April 1996). Available for download from http://www-library. itsi.disa.mil/tafim/tafim3.0/pages/volume6/v6_toc.htm.

FIPS 199 (February 2004). Standards for Security Categorization of Federal Information and Information Systems. Available at the NIST Web site: www.nist.gov.

IEEE Std 1220-1998 (December 1998, copyrighted January 1999). IEEE Standard for Application and Management of the Systems Engineering Process. IEEE: New York, NY. (Revision of IEEE Std 1220-1994.)

Information Systems Security Handbook, Release 1.0 (February 28, 1994). National Security Agency, Central Security Service. Only available for official USG use.

MIL-STD-499A and MIL-STD 499B, U.S. Department of Defense Systems Engineering Standards (May 1974 and May 1991).

Office of Management and Budget's Federal Enterprise Architecture Program, Management Office publication (June 2003).The Business Reference Model Version 2.0. Available at the Federal Enterprise Architecture Web site: http://www.feapmo.gov/resources/fea_brm_release_document_rev_2.pdf.

NIST SP 800-35, Guide to Information Technology Security Services (October 2003). Available at the NIST Web site: www.nist.gov.

SP 800-53, Recommended Security Controls for Federal Information Systems" (February 2005). Available at the NIST Web site: www.nist.gov.

NIST SP 800-59, Guideline for Identifying an Information System as a National Security System (August 2003). Available at the NIST Web site: www.nist.gov.

NIST SP 800-60 Version 2.0, Volume 1: Guide for Mapping Types of Information and Information Systems to Security Categories (June 2004). Available at the NIST Web site: www.nist.gov.

NIST SP 800-60 Version 2.0, Volume 2: Appendixes to Guide for Mapping Types of Information and Information Systems to Security Categories (June 2004). Available at the NIST Web site: www.nist.gov.

Sage, Andrew P. and James E. Armstrong (1999). *Introduction to Systems Engineering: Methods and Technologies for the Engineering of Trustworthy Systems.* John Wiley & Sons, Custom Textbook: New York.

Taylor, Stephen (1996). BPR Is Legacy of Pentagon's Troubled CIM Program. © Copyright 1996 Enterprise Reengineering. Available at: http://www.reengineering.com/articles/sept96/CIMstory.htm.

3

ISSE Model Phase 2: Define System Security Requirements

Introduction

The phases in the Information Systems Security Engineering (ISSE) life-cycle model are:

1. Discover Information Protection Needs. Ascertain why the system needs to be built and what information needs to be protected.
2. **Define System Security Requirements. Define the system in terms of what security is needed.**
3. Define System Security Architecture. Define the security functions needed to meet the specific security requirements.
4. Develop Detailed Security Design. Based on the security architecture, design the security functions and features for the system.
5. Implement System Security. Following the documented security design, build and implement the security functions and features for the system.
6. Assess Security Effectiveness. Assess the degree to which the security of the system, as it is defined, designed, and implemented, meets the security needs.

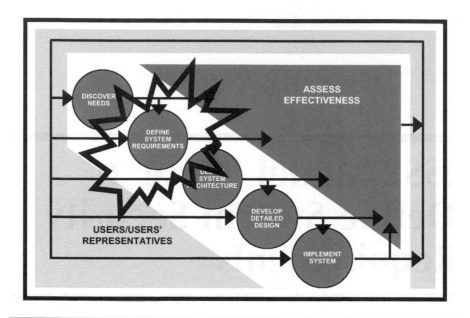

Figure 3.1　ISSE model: Define security requirements. (*Source:* Adapted from IATF, p. 3-2.)

In this chapter, the focus is on Phase 2 of the ISSE model: Defining System Security Requirements (Figure 3.1). This activity expands on Phase 1, Discovering Information Protection Needs, by specifically establishing a context for the target system. The activities provide an end result that is an **abstract** view of the functional security aspects of the system. This view is for system engineers and architects so they will know what is intended for the design of the system in Step 3, Defining the System Security Architecture.

Before beginning, take a minute to think about how you would answer the following question:

What is so important about defining requirements?

According to an article entitled "Software's Chronic Crisis" by W. Wayt Gibbs (1994), there is a very real problem with large software developments projects. The article states that:

- Out of every eight large systems development efforts started, two will be canceled; and 75 percent of those delivered will have operating failures (system does not function as intended or is not used at all).

- The average software development project takes 50 percent longer than planned.
- An IBM survey of 24 leading software companies revealed that 55 percent of projects cost more than expected, 68 percent overran their schedules, and 88 percent require substantial revisions.

The reasons why these failures exist can be attributed to the following risks (Department of Energy Requirements Management Awareness, not dated, p. 2):

- Starting projects with no or poor requirement specifications
- Changing requirements midstream
- Adding requirements without conducting a risk analysis to determine impact on project plans
- Adding and changing requirements without re-estimating the cost of the project
- Lack of requirements configuration management

System requirements are not rigid and set. The important element is that the system requirements address all functions the system is expected to perform so that risks can be avoided. A good requirements document can be the critical element that provides the integrity of the system and the customer a product that has the right functionality to meet the mission and business needs.

Defining system security requirements is equivalent to the Systems Engineering (SE) activity, Define System Requirements. In the SE process, the system is defined in terms of functional characteristics and operational concepts. The requirements phase describes what the system will be able to do and the system functions that should be allocated to the target system or external or existing systems. Note that some of the mission or business functions are allocated to the system, while others are allocated to external or existing systems. This is the essential difference between mission and business requirements and system requirements. The same is true for information protection requirements, which are a subset of all the requirements.

In the ISSE process, the Information Systems Security Engineering Professional (ISSEP®) identifies one or more solution sets that can meet the information protection needs expressed by the customer and documented in the Information Management Plan (IMP). The ISSEP allocates mission or business information management needs to the solution sets. The solution sets include the target system and external or existing systems. McAllister (2003) depicts this process in Figure 3.2. What is important is the focus of defining the requirements based not only on the target system,

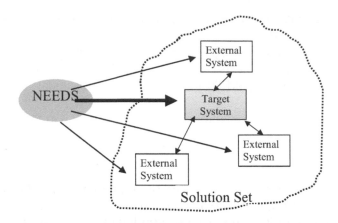

Figure 3.2 Needs to solutions sets. (*Source:* Adapted from McAllister, 2003.)

but also interconnections to other external outside systems or legacy systems.

The inputs needed for this phase include the customer's defined IMP, which are derived from the Information Management Model (IMM) and the Information Protection Policy (IPP). The IMM is the source document describing the customer's needs based on identifying users, processes, and information. The IPP contains the threats to the information management and the security services and controls needed to counter those threats. The IPP is the source document that will be most useful for the ISSE when defining the needed security functionality.

At the end of the phase, the ISSE outputs will be a definition of the solution set that includes a System Security Concept for the target system. As this point, the solution set includes a description of the information management operations and the information protection needs from Phase 1. As shown in Figure 3.3, the System Security Concept includes the following documents: the System Security Context, System Security Requirements (what the system security is to accomplish), and the Preliminary System Security Concept of Operations (CONOPS).

A system CONOPS (or a system security CONOPS) is a narrative discussion of how a system is intended to operate. It is written from a user perspective and captures all aspects of the system operation. It should include both short- and long-term goals and objectives. A successful CONOPS is one that can be used to quickly provide a comprehensive overview of all system goals and operational concepts.

Chapter 1 discussed the concepts of the problem set and the solution set. As we define the system security requirements, it is important to

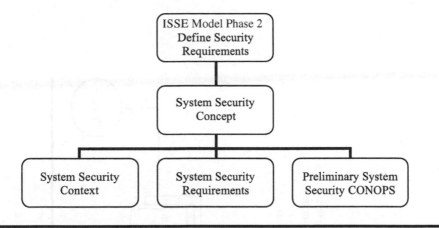

Figure 3.3 System security concept elements.

realize that there may be more than one system in the solution set, and each and every need is either allocated to one of the systems or other external or existing systems prior to deciding that the need will not be satisfied. If the decision is made that the need cannot be met, this should be documented, coordinated, and agreed to by the customer.

McAllister (2003) notes that when defining the needs for a target system within the context of a solution set, the ISSE should define the:

■ Responsibilities of the target system
■ Responsibilities of existing or external systems
■ Relationships between target and external systems

The major focus of this phase is to define what security will be required for the entire system, including items such as the security functions it needs to perform and whether it will need to interact with other systems in the solution set. An example of an external system is public key infrastructure. While the systems engineer is defining the system requirements, the ISSEP must be involved and working alongside the SE to provide the security input.

This chapter begins by briefly explaining the SE activity associated with defining system requirements. An outline of the major activities and theories discussed in this chapter are shown in Figure 3.4. Although we have separated the material into system requirements followed by system security requirements, the activities and concepts are similar. When looking at the requirements development through the lens of the ISSEP, the focus is on including security in the process.

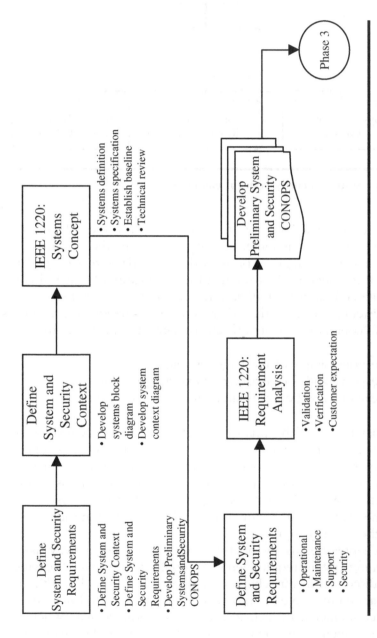

Figure 3.4 Define system and security requirements.

When defining the SE system requirements, the first step is to begin the tasks involved in documenting the System Context and the Preliminary System CONOPS. The Preliminary System CONOPS and the System Context identify the system environment and the allocation of system functions for that environment. It also includes a preliminary look at the operational aspects of the proposed system. The system requirements define what the system is to accomplish. The second section explains the ISSE activity, defining system security requirements. The security component must be included in this design phase, so the ISSEP is responsible for defining the system *security* context, the *security* CONOPS, and the *security* requirements.

Systems Engineering Activity: Defining System Requirements

The objective of defining the system requirements activity is to establish the definition of the system with a focus on system elements required to meet the operational requirements. The activities are based on the identified need and lead to the definition of a system in functional terms. The process is evolutionary in nature, beginning with this activity that defines the system level. In the architecture phase, the definition will include the subsystem level, major components, and interfaces with other systems. The set of requirements at this point are allocated to the system(s) as a whole. The goal is to describe **the system requirements** at a broad level of the system hierarchy (not how the system requirements will operate).

This section is divided into three topics. As shown in Figure 3.5, the System Context is the first topic, which includes models that can be helpful in defining the system context. The second topic discusses the System Requirements, and the final topic explores the Preliminary System CONOPS.

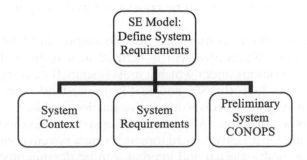

Figure 3.5 SE model system requirements.

Defining the System Context

Systems are complex and can be difficult to describe. Remember that systems are defined as a combination of elements or components that form a complex or unitary whole. The system context is the result of SEs (and ISSEPs) translating the requirements into system parameters and possible measurement concepts that meet the defined requirements. An example of a system context is the DoD Net-Centric Data Strategy discussed in Chapter 1.

How does one describe a system so that it can be understood by others? There are several models that can be helpful in communicating a system's structure and behavior.

The first and probably most simple is the block diagram, as shown in Figure 3.6. The main purpose of the block diagram is to structure the system requirements into functional terms. However, in this early stage of defining the system, the block diagram identifies the major system level (or top-level) requirements that need to be performed by the system to accomplish its mission. In the architecture phase, these system requirements will be analyzed and written as system functions. The functional blocks can then be decomposed into a hierarchical block diagram, typically called a Functional Flow Block Diagram (FFBD). What is key at this level of the process is identifying the system requirements in an easy to manage form. A flow block diagram is just an example of how it can be accomplished. Note that the characteristics of how a system, subsystem, and its components are modeled using FFBD is discussed in Chapter 4, "Defining System Security Architecture."

Another type of SE model is the system context diagram shown in Figure 3.7. This diagram represents all external entities the system may interact or interface with, whether directly or indirectly. The diagram pictures the system at the center, with no details of its subsystem or components, but is surrounded by all interfacing systems or environments. The goal of a system context diagram is to bring attention to external factors and systems that should be considered in the requirements/design of the system.

Defining the system context can also be helpful in formulating operational scenarios. When a system is defined in a manner that indicates the different conditions under which it must operate (i.e., using operational scenarios), it can help the SEs and ISSEPs understand more about what the system is required to do to meet the mission needs.

Using a block diagram, the system, its subsystems, and its components can be identified in an easy to read format. Using a system context diagram, the interfaces, both external and internal, can be documented. If working in the DoD environment, the ISSEP must define the system context in

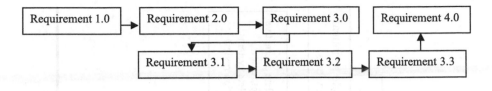

Figure 3.6   System requirements flow block diagram.

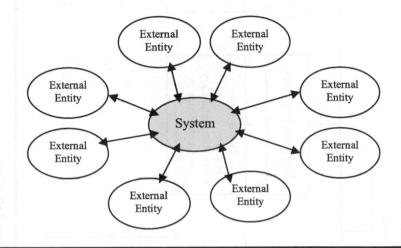

Figure 3.7   System context diagram.

terms of the local computing environment, enclave boundary, network and infrastructure, and the supporting infrastructures. In the next topic we look at how to define the system requirements.

Note: For the ISSEP candidate, the following information on IEEE 1220 is for background purposes only. It is included for those not well versed on SE principles and because the IEEE standard can be helpful in gaining another SE perspective on defining the system context.

IEEE 1220: 5.1.1.1 System Concept

The system concept is one element of the system definition activities, which are shown in Figure 3.8. IEEE 1220 explains the system concept as "For precedented system developments, with incrementally improved or evolutionary growth products, the enterprise should refine established system definitions and product-line strategies to satisfy the market opportunity or customer order. For unprecedented systems where the concept is not already defined, the enterprise should create and evaluate candidate alternative concepts that would satisfy a market opportunity or customer

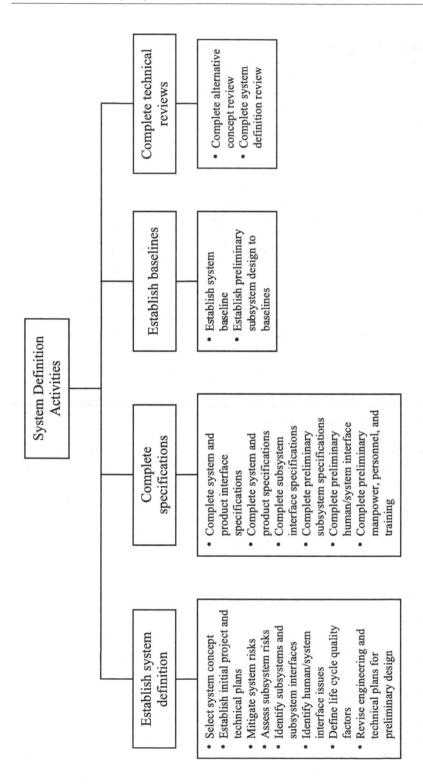

Figure 3.8 System definition activities (based on information from IEEE 1220).

order" (pp. 18–19). Important to this definition is the connection of business needs (e.g., market opportunity or customer order) for defining the system concept.

During this phase of the process, one or more of the alternate system concepts should be selected for further system definition. When considering the different concepts, the SE identifies and assesses the risks associated with each alternative system concept. If appropriate, the SE may also complete preliminary system and product specifications and interface specifications for each viable alternative.

Define System Requirements

Regardless of the type of system development, the project began because of a business or mission need. This need is decomposed into requirements. The goal of the project is to design, develop, and implement those requirements to meet the business or mission needs. SEs should track the requirements throughout the life cycle of the project; this is called requirements management. At each stage of the process, the requirements are checked and modified to make sure the project is meeting its intended goals.

According to DoE (2000) "Guidelines for Requirements Management," some best practices for requirements management include:

- "The project team understands and follows an appropriate life cycle.
- Customers, users, and all important stakeholders are involved.
- Good communication occurs during the process of deriving requirements.
- Difficulties that stem from the inherent complexity of the product or the computing environment are addressed early on.
- A prototype or early version of the software system in addition to a specification document is developed so that requirements can be better defined before they are baselined. (*Note:* These should be considered as tools for conducting requirements analysis and should not serve as the design; i.e., they simulate but do not actually perform the operations.)
- A list of requirements is maintained in a database where they are more easily managed.
- A requirements configuration management process is implemented.
- Requirements are not added or changed without (1) conducting a risk analysis to determine impact on project plans, and (2) re-estimating the cost and schedule of the project.
- Some operational capabilities are delivered during the development process with the intention to add the remaining or new requirements" (p. 11).

In this topic, we look at two models of defining system requirements. Although the first model is more academic in nature, it includes several key points that are pertinent to the SE model of defining system requirements. The second model is from the IEEE 1220 Systems Engineering Standard and provides another viewpoint of defining requirements.

Note to ISSEP candidate: It is unlikely that exam questions will focus on these theoretical models. Those with an academic SE background should recognize these concepts as they are germane to the field. They are included in this chapter to provide background information, especially because many of the terms are common in subsequent SE and ISSE activities.

The first approach by Blanchard and Fabrycky (1998) defines two types of system requirements: (1) Operational Requirements and (2) Maintenance and Support Requirements. Operational Requirements include the following:

- *Operational distribution or deployment.* The number of customer sites where the system will be used, the geographic distribution and deployment schedule, and the type and number of system components at each location.
- *Mission profile or scenario.* Identification of the prime mission for the system, and its alternate or secondary mission. What is the system to accomplish and what functions must be performed in responding to the need? This can be defined through a series of operational profiles, illustrating the dynamic aspects required in accomplishing a mission.
- *Performance and related parameters.* Definition of the basic operating characteristics or functions of the system. This refers to parameters, such as range, accuracy, rate, capacity, throughput, power output, size, and weight. What are the critical system performance parameters needed to accomplish the mission at the various sites? How do these parameters relate to the mission profile(s)?
- *Utilization requirements.* Anticipated usage of the system and its components in accomplishing the mission. This refers to hours of equipment operation per day, on-off cycles per month, etc.
- *Effectiveness requirements.* System requirements to include cost/system effectiveness, operational availability, dependability, reliability mean time between failure (MTBF), failure rate, readiness rate, maintenance downtime (MDT), mean time between maintenance (MTBM), facility use, personnel quantities and skills levels, etc. Given that the system will perform, how effective or efficient must it be?
- *Operations life cycle (horizon).* The anticipated time duration that the system will be operational. How long will the system be in

use by the customer? Although this may change, a baseline must be established at the beginning.

■ *Environment.* Definition of the environment in which the system is expected to operate in an effective manner. Examples are temperature, shock and vibration, noise, humidity, arctic or tropics, etc. To what will the system be subjected during its operational use and how long? (p. 50–52)

Identifying the Maintenance and Support Requirements is an integral aspect of SE. The maintenance concept evolves from the definition of system operational requirements and defines the follow-on requirements for system support based on the results of the supportability or logistic support analysis or its equivalent.

The maintenance concept evolves into a detailed maintenance plan. The system Maintenance and Support Requirements include the following (Blanchard and Fabrycky, 1998, p. 53–57):

■ *Levels of maintenance.* Corrective and preventive maintenance may be accomplished on a system itself at the site where the system is being used, in an intermediate shop near the customer site, or at a manufacturer's plant facility. Maintenance level pertains to the division of functions and tasks for each area where maintenance is performed. Anticipate frequency of maintenance, task complexity, personnel skill-level requirements, special facility needs, etc.

■ *Repair policies.* Within the constraints, there may be several possible policies specifying the extent to which repair of a system component will be accomplished.

■ *Organizational responsibilities.* The accomplishment of maintenance may be the responsibility of the customer, the producer, a third party, or a combination thereof.

■ *Logistic support elements.* As part of the definition of the initial maintenance concept, criteria must be established relating to the various elements of logistic support. These elements include supply support, test and support equipment, personnel and training, transportation and handling equipment, facilities, data, and computer resources.

■ *Effectiveness requirements.* This constitutes the effectiveness factors associated with the support capability. The effectiveness requirements applicable to the support capability must complement the requirements for the overall system.

■ *Environment.* This refers to the definition of the environment as it pertains to maintenance and support.

The second model is from IEEE 1220. Figure 3.9 shows the activities associated with determining system requirements — each item must be defined in order to create the requirements baseline. A brief overview of each step is also provided. Because the ISSEP will be working directly with the SE, the ISSEP should be aware of these concepts so he or she has an understanding of what the SE is identifying and documenting.

Define Customer Expectations (Task 6.1.1)

If available from the customer, several documents such as functional or design verification can feed into the requirements analysis. Defining the customer expectations is one of the first activities. During this activity, the system engineer helps the customer to define what type of system product is required, the life-cycle processes, and the desired level of effort necessary to accomplish the functional requirements. This also includes having the customer identify the performance requirements for each function. An aspect of the customer expectations is the costs involved, such as financial, schedule, and technology costs. One of the responsibilities of the system engineer is to help the customer analyze their requirements in a realistic manner.

Define Constraints (Tasks 6.1.2 and 6.1.3)

Because constraints, whether they are project, enterprise, or external, can impact the design or acquisition solutions, it is important to identify the constraints in these beginning steps. Project constraints include the resource allocations to the project and any externally imposed deliverable time frames. For example, customers may have quality management constraints that will dictate how the projects can operate. Enterprise constraints include any organizational policies, procedures, standards, or guidelines that govern system development and procurement. It may also include specific metrics or documentation procedures. External constraints include national and international laws and regulations, compliance with industry-wide standards, as well as ethical and legal considerations. Other constraints might include:

- Management decisions
- Enterprise specifications, standards, or guidelines
- Established life-cycle process capabilities
- Financial and human resource allocations to the technical effort and training needed for personnel
- Competitor product capabilities

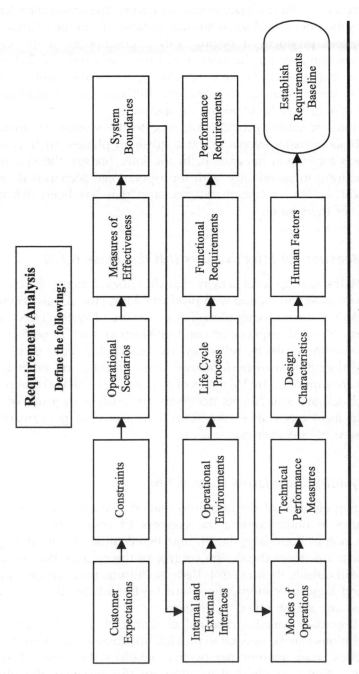

Figure 3.9   Requirement analysis steps (based on information from IEEE 1220).

Define Operational Scenarios (Task 6.1.4)

In the next step, defining operational scenarios, the customer identifies and defines the operational scenarios that indicate the range of anticipated uses of system products. It begins with a description of the general operating environment for the system and the environmental factors that may have an impact on the system. Specific operational scenarios are then described in users' language to depict the full range of circumstances in which the system may be expected to operate.

Operational scenarios provide guidance to the system designers and form the basis of major events in the acquisition phases, such as testing the products for system integration. In the later phases, the system will need to perform in accordance with the operational scenarios described at this point — not an operational scenario that has been defined or adapted to fit the system.

Define Measures of Effectiveness (MOEs) (Task 6.1.5)

Defining MOEs is a top-level activity that describes a metric the customer will use to measure satisfaction with products during the acquisition phase. To define MOEs, the customer identifies a measure of system effectiveness that will reflect overall expectations and satisfaction, such as performance, safety, operability, usability, reliability, maintainability, ease of use, cost to train, workload, human performance requirements, and other factors. The MOEs are supported by Measures of Performance (MOPs) that provide lower-level design requirements necessary to satisfy a measure of effectiveness. In most cases, there are several measures of performance for each measure of effectiveness.

Define System Boundaries (Task 6.1.6)

A challenging element of defining information domains and information infrastructures is understanding the concept of system boundaries. To define the system boundary, the SE and ISSEP must identify the system elements that are under the design control of the organization as well as those that fall outside their control. Because information can exist in both physical and logical locations, there can be boundaries that encompass both or just one specific type of location.

If the boundary contains external elements, then a different set of security solutions may be needed to provide adequate protections. Looking at boundaries from another perspective involves the issue of several boundaries within one physical location. In this instance, the physical location might be considered a boundary that includes logical boundaries associated with different levels of information. Although there can be many different scenarios, the ISSEP must make an effort to understand and define the security boundary for the system.

For example, a Federal agency (Figure 3.10) has main headquarters in Washington, D.C., but also interfaces with field offices throughout the United States. How would you define the boundary? Would you consider each physical location a boundary? Would the information processed in one field office need to be available to another field office? What type of security requirements would be needed between the field offices? Between headquarters and the field office? What would drive the boundary decision?

Define Interfaces (Task 6.1.7)

Defining the functional and design interfaces includes the external and higher-level systems, platforms, humans, and products in quantitative terms. Interfaces with existing or future external systems need to be defined as they may place requirements on the system. In some cases, the success of the system is based on its ability to interface with external or current fielded systems.

Define Utilization Environments (Task 6.1.8)

The identification of the environments that will be utilized ties in with defining operational scenarios. All environmental factors that might affect system performance should be identified and defined, such as weather conditions, temperature ranges, topologies, and time of day factors.

Define Life-Cycle Process Concepts (Task 6.1.9)

Based on the outputs of these initial tasks, the life-cycle process requirements are defined. These include defining the tasks necessary to develop, produce, test, distribute, operate, support, train, and dispose of system products under design and development. Subtasks include:

- *Manpower:* identifying the required job tasks and associated workload used to determine the staffing level needed to support the system life-cycle processes.
- *Personnel:* identifying the skills needed by the personnel who will support the system life-cycle processes.
- *Training:* identifying the training necessary to provide the personnel with the appropriate knowledge and skills to support the system life-cycle processes.

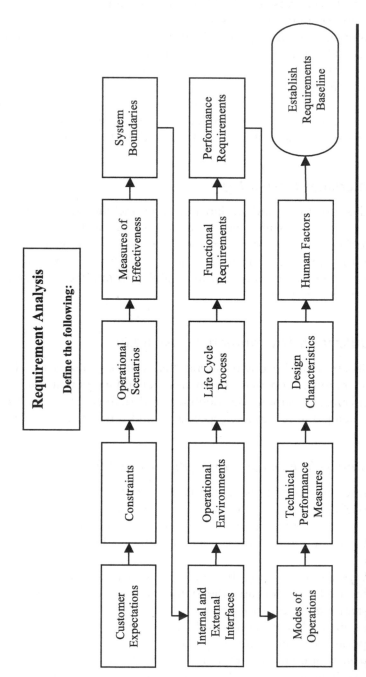

Figure 3.10 Defining boundaries.

- *Human engineering:* identifying the human cognitive, physical, and sensory characteristics of the personnel who will support the system life-cycle processes.
- *Safety:* identifying any potential system design features that create significant risks of death, injury, or acute chronic illness, disability, or reduce job performance of personnel who will support the system life-cycle processes.

At this point in the process, another life-cycle impact to consider is the cost factors related to implementing and maintaining system components. For example, the customer wants all workstations to have the function of read/write DVD drives. What are the security considerations for having this component functionality?

Define Functional Requirements (Task 6.1.10)

The customer performs the *functional context analysis* for the purpose of defining what the system should be able to do. The functional requirements are an important part of the overall system requirements analysis because they identify the different functions that the system will need to perform in order to meet the documented mission/business needs. Functional requirements define elements such as quantity (how many), quality (how good), coverage (how far), timelines (when and how long), and availability (how often).

One method of analyzing functional requirements is to use Functional Flow Block Diagrams (FFBDs). More information on functional requirements and FFBDs is provided in Chapter 4, "Defining System Security Architecture."

Define Performance Requirements (Task 6.1.11)

Once the functions have been identified, the SEs and customer (and if appropriate the ISSEP) agree on how well the system functions (as identified in Task 6.1.10) must perform. Once it has been decided what functions the system must perform, the next step is to determine how well the system functions must perform. It may be helpful to establish this from the beginning of Task 6.1.10 — that is, every time a functional requirement is identified, a corresponding performance requirement is also defined.

Performance requirements include speed, throughput, accuracy, humidity tolerances, mechanical stresses such as vibrations or noises, etc. Other performance requirements might be quality factors such as availability, reliability, or maintainability.

Define Modes of Operations (Task 6.1.12)

It may be useful to define the various modes of operation for the system or its components. During the design phase, the SEs document in which mode the system is planned to operate. The customer defines the various modes of operation for the system or components. Modes of operation include a training mode, pre-production mode, or full operation mode. Specific conditions that determine the mode of operation, such as mission, operational, environmental or configuration, should also be defined.

Define Technical Performance Measures (Task 6.1.13)

Technical Performance Measures (TPMs) are key indicators of system performance. TPMs should be identified early in the system development life cycle and continually monitored throughout the project as a method of managing the risks associated with system design and development. Thus, they should be limited to critical MOEs that will put the project at risk, such as cost, schedule, or performance issues. Appropriately selected TPMs can be used to assess conformance to requirements, assess conformance to levels of technical risk, trigger developments of recovery plans for identified deficiencies, and examine marginal cost benefits of performance in excess of requirements.

Define Design Characteristics (Task 6.1.14)

Defining design characteristics includes identifying the required design characteristics, such as color, size, or weight for the system or components.

Define Human Factors (Task 6.1.15)

The definition of human factor considerations includes factors that may affect operation of the system or component, such as design space, eye movement, or ergonomics.

Establish Requirements Baseline (Task 6.1.16)

The output of the system requirement definitions are recorded in a requirements baseline. The requirements baseline is viewed in three forms (IEEE 1220-1998):

1. *Operations:* describes how the system will serve the users. It defines who will operate and support the system and its life-cycle processes, and how well and under what conditions the system products are to be used.
2. *Functional:* describes what the system products need to do to produce the desired behavior described in the operational view.
3. *Design:* describes the design considerations of the system or components development and establishes requirements for technologies and for design interfaces among equipment and among humans and equipment.

Using the IEEE 1220 requirements analysis model, the final step for the SE is to present the requirements baseline to the customer and ensure that the requirements baseline meets the customer's expectations. The customer should verify whether the technical requirements will adequately represent the customer's needs, requirements, and whether constraints have been properly identified.

Define Design Constraints

As part of system requirements, the SE also identifies any design constraints. Design constraints define factors that limit design flexibility, such as environmental conditions, shock vibration, internal or external threats, regulatory or procedural requirements, etc. Although design constraints are handled later in the development process, it is not too soon to be aware of their impact while defining the system requirements.

One of the benefits of identifying design constraints at this early stage is to assist in eliminating options that are not feasible. Therefore, more time can be spent on realistic approaches.

A final comment on system requirements is that the SE must be careful not to state an implementation when specifying requirements. For example, "develop a database" is an implementation for design; "provide the ability to sort" is a requirement that may need the implementation of a database. Stating the implementation in a requirements specification may cause a design that would not be the best solution or cause other requirements to be overlooked. One solution to determining whether the requirement is truly a requirement or an implementation is to ask "why" a requirement is needed (DoE Requirements Management, p. 11).

The next topic explains the Preliminary System CONOPS, which can be a useful tool in explaining many of the technical concepts to the customer or user base.

The Preliminary System Concept of Operations (CONOPS)

The Preliminary System CONOPS is the first step in compiling the system context and system requirements into an initial document. The purpose of a System CONOPS is to bridge the gap between the user's needs and visions and the developer's technical specifications. The CONOPS is different from the system specifications, which is a formal statement of what the system must do <u>and</u> is written for the developers.

According to Fairley and Thayer (1996), a CONOPS is a user-oriented document that describes system characteristics for a proposed system from the users' viewpoint. IEEE Std 1362-1998 (1998) defines the CONOPS as an opportunity to communicate, in written form, the overall quantitative and qualitative system characteristics to the user, buyer, developer, and other organizational elements. It describes the existing system, operational policies, classes of users, interactions among users, and organizational objectives from an integrated systems point of view. The CONOPS should describe, in user's terminology, what the system should do to meet the users' needs for the system.

Kossiakoff and Sweet (2003) define the CONOPS as an extension of the operational requirements that adds constraints and expresses the customer's expectation for the anticipated system development. They identify four components of a CONOPS (p. 147):

1. Mission descriptions, with success criteria
2. Relationships with other system or entities
3. Information sources and destinations
4. Other relationships or constraints

The CONOPS defines the general approach, not a specific implementation, to the desired system. In this way, the CONOPS clarifies the intended goal of the system.

According to IEEE Std 1362-1998, the CONOPS provides the following:

■ "A means of describing a user's operational needs without becoming bogged down in detailed technical issues that shall be addressed during the systems analysis activity.
■ A mechanism for documenting a system's characteristics and the user's operational needs in a manner that can be verified by the user without requiring any technical knowledge beyond that required to perform normal job functions.
■ A place for users to state their desires, visions, and expectations without requiring the provision of quantified, testable specifications. For example, the users could express their need for a highly

reliable system, and their reasons for that need, without having to produce a testable reliability requirement. [In this case, the user's need for high reliability might be stated in quantitative terms by the buyer prior to issuing a Request for Proposal (RFP), or it might be quantified by the developer during requirements analysis. In any case, it is the job of the buyer and/or the developer to quantify users' needs.] (p. iii)"

An important ingredient of a CONOPS is that it should not reflect design detail. The design of the system starts to occur in Phase 3, Designing the System Architecture. Although it is not supposed to happen, in some instances it may not be possible to exclude some system design from the preliminary CONOPS. Thus, the SE and ISSEP should remain flexible in their approach. If necessary, the CONOPS can contain design strategies that are helpful in clarifying operational details of the proposed system.

The next section discusses how the ISSE model fits into defining system requirements. The elements are similar to the SE activities but involve the security influence. The role of the ISSEP is to ensure that a Preliminary Security CONOPS is documented, reviewed, and agreed to by the customer. What is important is for the ISSEP to analyze the customer's security requirements for the system environment and functions.

ISSE Activity: Defining System Security Requirements

Regardless of which framework is used to define the system context and system requirements, the ISSEP should have a complete understanding of what is required from the system to meet the customer's missions. For ISSEPs to define the **system security requirements**, they need to understand what will be inside the network, what will be outside the network, and any relationships and interfaces to other systems.

The system security context, system security requirements, and the preliminary security CONOPS are coordinated with the ISSEP, SE, the customer, and the owners of external systems. As shown in Figure 3.11, these three items are the main topics of this section. To begin, we look at how to define the system security context.

Define the System Security Context

When defining the system security context, the ISSEP determines system boundaries and interfaces with other systems and allocates security functions to target or external systems (Figure 3.12). This process is similar to how the SE defines the system context. The ISSEP also defines data flows

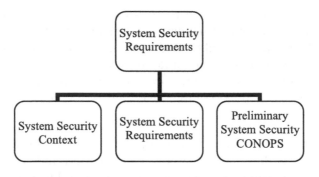

Figure 3.11   ISSE model system security requirements.

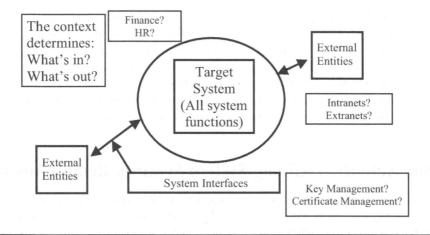

Figure 3.12   System context. (*Source:* Adapted from McAllister, 2003.)

between the target and any external systems and identifies the protection needs associated with those flows. Information management needs and information protection needs are allocated to the target system and to external systems. Note that allocations to external systems are assumptions that must be accepted by those system owners (IATF, Sec. 3.3.2).

If there are external network connections or interfaces for the enclave, they need to be documented, as well as listing any specific functions that will be needed for those connections. For example, if the system context document from the SE identifies and documents data flows between the target and external systems, the ISSEP in the system security context must document any information protection needs associated with those flows. Typically, the ISSEP will work along side the SE while the system context information is being defined to gain a clear understanding of the information flow.

As an example, the security context for an application might be used to establish a context in which authentication and authorization actions are carried out. The ISSEP would designate that the developer must create a security context for the application development effort. As such, the ISSEP would define users, groups, and rules that apply to the developers who are working on the project.

Define System Security Requirements

The system security requirements specify what security a system must perform, without specifying its design or implementation. The system security requirements must clarify and define security functional requirements and design constraints. The ISSEP works with SEs to define system security requirements, system security modes of operation, and system security performance measures. Together, the SE and ISSEP ensure that the requirements are understandable, unambiguous, comprehensive, and concise.

Any performance requirements and residual design constraints identified in the Information Management Plan are carried forward as part of the system security requirements document. Design constraints are not independent of implementation but represent design decisions or partial system design. In the system security requirements document, the design constraints should be identified separately from system interface requirements, which must be documented, including any that are imposed by external systems. Design constraints define factors that limit design flexibility, such as environmental conditions or limits, defense against internal or external threats, and contract, customer, or regulatory standards. When the system security requirements are approved, they are documented to give designers a baseline for system security development (IATF, p. 3-9).

DoD Directive 8500.1 (2002) is very clear about the policy for defining security requirements for systems: "Information assurance requirements shall be identified and included in the design, acquisition, installation, operation, upgrade, or replacement of all DoD information systems in accordance with 10 U.S.C. Section 2224, Office of Management and Budget Circular A-130, Appendix III, DoD Directive 5000.1 (references (a), (j) and (k)), this Directive, and other IA-related DoD guidance, as issued" (Section 4.1, p. 3).

Once the security context and security requirements have been identified, the ISSEP can present this information to the customer. When they are approved, they are documented to give designers a baseline for system security development.

Define the Preliminary System Security CONOPS

A preliminary security CONOPS describes, from the customer's perspective, what information management and information protection functions the system will need to perform and support the mission. The preliminary security CONOPS does not define step-by-step procedures; it defines the interface or reliance of mission/business needs with other systems and the products and services they deliver.

Because the customer is most familiar with the overall operations, the ISSEP should coordinate directly with the customer to develop the preliminary system security CONOPS. To begin, the ISSEP works with the customer to identify security operations, support, and management concepts and issues for the system under design and development. The security CONOPS is used by the SE in the system design/architecture phase as an aid for improving communications and understanding between the operational and engineering communities involved in the program.

The *ISSE Handbook* (1993, p. 3-43) describes how the analysis of security operations can be applied over the entire life cycle and should focus on:

- Defining the people, automated links, and other environmental elements that interact with the system — both directly and over remote/external interfaces within the total system and mission environment
- The roles they may play (e.g., personnel roles might include system users, system maintainers, system managers and administrators, postulated threat agents — while automated roles might be data sources, data sinks, operators for remote application functions or originators of network servicing command, etc.)
- Determining the manner and modes through which they might interact with the operational system in its mission environment

The security operations analysis is concerned with defining and reviewing likely security system operational scenarios. Typical items to consider include (*ISSE Handbook,* p. 3-43):

- System start-up and shutdown under normal and abnormal conditions
- System, human, and environmental responses to error conditions or security incidents
- Sustained operations under one or more pre-planned degraded (fallback) modes for system/component malfunction
- Security incident or natural disaster response/recovery modes (i.e., recovery related to a computer virus event)

- System responses to critical and common external and internal events
- Any site/environment unique scenarios (either on an individual basis, or by classes of sites/environments) if multiple systems will be deployed
- System behavior and interactions with the environment, and with human and external automated interfaces in the course of normal mission applications

Issues that should be considered by the ISSEP include those aspects of the overall Security CONOPS needed to perform key security analysis. At a minimum, these would usually include (*ISSE Handbook*, p. 3-44):

- The sensitivity levels of data the system will be expected to handle
- The approximate volume of data at each level
- The clearance levels and functional capabilities and privileges associated with system users (both human and automated), in any major classes of roles that may be applicable (e.g., help desk support, network system administrator, etc.)
- The identity of system users (including USG direct-hires, contractors, academic/research communities, other USG agencies, foreign entities, etc.)
- The sensitivity levels associated with interfaces to other systems, and the degree of mission criticality
- The interaction of technical and non-technical security enforcement mechanisms, from information system security and any other disciplines (e.g., physical security or personnel security) that are applied to jointly share the responsibility for day-to-day security system operation

The ISSEP also ensures that the preliminary system security CONOPS covers all of the customer's functionality, missions, or business needs and addresses the inherent risk in operating the system.

An article written by Darwin Ammala (2000) expresses how important a security CONOPS was to the design of a Navy project. He noted that "traditional software projects have been undertaken with less than complete understanding of requirements. The CONOPS document is a stride toward allowing the user's views to be heard, and allowing the developer to demonstrate to the users that their needs are understood and acknowledged."

Due to the complexity and knowledge needed to provide systems with security, Ammala notes that security-relevant software engineering would benefit from a more thorough and well-understood collection of requirements that included security requirements. This would ensure that the right product is being built correctly and with security in mind. Since the CONOPS document is written in user language it is an ideal vehicle for this purpose. The full set of CONOPS documents would represent the user requirements for the entire system. With these documents, refining requirements and creating the system requirements specification, software requirements specification, and security requirements specification could begin. The full article is available online at: http://www.stsc.hill.af.mil/crosstalk/2000/08/ammala.html.

Final Deliverable of Step 2

The final outcome or "deliverable" from the SE activities is the system context, system requirements, and the preliminary system CONOPS. The deliverable from the ISSE activity is the Preliminary System Security CONOPS, the System Security Context, and the System Security Requirements.

As an example of how a system requirements document might look, a template for documenting the System Requirements is outlined in Figure 3.13 (template is based on the Department of Energy [DoE] System Requirements template). The DoE template can be downloaded from the DoE Web site (see References section for Web site address).

Summary

At this point in the system design and development process, a preliminary concept of the system is defined, the preliminary requirements and functions have been established, and the system requirements have been identified. During this phase, the ISSEP ensures that the selected solution set meets the mission or business security needs, coordinates the system boundaries, and ensures that the security risks are acceptable.

The ISSEP documents and presents the system security context, system security requirements, and the preliminary security CONOPS to the customer and gains concurrence. The system security context documents the security allocations and specified data flows between the system and external systems and how they are controlled. The system security requirements clarify and define security functional requirements and design constraints. Functional requirements define items such as quantity, quality, timelines, availability, etc. Any performance requirements and design constraints are carried forward as part of the system security requirements document. Although it may seem early in the process, the ISSEP should

---

System Requirements Template

Section I: Overview
- Objectives
- Scope
- References
- Outstanding Issues

Section II: Current Environment
- Organization Profile
- Business Functions
- Component or System Description
- Deficiencies

Section III: Requirements
- Goals
- Input and Output Requirements
- Data Requirements
- Functional Requirements
- Performance Requirements
- Systems and Communication Requirements
- **System Security Requirements***
- Back up and Recovery Requirements
- Support Considerations
- Hardware Requirements
- Software Requirements
- Usability Requirements

Section IV: Technical Requirements
- Development Requirements
- Technical Specifications
- Design Constraints

Figure 3.13   System requirements template.
*The definition for System Security Requirements is "Provide details of the security classification of the data handled by the system, special handling required for the data, and the types and levels of protection and control required for user access to the data. This section should also detail telecommunications security aspects, e.g., workstation/server, network, system, dial-up access, etc." (DoE Template, p. 3-2).

also get the system security requirements accepted by the individuals responsible for the Certification & Accreditation (C&A) of the system. If those responsible for C&A have already agreed to the security requirements, the final C&A process can be easier and quicker to complete. Thus, the ISSEP should ensure that the Certifier and Accreditor have reviewed and accepted the documentation from this phase. More information on C&A is provided in Chapters 8 and 9.

In the next phase, Defining the Security Architecture, the system blueprint is defined; which is based on the system and security requirements defined in this phase. The security architecture activities provide a common level of understanding and a common basis for the design and implementation of the system.

References

Ammala, Darwin (2000). A New Application of CONOPS in Security Requirements Engineering. STSC Cross Talk, August 2000 Issue. Available from http://www.stsc.hill.af.mil/crosstalk/2000/08/ammala.html.

Blanchard, Benjamin S. and Wolter J. Fabrycky (1998). *System Engineering and Analysis, 3rd edition*. Prentice Hall: Upper Saddle River, NJ.

DoD Directive No. 8500.1 (October 2002). Information Assurance. (Certified Current as of November 21, 2003.) Available from www.dtic.mil/whs/directives.

DoD Directive No. 8500.2 (February 2003). Information Assurance Implementation. Available from www.dtic.mil/whs/directives.

DoD 5000.2M (February 1991). Defense Acquisition Management Documentation and Reports. Available from www.dtic.mil/whs/directives.

DoD 5200.1-R (January 1997). Information Security Program. Available from www.dtic.mil/whs/directives.

DoE G 200.1-1A (September 2002). Systems Engineering Methodology Version 3: The DOE Systems Development Lifecycle (SDLC) for Information Technology Investments. Department of Energy, Office of the Chief Information Officer. This document and associated process guides, checklists, and templates can be found at Web site http://cio.doe.gov/ITReform/sqse.

DoE Document SQAS19.01.00—2000 (April 2000). Guidelines for Requirements Management. http://cio.doe.gov/ITReform/sqse/download/_Toc479150598.

DoE (1998). Requirements Specification Template. http://cio.doe.gov/ITReform/sqse/download/reqspc.doc.

DoE (not dated). Requirements Management Awareness. http://cio.doe.gov/ITReform/sqse/download/rm_aware.doc.

Fairley, R. and R. Thayer (1996). The Concept of Operations: The Bridge from Operational Requirements to Technical Specification, *Software Engineering*, M. Dorfman and R. Thayer, Eds. IEEE Computer Society Press.

Faulconbridge, R. Ian and Michael J. Ryan (2003). Managing Complex Technical Projects: A Systems Engineering Approach. Artech House: Norwood, MA.

Gibbs, W. Wayt (1994). Software's Chronic Crisis, Trends in Computing. *Scientific American*, September 1994, p. 86

IAEC3186 (February 2002). Introduction to Information Systems Security Engineering, ISSE Training, student guide.

IEEE Std 1220-1998 (December 1998, copyrighted January 1999). IEEE Standard for Application and Management of the Systems Engineering Process. IEEE: New York, NY. (Revision of IEEE Std 1220-1994)

IEEE Std 1362-1998 (Approved March 1998, Published December 1998). IEEE Guide for Information Technology — System Definition — Concept of Operations (CONOPS) Document. IEEE: New York, NY.

Information Assurance Technical Framework (IATF), Version 3.1 (September 2002). National Security Agency, Information Assurance Solutions, Technical Directors; Fort Meade, MD.

Information Systems Security Engineering Handbook, Release 1.0 (February 28, 1994). National Security Agency, Central Security Service. Only available for official USG use.

Information Technology Laboratory (ITL) Bulletin (December 2003). Security Considerations in the Information System Development Life Cycle. NIST: Gaithersburg, MD. Available from www.csrc.nist.gov/publications/nistpubs/index.html.

Kossiakoff, Alexander and William N. Sweet (2003). *Systems Engineering: Principles and Practice.* John Wiley & Sons: Hoboken, NJ.

Loscocco, Peter and Stephen Smalley (February 2001). Integrating Flexible Support for Security Policies into the Linux Operating System. Available from http://www.nsa.gov/selinux/papers/slinux/slinux.html.

McAllister, Richard (2003). System Security Architecting-Defining Systems. Slide presentation available by request (rmcall@sparta.com).

NSTISSP No. 11, Revised Fact Sheet (July 2003). National Information Assurance Acquisition Policy. CNSS: Fort Meade, MD. Available from www.nstissc.gov.

4

ISSE Model Phase 3: Define System Security Architecture

Introduction

The phases in the Information Systems Security Engineering (ISSE) life-cycle model are:

1. Discover Information Protection Needs. Ascertain why the system needs to be built and what information needs to be protected.
2. Define System Security Requirements. Define the system in terms of what security is needed.
3. **Define System Security Architecture. Define the security functions needed to meet the specific security requirements.**
4. Develop Detailed Security Design. Based on the security architecture, design the security functions and features for the system.
5. Implement System Security. Following the documented security design, build and implement the security functions and features for the system.
6. Assess Security Effectiveness. Assess the degree to which the security of the system, as it is defined, designed, and implemented, meets the security needs.

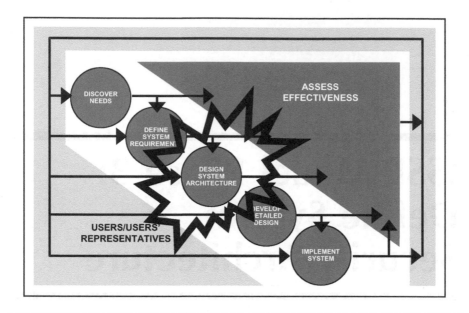

Figure 4.1   ISSE model: Define security architecture. (*Source:* Adapted from IATF, p. 3-2.)

When developing a new system or performing major modifications to an existing one, the architecture phase represents the initial steps of defining the functional and physical characteristics of the new system. IEEE Standard 1471:2000 defines architecture as the fundamental organization of a system embodied in its components, their relationships to each other, to the environment, and the principles guiding its design and evolution. This chapter focuses on Phase 3 of the ISSE model: Defining System Security Architecture (Figure 4.1).

Prior to this point, the need for the system was established (Phase 1) and the requirements were identified (Phase 2). This phase is the next step in the ISSE model and leads to a further commitment of how the system's security features and components will operate. The same architecture concepts apply for designing both the system and security architecture — the functional and component characteristics of the system and its security are defined. Following this phase, the system designers will use what is established in the architecture documents to "design" how the components will work as a system.

Figure 4.2 identifies the activities involved in defining the system and security architecture. The system requirements and the system security requirements defined in Phase 2, such as the security context and security requirements, are the inputs for this activity. The Phase 2 requirements

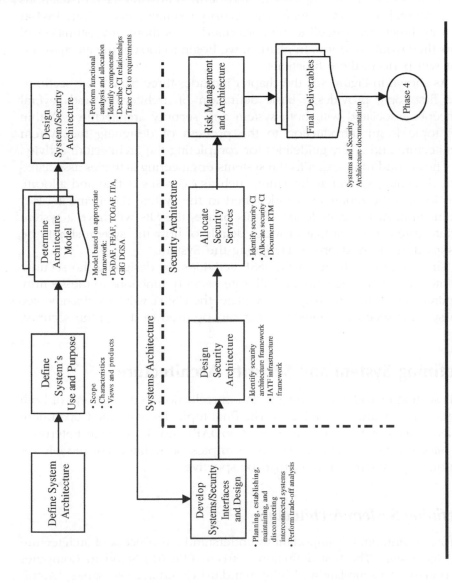

Figure 4.2 Defining system and security architecture.

were built on the outcome of the Phase 1 activities, where the protection needs were defined based on the customer's mission and business goals. In the Phase 2 requirement documents, the Systems Engineers (SEs) and the Information Systems Security Engineering Professionals (ISSEPs) identified the scope of existing systems and defined any interface or relations with external or legacy systems. The security requirements indicated **what** security functions needed to be performed — without any definition of **how** they would perform. In phase 3, we begin to look at the mechanisms that will perform these functions.

As shown in Figure 4.3, the chapter includes three main topic sections. The first topic provides a basic definition of architecture and several concepts associated with both system and security architectures. Within this topic is an introduction to the process of designing the system architecture and a few guidelines for completing the architecture activity.

The second topic explains the systems engineering activities associated with designing system architecture, such as how SEs define and allocate functions to the requirements identified in the system requirements documentation. At the completion of this phase, the SEs will have a system architecture document that provides details of how the system should be designed in the next phase, Designing the System.

The final topic discusses the ISSE activities for designing the security architecture. ISSEPs identify and allocate security functions to the security requirements. When this phase is complete, the ISSEPs will have documented the systems security architecture that can be used to design the security.

Defining System and Security Architecture

This section provides an overview and introduction to the concept of both system and security architectures. The final topic discusses the Department of Defense Architecture Framework (DoDAF) and the Federal Enterprise Architecture Framework (FEAF) as examples of architectural models for information systems from a broad perspective.

Defining System Architecture

Before beginning, it is important to understand the concept of architecture and its design. The first definition is from IEEE 610 Standard Computer Dictionary: A Compilation of IEEE Standard Computer Glossaries: "Architecture is the structure of components that comprise a system, their relationships, and the principles, rules, and guidelines governing the design and evolution of the components and their relationships" (p. 10). An architectural design is the "process of defining a collection of hardware

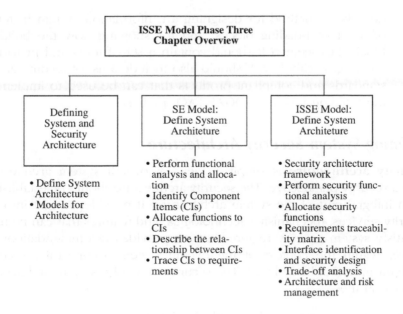

Figure 4.3   Architecture chapter overview.

and software components and their interfaces to establish the framework for the development of a computer system" (p. 10).

The Open Group Architectural Framework (TOGAF) (2003) provides a framework for developing enterprise architecture and includes the following definitions:

- **Architecture** has two definitions: (1) A formal description of a system, or a detailed plan of the system at component level to guide its implementation. (2) The structure of components, their interrelationships, and the principles and guidelines governing their design and evolution over time.
- An **architecture description** is a formal description of an information system, organized in a way that supports reasoning about the structural properties of the system. It defines the components or building blocks that make up the overall information system, and provides a plan from which products can be procured, and systems developed, that will work together to implement the overall system. It thus enables you to manage your overall IT investment in a way that meets the needs of your business.
- An **architecture framework** is a tool, which can be used for developing a broad range of different architectures. It should

describe a method for designing an information system in terms of a set of building blocks, and for showing how the building blocks fit together. It should contain a set of tools and provide a common vocabulary. It should also include a list of recommended standards and compliant products that can be used to implement the building blocks. (TOGAF FAQ, p. 1–2)

Defining System Security Architecture

Security architecture is simply a view of overall system architecture from a security perspective. The security architecture should be established as an integral part of the system architecture. It provides insight into the security services, mechanisms, technologies, and features that can be used to satisfy system security requirements. It provides recommendations on where, within the context of the overall system architecture, security mechanisms should be placed. The security view of a system architecture focuses on the:

- System security services and high-level mechanisms
- Allocation of security-related functionality
- Identified interdependencies among security related components, services, mechanisms, and technologies, while at the same time reconciling any conflict among them

The security (and information assurance) architecture consists of those attributes of the architecture that deal with the protection or safeguarding of operational assets, including information assets. Because security is an inherent property, the security architecture cannot be addressed independently of the rest of the architecture, instead it must be fully integrated with it (DoDAF, Workbook).

The security architecture is only one aspect of the enterprise or system architecture, which may also include network architecture or physical connectivity architectures. Keep in mind that there are many different systems, and thus there are different architectures. Ultimately, the goal of designing a system and security architecture is to provide a tool that will facilitate the functions and components of the system into the design and development phases.

Guidelines for Designing System Architectures from DoDAF and FEAF

Note: For the ISSEP® candidate, the following sections define and expand on the DoD Architectural Framework (DoDAF) and the Federal Enterprise

Architecture Framework (FEAF). Both are included to provide an introduction to ISSEPs operating in the defense and federal arena. Although the DoDAF and FEAF are provided for background and reference purposes only, they can be helpful in expanding your perspective on architectural theories.

DoD Architectural Framework

The DoD Architectural Framework (DoDAF, 2003) also provides guidance on defining architectures: "Architecture is a representation of a defined domain, as of a current or future point in time, in terms of its component parts, what those parts do, how the parts relate to each other, and the rules and constraints under which the parts function. What constitutes each of the elements of this definition depends on the degree of detail of interest" (p. 1-2). The DoD Architectural Framework (DoDAF) upgraded the C⁴ISR Architecture Framework (1997), which revised the **Technical Architectural Framework for Information Management (TAFIM) (1994)**. [C⁴ISR is an acronym for Command, Control, Communications, Computers, Intelligence, Surveillance, and Reconnaissance.]

The DoDAF notes the difference between an architecture *description* and an architecture *implementation.* The architecture description is a representation or blueprint of a current or necessary real-world configuration of resources, rules, and relationships. Once the blueprint enters the design, development, and acquisition process, the architecture description is then transformed into a real *implementation* of capabilities and assets in the field. The DoDAF does not address this blueprint-to-implementation transformation process. According to this description, in this phase, the SEs and ISSEPs are only compiling the architecture description.

Although the following information is derived from the DoDAF, and thus has a military slant, the concepts provide the ISSEP with an overall perspective of system architecture. Another reason why the DoDAF is important is its focus on aligning itself with the Federal Enterprise Architecture (FEA) Reference Models, which are discussed later. Therefore, even if the ISSEP is working directly with a Federal agency, the DoDAF can still provide an outline for designing system architectures.

Prior to adopting a single DoD Architectural Framework, each military service, major command, etc. used its own methodology for describing and developing system architectures. These different models made it difficult for SEs to exchange information and ensure joint interoperability. With the increasing emphasis on joint operations and interoperability, the DoDAF was implemented to provide a common DoD-wide approach to portraying architecture information.

Figure 4.4 DoDAF architecture views.

In the DoDAF there are three major perspectives (or views) that logically combine to describe architecture (Figure 4.4). Each of the three architecture views has implications on which architecture characteristics are to be considered, although there is often some degree of redundancy in displaying certain characteristics from one view to another.

The three DoDAF architecture views are:

1. *Operational architecture view.* A description of the tasks and activities, operational elements, and information flows required to accomplish or support a military operation.
2. *Systems architecture view.* A description, including graphics, of systems and interconnections that provide for or support warfighting functions.
3. *Technical Standards architecture view.* The minimal set of rules governing the arrangement, interaction, and interdependence of system parts or elements, whose purpose is to ensure that a conformant system satisfies a specified set of requirements.

Because the views provide different perspectives on the same architecture, it is expected that, in most cases, the most useful architecture description will be an "integrated" version. An integrated architecture description "often can provide closer linkage to the planning, programming, and budgeting process and to the acquisition process, and can provide more useful information to those processes" (C⁴ISR, p. 2-2). For the views to be integrated, the architecture must provide clearly defined linkages among its various views.

These linkages are needed to provide a cohesive audit trail from the system operational requirements and measures of effectiveness to the supporting systems and their characteristics; and, the specific technical criteria governing the acquisition and development of the supporting systems. Figure 4.5 illustrates some of the linkages that serve to describe the interrelationships among the three architecture views.

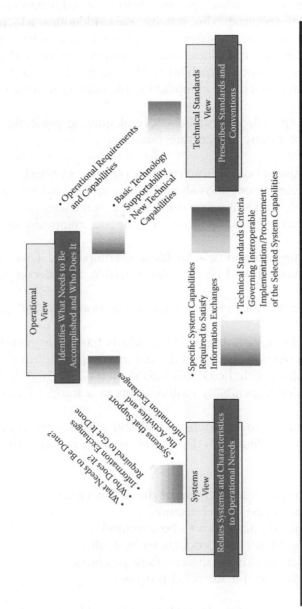

Figure 4.5   DoDAF fundamental linkages between views. (*Source:* From DoDAF, Vol. 1, p. ES-1.)

Interoperability is a typical architecture focus that demonstrates the criticality of developing these inter-view relationships. The operational view describes the nature of each need's information exchange in detail sufficient to determine what specific degree of information-exchange interoperability is required. The systems view identifies which systems support the requirement, translates the required degree of interoperability into a set of system capabilities, and compares current and proposed implementations with those capabilities. The technical view articulates the criteria that should govern the compliant implementation of each required system capability.

The DoDAF (p. 5-1–5-2) outlines several guiding principles that can be of importance to any architecture process:

- Architecture should be built with a purpose in mind.
- Architecture descriptions should be as simple and straightforward as possible and still achieve the stated purpose.
- Architectures should facilitate, not impede, communication among humans.
- Architectures should be relatable and comparable across the DoD.
- Architectures should be modular, reusable, and decomposable.

The guidance includes the following suggestions (DoDAF, p. 5-2):

- Provide the appropriate set of products based on intended use.
- Use the common terms and definitions as specified in the DoDAF.
- Be compliant with the Global Information Grid (GIG) Architecture.
- Describe interoperability requirements in a standard way.

There are six fundamental steps to building architectures in accordance with the Framework. Figure 4.6 depicts this six-step process. The six steps are:

1. Determine the intended use of the architecture.
2. Determine scope of architecture.
3. Determine characteristics to be captured.
4. Determine views and products to be built.
5. Gather data and build the requisite products.
6. Use architecture for intended purpose.

The *Desktop* volume of the DoDAF provides guidance on development, use, and incorporating security into the architecture, which is discussed later in this chapter under the ISSE security architecture activities.

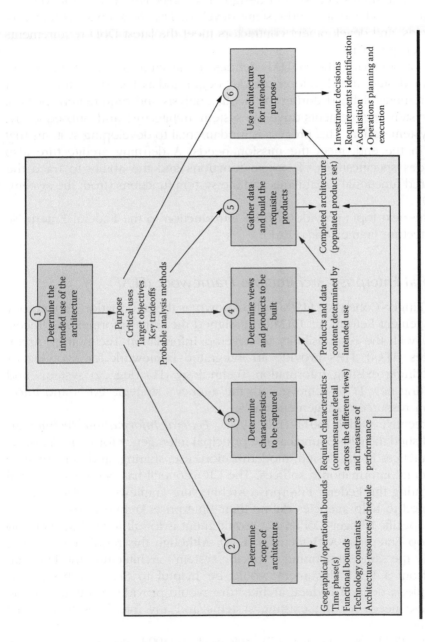

Figure 4.6   Six-step process of building the architecture. (*Source:* **From DoDAF, p. 5-5.**)

Those working in the DoD environment need to be aware of the DoDAF as this will be the mandated architectural military standard for future acquisitions and system design. The objective of the DoDAF is to ensure that architectures and systems developed by DoD service commands, agencies, and development contractors meet the latest DoD requirements for interoperability.

As a summary, the DoDAF defines architecture as occurring before system design and development can begin and is based on the system requirements defined during the needs analysis and requirement phases. The system requirements drive the system architecture and, subsequently, the system design. This process is fundamental to developing systems that will, in the end, meet the mission needs. A defining architecture also provides specifications of system functions and the ability to trace the required functional capabilities and the system functions (from the systems view).

The next topic provides a brief introduction to the Federal Enterprise Architecture Framework (FEAF).

Federal Enterprise Architecture Framework (FEAF)

The Clinger–Cohen Act (1996), also known as the Information Technology Management Reform Act (ITMRA) assigned the Chief Information Officers (CIO) with the responsibility to develop Information Technology Architectures (ITAs). ITAs provide an integrated framework for evolving or maintaining existing Information Technology (IT) (legacy) systems and acquiring new IT to achieve both the agency's strategic goals and information resource management goals.

Executive Order 13011 (July 1996), *Federal Information Technology*, established the CIO Council as the principal interagency forum for improving practices in the design, modernization, use, sharing, and performance of Federal information resources. The CIO Council has been instrumental in creating the Federal Enterprise Architecture Framework (FEAF) that is designed to help agencies define their Enterprise Architectures.

A specific Clinger–Cohen Act requirement is for all federal agencies to develop Enterprise Architectures (EAs). Although this requirement is not exactly the same as defining a specific system's architecture, the information from a FEAF document would be helpful to SEs and ISSEs. For example, a defined Federal architecture would provide an outline of the business needs for the existing systems and any interfaces to external systems.

The FEAF (see Figure 4.7), released in 1999, consists of various approaches, models, and definitions for communicating the overall organization and relationships of architecture components required for developing

> **Why develop a Federal Enterprise Architecture Framework?**
>
> A Federalwide collaboration tool is needed to collect common architecture information and build a repository for storing this information. A Federal Enterprise Architecture Framework is such a tool and repository. The Framework allows the Federal Government to accomplish the following:
>
> - Organize Federal information on a Federalwide scale
> - Promote information sharing among Federal organizations
> - Help Federal organizations develop their architectures
> - Help Federal organizations quickly develop their IT investment processes
> - Serve customer needs better faster, and cost effectively

Figure 4.7   Purpose of FEAF. (*Source:* From CIO Council, FEAF, 1999, p. 3.)

and maintaining the Federal Enterprise Architecture. FEAF is a strategic information asset structuring that helps agencies to define the:

- Business
- Information necessary to operate the business
- Technologies necessary to support the business operations
- Transitional processes for implementing new technologies in response to the changing needs of the business.

The framework is a conceptual model that begins to define a documented and coordinated structure for cross-cutting businesses and design developments in the government. Collaboration among the agencies with a vested interest in a Federal segment will result in increased efficiency and economies of scale. Agencies should use the framework to describe segments of their architectures (FEAF, p. 2).

The CIO Council chose a segment architecture approach that allows critical parts of the overall Federal Enterprise, called architectural segments, to be developed individually, while integrating these segments into the larger Enterprise Architecture.

The Clinger–Cohen Act also requires Federal organizations to define measures of performance for evaluating the impact and progress of their information systems. Integrated architecture descriptions are essential to meet this requirement. For example, systems and/or system attributes (identified in the systems architecture view) and their "measures of performance" must be assessed with respect to the utility they provide to the missions (identified in the operational architecture view in terms of "measures of effectiveness"). Similarly, systems must also be assessed with respect to the standards and conventions that apply and are identified in the technical architecture view (C⁴ISR, p. 2-8).

More information on the Enterprise Architecture concept is provided in Appendix B.

The FEAF document is available on the CIO Council Web site (www.cio.gov).

System Engineering Activity: Designing System Architecture

As shown in Figure 4.8, during this phase the SE is responsible for analyzing design constraints and designing the architecture. This includes performing a "functional analysis and allocation." A functional analysis and allocation translates requirements into functions, identifies components and allocates functions to the components, defines the relationship among the components, and traces all of the system requirements and functions to the elements until all requirements and functions are addressed.

Although it may sound simple, allocating functions to components can be complex. This is because components are usually a collection of properties of elements that, when combined, provide the needed system function. For example, the SE should not just assign any off-the-shelf hardware component to the application server function. The SE must decide which hardware component is the most appropriate based on capabilities such as speed, durability, reliability, etc. There are additional challenges if the combination of components cannot meet all the mission and business needs. In these situations, the SE may need to conduct a trade-off analysis. This involves a further analysis of what can or cannot

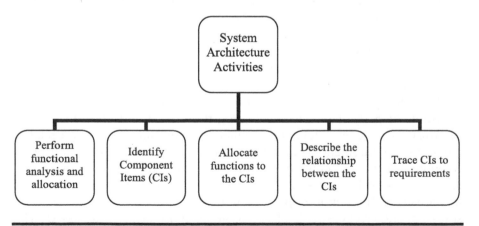

Figure 4.8   System architecture activities.

be done, and yet get closest to meeting the mission needs. During this type of analysis, the ISSEP must ensure that the SEs do not trade off security functions to meet other system functions. The end result of these activities is the detailed system architecture.

In the previous phase, the system requirements were documented into the System Concept of Operations (CONOPS). The CONOPS was an abstract of the customer's needs for hardware, software, people, facilities, data, etc. Once the functional requirements have been defined at the higher level (as done in Phase 2, Define System Requirements), SEs begin to analyze and allocate those requirements into functions — that is, they conduct the "functional analysis and allocation."

Perform Functional Analysis and Allocation

Functional Analysis

Functional analysis is the process of translating system requirements into detailed function criteria. The **functions** generally include the actions and sequence of actions necessary to meet each system requirement. The outcome of the functional analysis is a verification that the elements of a system-level functional architecture are defined sufficiently to allow for synthesis in the design phase.

The basics elements of functional analysis are to:

- Develop concepts and alternatives that are not technology or component bound.
- Model possible overall system behaviors that are needed to achieve the system requirements.
- Decompose functional requirements into discrete tasks or activities — the focus is still on functions not technology or components.
- Create a hierarchical outline of the functions and sub-functions that can be used to trace the functions to the requirements.
- Use a top-down approach with some bottom-up verification.
- Allocate functions to components in the system architecture.

The functional analysis breaks down higher-level functions (identified through requirements analysis) into lower level functions. Essentially, the previously defined requirements are first defined as high-level functions needed to meet the requirements. The high-level functions are then analyzed to identify the lower-level functions that are necessary to achieve the higher-level functions. This analysis includes candidate system architectures, function and process, internal and external interfaces, elements, components, information transfers, environments, and users/accesses.

To begin, the SE starts with an abstract of the customer needs and works down to identify the requirements for items such as hardware, software, people, facilities, and information. The process includes the following tasks:

■ Express the overall function for the design in terms of the conversion of inputs into outputs.
■ Decompose the overall function into a set of essential sub-functions.
■ Identify alternative functions.
■ Draw a block diagram showing the interactions between sub-functions.
■ Draw or outline the system boundary.
■ Search for appropriate components for performing the sub-functions and their interactions.

As an example, what would be the high-level function(s) and sub-functions for the following system requirement?

> The remote telecommuting office 60 miles from headquarters must automatically connect to the e-mail server from 5:00 a.m. to 8:00 p.m., Monday through Friday. All other times and connections must be determined on a case-by-case basis with the approval of the system owner.

If the requirement specified the following performance, how would the functions change?

> The remote telecommuting office 60 miles from headquarters must automatically connect to the e-mail server from 5:00 a.m. to 8:00 p.m., Monday through Friday **with a minimum 128 kbps transfer and has an alternate link if the primary link is not available for more than 120 seconds**. All other times and connections must be determined on a case-by-case basis with the approval of the system owner.

How would the functions change when the ISSEP adds the security requirement?

> The remote telecommuting office 60 miles from headquarters must automatically connect to the e-mail server from 5:00 a.m. to 8:00 p.m., Monday through Friday with a minimum 128 kbps transfer and has an alternate link if the primary link is not available for more than 120 seconds **and uses encryption**

modules that are in accordance with FIPS 140. All other times and connections must be determined on a case-by-case basis with the approval of the system owner.

In many situations, the functional analysis will identify new requirements or refine those that were previously defined. Thus, there should be a method or procedure to provide feedback into the process as necessary. These feedback inputs should not be viewed as slowing or inhibiting the process, but rather as something that can enhance the synergy necessary to bring out important SE design issues. It is also easy to see the importance of adequately defining the requirements during Phase 2.

Some functional analysis and allocation tools are:

- Functional hierarchy diagram
- Functional flow block diagram (FFBD)
- Timeline analysis diagram

Next is a description of these tools.

Functional Hierarchy Diagram

A functional hierarchy diagram is used to model the hierarchy of functions that the system is responsible for performing, the sub-functions that are needed by those functions, and any business processes that are used to invoke those sub-functions. The goal of the functional hierarchy diagram is to show all of the function requirements and their groupings in one diagram.

Figure 4.9 is a simple example of a functional hierarchy diagram. It has the form of a tree, with a branch structure representing the relationship between components at successive layers. The top level is a single block representing the system, the second level consists of blocks representing

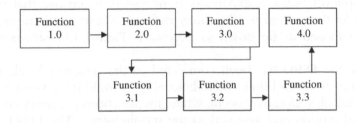

Figure 4.9   Simple functional hierarchy diagram.

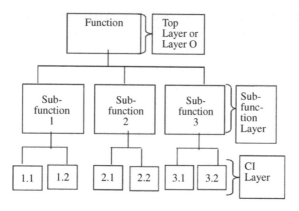

Figure 4.10 Functional hierarchy diagram.

the subsystems, and the third level separates each subsystem into the components. Figure 4.10 shows more elaboration and includes the function, sub-function, and component levels. At each level, lines connect the blocks so that the "child block (or subordinate)" is shown as a subset of the "parent block."

The system-level functions are assigned numbers, and those numbers are continued through the lower-level functions. This provides the ability to "trace" back the lower level functions (i.e., Functions 3.1, 3.2, and 3.3) to the original higher-level functions (i.e., Function 3.0).

Functional Flow Block Diagrams

Functional flow block diagrams (FFBDs) represent an approach used for functional decomposition, sequencing, and showing a logical flow. The main purpose of FFBDs is to structure the system requirements into functional terms. The FFBD identifies the major system-level (or top-level) functions that must be performed by the system to accomplish its mission. Each top-level block is expanded as necessary to ensure that the functionality of the system is adequately defined. These requirements should be decomposed as far down as necessary. Figure 4.11 shows a simple FFBD.

Once the FFBD has been completed to the required level, all major system functions and their interrelationships should have been identified. Functional allocation may occur, where the functions are grouped together in logical groups and assigned to the requirements. The FFBD provides a framework within which preliminary design can be conducted (Faulconbridge and Ryan, 2003).

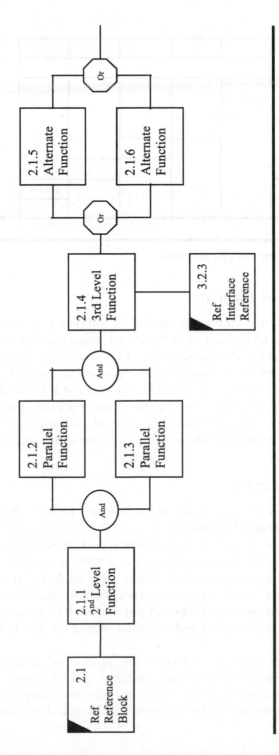

Figure 4.11 Functional flow block diagram example.

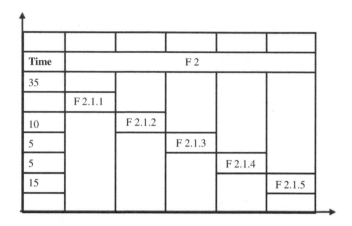

Figure 4.12   Timeline analysis diagram.

Timeline Analysis Diagram

When time is critical to the performance of a function, system engineers perform a timeline analysis to show functions, sequences, and their timing. The "timeline diagram" (Figure 4.12) provides a graphical view of whether the functions are to be accomplished in series or in parallel.

Creating a timeline diagram can help determine if it is possible to share resources in some instances; that is, the same resources can be utilized to accomplish more than one function. Also, the diagram may indicate if functions can be combined and integrated to minimize time or costs.

Functional Allocation

Allocation activities are performed in conjunction with functional analysis activities. **Functional allocation** is when SE's allocate performance and design requirements to each system function and sub-function. The result is a description of the functions in terms of what is needed and also in terms of the performance required. These derived functions need to be stated in sufficient detail to permit allocation to hardware, software, procedural data, or personnel. Special personnel skills or unusual design requirements are also defined and included during the functional analysis and allocation.

Functional allocation also refers to the process of grouping or combining similar functions and requirements into logical divisions. The grouping of similar functions helps the SEs determine the design of the major subsystems and ultimately the components required to make up the system.

Essentially, functional analysis and allocation allows for a better understanding of what the system has to do, in what ways it can do it, and to some extent, the priorities and conflicts associated with lower-level functions. It can provide information essential to optimizing physical solutions, which involves identifying and allocating components.

Identifying and Allocating Components

The process of translating functional design into physical design includes identifying components that will perform the system functions and then allocate those components to one or more functions. The components are typically referred to as **configuration items (CIs)** and are selected and designed to perform the group of functions assigned to them. The assignment or allocation of functions to physical CIs is the major focus of requirements allocation (Faulconbridge and Ryan, 2003).

One of the earlier tasks was to create a block diagram that outlined the system functions in a general view. In Figure 4.13, the block diagram shows (in very basic form) an information system, subsystem, and a few components. In this example, Function 1 would be to provide hardware CIs that will enable the information to be stored and transmitted between two external locations. Thus, a simple outline shows a need for a server to store the information and a router to forward the external transmissions.

Describe the Relationship Between the CIs

To define architectures accurately, one must also define any interfaces or relationships between the CIs. "When a new system, application, or database is deployed into a new environment, it is inevitable that the stakeholders will need to define, design, and implement interfaces to other applications, systems, and databases that exist in the enterprise architecture. Knowing what needs to be interfaced, how it needs to be interfaced, and when an interface is required are all imperative for the architecture" (DoDAF, p. 4-3).

During the selection of CIs, the relationship and interfaces between the CIs must be identified. The identification of the interfaces and any communication channels needed between them is a critical part of the architectural design, especially because the interfaces between the subsystems can indicate whether the system is successful. However, they also place constraints on the system design (and security design as we will see in the ISSE model section).

One method of documenting interfaces is to produce an Interface Control Document (ICD) that provides, in sufficient detail, the interfaces

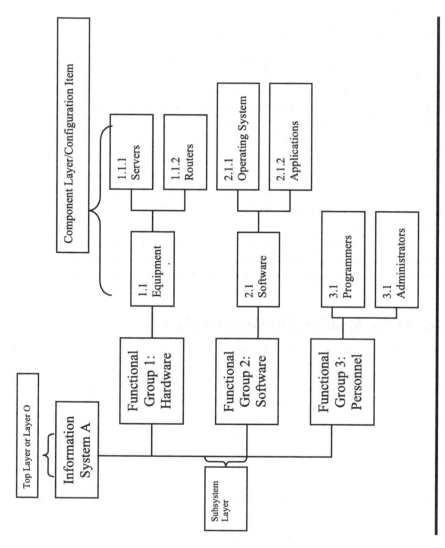

Figure 4.13 Function and CI diagram.

and relationships between the subsystems. The FFBD can be rearranged to also show the interfaces, as shown in Figure 4.14.

Faulconbridge and Ryan (2003) identify the following types of interfaces that can exist: physical, electronic, electrical, software, and environmental. Based on Figure 4.14, what would need to be documented as the interfaces between the router CIs? The answer will depend on the system, but questions to consider are how many routers, communications media, location of the routers within and external to the building, sensitivity of information systems A and B, etc.

Trace Functions and Components to Requirements

Traceability, a key concept in SE, is the process of ensuring that system requirements have been addressed in the system design. Forward traceability is derived from the system requirements to the system specification. Backward traceability is from the system specification to the system design. It can be used to ensure that additional requirements have not crept into the system specification during the design process. The concept of traceability is used at various points in the design and development phases to make sure the system is meeting the expected requirements.

The addition of requirements during the design and development phase is often referred to as "scope creep." SEs and ISSEPs must be on the alert for new requirements because additional unapproved requirements can compete with approved requirements for valuable design space and may reduce the performance of the system. Also, extra requirements can add to the cost and schedule associated with the system design and development — and may not add to the system's ability to meet the customer's mission needs. For the ISSEP, additional unapproved requirements can also affect the security stance of the system and cause further security controls, which may in turn also affect the performance of the system.

More information on traceability and creating a requirements traceability matrix is provided in the next section on the specific ISSE activities and tasks for defining the security architecture.

Once the definition of key system functions are identified, an internal review provides the SE team with the opportunity to collaborate, refine, and verify that all functions and interfaces are identified. The responsibilities of the SE in designing the system architecture also apply to the ISSEP. The ISSE, however, must focus on the security aspects of the architecture design and provide needed input to ensure that the system **security** requirements are included. The next section discusses the activities involved in designing the security architecture.

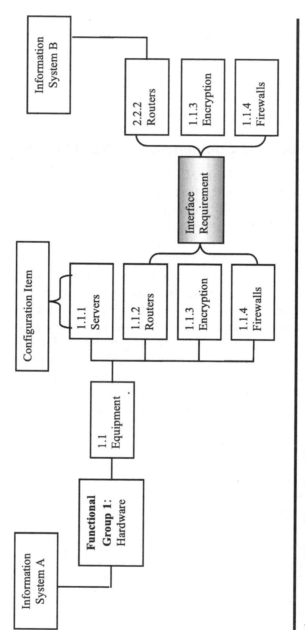

Figure 4.14 CI and interface diagram.

ISSE Activity: Define the Security Architecture

The role of the ISSEP during this phase is to define the security architecture in coordination with the SEs defining the system architecture. This includes allocating security services to the functions, identifying security mechanisms and components, defining the relationships between the security components, and analyzing any constraints to the security functions.

When defining the architecture for a secure system, the ISSEPs perform the following activities:

- Review the system decomposition of subsystems and components identified by the SEs.
- Perform a security functional analysis and allocation based on the security requirements.
- For each subsystem, choose a security component that matches its style and meets the security requirement.
- Examine the relationships between subsystems and identify the communication channels between the entities.
- Choose communication security components that will enforce the security requirements for each interface.
- If the implementation of a security component will place a constraint on the system, document it as a system constraint.
- Document the rationalization of how the security components and their integration will meet the security requirements.

In this phase, previously documented information is used to define the security functions and to choose the security components that will perform the security functions — this process is the core element of designing the security architecture. The difference between defining the security requirements and defining the security architecture is shown in Figure 4.15. That is, the target systems will now be defined.

The security architecture describes how the system will be put together to satisfy the security requirements. It is a design overview, describing the security functions and relationships between key elements of the system, such as hardware, operating systems, applications, networks, and other required components. It should describe how the functions in the system will follow the security requirements during the design and development process. For example, if the security requirements specify that the system must have a given level of assurance as to the correctness of the security controls, the security architecture must prescribe how these specifications will be met during the design and development process.

At this stage in the ISSE model, it is important for the ISSEP to explain to the customer that the security requirements are not added steps to the

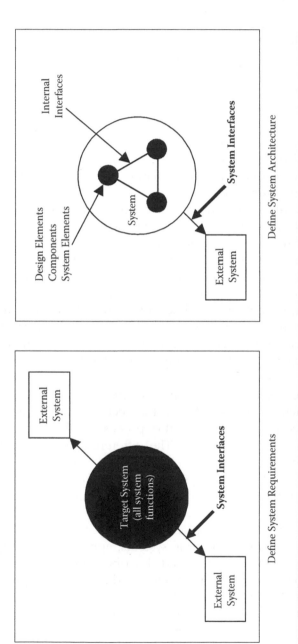

Figure 4.15 Define system requirements and system architecture. (*Source:* From IATF, 2002, p. 3-10.)

design or development process. Instead, it is the specifications outlined in the security architecture that influence all further design and development processes. Thus, the security architecture should outline high-level security issues, such as the system security policy, the level of assurance required, and any potential impacts security could have on the design process.

The security architecture should include a definition of expected residual risk and any expected failure in achieving full compliance with the system security requirements. The output of this phase is the detailed system security architecture, which translates into a stable, productive, cost-effective security design during Phase 4, Develop Detailed Security Design.

In theory, defining the security architecture sounds easy. In reality, there are always challenges to overcome. These "challenges" usually indicate that the SEs, ISSEPs, and maybe even the customer will need to make trade-offs (modifications) to the needs or requirements. When trade-offs must be made, the ISSEP must also reevaluate the risk management strategy. Because the ability to make the right trade-off choices is a critical factor in the ISSEP process, it will be discussed in more detail later in this section.

As shown in Figure 4.16, this section begins with an example of a security architecture framework that could be used by ISSEPs to develop the security architecture. Just as in the SE activities, the ISSEP also conducts a security functional analysis and allocation. This also includes a requirements traceability matrix for matching security functions to security requirements. An important aspect of the security architecture is reviewing the system

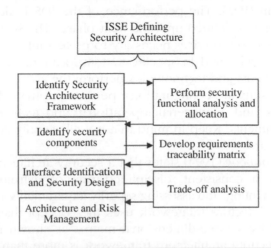

Figure 4.16   ISSE security architecture activities.

interfaces and defining the security functions. This is significant because many threats take advantage of vulnerabilities in a system's connection to external networks or entities. The final topic discusses the role of risk management in defining the architecture and why the ISSEP might need to conduct a preliminary risk assessment before continuing to the design phase.

As a first step, the ISSEP may want to review the documentation from the first two phases, such as the Information Management Plan (IMP) and, specifically, the Information Protection Policy (IPP). These documents provide an analysis of the customer's needs (not wants) that relate to the mission and business needs. If any security design constraints were identified in these documents, the ISSEP should reexamine the constraints for any effect on the security architecture.

If this is a legacy system, the ISSEP would also consider what security mechanisms are currently in place — this information should have been documented in the System Security Concept of Operations during Phase 2. If security components do not currently exist or are not implemented correctly or effectively, the ISSEP considers adding new security components to the system.

Define System Security Architecture

The system security architecture defines where the security functions and components are located within the system. The security components are not defined in detail, but rather in general high-level terms. For example, the security component needed for the requirement may be an intrusion detection system (IDS). The performance of the IDS is defined, but the specific brand is not defined until the next phase. The security functions, in the form of security services necessary to protect information, can now be appropriately allocated in specific system locations. Various types of security components and technologies perform the security services, such as hardware or software configurations; personnel, physical, and environmental controls; and, managerial, operational, and technical policy and procedure documents. Keep in mind that not all security components are technical in nature.

The ISSE Handbook (1994) states that a security architecture framework should provide a consistent, disciplined way of defining, organizing, applying, documenting, and assessing security requirements and technology. The security architecture framework uses the concept that a system can be represented by a three-dimensional matrix, as shown in Figure 4.17. Although the security architecture framework is more than ten years old, the concepts remain helpful to the ISSEP in understanding the role of the security architecture.

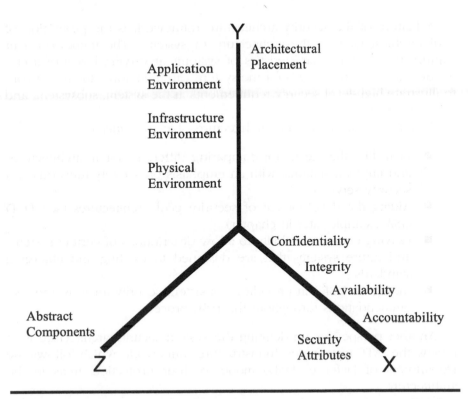

Figure 4.17   Security architecture framework. (*Source:* From ISSE Handbook, 1994, p. F-21.)

"The three dimensions of the matrix capture the architectural structure of a system, the architectural placement of resources and services, and the security attributes of the system. As shown in Figure 4.18, each cell in the three-dimensional matrix can contain a variety of information such as requirements, mechanisms, standards, and specifications of the security attributes such as assurance, cost, and security management responsibilities" (*ISSE Handbook,* p. F-21).

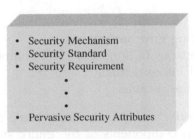

Figure 4.18   Security architecture framework cell.

A feature of the security architecture framework is the promotion of a hierarchical view of the architecture of systems. The framework can capture the security characteristics of systems at varying levels of architectural abstraction. Designs for the system can then apply the framework to illustrate high-level security requirements at the system, subsystem, and component levels.

A summary of the security architecture objectives include:

- Providing the means for comparing different system architectures and implementations, with an emphasis on security functions and security services
- Aiding the development of security goal architectures (see DoD GSA example later in chapter)
- Leaving enough flexibility to allow descriptions of current systems and future systems that are designed to existing and emerging standards
- Aiding an ISSEP in providing consistent security analysis and recommendations throughout the ISSE process

Another perspective on defining the system security architecture is to review the IATF Information Infrastructure framework, which follows the Department of Defense (DoD) model of four protection areas in the architecture.

IATF Information Infrastructure

The IATF provides a framework, the "Information Assurance Framework," as an example of how to define an information system infrastructure including the interfaces it has with other components or systems and its environment. Whether the ISSEP uses this or some other type of framework, it is a good idea to use some methodology to divide the information system into reasonable areas.

The Information Assurance Framework separates the information system into four areas:

1. Local Computing Environments
2. Enclave Boundaries (around the local computing environments)
3. Networks and Infrastructures
4. Supporting Infrastructures

Although the framework considers four areas, the areas are not considered separate, but rather as components of the entire system.

Figure 4.19 is an example of the **local computing environment**, which contains servers, client workstations, operating system, and appli-

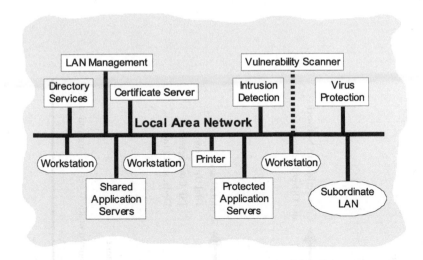

Figure 4.19 Local computing environment. (*Source:* **From IATF, 2002, p. 1-7.**)

cations. Most organizations have some version of a local computing environment already in existence, sometimes referred to as a legacy system. The legacy system may contain commercial-off-the-shelf (COTS) applications, government-off-the-shelf (GOTS) applications, or custom-developed applications.

Security of the local computing environment focuses on protecting the servers and client workstations, the operating system, applications, and any host-based monitoring capabilities, such as intrusion detection or anti-virus capabilities.

An **enclave boundary** is a collection of local computing devices, regardless of physical location, that are interconnected via local area networks (LANs) and governed by a single security policy. Shown in Figure 4.20, enclaves typically contain multiple LANs with computing resource components such as servers, client workstations, applications, communication servers, printers, and local routing/switching devices. An enclave is defined as an environment under the control of a single authority with personnel and physical security measures.

Because security policies are unique to the type or level of information being processed, a single physical facility may have more than one enclave present. If there are local and remote devices that access the enclave's resources, they must also meet the security policies of that enclave. An enclave may also span several geographically separate locations with dedicated connectivity via commercially purchased point-to-point communications, such as T-1 or T-3 connections or wide area network (WAN) connectivity, such as the Internet.

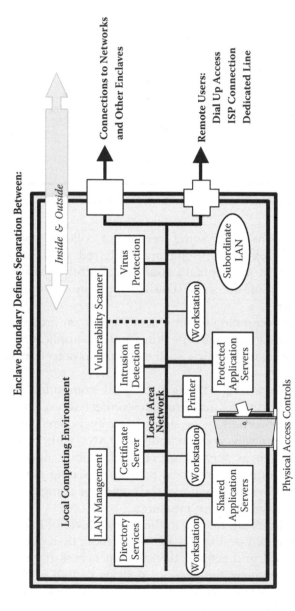

Figure 4.20 Enclave boundary. (*Source:* From IATF, 2002, p. 1-8.)

The point at which information enters or leaves the enclave (or organization) is considered the enclave boundary — it is the point at which the enclave's network service layer connects to another network service layer. Some external connections may be single-level connections where the enclave and connected network are at the same privacy level. Other external connections could have different privacy levels, such as a High-to-Low or Low-to-High transfer, where the enclave is at a higher or lower level than the connected network. Organizations may have connections to networks or enclaves that are outside their control, such as the Internet or other government agencies. In these situations, the enclave needs to protect its boundary with specific security services to ensure that the information entering does not affect the enclave's operation or resources. A variety of security mechanisms can be used, such as access controls, guards, one-way transfers, firewalls, and virus protections. Another security element to consider is the control of information leaving the enclave — it may be necessary to ensure that information leaving is authorized.

The ISSE strategy for defending an enclave boundary should include several defensive measures and security mechanisms to address remote access and interoperability. For example, the enclave perimeters must be established and equipped with professionally managed electronic access portals, which have security mechanisms providing effective access control and monitoring. The enclave boundaries would need intrusion detection capabilities to detect unauthorized access or other intrusion attempts. Other enclave protections include firewalls, remote access controls, guards, and anti-virus software. All of these security components need configuration and procedure guidelines and trained personnel — an anti-virus mechanism is not effective unless there is an anti-virus team ensuring definitions that are updated and distributed.

The **network and infrastructure** provide the network connectivity between enclaves. The terms typically associated with this include operational area networks (OANs), metropolitan area networks (MANs), and campus area networks (CANs). Figure 4.21 show several important components of the network infrastructure: the transport network, network management, domain name servers, and directory services. The transport networks move information between the nodes (e.g., routers, switches) via landline or wireless information transmission devices.

The three typical transport networks and services used by the USG are:

1. *Public/commercial networks.* This includes the Internet and networks that are owned by private industry, such as the public switched telephone network (PSTN), and wireless networks (e.g., cellular, satellite, wireless LAN, and paging networks).

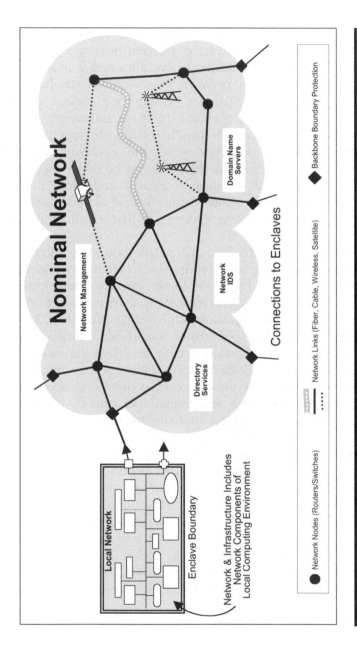

Figure 4.21 Network and infrastructure framework structure. (*Source:* From IATF, 2002, p. 1-10.)

2. *Dedicated network services.* The USG contracts directly with public network providers to provide dedicated network service.
3. *Government-owned and operated.* Several USG agencies own and operate their own private telecommunication networks.

The **supporting infrastructure** provides the foundation upon which security service mechanisms are used in the network, enclave, and computing environments. These security mechanisms are used to securely manage the system and provide security-enabled services. The supporting infrastructure provides security services for networks, client workstations, Web servers, operating systems, applications, files, and single-use infrastructure machines (e.g., Domain Name Server (DNS) and directory servers). The two areas addressed in the IATF are Key Management Infrastructure (KMI), which provides a unified process for the secure creation, distribution, and management of public key certificates, and Detect and Respond Infrastructures that provide the ability to detect and respond to intrusions.

DoD 8500.1 (2002, p. 3) states that "for IA purposes all DoD information systems shall be organized and managed in the four categories: Automated information system (AIS) applications, enclaves (which include networks), outsourced IT-based processes, and platform IT interconnections." Thus, if the ISSEP is working with a DoD customer, these specific categories must be identified and documented.

Once the security architecture framework has been determined, the next activity is to define the security functions based on the previously defined security requirements.

Security Functional Analysis and Allocation

The aim of security functional analysis and allocation is to ensure that the elements of the system-level functional architecture include the security functions in sufficient depth to allow for synthesis of the security solution in the following phase. The ISSEP must identify the high-level and low-level functions necessary to achieve the previously identified security requirements.

As noted in the DOE Systems Engineering Methodology (2002), some items to consider when conducting the security functional analysis and allocation are:

■ "Identify the users and organizations that will have access to the components.
■ Indicate what access restrictions they will have. All persons in a work area may not have the same security access level. Measures

should be taken to assure that sensitive materials and systems requiring protection are not accessed by unauthorized individuals.

■ Identify controls for the component, such as the user identification code for system access and the network access code for the network on which the product will reside.

■ Identify whether access restrictions will be applied at the system, subsystem, transaction, record, or data element levels. Classified information must be protected in accordance with Federal and agency directives.

■ Identify physical safeguards required to protect hardware, software, or information from natural hazards and malicious acts.

■ Identify communications security requirements (p. 175)."

The ISSEP can use the same tools defined in the SE activity to conduct the security functional analysis and allocation (i.e., functional hierarchy diagrams, functional flow block diagrams, and timeline analysis diagrams).

An example of decomposing the security requirements and security functions is shown in Figure 4.22. It begins with capturing all the security requirements from the earlier phases and charting them at the higher level. In addition to the derivation of requirements during functional analysis and allocation, the ISSEP needs to group and allocate the functions. Just as in the SE activity, the grouping of security functions may indicate an overlap or indicate where one security function could meet several security requirements.

Once the security functions have been defined and allocated, the next step is to identify the security components that will perform the security functions.

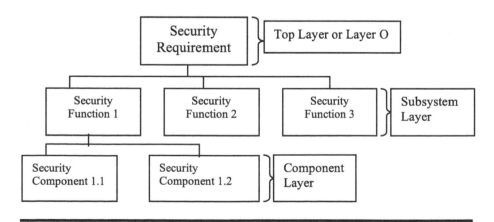

Figure 4.22 Security functional flow block diagram.

Identify Security Components, Controls, or Technologies

Chapter 4 of the IATF provides an overview of the widely used technical security controls. Although these controls will vary in capability, the basic principle of the control remains. Brief descriptions are provided here; for a full explanation, refer to IATF, p. 4-25 through 4-30 (2002).

- *Application layer guard.* The need for a separate mechanism to perform a gatekeeper function, checking the invocation of security features, gives rise to a need for security at the application layer. This gatekeeper has recently taken the form of an application layer guard that implements firewall mechanisms performing I&A functions and enforcing security policies, such as allowing or disallowing connections based on identification or requested protocol processing.
- *Application program interface (API).* It provides standard interfaces so that multiple vendors can provide interoperable solutions. APIs are a means of isolating a computing platform from the details of the implementation of cryptographic functions (both the actual algorithms and the hardware implementations).
- *Common data security architecture (CDSA).* The CDSA is a set of layered security services that address communications and data security problems in the emerging Internet and intranet application space.
- *Circuit proxy.* Circuit gateways are another type of proxy firewall. A circuit-level proxy becomes an intermediate connection point in a session between a client and a server.
- *CryptoAPI.* The Microsoft Cryptographic API provides services that enable application developers to add cryptography to their Win32 applications.
- *Cryptographic service providers (CSPs).* Both CDSA and CryptoAPI make use of the concept of CSPs, which are independent modules that perform the real cryptographic work. A CSP may implement one or more of the following cryptographic functions: bulk encryption algorithm, digital signature algorithm, cryptographic hash algorithm, unique identification number, random number generator, secure key storage, and custom facilities unique to the CSP.
- *File encryptors.* These provide confidentiality and integrity for individual files, provide a means of authenticating a file's source, and allow the exchange of encrypted files between computers.
- *Hardware tokens.* A number of hardware token approaches are available. The approaches range from a token that is an external memory device only to a token with significant levels of processing. One hardware token that is prominent in the Department of Defense (DoD) community is the FORTEZZA® Crypto Card.

■ *Intrusion and penetration detection.* Intrusion detection and response systems can protect either a network or individual client platforms. Effective intrusion detection systems detect both insider and outsider attacks.

■ *Internet Protocol Security (IPSec).* IPSec is the security framework standardized by the Internet Engineering Task Force (IETF) as the primary network layer protection mechanism.

■ *Internet Key Exchange (IKE) Protocol.* IKE was developed by the IETF as a standard for security attribute negotiation in an IP network. It provides a framework for creating security associations between endpoints on an IP network, as well as the methodology to complete a key exchange.

■ *Media encryptors.* Media encryptors protect the confidentiality and integrity of the contents of data storage media. They can also perform a role in maintaining the integrity of the workstation by verifying the Basic Input/Output System (BIOS) and ensuring that configuration and program files are not modified.

■ *Packet filter.* Packet filtering firewalls (also called screening routers) commonly operate at the network layer (Open Systems Interconnection [OSI] Layer 3). These firewalls check the IP and protocol headers against a set of predefined rules.

■ *PKI Certificate Management Protocol (CMP).* For managing public key material, the Internet community has developed the Internet X.509 PKI CMP. Management protocols are required to support online interactions between PKI components.

■ *Secure Socket Layer (SSL).* SSL exists just above the transport layer and provides security independent of application protocols, although its initial implementation was meant to secure the Hypertext Transfer Protocol (HTTP). This effort has migrated to the IETF as the Transport Layer Security (TLS) protocol, which provides data encryption, server authentication, message integrity, and optional client authentication for a TCP/IP connection.

■ *S/MIME.* S/MIME is a specification for adding security for e-mail in Multipurpose Internet Mail Extensions (MIME) format, supporting binary attachments as well as text. It offers authentication and confidentiality. The S/MIME specification is currently an Internet draft.

■ *SOCKS.* This protocol supports application-layer firewall traversal. The SOCKS protocol supports both reliable TCP and User Datagram Protocol (UDP) transport services by creating a shim-layer between the application and the transport layers.

■ *Stateful packet filter.* Stateful packet filters look at the same headers as do packet filters, but also examine the content of the packet. In addition, this technology is capable of dynamically maintaining information about past packets or transaction state information. Security decisions can then be based on this state information.

■ *Trusted computing base (TCB).* A trusted computer system is a system that employs sufficient hardware and software assurance measures to allow its use for simultaneous processing of a range of sensitive or classified information. Such a system is often achieved by employing a TCB. A TCB is the totality of protection mechanisms within a computer system, including hardware, firmware, and software, the combination of which is responsible for enforcing a security policy.

■ *Virus detectors.* Virus detectors can be used to protect a network or an individual client.

Additional Security Controls

Before concluding this section on security controls, it is important to note a new NIST Special Publication on security controls. NIST SP 800-53 (February 2005) "Recommended Security Controls for Federal Information Systems" is a part of a series of seven documents that provide a framework for selecting, specifying, employing and evaluating the security controls in Federal information systems.

Note to ISSEP: It is my understanding that draft publications will not appear on any ISSEP exam. However, it is important for ISSEs assisting Federal agencies to be aware of NIST publications, especially SP 800-53, since under Federal mandate it will become a FIPS standard. When finalized, "FIPS Publication 200, Minimum Security Requirements for Federal Information and Information Systems," will become a mandatory standard for Federal agencies in accordance with the Federal Information Security Management Act (FISMA) of 2002 (p. iv).

NIST SP 800-53 defines two important properties for security controls: robustness and flexibility.

Robustness is determined by two factors: the *strength of function* associated with the control and the *assurance in the effectiveness* of the control. Three levels of security control robustness are defined in SP 800-53: basic, enhanced, and strong.

■ "The *strength of function* associated with a particular security control is a relative measure of the effort (or cost) required to defeat a correctly implemented control and is not necessarily related to the cost of implementing such a control.

■ *Assurance in the effectiveness* of a security control is a function of the control's strength of function as well as the design of the control, the methodology used to construct the control (including the maturity of the processes employed during development), and the context in which the control is used. Assurance is based on these factors and the sophistication and degree of rigor applied during the security control verification process (pre-deployment and post deployment)" (SP 800-53, p. 6).

Flexibility allows organizations to tailor security controls to satisfy organizational security policies and to meet specific operational needs.

"The variable section of a security control is clearly identified by the keywords *assignment* or *selection* indicating the type of operation permitted. The assignment operation permits the specification of a parameter to be filled in when the security control is used. For example, the requirements for conducting information backup operations within an organization may vary widely. The assignment operation for information backups permits organizations to specify how often backups are to be conducted but provides a minimum period which is at least monthly. Where assignment operations are allowed, there is typically a lower bound (minimum value) or upper bound (maximum value) established for the variable portion of the security control. The selection operation permits the specification of items that are to be selected from a list given in the security control. For example, organizations may be asked to specify the type of alternate communications services that will be available on a contingency basis by selecting from a list of available options (i.e., long haul, short haul" (SP 800-53, p. 7).

NIST SP 800-53 provides a specific structure of three components for each security control: a *control objective* section providing the overall objective; a *control mapping* section listing source documents that have similar security controls; and a *control description* section providing specific security control requirements and details of each control. Based on the robustness level (basic, enhanced, or strong), a single control objective may have up to three security control versions. Security controls are also organized into *classes* and *families*. The three general classes of security controls (management, operational, and technical) correspond to the major sections of a security plan.

Table 4.1   Security Control Classes and Families

Class	Family Name	Identifier
Management	Risk Assessment	RA
Management	Security Planning	PL
Management	System and Services Acquisition	SA
Management	Security Control Review	CR
Management	Processing Authorization	PA
Operational	Personnel Security	PS
Operational	Physical and Environmental Protection	PE
Operational	Contingency Planning and Operations	CP
Operational	Configuration Management	CM
Operational	Hardware and Software Maintenance	MA
Operational	System and Information Integrity	SI
Operational	Media Protection	MP
Operational	Incident Response	IR
Operational	Security Awareness and Training	AT
Technical	Identification and Authentication	IA
Technical	Logical Access Control	AC
Technical	Accountability (including audit trails)	AU
Technical	System and Communications Protection	SP

Within NIST SP 800-53, security controls are identified by a standardized naming convention to uniquely identify each control. A two-character identifier indicates the respective family where the control resides, and a numeric identifier indicates the number of the control within the family. Table 4.1 lists the class, family name, and two-character family identifiers.

An example of a security control from Management, Operational, and Technical (NIST SP 800-53, p. 205):

Class: Management
Family: Security Planning
PL-5 ACCOUNTABILITY POLICY

CONTROL OBJECTIVE: Establish information system policy for accountability when organizational policy is not adequate to address system needs.

CONTROL MAPPING: [NIST 800-26: 17.1.1, 17.1.2; FISCAM: AC-4.3, SP-1.2; ISO-17799: 3.1.1]

PL-5.b BASIC CONTROL: An explicit accountability policy establishes the rules to be implemented to ensure that information system users can be held accountable for their actions as needed. Accountability policy elements are, for example: (i) purposes for accountability (e.g., deterrent, incident forensics, etc.); (ii) required granularity for accountability (e.g., to the granularity of individual users); and (iii) time period for which accountability information must be available (e.g., five years).

PL-5.e ENHANCED CONTROL: To be defined.

PL-5.s STRONG CONTROL: To be defined. (NIST SP 800-53, p. 79)

Class: Operational
Family: Contingency Planning and Operations
CP-1 CONTINGENCY PLAN

CONTROL OBJECTIVE: In accordance with organizational policy, an effective response to an information system disruption is enabled by developing a system contingency plan.

CONTROL MAPPING: [NIST 800-26: 9.2.1, 9.3.3; FISCAM: SC-3.1; ISO-17799: 11.1.1, 11.1.2, 11.1.3; DCID 6/3: Cont1; CMS: 5.2.1, 5.2.3, 5.2.5, 5.2.9, 5.4.4, 5.7.1, 5.7.2, 5.7.5, 5.8.1, 6.1.1, 6.1.2; DOD 8500: CODP-3]

CP-1.b BASIC CONTROL: A contingency plan is produced for the information system that is compliant with OMB policy and consistent with the intent of NIST SP 800-34. In addition, key affected parties approve the contingency plan for the system. The plan is reviewed once a year, reassessed, tested and, if appropriate, revised to reflect changes in hardware, software and personnel.

CP-1.e ENHANCED CONTROL (Add to basic control):

Plan includes checks to be performed and assigned responsibilities for conducting these checks to periodically ensure that the plan is being implemented as intended.

CP-1.s STRONG CONTROL: To be defined. (NIST SP 800-53, p. 175)

Class: Technical
Family: Identification and Authentication
IA-4 PASSWORD LIFE

CONTROL OBJECTIVE: In accordance with organizational policy, automated mechanisms are in place and detailed supporting procedures are developed, documented, and effectively implemented to ensure that passwords are changed and not reused. CONTROL MAPPING: [NIST 800-26: 15.1.6; FISCAM: AC-3.2; DCID 6/3: I&A2-e]

IA-4.b BASIC CONTROL: Mechanisms are implemented to enforce automatic expiration of passwords and to prevent password reuse. Passwords are changed at least [*Assignment: time period; typically sixty-ninety days*]. Passwords have a minimum life of [*Assignment: time period (e.g., one day)*]. Passwords are prohibited from reuse for a specified period of [*Assignment: number of generations; typically six*].

IA-4.e ENHANCED CONTROL (Add to basic control): Supporting procedures include checks to be performed and assigned responsibilities for conducting these checks to periodically ensure that the mechanisms are properly configured and the procedures are being correctly applied and consistently followed.

IA-4.s STRONG CONTROL: To be defined.

The end product is a documented outline of the architecture for the system security components that follow the security functions that meet the security requirements. To verify whether the components meet the requirement, the ISSEP prepares a requirements traceability document.

The next topic explains the requirements traceability concepts and provides two examples of how an ISSEP could document the requirements, functions, and components into a Requirements Traceability Matrix (RTM).

Requirements Traceability and the RTM

Gotel and Finkelstein (1994) define requirements traceability as the "ability to follow the life of a requirement, in both forwards and backwards direction, i.e., from its origins, through its development and specification, to its subsequent deployment and use, and through periods of ongoing refinement and iteration in any of these phases (p. 94)." All system security components, such as hardware, software, policies, and procedures, produced at different stages of the design and development process are connected to requirements. In addition, traceability provides the ability to show compliance with requirements, maintain system design rationale, show when the system is complete, and establish change control and maintenance mechanisms (Ramesh et al., 1995).

Kean (1997) notes that for any given project, a key milestone for traceability is to first determine and agree upon requirements traceability details. Initially, three important questions should be answered before embarking on any particular requirements traceability approach:

1. What needs to be traceable?
2. What linkages need to be made?
3. How, when, and who should establish and maintain the resulting database?

After answering these basic questions, the approach for tracing requirements can be made. One approach could be the use of general-purpose tools, such as hypertext editors, word processors, and spreadsheets, which are configured to support cross-referencing between documents. For large system development projects, an alternative approach could be the use of a dedicated workbench centered on a database management system that provides tools for documenting, parsing, editing, decomposing, grouping, linking, organizing, partitioning, and managing requirements.

In 1995, Ramesh et al. analyzed the use of requirements traceability at a DoD system development at McClellan Air Force Base. Although a formal methodology was not developed to implement traceability, information models were used to convey the semantics of the various types of traceability information being captured and used by the organization. The models identified various types of traceability information used in areas such as requirements management, design rationale capture, and allocation of requirements to system components and use of resources by various system components. It is included here as an example to show the ISSEP one idea of tracing requirements.

Figure 4.23 identifies the information captured for requirements management. For each requirement, the rationale behind its creation is maintained. The evolution of requirements is represented by linking derived requirements to their sources and identifying the change proposals that

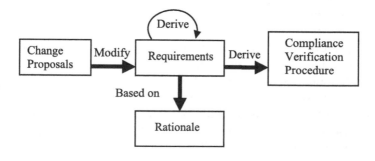

Figure 4.23   Requirements management model. (*Source:* Adapted from Ramesh et al., 1995.)

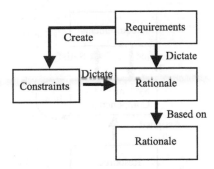

Figure 4.24 Design model. (*Source:* Based on Ramesh et al., 1995.)

modify requirements. Also, the compliance verification procedures (such as tests or simulations that need to be performed to ensure that a requirement is satisfied) are also identified (Ramesh et al., 1995). These beginning documentation requirements will be carried into the remaining steps of the model. For example, the change proposals are elements of a total configuration management plan (discussed further in Chapters 5 and 10). Also, the verification procedures documented now will be used to test the system and security functional in the development phase (discussed in Chapter 6).

Figure 4.24 identifies the information captured for relating requirements to design and system components. The constraints created by requirements need to be clearly identified and linked to their sources. Ramesh et al. noted that in the design phase (defined in the ISSE model as an architecture and design phase), the requirements or constraints that dictate design elements are identified. Further, the rationale behind major design decisions should be captured and linked to the design documentation

Figure 4.25 shows the linkages between requirements and system components. Ramesh et al. (1995) state that using an implementation model explains information about the *flow down* of requirements to system components. It can define how the flow is maintained as well as identifying how resources are assigned to system components.

This type of traceability provides a mechanism to identify the resources needed to satisfy specific requirements and the impact of changes on resources. The hierarchical breakdown of system components is also captured and is shown as an "is-a" link from and to system components. This linkage also indicates that a system component may be composed of *lower*-level components. Finally, the model shows that requirements can be related to various levels of system components.

If working in the DoD environment, one will also need to follow the Defense Information Technology System Certification and Accreditation

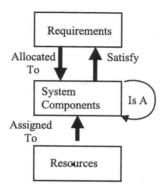

Figure 4.25 Implementation model. (*Source:* Based on Ramesh et al., 1995.)

Process (DITSCAP), which requires the ISSEP to prepare a Requirements Traceability Matrix (RTM). The objective of creating an RTM is to provide security traceability that ensures each security function or component is traceable to at least one security requirement.

Even if not working in the DoD environment, the RTM is a good ISSEP tool to verify whether the security requirements have been associated to appropriate security components and controls. The RTM can also be used during the C&A process to verify and validate requirements.

According to the DITSCAP model, the first step is to identify and analyze the mandatory directives and requisites to determine the system security requirements. The RTM is used to track the source of the requirement, the requirement statement, any related requirements, and a review method. Table 4.2 from DoD 8510.1-M is an example RTM.

The first column, the requirements number (REQ No.), shows the category of the requirement from a specific directive. The Requirement column describes the requirement in abbreviated form. The Review Method column identifies the review process for each requirement: I — Interview, D — Documentation Review, T — Test the scientific instrumented evaluation, and O — Observation (or demonstration of the security function) (DITSCAP, 2000, p. 48). The acronym DOIT may be helpful for remembering the types of review methods. The Comments column can be used to record findings or describe where to find the evidence needed to satisfy the requirement. More information on DISTCAP is provided in Chapter 8.

Another example of how to develop a RTM is shown in Table 4.3. This example is based on the Department of Energy's Requirements Traceability Matrix Template (DoE RTM, September 2002). Although the example does not relate directly to security, it can be easily modified to also include security requirements.

Table 4.2 Example of the Security Requirement Traceability Matrix (RTM)

REQ No.	Requirement	Source	Related Requirement	Review Method* I	D	O	T	Comments
	1.0 General							
	1.1 Fundamental Computer Security Requirements							
Fundamental 1	Requirement 1—SECURITY POLICY—There must be an explicit and well-defined security policy enforced by the system.	TCSEC, INTRO p. 3 TNI 2.2.1	DOJ 2640.2C-14	X	X	X		See FUND 2-6

* I = interview; D = documentation review; O = observation (or demonstration of the security function); and T = test the scientific instrumented evaluation.

Source: From DoD Directive 8510.1-M (2000), p. 49.

Table 4.3   Project Name: DoE Requirement Traceability Matrix (RTM)

Unique Number	Requirement	Source of Requirement	Software Reqs. Spec/ Functional Req. Doc.	Design Spec.	Program Module	Test Spec.	Test Case	Successful Test Verification	Modification of Requirement	Remarks
Objective 1:										

Source: From DoE Requirements Traceability Matrix (2002), p. 2-2.

The DoE RTM states that the matrix objective is used to "trace the requirements back to the project objectives identified in the Project Plan and forward through the remainder of the project life cycle stages (p. 21)." Place a copy of the matrix in the Project File. Expand the matrix in each stage to show traceability of work products to the requirements and vice versa. "The requirements traceability matrix should contain the following fields:

■ A unique identification number containing the general category of the requirement (e.g., SYSADM) and a number assigned in ascending order (e.g., 1.0; 1.1; 1.2)
■ The requirement statement
■ Requirement source (Conference; Configuration Control Board; Task Assignment, etc.)
■ Software Requirements Specification/Functional Requirements Document paragraph number containing the requirement
■ Design Specification paragraph number containing the requirement
■ Program Module containing the requirement
■ Test Specification containing the requirement test
■ Test Case number(s) where requirement is to be tested (optional)
■ Verification of successful testing of requirements
■ Modification field. If requirement was changed, eliminated, or replaced, indicate disposition and authority for modification" (p. 2-1)

Interface Identification and Security Architecture

An issue the ISSEP must consider is what impact the security function or component will have on the system functions and components and if it will adversely affect another internal or external component. In some instances, the choices the ISSEP makes to secure one subsystem may cause constraints in other subsystems. For example, using a Type II encryption device between two subsystems may cause performance degradation. The same can occur in the reverse; adding system components may affect the security requirements. Adding external interface connections to a system exponentially increases the complexity of the security. The SEs as part of their system architecture activities will define the functions needed for the interfaces. Once the system interfaces have been identified by the SE, the ISSEP reviews the interface control document to identify any security needs between the interface components.

The ISSEP should consider the physical location of the connections, whether the communication link between the two entities leaves the controlled space of a U.S. Government facility (i.e., traveling over unsecured Internet links), the information sensitivity level on both systems, etc. These types of critical questions must be considered during the architectural design of the system. Thus, communication between the ISSEPs and SEs must be constant to ensure that all parties understand how security affects the architecture definition.

If working with interconnections of DoD systems, the ISSEP needs to consider DoD Directive (DoDD) 8500.1 S4.14 (October 2002). This policy states that "All interconnections of DoD information systems shall be managed to continuously minimize community risk by ensuring that the assurance of one system is not undermined by vulnerabilities of interconnected systems" (p. 6).

Further, S.4.14.3 and S.4.14.4 clarify the interconnection with different security domains, other USG agencies, foreign nations, coalition partners, etc. It continues as "Interconnections among DoD information systems of different security domains or with other U.S. Government systems of different security domains shall be employed only to meet compelling operational requirements, not operational convenience. Secure configurations of approved IA and IA-enabled IT products, uniform risk criteria, trained systems security personnel, and strict configuration control shall be employed. The community risk shall be assessed and measures taken to mitigate that risk in accordance with procedures established by the Defense Information Systems Network (DISN) Designated Approving Authorities (DAAs) prior to interconnecting the systems" (p. 6).

"The interconnection of DoD information systems with those of U.S. allies, foreign nations, coalition partners, or international organizations shall comply with applicable international agreements and, whenever possible, DoD IA policies. Variations shall be approved by the responsible Combatant Commander and the DISN DAAs, and incorporated in the system security documentation. Information provided through these interconnections must be released in accordance with DoD regulations" (p. 7).

If ISSEPs will be working with Federal interagency interface connections, they should review NIST SP 800-47 (August 2002), "Security Guide for Interconnecting Information Technology Systems." SP 800-47 provides guidance for planning, establishing, maintaining, and terminating interconnections between information technology (IT) systems that are owned and operated by different organizations. The guide describes various benefits of interconnecting IT systems, identifies the basic components of an interconnection, identifies methods and levels of interconnectivity, and discusses potential security risks associated with interconnections.

SP 800-47 outlines a life-cycle approach for interconnecting information systems, with a focus on security. It defines the four phases of the interconnection life cycle as (NIST SP 800-47, 2002, p. ES-1):

- *"Planning the interconnection.* The participating organizations perform preliminary activities; examine all relevant technical, **security**, and administrative issues; and form an agreement governing the management, operation, and use of the interconnection.
- *Establishing the interconnection.* The organizations develop and execute a plan for establishing the interconnection, including **implementing or configuring appropriate security controls**.
- *Maintaining the interconnection.* The organizations actively maintain the interconnection after it is established to ensure that it operates properly **and securely**.
- *Disconnecting the interconnection.* One or both organizations may choose to terminate the interconnection. The termination should be conducted in a planned manner to avoid disrupting the other party's system. In response to an emergency, however, one or both organizations may decide to terminate the interconnection immediately."

An important element of defining the architecture is recognizing that various constraints will impact the selection of security functions and components. This is when it can be helpful to have a process to make decisions and also to explain to the customer how the decision was made. Sometimes, ISSEPs may find themselves in a precarious spot when having to explain to the customer that the security component must be included in the architecture and design — especially if the customer is a senior executive and does not want to delay the project, spend more money, etc. Having a rationale for explaining why the security requirement must be met with a specific component can be reassuring to the ISSEP who must insist on security.

Trade-Off Analysis

The process of analyzing alternatives and choosing the most appropriate solution is often referred to as *trade-off analysis*. This analysis must consider the different alternatives and balance the requirements with the solution. It is considered a decision-making tool and should be used to help SEs and ISSEPs make architectural and design decisions.

The Software Engineering Institute (SEI) at Carnegie Mellon University has developed an Architecture Tradeoff Analysis Method (ATAM^{SM}) for evaluating software system architectures relative to quality attribute goals. The focus is on achieving information systems that are secure, interoperable, portable, and reliable. The SEI states that using the ATAM will result in improved architectures by eliciting sets of quality requirements along multiple dimensions, analyzing the effects of each requirement in isolation, and then understanding the interactions of these requirements.

Although SEs and ISSEPs may not be familiar with this specific framework, the ATAM does provide good insight into the thought process of conducting a trade-off analysis that can be applied to a variety of architectural designs. For this reason, a brief overview of the ATAM is provided. However, those who are responsible for conducting formal trade-off analyses should refer to the Carnegie Mellon SEI Web site.

Note to the ISSEP candidates: The ATAM is provided for reference purposes only.

As shown in Figure 4.26, the first activity is to work with the project decision makers to identify the business needs, determine the quality attributes, identify the software architecture, and review other architectural approaches. This information is refined into operational scenarios and the architectural decision. An analysis of the scenarios and architecture is conducted to identify risks, non-risks, sensitivity points, and trade-off points. Identified risks are synthesized into a set of risk themes, which are then reviewed against the architecture and operational scenarios. The result of an ATAM is an out-brief presentation or a written report that includes the major findings of the analysis.

The elements of the report are:

■ Identification of the architectural styles
■ A hierarchical model of the requirements that describes the architecture with a focus on how it works with or meets the business drivers
■ Quality factors such as performance, availability, security, modifiability, and usability are elicited and prioritized
■ Operational scenarios are generated and mapped onto the architecture
■ Quality-attribute questions that were applied to the architecture and the responses to these questions
■ Identified risks and non-risks

The intent of the ATAM is to expose architectural risks that could inhibit the achievement of an organization's business or mission goals. Using the ATAM or a similar type of model can provide insight into how well the architecture satisfies particular goals, as well as how those goals interact with and trade off against each other.

At this stage of the ISSE process, as design decisions are being formulated, it may be necessary to begin noting information that will be needed during a trade-off analysis. However, it is expected that a true trade-off

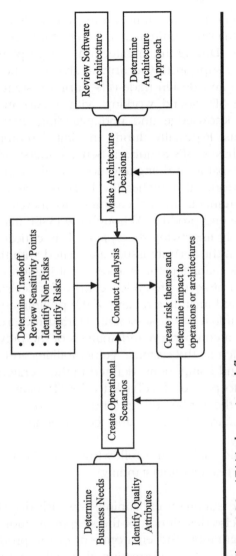

Figure 4.26 ATAM elements and flow.

analysis will be made in the next step; thus, more information on trade-off analysis is provided in Chapter 5: "Develop Detailed Security Design."

ISSE and Risk Management

Risks can be identified at any time during the ISSE process — during system security definition, requirements, architecture design, development, implementation, etc. During the architectural design phase, the identified risks can be used to support the security analyses of the system that may lead to architecture and design trade-offs during system development.

The more time SEs spend working with a customer on a specific project, the more knowledge and understanding they gain about the system requirements. Especially during the initial requirement, architecture, and design phases, SEs acquire a better understanding of what the system should be capable of doing and how, if minor modifications were made, it could perform at a higher level. Thus, it is typical for SEs to suggest new requirements to the customer to increase the customer's satisfaction with the end product. Although the ISSEP may also view these changes as ultimately improving the system, it is critical for the ISSEP to provide guidance on the security issues associated with the modifications. Thus, continual risk management is a key contribution of the ISSEP.

Usually, during a project's life cycle, security risk decisions follow major system milestones and include a review of the preliminary risk assessment or conducting the initial risk assessment. During the architecture phase, the ISSEP conducts a comparison and analysis of the previously identified risk information, such as the system's vulnerabilities and threats, with the security functions and components defined in the architecture. It is important for the ISSEP to provide feedback to the SE team and the customer to make sure that the further design and actual development does not begin until the security features and components are reviewed and accepted.

The ISSEP should include the following items in the risk analysis in sufficient detail for reader understanding:

- An executive summary explaining how risk decisions are made
- A clear, concise description of the system, including the current or future configuration and environment of the product or system
- A description of the information that will be processed on the system and the impact to the organization if the information was disclosed, modified, or unavailable
- A results statement of a vulnerabilities analysis

- The results of a threat analysis, including the likelihood of the threat occurring, and the impact to the organization if the threat disclosed, modified, or made the information unavailable
- A visual representation of the risk data, to include a representation model, such as a security risk plane (described next)
- List of management, operational, or technical controls
- Recommendations for additional security controls
- Any new decision review meeting minutes and presentations

Throughout the life cycle of the project, security risk analysis and reports should be linked together using a standard graphical representation and notation. One approach for presenting risk information is through a security risk plane model. Figure 4.27 shows an example of three security risk planes. The first risk plane (dated January 10) indicates three attacks — A1, A2, and A3. The next risk plane (dated March 5) implies that A1 was accepted during the previous assessment; A3 has been adjusted based on new information; and a new item called B1 has been added to the assessment. Item A2 does not show up in this assessment and therefore must have been mitigated during the design activities preceding this

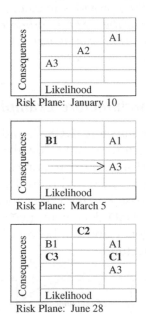

Figure 4.27   Risk plane example. (*Source:* Based on *ISSE Handbook,* 1994, Figure 3.7.2.4-1, p. 3-58.)

assessment. The third assessment (dated June 28) shows the addition of items C1, C2, and C3 during this last assessment phase.

The output and documentation from the security risk assessment should include:

- The identification of all possible scenarios, events, attacks, or vulnerabilities that could result in the inability of the system to maintain compliance with stated security requirements
- A ranked assessment of these items based on specific system consequences and the likelihood of occurrence
- A set of possible approaches to mitigate these items, including any possible impact on the program plan or operational requirements
- Recommendations for a course of action

Before moving into the preliminary design activities, the ISSEP must review the security architecture against previously defined risks. Again, ISSEPs must be integrated into the SE team so that security is included during all design and development decisions.

As a reference of security architecture, the DoD Goal Security Architecture document (April 1996) provides an example of the various elements that would be included. *For the ISSEP candidate, it is highly unlikely this will appear on the exam. However, it may be interesting to review an example, so it is included in this chapter.*

DoD Goal Security Architecture Example

The DoD Goal Security Architecture (DGSA, April 1996) identifies a generic information system architecture security view that refines the abstract local subscriber environment (LSE) and communication networks (CNs) into several elements (see Figure 4.28) and then defines four generic security architecture components based on the LSE elements and the CN. Although this information is from a DoD document, many of the principles can be applied to any Federal agency and can be very helpful in assisting ISSEPs design the security architecture.

Figure 4.28   Abstract security architecture view.

Included in the LSE are three generic functional elements:

1. End systems (ESs): for example, workstations, servers, telephones, radios, mainframes
2. Relay systems (RSs): for example, multiplexers, routers, switches, cellular nodes, message transfer agents
3. Local communications systems (LCSs): for example, rings, buses, wire lines

The distinction between end systems and relay systems is that end systems support users with direct human interfaces and personal or general applications, while relay systems are only indirectly accessible by users and the functionality is limited to information transfer relay. Some relay system functions may be performed in many communications protocol layers. Local communication systems (LCSs) serve to connect ESs and RSs within an LSE. Where necessary, the abstract CN can be refined to generic elements such as packet switches, routers, and transmission elements. An LSE may contain a single ES such as a workstation, a single RS such as a router, or combinations of ESs and RSs connected through LCSs. All physical elements of the information system architecture are either part of an LSE or are CNs.

When ISSEPs view this from a security perspective, it is not enough to consider only the physical information system elements. ISSEPs must also take into account the environment in which the elements are employed and the means through which they are managed. The resulting generic security architecture view includes four components to which security service allocations will be made:

1. *ESs and RSs:* information processing elements
2. *Security management:* security-related activities of information system management
3. *Transfer system:* LCS and CN elements and communications protocols used by them and by ESs and RSs
4. *Physical and administrative environment:* security related to environmental (physical) elements and personnel

Taken from the DGSA, Figure 4.29 illustrates a generic view of several LSEs joined by CNs. Each LSE is defined and bounded by the elements under user (organization) control, including the environment. LSEs exhibit all or parts of each of the four generic architecture components, while the CN only represents a part of the transfer system.

ESs and RSs are entirely contained within an LSE. Although Figure 4.29 shows ESs and RSs as separate generic components, in practice the same

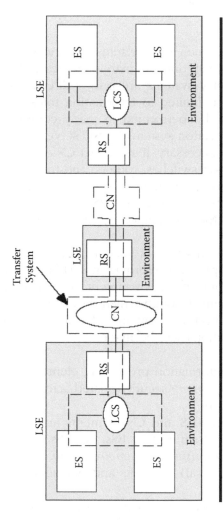

Figure 4.29 Generic security architecture view. (*Source:* **From DGSA, 1996, p. 3-3.**)

information system can combine both ES and RS functions, as necessary. LSE connections to CNs are only through RS functions.

The security management component is not illustrated in this figure but its functions are pervasive in the LSEs and extend to cooperate with CN management facilities. The transfer system component is shown within dashed lines. Although it includes all of the LCS and CN elements, it includes only those portions of the ESs and RSs that implement communications protocols.

The physical and administrative environment component (labeled collectively as *Environment* in Figure 4.29) represents all of the generic security services provided directly or indirectly by physical means (e.g., locked gates, guard dogs) or through administrative procedures (e.g., background investigations, issuance of badges) (DGSA, April 1996, p. 3-3).

The next step is to allocate the security services to the abstract security architecture components. The DGSA security services include authentication, access control, data availability, data integrity, data confidentiality, and non-repudiation. The next topics provide information on how these security services are allocated to functions and components.

CN Security Allocation

Because most DoD systems use common carrier services, the DGSA makes only a security service allocation of communications availability to CNs. CNs must provide an agreed level of responsiveness, continuity of service, and resistance to accidental and intentional threats to the communications service.

CN providers must employ various security services to protect the CN's own resources to ensure that the agreed availability will be maintained. However, ISSEPs should not rely upon the CNs for the confidentiality or integrity of the information they transfer. A failure by the CNs will result only in the delay, incorrect delivery, or non-delivery of otherwise adequately protected information.

LSE Security Service Allocations

All the security services are allocated to LSEs. The provision of security services for an entire LSE is accomplished by management, operational, and technical security controls.

End System and Relay System Security Service Allocations

Security service allocations are made to both ES and RS hardware and software. The hardware protects the software, and the software protects information being processed, transferred, or stored. Together, ES and RS hardware and software provide the security services of user identification and authentication, access control, data integrity, data confidentiality, non-repudiation, and availability.

Examples of end system security hardware components include:

- *Fault tolerance* — availability
- *Fault detection* — availability, integrity
- *Memory management* — strict isolation, integrity
- *Protected mode/multistate processors* — strict isolation, integrity
- *Majority logic* — availability, integrity
- *Multiprocessor architectures* — availability, strict isolation, integrity
- *TEMPEST* — confidentiality
- *QUADRANT* — availability, integrity

Examples of end system security software components include:

- Separation kernel
- Security contexts, including:
  - A unique identification for each security context
  - The identification of the information domain being supported
  - Hardware register values related to control of end system resources, including virtual memory and all devices in or attached to the end system
  - The authenticated identity of the user being served
  - The user's security attributes (permissions)
  - Data structures needed to operate security-related functions and other untrusted system applications
- Security-critical functions. The separation of security mechanisms from security policy enforcement and decisions is crucial to the flexibility of the end system security architecture. The Security Policy Decision Function (SPDF) is responsible for making all security policy decisions. The primary role of the SPDF is to isolate the rest of the end system software from knowledge of security policies. To illustrate this concept, consider an example of three enterprises with different, or even conflicting, security policies. The first is a DoD organization using a conventional DoD security policy. The second is a corporation with requirements for data integrity and data separation based solely on need-to-know authorization. The third is a university research laboratory that does not have any special security needs except a basic privacy-based access control policy. Without a policy-independent architecture, these three differing security policies would result in three different operating system implementations that could cause serious compatibility

problems for a vendor trying to support all three environments. Using the SPDF approach, any or all of the three policies could be supported by the same end system software. If necessary, the three enterprises could be served by the same end system or (using the transfer system) they could share information as necessary across different end systems. Examples of SPDF functions include authentication, audit, process scheduling, and device management and device controllers.

■ Trusted applications, such as databases, X Window Systems, or operating systems. (DGSA, April 1996, p. 4.1–4.18)

Security Management Security Service Allocations

Security management provides supporting services that contribute to the protection of information and resources in accordance with applicable information domain and information system security policies. All the security services are allocated to the security management component, but only indirectly. The function of the security management component is to support and control the other architectural components.

A complexity of security management emerges when the system will have multiple information domains. Traditional security management is based on the assumption that all users of an end system are subject to the same security policy, so that a single view of security management is sufficient for the entire end system. In today's interconnected systems, end systems that support multiple information domains must provide the ability to manage each information domain independently. The use of security services and security mechanisms shared among multiple information domains will require security management coordination at the end system level. Thus, an end system security policy is necessary to specify how the shared use of security functions and resources among information domains is accomplished. This end system policy also must be managed.

Examples of security management security services include (DGSA, April 1996, p. 5.1–5.9):

■ Member registration information
■ Member authentication criteria (e.g., strength of mechanism required)
■ Member authentication information
■ Member attributes (privileges) (e.g., access privileges, release authority for interdomain transfers)
■ Visible security label information (i.e., what label, if any, is attached to information that is printed or displayed)
■ Security service and security mechanism requirements for specific applications, including:

- Intradomain communications and interdomain information transfer
- The selection of events to be logged and/or remotely collected
- The enabling and disabling of audit trail logging of selected events
- The remote collection of selected audit records
- The preparation of security audit reports
■ Maintenance of the rules used to react to real or suspected security violations
■ The remote reporting of apparent violations of system security
■ Security administrator interactions
■ Determination and assignment of the target security protection for the service
■ Assignment and maintenance of rules for the selection (where alternatives exist) of the specific security mechanism to be employed to provide the requested security service
■ Negotiation (locally and remotely) of available security mechanisms requiring prior management agreement
■ Invocation of specific security mechanisms via the appropriate security mechanism function (e.g., for the provision of administratively imposed security services)
■ Interaction with other security service management functions and security mechanism management functions

Transfer System Security Service Allocations

Because security services are implemented within protected end systems and relay systems, most of the protections for the transfer of information are provided. However, the remaining security service allocations to the transfer system make it responsible for peer entity and data origin authentication, access control, non-repudiation, confidentiality, integrity, and availability of information in transfer. The protection of information being transferred enables the protected distribution of security-relevant information for security management as well as user information. The sharing of identification and authentication information, audit records, key management information, and policy and privilege management information among LSEs can be safely accomplished if the transfer system is protected.

Several elements needed to support the basic transfer system activities are (DGSA, April 1996, p. 6.1–6.9):

■ End system communications applications requests (e.g., through the GSS-API)
■ Additional information object use and maintenance (e.g., to access information for remote security administration maintenance, security protocol and algorithm operation, certificate processing)

- Maintenance and retrieval of security information from the X.500 Directory using the directory access protocol
- Management information processing for staged delivery secure messaging for both transmission and receipt of security association management protocol operations for establishment of interactive distributed security contexts, including security protocol operation, termination, and recovery, plus maintenance of security management information base entries for each security association established
- General-purpose management protocol operation to accomplish secure exchange of security information between distributed security management areas or network management information requested by network management systems
- X.509 certificates to carry appropriate security information, such as key management certificates
- User access control information for distributed operations
- Traffic and message keys
- Accumulated audit data, including records of distributed security context utilization
- Key management, encipherment, integrity, and signature algorithm identifiers, and security protocol objects
- End system access control information for distributed operations
- Encryption algorithm initialization information
- Security association configuration information
- Compromise action information (e.g., certificate revocation lists)
- Contingency plan parameters (e.g., auto-purge and security policy replacement actions under emergency conditions)

Physical and Administrative Environment Security Service Allocations

All security services are allocated to the physical and administrative environment architecture component. Reliance on people (i.e., administrative procedures) and the environment is an integral part of achieving total security for an information system. When products are designed and deployed in information systems, administrative and environmental conditions of their use must be met to complement the protection afforded by any hardware and software security mechanisms employed in those products. Sometimes, the specification of such conditions for the use of a component, facility, or system is referred to as *security doctrine*. The administrative and environmental security conditions of use specify how security requirements are to be met and, as such, are elements of the specific security architecture. As with any design aspect of a specific security architecture, there will be different types of administrative and environmental security allocations, each with different degrees of specificity, which eventually lead to the satisfaction of the required security services through the choice of appropriate security mechanisms. In the case of administrative and environmental security, security services are provided by physical, administrative, personnel, and operational security mechanisms (DGSA, April 1996, p. 7.1–7.4):

■ *Mechanisms for identification and authentication.* Authentication responsibilities are often shared between administrative, environmental, and technical (i.e., hardware and software) mechanisms. Probably the most common mechanism is the picture badge and the guard. The use of keys with locks, passwords, or cipher lock codes authenticates identity only to the extent of the probability that the presenter is a valid holder of the object or information. That probability is based on the administrative handling and physical protection of such mechanisms or information. The same considerations apply to the use of smart cards, cryptographic ignition keys, and other credentials that make no positive connection with the holder. In general, nonforgeable information bound to the holder is the strongest type of authentication mechanism. Security mechanisms for authentication depend upon system security administrators who perform the initial assignment of the badge or other credential to an individual.

■ *Mechanisms for access control.* The first line of protection for the LSE is through mechanisms that control access to the facilities (e.g., buildings, rooms) containing the ESs, RSs, and LCSs. The human security guard is one of the most familiar types of access control mechanisms. Key, combination, and cipher locks are common mechanisms of controlling access to facilities. The next line of protection involves the use of approved containers (e.g., combination safes and locking cabinets) for the protection of system assets. Finally, the components themselves may contain access control mechanisms such as power locks, two-person-control devices, and sealed housings.

■ *Mechanisms for confidentiality.* The major applications of administrative and environmental confidentiality mechanisms in LSEs involve video displays, printing devices, sounds, and non-video electromagnetic emanations. Users and security administrators can control when, where, and in whose presence video information is displayed. Video display emanations can be controlled through screen filters and shielded enclosures. Printer ribbon handling, copy counting, and labeling requirements can be controlled by users, operators, and system administrators. The control of trash and the destruction of paper and other media are important procedures. Paper shredders may be useful. Procedures for handling and mechanisms for erasure of persistent storage media can be critical to confidentiality. Sound insulation and sound masking can be used to control disclosure through conversations and machine noises. Electromagnetic emanations, either radiated or conducted, can be confined by shielding rooms and by filtering signal and power wiring using standard TEMPEST features. The presence of copiers and photographic equipment in LSEs requires careful control. Paper and other media devices should be properly wrapped prior to shipping or mailing.

■ *Mechanisms for integrity.* Integrity mechanisms are used in response to security policy requirements to protect information and other system assets from unauthorized modification. System components may have features that permit security diagnostic checking of hardware (e.g., through comparison of diagnostic known-answer tests with off-line security check mechanisms). Non-forgeable seals and protective coatings can be used on hardware components and subcomponents to detect or prevent alteration. Cryptographic and noncryptographic check value mechanisms can be used to ensure the integrity of software packages as delivered and as used. Regular inspections of facilities and system components are an important part of using integrity mechanisms. Devices used for integrity checking must be stored in protected areas. Software master copies and small system components must also be stored in protected areas while not in use. Protection from electromagnetic interference can be accomplished by filtering and shielding.

■ *Mechanisms for non-repudiation.* Non-repudiation mechanisms support security policy requirements for proof of delivery and proof of origin of information transactions. Non-repudiation mechanisms may include the contents of a transaction. For paper transactions, notary services and personal signatures are useful mechanisms in providing non-repudiation services. Non-repudiation mechanisms, such as hash coding of data and digital signatures, can be used to validate the source of software packages. Non-repudiation mechanisms could be used for verifying that hardware is unchanged from its manufactured state.

■ *Mechanisms for availability.* Availability mechanisms in communications networks and LSEs satisfy security policy requirements for availability of communications and processing resources. The ability of communications networks to provide timely and regular service depends on the total security architecture, implementation, and management of those systems. The techniques of redundancy, diversity, contingency reserves, and contingency planning play a large part in communications network availability. Within LSEs, the LCS must be similarly designed and protected to avoid failure outages. In general, the physical protection and integrity checking of the ESs, RSs, and LCSs will provide for their availability.

For examples of other security architectures, refer to the final section of the DGSA (April 1996).

Final Deliverable of Designing System and Security Architectures

The final deliverable for the SE is the system architecture document that provides details of how the system should be designed during Phase 4. It should define the results of the functional analysis and allocation, and provide a blueprint for the components of the system. The output for the ISSEPs will be the documented Systems Security Architecture that defines the outcome of the security functional analysis and allocation, and identifies the security components that will need to be designed and developed for the system.

Summary

The architecture of the system is the framework for designing an information system in terms of a set of building blocks and how the building blocks fit together. Security architecture is a view of the overall system architecture from a security perspective. It provides insight into the security services, mechanisms, technologies, and features that can be used to satisfy system security requirements. It provides recommendations on where, within the context of the overall system architecture, security mechanisms and components should be placed. The objective of the security architecture is to provide a tool that will communicate where security is necessary as the process moves into the design and development phases.

Important tasks in system and system security architecture are to conduct a functional analysis (translating system requirements into detailed design criteria) and functional allocation (grouping and allocating of functions). The main purpose of the functional analysis and allocation is to structure the system requirements into functional terms and identifiable components. It identifies the major system-level (or top-level) functions that must be performed by the system to accomplish its mission. A timeline analysis can be completed to determine whether the functions are to be performed in series or in parallel. Key tools in functional analysis and allocation include functional hierarchy diagrams, functional flow block diagrams (FFBDs), and timeline analysis diagrams.

When the ISSEP performs the security functional analysis and allocation, the goal is to ensure that the elements of the system-level functional architecture include the security functions in sufficient depth to allow for synthesis of solution in the following stage. The ISSEP can use the same tools defined in the SE activity to conduct the security functional analysis and allocation.

Traceability, a critical SE and ISSE concept, is the process of ensuring that system requirements have been addressed in the system design. If following DITSCAP, the ISSEP must prepare a Requirements Traceability Matrix (RTM). The RTM is a good tool to use in any environment to verify whether security functions and components have been associated to appropriate security requirements.

At the end of this phase, the SEs will have the system architecture documented. The ISSEP, in coordination with the SEs architectural document, will have defined the security architecture. These architectural plans are the basis for the next phase, designing the system and the security for the system.

References

Blanchard, Benjamin (1998). *Systems Engineering Management, 2nd edition*. John Wiley & Sons: New York, NY.

Chief Information Officers (CIO) Council (September 1999). Federal Enterprise Architecture Framework, Version 1.1. Available from: http://www.cio.gov/Documents/fedarch1.pdf.

DoD C4ISR Architecture Framework Working Group (December 1997). C4ISR Architecture Framework, Version 2.0. Available from: http://www.defenselink.mil/nii/org/cio/i3/AWG_Digital_Library/pdfdocs/fw.pdf.

DoD Directive No. 8500.1 (October 2002). Information Assurance. (Certified current as of November 21, 2003.) Available from www.dtic.mil/whs/directives.

DoD Directive No. 8500.2 (February 2003). Information Assurance Implementation. Available from www.dtic.mil/whs/directives.

DoD Technical Architecture Framework for Information Management, Volume 6: Department of Defense (DoD) Goal Security Architecture, Version 3.0 (DGSA, April 30, 1996). Available for download: http://www-library.itsi.disa.mil/tafim/tafim3.0/pages/volume6/v6_toc.htm.

DOE G 200.1-1A (September 2002). "Systems Engineering Methodology, Version 3 "The DOE Systems Development Lifecycle (SDLC) for Information Technology Investments." U.S. Department of Energy, Office of the Chief Information Officer. This document and associated process guides can be found at http://cio.doe.gov/ITReform/sqse.

DOE Requirements Traceability Matrix (September 2002). "Requirements Traceability Matrix Template." U.S. Department of Energy, Office of the Chief Information Officer. This document and associated process guides can be found at http://cio.doe.gov/ITReform/sqse.

Executive Order 13011 (July 1996). Federal Information Technology. Available at http://www.archives.gov/federal_register/executive_orders/1996.html

Faulconbridge, R. Ian and Michael J. Ryan (2003). *Managing Complex Technical Projects: A Systems Engineering Approach*. Artech House: Norwood, MA.

Gotel, O. and A. Finkelstein (April 1994). An Analysis of the Requirements Traceability Problem, in *Proceedings of the First International Conference on Requirements Engineering*, Colorado Springs, CO.

IEEE 610-1990 (September 1990). Standard Computer Dictionary: A Compilation of IEEE Standard Computer Glossaries. IEEE: New York, NY.

IEEE Std 1220-1998 (December 1998, copyrighted January 1999). IEEE Standard for Application and Management of the Systems Engineering Process. IEEE: New York, NY. (Revision of IEEE Std 1220-1994)

IEEE Std 1471-2000 (September 2000). IEEE Recommended Practice for Architectural Description of Software-Intensive Systems. IEEE: New York, NY.

Information Assurance Technical Framework (IATF), Version 3.1 (September 2002). National Security Agency, Information Assurance Solutions, Technical Directors: Fort Meade, MD.

Information Systems Security Engineering Handbook, Release 1.0 (February 28, 1994). National Security Agency, Central Security Service. Only available for official USG use.

Kean, Liz (1997). Requirements Tracing — An Overview. Available from: http://www.sei.cmu.edu/str/descriptions/reqtracing_body.html.

NIST SP 800-30 (January 2002), "Risk Management Guide for Information Technology Systems." Available at the NIST Web site: www.nist.gov.

NIST SP 800-47 (August 2002), "Security Guide for Interconnecting Information Technology Systems." Available at the NIST Web site: www.nist.gov.

NIST SP 800-53 (February 2005). Recommended Security Controls for Federal Information Systems. Available at the NIST Web site: www.nist.gov.

Office of Management and Budget (November 2000). Office of Management and Budget Circular No. A-130. Available from: www.whitehouse.gov/omb/circulars/a130/a130trans4.html.

Open Group, The (2003). The Open Group Architecture Framework (TOGAF), Version 8.1 Enterprise Edition. ©2003, The Open Group: San Francisco, CA.

Ramesh, Bala, Lt. Curtis Stubbs, Lt. Cmdr. Timothy Powers, and Michael Edwards (1995). Lessons Learned from Implementing Requirements Traceability. *CrossTalk: The Journal of Defense Engineering*, April 1995. Article available online at: http://www.stsc.hill.af.mil/crosstalk/1995/04/.

SEI ATAM (last modified February 2005). Architecture Tradeoff Analysis Method. Copyright 2005 by Carnegie Mellon University, available at http://www.sei. cmu.edu/architecture/ata_method.html.

U.S. Government Accounting Office (April 2003). U.S. GOA Executive Guide: Information Technology: A Framework for Assessing and Improving Enterprise Architecture Management, Version 1.1, Document #GAO-03-584G.

5

ISSE Model Phase 4: Develop Detailed Security Design

Introduction

The phases in the Information Systems Security Engineering (ISSE) life-cycle model are:

1. Discover Information Protection Needs. Ascertain why the system needs to be built and what information needs to be protected.
2. Define System Security Requirements. Define the system in terms of what security is needed.
3. Define System Security Architecture. Define the security functions needed to meet the specific security requirements.
4. **Develop Detailed Security Design. Based on the security architecture, design the security functions and features for the system.**
5. Implement System Security. Following the documented security design, build and implement the security functions and features for the system.
6. Assess Security Effectiveness. Assess the degree to which the security of the system, as it is defined, designed, and implemented, meets the security needs.

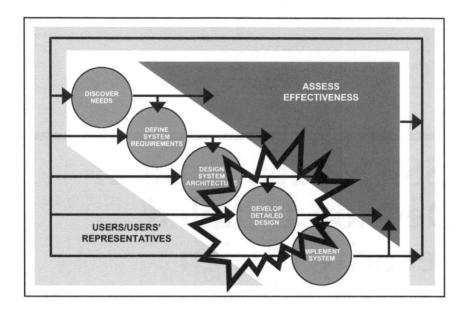

Figure 5.1   ISSE model: develop security design. (*Source:* Adapted from IATF, p. 3-2.)

This chapter focuses on Phase 4: Develop Detailed Security Design of the Information Systems Security Engineering (ISSE) Model. This phase is analogous to the systems engineering activity: Develop Detailed Design. As shown in Figure 5.1, following the formulation of the security architecture in Phase 3, the System Engineers (SEs) and Information Systems Security Engineering Professionals (ISSEPs) transform the architecture into a detailed written design and, if appropriate, begin the preliminary design of the system and security components.

In the architecture design phase, the ISSEP® developed an abstract view of the functional security aspects of the system; in this phase, the ISSEP brings together the previous elements into a formal document that explains how the system design will meet the security requirements. Figure 5.3 provides an outline of the activities involved in preparing the system and security design. The system security design document specifies the system and its components, but does not decide on specific components or vendors. The final selection of components and building the system in a secure manner is part of the next activity, Implement System Security.

As shown in Figure 5.2, there are two primary topics in this chapter: design activities for the SEs and those for the ISSEPs. The chapter begins by discussing the systems engineering process for the design phase,

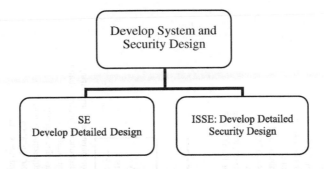

Figure 5.2 Chapter overview.

followed by a section defining the role of the ISSE team during the design phase. Within the ISSE topic is a brief introduction to Common Criteria (CC) and the development of CC profiles. In addition, a basic life-cycle plan is outlined to demonstrate how it fits into the security design document, which can also be referred to as the security specification document.

Systems Engineering Activity: System Design

The SE relies on the system architecture plans to define and finalize the system design. That is, the system design should follow what has been outlined as the subsystems or component items (CIs) in the architecture. The objective for the SE is to design the component parts of the system so they will fit together as an operating whole during the implementation phase. According to Kossiakoff and Sweet (2003), typical functional and component design activities include:

■ Analyzing component interactions and interfaces and identifying design, integration, and test issues
■ Analyzing detailed user interaction modes
■ Designing and prototyping user interfaces
■ Laying out preliminary design of all hardware and software components and interfaces
■ After review, implementing detailed hardware designs and software code
■ Building prototype versions of engineered components (p. 241–242)

It is assumed that the primary allocation of functions was accomplished in the earlier phases, but the definition of their interactions has not been

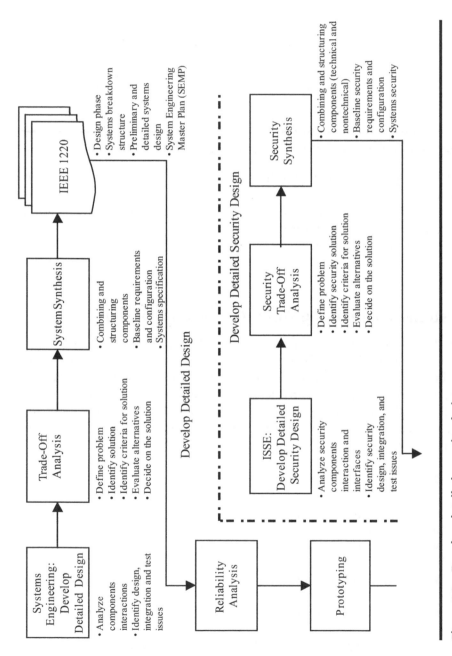

Figure 5.3   Develop detailed security design.

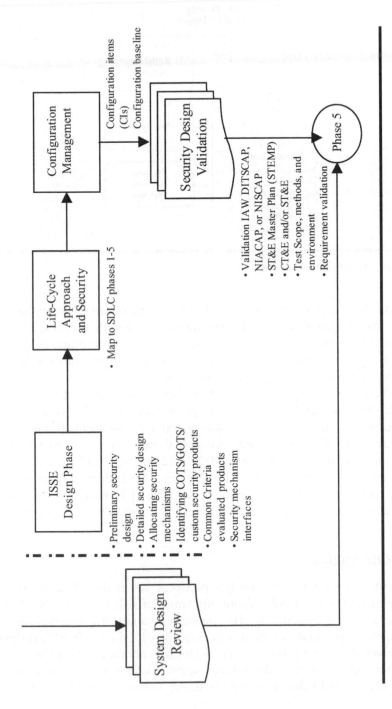

Figure 5.3 (continued)

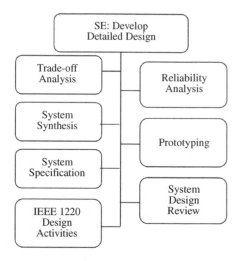

Figure 5.4 SE design activities.

finalized. Thus, a primary objective of the design phase is to finalize the interactions of components with one another and with the system environment. This final design includes aspects such as recommendations for acquisition of components, configuration of components, integration, and operation and maintenance of the components.

As shown in Figure 5.4, this section begins by defining two central elements of the design phase: the concept of trade-off analysis and system-level synthesis. The system specifications activity documents the technical requirements for the system and its components. The next topic reviews the design activities according to IEEE 1220:1998, IEEE Standard for Application and Management of the Systems Engineering Process. The final sections look at reliability analysis, the idea of prototyping the system components and subsystems, and conducting a final system design review.

Trade-Off Analysis

An important element of the design phase is when the SE analyzes the design constraints and thinks about any trade-offs that may be needed to meet the system requirements. The process of analyzing alternatives and selecting the appropriate solution is generically called a **trade-off analysis**. This analytical process involves considering the alternatives and balancing the requirements prior to selecting the appropriate solution. The trade-off analysis should help decision makers make decisions, not be a decision maker.

The steps involved in trade-off analysis include:

1. *Define the problem.* To select the appropriate solution, the requirements and the needs of the problem must be defined and documented precisely.
2. *Identify solutions.* This can be one of the most important steps in the trade-off analysis. It must identify the widest range of possible alternative solutions to maximize the chance of selecting the optimal solution to the problem. This is often referred to as **brainstorming**. During a brainstorming session, all possible alternatives are noted, regardless of the feasibility of the solution. The idea is to generate as many alternatives as possible.
3. *Identify criteria for deciding on a solution.* To determine the appropriate solution, criteria must be formulated that provide a measure that can be used to determine the effectiveness of the alternatives. Criteria can include but are not limited to items such as personnel limitations, time constraints, financial resources, information sensitivity, training issues, or security constraints. Once the criteria have been identified, they can be weighted based on their importance. For most systems, the criteria will have different values. For example, sensitivity of information would be weighted differently if it was considered Unclassified versus Secret. A good evaluation can be obtained by combining the assessment of how well an alternative meets a certain criterion with a measure of the significance of that criterion.
4. *Evaluate the alternatives.* The initial action is to eliminate the solutions that are not feasible, particularly because it can save time to eliminate alternatives that can be easily recognized as not reasonable to implement. The remaining feasible solutions should then be discussed and identified in sufficient detail so that everyone understands the impact of the solution. It may be necessary to obtain more information about the solutions to provide some differentiation among the alternatives.
5. *Decide on the solution.* Based on the evaluation of the alternatives, a decision is made as to the best possible solution.

Once the design constraints have been identified and adjusted for any trade-offs, a detailed system design is documented following the life-cycle phases discussed later in the chapter. This activity produces a detailed written document describing the system design. It must provide enough information about components and interface specifications so that the SEs can build the system or acquisition specialists can acquire the components to be built.

System Synthesis (Design)

According to Blanchard and Fabrycky (1998), the trade-off analysis leads to **synthesis**, which is the combining and structuring of components in such a way as to represent a feasible system configuration. At the synthesis point, the basic requirements are established, trade-off studies are completed, and a baseline configuration is developed to demonstrate the design concepts. *The synthesis is the design — it describes the build-to requirements for the system elements.* It defines, refines, and integrates the configuration items into a physical configuration that satisfies the system requirements. It is used in the development of preliminary concepts and to establish relationships among the various components of the system.

During the synthesis of the system, alternate configurations or architectures are developed and evaluated against the system requirements. Prototypes or models can be constructed to support trade-off analysis or valid alternatives. Synthesis takes these alternatives and develops the preliminary concepts and establishes the relationships between system elements. At this step in the process, synthesis establishes a system configuration that is representative of the final system form, sometimes referred to as the system specification document. The steps of conducting a system-level synthesis are shown in Figure 5.5.

The first step — identifying potential system solutions — uses the architectural options from the previous phase. Next, the SEs gather and review information about each solution, such as life-cycle significance, quality assurance, test and evaluation, or maintenance considerations. Based on this information, an evaluation of the possible solutions is conducted. Any discrepancies are noted and fed back to previous activities. The preferred solution is then chosen. The final step is to document the decisions and accompanying rationale in the system specifications.

System Specifications

The technical requirements for the system and its components are documented through a series of specifications called the system specifications. The **system specifications** is a document containing the functional baseline and results from various SE activities, such as the needs analysis, feasibility analysis, operational requirements, top-level functional analysis (which may lead to subordinate specifications), maintenance concept, system requirement analysis, and critical technical performance measures.

There are several different categories of system specifications, starting with Type A (System Specification) and continuing with Type B through Type E. Table 5.1 provides a brief description of each specification category. The categories were initially developed for the Department of

Table 5.1   System Specification Categories

Category	Type	Description
System specification	Type A	The technical, performance, operational, maintenance, and support characteristics for the entire system
Development specification	Type B	The technical requirements for any item below the system level where research, design, and development are accomplished
Product specification	Type C	The technical requirements for any item below the top system level that is currently in the inventory and can be procured off-the-shelf
Process specification	Type D	The technical requirements that cover a service that is performed on any component of the system
Material specification	Type E	The technical requirements that pertain to raw material, mixtures, or semi-fabricated materials used in the fabrication of a product

Defense but are used in generic terms throughout the systems engineering field.

The system specification document outlines what is to be achieved by the system and the minimum acceptable level of performance. The main product of synthesis is the refined system specification and a broad system solution for achieving the requirements. In Phase 3, we mentioned traceability, the process of ensuring that system requirements have been addressed in the system design. Forward traceability is from the system requirements to the system specification. Backward traceability is from the system specification to the system design, which ensures that additional requirements have not crept into the system specification during the design process. The system specifications must develop from the system requirements document, and SEs must ensure that these requirements are met in the system specifications document. The difference is that the system specifications is more detailed and provides more formal specifications of the requirements.

The system specifications are perhaps the most important of all SE design documents. The specifications become the source for all of the subordinate specifications that are produced at later stages through the design and development process. If the system specifications is firm, an effective foundation is formed for the remainder of the design and development effort. Errors or omissions in the system specifications flow into the remaining design effort. The later these errors are discovered, the

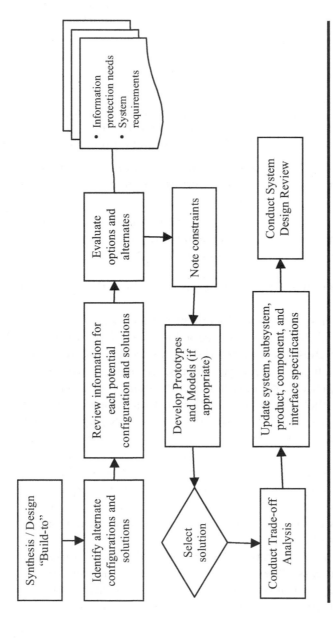

Figure 5.5 System-level synthesis.

more expensive and time consuming the rectification becomes (Faulcon-bridge and Ryan, 2003).

For background purposes of how another model defines the design phase, the next section provides a brief introduction to the system design activities outlined in the IEEE 1220 standard.

IEEE Systems Engineering Process: Design Phase

Note to ISSEP candidates: IEEE 1220 is not listed as an (ISC)[2] exam requirement; however, this standard is helpful in understanding the SE design phase activities.

IEEE 1220 states that during the system design phase, the organization should generate a System Breakdown Structure (SBS) to depict the hierarchy of products and processes that comprise the system architecture. The SBS should be used by the organization for development and control of planning packages and their conversion to work packages, sizing of work packages, configuration management, resource allocation, traceability of requirement changes, interface control, cost reporting, and event-based scheduling.

The SBS should also assign the life-cycle processes to the product and assembly levels and identify any personnel who need to support the life-cycle processes. IEEE 1220 states that "the manpower, personnel, and training specifications that define the knowledge, skills, abilities, availability, and training required for the humans who support the system, its subsystems, and components are developed to ensure that the system may be adequately operated and supported throughout its life cycle" (p. 15). Figure 5.6 depicts the various system elements and life-cycle processes that can be included in an SBS for a fully developed system. Figure 5.7 reflects the typical life-cycle phases of system development — system definition, subsystem definition, preliminary design, detailed design, and fabrication, assembly, integration, and test.

System Definition Level

During system definition stage, the SEs focus on products required to satisfy operational requirements. This includes establishing the system definition; beginning the specification for the system, product, subsystems, and interfaces; establishing the system baseline; and completing any technical review. Table 5.2 provides details of the IEEE 1220 events for this stage.

The documentation produced during system definition is required to guide subsystem development. The technical reviews should evaluate the

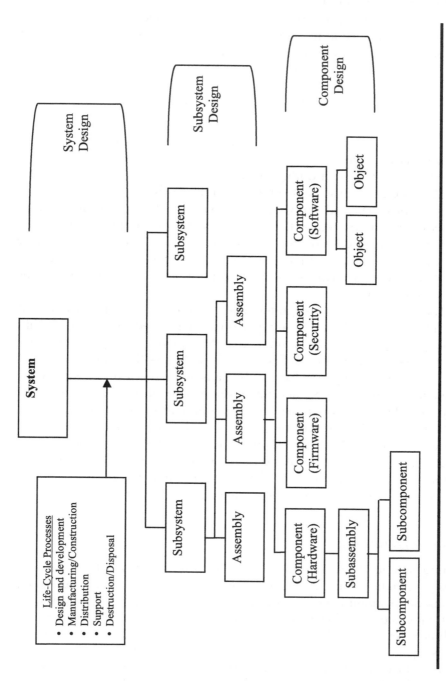

Figure 5.6 System breakdown structure.

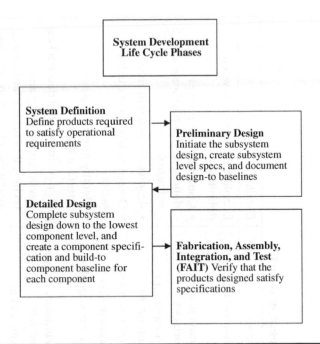

Figure 5.7 System development life-cycle phases.

maturity of the system development and the readiness to progress to subsystem definition. Note that this material was also discussed in Chapter 3, "Defining the System Requirements."

Preliminary System Design

The objectives of the preliminary system design phase are to initiate the subsystem design, create subsystem-level specifications, and document design-to baselines that will guide component development.

The major events in the preliminary system design reflect many of the system definition activities; however, the focus is on subsystems and components. Table 5.2 provides details of the IEEE 1220 events for the preliminary system design.

The enterprise uses the system architecture for the purpose of decomposing identified subsystem functions into lower-level functions and allocating functional and performance requirements to component-level functional and physical architectures. Each preliminary subsystem specification and preliminary design-to baseline should evolve into a subsystem specification and a design-to baseline, respectively. Preliminary component specification and build-to baselines should be defined for the components of the subsystem being developed. Final subsystem documents should

Table 5.2 System Definition, Preliminary Design, and Detailed Design Activities

	System Definition	Preliminary Design	Detailed Design
Establish definitions	Establish system definition: • Selection of system concept • Establish initial project and technical plans • Mitigate system risks • Assess subsystem risks • Identify subsystems and subsystems interfaces • Define life-cycle factors • Revise engineering and technical plans for preliminary design	Establish preliminary subsystem definitions: • Identify assemblies and assembly interfaces • Identify component and component interfaces • Mitigate subsystem risks • Assess component risks • Design for life-cycle quality factors • Complete preliminary drawings for each subsystem • Identify human/system interface issues • Revise engineering and technical plans for detailed design	Establish detailed subsystem definitions: • Complete component definition (for hardware and software) • Resolve component risks • Design in life-cycle quality factors • Identify human/system interface issues • Prepare integrated data package • Revise engineering and technical plans for fabrication, assembly, integration, and test

Complete specifications	• System, product, and subsystem interface specifications • System and product specifications • Preliminary subsystem specifications • Preliminary human/system interface specifications • Preliminary manpower, personnel, and training specifications	• Update system and product specifications • Complete subsystem and assembly specifications • Complete component interface specifications • Complete preliminary component specifications • Update human/system interface specifications • Update manpower, personnel, and training specifications	• Update system, product, subsystem, and assembly specifications • Complete component specifications (for hardware and software) • Update human/system interface specifications • Update manpower, personnel, and training specifications
Establish baselines	• Establish the system baseline • Establish preliminary subsystem design-to baselines	• Update system baselines • Establish design-to baselines • Establish preliminary build-to baselines	• Update system and design-to baselines • Establish build-to baselines
Complete technical reviews	• Complete alternate concept review • Complete system definition review	• Complete subsystem preliminary design reviews • Complete system preliminary design review	• Complete component detailed design reviews • Complete subsystem detailed design reviews • Complete system detailed design review

Source: Adapted from IEEE 1220.

include identification of recommended components and interfaces; resolution of sub-system-level risks; assessment of component risks; and design for quality factors, to include, as appropriate, the ability to assess production capability, ease of distribution, usability, supportability, ease of training, and disposal for each subsystem.

An important concept in system (and security) design (and life-cycle synthesis) is that of establishing system baselines, also called configuration baselines. A system baseline is the design of a system established at a beginning point in time that captures both the structure and details of a configuration. IEEE 1220 states that "the system baselines should include the system interface specifications, the product interface specifications, the system specifications, the product specifications, and the integrated database that captures the design, data, models, metrics, changes, design rationale, and other pertinent information on decisions or clarifications made to system requirements" (p. 21). The system baseline serves as reference for further activities. The configuration can be updated throughout the process but the initial baseline remains static so it can be used as a comparison to later versions.

The most widely used forms of configuration baselines are called functional, allocated, and product baselines. A *functional baseline* describes the system functional specifications as derived from system performance requirements during the concept definition phase. An *allocated baseline* is defined during the design phase as the allocation of functions to system components (or CIs) and is validated by analyses and tests. The result is a specification for each CI as well as the technical approach developed to specify the specified need or objective. The *product baseline* is established during the design phase in terms of detailed design specifications. It consists of product, process, and material specifications and engineering drawings (Kossiakoff and Sweet, 2003).

Detailed System Design

The objective of detailed system design is to complete subsystem design down to the lowest component level, and create a component specification and build-to component baseline for each component. The outputs of this stage are used to guide fabrication of pre-production prototypes for development testing. Each preliminary component specification and build-to baseline generated during preliminary design of the subsystem should evolve into a component specification and a build-to baseline, respectively. Final component documents should include identification of recommended parts and interfaces; resolution of component-level risks; and for each component, down to the lowest subcomponent, the design for quality factors, to include, as appropriate, the ability to assess production capability, ease of distribution, usability, supportability, ease of training, and disposal for each subsystem. Table 5.2 also provides details of the IEEE 1220 events for the detailed system design.

Fabrication, Assembly, Integration, and Test (FAIT) Stage

The purpose of the FAIT stage is to verify that the system, products, subsystems, assembly, and components that have been designed satisfy the specifications. The verification can be done by inspection, analysis, demonstration, or test. If specifications are not met, the architecture is reviewed for the purpose of resolving product deficiencies. More information on the FAIT stage activities is provided in Chapter 6.

Production and Customer Support Stages

Once the design stage has been completed, the SE reviews the planning documentation to ensure that deficiencies discovered during production, assembly, integration, and acceptance testing are corrected. Also, during customer support, the SE reviews the design plans to evolve the product to implement an incremental change, resolve product or service deficiencies, or implement planned evolutionary growth. The major events in these two stages of a product's life cycle are to produce system products, complete technical reviews, and provide customer service.

IEEE 1220 identifies the production and customer support events as:

- Produce system products:
  - Perform production inventory and control activities.
  - Produce and assemble consumer products.
  - Correct product- and process-design deficiencies.
  - Dispose of by-products and wastes.
- Complete physical configuration audits for components, subsystems, and the system.
- Provide customer support.
- Provide after-market products.
- Complete system evolution to make incremental changes, resolve product deficiencies, and exceed competitive products.

More information on production and customer support appears in Chapters 6 and 7.

This section briefly introduced the main activities outlined in IEEE 1220, which provides a framework for systems engineering that can be helpful for those without a background in SE.

The next topic looks at an important element of designing components — understanding how reliable the product or component will perform when implemented. Because a system, by definition, is composed of many elements that rely on each other to ensure the total system performance, an inefficient or ineffective component can disrupt the entire effectiveness of the system.

Component Reliability

Reliability has to do with the quality of measurement and the extent to which those measures have consistency or repeatability over a specified time period, with performance over time being a key factor. The IEEE Reliability Society defines reliability as a design engineering discipline that applies scientific knowledge to assure a product will perform its intended function for the required duration within a given environment. An important factor in determining reliability is to include in the design the ability to maintain, test, and support the product throughout each of the life-cycle phases.

When working on the design of a system, the reliability of an individual component can be a deciding factor, as well as how reliant the component will be once it is functioning in the system. To measure the reliability of a component, organizations may want to perform a reliability analysis or hire an outside specialist to conduct such an analysis. By using modeling techniques, a reliability analysis will analyze parameters such as temperature, stress, quality, packaging, and environment so that purchasers can understand the component's reliability. It can also show functioning aspects such as redundancy switch-over times, repair strategies, fault detection, and reboot and recovery time can be modeled to understand how each component affects system downtime.

A consideration for reliability analysis (see Table 5.3) is that the activity should be an ongoing process starting at the conceptual phase of the product or system design and continuing throughout all phases of the life cycle. The objective is to identify potential reliability problems as early as possible in the product life cycle. As is typical, it may never be too late to improve the reliability of a product, but changes to design are usually less expensive in the early part of the design process rather than once the product is manufactured and in service.

In large systems where a single component could affect the function and performance of the entire system, it may be necessary to conduct some type of reliability analysis on the component. This type of study can help SEs identify the best component for the system before large amounts of money and time have been devoted to the wrong component.

Table 5.3 Background Information on Reliability Standards

Background Information on Reliability Standards

The U.S. Department of Defense standard MIL-HDBK-217 was the original reliability standard for predicting the reliability of electronic devices (latest version, released in 1995, is MIL-HDBK-217F-2). It is used by commercial companies and the defense industry and is accepted and known worldwide. MIL-HDBK-217 provided two reliability prediction methods: the *parts count* method and the *part stress* method. The parts count method provides a simpler reliability math approach that is normally used during the early design phase when detailed information, such as quality, quantity, and environment, is not available, or a rough estimate of reliability is all that is required. Examples of information needed include quality, quantity, and environment. The part stress method is more complex and requires detailed information regarding the device, such as temperature conditions and electrical stress. The part stress method is used when the actual hardware and circuits are being designed and can provide a more accurate estimate of failure rate.

AT&T Bell Laboratories/Bellcore modified the equations in MIL-HDBK-217 to better represent what their equipment was experiencing in the field. From this modification, the Telcordia SR-332 reliability prediction model was developed. The main concepts in MIL-HDBK-217 and Telcordia are very similar, but Telcordia added the ability to take into account burn-in, field, and laboratory testing. This added ability has made the Telcordia standard very popular with commercial organizations. The current version of Telcordia is Issue 1, and follows Bellcore Issue 6 in order of release. Telcordia Issue 1 was released in May 2001. Telcordia SR-332 also supports the ability to perform a *parts count* or *part stress* analysis, but in the Telcordia standard, these different calculations are referred to as Calculation Methods. Telcordia offers ten different Calculation Methods. Each of these methods is designed to take into account different information. This information can include stress data, burn-in data, field data, or laboratory test data. Based on both of these standards vendors have created software tools to assist in reliability analysis.

Another aspect in determining the most appropriate component for the system design is to create a prototype of the item. The next topic briefly explores how prototypes fit into the design phase. Note that prototypes are also covered in the ISSE section of this chapter.

Prototyping

Up to this point, the system design has been abstract and theoretical in nature; the assessments have been based on concepts, analyses, drawings, and related documentation. It may be necessary to verify the concepts and design configuration through the use of actual system components. **Prototyping** is the iterative process of combining and integrating the system components, such as hardware, software, and logistic support, into the proper system configuration and evaluate whether it meets the system requirements. Simply stated, the objective is to build a simplified version of the system (the prototype), review it, and use the feedback to build a second, better version.

Blanchard and Fabrycky (1998) point out three types of prototyping models:

1. *Engineering model.* Represents a working system, or an element of the system, that will exhibit the functional performance characteristics defined in the specifications. It can be developed in either the preliminary system design stage or in the detail design stage and its primary function is to verify the technical feasibility of an item.
2. *Service test model.* Represents a working system, or an element of the system, that reflects the end product in terms of functional performance and physical dimensions. It is similar to the operational configuration except that substitute components can be used to simulate those contained in the design. Typically, the service test model would be designed in the detail design stage to verify the functional performance–physical configuration interface.
3. *Prototype model.* Represents the production configuration of a system in all aspects of form, fit, and function except that it has not been fully qualified in terms of operational and environmental testing. The prototype may evolve from the results of the engineering model and the service test model. The prototype would be designed in the detail design stage and would contain the required equipment, software, and associated logistic support. The prototype would be evaluated before entering the production or construction phase to verify whether the design requirements are met.

Some prototyping models can assist SEs in verifying the technical concepts and various system design approaches. Prototyping is intended to identify any noncompliance with the specifications so they can be corrected before production and operation begin. The ISSE section contains more information on prototypes. The next topic addresses the final element in the SE design phase: conducting a system design review.

System Design Review

At the end of the design stage, the SE should conduct some type of formal review. The goal of the System Design Review (SDR) is to verify the conceptual design against activities conducted in the preliminary and detailed system design. The system specifications are reviewed against the system requirements and the system architecture. The reviewed and approved system specifications are then used to establish the functional baseline from which the remainder of the design will follow. The functional system baseline, with its approved changes, represents the current configuration of how the system will be developed. Throughout the system development life cycle, it serves as the description of the required functional characteristics for the system.

The SDR should provide a formalized check of the proposed system, subsystem, and component design against the system requirements. If there are problem areas, discussions and corrective action must be taken before moving into the next phase — developing and implementing the system.

System Engineering Management Plan (SEMP)

During the latter stages of conceptual design, a comprehensive Systems Engineering Management Plan (SEMP) is developed. The objective of the SEMP is to ensure the implementation of a program that will lead to a well-coordinated and integrated product output. The SEMP should provide an integration of documents from previous activities and any design-related tasks necessary to enhance the integration and implementation activities. More information on the development of a SEMP is provided in the Technical Management domain.

The next section of the chapter integrates the security activities into the design of the system. The ISSEP must focus on the security aspects of the design and provide needed input to ensure that the system security requirements are included during the initial design integrations. The ISSEP is responsible for validating that the design includes the security components and they are functioning as intended. During the design process, the ISSEP can create a security prototype, a system security specification document, and conduct a final verification and review that ensures the security design meets the system security requirements.

ISSE Activity: System Security Design

Following a similar format to the systems engineering process, during this activity in the ISSE model, the ISSEP analyzes the security design constraints and adjusts for any trade-offs. This information is then written in detailed system security specifications that follows the life-cycle phases. Similar to the SE process, the ISSEP must provide enough information about the components and interface specifications in the system security specifications so that the security components of the system can be built or acquired.

Chapter 1 discussed the two primary threads in the process of designing and developing a system, regardless of whether it is to be built or acquired. The first is the identification of **what** functions the system must perform, and the second is a determination of **how** the system will perform these functions. At various times in the life-cycle process, one thread may dominate the other but both are always evident in each phase. The "what" issues — discover needs, define requirements, and define the architecture — primarily occur during the requirement phases. The "how" issues — design system, implement system, and assess effectiveness — are considered part of the implementation functions. As mentioned, the critical connection between these two threads is made in this fourth phase, designing the system. This is the point at which all of the critical up-front need requirements and analysis work is melded into the design of the system.

This is, of course, the idyllic world setting, one where the process works smoothly and as intended. However, what can happen in the real world is that mission statements are adjusted or changed, requirements change, security mechanisms are out of date (i.e., technology advances have superseded the original concept), personnel change, etc. Thus, an important consideration for the ISSEP during this phase is to understand that the process of the security design is iterative. It is changeable, adaptive, and extends over the life cycle of a system, so it is an ongoing process. In addition, as the various team members gain more knowledge, the newly found information will improve the efficiency of the process.

For some projects, the requirements will be based on making major modifications to an existing system instead of designing a new system. It is well known that attempting to incorporate security onto an existing, legacy system is challenging. Modifying an existing system places several constraints on all of the ISSE phases and most importantly the design phase. In projects where there is a legacy system, the ISSEP should have defined the architecture of the existing system during the early phases and identified any existing security mechanisms. During the design phase, the ISSEP allocates the new security services in such a way as to not disrupt the existing security mechanisms. The issues involved in working with legacy systems cannot be simply stated. Each project has its own issues, not the least of which is keeping the system operating while making changes. This is why the ISSEP may find that although there are challenges when designing new systems, there is more flexibility and control over the security design.

As shown in Figure 5.8, there are several topics in this section. The first topic discusses when and how the ISSEP conducts a trade-off analysis. The security synthesis is the configuration design for how security components will be developed to create a system with security as a focal

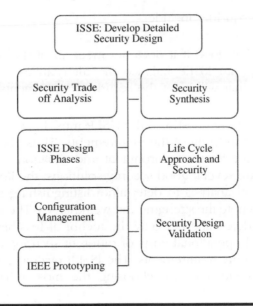

Figure 5.8 ISSE security design activities.

point. The next topic explores the various phases of the ISSE design, such as how to create the preliminary security design and the detailed security design documentation. This also includes reviewing the allocation of the security mechanisms and initiating the initial assessment of whether security components can be obtained using commercial off-the-shelf (COTS) products or must be custom built. When evaluating COTS products, the ISSEP should also review the Common Criteria (CC) protection profiles for products. A brief overview of the CC is included in this topic. Chapter 15 takes a more detailed look at the CC. As part of the design phase, the ISSEP begins to document the configuration management plan. This ensures that any significant changes during development are evaluated and that the security design has not been compromised. The final two topics discuss how the ISSEP validates the security design and, if appropriate, may develop a prototype to validate the security design.

Conducting the Security Trade-Off Analysis

During the design phase, the ISSEP may realize that the requirements are not achievable (whether it is theoretically not possible or more typical causes such as financial or time constraints) or several solutions seem equally good.

Questions to consider include:

- Is a solution good if it does not meet all of the requirements?
- How does an ISSEP balance the alternatives and make sound decisions that will meet the security requirements?

When answering these questions, the ISSEP must keep in mind that good solutions may not meet all of the requirements. Thus, they may be good, but not appropriate for the environment and situation.

When there are several good security solutions, the ISSEP can conduct a security trade-off analysis to determine distinguishing characteristics of the solutions and note the strengths and weaknesses. The trade-off analysis is conducted to determine not only the technical feasibility, but also the development and operational costs of different security architectures that will meet the security requirements. The ISSEP evaluates the analysis and provides recommendations for choosing the most reliable and secure alternative.

A greater challenge is when the requirements cannot be met by any current solutions. In this case, the ISSEP must determine which solution will come closest to meeting the security requirements. Important to this process is the ISSE team working closely with the SE team and the customer to review or revise the original system and security requirements. If revisions are necessary, the ISSEP must provide guidance on whether the adjustments allow more risks to the system than are acceptable.

Security Synthesis

Similar to the system engineering model, the ISSEP will structure the security configuration items into a synthesis — a combination and structuring of the components in such a way as to represent a feasible system security configuration. Once this configuration is established, the ISSEP documents this information in the system security specifications. The synthesis, including incorporating any changes, provides the preferred design considerations that will lead to the establishment of the functional security baseline.

During Phase 4, the ISSEP works with other team members to combine all of the previous efforts into a written synthesis (design) document. This security design document, also called the system security specifications, must be specific enough so that during the next phase the security functions can be built or acquired and then implemented. The IATF (2002) provides the following as important aspects of the ISSEPs effort during this phase:

- Components include both technical and non-technical mechanisms (e.g., doctrine).
- Design must satisfy customer-specified design constraints.
- Trade-offs must consider priorities, cost, schedule, performance, and residual security risks.
- Risk analysis must consider the interdependency of security mechanisms.
- Design documents should be under strong configuration control.
- Failures to satisfy security requirements must be reported to C&A authorities.
- Design should be traceable to the security requirements.
- Design should project the schedule and cost of long-lead items and life-cycle support.
- Design should include a revised security CONOPS (p. 3-12).

In the Develop Detailed Security Design phase, the ISSEP also reviews how well the selected security services and mechanisms counter the threats identified in the IPP by performing an interdependency analysis to compare desired to effective security service strengths. Once completed, the risk assessment results, particularly any identified mitigation needs and residual risk, are documented and shared with the customer to obtain concurrence" (*ISSE Handbook*, 1994, p. 3-12).

The design phase involves interactions between various players, such as SEs, acquisition specialists, ISSE teams, and possibly between systems and component engineers within the teams. While design decisions are being formulated, the ISSE team must have continual involvement with all team members. The ISSEP brings to the discussion an understanding of the organization's mission, its security requirements, various security components, and the security architecture considerations. Based upon the ISSEPs expertise and knowledge, risk management decisions can also be made during the design phase. Another important element for the ISSEP is to make sure the final written design documentation meets the organization's Certification and Accreditation (C&A) requirements, whether it follows DITSCAP, NIACAP, or the NIST process (C&A is discussed further in Domain 2, Chapters 8 and 9).

An important aspect of documenting the security design is presenting a rationale as to why and how it meets the security requirements. Although independent analysis and evaluation should still be conducted (i.e., independent verification and validation [IV&V] studies), it is necessary for the design team, including the ISSE team, to develop a strong rationale for the system's security posture and include it in the design document. This information can also be helpful when beginning a system security plan and should transfer easily from the design document.

ISSE Design Phases

The objectives of the system security design phase are to complete the top-level security design of the overall system, define the security configuration items (CIs) that will work within the system, and design and approve the system security specifications. Just as in the IEEE model, the ISSE design phase includes the Preliminary Security Design and the Detailed Security Design Phases.

Preliminary Security Design Phase

During the preliminary security design, security system-level design requirements and specifications are translated and allocated to the configuration item level. According to the *ISSE Handbook*, a preliminary design review is conducted to:

- Determine whether there are any system level requirements that have not been considered or fully satisfied by the individual CIs.
- Ensure that the issues for the system CIs, functional areas, and subsystems are resolved or address remaining issues.
- Review risk management actions and results of risk closure activities to ensure an acceptable level of risk.
- Assess the integration of the physical architecture of the system and to ensure that internal and external interfaces and interoperability requirements have been defined
- Confirm that the integrated system design meets the security functional baseline requirements and user requirements (p. 2-22).

ISSEP contributions during this phase include participation in activities such as the following (*ISSE Handbook*):

- Continued review and refinement of all areas considered in the previous phase, with particular attention to the definition of appropriate CI-level and interface specifications
- Survey of existing inventory of security solutions for a match to needed CIs
- Examination of technical rationales for the proposed preliminary design review level security solutions
- Verification that CI specifications satisfy system security requirements
- Continued inputs to C&A process activities as required
- Participation in the collective, multidisciplinary examination of all system issues (p. 2-23)

Detailed Security Design Phase

The objective of the detailed security design phase is to complete the design of the CIs requiring development. The conclusion of this phase is the system Critical Design Review (CDR). The CDR is conducted to (*ISSE Handbook*):

- Determine any system problems or issues that were not resolved by the individual CIs.
- Determine the compatibility of the system with interfacing systems.
- Determine the detailed system and CI designs are complete and include all relevant products and processes.
- Determine that system design requirements, interface requirements, and design constraints are consistent with and supported by available verification results.
- Complete, as required, the establishment of allocated baselines for all CIs (p. 2-23).

ISSE activities during this phase include (*ISSE Handbook*):

- Security design support, through inputs on feasible security solutions or review of detailed design materials such as software program specifications and engineering drawings
- Examination of technical rationales for the proposed component level security solutions
- Support generating and verifying information security test and evaluation requirements
- Tracking of, or participation in, application of security assurance mechanisms related to the design/development
- Verification that the set of CI designs and their associated interface designs collectively satisfy system-level security requirements
- Completion of most input to the life-cycle security support approach, including security inputs to training plans and emerging training materials
- Reviewing and updating the security risk and threat projections, and reviewing any changes to the requirements set
- Inputs to the C&A process activities, as required
- Participation in the collective, multidisciplinary examination of all system issues (p. 2-24)

The IATF document defines the role of the ISSEP during the development of the detailed security design as five primary activities:

- Allocating security mechanisms to system security design elements
- Identifying candidate commercial off-the-shelf (COTS)/government off-the-shelf (GOTS) security products
- Identifying custom security products
- Qualifying element and system interfaces (internal and external)
- Developing specifications (e.g., Common Criteria protection profiles) (p. 3-11 to 3-12)

The next section provides more details on each of these ISSEP responsibilities.

Allocating Security Mechanisms

In the previous phase, the ISSEP conducted a security function analysis and allocation to complete the security architecture. During the initial design phase, the ISSEP should consider conducting another examination (or review) of the security design constraints, as identified in the discover needs activity, for any effect on the security architecture and thus the security mechanisms.

During the design phase, the ISSEP must also consider the nontechnical security mechanisms, such as writing security policies, how to ensure the enforcement of security policies, awareness briefings, and training. As appropriate, the ISSEP should ensure that the nontechnical mechanisms are allocated appropriately in the design documentation and outlines.

As part of reviewing the security function allocations, the ISSEP should review the previously conducted analysis of the security mechanisms and their interactions, especially in terms of the required strength of the security services. The combining of security mechanisms is sometimes referred to as a security service. For example, a trained firewall administrator combined with specific firewall software can be considered a firewall security service. Because various types of security mechanisms can perform security services, the role of the ISSEP is to verify that the most appropriate corresponding sets of mechanisms match the security needs.

Identifying COTS/GOTS/Custom Security Products

When deciding on security products, the ISSE team must balance factors such as operational function and performance, cost, schedule, and risk. The trend within the U.S. Government has been to buy IT and IT security products based on a prioritized hierarchy of:

1. Commercial-off-the-shelf (COTS) products
2. Government-off-the-shelf (GOTS) products
3. Custom-developed products

Although operational function and performance should be the deciding factor, in many situations, decisions are based primarily on lowest cost. Although this is not desirable, the reality is that many organizations simply lack appropriate funding to purchase the best-performing product or the most secure product. So, although it looks easy to make these types of decisions, in reality it is not always easy to accomplish.

When reviewing COTS products, trade-offs will be needed. Typically, selected products will have some or even most of the features wanted, but it is not usual for a COTS product to offer all the security features that may be needed. This can be a major element of the trade-off analysis — deciding whether to buy a commercially available product or custom-design a product.

For example, buying a COTS intrusion detection system (IDS) is less costly than designing and developing one's own. Imagine the costs involved in the design requirements, programming needs, and testing of an IDS product. Therefore, the ISSEP will need to conduct a trade-off analysis. For example, one of the security requirements for the IDS is to have an audible alert when a specific event occurs. If the COTS product provides a visual alert versus an audible alert, the ISSE team would need to evaluate whether this alert feature was acceptable. Essentially, the question revolves around whether the ISSEP is assured that the product will still meet the security requirement or is the compromise acceptable. If the requirement is to have an audible alert, the ISSE team will need to consider other options, such as identifying another product (which will necessitate other trade-offs), ask the vendor to add an audible alert, or have internal programmers modify the current software code or create an add-on feature (both modifying the software and adding on features to software can be challenging, especially because the vendor may not be willing to give the original source code). Caution is necessary here because either of these actions can invalidate the product's maintenance and service agreements.

During the design phase, decisions regarding whether to purchase a COTS product or to custom-develop a product are usually considered recommendations. The final decision is often made during the next activity, implementation. When possible, the ISSEP should recommend a set of options indicating the various security features and any security trade-offs imposed for each product. During the implementation stage, it is helpful and more efficient to have several options (versus one product) already evaluated and identified. More information on government-evaluated products is provided in the Common Criteria section.

Identifying Security Mechanism Interfaces

Systems use different security mechanisms to meet the security requirements. In situations where the security mechanisms must interact, an interface protocol must be established and rules must be written to allow this interaction to operate in a secure manner. This can be an interesting issue for the ISSE, especially if it is a new system interfacing with a legacy system.

As an example, consider a new building on a military base compound that will provide mini-mart grocery store-type services, such as foods, snacks, and soda. The manager of the mini-mart wants to have an Internet and e-mail connection using the military base services. The current require-ment is to install a wireless connection for the manager to connect to the mail server located in the main building. How would you determine the security services needed for this new building and the wireless system requirement? Would it be different if it were a controlled access building with dedicated landline telecommunication connections? As part of the answer, the ISSEP must consider how any new security mechanisms designed for the wireless system must work (interact) with the existing telecommunication services, taking into account the original security requirements for the mail server in the main building. In this type of scenario, the ISSEP must consider the design of the interface mechanism between the different security mechanisms and provide an acceptable solution to both parties.

Designing interfaces between security mechanisms can become par-ticularly significant when individual systems have different security strat-egies, security requirements, and constraints for operation within their own local environments. It is also important when a new connection may cause some additional security or other adverse impact on the existing system or infrastructure. This may require the ISSEP to suggest trade-offs on some of the functional requirements. Using the mini-mart example, the ISSEP may have to negotiate for the use of bringing in a landline connection and not using the wireless system for connectivity.

Developing Specifications: Common Criteria Profiles

Developing a Common Criteria (CC) profile is one of the items recom-mended by the IATF document. The CC evaluates software systems based on both functionality and assurance in terms of integrity, confidentiality, and availability.

The CC is an international standard to evaluate IT security products. In 1993, the sponsoring agencies for the United States, Canada, and European criterion started the CC project with the goal of creating a single IT security evaluation criterion. In 1996, the first version was released for public review. In 1998, Version 2 was released; and in 1999, this modified version (v2.1) became the ISO International Standard 15408. It began as an update on the *U.S. Federal Criteria,* which expanded on the ITSEC by giving more guidance in the definition of evaluation classes but retaining some degree of flexibility. The U.S. Federal Criteria kept the linkage between function and assurance in the evaluation classes and tried to overcome the rigid structure of the Orange Book by adding *Protection Profiles*. The CC is the outcome of efforts to develop criteria that can be useful within the international community. It leaves the total flexibility of ITSEC and follows the U.S. Federal Criteria by using protection profiles and predefined security classes.

An important point about the CC is that in May 2000, the international community (i.e., Australia, Canada, Finland, France, Germany, Greece, Israel, Italy, Netherlands, New Zealand, Norway, Spain, the United Kingdom, and the United States) agreed to the Common Criteria Recognition Agreement (CCRA). The CCRA established that each country would accept the results of CC evaluations performed by other member nations for Evaluation Assurance Levels 1 through 4. For example, a U.S. software vendor could ask the British CC laboratory to conduct the security evaluation and the United States will accept the rating. Although there has been some discourse about whether some of the countries are considered trustworthy to each other, the spirit of the agreement specifically states that "the Participants plan to recognize the Common Criteria certificates which have been authorized by any other certificate authorizing Participant in accordance with the terms of this Arrangement and in accordance with the applicable laws and regulations of each Participant" (CCRA, May 2000, p. 5). Thus, in order for the CC to be an international standard, each country must accept the trust of each other country.

According to the Common Criteria User Guide (CESG/NIST, 1999), a protection profile is an independent statement of security requirements that is shown to address threats that exist in a specified environment. For the United States Government (USG), it would be appropriate to use a protection profile when the USG wishes to specify security requirements for a class of security products, such as firewalls, IDSs, etc.

A protection profile includes the following information:

- *Introduction.* Descriptive elements, such as the name of the protection profile and an overview.
- *Target of evaluation (TOE) description.* Identification of the information protection problem that needs to be solved.
- *TOE Security Environment.* A listing of the assumptions about the organizations, threats that exist, and organizational security policies.
- *Security objectives.* A listing of the security objectives for the TOE and for the environment.
- *IT security requirements.* A listing of the security requirements for the IT environment.

- *TOE functional requirements.* Establishes the protection boundary that must be provided by the product, so that expected threats can be countered.
- *TOE development assurance requirements.* Identifies the requirements for all phases of development, from the initial design through implementation.
- *TOE evaluation assurance requirements.* Specifies the type and intensity of evaluation.
- *Rationales.* Fundamental justification (threat/environment/usage) of the protection profile and some guidance on and the security policies that can be supported by the product conforming to the profile.

Table 5.4 is from the http://niap.nist.gov/cc-scheme/PPRegistry.html Web site and provides a listing of protection profiles that have already been developed for USG agencies.

Protection profiles are needed when setting the standard for a particular product type. Government agencies, consumers, or developers can set these standards. They are also used to create specifications for systems or services and as the basis for procurements (CESG/NIST, 1999, p. 12).

The use of protection profiles to define information assurance requirements is part of the National Information Assurance Partnership (NIAP) program. NIAP is a collaboration between the National Institute of Standards and Technology (NIST) and the National Security Agency (NSA) in fulfilling their respective responsibilities under federal law (Computer Security Act of 1987). By combining the IT security experience of both agencies, NIAP serves to promote the development of technically sound security requirements for IT products and systems and appropriate measures for evaluating those products and systems. More information on protection profiles and NIAP is available from the http://niap.nist.gov/ Web site. NIAP invites helpful comments and suggested improvements on protection profiles that have been developed and those currently in the development process. The protection profiles are also posted on the Information Assurance Technical Framework (IATF) Web site at http://www.iatf.net/protection profiles/.

During the design phase of the ISSE model, the ISSEP would assist in the development of the protection profile or review of current protection profiles. If the first phases of the ISSE model have been followed, the ISSEP will transfer much of the information already gathered to document the protection profile. Although there may be a tendency to view this as just another bureaucratic paper exercise, when deciding on products, having a protection profile can help the ISSEP understand the CC evaluation rating for any COTS products. More detailed information on CC is provided in Chapter 15.

Table 5.4 NIAP CC Overview

NIAPCC Overview

"The following products have been evaluated and certified in accordance with the provisions of the NIAP Common Criteria Evaluation and Validation Scheme and the Common Criteria Recognition Arrangement (CCRA). Products and profiles on this list have been evaluated at accredited and licensed/approved evaluation facilities in the U.S. or in one of the other countries participating in the CCRA for conformance to the Common Criteria for IT Security Evaluation (ISO Standard 15408).

Common Criteria certificates issued for IT products apply only to the specific versions and releases of those products and profiles and are valid only in conjunction with complete certification/validation reports.

Certificates are not endorsements of IT products by NIST, NSA, or any other organization that recognizes or gives effect to the certificate. No warranty of the IT product by NIST, NSA or any other organization that recognizes or gives effect to this certificate, is either expressed or implied."

Defend the Network and Infrastructure	Defend the Enclave Boundary	Defend the Computing Environment	Supporting the Infrastructure (PKI, Detect, Mgmt)
Switch and Routers PP	Firewall PP	Operating System PP	Network Mgt
Routers PP	VPNs PP	Biometrics PP	Certificate Mgt PP
WLAN PP	Remote Access PP	Secure Messaging PP	Key Recovery PP
	Mobile Code PP	Tokens PP PP	Smart Code
	Multiple Domain Solutions PP	Single Level Web Server PP	PKI/KMI PP PP
	Guards PP	Mobile Code PP	IDS PP
		Peripheral Switch PP	Miscellaneous PP

Notes:

PP = There is a *Validated U.S. Gov't PP* available for this technology category of product type. However, it should not be inferred that every product listed within this technology category necessarily meets the PP. You can be redirected to the PP page for the given technology by clicking on the red or black PP icon.

PP = There is a *draft U.S. Gov't PP* available for this category of product type. However, it should not be inferred that every product listed within this product type necessarily meets the PP. Draft PPs can be in various stages of development, i.e., being written or vetted, or in evaluation in a NIAP CCEVS CCTL. You can be redirected to the PP page for the given technology by clicking on the red or black PP icon.

PP = There is a *Validated non-U.S. Gov't PP* available for this technology category."

Life-Cycle Security Approach and the System Security Design Document

Although the life-cycle security approach can be considered during any of the ISSE activities, it is usually in this phase that the ISSEP documents how the design and development of the system will follow a life-cycle approach model. The ISSEP begins by working with the customer and, as appropriate, other team members to define a comprehensive security approach for the full life cycle of the system.

There are various models for defining the phases in a life cycle. For example, the U.S. Army Corps of Engineers (CECI-P Engineer Regulation 25-1-2, 1999) established the Life Cycle Management of Information Systems (LCMIS) in May 1999. The IEEE 1220 standard also identifies life-cycle phases. Table 5.5 is an attempt to match the basic life-cycle steps outlined in the SDLC, IEEE 1220, LCMIS, and ISSE model.

Essentially, if an organization has adopted a specific life-cycle model, they will find that many of the ISSE activities can be incorporated into their own model. There is no need for the ISSEP to perform duplicate work in defining specific life-cycle activities versus specific ISSE activities.

Table 5.5   Life-Cycle Phases and ISSE Activities

SDLC Phases	IEEE 1220 Phases	LCMIS Phases	ISSE Activities
Phase 1: Initiation	Development	Mission Need Identification	Discover information protection needs
		Concept Exploration and Definition	Define system security requirements
			Define system security architecture
Phase 2: Development or Acquisition	Manufacturing, Test	Demonstration and Validation	Develop detailed security design
Phase 3: Implementation Phase 4: Operation or Maintenance	Distribution, Operations, Support, Training	Development/ Deployment Operations and Support	Implement system security Assess security effectiveness
Phase 5: Disposal	Disposal		

Although the terms can be used differently, the work completed in each ISSE activity will usually match activities in most life-cycle models.

If the activities do not match, the ISSEP may need to add some specific elements into the design document to ensure that all phases of the life cycle will be addressed. As an example, some life-cycle models specifically ask for training and disposal/destruction policies to be written into the system design document. Thus, in these situations, the ISSEP would need to add information into the design document on how these activities will be accomplished for the system.

When looking at life-cycle phases, one of the "tools" to manage the system at each phase is configuration management. The next topic explains the importance of configuration management to life-cycle phases and security.

Configuration Management and the Life-Cycle Security Approach

Thus far we have separated the development of a new, complex system into manageable activities where each activity has evolved to define more specific system and security requirements and specifications. Configuration Management (CM) is the ISSE process used to maintain the continuity and integrity of the security design throughout the development, integration, and implementation phases. Although CM occurs during all phases of the ISSE model, before beginning the implementation phase there must be a CM plan that will manage the changes occurring during design integration.

Configuration is described as a collection of the products' descriptive and governing characteristics. These can be expressed in functional terms such as what performance the product is expected to achieve and in physical terms such as what the product should look like and consist of when it is completed. In design terms, it is the technical description needed to build, test, accept, operate, install, maintain, and support the system.

CM is a management process that applies technical and administrative direction to a component during the development, production, and operational phases. It is applicable to hardware, software, services, and technical documentation, and is an integral part of life-cycle management.

Two common terms used in CM are "configuration item (CI)" and "configuration baseline." In the design and implementation phases, the CI is used to define a component or system element. A CI is considered a fundamental building block of the system and is usually designed by a single organization and must interface with other building blocks. During the design phase, these interfaces or interactions are supposed to be outlined and defined; during the implementation phase, the CI (or building block) interactions must be integrated and controlled to ensure proper operation within the system as a whole. Because of the different processes in system design, it is typical for engineers to distinguish between Hardware Configuration Items (HWCIs) and Computer Software Configuration Items (CSCIs). Entire books have been written about the complexity of computer software design and development. The focus here is on what the ISSEP must consider in the design of CSCI. However, ISSEPs who will be working on large software design and integration projects are strongly encouraged to review the bibliography for additional resources on secure software design.

A critical part of a CM plan is the interface management plan that describes how the CIs will work together to become the required system. A primary condition for an effective CM plan is to define how the interface of CIs will occur. A secondary condition of the CM plan is to outline the involvement needed from CI vendors or owners so that combining the units will produce a successful whole. In some instances, it may be necessary or required to have formal approval procedures agreeing on how the CIs will be interfaced. Refer to NIST SP 800-47 (August 2002), "Security Guide for Interconnecting Information Technology Systems," for more information on how to develop interface agreement procedures.

Another aspect of a CM plan is to determine how change control will be managed. Change is natural and expected; however, it must be managed, especially for security considerations. To help minimize the impact of change, the ISSE team should be instrumental in designing flexibility into the system. Having a flexible design that can accommodate changes without major disruption will prove a valuable asset during the implementation and operation phases. Note that more information on CM is provided in the technical management chapter.

The next section provides an overview of software design and security. If an ISSEP is assigned a project that supports a software design program, the ISSEP should review additional readings regarding best practices of verifying how security should be included throughout the process. *Note to the ISSEP candidate:* The specifics of secure software design is not currently mentioned in the (ISC)2 study guide.

Software Design

Typically, ISSEPs are not required to be expert programmers or know the inner workings of application code such as C++ or how to develop Web code using Java. However, ISSEPs may be the ones responsible for ensuring that security is included in such developments; thus, they should know the basic procedures and concepts involved during the design and development of software programming. Essentially, if the ISSEP must "manage" the software development process to verify that security is included, then he or she should understand the fundamental concepts of programming developments and the security strengths and weaknesses of various application development processes.

The generic use of word "software" could describe operating system software (the software that manages the operations of a computer system) or application software (the software that provides functionality for the user such as word processing programs). During the 1960s, the development and maintenance of software for a computer system made up the predominant cost of a systems project — almost 75 percent. Because of the expenses associated with software development, industry research began to provide the best methods of reducing costs, which subsequently led to the discipline of software engineering. **Software engineering** simply stated that software products had to be planned, designed, constructed, and released according to engineering principles. It included software metrics, modeling, methods, and techniques associated with the system design before it was developed, and tracking project progress through the entire development process. By the 1980s, the software engineering field had developed structured methods and modeling that culminated in the acceptance of object-oriented programming in the 1990s.

> It is a well-known fact in computer security that security problems are very often a direct result of software bugs. That leads security researchers ... to pay lots of attention to software engineering. The hope is to avoid the ever-present penetrate-and-patch approach to security by developing more secure code in the first place.
>
> —McGraw and Felton, 1999

Since the beginning, software development has faced numerous problems that could result in higher costs and lower quality. In fact, budget and schedule overruns are two of the largest problems for software design and development. Software is a major element and performs critical functions in information systems; thus, understanding the design of software is an important task for the ISSE. It is not the same as system design and requires a different knowledge and skills set, especially from a security standpoint.

The following information is excerpted from the chapter I wrote for the *Official (ISC)² Guide to the CISSP Exam* (Hansche et al., 2004). The environment in which software operates is fundamental to computer operations. This environment begins with the hardware resources, such as the central processing unit (CPU), memory, input/output (I/O) requests, and storage devices. The operating system is responsible for controlling these resources and providing security mechanisms to protect them. The applications employed by the end users make requests or calls to the operating system to provide the required computer services. In some applications, there are security features built into the software that allow the users more control over their information, such as access controls or auditing capabilities. There are also vulnerabilities that can be introduced into the application, such as when a buffer overflow attack takes advantage of improper parameter checking within the application.

Application development procedures are absolutely vital to the integrity of systems. If applications are not developed properly, data can be processed in such a way that the integrity of the data is corrupted. The integrity of the application software itself must be maintained, both in terms of change control and attack from malicious software such as viruses. Also, if confidentiality is required for data, encryption mechanisms and file access controls should be built into the programming code from the beginning and not added on as an afterthought.

Information systems are becoming more distributed and open, with a substantial increase in the sharing of resources. Increased sharing requires that all resources be protected against unauthorized access. Many of these safeguards are provided through software controls, especially operating system mechanisms. Therefore, the operating system must offer controls that protect the computer's resources. In addition, the relationship between applications and the operating system is important. Controls must be included in operating systems so that applications cannot damage or circumvent the operating system controls. If there is a lack of application software protection mechanisms the operating system and critical computer resources can be open to corruption and attack.

Some of the main security requirements for applications and databases are to ensure that only valid, authorized, and authenticated users can access the data; permissions related to use of the data are controlled; the software provides some type of granularity for controlling the permissions; encryption is available for protecting sensitive information such as password storage; and audit trails can be implemented and reviewed.

Essentially, security in operating systems, applications, and databases focuses on the ability of the software to enforce controls over the storage and transfer of information in and between objects. Remember that the underlying foundation of the software security controls is the organization's security policy. The security policy reflects the security requirements of the organization. Therefore, if the security policy requires that only one set of users can access information, the software must have the capability to limit access to that specific group of users. Keep in mind that the ability to refer to a system as secure is based upon the reliable enforcement of the organization's security policy (Hansche et al., 2004, pp. 227–228).

There are several software development models, such as the waterfall, spiral, prototype, Capability Maturity Model®, and the object-orienting model. Regardless of which software development model is used, there are typical phases that must be included. These basic phases, including the corresponding security activities are shown in Table 5.6.

When implementing security in an application program environment, it is important to consider security throughout the entire life-cycle process, especially in the requirements and design phases. Viega and McGraw (2002, p. 92) identified ten principles for building secure software. The goal of the principles is to identify and to highlight the most important objectives when designing and building a secure system.

> *"90/10" Strategy — Avoid 90 percent of the potential problems by following these ten guidelines.*
> 1. *Secure the weakest link.*
> 2. *Practice defense in depth.*
> 3. *Fail securely.*
> 4. *Follow the principle of least privilege.*
> 5. *Compartmentalize.*
> 6. *Keep it simple.*
> 7. *Promote privacy.*
> 8. *Remember that hiding secrets is hard.*
> 9. *Be reluctant to trust.*
> 10. *Use your community resources.*

Although ISSEPs may not typically manage a specific software design and development project, they should know the basic procedures and concepts involved during the design and development of software programming.

Security Design Validation

A final step in the ISSE design phase is to validate the security design. The objective of validation is to ensure that the overall system security specifications comply with the system security requirements. Although validation can occur at various levels throughout the ISSE process, if any specific components or the interface of subsystems have been designed during this phase, it is necessary for some type of validation to occur. This is also related to the DITSCAP/NIACAP phase 3 activity.

Table 5.6 Software Development Phases and Security Activities

Software Development Phases	Related Software Activities	Related Security Activities
Project initiation and planning	Identify user needs; evaluate alternatives; select/approve approach.	Identify security needs; conduct an initial risk analysis, identify the security framework.
Functional requirements definition	Prepare project plan; develop functional requirements; preliminary test plan; select acquisition strategy; establish formal functional baseline.	Select configuration, access, and audit controls; define security requirements; define the preliminary security test plan; include security requirements in request for proposals and contracts; ensure that functional baseline has security requirements outlined.
System design specifications	Develop detailed design; update testing goals and plans; establish formal baseline/quality controls and requirements.	Define security specifications; update security test plan; and include security area in formal baseline documentation and quality assurance documentation.
Build (develop) and document	Construct source code from detailed design specifications; perform and evaluate unit tests; implement detailed design into final system.	Write or procure and install security related code; perform unit tests and evaluate security related code; ensure approved security components in formal baseline are included.
Acceptance	Test system components; validate system performance; install system; prepare project manuals; perform acceptance test; accept system.	Test security components; test security in integrated system; install security code with necessary modifications; document security controls; conduct acceptance test; and accept/verify project security.
Transition to production (installation)	System is transitioned from acceptance to live production; training new users.	Obtaining security accreditation; verify data conversion and data entry are controlled; accept risk level.

Table 5.6 (continued)   Software Development Phases and Security Activities

Operations and maintenance support (post-installation)	Monitoring the performance of the system and ensuring continuity of operations.	Periodic risk analysis and re-certification is required; verify that any changes to the system do not disable or circumvent the security features.
Revisions and system replacement	Baselines should be updated; future plans and procedures are designed.	Revisions include security planning and procedures to avoid future problems.

The documentation for security verification and validation usually begins in the design phase. However, in some instances, security test planning begins in the conceptual phase when security requirements are initially established. Essentially, if a security requirement is specified, there should be a method of evaluating and validating that the final system has met the requirement. Thus, considerations for test and evaluation are an integral part of all phases but should not be documented later than the design phase.

The security design will be validated against an initial test plan. In the SE model, this initial test plan is called a Test and Evaluation Master Plan (TEMP). In the DITSCAP/NIACAP framework, this is Certification Test and Evaluation (CT&E) or Security Test and Evaluation (ST&E) plans and procedures. Typically, a TEMP as shown in Table 5.7 includes the requirements for test and evaluation, the categories of the tests, the procedures for accomplishing testing, the resources required, and associated planning information, such as schedules and responsibilities. One of the primary goals of the TEMP is the integration of the various test requirements for the overall system, especially the security requirements, which may require different tests than functional requirements.

The system and nontechnical controls associated with each system site should also be tested to ensure that adequate security protection is provided. For example, a nontechnical control may be training the employee who monitors a new IDS. The employee is expected to respond to a certain type of event in a specific manner, such as blocking an IP address at the firewall. To test whether the employee is indeed able to respond to the event, it is necessary to either simulate the event in a closed environment or conduct a live test that will monitor the employee's behavior. Federal agencies typically perform verification tests through operational demonstrations, testing, inspection, and analyses that are designed to determine how well the security controls have been implemented and are being used.

Table 5.7   Test Plan Elements

Element	Description
Test Scope	
Features to be tested	Identify all features and combinations of features that will be tested.
Features not to be tested	Define all features and significant combinations of features that will not be tested.
Test Methodologies	
Testing approach	Specify the types of tests required, such as regression, stress, and pilot. Define the major activities, techniques, and tools that are used to test the features.
Test data	Document the sources of test data, including how the identified test data will ensure adequacy of testing.
Test documents	Identify test documents created throughout the project life cycle, such as test cases, acceptance test plans, integration test plans, etc.
Requirements validation	Defines how tests and test results will be matched to documented system requirements.
Control procedures	Identify the procedure for identifying, recording, and tracking test results to closure, including any change control procedures.
Test phases	Identify test phases, such as unit, integration, system, acceptance, and prototype testing.
Definition	For each phase, identify the process or scenario involved in performing the activities in the phase.
Participants	Specify the individual or group responsible for conducting the test phase.
Sources of data	Identify the source and type of data for the test phase.
Entrance and exit criteria	Describe how test results are evaluated; explain the criteria for test sufficiency.
Requirements	Specify requirements that are validated in the phase.
Work products	Identify the work products that are initiated and/or completed in this phase.

Table 5.7 (continued)   Test Plan Elements

Element	Description
Test Environment	
Hardware	Describe the hardware requirements.
Software	Describe the software requirements.
Location	Define the location of the testing, including any office and space requirements.
Staffing and training	Define any staffing or training needs to conduct the tests.
Schedule	Document a detailed schedule of testing activities and responsibilities.

To be as objective as possible, this validation should include participation by individuals outside the design team. Outsiders do not have the same investment (i.e., technical or emotional) and provide a fresh viewpoint on whether the design will meet the functional requirements. During the design phase, the role of the ISSEP is to ensure that security is included in the TEMP or if necessary, develop a Security Test and Evaluation Master Plan (STEMP).

In addition to validating the security design, the TEMP in combination with follow-on system verification and validation documents, such as test plans and test procedures, can provide security requirements *verification*. Verification can be done through a variety of analysis, such as demonstration, test, and inspection. These analyses are used to provide information to evaluate risk, such as whether the system has met security specification requirements, product and process capabilities, proof of concept, or warranty compliance.

Validation is a critical activity to perform before moving to the next phase of integrating components into a system. For example, when a design has only been documented, it may be necessary to convert its design to a physical component — prototyping — and test whether the design will actually result in the required performance. How prototyping fits into the ISSE model is discussed in the next topic.

Prototyping for the ISSE Process

During the system design phase, the ISSEP may verify the documented security concepts and design configurations through the use of a physical working model or prototype. A prototype is defined as a partially functioning implementation of the design that has not been fully qualified for operational use. It can be software, hardware, or a combination of both.

The ISSEP can use the prototype to help define requirements and validate design concepts. It can be an experimental model of a system, system component, or system function that contains enough capabilities to establish or refine requirements or to validate critical design concepts.

Take the example of an electronic mail guard system. The ISSEP reviews the NIAP protection profile and security targets by several vendor products that have already been evaluated. If the security design calls for a guard system that has already been evaluated, the ISSEP might strongly recommend that the client prototype the guard system in a test environment to verify whether it will meet the security specifications. If the component can be validated to the security design requirements during this phase, time and effort can be utilized more effectively when the component is integrated into the entire system during the implementation or integration phase.

Once the ISSEP has determined that a prototype is needed, the development efforts of the prototype must be planned. Clearly, it is not the same as the formal development efforts; but in order for the prototype to match the system design, the effort should be planned according to the design specifications. Once the prototype is assembled, the ISSEP conducts an evaluation to determine the strengths and weaknesses inherent in its functionality or design. The ISSEP discusses the results with the development team to improve the requirements or design of the real system, with a special emphasis on any security-related issues. If necessary, additional prototypes can be developed.

Figure 5.9 from the *ISSE Handbook* (1994) illustrates the design prototype development process. It shows the five major efforts of the prototype process:

1. evaluate the need
2. plan the effort
3. build the prototype
4. use the prototype
5. monitor the prototype's application

Unless specifically developed for operation, prototypes are usually discarded once the purpose has been achieved. Table 5.8 identifies features often prototyped during development.

Whether using a prototype or another process, one of the final steps of the design phase is to validate the design. During security validation,

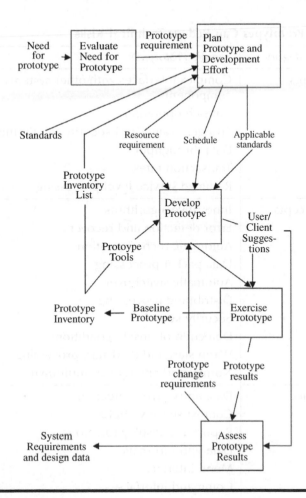

Figure 5.9   Developing design prototypes. (*Source:* From *ISSE Handbook,* 1994, p. F-17.)

the ISSEP determines whether the component parts when combined will meet the security requirements for the entire system.

Throughout the design process, the ISSEP is balancing the security requirements alongside the system requirements. This involves managing the risk at all times and, if necessary, performing a risk assessment to determine whether the design will provide the necessary control to counter the threats to the system. Risk management is discussed in detail in Chapter 10, "Technical Management." However, the next topic defines how it relates to the design phase.

Table 5.8 Prototypes Can Reduce Technical Risks

Prototype Category	Sample Prototypes
Requirements definition	Complex interfaces with other systems and system components Fail-safe operations Stringent safety and security requirements Data throughput Transaction rates Reduced service level processing
Design concepts	Innovative algorithms Error detection and recovery Automatic reconfiguration Data packet processing Automatic switchover Distributed processing Security kernels Detection of unsafe conditions Warm start and cold start processing Normal and emergency shutdown
User interface	Data entry error detection Context sensitive help Report and display functions Data entry formats Menu interface Command interface Tutorial assistance
Data management	Online transaction protocol Security violations Data privacy constraints Password control Database recovery Multi-user data locking Batch transaction processing Data archiving and purging Data distribution Database reorganization File access methods

Source: From *ISSE Handbook,* 1994, p. F17–F18.

ISSE Design and Risk Management

During the design phase, the ISSEP may choose to perform a risk analysis on the prototype or other design models. To assess risk, the system should be as realistic a working model as possible. A challenge for the ISSEP during the design process is trying to establish or emulate an environment in which the system will operate, especially because it is not known with certainty what that will be and how it may vary during the system lifetime. Thus, to the extent possible, the ISSEP should evaluate the risk based on several environmental scenarios. This will help the ISSEP understand the level of risk that may be introduced into the system and assess whether the security controls are mitigating the risk to an acceptable level.

Residual risk is the risk that remains after the implementation of new or enhanced controls. The residual risk can be accepted by the approving authority. During the design phase, the ISSEP must note whether any residual risk might exist for the component or the system. Senior management must closely monitor the residual risk to ensure that changes to the environment, system, etc. do not affect the impact of the risk or increase the risk beyond an acceptable limit.

Final Deliverables of Step 4

The final outcome or "deliverable" for the SE is the system specification document that outlines the system functional baseline and includes:

- Results from the needs analysis and feasibility analysis
- Operational requirements
- Top-level functional analysis
- Maintenance concept
- System requirement analysis
- Critical technical performance measures

The outcome for the ISSEPs will be the documented systems security specifications that define the security functional baseline. Just as in the SE model, the ISSEP may need to create several security specification documents, such as

- Security development specification
- Security product specification
- Security process specification
- Security material specification

Once completed, these documents are version controlled to manage and document changes.

During the latter stages of the design phase, a comprehensive System Engineering Management Plan (SEMP) is developed. The goal is to ensure the implementation of a program that will lead to a well-coordinated and integrated product output. The SEMP provides an integration of documents from previous activities and any design-related tasks necessary to enhance the integration and implementation activities. Managing the security elements would be included in the SEMP or can be provided as separate documentation.

A Configuration Management plan is developed that explains how to create an initial baseline to use as a comparison when changes are made. A Testing and Evaluation Management Plan (TEMP) is created to provide a framework for testing the components of the system. Again, security can be included in these plans or written as individual security documents that are combined with the other plans.

Summary

This chapter focused on designing the system — how SEs and ISSEPs take the system and security requirements defined in the architectures and create the system and security specifications. In the first section, the SE process outlined some key factors of the design phase, such as the trade-off analysis. The trade-off analysis involves considering the alternatives and balancing the requirements prior to selecting the appropriate solution. It is considered a tool that can help SEs, ISSEPs, and the customer make the best decisions.

The trade-off analysis leads to synthesis — the combining and structuring of components in a manner to represent a viable system configuration. The synthesis is the design — it defines the build-to requirements for the system elements. The synthesis activity defines, refines, and integrates the configuration items into a physical configuration of the system that will satisfy the system requirements. It is used in the development of preliminary concepts and to establish relationships among the various system and subsystem configuration items. At this point in the process, the basic requirements have been established, trade-off studies have been completed, and a baseline configuration has been developed to demonstrate the design concepts.

The IEEE 1220 standard outlines three major system development levels: system definition, preliminary design, and detailed design. During the system definition, the customer establishes the definition of the system with a focus on system products required to satisfy operational requirements. The preliminary system design phase initiates subsystem design and creates subsystem level specifications and design-to baselines to guide component development. In the detailed system design, a complete subsystem is designed down to the lowest component level, a component specification is created, and a build-to component baseline is established for each component.

One of the final steps in the design phase is to conduct the System Design Review (SDR) to validate the conceptual design against activities conducted in the preliminary and detailed system design. Essentially, the system specifications are reviewed against the system requirements and the system architecture.

Similar to the SE model, the ISSEP structures the security configuration items into a synthesis — a structuring of the components to characterize a practical system security configuration. Once this configuration is established, the ISSEP documents this information in the system security specifications. The synthesis leads to the establishment of the functional security baseline, which is used in Phase 5 to develop and integrate the security components into the system.

Just as in the IEEE model, the ISSE design phases include the preliminary security design phase and the detailed security design phase. ISSEP contributions during this phase include participation in activities such as the following:

- Review and refinement of all areas with particular attention to the definition of appropriate component item level and interface specifications
- Survey of existing inventory security solutions for a match to needed component items
- Assessment of technical and nontechnical rationales for the proposed preliminary design review level security solutions
- Validation and verification that component item specifications satisfy system security requirements
- Continued inputs to certification and accreditation process activities as required
- Participation in the collective, multidisciplinary examination of all system security issues

Although the life-cycle security approach can be considered during any of the ISSE activities, it is usually in this phase that the ISSEP documents how the design of the system will follow a life-cycle approach model. As part of the life-cycle, the ISSEP assists in deciding on a security product by balancing factors such as operational function and performance, cost, schedule, and risk. This will require the ISSEP to review COTS, GOTS, or decide on custom building the products.

A final step in the ISSE design phase is to validate the security design, which ensures the overall security specifications comply with the security requirements. Validation can be accomplished through the use of a physical working model, such as a prototype. The ISSEP uses the prototype to define requirements and validate design concepts. During the next phase, the SE and ISSEP begin to develop and build the components into a functioning system.

References

Blanchard, Benjamin (1998). *Systems Engineering Management, 2nd edition.* John Wiley & Sons: New York, NY.

Blanchard, Benjamin S. and Wolter J. Fabrycky (1998). *System Engineering and Analysis, 3rd edition.* Prentice Hall: Upper Saddle River, NJ.

CESG/NIST (1999). Common Criteria for IT Security Evaluation: User Guide. Published by CESG in the United Kingdom, NIST in the United States. Available for download at www.commoncriteria.org.

Clements, Paul, Rick Kazman, and Mark Klein (2002). *Evaluating Software Architectures: Methods and Case Studies.* Addison-Wesley: Boston, MA.

Common Criteria (May 2000). "Arrangement on the Recognition of Common Criteria Certificates in the field of Information Technology Security." Available at: www.commoncriteriaportal.org/public/files/cc-recarrange.pdf.

CECI-P, Engineer Regulation 25-1-2. (August 1999). Life Cycle Management of Information Systems (LCMIS). Department of the Army, U.S. Army Corps of Engineers, Washington, D.C. Available for download at http://www.usace.army.mil/ci/lcmis/lcmdocs.html#adobe.

DoD Instruction 5200.40 (December 1997). DoD Information Technology Security Certification and Accreditation Process (DITSCAP). Available at http://www.dtic.mil/whs/directives/index.html.

Faulconbridge, R. Ian and Michael J. Ryan (2003). *Managing Complex Technical Projects: A Systems Engineering Approach.* Artech House: Norwood, MA.

Hansche, Susan, John Berti, and Chris Hare (2004). *Official (ISC)² Guide to the CISSP Exam.* CRC Press/Auerbach: Boca Raton, FL.

Herrmann, Debra S. (2002). *A Practical Guide to Security Engineering and Information Assurance.* CRC Press: Boca Raton, FL.

IAEC3186 (February 2002). *Introduction to Information Systems Security Engineering,* ISSE Training, student guide.

IEEE Std 1220-1998 (December 1998, copyrighted January 1999). IEEE Standard for Application and Management of the Systems Engineering Process. IEEE: New York, NY. (Revision of IEEE Std 1220-1994.)

ISO/IEC 15408 (2000). The Common Criteria. It can be purchased through the ISO Web site: http://www.iso.ch/iso/en/ISOOnline.frontpage.

Information Systems Security Engineering Handbook, Release 1.0 (February 28, 1994). National Security Agency, Central Security Service. Only available for official USG use.

Information Assurance Technical Framework (IATF), Version 3.1 (September 2002). National Security Agency, Information Assurance Solutions, Technical Directors; Fort Meade, MD.

Kossaikoff, Alexander and William N. Sweet (2003). *Systems Engineering: Principles and Practice.* John Wiley & Sons: Hoboken, NJ.

McGraw, Gary and Ed Felton (1999). *Securing Java: Getting Down to Business with Mobile Code.* John Wiley & Sons: New York, NY.

NIST SP 800-30 (January 2002). Risk Management Guide for Information Technology Systems. Available at the NIST Web site: www.nist.gov.

NIST SP 800-47 (August 2002). Security Guide for Interconnecting Information Technology Systems. Available at the NIST Web site: www.nist.gov.

NIST SP 800-53 (February 2005), Recommended Security Controls for Federal Information Systems. Available at the NIST Web site: www.nist.gov.

NSTISSI No. 1000 (April 2000). National Information Assurance Certification and Accreditation Process (NIACAP). Available at http://www.nstissc.gov/html/library.html.

Web Sites

http://niap.nist.gov/cc-scheme/PPRegistry.html for Common Criteria protection profile listing

http://www.sei.cmu.edu/ata/ata_method.html for Architecture Tradeoff Analysis Method (ATAM) by CE SEI

http://www.ewh.ieee.org/soc/rs/Reliability_Engineering/index.html for IEEE information

http://www.iatf.net/protection profiles/

http://niap.nist.gov/

Capability Maturity Model® is a registered trademark of the Software Engineering Institute at Carnegie Mellon University.

Software Design and Development Bibliography

Anderson, Ross (2001). *Security Engineering.* John Wiley & Sons: New York, NY.

Atluri, Vijay and Pierangela Samarati (2000). *Security of Data and Transaction Processing.* Kluwer Academic Publishers: New York, NY.

AlBanna Sami J. and Joe Ohsterhaus (1998). Meeting the Software Challenge: A Model for IS Transformation, *Information Systems Management Journal,* Winter issue.

Barman, Scott (2001). *Writing Information Security Policies.* New Riders Publishing: Indianapolis, IN.

Blakeley, Jose A. (1996). OLE DB: A Component DBMS Architecture, in *Proceedings of the 12th International Conference on Data Engineering (ICDE '96).* Published on the Web site: http://www.computer.org/proceedings/icde/7240/72400203.pdf.

Blakley, Bob (2000). *CORBA Security: An Introduction to Safe Computing with Objects*. Addison-Wesley: Reading, MA.

Brooks, Frederick P. (1995) (first edition 1974). *The Mythical Man-Month: Essays on Software Engineering, Anniversary Edition (2nd edition)*. Addison-Wesley: Reading, MA.

Castano, Silvano, Maria Grazia Fugini, and Giancarlo Martella (1994). *Database Security*. Addison-Wesley/ACM Press Books: New York, NY.

Dean, Drew, Edward W. Felten, and Dan S. Wallach (1996). Java Security: From HotJava to Netscape and Beyond, in *1996 IEEE Symposium on Security and Privacy*, Oakland, CA.

Forcht, Karen Anne (1994). *Computer Security Management*. Boyd & Fraser Publishing Company: Danvers, MA.

Gollman, Dieter (1999). *Computer Security*. John Wiley & Sons: West Sussex, England.

Grimes, Roger A. (2001). *Malicious Mobile Code: Virus Protection for Windows*. O'Reilly Computer Security: Cambridge, MA.

Harley, C. David, Robert Slade, David Harley, Urs E. Gattiker, and Eugene H. Spafford (2002). *Viruses Revealed*. McGraw-Hill Osborne Media: Berkeley, CA.

Heiser, Jay (2002). Combating Nonviral Malware: Trojans, Sniffers and Spyware, Oh My! *Information System Security*, May 2002.

Henry, Paul (2000). Covert Channels Provided Hackers the Opportunity and the Means for the Current Distributed Denial of Service Attacks. A White Paper for CyberGuard Corporation: Ft. Lauderdale, FL. © CyberGuard Corporation, 2000.

Hurley, Edward (2002). The Lexicon of Viruses, Worms and Malicious Code. SearchSecurity.com, November 19, 2002. http://searchsecurity.techtarget.com/originalContent/0,289142,sid14_gci864280,00.html.

Inmon, W.H. (1996). *Building the Data Warehouse, 2nd edition*. John Wiley & Sons: New York, NY.

Kelley, Al, Ira Phol, and Carter Shanklin (1992). *C by Dissection: The Essentials of C Programming*. Addison-Wesley Publishing: Reading, MA.

Kotz, David and Robert S. Gray (1999). Mobile Agents and the Future of the Internet, articles from the Thayer School of Engineering, Dartmouth College: http://www.cs.dartmouth.edu/~dfk/papers/kotz:future2/.

McGraw, Gary and Ed Felton (1999). *Securing Java: Getting Down to Business with Mobile Code*. John Wiley & Sons: New York, NY.

Neumann, Peter G. (1995). *Computer-Related Risks*. Addison-Wesley: Reading, MA.

Olivier, Martin S. and Sebastian H. von Solms (1994). A Taxonomy for Secure Object-Oriented Databases. *TODS*, 19(1), 3–46. http://dblp.uni-trier.de/db/journals/tods/OliverS94.html.

Pfleeger, Charles P. (1997). *Security in Computing*. Prentice Hall: Upper Saddle River, NJ.

Paulk, Mark C. (1996). Effective CMM-Based Process Improvement. © 1996 by Carnegie Mellon University. ftp://ftp.sei.cmu.edu/pub/cmm/Misc/effective-spi.pdf.

Ramachandran, Jay (2002). *Designing Security Architecture Solutions*. John Wiley & Sons: New York, NY.

Rowland, Craig H. (1996). Covert Channels in the TCP/IP Suite. *First Monday,* peer-reviewed journal on the Internet. http://www.firstmonday.dk/issues /issue2_5/rowland/.

Samarati, Pierangela and Ravi Sandhu, Editors (1999). *Database Security: Status and Prospects.* Kluwer Academic Publishers: New York, NY.

Slade, Robert (1996). *Robert Slade's Guide to Computer Viruses: How to Avoid Them, How to Get Rid of Them, and How to Get Help.* Springer Verlag: New York, NY.

Sommerville, Ian (2000). *Software Engineering, 6th edition.* Addison-Wesley: Reading, MA.

Theriault, Marlene, William Heney, and Debby Russell (1998). *Oracle Security.* O'Reilly & Associates Press:

Theriault, Marlene and Aaron Newman, (2001). *Oracle Security Handbook: Implement a Sound Security Plan in Your Oracle Environment.* Osborne McGraw-Hill.

Viega, John and Gary McGraw (2002). *Building Secure Software: How to Avoid Security Problems the Right Way.* Addison-Wesley, Pearson Education Corporate Sales Division: Indianapolis, IN.

Wiener, Lauren Ruth (1993). *Digital Woes: Why We Should Not Depend on Software.* Perseus Publishing: Cambridge, MA.

6

ISSE Model Phase 5: Implement System Security

Introduction

The phases in the Information Systems Security Engineering (ISSE) life-cycle model are:

1. Discover Information Protection Needs. Ascertain why the system needs to be built and what information needs to be protected.
2. Define System Security Requirements. Define the system in terms of what security is needed.
3. Define System Security Architecture. Define the security functions needed to meet the specific security requirements.
4. Develop Detailed Security Design. Based on the security architecture, design the security functions and features for the system.
5. **Implement System Security. Following the documented security design, build and implement the security functions and features for the system.**
6. Assess Security Effectiveness. Assess the degree to which the security of the system, as it is defined, designed, and implemented, meets the security needs.

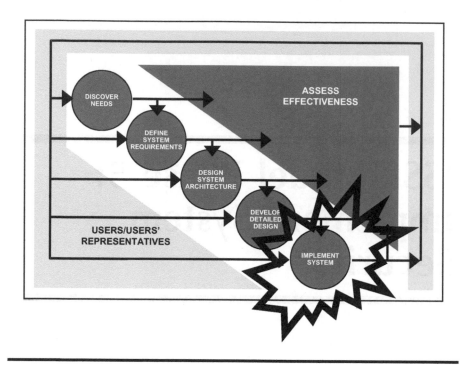

Figure 6.1   ISSE model: security implementation. (*Source:* Adapted from IATF, p. 3-2.)

This chapter focuses on Phase 5 of the ISSE model: Implementing System Security (Figure 6.1). This is equivalent to the Systems Engineering activity, Implement System. All of the previous activities have focused on and led up to the abstract design and working models of the system. In the implementation phase, or what is more realistically called the *integration phase,* the system evolves from the systems specifications (design) to the tangibles, including hardware, firmware, software, and the people necessary to develop and implement the system. **System implementation** is the process of making the new system available to a prepared set of users (deployment) and positioning ongoing support and maintenance of the system at the customer's site (the transition).

In this activity, the components are integrated into a whole system, then tested, evaluated, and accepted by the customer. The role of the Information Systems Security Engineering Professional (ISSEP®) during this phase is to ensure that the security mechanisms designated in the security specifications are integrated into the functional operation of the system. One of the first ISSE implementation activities is to review both the security requirements and the security specifications to identify any concerns associated with the integration of the proposed security mechanisms. It is important to remember that all U.S. Government (USG) systems must be assessed for security effectiveness and approved (through a Certification & Accreditation process) before the completed system can become operational; this will occur in the final implementation activity.

The Information Assurance Technical Framework (IATF, 2002) defines the system implementation activities as acquiring, integrating, configuring, testing, documenting, and training. During this phase, the system is moved from design to operations and concludes with a final system effectiveness assessment. The final assessment involves presenting evidence that defines what the system is intended to do and how the system complies with the requirements and satisfies the mission needs. Final issues involving any of the systems engineering primary functions must be considered and any interdependency or trade-off issues resolved.

An important element of this phase is to actually deploy the system, which consists of:

- Executing all steps necessary to educate the users of the new system
- Placing the newly developed system into production
- Confirming that all data required at the start of operations is available and accurate
- Validating that business functions that interact with the system are functioning properly

Also, one of the final activities is to transition the system support responsibilities from system development to a system support and maintenance mode of operation. This includes transferring ownership of the system from the project team to the customer.

Figure 6.2 provides an overview of the two primary topics in this chapter and their associated implementation activities. The chapter begins by explaining the role of system engineering during system implementation. The second section focuses on the ISSE model and role of the ISSEP during the implementation phase. The final section discusses the role of risk management during the implementation and evaluation phase.

Systems Engineering Activity: System Implementation

The systems engineering phase for implementation is also called the construction, integration, and validation (or evaluation) phase. The objective is to assemble and integrate (also called construction and production) the engineered components of the new system into an effective operating whole. It also involves testing and evaluating the system to ensure that it meets all of its operational requirements. The goal is to qualify the systems

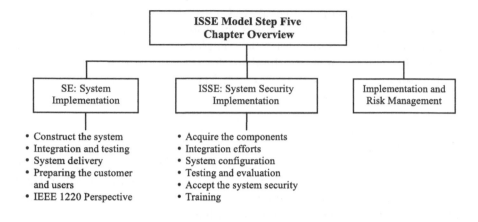

Figure 6.2 Chapter overview.

engineering design for release to production and operational use. Figure 6.3 outlines the Systems Engineer (SE) implementation activities and tasks in more detail.

Following the establishment of the functional baseline (which follows the successful completion of detail design and development), the system is ready for construction and production. Construction is the building of the system using the previously defined components and subsystems. Production refers to the manufacturing or purchase of the components and subsystems that will comprise the entire system.

An important consideration during the construction and production stage is whether the system is designed to be only one system or will it need to be replicated in various locations. Although a system can demonstrate a certain level of effectiveness during testing, it is another challenge to ensure that additional replicas of the system will exhibit the same characteristics.

Issues that should be addressed during construction/production of the system include:

- *Plant requirements.* Type and size of any plant to produce and construct the system
- *Personnel resources.* Including skills required by personnel and any training programs needed
- *Schedule development.* Planning documents of who, when, where, and how construction/production will occur

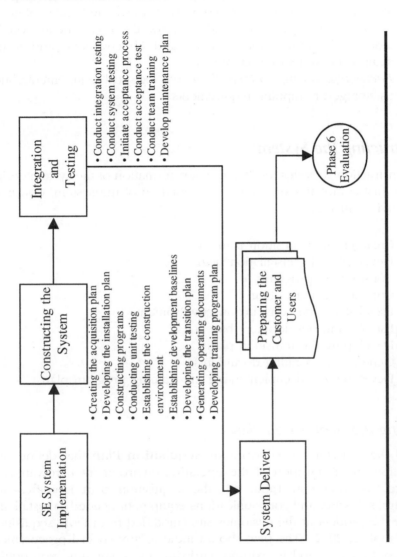

Figure 6.3 SE implementation activities.

- *Material availability, ordering, and handling.* Complete list of materials needed, ordering procedures, shipping requirements, and storage requirements
- *Process control.* How the process will be managed
- *Documentation of construction processes.* Document the step-by-step procedures of how the system was constructed and configured
- *Assembly, inspection, and testing.* How the components will be assembled, verified for accuracy and effectiveness, and tested against the system requirements
- *Packaging, storing, and handling.* Any logistical requirements, such as storage or shipping requirements

Constructing the System

The construction activities result in the transformation of the system design into the first complete executable representation of the system. Construction activities include:

- Creating the acquisition plan
- Developing the installation plan
- Constructing programs
- Conducting unit testing
- Establishing the construction environment
- Establishing development baselines
- Developing the transition plan
- Generating operating documents
- Developing and implementing the training program plan

Creating the Acquisition Plan

One of the first steps is to create an **Acquisition Plan** that defines the acquisition and installation of the operating environment hardware and software. As shown in Table 6.1, the acquisition plan identifies any hardware, software, and communications equipment needed to install and operate the product at the customer site (modified from DoE Acquisition Plan Template, 2002). The plan should indicate any special procurement necessary to accommodate existing hardware and communication equipment with which the new system will interface. A challenge for project managers is to determine sufficient lead-time to accomplish all procurement, delivery, testing, and installation processes. Because some procurement may

Table 6.1 Acquisition Plan Elements

Element	Description
Strategy Development Factors	This section should describe the development factors, constraints, and selection method to obtain equipment. It should identify the factors, such as size, speed, availability, etc., and any impact on the selection of a specific strategy.
Existing products	If applicable, describe the ability of currently used products to meet the requirements.
Constraints	Identify any constraints that may affect the acquisition process, such as Federal regulations, budget, required approvals, lead times, etc.
Method of acquiring new products	Identify the method(s) by which new products will be obtained, such as GSA schedules, Request for Proposals, sole sourcing, and lease versus buy.
Selected Acquisition Strategy	This section should outline the acquisition strategy chosen to meet the system requirements.
Method of acquiring the products	Describe the method chosen and give the rationale used.
Regulations	Identify the regulations that support the acquisition.
Source of Funds	Identify the source(s) of funds for the acquisition.
Approvals	Identify who must approve the strategy.
Lead time	Identify the project lead times and date the product must be available and operational for each phase of the acquisition process.
Procurement schedule	Provide schedule information of the relevant procurement activities.
Hardware Specifications	This section should address hardware compatibility and also describe the type of processing equipment, communications, special equipment, support services, and site preparation required.
Hardware compatibility	Identify any hardware compatibility issues that may impact the acquisition process, such as hardware, vendors, versions, software operating system, etc.

Table 6.1 (continued)   Acquisition Plan Elements

Element	Description
Processing equipment	Identify the requirements needed to run the proposed system, such as type, size, speed, intended site, and quantity of the equipment. Also, manuals needed for setup, operations, or maintenance should be specified.
Communications	Outline a description of the communications equipment and any related software, services, and facilities required by the system.
Special equipment	Identify any special equipment that must be acquired, such as emergency power generators, etc.
Support services	If applicable, identify the support services, such as repair, maintenance, or training, required to install and maintain the hardware and software.
Site preparation	Identify the customer sites requiring modification in order to receive the computer or communications equipment, hardware, or software.
Software Specifications	This section should describe the required capabilities, features, and capacity of the software.
Required capabilities and features	List the required capabilities of the software.
Capacity	As much as possible, estimate the volumes of data that will be handled after the system is running for several years.
Documentation	Identify the manuals necessary for proper installation and operation of the software.
Training program	Identify the training of users of software, including any follow-up training.
Maintenance features	Identify the vendor's method of supporting errors or bugs in the software, and also any agreements for revisions or updates to the software.
Sources	Identify the potential sources of products, such as the manufacturer and distributor names, lead times, and estimated costs.

Source: Adapted from DoE Acquisition Plan Template, 2002.

be out of the control of the design and development team, a contingency plan should be developed for how to deal with needed resources that may not be available or do not meet the required specifications.

Components can be purchased, leased, or in some situations borrowed (i.e., other government agencies may have excess resources to share). The SE team reviews the selection of components based on factors such as cost, availability, expected life cycle, and how they will fit into the overall system. Other factors may include how the component will affect reliability, risk to system performance if the component's performance is marginal, and future availability of the component or substitutes.

One primary consideration is cost, especially for technology products that have limited life cycles. For example, organizations may find it is cost effective to lease instead of buy hardware. For some leasing costs less money and eliminates the risk of the technology becoming obsolete before it is paid for. The idea of leasing equipment is that if executed properly, it can provide flexibility to the organization and shift the technology risk to the leasing agent. The leasing agent benefits from the leased arrangement by receiving higher compensation for taking the risk. Therefore, the organization pays more for the leased equipment but benefits by having the ability to quickly update its technical abilities without a large investment.

Leasing can also increase cash flow for an organization. Instead of an initial large output of money to purchase the equipment, the cost is spread over a predetermined time period. For example, it may cost $20,000 to buy equipment; however, it may cost $7000 per year for three years to lease the equipment. Thus, the initial outlay of cash each year would be less. For some organizations this reduced initial cost may allow other purchases, such as security services or training for employees. Table 6.2 provides a brief comparison of buying versus leasing hardware equipment.

Table 6.2   Buying versus Leasing

Buying Equipment	Leasing Equipment
It is worth the investment when you plan to keep something for a long time	IT equipment has a typical life span of 2 to 5 years (although some equipment is only 2 to 3 years)
No interest component	Typically includes an interest component or higher premium
Management of assets does not require specific controls	Management of assets must be highly controlled

Hennigan (2002) provides the following guidelines that a manager can use to make decisions about buying or leasing hardware:

- Useful life of the hardware within the organization and in the marketplace
- Expected end-of-lease action (e.g., return, renew, purchase)
- Possible pre-end-of-lease actions (e.g., termination, upgrade)
- Organization's asset management capabilities

Note that the specific terms and end-of-lease details for each transaction will ultimately determine the cost of that flexibility. In some situations, it may be necessary to have a mixture of purchased and leased hardware. On the other hand, there may be additional security requirements that would not allow the option of leasing hardware. For example, the leasing contract might include a maintenance agreement to repair or replace all equipment. If the equipment will process classified information and part of the security requirement is to limit access by maintenance personnel, the maintenance agreement would not be cost effective. Thus, leasing would not be cost effective.

A consideration for the leasing of equipment is asset management. For example, an organization leases 100 laptops for a three-year time period. Based on your own experience, how would you answer the following questions: At the end of the three years, how many laptops will the organization be able to account for? How many laptops will be located in a storage closet and lost to the inventory count? How many laptops will be lost or misplaced by employees? What about accessories, such as external disk drives, battery replacements, power cords, etc.? It is easy to see that if an organization chooses leasing as an option, it must have asset management controls and personnel in place to track the inventory.

Developing the Installation Plan

In large programs, the team should develop an **Installation Plan** that specifies the requirements and procedures for the full-scale installation of the product at the customer site. The plan would address the installation of any hardware, software, firmware, and communications equipment needed to operate the product at the customer site. An important consideration is whether the system will operate in various customer sites. If so, the installation plan should include each site's requirements for continuity of operations, level of service, and the needs of the project team, users, maintenance personnel, and management. For small- and medium-sized projects that have limited procurement and installation requirements, the acquisition and installation plans could be combined into one document.

Constructing Programs

Systems requiring custom development of software would begin with the development of the source code. The code should follow the requirements developed in the system design phase and those outlined in the configuration management plan. Regardless of the platform, construction of the code should follow a consistent set of coding practices and error prevention procedures. This promotes the efficient development of reliable and maintainable code. Source code can be developed in a sequence of units based on a plan that accounts for factors such as criticality, difficulty, integration and test issues, and needs of the customers.

For COTS (commercial-off-the-shelf) products, the SE team may have to adapt and integrate the product so that it will work within the customer's environment. The typical solution is to adapt COTS software products through the use of wrappers, bridges, or other "glueware" (Generic Language Universal Environment [GLUE] uses open Internet standards to integrate, connect, and extend enterprise applications). It is important to note that adaptation does not imply modification of the COTS product. Adaptation can be a complex activity requiring technical expertise at specific COTS component levels. Thus, adaptation and integration must take into account interactions among custom components, COTS products, any nondevelopmental item components, any legacy code, and the architecture, including infrastructure and middleware elements.

Conducting Unit Testing

For software components, a traceability check of the code against the requirement specifications helps ensure that the component satisfies all requirements and does not include inappropriate or extraneous functionality. The SEs would expand the Requirements Traceability Matrix (RTM) developed in the requirements phase to include the source and object code to the requirements.

To verify whether software code is meeting the requirements, the SEs should conduct structured walkthroughs of the expanded RTM and completed units to ensure that the code is accurate, logical, internally well documented, complete, and error-free. For large or complex projects, code inspections may be a more effective method of removing defects and identifying areas where defects may occur. Code inspection is an analysis technique that relies on visual examination of code to detect errors, violations of development standards, and other problems. Code inspections should be conducted at successive stages of code production, especially when several developers or different teams produce code.

Another type of validity testing is to conduct **unit tests**, which are used to verify the input and output for each completed module. Unit tests can indicate the validity of the function or sub-function performed by the module and show traceability to the design. During unit testing, each module is tested individually and the module interface is verified for consistency with the design specification. All important processing paths and error-handling paths through the module are tested for expected results.

An important mantra of software development is: **test, test, test**. Some even suggest writing unit tests before writing the code. Test everything you can, and test it often. The reality of testing is that in today's programming environment, when deadlines are tight and management wants it now, it is difficult to test exhaustively. Another obstacle to adequate unit testing is the start-up costs to design and implement an acceptable unit-testing framework. To overcome this, management and the SE team must work together to plan for adequate testing in an efficient manner.

Establishing the Construction Environment

As part of constructing the system, the SE team establishes the construction environment for assembling and installing the hardware, software, communications equipment, and other items required to support the construction effort. When the installation of the equipment or software is complete, the SEs conduct tests to verify the operating characteristics and functionality of the hardware and software. At this point, the ISSEP also verifies whether the security software and procedures have been activated and are operational.

In some situations, the operational environment is also the construction environment. If this occurs, it may be necessary to alter the operational environment to accommodate an infrastructure of purchased hardware and software for use during construction and testing. Before the new system is integrated into the operational environment, it should be tested to verify that it performs as specified, is acceptable and predictable in the customer's environment, meets the system requirements, and is compatible with other hardware/software interfaces.

At this point, the project team members who will use the hardware or software may need to obtain training, such as attending vendor training sessions or customized in-house training. This should follow a previously established training program that describes how the system is to be used. The training program plan is discussed in the topic, Develop Training Program Plan.

Establishing Development Baselines

One aspect of the construction activity is to establish a development baseline. A **development baseline** is an approved build of the product and can be a single component or a combination of components. The first development baseline is established after the first build is completed, tested, and approved by the SEs, ISSEPs, project manager, or customer. The baseline should be reproducible. Any later versions of the development baseline should also be approved, and the approved development baseline for one build supersedes that for its predecessor build.

The types of internal tests to conduct on builds include regression, functional, performance, and reliability:

- *Regression tests* (sometimes referred to as verification testing). They are designed to verify that capabilities in earlier builds continue to work correctly in subsequent builds. For software that has been modified, it retests the application to ensure that bugs have been fixed, previously working functions have not failed as a result of the changes, and newly added features have not created problems with previous versions.
- *Functional tests.* Focus is on verifying that the build meets its functional and data requirements and correctly generates each expected display and report.
- *Performance tests.* Used to identify the performance thresholds of each build.
- *Reliability tests.* Used to identify the reliability thresholds of each build.

Once the first development baseline is established, any changes to the baseline must be managed under the change control procedures described in the Configuration Management Plan. Configuration management is discussed in more detail in Chapter 10. Approved changes to a development baseline must be incorporated into the next build of the product and the revisions noted in affected work documents (e.g., Requirements Specification, System Design Document, and Program Specifications).

Developing the Transition Plan

Successful transition from the construction phase to full operational use of the system depends on planning for the transition before it is installed in its operational environment. The transition requirements for the SEs are to plan for the transition, quantify the operational needs associated with the system, and describe the procedures that will be used to perform the transition.

The **Transition Plan** describes the detailed plans, procedures, and schedules that will guide the transition process. Table 6.3 is an example of information documented in a transition plan.

The following should be considered in the preparation of a Transition Plan:

- Do the operational scenarios describe the functions to be performed by the operational support staff, maintenance staff, and users?
- How many of the operational and maintenance staff or users will require training?
- Is the release process clearly defined? For example, if development is incremental, the release documentation should define the particular process, schedule, and acceptance criteria for each release.
- Is it necessary to transfer operational data? How will it be accomplished?
- What are the procedures to detect problems? What are the resolution procedures?
- Have the configuration management procedures for the operational system been defined?
- What is the scope and type of support that SEs or ISSEPs will need to provide during the transition period?
- Which organizations and individuals will be responsible for each transition activity?
- Are there additional products and support services that must be implemented for either day-to-day operations or enhancement of operational effectiveness?

Generating Operating Documents

Another activity in the construction phase is the development of **operating documentation** such as user manuals. A users manual should provide information needed to access, navigate, and operate the system or a specific component. The manual can be organized functionally, that is, the information is presented the same way the product works. This can be helpful to users trying to understand the flow of menus, functions, and various options.

The purpose of operating documents is to describe the functions and features of the product from the user's point of view. For a large project, these include user's manual or online help screens, developer's reference

Table 6.3   Transition Plan Elements

Element	Definition
Plan Objectives	Briefly describe the objectives of this plan, such as scheduling the transition from testing to operational status, identifying staffing and training needs for system operation and maintenance, and planning for data migration.
Outstanding Issues	State any project planning issues or problems relevant to transition planning that are known as of this plan revision.
System Support Resources	
Facilities	Describe the facilities needed to support the deliverable system, such as safety and security requirements, special power needs, cabling, and room construction.
Hardware	Describe the hardware needed to support the deliverable system.
Software	Describe any software needed to support the deliverable system.
Documentation	List any hardware, software, or additional documentation needed to support the deliverable system.
Personnel	Describe the number of personnel (including the project team) needed to accomplish the transition, maintenance, and support of the deliverable system. If appropriate, list the level of expertise, security clearances, or special skills needed during the transition.
Training	Estimate the training requirements for operational staff, support and maintenance staff, and users.
Operational scenarios	Develop detailed operational scenarios that will need to be performed by the operational, support, and maintenance staff and users. Explain how each scenario will impact transition planning, and describe any specific transition procedures that result from these scenarios.
Transition Planning	
Release process	Document the release process for the deliverable system.
Data migration	Describe any data that must be transferred into the deliverable system.

Table 6.3 (continued)   Transition Plan Elements

Element	Definition
Problem resolution	Specify procedures for identifying, tracking, and resolving problems with the operational system.
Transition schedule	Develop a detailed schedule for transition, including roles and responsibilities. Address transition through the development, operation, maintenance, and support phases of the system product.

Note: Based on DoE Transition Plan Template, 2002.

manual, systems administrator manual, database administrator manual, or operator manual. For small projects, a quick reference guide or card may be more appropriate than a full-scale user's manual. A quick reference guide might explain logon or logoff procedures or commands for frequently used functions. Also, different types of users, such as system administrators, will require different types of information. Thus, it may be necessary to use a modular approach to developing operating documentation that will accommodate the needs of different users.

Developing a Training Program Plan

The final activity in the construction phase is to develop a **training program** that defines the training needed for users to implement and operate the system successfully. A sample training plan is shown in Table 6.4. Typically, a training plan identifies the fundamental elements of how and what training needs to be conducted and who should receive the training (e.g., system owner, operational or maintenance staff, system administrators, or users). For example, systems containing new hardware or software should plan to have the operational personnel attend hands-on training in a nonoperational environment before bringing the new equipment or software into daily operation.

Once the components have been constructed, the next step is to integrate the system into the operational environment and conduct testing to ensure that the system is operating in its environment as expected.

Integration and Testing Phase

During this activity, components are integrated and tested to determine whether the system meets predetermined functionality, performance, quality, interface, and security requirements. Activities concentrate on interfaces between and among components of the system, such as functional

Table 6.4 Training Plan Elements

Element	Definition
Training program	Describe the general work environment, skills for which training is required, training audience, and time frame in which training must be given.
Roles and responsibilities	Identify the roles and responsibilities of the training staff, such as course designers/developers and course presenters/instructors.
Training evaluation	Define how training evaluation will be performed.
Training strategy	Describe how the training will be delivered, such as classroom or computer-based training, and the training schedule, such as duration, sites, and dates.
Training sources	Identify the source or provider for the training, such as course developed in-house or contracted to external training agencies.
Pilot Class	If developed in-house, once the training is developed, it should be presented to a test group and then revised based on recommendations from the pilot audience.
Dependencies/ constraints/ limitations	Identify all known dependencies, constraints, and limitations that could affect training.
Training resources	Identify all of the essential resources associated with the training, such as hardware or software needs, instructor availability, training time estimates, projected level of effort, system documentation, and other resources required to familiarize the trainer with the system, produce training materials, and provide the actual training.
Training environment	Describe the equipment and conditions required for the training.
Training materials	Describes the types of training materials required for the training, such as overhead projectors, handouts, workbooks, manuals, computerized displays, and demonstrations.
Update/revise training materials	Based on changes to the system, training materials must be subjected to the same kind of configuration management process as the other system documentation.

Source: Based on DoE Training Plan, 2002.

correctness, system stability, overall system operability, system security, privacy and sensitive information control, and system performance requirements (e.g., reliability, maintainability, and availability). When performed incrementally, integration and testing will provide feedback on quality, errors, and design weaknesses early in the integration process (DoE G 200.1-1A, 2002).

Once the product is fully integrated, system testing is conducted to validate that the system will operate in its intended environment, that it satisfies all user requirements, and is supported with complete and accurate operating documentation.

The integration and testing activities include:

- Conduct integration testing
- Conduct system testing
- Initiate acceptance process
- Conduct acceptance test team training
- Develop maintenance plan

Conduct Integration Testing

Integration testing is a formal procedure that is planned and coordinated with the completion dates of the components or units. At this point in the process, the components — whether they are COTS or custom built — are assembled into one product. Each assembly should be tested according to an Integration Test Plan. Using an incremental approach, each component and its integration can be verified — and corrections can be made at the component level and tested again.

Two techniques for conducting integration testing are "bottom-up" and "top-down." The bottom-up approach combines one or more modules into a build, tests the build, and then integrates the build into the structure. Usually, the build will contain a set of modules that performs a major function of the system. In the top-down approach, all modules that comprise a major function are integrated, which allows an operational function to be demonstrated prior to completion of the entire system. Most integration test plans will use both a bottom-up and top-down approach. Results from the integration tests should be documented in the Testing and Evaluation Master Plan (TEMP). When the integration tests have been conducted, a complete system test is scheduled. The TEMP is discussed further in Chapter 10.

Conduct System Testing

Once the system is completely integrated, system testing is done to validate that the system meets all requirements. System testing should follow the TEMP and the results should be documented in the TEMP.

The system test bed should match as closely as possible the actual production system. In some instances, an independent evaluator is brought in to assure that the system performs as expected and that each function executes without error. For smaller, less complex projects, the project team will most likely conduct the system test.

Prior to beginning any formal testing, an appropriate period of time must be designated for test preparation. Planning for testing considers people, tools, facilities, schedule, and capital resources required to test both individual components and the entire system.

Blanchard (1998) states that proper testing and evaluation conditions must be established to ensure effective results. Further, he notes that to simulate a realistic environment, the following factors must be addressed:

- *Selection of test item.* The system selected for test should represent the most up-to-date design or production configuration.
- *Selection of test site.* The system should be tested in an environment that will be characteristic of user operation, such as temperature changes or motion changes.
- *Testing procedures.* The fulfillment of test objectives usually involves the accomplishment of both operator and maintenance tasks, and the completion of these tasks should follow formal approved procedures.
- *Test personnel.* This includes the individuals who will actually operate and maintain the system throughout the test; and supporting engineers, technicians, data recorders, analysis, and administrators who provide assistance in conducting the overall test program. It is recommended that personnel selected for operation and maintenance testing be representative of the user community in terms of skill levels and supporting training needs.
- *Test and support equipment and software.* The accomplishment of system operational and maintenance tasks may require the use of ground handling equipment, test equipment, software, or a combination thereof. Only those items that have been approved for operation should be used.
- *Supply support.* This includes all spares, repair parts, consumables, and supporting inventories necessary for the completion of system test and evaluation. A realistic configuration is desired.
- *Test facilities and resources.* System testing may require the use of special facilities, test chambers, capital equipment, environmental controls, special instrumentation, and associated resources. These facilities and resources must be properly identified and scheduled.

If errors are discovered, the test team leader reviews the problem and determines the severity and necessary subsequent action. If minor, the problems can be corrected and regression tested by the developers during the time frame allotted for the system test. An important consideration is to verify that any corrections or changes to the system are included and controlled under the configuration management plan. If there are problems during the testing, the SE, ISSEP, or testing team can suspend or terminate the system test procedures. The tests would be rescheduled once the problems have been satisfactorily resolved.

During the system test, the test team may ask users of the system to participate. This can provide an early indication of any problems from the user's perspective and also give insight into the type and level of user training that will be needed. When the system tests have concluded, the next step is to move the system into the acceptance phase.

Initiate Acceptance Process

Following the successful completion of system testing, the acceptance process is begun to officially accept new or modified systems. For the system to move into the initial acceptance phase, the system must be fully operational, meet the project requirements, and have satisfied the mission needs. The acceptance process can be initiated by completing a pre-acceptance checklist. This type of checklist can ensure that all necessary pre-acceptance activities have been completed and that the required operating documents have been developed and approved.

Activities of a pre-acceptance checklist might include (adapted from DoE Pre-Acceptance Checklist, 2002):

- The Acceptance Test Plan is approved by the system owner, user, and other project stakeholders prior to conducting any acceptance tests.
- Copies of system documents have been provided to the support staff.
- The security checklist has been completed by the system owner and forwarded to the site's information system security officer.
- Criteria for determination of mission essentiality have been reviewed and a determination made for the system.
- If mission essential, a Continuity of Operations Plan is in place. The plan has been reviewed and approved by the appropriate organizations and personnel.
- Support staff has been identified for the project, including hotline support.
- An operational analysis of the project has been done for support issues.

- An Acceptance Test Plan has been reviewed to ensure the plan reflects the current version of the system requirements.
- The approved Acceptance Test Plan is placed in the configuration management plan.
- Operating documents and other test materials have been provided to the Acceptance Test Team prior to the start of acceptance test training.
- The acceptance test team is trained, if necessary.
- The project plan has been updated to include any revised estimates of resources, cost, and schedule.
- A structured walkthrough has been conducted to ensure that the project plan reflects the project's current status and adequately estimates the resources, costs, and schedule for the installation and acceptance stage.
- An in-stage assessment has been conducted.
- An integration and testing stage exit has been conducted.

Note that for the ISSEP, a pre-acceptance security issues checklist helps to ensure that security issues were addressed and completed by the system owner, as appropriate. The items contained in the pre-acceptance security checklist are shown in the ISSE section of this chapter.

Conduct Acceptance Test Team Training

If necessary, training may be required for the personnel performing the acceptance testing. The level of training depends on the testers' familiarity with the product and the platform on which the product will run.

Develop Maintenance Plan

Transitioning the system support responsibilities involves changing from a system development to a system support and maintenance mode of operation, with ownership of the new system moving from the development team to the customer. The **Maintenance Plan** is a documented statement outlining the maintenance process for the accepted system.

Key features of the maintenance plan include:

- Determining the scope of the maintenance effort
- Identifying anticipated maintenance requirements
- Identifying the process and tools
- Quantifying the personnel and resources needed for the maintenance effort

The maintenance process is a natural outgrowth of many of the configuration management procedures. Therefore, part of the maintenance plan is coordinating maintenance efforts with the configuration management plan. Depending on what is needed, the maintenance process can be tailored to the type of maintenance being performed and can be divided in several different ways, such as corrections or enhancements.

When defining the maintenance plan, keep in mind the following issues:

- External or regulatory changes to the product
- Internal changes to support new requirements
- Requirements deferred from current projects to later releases
- Wish-list of new functions and features
- Expected upgrades for performance, adaptability, or connectivity
- New lines of business that must be supported
- New technologies that must be incorporated

Following the completion of the integration and testing activities, the system is ready for delivery to the customer.

System Delivery

All of the previous construction, integration, and testing activities have led to the final item: delivering the fully tested version of the system. In planning for system delivery, the SEs should consider:

- Conducting a final audit of the physical configuration to verify that the system and its documentation are ready for delivery
- Notifying the user community of the delivery date and plans
- Developing an archival version of the system for backup

The final step is to perform the installation and training at the user facility.

An important difference between this activity and other SE activities is that most, if not all, activities up to this point have been performed in safe, protected, and secure environments. Once the system goes live, this is no longer the case. Any problems after live deployment could result in operational and financial impacts to the customer. The SE team, through careful planning, execution, and management of the processes, ensures a successful system or at a minimum reduces the likelihood of difficulties occurring during delivery. In addition, a good SE team develops appropriate contingency plans in the event a mishap does occur.

Part of the final documentation associated with this step is to provide the customer with some type of "version document." A version document provides information related to or important to the version or release of the system being delivered. This includes information such as the system name, date delivered, version number, release number, brief description of functionality delivered in the modification, and prerequisite hardware and software with its associated version and release numbers. If the system will be released in differing versions, one central document should contain the various release information.

The next topic focuses on the IEEE 1220 methodology for system implementation activities. *Note to ISSEP candidate:* This is provided as background reference material to give a different perspective on the titles and descriptions of system implementation.

IEEE 1220 Perspective on System Implementation Activities

For another perspective on some of the activities and terms a SE may use, some brief information on the IEEE implementation activities is provided. According to IEEE 1220 (1998), one of the first activities of the implementation phase is the Fabrication, Assembly, Integration, and Test (FAIT) stage.

Fabrication, Assembly, Integration, and Test (FAIT)

The purpose of FAIT is to resolve product deficiencies when specifications for the system, product, subsystem, assembly, or component are not met, as determined by inspection, analysis, demonstration, or test. Remember that in the design phase, the system specifications were defined and a functional baseline was created. The purpose of the FAIT stage is to continue the process to the system and subsystem level to verify that the products designed satisfy specifications.

IEEE 1220 identifies the major activities of the FIAT stage as:

- Conduct system integration and test:
  - Fabricate hardware components, implement software components
  - Assemble, integrate, and test components and assemblies
  - Assemble, integrate, and test subsystems and products
  - Establish life-cycle processes
  - Analyze, fix failures and deficiencies, and retest
  - Update all specifications and baselines
  - Revise engineering and technical plans for production

- Complete technical reviews for component, subsystem, and system test readiness
- Complete audits for component, subsystem, and system functional configuration
- Complete production approval reviews for components, subsystems, and system

During FAIT, the customer begins integration activities with a focus on combining the lower-level elements to result in a functioning higher-level element. The test activities verify that system requirements are met. To test the system, the SE team first tests the components and then tests at each level up to, and including, the total system. The SE team progressively assembles and integrates subcomponents into complete components, components into assemblies, assemblies into subsystems, subsystems into products, and then, where meaningful, products and their life-cycle processes and services into a complete system.

At each level of assembly and integration, the components, assemblies, subsystems, products, and system should undergo testing. Testing should ensure operational effectiveness, ease of use, ease of training, interface conformance, compliance with specified requirements, level of production is met, and supportability. When a subcomponent, component, assembly, subsystem, or product does not satisfy its requirements, the SE analyzes the deficiency to determine the cause of the problem and, when necessary, retests the product.

IEEE 1220 states that a system-level production approval review shall be completed by the organization after completion of product functional configuration audits to demonstrate that the total system (i.e., people, products, and processes) has been verified to satisfy specification and baseline requirements for each system level, and to confirm readiness for production, distribution, operations, support, training, continuing improvement (if applicable), and disposal.

IEEE 1220 states that the organization should confirm the following:

- "Issues for the components, assemblies, subsystems, products, and life-cycle processes and services are resolved;
- Test procedures for components, assemblies, subsystems, and products were completed and were accurate;
- The system and products were confirmed ready for test;
- Tests were conducted in accordance with established procedures;
- An audit trail from design reviews, held after detailed design, is established with changes substantiated, and all component, subsystem, and system products meet specification requirements;
- Risk-handling procedures are satisfactory for production;
- Evolutionary development requirements and plans have been refined;

■ Planning is complete and procedures, resources, and other requisite people, products, and processes are available (or programmed to be available) to initiate production, distribution, operations, support, training, disposal, and evolutionary development (if any) (p. 31–32)."

Preparing the Customer and Users

A final element of the SE implementation activity is an important and often overlooked activity — prepare the customer and the users for the changes brought about by the new system. During the implementation process, it is necessary to ensure that the customer and users are in the best position to utilize the system once deployment efforts have been validated, which is usually accomplished by delivering training.

Training is often the first exposure the customer and users will have to the new system. To create a positive experience, training should be well designed and delivered by professionals. Another important aspect for the customer and user is to understand transition needs and to make appropriate plans for changes that might impact their daily business schedule. For example, if the transition occurs on the weekend prior to a monthly batch file, users should be aware of how the transition will impact their schedule and ability to perform their duties on a timely basis, which may include appropriate contingency planning.

Once the system has been implemented, it moves into the product and customer support stages. According to IEEE 1220, the important activities at this point are to correct deficiencies discovered during production, assembly, integration, and acceptance testing of products or life-cycle process products. As part of this process, customer support should address any incremental changes, resolve product or service deficiencies, or assist with implementing any evolutionary system plans.

IEEE 1220 identifies the following as the major customer support activities:

■ Provide customer support, including support and service for "after-market" products
■ Complete system evolution, to include:
  – Make incremental changes
  – Resolve product deficiencies
  – Exceed competitive products

Due to the complexities involved in system implementations, the communication of planned deployment activities to all parties involved in the project is critical. The transition must be planned for, managed well, and effectively communicated to ensure success.

Is the System Really Ready?

"Damn the torpedoes, full speed ahead!" Although this might have worked for Admiral Farragut in 1864, the lead of the SE team may be better served by knowing when to hold the line. To help ensure a successful deployment, the team should have points where the process can be frozen and problems can be addressed. These "go/no-go" points can ensure that the final implementation is not riddled with problems.

One final thought on implementation: does the system need to be perfect before deployment? If so, who defines perfection? This is a critical question that must be discussed between the customer and SE team. It can also lead to the security aspects: what if the system is ready, but security has not been tested or cannot be tested until fully operational? Does the ISSEP have the responsibility for the "go" sign? Who has the final authority on the Certification and Accreditation activities?

To answer some of these security-related questions, the next section of this chapter looks at the ISSE responsibilities and activities to ensure that security is included as part of the system integration, testing, and delivery. The role of the ISSEP is to work with the SE team during all activities and verify that the security components, when integrated, meet the security requirements and are functioning as intended.

ISSE and System Security Implementation

The IATF (2002) states that the role of the ISSEP during systems security implementation involves the following:

- "Providing inputs to the Certification and Accreditation (C&A) activities.
- Verifying that the system as implemented does protect against the threats identified in the original threat assessment.
- Tracking of, or participation in the application of information protection assurance mechanisms related to system implementation and testing practices.
- Inputs to and review of evolving system life-cycle support plans, operational procedures, and maintenance training materials.
- A formal information protection assessment in preparation for the final system effectiveness assessment.
- Participation in the multidisciplinary examination of all system issues (p. 3-13)."

During this phase, the objectives and activities differ remarkably from the earlier requirements and design phases. An important difference involves the personnel responsible for implementing the system. For example, separate or new team members may engage in the process to carry out the technical effort. Although integration efforts are planned to run smoothly, complex systems with evolving technology will inevitably incur snags. Thus, the integration effort requires teams with the best technical expertise to carry out the requirements of the design teams. The role of the ISSEP is to work with all personnel to ensure that the path to system integration does not lose a security focus.

Take a look at an example of a potential security incident.

> The "development team" still in the safety of the non-production environment configures the system, tests the system, and approves it as ready for deployment. The system is handed to the "integration team" for setup at the customer site. During the setup, a software component does not execute using a user account, but it does work using an administrator-privileged account. To get the system operational within the restricted time period, the integration team gave all users low-level administrator privileges so that the software component would execute.

This type of scenario raises some important questions. What is the risk of having regular user accounts with administrator privileges? Would the event be noticed in the evaluation phase before the system was released for operation? How can an ISSEP ensure that the integration team followed procedures and did not give users administrative privileges? What is the responsibility of the ISSEP to conduct a final security assessment?

In this section, we attempt to answer these questions by discussing in further detail the ISSEP's role in ensuring that the security of the system does not get compromised during the final deployment and acceptance phases.

The ISSE implementation activities (Figure 6.4) include:

- Acquire the security components
- Secure integration efforts
- Secure system configuration
- Security testing and evaluation
- Accept the security of the system
- System security documentation
- Training to ensure secure operation

Figure 6.4 ISSE implementation activities.

Acquire the Security Components

During the design phase, security components were identified. The component's description included a listing of possible vendors and rationale as to how that component would meet the security requirements. Also during the design phase, a prototype of the security components may have been tested in either a stand-alone environment or with a few select interfaced components. During the integration activity, all of the security components for the system will be procured and brought together.

Just like other system components, the security components can be purchased, leased, or, in some situations, borrowed (i.e., other government agencies may have excess resources to share). The ISSEP reviews the selection of security components based on factors such as cost, availability, expected life cycle, and how they will mitigate the risk of the overall system. Other factors may include how the security component will affect reliability, risk to system performance, and future availability or modifications expected of the component.

An important aspect of leasing security components is life-cycle management. All aspects of the life cycle should be considered, including the expected life of the component and the system it is deployed in, as well as the type of disposal needed for the equipment. Disposal of equipment is a prime consideration for security requirements. In USG systems processing national security information, for example, the requirement for disposal of equipment may include total destruction depending on the equipment and classification level. Thus, in systems processing information at high sensitivity levels, leasing would not be a good option.

If components are acquired through an outside vendor, one type of security control is to use the *blind buy* approach. A blind buy conceals the identity of a developer or owner. For example, a federal agency will purchase a component from a preselected vendor, but the vendor does not know the location within the agency where the product will be implemented. Also, a federal agency may select a secure contractor to purchase items to ensure that the vendor or shipper will not know who is obtaining the component.

Components that cannot be procured must be built. Although some organizations might actually build the hardware based on purchased components, it is usually software components that must be customized, especially to add security to the system. As discussed in Chapter 5, the design of software can be costly and time consuming; thus, it must be managed well. In the implementation activity, it is expected that custom-designed software will have already been through prototype development and initial tests for compatibility and security performance. If a security component prototype was not initially developed during the design phase, it should be done before the prototyping of all components occurs.

Remember that prototyping, whether it is a hardware or software component, is a technique in which a preliminary version of the product is developed and implemented as required. It is then tested and evaluated for technical feasibility, interface issues, system user or operator issues, and security requirements. During the integration phase, the entire system may be subject to prototype activity. In this situation, a preliminary implementation of the system will be developed that later serves as a model for the final, completed version of the system.

Regardless of whether security components are purchased, leased, or custom built, they should be verified as corresponding to the security design specifications, and the ISSEP verification should be formally documented. If the security components are different from the design, this deviation must be evaluated for impact on the achievement of not only functional design and mission or business objectives, but also the security requirements and design.

The next topic provides an overview of Federal guidance from the National Institute of Standards and Technology (NIST) regarding the acquisition of security components.

NIST Special Publication (SP) 800-23

In August 2000, NIST published Federal guidance for purchasing and using components in sensitive unclassified systems. The purpose of SP 800-23 is to provide guidelines for Federal organizations' acquisition and use of security-related IT products. Table 6.5 provides a summary of the SP 800-23 acquisition recommendations.

For national security systems, the Committee of National Security Systems (CNSS) published National Security Telecommunications and Information Systems Security Policy (NSTISSP), Number 11 as a mandatory requirement when purchasing security components.

NSTISSP, Number 11

In January 2000, NSTISSP Number 11, "National Policy Governing the Acquisition of Information Assurance (IA) and IA-Enabled Information Technology Products," was released. NSTISSP Number 11 applies to national security systems. The policy states that:

> "IA shall be considered as a requirement for all systems used to enter, process, store, display, or transmit national security information. IA shall be achieved through the acquisition and appropriate implementation of evaluated or validated GOTS or COTS IA and IA-enabled IT products. These products should provide for the availability of the systems; ensure the integrity and confidentiality of information, and the authentication and non-repudiation of parties in electronic transactions. Effective January 2001, preference shall be given to the acquisition of COTS IA and IA-enabled products, which have been evaluated and validated, as appropriate in accordance with Common Criteria (CC), NSA/NIST NIAP Evaluation and Validation Program, or the NIST FIPS validation program. By July 2002, the acquisition of all COTS IA and IA-enabled IT products to be used on the systems specified (national security systems) shall be limited only to those which have been evaluated and validated in accordance with the criteria, schemes, or programs specified (CC, NIAP, or NIST FIPS)."

> —NSTISSP No. 11, 2000, p. 2-3

This policy is also discussed in Chapter 13. As of publication date, both NSA and NIST have adopted the CC evaluations for IT system

Table 6.5   Acquisition Guidelines for Security Components

Guidelines	Description
Federal departments and agencies should understand the concept of computer security assurance.	Computer security assurance provides a basis for one to have confidence that security measures, both technical and operational, work as intended. Varying degrees of assurance are supported through methods such as conformance testing, security evaluation, and trusted development methodologies. Assurance is not a guarantee that the measures work as intended; it is closely related to areas of reliability and quality.
Federal departments and agencies should be aware of how assurance in the acquired products supports security.	Assurance in individual product components contributes to overall system security assurance — but it neither provides a guarantee of system assurance nor, in and of itself, the security of a system. Use of products with an appropriate degree of assurance contributes to security and assurance of the system as a whole and thus should be an important factor in IT procurement decisions. For a security product, system, or software, a combination of measures for such areas as security functionality, sound development and operational practices, and periodic inspection and review need to be addressed as well.
Federal departments and agencies should be knowledgeable of the many approaches to obtaining security assurance in the products they procure.	There are a number of ways that security assurance in products and systems is achieved/determined, such as: NIST, NSA, or other conformance testing and validation studies; testing and certification; evaluation and validation; advanced or trusted development techniques; performance track record/user's experiences; warranties, integrity statements, and liabilities; and secure distribution.

Table 6.5 (continued) Acquisition Guidelines for Security Components

Guidelines	Description
Federal agencies should specifically be aware of the benefits that can be obtained through testing of commercial products against customer, government, or vendor-developed specifications.	Two government programs are of particular interest — the National Information Assurance Partnership (NIAP) Common Criteria Evaluation and Validation Program and the NIST Cryptography Module Validation Program (CMVP). The NIAP program focuses on evaluations of products against a set of security specifications. The CMVP program focuses on security conformance testing of a cryptographic module against FIPS 140-1, Security Requirements for Cryptographic Modules and related Federal cryptographic algorithm standards.
Federal departments and agencies should acquire and use products appropriate to their risk environment and the cost-effective selection of security measures. Agencies should develop policies for the procurement and use of evaluated products as appropriate. When selecting products, agencies need to consider the threat/risk environment, cost-effectiveness, assurance level, and security functional specifications, as appropriate.	A listing of products that have been validated under the NIAP CC can be found via http://niap.nist.gov. At the time of publication, no CC protection profiles have been designated as mandatory and binding by the Secretary of Commerce. It is NIST's intent to issue protection profiles (when appropriate) as technical security guidelines to the Federal community.
Federal agencies should give substantial consideration in IT procurement and deployment for IT products that have been evaluated and tested by independent and accredited laboratories against appropriate security specification and requirements.	The ultimate goal in purchasing a system is to obtain the necessary functionality and performance within cost and time constraints. Moreover, performance includes dependability and reliability — directly impacted by security considerations. In general, third-party testing and evaluation provides a significantly greater basis

Table 6.5 (continued)   Acquisition Guidelines for Security Components

Guidelines	Description
	for customer confidence than many other assurance techniques. Yet, it is important to note that purchasing an evaluated product simply because it is evaluated and without due consideration of applicable functional and assurance requirements, may be neither useful nor cost effective. IT users need to consider their overall requirements and select the best products accordingly.
Federal departments and agencies need to address how products are configured and integrated properly, securely, and subject to the managerial operational approval process so as to help ensure security is appropriately addressed on a systemwide basis.	The overall assurance level of a system as a whole may be different (usually lower) than the assurance level of individual components. While product assurance is a crucial and necessary input into the system security process, all the usual policies, controls, and risk management processes must also be in place for a system to operate in a reasonably secure mode. These are typically specific configuration settings that must be employed for the product to operate in the security manner desired. In addition, much attention must be paid to combining such products in order to provide an appropriate security solution for a given risk and threat environment. Thus, in addition to employing products with appropriate security capabilities and assurance, review of the security of a system from a systemwide perspective supports the managerial operational approval process.

Source: From NIST SP 800-23, 2000, p. 2-6.

products and the Cryptography Module Validation Program (CMVP) for cryptographic products.

A limitation of NSTISSP Number 11 (2000) is that it does not provide guidance on how to compose compliant products into secure systems. CNSS released an Information Assurance Advisory Memorandum, CNSSAM 1-04 (July 2004), "Security through Product Diversity."

The CNSSAM 1-04 recommendation is for USG agencies and departments to use a multi-layer approach to security when developing and deploying security solutions. An example of a multi-layer approach is a defense-in-depth solution. When possible, compliant products should also be acquired from a diverse group of vendors because inadvertent or deliberate vulnerabilities present in one vendor's products can be offset by the security afforded by products acquired from other vendors. When agencies combine product layers and diversity for both software and hardware, the overall security of the systems will be enhanced. This policy is also discussed in Chapter 13.

Secure Integration Efforts

Security components, regardless of acquisition method, must be integrated into the system based on the planned architecture and design. During the integration, any incompatibility with existing (legacy) components must be resolved. The focus is on constructing, assembling, and integrating the security components into a complete working system that can be evaluated for the effectiveness of both technical and security capabilities.

For most systems, the integration process is the first time that components are linked to one another and made to perform as a whole system. Thus, an important element of integration is the interaction and interface between the components. The ISSE team ensures that connections do not introduce any unexpected risk.

Despite best efforts, the integration may disclose unexpected incompatibilities. Sometimes the integration team will resolve problems through quick fixes or work-around solutions. This can be a critical moment for the ISSEP to engage, especially because many work-around or quick fix solutions bypass the intended security controls. If this occurs, the ISSEP must insist that security requirements NOT be put aside due to time or budget constraints. If time limitations cannot be managed, the ISSEP may need to inform the customer that other trade-offs are necessary until the security requirements can be met.

When there are time constraints to get the system operational, the role of the ISSEP is to assess the risks and then help the customer understand the risks. It may be necessary to explain that the system will not be accredited or authorized to operate until the risks are mitigated. For example, an agency schedules a software transition for all system servers during a weekend in order to minimize disruption of network services to employees. The work is scheduled to begin on Friday after close of business and must be completed by Sunday evening at 8:00 p.m. During the last few hours of integration, the team cannot accurately configure the firewall to work with the new software. The team is unable to restrict access from the Internet, which leaves the file server vulnerable to attack. The question is: how likely is an attack on this vulnerability and what is the impact to the agency if the information on the file server is disclosed, modified, or unavailable?

The integrators, not thinking about the security implications, might allow the system to remain in operation until Monday morning and figure out the firewall problems sometime on Monday after operations have begun. As the ISSEP for this system, would that be acceptable? What should an ISSEP recommend? One answer might be to allow operation for internal processing but block Internet access until the firewall can be correctly configured and tested. There may be other options, depending on the situation, but what is most important is that the ISSEP is aware of the vulnerability and is involved in ensuring that the integration of the new software component does not bypass any security requirements.

A challenging management issue can occur during integration that will require careful handling by the SEs and ISSEPs. Once the system has been integrated, it is probably the first time that management at the customer site will view the entire system and its functionality. It is at this point that the customer's management may want to suggest or impose additional or different design features into the system.

You may have heard this before: wouldn't it be great if the system could be modified to... (insert word for added functionality)? As part of the integration, the SEs and ISSEPs must keep the scope of the design under control. One method of working with the customer at this time is to listen, document the request, and explain that it cannot be done at this point, but the request will be reviewed by the team once the system is completely operational.

A customer's "additions" or "changes" can also be a challenge for those working on a system under some type of contract. This is commonly referred to as "scope creep" — it occurs once a contract has been signed that indicates original requirements and then the customer subsequently requests additional capabilities. Scope creep almost always add delay and additional cost to a project. Although the capabilities may make it a better product, it is important to control these additional efforts or renegotiate the terms of the contract in order to make adjustments for any cost or time delays.

Another issue is how to handle the failure of a component or subsystem during integration. The customer may be especially critical and attempt to intervene to solve the problem. If this should occur, all design and development teams, including the ISSEP, must assure the customer that the program management and engineering teams have complete control over the design and can resolve any issues.

During the integration activity, the ISSEP should perform a final verification that confirms that the evaluation criteria for the security components measure the desired level of security and that the security components meet those criteria. The ISSEP ensures that both system and security components acquired and integrated into the system meet the security design and requirements, as well as any federally mandated requirements.

Secure System Configuration

Most COTS and GOTS products, especially software, require specialized security and operational configurations. Although software vendors have become more conscious of enabling security features within their products, many still deliver software with default settings that disable security features. Because this default openness is still the norm, most Federal agencies will need to enable and configure many of the security features before deployment.

Therefore, during system integration, the ISSEP helps configure the components to ensure that the security features are enabled and the security parameters are set to provide the required security services. Once the security configuration for the system has been established, any differences in settings must be recorded and approved following configuration management or waiver procedures.

The configuration management output during the integration phase verifies that the configuration baseline outlined during the design phase still matches the system following integration. Simply stated, changes made to component items or baselines must be documented and the configuration management plan must be updated to reflect those changes.

Examples of software security configurations for COTS products are the "gold standard guidelines" published by the National Security Agency (NSA). The NSA, in coordination with other Federal and private-sector organizations, has developed and distributed security configuration guidance for software such as Microsoft Windows and Cisco products. These guides are used throughout government as security baselines for IT products. The guidelines are available from the NSA Web site (www.nsa.gov/) under Security Recommendation Guides.

Security Test and Evaluation

There are several types of Security Testing and Evaluations (ST&Es) that occur during the integration phase. The most common is functional testing, which demonstrates whether a system behaves according to its specifications and produces specified outputs when inputs are introduced. Additional types of ST&E include penetration testing, cryptographic verification testing, security Independent Verification & Validation (IV&V), security assurance analysis methods, and TEMPEST testing. In some cases, reliability testing and analysis can be used to determine whether the security mechanisms of a system are implemented as designed and are adequate for the real-life environment.

The ISSEP should write test procedures that reflect the results expected during the design of the system. Essentially, during the design phases, the ISSEP develops the ST&E criteria and documents it in the Test and Evaluation Master Plan (TEMP). If this is not done early in the process, the results of the ST&E may not meet the correct requirements. The test team should know what test expectations would be considered acceptable before conducting the tests.

For example, the expected test results might be stated as "During an unplanned power outage at various times during the day, the backup power supply will automatically initiate for all primary server components." The TEMP requirements would be written as "Four tests that shut down power will be completed to indicate how the system will respond. During all tests, backup power must automatically begin with no time delay."

The test team might document the results as follows:

1. Monday, July 7, main power source shut at 8:05 a.m. Backup power initiated immediately with no delay in power to all primary servers.
2. Monday, July 7, main power source shut at 3:25 p.m. Backup power initiated immediately with no delay in power to all primary servers.
3. Monday, July 7, main power source shut at 8:00 p.m. Backup power initiated immediately with no delay in power to all primary servers.
4. Tuesday, July 8, main power source shut at 2:25 a.m. Backup power did not initiate, causing a total shutdown of all primary servers.

If the test expectations had not been previously established, the testing team might have accepted results after the second or third test, which could have led to accepting faulty components. Also, because the test was established over several time frames, it may indicate other problems that might occur during the same time period.

Although it may seem obvious, test reports should document both positive and negative results. No team will want negative results, but all results must be recorded in the original test results documentation. Even if the problems were fixed, the original results must still be documented.

NIST SP 800-42 (October 2003), "Guideline on Network Security Testing," provides guidance on network security testing, which is defined as "activities that provide information about the integrity of an organization's networks and associated systems through testing and verification of network-related security controls" (p. 1-3).

SP 800-42 outlines the objectives of the ST&E as:

- "Uncover design, implementation, and operational flaws that could allow the violation of security policy
- Determine the adequacy of security mechanisms, assurances and other properties to enforce the security policy
- Assess the degree of consistency between the system documentation and its implementation

The scope of an ST&E plan typically addresses computer security, communications security, emanations security, physical security, personnel security, administrative security, and operations security (p. 2-2)."

The role of the ISSEP during test planning is to assess the need for security requirements to be placed on the various elements of the test. For example, if the system (once operational) will be used in an environment processing classified information, should the test environment actually use classified information? In most cases, a test environment should not use real-life data; therefore, classified information would not be used. In this instance, the ISSEP would verify and ensure that classified information is not needed or utilized during the ST&E.

Once test preparations have been completed, the next step is to begin testing the system. The system is operated in its specified manner and the TEMP is followed, including the security test plans. Throughout the testing process, data should be collected and analyzed for comparison with the initial requirements.

Security questions during the testing and evaluation phase include:

- Did the security of the system perform as intended?
- Did the security of the system accomplish the security mission or objective?
- What is the effectiveness of the security mechanisms?

- Did the security mechanisms meet all of the requirements covered in the TEMP?
- Does the system configuration meet all of the security requirements?

Another type of security testing is **verification and validation**. It contains many of the same elements of testing and evaluation, but different terms are used and a different slant is taken.

Verification ensures that the integration and implementation of the system satisfy the requirements as stated and documented in the requirements. Verification answers the following question: *Did you build the system right?* Verification can reveal problems such as poorly executing software code, unreliable hardware components, or issues with interface or interactions between components. From a security standpoint, one aspect of verification might be: Did we build a system that has no more than the level of security risk we specified as acceptable?

Validation ensures that the stated system requirements satisfy the real-world needs. Validation answers the question: *Did you build the right system?* Validation can reveal problems in requirements analysis where the system meets all of its written specifications but, unfortunately, does not meet a key operational need or constraint. From a security standpoint, one aspect of validation might be: Did we ask for a system with the right amount of security risk — that is, is the expected, specified security risk really acceptable for the system's real-world operating environment? Is the specified security risk too high (under-specified) for the threats faced by the system? Or conversely, is the risk really over-specified and lower than actually needed? If so, is the over-specification benign, or is it causing trade-off balance problems with other requirements that might lead us to allow more security risk in order to achieve better results in some other system capability area? (*ISSE Handbook*, 1994, p. 3-53).

The role of the ISSEP during this evaluation is to participate in developing and reviewing plans for the security-relevant verification of the system. The ISSEP should directly participate in, or at least track and advise, security verification and validation as it is executed over the system development life cycle. This information can be documented in the Security Engineering Management Plan (SEMP), the TEMP, or other Test Plans and Procedures generated during the development life cycle. Again, this activity should begin early in the design phase (Phase 4) and should include when and how the system should be tested for compliance with the security requirements.

Depending on the situation, the ISSEP may actually conduct or witness the security testing being performed. In other cases, the ISSEP will be responsible for reviewing the results of the test and evaluation. In either role, it is important that the ISSEP is part of the testing process and verifies whether security requirements have been met.

The ISSEP may also assist in the development of test cases to exercise the functionality and performance of a specific component or the entire system. Techniques for security testing usually involve selecting scenarios or action/reaction arrangements. Although the input is usually controlled in this type of testing, it does allow for a specific type of output to test the component or system. Parameters can be selected for security testing to view how the system will respond at its boundaries. For example, this might include improper inputs or exceptional requests to the system to test for denial-of-service attempts.

Based on the ST&E results, a final security test report is prepared. This report should reference the initial test-planning document (i.e., the TEMP), describe the test conditions, outline the test procedures that were followed, identify data sources, provide results of the analysis, and define any recommendations for improvements. Remember that if the system requires changes, the changes must be included in the configuration management document.

Accept the Security of the System

Once the security components have been evaluated, the next step is to accept that the security components are operational and meeting the security requirements for the system. Preparing for system security acceptance is an activity that ensures everything is in place to begin the acceptance process activities. A preliminary security acceptance checklist can help the ISSEP verify that the security requirements have been met and all necessary security activities have been completed.

Items on a security checklist might include (adapted from DoE 2002 Pre-Acceptance Checklist, 2002):

■ The system sensitivity and essentiality has been identified as either classified, sensitive unclassified, and/or mission essential.
■ The system owner, based on a risk analysis and/or assessment, established security objectives.
■ The project team specified security requirements.
■ System design features enforce the security requirements.
■ Testing was conducted to verify that the security design features were incorporated into the system and the results were recorded.
■ Appropriate data set and file protection rules, authorities, and user identification codes were established by the system owner or as mandated by higher authority.
■ Access control protection was incorporated into the system.

- All manufacturer generic, test team, temporary, and superfluous passwords were deleted from the system.
- All privacy, freedom of information, sensitivity, and classification considerations were identified, resolved, and established.
- An approved Security Plan was developed.
- The system owner has provided the required information to the Information System Security Officer.
- For classified systems, the security test plan was approved. For unclassified systems, the computer security and privacy plan was approved.
- The security test was successfully completed.
- For classified systems, the software product was certified by the owning organizations.

System Security Documentation

Throughout all the phases, there is some type of documentation that indicates the status of the system. In addition to the fact that all systems are subject to auditing, which requires specific documentation, it is good management practice to document what has been accomplished and what needs to be accomplished. Although documenting activities may be viewed as tedious and time consuming, it is important to the success of the program.

There are as many methods of documenting information as there are document requirements. For example, systems can be drawn using computer-modeling software and management plans can be outlined in spreadsheet format. Also, with the advent of document sharing among remote team members, many employees can contribute to the same document. U.S. Government agencies have developed specific manuals and handbooks that provide design standards. Thus, the ISSEP must be sure to ask whether there are specific agency documentation guidelines that must be followed for SE and ISSE activities.

The role of the ISSEP in documentation will vary, depending on the project. For some projects, the ISSEP will be responsible for creating and maintaining all documentation, while on other projects the ISSEP will play an advisory role and only review and comment on documentation. One documentation role that must be assigned is that of the person responsible for ensuring that documentation follows strict version control procedures. If necessary, the ISSEP, along with the project manager, should insist on the establishment of mechanisms for version control and guarantee that this important responsibility is assigned and that version control procedures are followed.

As a final step in the documentation of the integration phase, the ISSEP ensures that all the documentation necessary for Certification and Accreditation (C&A) is completed and ready for use during the next phase. This documentation will include integration and test reports showing any variations to specifications. The ISSEP may also be asked to work on or verify the system security plan for the newly integrated system.

Training for Secure Operations

Training materials and instruction should address operational policy and technical abilities as it pertains to the system, the security of the system, and system limitations as well as functions. Although there may be many training requirements, looking at it from a security perspective involves defining the tasks required to administer (operate), maintain, and use the new system in a secure manner.

During the integration phase, it may be necessary to have operational-level employees (i.e., those who have not been involved in the design and development) use the system with or without instructions. Their performance on the system can be a strong indication of what will be needed for training employees on how to operate or use the system.

A training program plan includes items such as:

- Which personnel need training and their specific requirements (i.e., who needs to be trained and what are their current skill levels?)
- Instructional design capabilities
- Types of training mediums (i.e., instructor led versus technology based)
- Training materials
- Training equipment
- Training facilities
- How much money is available for training

Far too often in projects, security training is not given a specific budget line item and is therefore not built into the cost of the system design and development. If specific security mechanisms will require specialized training, management must include enough resources to provide that training. The role of the ISSEP, especially when it concerns security components, is to ensure that the program plan includes training as a budget consideration.

The final step in the ISSE integration activities is to transfer the responsibility for security of the system to the customer. At this point, the system will now be operated and maintained by the customer, including the secure operation of the system.

ISSE and Risk Management

There are many critical points in the ISSE process and the development life cycle of the system when the level of risk must be evaluated. At the integration phase, the risk management plans should have already been incorporated into existing security-related or other program plans. Therefore, during integration, the ISSEP should lead or participate in the continuing risk assessment of the system.

It should be noted that "official acceptance of the system" and "official approval to authorize processing (accreditation)" are different concepts. The approval to authorize processing is a separate decision based on system risks as the system is installed in a specific operational environment. More discussion on system authorization (accreditation) is provided in Domain 2.

Final Deliverable of Phase 5

The final outcome or deliverable for the SE consists of (1) the acquisition plan, (2) the installation plan, (3) conducting unit tests, (4) establishing a development baseline, (5) creating a transition plan, (6) creating operating documents, and (7) developing a training plan. Also during this activity, the following integration and testing activities are completed: conducting integration testing, conducting system testing, initiating the acceptance process, and developing a maintenance plan.

The outcome for the ISSEPs will be to ensure that the security of the system does not get compromised during the final deployment and acceptance phases. The ISSEP's responsibilities are similar to those of the SE, with an emphasis on security — acquiring security or system components that can be integrated in a secure manner, configuring the components in a secure manner, and testing and evaluating the system to verify that it meets the security requirements. The ISSEP also accepts the security of the system and either produces or ensures that system documentation includes security elements and verifies that appropriate training is included so the system can be operated, maintained, and used in a secure manner.

The final activity for both the SE and ISSEP is to deliver the system to the customer and transfer the operational and maintenance responsibilities to the customer.

Summary

The integration phase is when all of the previous activities are combined to produce a secure and functioning system in an operational environment.

During this phase, one of the first steps is to create an acquisition plan that defines the acquisition and installation of the hardware, software, and communications equipment needed to operate the system at the customer site. In large programs, the team may develop an installation plan that specifies the requirements and procedures for the full-scale installation of the system at the customer site. During the construction and integration phase, unit testing can be used to verify the input and output for completed modules. After the first build is completed, tested, and approved, the development baseline is established.

Other SE requirements are to plan for the transition, quantify the operational needs associated with the system, and describe the procedures that will be used to perform the transition. The transition plan describes the detailed plans, procedures, and schedules that will guide the transition process. Once the product is integrated, system testing is conducted to validate that the system will operate in its intended environment, user requirements have been satisfied, and complete and accurate operating documentation is available. The final activity in the construction phase is to develop a training program plan that outlines what employees need to know to operate and use the system successfully.

During the integration and implementation phase, the ISSEP monitors the system security aspects of interfaces, acquisition, integration, configuration, documentation, and training. During test and evaluation, unexpected vulnerabilities may be revealed. These must be documented as risks to the system, and possible mission impacts associated with these vulnerabilities must be evaluated.

The ISSEP continues coordination with the Certifiers and Accreditors to ensure the completeness of the required documentation. The ISSEP also monitors tasks to ensure that the security design is implemented correctly. To accomplish this, the ISSEP should observe and participate in testing and analyze test and evaluation results.

One of the final outputs during this task is to conduct or update a risk analysis. Based on the results of the assessment, strategies may need to be developed that will mitigate identified risks and the ISSEP will identify possible mission impacts and advise the customer and also the customer's Certifiers and Accreditors.

After all of these activities, the system should now be operational at the customer site. The SE and ISSEP review any final issues with the customer and hand over the responsibility of the system to those responsible for operating and maintaining the system. The final activity in the IATF ISSE model discussed in the next chapter is to assess how effective the security mechanisms are for the system and meeting the security requirements. Although this is seen as an ongoing activity throughout the analysis, design, and development phases, a final assessment can provide a debriefing and learning experience for all team members.

References

Blanchard, Benjamin (1998). *Systems Engineering Management, 2nd edition.* John Wiley & Sons: New York, NY.

Blanchard, Benjamin S. and Wolter J. Fabrycky (1998). *System Engineering and Analysis, 3rd edition.* Prentice Hall: Upper Saddle River, NJ.

DOE G 200.1-1A (September 2002). Systems Engineering Methodology Version 3: The DOE Systems Development Lifecycle (SDLC) for Information Technology Investments. Department of Energy, Office of the Chief Information Officer. This document and associated process guides, checklists, and templates can be found at Web site http://cio.doe.gov/ITReform/sqse.

DoE (2002). Acquisition Plan Template. http://cio.doe.gov/ITReform/sqse/download/reqspc.doc.

DoE (2002). Transition Plan Template. http://cio.doe.gov/ITReform/sqse/download/transpln.doc.

DoE (2002). Training Plan Template: http://cio.doe.gov/ITReform/sqse/download/traintem.doc.

DoE (2002). Pre-Acceptance Checklist. http://cio.doe.gov/ITReform/sqse/download/preacpt.doc.

Faulconbridge, R. Ian and Michael J. Ryan (2003). *Managing Complex Technical Projects: A Systems Engineering Approach.* Artech House: Norwood, MA.

Hennigan, Peter (2002). Leasing Hardware: Options and Benefits. ©2002 Tech-Republic, Inc. Available at http://www.zdnet.com.au

IAEC3186 (February 2002). Introduction to Information Systems Security Engineering, ISSE Training, student guide.

IEEE Std 1220-1998 (December 1998, copyrighted January 1999). IEEE Standard for Application and Management of the Systems Engineering Process. IEEE: New York, NY. (Revision of IEEE Std 1220-1994)

Information Systems Security Engineering Handbook, Release 1.0 (February 28, 1994). National Security Agency, Central Security Service. Only available for official USG use.

Information Assurance Technical Framework (IATF), Version 3.1 (September 2002). National Security Agency, Information Assurance Solutions, Technical Directors: Fort Meade, MD.

Kossiakoff, Alexander and William N. Sweet (2003). *Systems Engineering: Principles and Practice.* John Wiley & Sons: Hoboken, NJ.

MIL-HDBK-217F-Notice 2 (1995). Reliability Prediction of Electronic Equipment. Defense Printing Service: Philadelphia, PA.

NIST SP 800-23 (August 2000). Guidelines to Federal Organization on Security Assurance and Acquisition/Use of Tested/Evaluated Products: Recommendation of the National Institute of Standards and Technology. Published by: Computer Security Division, NIST: Gaithersburg, MD.

NIST SP 800-30 (January 2002). Risk Management Guide for Information Technology Systems. Available at the NIST Web site: www.nist.gov.

NIST SP 800-42 (October 2003). Guideline on Network Security Testing. NIST Publications, Computer Security Division, NIST: Gaithersburg, MD. Available at the NIST Web site: www.nist.gov.

NSTISSP, Number 11 (January 2000). National Policy Governing the Acquisition of Information Assurance (IA) and IA-Enabled Information Technology Products.

NSTSSC Secretariat (I42). NSA: 9800 Savage Road, Fort Meade, MD.

Web Sites

http://www.isograph-software.com/rwbovertel.htm for information on reliability analysis.

http://www.relexsoftware.com/resources/prmodels.asp for information on reliability analysis.

http://www.nsa.gov/ for Microsoft and Cisco security recommendation guides.

http://www.mockobjects.com for creating and using mock objects.

7

ISSE Model Phase 6: Assess Security Effectiveness

Introduction

The phases in the Information Systems Security Engineering (ISSE) life-cycle model are:

1. Discover Information Protection Needs. Ascertain why the system needs to be built and what information needs to be protected.
2. Define System Security Requirements. Define the system in terms of what security is needed.
3. Define System Security Architecture. Define the security functions needed to meet the specific security requirements.
4. Develop Detailed Security Design. Based on the security architecture, design the security functions and features for the system.
5. Implement System Security. Following the documented security design, build and implement the security functions and features for the system.
6. **Assess Security Effectiveness. Assess the degree to which the security of the system, as it is defined, designed, and implemented, meets the security needs.**

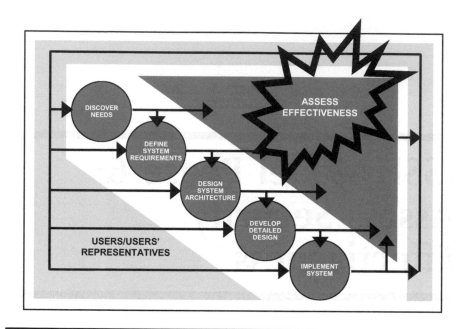

Figure 7.1   ISSE model. *Source:* From IATF, p. 3-2.)

The focus of this chapter is the sixth phase of the ISSE model: Assessing Security Effectiveness (see Figure 7.1). This is equivalent to the Systems Engineering (SE) activity, Assessing System Effectiveness. Important to the ISSE model, and system security planning in general, is having a plan that includes mechanisms for assessing and evaluating the status of the system from a security perspective.

The chapter (Figure 7.2) begins by explaining the role of system engineers (SEs) during a system assessment. Part of this assessment involves comparing how well the system performs with similar systems. The second section discusses the effectiveness of the ISSE activities throughout the design, development, and implementation of the system. An important consideration of assessment, whether directly related to the SE or ISSE activities, is the concept of assessment as an ongoing process that occurs throughout the system's life cycle.

A common approach to assessment is to conduct a review of the processes that organizations use to produce systems or components. When viewing it from the perspective of improvement, a **process** can be defined as a leverage point for an organization's sustained progress. This chapter reviews several tools that can be used to assess processes as well as products.

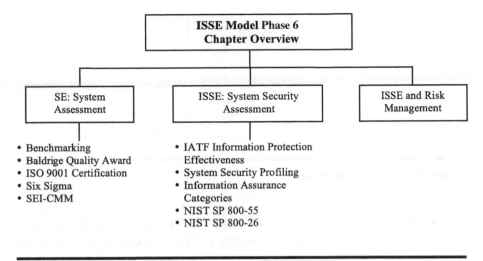

Figure 7.2   Chapter overview.

System Engineering Activity: System Assessment

As stated by Blanchard (1998):

> Where are we today? How do we compare with the competition (relative to both product and organization)? Where would we like to be in the future?

Once the system is operational, the SEs should review what was and was not successful in bringing the system online and its operational effectiveness. The assessment should review both the technical characteristics of the system and any organizational issues related to policies or procedures that have been implemented to operate and maintain the system.

As shown in Figure 7.3, there are several process improvement tools available. These include:

- *Benchmarking capability.* Benchmarking can provide a point of reference by which measurements can be made.
- *Baldrige Criteria for Performance Excellence.* The focus is on performance excellence of the entire organization in an overall management framework. The objective is to identify and track all important organizational results, such as customer, product or service, financial, human resources, and organizational effectiveness.

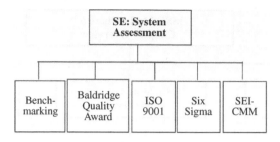

Figure 7.3   SE assessment tools.

- *ISO 9001:2000.* It is a product/service conformity model for guaranteeing equity in the marketplace. The concentration is on fixing quality system defects and product/service nonconformities.
- *Six Sigma.* It concentrates on measuring product quality and improving process engineering. The goal is to improve processes and cost savings.
- *SEI-CMM.* To improve and control development, the Software Engineering Institute (SEI) has designed and developed various Capability Maturity Models (CMM)®. CMMs provide integrated process models that organizations can use to improve the processes used to design and develop systems, software, etc.

Each assessment tool offers a different emphasis in helping organizations improve performance and increase customer satisfaction by reviewing their processes. For most organizations, it is not a matter of adopting one of the process/quality options, but rather deciding which one to do first, second, or third. The decision will ultimately be based on the organization's needs at that point in time and whether the organization views the tools as a valuable investment to their business. For example, some government proposal requests require the winning bidder to be ISO or CMM certified.

Note to ISSEP® candidates: As of this publication date, the (ISC)² ISSEP exam requirements only lists the SEI-CMM process assessment tool. Because the other tools are used by various government contractors, a brief overview is included as reference information.

Benchmarking

Benchmarking is a tool for improving performance by learning from best practices and processes that have been successful. It involves looking outside your own organization to examine how others achieve their performance levels and what processes they use to reach those levels. The Benchmarking Network (2002) states that benchmarking is the most cost-effective way of introducing best practices to your organization. This is achieved by organizations taking the time to document their processes, researching how similar processes are performed, and analyzing the strengths and weaknesses of their processes compared to others.

The basic steps of benchmarking are:

1. *Create a benchmarking plan.* This involves developing a plan for the benchmarking activity. It should be based on a definition of the organization's goals for the product. It should also identify the steps that must be accomplished to progress from the current status to a desired level of performance.
2. *Understand in detail your own processes.* This includes assessing the current process, identifying problem areas, and developing recommendations for process or product improvement.
3. *Analyze the processes of others.* Analyze major competitors for their performance outcomes.
4. *Compare your own performance with that of others.* Based on their objectives and your objectives, how do your processes compare? How does the competitor perform similar processes?
5. *Identify the proposed changes necessary to improve your own processes or products.*
6. *Implement the steps necessary to close the performance gap.* If your processes need changing, review the potential impact of the proposed changes and incorporate modifications as appropriate.

In addition to creating benchmarks for processes, organizations can also create benchmarks for products. For example, the Internet Engineering Task Force (IETF) has a benchmarking working group that creates baseline performances for products. The goal of the Benchmarking Methodology Working Group (BMWG) is to make recommendations concerning the measurement of the performance characteristics of various internetworking technologies (BMWG Charter, 2003).

As stated in the BMWG charter, each recommendation will describe the class of equipment, system, or service being addressed; discuss the performance characteristics that are pertinent to that class; clearly identify a set of metrics that aid in the description of those characteristics; specify the methodologies required to collect said metrics; and finally, present the requirements for the common, unambiguous reporting of benchmarking results. Because the demands of a particular technology may vary from deployment to deployment, a specific non-goal of the BMWG is to define acceptance criteria or performance requirements. In addition, the BMWG provides a discussion forum regarding the advancement of measurements designed to provide insight on the operation of internetworking technologies.

A BMWG example is a Request for Comments (RFC) document that provides methodologies for the performance benchmarking of firewalls. RFC 2647, "Benchmarking Terminology for Firewall Performance," (1999) discusses and defines a number of tests that can be used to describe the performance characteristics of firewalls. In addition to defining the tests, the document also describes specific formats for reporting the results of the tests. Within the RFC 2647, an example of a benchmarking test that can be conducted for firewalls is to test for connection establishment. It states:

> Connection establishment. *Definition*: The data exchanged between hosts, or between a host and the Device Under Test/System Under Test (DUT/SUT) to initiate a connection. *Discussion*: Connection-oriented protocols like TCP have a pro-scribed handshaking procedure when launching a connection. When benchmarking firewall performance, it is important to identify this handshaking procedure so that it is not included in measurements of bit forwarding rate or Unit of Transfers (UOTs) per second. Testers may also be interested in measurements of connection establishment time through or with a given DUT/SUT. RFC 2647, 1999, Section 3.8

Although benchmarking is an option available to assess SE processes or products, it can also be applied to assess ISSE processes or products. There are many organizations and consultants dedicated to the field of benchmarking that can help analyze systems and processes for improving performance.

Baldrige Criteria for Performance Excellence

In 1987, The Malcolm Baldrige National Quality Award was created by Public Law 100-107. The Award is named for Malcolm Baldrige, who served as Secretary of Commerce from 1981 until his death in 1987. Secretary Baldrige, during his tenure at Commerce, made continual efforts to push the concept of quality management to U.S. corporations. He believed quality management was key to U.S. prosperity and long-term strength.

From a historical viewpoint, during the 1970s and early 1980s, many key U.S. industries began to face international competition for its products or services. Because of this competition, the U.S. Government (USG) began to encourage companies to review the quality of their products and organizational processes so that the United States could produce products that would be competitive in an international market. PL 100-107 highlights some of the quality-oriented principles the USG wanted U.S. companies to adopt.

An overview of PL 100-107 (1987, Section Findings and Purpose) includes:

1. "The leadership of the United States in product and process quality has been challenged strongly (and sometimes successfully) by foreign competition, and our nation's productivity growth has improved less than our competitors' over the last two decades.
2. American business and industry are beginning to understand that poor quality costs companies as much as 20 percent of sales revenues nationally and that improved quality of goods and services goes hand in hand with improved productivity, lower costs, and increased profitability.
3. Strategic planning for quality and quality improvement programs, through a commitment to excellence in manufacturing and services, are becoming more and more essential to the well being of our Nation's economy and our ability to compete effectively in the global marketplace.
4. Improved management understanding of the factory floor, worker involvement in quality, and greater emphasis on statistical process control can lead to dramatic improvements in the cost and quality of manufactured products.
5. The concept of quality improvement is directly applicable to small companies as well as large, to service industries as well as manufacturing, and to the public sector as well as private enterprise.
6. In order to be successful, quality improvement programs must be management-led and customer-oriented, and this may require fundamental changes in the way companies and agencies do business.
7. Several major industrial nations have successfully coupled rigorous private-sector quality audits with national awards giving special recognition to those enterprises the audits identify as the very best; and
8. A national quality award program of this kind in the United States would help improve quality and productivity by:
   a. Helping to stimulate American companies to improve quality and productivity for the pride of recognition while obtaining a competitive edge through increased profits;
   b. Recognizing the achievements of those companies that improve the quality of their goods and services and providing an example to others;

    c. Establishing guidelines and criteria that can be used by business, industrial, governmental, and other organizations in evaluating their own quality improvement efforts; and

    d. Providing specific guidance for other American organizations that wish to learn how to manage for high quality by making available detailed information on how winning organizations were able to change their cultures and achieve eminence."

The National Institute of Standards and Technology (NIST), a division of the U.S. Commerce Department, manages the Baldrige National Quality Program in close cooperation with the private sector. Each year, the U.S. President gives the Baldrige Award to businesses (manufacturing and service, small and large) and education and healthcare organizations. It provides a framework for designing, implementing, and assessing a process for managing all business operations. Candidates must apply for the award and be judged outstanding in seven areas: leadership, strategic planning, customer and market focus, information and analysis, human resource focus, process management, and business results.

The USG created the Baldrige Award to enhance U.S. competitiveness in the international marketplace, promote quality awareness, recognize quality achievements of U.S. organizations, and provide a vehicle for sharing successful strategies. Since 1988, more than 60 companies have received the Malcolm Baldrige National Quality Management Award.

The next tool is the ISO 9001 (2000) quality management standards. Organizations can use the ISO 9001 to help determine what is needed to maintain an efficient quality conformance system that is recognized world-wide.

ISO 9001 (2000)

The International Organization for Standardization (ISO) technical committee first published the quality management series in 1987. ISO 9001:2000 specifies requirements for quality management and is a continuation of the ISO 9000 series. The ISO provides supporting documents to assist users in implementing the ISO 9001 standard, which is now the only ISO 9001 certification standard (from the 1994 versions of ISO 9001, ISO 9002, and ISO 9003).

Organizations can achieve the ISO 9001 by:

■ Establishing and documenting a quality system
■ Implementing requirements for management that ensure support of quality and customer satisfaction, an establishment of a quality

policy that is carried out and controlled, and performance of management reviews of the quality system
■ Providing quality resources, personnel, infrastructure, and environment
■ Controlling realization planning, customer processes, product development, purchasing function, operational activities, and monitoring devices
■ Performing remedial processes, monitoring and measuring quality, controlling nonconforming products, analyzing quality information, and making quality improvements

ISO 9001 is based on eight quality management principles that can be used as a framework to guide organizations toward improved performance (Table 7.1). The guidance for this framework is included in the ISO 9001 documentation. *Note to ISSEP candidate:* A brief overview of each principle is provided for reference purposes only. The information is derived directly from the ISO 9001 standard.

Customer focus (Principle 1) is more than recognizing customer satisfaction as a primary project goal. Without customers, an organization's

Table 7.1   ISO 9001 Quality Management Principles

ISO 9001 Quality Management Principles
• Principle 1 - Customer focus. Organizations depend on their customers and therefore should understand current and future customer needs, should meet customer requirements and strive to exceed customer expectations.
• Principle 2 – Leadership. Leaders establish unity of purpose and direction of the organization. They should create and maintain the internal environment in which people can become fully involved in achieving the organization's objectives.
• Principle 3 - Involvement of people. People at all levels are the essence of an organization and their full involvement enables their abilities to be used for the organization's benefit.
• Principle 4 - Process approach. A desired result is achieved more efficiently when activities and related resources are managed as a process.
• Principle 5 - System approach to management. Identifying, understanding, and managing interrelated processes as a system contributes to the organization's effectiveness and efficiency in achieving its objectives.
• Principle 6 - Continual improvement. Continual improvement of the organization's overall performance should be a permanent objective of the organization.
• Principle 7 - Factual approach to decision making. Effective decisions are based on the analysis of data and information.
• Principle 8 - Mutually beneficial supplier relationships. An organization and its suppliers are interdependent and a mutually beneficial relationship enhances the ability of both to create value. (ISO/TC 176/SC 2/N544R)

very existence is questionable, so it is incumbent upon the organization to know who the customers are and understand their present and future needs. It is the responsibility of project managers to ensure that project objectives strive to accommodate the customer needs and expectations. During the course of any project, decisions will be made to balance the various trade-offs in time, cost, or product quality. Those decisions should consider the potential impacts with respect to customer requirements and expectations. Any revision in objectives should be documented in the project management plan.

An organization's direction and purpose are established through *leadership* (Principle 2). This is projected in the choice of project leadership and should foster an environment that keeps personnel engaged in meeting the project and organizational objectives. The project manager who demonstrates good leadership will minimize problems that could lead to idle or disillusioned staff. However, the project manager must be granted the authority commensurate with his or her responsibilities. It would be difficult to be an effective leader and ensure that the quality management system is established, implemented, and maintained if the project manager does not have the authority to make meaningful decisions.

People (Principle 3) are what make a project happen. Their abilities and competencies shape the likelihood of success. To engage their abilities and improve performance, the organization should ensure they have the tools, knowledge, and materials to do so. As with the project manager, staff involved with the project must have well-defined duties and the authority to carry them out. The duties should be well defined and on par with the person's competency.

When defined as a collection of *processes* (Principle 4), the relationships and objectives between tasks have greater clarity, enabling resources to be managed more efficiently. To reap continuing benefits beyond the current project, the pros, cons, and wisdom gained in developing and managing the processes should be documented for future reference. Likewise, documentation and advice from past projects should be referenced prior to commencing a new project.

Throughout the chapters in this domain, there have been discussions of many SE and ISSE processes or activities that are used to design and develop systems. The ISO 9001 approach for processes (Principle 4) provides another viewpoint. For example, the standard stresses the importance of identifying, implementing, managing, and continually improving the effectiveness of the processes that are necessary for the quality management system. It also emphasizes the management of the process interactions in order to achieve the organization's objectives. As noted in Figure 7.4 (based on ISO ISO/TC 176/SC 2/N544R), a process is composed

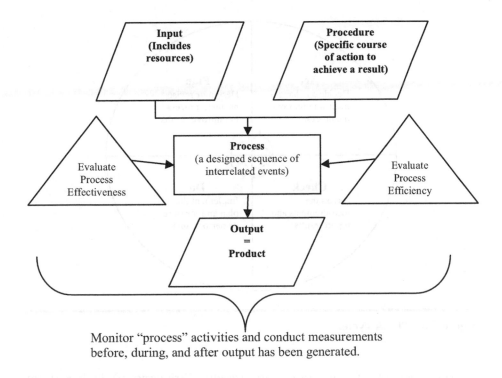

Monitor "process" activities and conduct measurements before, during, and after output has been generated.

Figure 7.4   Process evaluation.

of inputs and procedures that result in an output or product. Before, during, and after the process, there are measurements to take that will assist in determining whether the "process" provided efficiency (i.e., where results achieved versus resources used) and effectiveness (i.e., was the desired result achieved).

Taken as a whole, the collection of processes within a project can be viewed as a *system* (Principle 5) and managed as such. Each task, or process, will have defined inputs and outputs. Thus every task will depend upon other tasks that have been completed, run concurrently, or have yet to be done. This includes administrative processes that may fall outside the project but upon which the project relies (e.g., procurement or a travel section). To manage these dependencies as a system, communication paths and links for each task must be determined or defined. Links could define the dependencies among the tasks and the relevant timing of those dependencies. There are many tools available to a project manager to assist in defining project "system" relationships. The more common tools and methods are presented in Chapter 10.

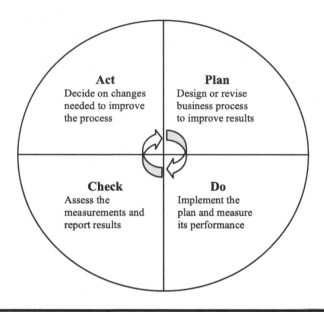

Act
Decide on changes
needed to improve
the process

Plan
Design or revise
business process
to improve results

Check
Assess the
measurements and
report results

Do
Implement the
plan and measure
its performance

Figure 7.5   PDCA cycle.

The concept of *continual improvement* (Principle 6) is based on experience. First we try something; if it does not work, we try it again from a slightly different approach. With each failure and success, we learn and remember the process that yielded the best results. The cycle is repeated until the goal is reached. It is not unlike a baby learning to walk. After the initial step, the oversized head lurches forward with the feet frantically trying to keep up. Although the goal may be reached, thumping ungracefully headfirst, repeated attempts slowly refine the process until a quality walk is achieved. Quality management captures this with the phrase, "Plan-Do-Check-Act" (PDCA).

A task is planned, it is implemented, the performance evaluated, and then changes incorporated. This is done not once, but on a continual, reiterative basis to ensure a graceful completion rather than finishing with a thump. The PDCA cycle is shown in Figure 7.5. It was first developed in the 1920s by W. Shewhart, but was later popularized by W. Edwards Deming and is often referred to as the Deming Cycle. Deming recommended that business processes be placed in a continuous feedback loop so that managers can identify and change the parts of the process that need improvements.

The Note in Clause 0.2 of ISO 9001 explains that the PDCA cycle applies to processes as:

- *Plan.* Establish the objectives and processes necessary to deliver results in accordance with customer requirements and the organization's policies.
- *Do.* Implement the processes.
- *Check.* Monitor and measure processes and product against policies, objectives and requirements for the product and report the results.
- *Act.* Take actions to continually improve process performance.

Within the ISO 9001 quality management system, the PDCA is a dynamic cycle that can be deployed within each of the organization's processes and to the system of processes as a whole. It is a part of all aspects of a life cycle from the planning, needs analysis, design, development, implementation, operation, and other quality management system processes.

Performance evaluation is the pivotal step that allows improvement. It tells how well the process is working and what will make it work better. However, an evaluation is only as good as the data provided. Relevant and reliable data provide the *factual basis to make decisions* (Principle 7). Decisions and adjustments to the project management plan should be documented along with the corresponding performance data and evaluation.

Mutually beneficial supplier relationships (Principle 8) essentially mean that a project manager should know a supplier's capabilities and requirements, and vice versa. If a project planner understands the supplier's needs, then better specifications can be written. Understanding a supplier's capabilities translates into more realistic specifications and delivery timelines. Similarly, suppliers are more likely to help create value if they are aware of how they contribute to the project processes. They may also bring additional experience and expertise to the project.

In summary, the focus of the ISO 9001 standard is on quality management of systems implemented by any organization in any sector of activity. It applies to the processes that an organization employs to realize its products or services — the way the organization accomplishes its work and meets the customers' requirements.

The next topic reviews the Six Sigma approach to assessment.

Six Sigma

Six Sigma is a disciplined, focused approach of quality principles and techniques designed to eliminate defects in any process, whether it is for a component or a system. Motorola formulated Six Sigma in the 1980s to address the emerging competitive international marketplace for electronic products. For Motorola to establish itself as a company with quality products at a competitive price, Motorola's CEO at the time, Bob Galvin, started the company on a quality path known as Six Sigma. Since then, several other large companies have adopted the Six Sigma principles. In addition, the USG has recently promoted the use of Six Sigma by government contractors developing products for the Department of Defense (DoD).

Sigma is the Greek letter used by statisticians to measure the variability in any process. To achieve the "six" sigma level, a process must not produce more than 3.4 defects per million opportunities. A defect is defined as anything outside of customer specifications. To achieve the highest quality level, two possible Six Sigma methodologies have been established. Defined in Table 7.2, the first improvement system, "Define, Measure, Analyze, Improve, Control (DMAIC)," is implemented to find incremental improvement when existing processes fall below specification. The second, defined in Table 7.3, "Define, Measure, Analyze, Design, Verify (DMADV)," is an improvement system to develop new processes or products at Six Sigma quality levels.

Both processes can be executed by trained in-house technical leaders, known as Six Sigma green belts, black belts, or master black belts. These "change agents" provide the key to successfully implementing Six Sigma processes in the organization.

Table 7.2   Six Sigma DMAIC

Define, Measure, Analyze, Improve, Control = DMAIC

<u>Define</u>. Define the project goals and customer deliverables.
<u>Measure</u>. Measure the existing system and process to determine current performance.
<u>Analyze</u>. Analyze he system to identify ways to eliminate the gap between the current performance of the system or process and the desired goal.
<u>Improve</u>. Improve the system and process by eliminating defects.
<u>Control</u>. Control the system and future process performance.

Table 7.3   Six Sigma DMADV

Define, Measure, Analyze, Design, Verify = DMADV

<u>Define</u>. Define the project goals and customer deliverables.
<u>Measure</u>. Measure and determine current needs and specifications.
<u>Analyze</u>. Analyze the process options to meet the customer needs.
<u>Design</u>. Design the process to meet the customer needs.
<u>Verify</u>. Verify the design performance and ability to meet customer needs.

Some view the current popularity of Six Sigma as a management fad that will soon run its course. However, leading-edge organizations are applying the Six Sigma strategy and seeing savings in cost and time schedules, as well as improving the quality of the end product. Thus, it might become a mainstay of the process improvement tools.

The next topic explains the SEI-CMM model for assessing development and organizational processes.

Software Engineering Institute Capability Maturity Models (SEI-CMM)

The Capability Maturity Models (CMMs) contain the essential elements of effective processes for one or more bodies of knowledge. They are designed to provide guidance that encourages process improvement in organizations of any structure. The CMM documentation states that "an *assessment* is an appraisal that an organization does to and for itself for the purposes of process improvement" (CMMI-SE/SW/IPPD/SS, 2002, v1.1, p. 25).

According to the SEI Web site (2005), the following reflects the SEI's goals in developing CMMs:

- Addressing software engineering and other disciplines that affect software development and maintenance
- Providing integrated process improvement reference models
- Building broad community consensus
- Harmonizing with related standards
- Enabling efficient improvement across disciplines relevant to software development and maintenance

Since 1991, the SEI has developed six CMM products. Some are recently developed and others are previous models combined. Currently, the SEI is involved in developing, expanding, and maintaining three CMMs:

1. *CMMI®:* Capability Maturity Model Integration
2. *P-CMM:* People Capability Maturity Model
3. *SA-CMM:* Software Acquisition Capability Maturity Model

A relevant SE legacy CMM was the Systems Engineering CMM (SE-CMM). The SE-CMM was designed for judging the essential elements of the SE process in an organization. In 2000, the best SE-CMM principles and practices were incorporated into CMMI.

The purpose of the CMMI is to provide guidance for improving an organization's processes and ability to manage the development, acquisition, and maintenance of products or services. CMMI places proven approaches into a structure that helps organizations appraise their organizational maturity or process area capability, establish priorities for improvement, and implement these improvements (CMMI-SE/SW, 2001, v1.1, p. 1).

Within the CMMI, the four bodies of knowledge or disciplines available are systems engineering, software engineering, integrated product and process development, and supplier sourcing. The systems engineering discipline covers the development of total systems, which may or may not include software. SEs focus on transforming customer needs, expectations, and constraints into product solutions and supporting these product solutions throughout the life of the product. The SE discipline model contains four primary process areas: process management, project management, support, and engineering (CMMI-SE). Table 7.4 provides a definition of each CMMI process area. A process area is a cluster of related practices in an area that, when performed collectively, satisfy a set of goals considered important for making significant improvement in that area. Although process areas have been grouped in a particular manner,

Table 7.4 Four CMMI Process Areas

Process	Description
Process management	Contains the cross-project activities related to defining, planning, resourcing, deploying, implementing, monitoring, controlling, appraising, measuring, and improving processes
Project management	Covers the project management activities related to planning, monitoring, and controlling the project
Support	Covers the activities that support product development and maintenance, such as processes used in the context of performing other processes, processes targeted toward the project, and processes that apply more generally to the organization
Engineering	Covers the development and maintenance activities shared across engineering disciplines, such as systems engineering and software engineering
	The CCMI engineering process areas include Requirements Development, Requirements Management, Technical Solution, Product Integration, Verification, and Validation.

process areas often interact and have an effect on one another regardless of their defined group.

All CMMI models with a continuous representation (versus staged representation) reflect "capability levels" in their design and content. Capability levels focus on growing the organization's ability to perform, control, and improve its performance in a process area. Capability levels enable the organization to track, evaluate, and demonstrate progress as it improves processes associated with a process area. Capability levels build on each other, providing a recommended order for approaching process improvement. Table 7.5 defines the six CMMI capability levels designated by the numbers 0 through 5 (based on information from CMMI-SE/SW/IPPD/SS, 2002, v1.1).

Table 7.5 CMMI Capability Levels

Level		Focus and Key Process Area
0	Incomplete	An incomplete process is either not performed or partially performed. One or more of the specific goals of the process area are not satisfied.
1	Performed	A capability level 1 process is characterized as a "performed process." A performed process is a process that satisfies the specific goals of the process area. It supports and enables the work needed to produce identified output work products using identified input work products.
2	Managed	A managed process is a capability level 1 process that is also planned and executed in accordance with policy, employs skilled people having adequate resources to produce controlled outputs, involves relevant stakeholders; is monitored, controlled, and reviewed; and is evaluated for adherence to its process description. Management of the process is concerned with the institutionalization of the process area and the achievement of other specific objectives established for the process, such as cost, schedule, and quality objectives.
3	Defined	A defined process is a capability level 2 process that is tailored from the organization's set of standard processes according to the organization's tailoring guidelines, and contributes work products, measures, and other process-improvement information to the organizational process assets.

Table 7.5 (continued) CMMI Capability Levels

Level		Focus and Key Process Area
4	Quantitatively managed	A quantitatively managed process is a capability level 3 process that is controlled using statistical and other quantitative techniques. Quantitative objectives for quality and process performance are established and used as criteria in managing the process. The quality and process performance are understood in statistical terms and are managed throughout the life of the process.
5	Optimizing	An optimizing process is a capability level 4 process that is changed and adapted to meet relevant current and projected business objectives. An optimizing process focuses on continually improving the process performance through both incremental and innovative technological improvements. Process
		improvements that would address root causes of process variation and measurably improve the organization's processes are identified, evaluated, and deployed as appropriate. These improvements are selected based on a quantitative understanding of their expected contribution to achieving the organization's process-improvement objectives versus the cost and impact to the organization. The process performance of the organization's processes is continually improved.

Benchmarking, Baldrige, ISO 9001, Six Sigma, and CMM

Depending on the project and the organization, models can be combined to fit the specific design and development process. For example, an application may need a certain set of activities to take place to achieve success or the organization may require certain standards or processes to meet industry or government requirements.

Through these tools and others, the process improvement community has established an effective means of modeling, defining, and measuring the maturity of the processes used by organizations developing and maintaining IT systems. Although these assessments for improving processes are different, they are also compatible. As such, each may have a place in the management system of an organization.

The next section reviews the assessment tools and concepts available to the ISSEP.

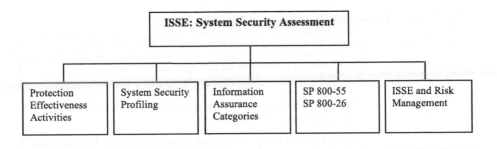

Figure 7.6   ISSE assessment tools.

ISSE and System Security Assessment

Assurance is a measure of confidence that the security architecture and features of a component item, product, or system accurately reflect the intended security. Assurance mechanisms are techniques that can be applied during the design, development, implementation, and evaluation of a product or system. Assurance planning identifies what assurance evidence is needed, what assurance mechanisms are used to produce the evidence, and what level of effort is applied for each mechanism.

To add the security goals into the definition, assurance can be defined as those measures intended to protect and defend information and information systems by ensuring their *confidentiality, integrity, availability, authentication*, and *non-repudiation*. This includes providing for restoration of information systems by incorporating protection, detection, and reaction capabilities. For national security systems, system security assessment is a vital part of systems engineering that helps, in part, meet overall system security requirements.

This section outlines several assessment tools as shown in Figure 7.6. It includes the IATF information protection effectiveness activities, system security profiling, six categories of information assurance, and two NIST special publications. The final topic reviews the role of risk management and assessment.

Information Protection Effectiveness Activities

Based on the IATF (2002) guidelines, the Assess Information Protection Effectiveness activity spans the entire ISSE process. Table 7.6 provides a summary of the assessment tasks associated with each of the ISSE activities.

The assessment tasks have been included in the chapters for each of the individual ISSE phases. However, for summary purposes, they are combined here into one listing (based on IATF, 2002, Appendix J, p. J-1-4).

Table 7.6   Assessment Tasks by ISSE Activity

ISSE Activity	*Assess Information Protection Effectiveness Task*
Discover information protection needs	Present an overview of the process.
	Summarize the information model.
	Describe threats to the mission or business through information attacks.
	Establish security services to counter those threats and identify their relative importance to the customer.
	Obtain customer agreement on the conclusions of this activity as a basis for determining system security effectiveness.
Define system security requirements	Ensure that the selected solution set meets the mission or business security needs.
	Coordinate the system boundaries.
	Present security context, security CONOPS, and system security requirements to the customer and gain their concurrence.
	Ensure that the projected security risks are acceptable to the customer.
Design system security architecture	Begin the formal risk analysis process to ensure that the selected security mechanisms provide the required security services and to explain to the customer how the security architecture meets the security requirements.
Develop detailed security design	Review how well the selected security services and mechanisms counter the threats by performing an interdependency analysis to compare desired to effective security service strengths.
	Once completed, the risk assessment results, particularly any mitigation needs and residual risk, will be documented and shared with the customer to obtain their concurrence.
Implement system security	The risk analysis will be conducted/updated.
	Strategies will be developed for the mitigation of identified risks.
	Identify possible mission impacts and advise the customer and the customer's Certifiers and Accreditors.

Source: From IATF, 1994, p. 3-15 to 3-16.

- Phase 1: Discover Information Protection Needs:
  - Provide and present documented information protection needs to the customer.
  - Obtain concurrence from the customer in the information protection needs.
- Phase 2: Define System Security Requirements:
  - Provide and present security context, security CONOPS, and system security requirements to the customer.
  - Obtain concurrence from the customer in system security context, CONOPS, and requirements.
- Phase 3: Define System Security Architecture:
  - Ensure that the selected security mechanisms provide the required security services.
  - Explain to the customer how the security architecture meets the security requirements.
  - Generate risk projection.
  - Obtain concurrence from the customer in the security architecture.
- Phase 4: Develop Detailed Security Design:
  - Conduct design risk analysis.
  - Ensure that the selected security design provides the required security services.
  - Explain to the customer how the security design meets the security requirements.
  - Explain to the customer, and document, any residual risks of the design.
  - Obtain concurrence from the customer in the detailed security design.
- Phase 5: Implement System Security
  - Monitor to ensure that the security design is implemented correctly.
  - Conduct or update risk analysis.
  - Define the risks and possible mission impacts and advise the customer and the customer's Certifiers and Accreditors.

The next topic outlines security profiling as an assessment tool. It is also referred to as *benchmarking* and has characteristics similar to that of the SE benchmarking tool.

System Security Profiling

The *ISSE Handbook* (1994) describes another method of assessing the success of the ISSE process — the system security profile or benchmarking.

The goals of creating a security profile are to provide information not readily available and assist the SEs by providing data for security risk mitigation and risk management. It can also be used to address uncertainties arising during applications of the ISSE process or from a situation in which the ISSE model or activities were not deliberately or continuously applied during the SE and acquisition process.

As an example, a system security profile can be used when an ISSEP is assigned mid-way through the system design phase and must assess the security strengths and weaknesses of the design. The ISSEP may need to quickly develop a security benchmark and institute a plan for including ISSE activities in the remaining phases of the project. Another example is when an ISSEP is asked to provide a security profile or security benchmark of a current (or legacy) system.

The *ISSE Handbook* (1994) outlines the system security profiling activities as:

- Study the available system documentation.
- Design security relevant scenarios and begin to generate potential attacks against the system.
- If testing is appropriate, assemble a representative system configuration in a non-operation environment. Configuration testing verifies the operational connectivity of the configuration and consistency with the system specifications. Security mechanism testing verifies a consistency with the system's security paradigm. Attack testing then attempts to circumvent the security mechanisms the profile customer has identified as critical to the system's security.

The results from any testing or document analysis are recorded in a security profile. Because there are usually time constraints, the testing and analysis will only provide a snapshot or overview of the system's security.

Questions to consider when creating a system security profile include (*ISSE Handbook*):

- Who is the security profile customer?
- To whom will the security profile be delivered?
- Is the customer interested in receiving a profile?
- What is the purpose of the profile?
- When is the profile information needed?
- Are there knowledgeable system people available to help in the analysis?
- Is testing information desired in the profile?
- Can the requestor supply the (any) equipment?

- When will the equipment be available?
- Are there people familiar with the configuration to help set up this equipment?
- Does the customer have a classification guide for system vulnerabilities?
- What type of feedback/review does the customer want?
- Is the customer interested in sharing the profile information with other government organizations? (p. F-29)

The answers to these questions will help tailor the system security profiling process to meet the customer's needs, establish the scope of the security profile, and focus attention on the issues that are important to the customer. The system security profiling may take the form of a quick security vulnerability assessment accomplished through a time-limited penetration attack, or an assessment of the system architecture from a security point of view.

A system security profiling team can include the system integrator, security evaluation experts, product developers, and system analysts. However, because security profiling can occur at any point in the engineering or acquisition process, the team must be flexible to meet the specific security needs at that moment and for that project.

Identification of security capabilities and weaknesses is the essential element of a security profile. It is not used to displace SE activities. The next topic explains the six information assurance categories.

Six Categories of Information Assurances

The ISSEP should be aware that many information system security assurances are related to, and in many cases, the same techniques used in the SE field, such as software quality assurances and reliability engineering. The focus for the ISSEP is to make sure the SE assurances are coordinated with the security needs of the system.

According to the *ISSE Handbook* (1994, p. F-30 to F-37), there are six general categories of information system security assurances:

1. Processes (can be obtained by the way the system is built)

Process mechanisms are those assurance mechanisms that involve how a system or product is designed, developed, shipped, and maintained. The ISSE process is an assurance mechanism that integrates security into a system.

Process mechanisms include:

- *Configuration management.* Technique to measure the security features of a system through the control of changes made to the hardware, software, firmware, documentation, etc. throughout its development and operational life.
- *Life-cycle controls.* Controls that affect the life cycle include procurement/acquisition procedures, development procedures, shipping and handling procedures, and maintenance procedures.
- *Program reviews.* Managerial and technical meetings held at various program milestones to gather information and make decisions. Three broad type of program reviews include:
  - *Contractual review.* Covers the cost, schedule, and technical status
  - *Internal management review.* Emphasizes the security status of the program in relation to cost, schedule, and technical issues
  - *Security evaluation review.* Provides a means to maintain the quality of security evaluation
- *Independent Verification and Validation (IV&V).* Verification ensures that the output of a given phase of the development process fulfills the requirements. Validation is the process of evaluating the suitability of the output relative to the customer's reasonable expectations. Independent indicates that an outside source conducted the verification and validation activities.
- *Correspondence and formal methods.* The use of correspondence as an assurance mechanism is to provide a refinement of how a system specification correctly implements the more abstract specification. It is employed by the system developer as a means of communicating to independent system evaluators that the implemented system has met its security requirements. It is used when a system reaches a level of complexity that a single analyst cannot reasonably understand all aspects of system development and a high assurance is necessary.

2. Properties (can be obtained by the way the system is built)

Property mechanisms are those that involve the structure or characteristic that system or product components must have to convince the developers and evaluators that the system or product is implemented correctly. This includes items such as redundancy, modularity, traceability, mature technology, alarm philosophy/fail-safe design, physical integrity/tamper resident-evident, environment, distribution/installation, modularization, etc.

3. Analysis (can be obtained by an analysis of system descriptions for conformance to requirements and vulnerabilities)

This consists of mechanisms examining a description of an aspect of the system or product and not the physical entity itself. Different aspects of system and products that should be considered include covert channels, cryptography, key and privilege management, system architecture, TEMPEST, etc.

4. Testing (can be obtained by testing the system itself to determine operating characteristics and to find vulnerabilities)

These are the mechanisms that involve exercising an actual implementation of a system or product to determine certain characteristics of its operation. Testing yields relatively weak conclusions about the behavior of a system or product because test coverage is so small. Testing cannot show the absences of vulnerabilities in a system; it can merely confirm the presence of some vulnerability. Even so, testing can be useful because the conclusions are drawn from something that is much closer to way the system or product is built versus the use of descriptions in analysis.

There are two major types of testing:

1. *Functional testing.* Includes testing that is concerned with demonstrating that a system or product behaves according to its specifications.
2. *Penetration testing.* After functional testing is completed, penetration testing can determine if there are other ways to break into the system or product and violate its security requirements.

5. Guidance (can be obtained by the way the system is built)

The documentation that tells a system or product owners, administrators, or users how to securely operate the system or product. It may include a security features user's guide or Common Criteria evaluation information.

6. Fielded Systems Evaluation (can be obtained by operational experience and field evaluation of the system)

Once the system is deployed and operational, fielded system evaluations verify whether the security controls are performing as intended.

The next topics briefly outline three of the NIST Special Publications (NIST SPs) that relate to assessing the security of systems and security components. *For the ISSEP candidate:* these are not currently listed on the (ISC)² exam requirements; however, they may be helpful in understanding the NIST viewpoint toward security assessment.

NIST SP 800-55

NIST SP 800-55 (July 2003), "Security Metrics Guide for Information Technology Systems," provides guidance to Federal agencies on how to measure information technology (IT) security performance. The guidance is intended to support several existing laws, rules, and regulations that cite regulations for measuring IT performance in general and IT security performance in particular. For example, in 2002, the Federal Information Security Management Act (FISMA) specifically mandated that security control objectives and techniques for systems and programs must be reviewed and reported annually to the Office of Management and Budget (OMB). FISMA requires Federal agencies to demonstrate that they are meeting applicable security requirements and agencies must document the actual level of performance based on the results of annual security program reviews. Table 7.7 provides a brief comparison of SP800-55 and CMMI levels.

NIST SP 800-55 provides guidance on how organizations, through the use of metrics, can identify the adequacy of in-place security controls, policies, and procedures. The development and implementation of a security metrics program is based on and builds upon the annual security program reviews.

NIST SP 800-55 (2003, p. 2) states that a security metrics program within an organization should include four interdependent components:

1. A foundation of *strong upper-level management support.* This is critical not only for the success of the security program, but also for the implementation of a security metrics program.
2. *Practical security policies and procedures* backed by the authority necessary to enforce compliance.
3. Developing and establishing *quantifiable performance metrics* that are designed to capture and provide meaningful performance data.
4. The security metrics program itself must emphasize *consistent periodic analysis* of the metrics data.

The success of an information security program implementation should be judged by the degree to which meaningful results are produced. A comprehensive security metrics analysis program should provide substantive justification for decisions that directly affect the security posture of an organization, such as budget and personnel requests. One of the goals

Table 7.7   What NIST SP 800-55 and CMM Have in Common

What do SP 800-55 and CMM have in common?
NIST SP 800-55 states that "a program's maturity is defined by the existence and institutionalization of processes and procedures. As a security program matures, its policies become more detailed and better documented, the processes that it uses become more standardized and institutionalized, and it produces data that can be used for performance measurement in greater quantity. According to NIST SP 800-26, the security program progresses from having policies (Level 1) to having detailed procedures (Level 2), implementing these procedures (Level 3), testing compliance with and effectiveness of the procedures (Level 4), and finally fully integrating policies and procedures into daily operations (Level 5)." (SP 800-55, p. 11)
"The types of metrics (implementation, efficiency and effectiveness, and impact) that can realistically be obtained and that can also be useful for performance improvement depend on the maturity of the security control implementation. Although different types of metrics can be used simultaneously, the primary focus of IT security metrics shifts as the implementation of security controls matures. When security controls have been defined in procedures and are in the process of being implemented, the primary focus of metrics will be on the level of implementation of security controls. Examples of implementation metrics that are applied at this level of maturity are the percentage of systems with approved security plans and the percentage of systems with password policies configured as required. When a system progresses through Level 1 and Level 2, the results of these metrics will be less than 100 percent, indicating that the system has not yet reached Level 3. When the metrics implementation results reach and remain at 100 percent, it can be concluded that the system has fully implemented security controls and has reached Level 3." (SP 800-55, p. 12)

of IT security metrics is to progressively (Figure 7.7) measure implementation, efficiency, effectiveness, and the business impact of IT security activities within organizations or for specific systems (NIST SP 800-55, p. 3).

NIST SP 800-55 identifies six phases (Figure 7.7) that provide organizations with an effective security metric for assessing the performance of security controls. The six SP 800-55 security metric implementation phases are defined as:

■ *"Prepare for Data Collection.* Phase 1 of the process, *Prepare for Data Collection*, involves activities that are key for establishing a comprehensive IT security metrics program, including the IT security metrics identification, definition, development, and selection activities, and developing a metrics program implementation plan. After the metrics have been identified, specific implementation steps should be defined on how to collect, analyze, and report the

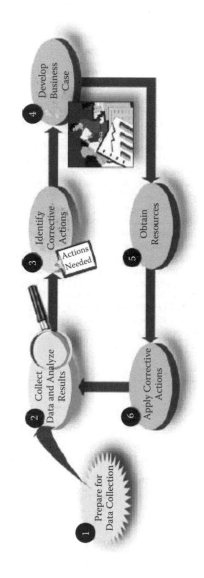

Figure 7.7   Six phases of implementing a security metric program. (*Source:* From NIST SP 800-55, 2003, p. 24.)

metrics. These steps should be documented in the Metrics Program Implementation Plan (p. 24).

■ *Collect Data and Analyze Results.* Phase 2 of the process, *Collect Data and Analyze Results,* involves activities that are essential for ensuring that the collected metrics are used to gain an understanding of system security and to identify appropriate improvement actions (p. 25).

■ *Identify Corrective Actions.* Phase 3 of the process, *Identify Corrective Actions,* involves the development of a plan that will provide the roadmap of how to close the implementation gap identified in Phase 2 (p. 26).

■ *Develop Business Case and Obtain Resources.* Phases 4 and 5, *Develop Business Case* and *Obtain Resources,* respectively, address the budgeting cycle required for obtaining resources required for implementing remediation actions identified in Phase 3. The steps involved in developing a business case are based on industry practices and mandated guidance, including OMB Circular A-11, the Clinger-Cohen Act, and the Government Paper Reduction Act. The results of the prior three phases will be included in the business case as supporting evidence (p. 27).

■ *Apply Corrective Actions.* Phase 6 of the process, *Apply Corrective Actions,* involves implementing corrective actions in technical, management, and operational areas of security controls. After corrective actions are applied, the cycle completes itself and restarts with a subsequent data collection and analysis. Iterative data collection, analysis, and reporting will track progress of corrective actions, measure improvement, and identify areas for further improvement. The iterative nature of the cycle ensures that the progress is monitored and the corrective actions are affecting system security control implementation in an intended way. Frequent performance measurements will ensure that if corrective actions are not implemented as planned, or if their effect is not as desired, quick course corrections can be made, internally to the organization, therefore avoiding problems being discovered during external audits, C&A efforts, or other similar activities (p. 28).

An important consideration when determining IT security metrics is to ensure that the metrics are based on IT security performance goals and objectives. IT security performance goals state the desired results of a system security program implementation, such as:

"all general support systems and major applications must be certified and accredited." The IT security performance objective enables accomplishment of the goal by identifying practices defined by security policies and procedures that direct consistent implementation of security controls across the organization, such as "system owners are responsible for certifying and accreditation all major applications under their control."

To provide a comprehensive framework for organizations, NIST has made an effort to link its publications together. In this fashion, SP 800-55 provides examples of metrics based on the critical elements and security controls and techniques contained in NIST SP 800-26, "Security Self-Assessment Guide for Information Technology Systems." Refer to Appendix C for examples of how the security topics and questions in SP 800-26 can be combined into a security matrix.

NIST SP 800-26

NIST SP 800-26 (Revised April 2005), "System Questionnaire with NIST SP800-53 References and Associated Security Control Mappings," provides a method for agency officials to determine the current status of their information security programs and, where necessary, establish a target for improvement. NIST SP 800-26 is a questionnaire that contains specific control objectives and techniques against which an unclassified system or group of interconnected systems can be tested and measured. A primary goal of the document was to provide a standardized approach to assessing a system.

NIST SP 800-26 builds on the *Federal IT Security Assessment Framework (2000)* developed by NIST for the Federal Chief Information Officer (CIO) Council. The Framework established the groundwork for standardizing on five levels of security status and criteria agencies could use to determine if the five levels were adequately implemented. NIST SP 800-26 provides guidance on applying the Framework by identifying IT security topics that affect the security posture of an organization.

The security topics in the questionnaire are separated into three control areas: management (five control areas), operational (nine control areas), and technical (three control areas). This division of control areas complements other NIST documents, such as: SP 800-12, *An Introduction to Computer Security: The NIST Handbook* (Handbook); SP 800-14, "Generally Accepted Principles and Practices for Securing Information Technology Systems" (Principles and Practices); and NIST SP 800-18, "Guide for Developing Security Plans for Information Technology Systems" (Planning Guide).

The introduction of NIST SP 800-26 (2001, p. 1) explains the need for self-assessments as:

"A self-assessment conducted on a system (major application or general support system) or multiple self-assessments conducted for a group of interconnected systems (internal or external to the agency) is one method used to measure information technology (IT) security assurance. IT security assurance is the degree of confidence one has that the managerial, technical and operational security measures work as intended to protect the system and the information it processes. Adequate security of these assets is a fundamental management responsibility. Consistent with Office of Management and Budget (OMB) policy, each agency must implement and maintain a program to adequately secure its information and system assets. Agency programs must: 1) assure that systems and applications operate effectively and provide appropriate confidentiality, integrity, and availability; and 2) protect information commensurate with the level of risk and magnitude of harm resulting from loss, misuse, unauthorized access, or modification."

To measure the progress of effectively implementing the needed security control, five levels of effectiveness are provided for each answer to the security control question. The levels are (SP 800-26, 2001, p. 10):

> *Level 1:* control objective documented in a security policy
> *Level 2:* security controls documented as procedures
> *Level 3:* procedures have been implemented
> *Level 4:* procedures and security controls are tested and reviewed
> *Level 5:* procedures and security controls are fully integrated into a comprehensive program

As an example, the first section of the questionnaire focuses on the management control for managing the risk for a system. The questions for Section 1 Risk Management include (p. A-5 to 6):

1.1 Critical Element: Is risk periodically assessed?
    1.1.1 Is the current system configuration documented, including links to other systems?
    1.1.2 Are risk assessments performed and documented on a regular basis or whenever the system, facilities, or other conditions change?
    1.1.3 Has data sensitivity and integrity of the data been considered?
    1.1.4 Have threat sources, both natural and manmade, been identified?

1.1.5 Has a list of known system vulnerabilities, system flaws, or weaknesses that could be exploited by the threat sources been developed and maintained current?

1.1.6 Has an analysis been conducted that determines whether the security requirements in place adequately mitigate vulnerabilities?

1.2 Critical Element: Do program officials understand the risk to systems under their control and determine the acceptable level of risk?

1.2.1 Are final risk determinations and related management approvals documented and maintained on file?

1.2.2 Has a mission/business impact analysis been conducted?

1.2.3 Have additional controls been identified to sufficiently mitigate identified risks? In 2003, NIST released the "Automated Security Self-Evaluation Tool (ASSET)" to automate the completion of the SP 800-26 questionnaire. In addition, there are several other vendors that have released automated tools to assist in completing an annual assessment using the SP 800-26 as the guideline.

NIST SP 800-42

NIST SP 800-42 (October 2003), "Guideline on Network Security Testing," provides guidance on network security testing and stresses the need for an effective security testing program within Federal agencies. Network testing is defined as those "activities that provide information about the integrity of an organization's networks and associated systems through testing and verification of network-related security controls on a regular basis" (NIST SP 800-42, p. 1-3). The primary reason for testing the security of an operational system is to identify potential vulnerabilities and subsequently repair them. NIST SP 800-42 states that:

> Testing serves several purposes. One, no matter how well a given system may have been developed, the nature of today's complex systems with large volumes of code, complex internal interactions, interoperability with uncertain external components, unknown interdependencies coupled with vendor cost and schedule pressures, means that exploitable flaws will always be present or surface over time. Accordingly, security testing must fill the gap between the state of the art in system development and actual operation of these systems. Two, security testing is important for understanding, calibrating, and documenting the operational security posture of an organization. Aside from development of these systems, the operational and

security demands must be met in a fast changing threat and vulnerability environment. Attempting to learn and repair the state of your security during a major attack is very expensive in cost and reputation, and is largely ineffective. Three, security testing is an essential component of improving the security posture of your organization. Organizations that have an organized, systematic, comprehensive, ongoing, and priority driven security testing regimen are in a much better position to make prudent investments to enhance the security posture of their systems (p. ES-1).

NIST specifically recommends the following for testing (NIST SP 800-42):

- Make network security testing a routine and integral part of the system and network operations and administration.
- Test the most important systems first.
- Use caution when testing.
- Ensure that security policy accurately reflects the organization's needs.
- Integrate security testing into the risk management process.
- Ensure that system and network administrators are trained and capable.
- Ensure that systems are kept up-to-date with patches.
- Look at the big picture.
- Understand the capabilities and limitations of vulnerability testing (p. ES2-3).

In most cases, there are network systems that should be tested before testing general staff and related systems (Figure 7.8). Thus, the primary focus of SP 800-42 is toward the testing of Category 1 systems, which are defined as the sensitive systems that provide security for the organization or that provide other critical functions. These include:

- Firewalls, both internal and external
- Routers and switches
- Related network-perimeter security systems such as intrusion detection systems
- Web servers, e-mail servers, and other application servers
- Other servers, such as for Domain Name Service (DNS) or directory servers or file servers (CIFS/SMB, NFS, FTP, etc.)

Category 2 systems are generally all other systems, such as desktops, stand-alones, and mobile client systems. It usually indicates those systems are protected by firewalls, etc., but must still be tested periodically.

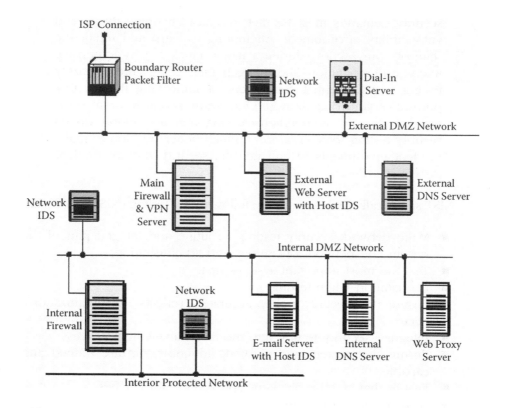

Figure 7.8 Examples of mission-critical systems for initial testing.

Evaluation of system security can and should be conducted at different stages of system development. Network security testing typically fits into the system development life cycle during the implementation and operational stages. During the implementation stage, Security Testing and Evaluation (ST&E) should be conducted on particular parts of the system and on the entire system as a whole. ST&E is an examination or analysis of the protective measures that are placed on an information system once it is fully integrated and operational.

Once a system is operational, it is necessary to assess whether the system is operating according to its security requirements. Operational testing needs to include both the actions of people who operate or use the system and the functioning of technical controls.

Security testing provides insight into other system development life-cycle activities such as risk analysis and contingency planning.

Examples of operational tests are listed in Table 7.8. It also includes several of the strengths and weaknesses for each type of test. Table 7.9

Table 7.8 Comparison of Testing Procedures

Type of Test	Strengths	Weaknesses
Network scanning	Fast (as compared to vulnerability scanners or penetration testing) Efficiently scans hosts, depending on number of hosts in network Many excellent freeware tools available Highly automated (for scanning component) Low cost	Does not directly identify known vulnerabilities (although will identify commonly used Trojan ports [e.g., 31337, 12345, etc.]) Generally used as a prelude to penetration testing, not as final test Requires significant expertise to interpret results
Vulnerability scanning	Can be fairly fast, depending on number of hosts scanned Some freeware tools available Highly automated (for scanning) Identifies known vulnerabilities Often provides advice on mitigating discovered vulnerabilities High cost (commercial scanners) to low cost (freeware scanners) Easy to run on a regular basis	Has high false positive rate Generates large amount of traffic aimed at a specific host (which can cause the host to crash or lead to a temporary denial of service) Not stealthy (e.g., easily detected by IDS, firewall, and even end users [although this may be useful in testing the response of staff and altering mechanisms]) Can be dangerous in the hands of a novice (particularly regarding DoS attacks) Often misses latest vulnerabilities Identifies only surface vulnerabilities
Penetration testing	Tests network using the methodologies and tools that attackers employ Verifies vulnerabilities	Requires great expertise Very labor intensive Slow, target hosts may take hours/days to "crack"

Table 7.8 (continued) Comparison of Testing Procedures

Type of Test	Strengths	Weaknesses
	Goes beyond surface vulnerabilities and demonstrates how these vulnerabilities can be exploited iteratively to gain greater access Demonstrates that vulnerabilities are not purely theoretical Can provide the realism and evidence needed to address security issues Social engineering allows for testing of procedures and the human element network security	Due to time required, not all hosts on medium- or large-sized networks will be tested individually Dangerous when conducted by inexperienced testers Certain tools and techniques may be banned or controlled by agency regulations (e.g., network sniffers, password crackers, etc.) Expensive Can be organizationally disruptive
Password cracking	Quickly identifies weak passwords Provides clear demonstration of password strength or weakness Easily implemented Low cost	Potential for abuse Certain organizations restrict use
Log reviews	Provides excellent information Only data source that provides historical information	Cumbersome to manually review Automated tools not perfect can filter out important information
File integrity checkers	Reliable method of determining whether a host has been compromised Highly automated Low cost	Does not detect any compromise prior to installation Checksums need to be updated when system is updated Checksums need to be protected (e.g., read-only CD-ROM) because they provide no protection if they can be modified by an attacker

Table 7.8 (continued) Comparison of Testing Procedures

Type of Test	Strengths	Weaknesses
Virus detectors	Excellent at preventing and removing viruses Low/medium cost	Require constant updates to be effective Some false positive issues Ability to react to new, fast replicating viruses is often limited
War Dialing	Effective way to identify unauthorized modems	Legal and regulatory issues, especially if using public switched network Slow
War Driving	Effective way to identify unauthorized wireless access points	Possible legal issues if other organization's signals are intercepted Requires some expertise in computing, wireless networking, and radio engineering

Source: From SP 800-42, 2003, p. 3-19 to 3-20.

describes a general schedule and list of evaluation factors for testing categories.

There are three factors organizations can use to determine which type of test to conduct and how often. NIST SP 800-42 defines them as:

1. *Prioritization process based on the security category.* Using FIPS 199, determine the security category based on low, medium, or high.
2. *Cost of conducting tests.* Cost will depend on size of the system, complexity of the system, level of human interaction required, and feasibility of selecting a sample for conducting the test and the size of the sample needed.
3. *Benefit to the overall organization's systems.* Need to ensure that the cost of performing the testing does not exceed its value to the organization.

Security testing results should be documented and made available to staff involved in other IT and security-related areas. NIST SP 800-42 (2003, pp. 2–4) notes that the results of security testing can be used in the following ways:

Table 7.9 Summarized Evaluation and Frequency Factors

Test Type	Category 1 Frequency	Category 2 Frequency	Benefit
Network scanning	Continuously to quarterly	Semi-annually	Enumerates the network structure and determines the set of active hosts and associated software. Identifies unauthorized hosts connected to a network. Identifies open ports. Identifies unauthorized services.
Vulnerability scanning	Quarterly or bimonthly (more often for certain high-risk systems), when the vulnerability database is updated	Semi-annually	Enumerates the network structure and determines the set of active hosts and associated software. Identifies a target set of computers to focus vulnerability analysis on. Identifies potential vulnerabilities on the target set. Validates that operating systems and major applications are up-to-date with security patches and software versions.
Penetration testing	Annually	Annually	Determines how vulnerable an organization's network is to penetration and the level of damage that can be incurred. Tests IT staff's response to perceived security incidents and their knowledge of and

Table 7.9 (continued)   Summarized Evaluation and Frequency Factors

Test Type	Category 1 Frequency	Category 2 Frequency	Benefit
			implementation of the organization's security policy and system's security requirements.
Password cracking	Continuously to same frequency as expiration policy	Same frequency as expiration policy	Verifies that the policy is effective in producing passwords that are more or less difficult to break. Verifies that users select passwords that are compliant with the organization's security policy.
Log reviews	Daily for critical systems (e.g., firewalls)	Weekly	Validates that the system is operating according to policies.
Integrity checkers	Monthly and in case of suspected incident	Monthly	Detects unauthorized file modifications.
Virus detectors	Weekly or as required	Weekly or as required	Detects and deletes viruses before successful installation on the system.
War dialing	Annually	Annually	Detects unauthorized modems and prevents unauthorized access to a protected network.
War driving	Continuously to weekly	Semiannually	Detects unauthorized wireless access points and prevents unauthorized access to a protected network.

Source: From SP 800-42, 2003, p. 3-21.

- As a reference point for corrective action
- In defining mitigation activities to address identified vulnerabilities
- As a benchmark for tracing an organization's progress in meeting security requirements
- To assess the implementation status of system security requirements
- To conduct cost/benefit analysis for improvements to system security
- To enhance other life-cycle activities, such as risk assessments, C&A, and performance improvement efforts (p. 2-4)

Security evaluation activities include, but are not limited to, risk assessment, certification and accreditation (C&A), system audits, and security testing at appropriate periods during a system's life cycle. These activities are geared toward ensuring that the system is being developed and operated in accordance with an organization's security policy.

This section highlighted the assurance mechanisms that the ISSEP has available. The size and complexity of the system or product and Federal requirements will all play a role in determining which mechanisms should be used and how often the techniques will be needed during the design, development, implementation, operation, and maintenance phases. The overriding goal of the assurance mechanisms is to ensure that the security requirements for the system or product have been met throughout the life cycle.

ISSE and Risk Management

Typically, an information system will continually be expanded, revised, updated, its components changed, and its software applications replaced with newer versions. Also, changes in personnel and system staff will occur, and security policies and procedures will likely change during the system's life cycle. These changes mean that new risks will become known and risks that have been previously mitigated may again become a concern. Thus, the risk management process is ongoing and will evolve during the system's life cycle.

NIST SP 800-30 (2002) states that Federal agencies must repeat the risk assessment process at least every three years, which is also mandated by OMB Circular A-130. SP 800-30 also states that agencies are responsible for conducting annual reviews to determine the effectiveness of security in IT systems. Thus, the three-year mandate should not be interpreted literally. Risk management should be conducted and integrated on a regular basis throughout the IT system's life cycle — not because it is required by law or regulation, but because it is good practice and helps to ensure the organization's business objectives or mission. There should be a specific schedule for assessing and mitigating mission risks, but the periodically performed process should also be flexible enough to allow changes where warranted, such as major changes to the IT system from new technologies or when the processing environment changes due to new policies and regulations.

NIST SP 800-30 also identifies some key success factors of a risk management program, including:

- Senior management's commitment
- Full support and participation of the IT team
- Competence of the risk assessment team (it must have the expertise to apply the risk assessment methodology to a specific site and system, identify mission risks, and provide cost-effective safeguards that meet the needs of the organization)
- Awareness and cooperation of members of the user community who must follow procedures and comply with the implemented controls to safeguard the mission of their organization
- An ongoing evaluation and assessment of the IT-related mission risks.

SP 800-30 is also discussed in Chapter 14.

Final Deliverable of Phase 6

There are no specific deliverables to this phase, although updates and revisions to previously documented information may be necessary.

Summary

This chapter focused on the mechanisms and techniques of assessing system effectiveness and system security effectiveness. The objective is to assess how well the whole system, after deployment, is effectively operating and also to review the processes used during the analysis, design, and development phases.

A necessary element of assessments is to have mechanisms in place or planned that will:

- Provide for assessing the current state of the system
- Determine how the system compares with similar systems
- Determine and define specific goals and objectives for future developments

It is important for the ISSEP to understand that assessment is an ongoing process during each phase and continues throughout system operation and maintenance.

Assessments should review both the technical characteristics of the system and any organizational issues related to policies or procedures implemented to operate and maintain the system. One of the options available is to establish a benchmark of the system, which basically allows organizations to define their own system and then compare it to other systems. Other assessment tools are quality and performance indicators such as the Baldrige Criteria for Performance Excellence, ISO 9001 certification, Six Sigma, and SEI CMMI. All provide performance and quality criteria with the goal of helping organizations improve processes to create quality systems that improve performance and increase customer satisfaction. For most organizations, it is not a matter of using just one assessment mechanism, but rather to evolve to using each one.

For the ISSEP, assurance is a measure of confidence that the security architecture and features of a component item, product, or system accurately reflect the intended security requirements. Like benchmarking, system security profiling is a technique used to establish and document the security posture of the system. It can address uncertainties resulting from questions on how the ISSE process was used or when the ISSE process was not deliberately or continuously applied in the SE process.

The IATF information assurance categories can be helpful in creating the system security profile. The six categories are:

- Reviewing system processes
- Evaluating the properties (structure or characteristics) of the system
- Analyzing a description of the system
- Conducting tests to verify the security requirements
- Reviewing security guidance documentation for users, etc.
- Conducting evaluations of fielded systems.

Several of the NIST guidelines can be helpful in conducting security assessments. The goal of the NIST documentation is to provide a standardized approach and framework for organizations to use when building and implementing information system security programs. As part of this framework, NIST SP 800-55 provides guidance on how organizations can identify the adequacy of in-place security controls, policies, and procedures by using metrics. The development and implementation of a security metric program is based upon and builds upon the annual security program reviews. NIST SP 800-26 provides a method for organizations to conduct the annual security program review. It is a questionnaire that contains specific control objectives and techniques against which systems can be tested and measured. Finally, NIST SP 800-42 (2003) provides guidance on network security testing and stresses the need for an effective security testing program within Federal agencies.

Security assessments should be applied during the design, development, implementation, maintenance, and operation of a product or system — throughout the entire life cycle. The goal of conducting assessments is to ensure that security requirements for the system are in place throughout each of the life-cycle phases and ultimately to provide organizations with an organized, systematic, comprehensive, ongoing, and priority-driven information system security program.

References

CMU/SEI-2002-TR-011, ESC-TR-2002-011 (March 2002). Capability Maturity Model® Integration (CMMI^{SM}), Version 1.1 for Systems Engineering, Software Engineering, Integrated Product and Process Development, and Supplier Sourcing (CMMI-SE/SW/IPPD/SS, V1.1). Software Engineering Institute at Carnegie Mellon University: Pittsburgh, PA.

CMU/SEI-2002-TR-002, ESC-TR-2002-002 (2001). Capability Maturity Model® Integration (CMMI^{SM}), Version 1.1 for Systems Engineering and Software Engineering (CMMI-SE/SW, V1.1), Staged Representation. Software Engineering Institute at Carnegie Mellon University: Pittsburgh, PA.

Federal Chief Information Officer (CIO) Council (November 2000). *Federal IT Security Assessment Framework,* developed by NIST for the CIO Council. Available at the NIST Web site: http://csrc.nist.gov/organizations/guidance/framework-final.pdf.

Information Systems Security Engineering Handbook, Release 1.0 (February 28, 1994). National Security Agency, Central Security Service. Only available for official USG use.

IAEC3186 (February 2002). Introduction to Information Systems Security Engineering, ISSE Training, student guide.

IETF RFC 2647 (August 1999). Benchmarking Terminology for Firewall Performance. Available at http://www.ietf.cnri.reston.va.us/rfc/rfc2647.txt.

ISO/TC 176/SC2 (December 2000). Quality Management and Quality Assurance. International Organization for Standardization: Geneva, Switzerland.

ISO/TC 176/SC 2/N544R (May 2001). Guidance on the Process Approach to Quality Management Systems. Available at http://www.iso.ch/iso/en/iso9000-14000/iso9000/2000rev9.html.

Information Assurance Technical Framework (IATF), Version 3.1 (September 2002). National Security Agency, Information Assurance Solutions, Technical Directors: Fort Meade, MD.

MIL-HDBK-217F-Notice 2 (1995). Reliability Prediction of Electronic Equipment. Defense Printing Service: Philadelphia, PA.

NIST SP800-12 (March 1995). *An Introduction to Computer Security: The NIST Handbook.* NIST Publications, Computer Security Division, NIST: Gaithersburg, MD. Available at http://csrc.nist.gov/publications/nistpubs/index.html.

NIST SP 800-14 (September 1996). Generally Accepted Principles and Practices for Securing Information Technology Systems. NIST Publications, Computer Security Division, NIST: Gaithersburg, MD. Available at http://csrc.nist.gov/publications/nistpubs/index.html.

NIST SP 800-18 (December 1998). Guide for Developing Security Plans for Information Technology Systems. NIST Publications, Computer Security Division, NIST: Gaithersburg, MD. Available at http://csrc.nist.gov/publications/nistpubs/index.html.

NIST SP 800-23 (August 2000). Guidelines to Federal Organization on Security Assurance and Acquisition/Use of Tested/Evaluated Products: Recommendation of the National Institute of Standards and Technology. NIST Publications, Computer Security Division, NIST: Gaithersburg, MD. Available at the NIST Web site: www.nist.gov.

NIST SP 800-26 (November 2001). Security Self-Assessment Guide for Information Technology Systems. NIST Publications, Computer Security Division, NIST: Gaithersburg, MD. Available at the NIST Web site: www.nist.gov.

NIST SP 800-30 (January 2002). Risk Management Guide for Information Technology Systems. NIST Publications, Computer Security Division, NIST: Gaithersburg, MD. Available at the NIST Web site: www.nist.gov.

NIST SP 800-42 (October 2003). Guideline on Network Security Testing. NIST Publications, Computer Security Division, NIST: Gaithersburg, MD. Available at the NIST Web site: www.nist.gov.

NIST SP 800-55 DRAFT (July 2003) Security Metrics Guide for Information Technology Systems. Published by: Computer Security Division, NIST: Gaithersburg, MD. Available at the NIST Web site: www.nist.gov.

NIST SP 800-26 (Revised April 2005). System Questionnaire with NIST SP 8000-53, Recommended Security Controls for Federal Information Systems References and Associated Security Control Mappings. NIST Publications, Computer Security Division, NIST: Gaithersburg, MD. Available at the NIST Web site: www.nist.gov.

NSTISSP, Number 11 (January 2000). National Policy Governing the Acquisition of Information Assurance (IA) and IA-Enabled Information Technology Products. NSTSSC Secretariat (I42) NSA: 9800 Savage Road, Fort Meade, MD.

Paulk, Mark C. (1996). Effective CMM-Based Process Improvement. © 1996 by Carnegie Mellon University. Available at ftp://ftp.sei.cmu.edu/pub/cmm/Misc/effective-spi.pdf.

Public Law 100-107 (signed into law on August 20, 1987). The Malcolm Baldrige National Quality Improvement Act of 1987. A paper copy of this document will be mailed if requested from nqp@nist.gov.

Pyzdek, Thomas (2003). *The Six Sigma Handbook, Revised and Expanded: The Complete Guide for Greenbelts, Blackbelts, and Managers at All Levels, 2nd edition.* McGraw-Hill: New York, NY.

Software Engineering Institute at Carnegie Mellon (March 2002). Capability Maturity Model® Integration (CMMI℠), Version 1.1 for Systems Engineering, Software Engineering, Integrated Product and Process Development, and Supplier Sourcing (CMMI-SE/SW/IPPD/SS, V1.1). Carnegie Mellon University: Pittsburgh, PA.

Technical Report, CMU/SEI-95-TR-015, ESC-TR-95-015 (October 1995). The Unified Information Security (INFOSEC) Architecture by Fred Maymir-Ducharme, P.C. Clements, Kurt Wallnau, and Robert W. Krut, Jr., Software Engineering Institute: Carnegie Mellon University, Pittsburgh, PA. Available at http://www.sei.cmu.edu/pub/documents/95.reports/pdf/tr015.95.pdf.

Web Sites

http://www.isograph-software.com/rwbovertel.htm for information on reliability analysis.

http://www.relexsoftware.com/resources/prmodels.asp for information on reliability analysis.

http://www.nsa.gov/ for Microsoft and Cisco security recommendation guides.

http://www.ietf.cnri.reston.va.us/html.charters/bmwg-charter.html for IETF Benchmarking Methodology Working Group information.

http://www.benchmarkingnetwork.com/ for information on benchmarking.

http://www.isixsigma.com/library/.

http://www.quality.nist.gov/index.html for information on Baldrige Quality Award Program.

http://csrc.nist.gov/asset/#ASSET for information on ASSET, the NIST automatic assessment tool.

http://www.sei.cmu.edu/cmm/cmms/cmms.html for information on Capability Maturity Model.

*CMM and Capability Maturity Model are registered in the U.S. Patent and Trademark Office. CMM Integration: CMMI is a service mark of Carnegie Mellon University.

ISSE Domain 2

CERTIFICATION AND ACCREDITATION

This domain is separated into two chapters. Chapter 8 covers the DoD Information Technology System Certification and Accreditation Process (DITSCAP) and the National Information Assurance Certification and Accreditation Process (NIACAP). Chapter 9 provides an overview of NIST Special Publication 800-37, "Guide for the Security Certification and Accreditation of Federal Information Systems."

Technological advances allow Federal Information System (IS) users to access and process information at various locations virtually anywhere in the world. An important result of this progress is the increased distribution of information and processes, which allows information to flow across multiple systems. It does not matter if users access the system through a local area network (LAN), a wide area network (WAN), or as remote users through a variety of mechanisms including Virtual Private Networks (VPNs) or virtual LANs (VLANs). The challenge for the U.S. Government (USG) and thus the information assurance practitioners is to provide and **ensure** an effective level of protection in this distributed and interconnected environment.

At the same time, it is necessary to meet the mission and functional needs of the organization and to do this, regardless of budget constraints, while taking into account the required security controls. Certification and Accreditation (C&A) is one of those processes that assist agencies in meeting and verifying that required protection needs are implemented and operational.

Contributors and Reviewers

Susan Hansche contributed, reviewed, edited, and finalized the material in this domain. She would like to thank the following individuals for also contributing and reviewing some or all of the material in this domain:

> **Robert B. Batie**, CISSP, ISSAP, ISSEP, CISM, contributed the initial research and draft of the DITSCAP material. He is a Security Engineering Manager for Raytheon NCS, St. Petersburg, Florida.
>
> **Larry L. Buickel**, CISSP, provided review and edits. Larry is an enterprise security consultant with Graphic Example Technologies, Inc., Austin, Texas.
>
> **K. Greg Duncan,** CISSP, contributed the initial research and draft of the NIST SP 800-37 material and reviewed the DITSCAP/NIACAP chapter. He is a Senior Information Assurance Engineer for Booz, Allen & Hamilton, McLean, Virginia.
>
> **Raed H. Hammad,** CISSP, contributed the initial research and draft of the NIACAP material. He is a Senior Information Security Analyst for Northrop Grumman Information Technology — Federal Enterprise Solutions of Herndon, Virginia.
>
> **Steven Rodrigo**, CISSP, provided a review of the DITSCAP, NIACAP, and NIST SP 800-37 material. He is a Senior Systems Security Analyst at Tenacity Solutions, Herndon, Virginia.

8

DITSCAP and NIACAP

Introduction

Although it may seem like the United States Government (USG) is facing new challenges in creating a security management framework that addresses regulations and policy controls, it is not. For quite some time, the USG has provided Federal policies and regulations to manage Federal information resources — including C&A policies, standards, and guidance such as the DoD Information Technology System Certification and Accreditation Process (DITSCAP); the National Information Assurance Certification and Accreditation Process (NIACAP); and NIST Special Publication 800-37, Guide for the Security Certification and Accreditation of Federal Information Systems. The benefits of these processes are to reduce risk through the use of a standard approved process and to reduce documentation and training through standard forms and a single procedure. Before looking at the DITSCAP/NIACAP standards, first we will look at the C&A policy requirements.

The E-Government Act (Public Law 107-347) (December 2002) recognized the importance of information security to the economic and national security interests of the United States. Title III of the E-Government Act, entitled "Federal Information Security Management Act" (FISMA), requires each federal agency to develop, document, and implement an agency-wide information security program to provide information security for the information and information systems that support the operations and assets of the agency, including those provided or managed by another agency, contractor, or other source. FISMA, along with the Paperwork Reduction

Act of 1995 and the Information Technology Management Reform Act of 1996 (Clinger-Cohen Act), explicitly emphasizes a risk-based policy for cost-effective security.

In support of this legislation, the Office of Management and Budget (OMB) requirements of Circular A-130 call for all information systems (IS) that operate to have their relevant management, operational, and technical controls assessed and accredited. Circular A-130 requires executive agencies within the federal government to (1) plan for security, (2) ensure that appropriate officials are assigned security responsibility, (3) periodically review the security controls in their information systems, and **(4) authorize system processing prior to operations and, periodically, thereafter**. Specifically, it states that the authorization (i.e., accreditation) of a system to process information, granted by a management official, provides an important quality control. By authorizing processing in a system, the Designated Approving Authority accepts the risk associated with it. More information on the OMB and Circular A-130 can be found in Chapter 11.

It is important to note that although the intent of DITSCAP and NIACAP was to standardize the process, the material was developed with adaptability to relate to multiple organizations. Users of DITSCAP/NIACAP are encouraged to make process modifications to meet the specific needs of their agency. The processes are not meant to have agencies change the way they do business, but rather to offer a common reference point and guidance to ensure that systems with security interests are operating in a secure computing environment.

In this chapter, the Information Systems Security Engineering Professional (ISSEP®) can expect to gain an understanding of the need for C&A, knowledge of DITSCAP and NIACAP, and how to use these processes to accredit USG information systems. To show knowledge and comprehension of C&A, the ISSEP should be able to describe the DITSCAP/NIACAP phases and explain the key roles in the C&A process. In addition, from an analysis perspective, the ISSEP should be able to differentiate the applicability of USG regulations with respect to C&A.

Note that DITSCAP and NIACAP operate on the same principles; thus, in this chapter, the activities of the two standards are combined. If there are specific differences between the two requirements, they are noted.

Note to ISSEP candidates: Questions refer to both and can be worded such as "According to DITSCAP and NIACAP, the negotiation activities include...." Although the (ISC)² exam requirements do not currently list NIST SP800-37 as a required study document, it has been adopted by Federal agencies for C&A activities related to systems processing unclassified information. Because of this, it is included as a separate chapter. ISSEP candidates are encouraged to watch the exam requirements for inclusion of this policy.

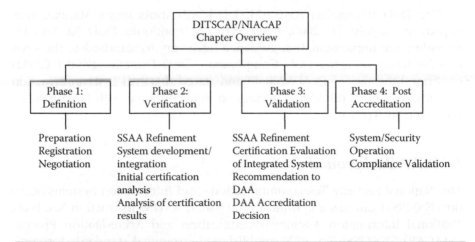

Figure 8.1 Chapter overview.

This chapter represents the essentials of DITSCAP and NIACAP as shown in Figure 8.1. It starts with an overview of the two models and a few key definitions that can be helpful in understanding the various phase activities and tasks. It continues with an explanation of the four distinct DITSCAP/NIACAP phases and highlights the activities that should be completed during each phase of the C&A process. Keep in mind that this chapter provides summary information. If the ISSEP candidate wishes to review more detailed information, refer to DoD 8510.1-M, DITSCAP Application manual, and NSTISSI No. 1000.

DITSCAP and NIACAP Overview

To gain a better understanding of DITSCAP and NIACAP, a brief background and overview is provided for each. In addition, a few key terms are defined.

DITSCAP Background

In December 1997, DoD Instruction 5200.40, "DoD Information Technology Security Certification and Accreditation Process (DITSCAP)," was released. It created the C&A process for security of unclassified and classified information systems. This standard C&A process is designed to meet the policies defined in DoD Directive 5200.28 (now 8500.1); Public Law (P.L.) 100-235 (1987), "Computer Security Act of 1987"; OMB A-130, Appendix III; and DoD Directive 5220.22.

The DoD Instruction 8510.1-M, DITSCAP Applications Manual, was approved on July 31, 2000. DoD 8510.1-M continues DoD 5200.40 by providing the implementation guidance necessary to standardize the C&A process throughout the DoD Components. DoD Directive 8500.1 (2002) confirmed the use of DoD 5200.40 and stated that "All DoD information systems shall be certified and accredited in accordance with DoD Instruction 5200.40" (p. 6).

NIACAP Background

The National Security Telecommunications and Information Systems Security (NSTISS) Committee in August 2000 issued NSTISS Instruction No. 1000, "National Information Assurance Certification and Accreditation Process (NIACAP)." NSTISSI No. 1000 establishes the minimal standards for certifying and accrediting IT systems with a national security interest. The primary purpose of NIACAP is to protect and secure the national security systems and other elements that make up the Civilian Government infrastructure. NSTISS has since been renamed the Committee of National Security Systems (CNSS).

DITSCAP/NIACAP Definition

DITSCAP/NIACAP establishes a standard process, set of activities, general tasks, and management structure to certify and accredit systems that will maintain the Information Assurance (IA) and security posture of a system or site. For DITSCAP, this is the Defense Information Infrastructure (DII). For NIACAP, this is USG national security systems. Although the original intent of NIACAP was to address the C&A of classified Federal systems (not DoD systems), the process was authored with an aim at adaptability and is often used to certify and accredit systems of multiple classification levels and computing environments. These processes focus on an enterprisewide view of the information system in relation to the organization's mission and the business case. They are designed to certify that the information system meets documented accreditation requirements and will continue to maintain the accredited security posture throughout the system life cycle.

The first item for the ISSEP to remember is that in accordance with (IAW) DoD 8500.1, the implementation of DITSCAP is mandatory for all systems that process both DoD classified and unclassified information; and under NSTISSP No. 6 (April 1994), "National Policy on Certification and Accreditation of National Security Telecommunications and Information Systems," NIACAP is mandatory for all systems that process USG classified information.

There are three types of accreditation:

1. *System accreditation:* evaluates a major application or general support system.
2. *Site accreditation:* evaluates the application and systems at a specified, self-contained location.
3. *Type accreditation:* evaluates an application or system that is distributed to a number of different locations. For type accreditation, the System Security Authorization Agreement (SSAA) must be prepared and shipped to every site, along with the hardware and software. After installation, the site will include the SSAA in its site accreditation package. Each site is not required to repeat the baseline tests that were conducted during the type accreditation effort.

To achieve C&A, DITSCAP/NIACAP activities are designed to support an infrastructure-centric approach, with a focus on the mission, environment, and architecture. For a system in development, the intent of the phases is to define, verify, validate, accredit, and monitor information systems with the following specific objectives:

■ Identify appropriate security requirements (Definition, Phase 1).
■ Design the information system to meet those requirements (Validation, Phase 2).
■ Test the design against the same requirements (Verification, Phase 3).
■ Monitor the accredited system for changes (Post Accreditation, Phase 4).

DITSCAP/NIACAP supports the evaluation of mission requirements versus risk requirements. According to DoD 8510.I-M, the nine characteristics include:

1. *"Tailorable.* The process applicable to any system regardless of the system status in its life cycle or shift in program strategy (grand design, incremental, or evolutionary).
2. *Scalable.* The process is applicable to systems differing in security requirements, size, complexity, connectivity, and data policies.
3. *Predictable.* The process is uniformly applicable to any system. It minimizes personal opinion and subjectivity.
4. *Understandable.* The process provides the participants with a consistent view of the security requirement compliance of the system.
5. *Relevant.* The process facilitates the identification of security requirements and solutions that are achievable.

6. *Effective.* The process results in and maintains an accreditation for the target system.
7. *Evolvable.* The process allows for incorporating lessons learned, changes in security policy and technology, in a manner that meets the schedule of the mission.
8. *Repeatable.* The process provides corresponding results when applied or reapplied to similar IS.
9. *Responsive.* The process accommodates timely responses essential for supporting emergent Military Department (MILDEP) and national operational requirements and priorities (p. 24)."

Definitions

The following provides a brief definition of a few key terms directly related to C&A activities.

Certification

DoD 8510.1-M (2000, p. 9) defines certification as "the comprehensive evaluation of the technical and non-technical security features of an IS and other safeguards made in support of the accreditation process, to establish the extent to which a particular design and implementation meets a set of specified security requirements."

Accreditation

Accreditation is defined as "the formal declaration by a Designated Approving Authority (DAA) that an IS is approved to operate in a particular security mode using a prescribed set of safeguards at an acceptable level of risk" (DoD 8510.1-M, 2000, p. 8).

Program Manager

The *program manager* indicates the manager currently responsible for the system. The program manager does not necessarily indicate the system owner, system manager, or the system user representative; it is the person designated in the C&A process as the person responsible for the system.

Designated Approving Authority (DAA)

The Designated Approving Authority (DAA — Accreditor) is the official with authority to formally assume responsibility for operating an automated information system (AIS) or network at an acceptable level of risk.

Security Manager

Sometimes called the Information Systems Security Manager (ISSM) or the Information Systems Security Officer (ISSO), the *security manager* usually conducts or assists with the risk assessment and preparation of C&A documentation.

Certification Agent (CA)

The *certification agent* (CA) is responsible for making the technical judgment of a system's compliance with stated security requirements. The CA signs the certification package and prepares the accreditation package.

User Representative

The interface to the user community is through a *user representative* who represents the interests of the users in all C&A issues. The user representative should provide the common voice in identifying the users' roles, responsibilities, and capabilities. The user representative should, at a minimum, review and approve the security requirements, assurance factors, certification results, and any proposed security features.

System Security Authorization Agreement (SSAA)

The SSAA is the cornerstone of DITSCAP/NIACAP and serves as the tracking document for C&A activities. The SSAA consists of multiple sections and appendices that outline the operation and features of the system. It is considered a binding agreement as to the level of security on a system. Also, during development and post accreditation, the SSAA serves as the baseline security configuration document for the system. The SSAA can also be used to identify all relevant costs associated with the C&A process.

The DITSCAP/NIACAP model includes four well-defined phases, running from the initial concept throughout the system's life cycle, commonly referred to as the "cradle-to-grave" concept. The four phases are:

> *Phase 1: Definition.* This phase occurs at the initiation of the project or at the initial C&A effort of a legacy system. It entails the definition of activities, practices, and procedures to certify, accredit, and maintain the security posture of an information system. Phase 1 activities verify the system mission, environment, and architecture, and identify threats. The levels of effort are defined and the DAA and Certification Authority are identified. The security of the system

is defined and documented in the initial SSAA. The end product of Phase 1 is a documented agreement between the C&A team (i.e., program manager, DAA, Certifier, security manager, and user representative) on the approach and results of Phase 1 activities.

Phase 2: Verification. Based on the security defined in Phase 1, the verification phase ensures that the design of the system meets all of the requirements identified in the SSAA. An important activity in the verification phase is to confirm that the evolving system development and integration complies with the agreements between role players documented in the first phase. Phase 2 solidifies the SSAA, which serves as a focal point of the C&A process. The C&A agreements are documented in the SSAA and used to channel and document the results.

Phase 3: Validation. In this phase, the activities provide a sanity check through security tests, government acceptance testing, and operational tests and evaluations. Validation begins once the system has been fully integrated. This phase confirms that the system is in compliance with the SSAA. The intent of this phase is to produce the appropriate documentation and results to support the DAA in the accreditation decision. Validation culminates in an Approval To Operate (ATO).

Phase 4: Post accreditation. Post accreditation follows the system from integration or installation and continues through its operational life until its ultimate retirement. The final phase includes activities to monitor system management, configuration, and changes to the operational and threat environment to ensure that an acceptable level of residual risk is preserved. Security management, configuration management, and periodic compliance validation reviews are conducted. Changes to the system architecture, environment, or operations may warrant beginning a new C&A cycle. The final phase continues until reaccreditation, which is required every three years or until the system has been removed from service.

The cyclical nature of the DITSCAP/NIACAP process and its required inputs and milestones are detailed in Figure 8.2. The remainder of the chapter defines in more detail the activities and tasks of each phase.

Phase 1: Definition

Phase 1 initiates the C&A process by acquiring or developing the information necessary to understand the system and then, using that information,

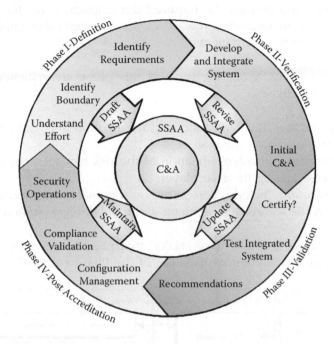

Figure 8.2   DITSCAP/NIACAP phases.

to plan the C&A tasks. The system can be either a modification to an existing system caused by change in mission need, operational requirements, or business case, or a new information system fulfilling a new mission.

Phase 1 activities verify the system mission, environment, and architecture; identify the threat; define the levels of effort; and, identify the key members and organizations that will be responsible for C&A. It ends with a documented agreement between the various parties that becomes a one part of the Security System Authorization Agreement (SSAA). The SSAA is fundamental to all phases of the C&A process and is discussed throughout the chapter.

The objectives of Phase 1 are to:

■ Define the level of effort for the C&A.
■ Identify and agree on the intended system mission, security requirements, and C&A boundary effort.
■ Identify, assign, and agree on the resources required for the principle C&A roles and responsibilities.
■ Review, define, and understand the system's mission, architecture, and environment.

- Define and prepare the required documentation for the C&A.
- Produce an agreement (i.e., SSAA) on the method of implementing the security requirements.

As shown in Figure 8.3, the goals of this phase are achieved through three primary activities:

1. *Preparation.* Involves collecting information and gathering documentation about the system.
2. *Registration.* Involves initiation of the risk management agreement process among the role players.
3. *Negotiation.* Includes agreement on the implementation strategy to satisfy the security requirements identified during system registration.

Each of these activities have "tasks" that need to be completed. The next topics provide further explanation of the Phase 1 activities and tasks.

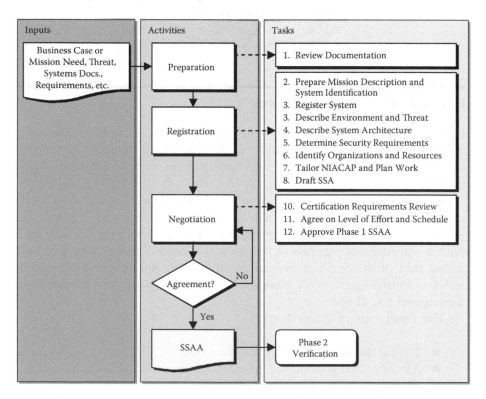

Figure 8.3   Phase 1 overview.

Preparation Activity

The **preparation** activity involves the collection of information and documentation about the system. For a system development the C&A team collects information on the capabilities and functions the system will perform, the desired interfaces and the associated data flows, the information to be processed, hardware and software considerations, operational organizations that will be supported, and anticipated operational threats. If the system is already in operation, the review may include additional information, such as how the system is performing, existing hardware and software applications, how interfaces and data flows are controlled, etc.

DoD 8510.1-M (2000, p. 35) notes that the gathering of information can be done by reviewing and analyzing a variety of sources, including the:

- Business case
- Mission need statement
- System specifications
- Architecture and design documents
- User manuals
- Operating procedures
- Network diagrams
- Configuration management documentation
- Threat analysis
- Federal and organizational IA and security instructions and policies

Once this initial document review and preparation activity has been completed, the next activity in Phase 1 is the *registration activity*.

Registration Activity

The **registration** initiates the risk management agreement process among the key players of the C&A process, such as the approving authority, systems owners, and certifiers. The information gained from the Preparation activity is evaluated and applicable IA requirements are determined. The risk management and vulnerability assessment actions begin and the level of effort required for C&A is determined and planned. Registration begins with preparing the system description and identification, and it concludes with preparing an initial draft of the SSAA.

The eight registration tasks guide the evaluation of information necessary to address the risk management process in a repeatable, understandable, and effective manner. The requirements and level of effort are guided by the degree of assurance needed. Registration tasks consider security services such as integrity, availability, confidentiality, and account-ability. Registration tasks also consider the system development approach, system life-cycle stage, existing documentation, and system business func-tions. Finally, the registration tasks take into account the environment (including the threat assessment), architecture, users, data classification and categories, external interfaces, and mission criticality.

It is necessary to complete the eight tasks in Table 8.1 during the registration activity. A brief definition of each task is provided.

Registration Task 1: Prepare Business or Operational Functional Description and System Identification

As defined in DoD 8510.1-M (2000), "The system and functional description and system identification task describes the system mission and functions, system capabilities and Concept of Operations (CONOPS). While the details of the system may not be clear at the outset of system development, the mission needs should provide a starting point. From the information obtained, the system's general concept and boundaries should be fairly well understood. In either developing or obtaining the system description, knowing what is not part of the system is as important as knowing what is part of the system (p. 40)."

The description and identification will include (DoD 8510.1-M):

- *System identification.* Identify the system being developed or enter-ing the C&A process.
- *System description.* Describe the system, focusing on the informa-tion security relevant features of the system.
- *Functional description and capabilities.* Describe the system clearly delineating what functions are expected in the fully accredited system.
- *System capabilities.* Clearly define the capabilities expected in the fully accredited system and the mission for which it will be used.
- *System criticality.* Define the system criticality and the acceptable risk for the system in meeting the mission responsibilities.
- *Classification and sensitivity of data.* Define the type and sensitivity of data processed by the system.
- *System users.* Define the users' security clearances, their access rights to specific categories of information processed, and the actual information that the system is required to process.

Table 8.1 Phase 1 Registration Tasks

Task	Action
1	Registration begins with preparing the business, mission, or operational functional description as well as system description and system identification. The information collected during the preparation activity is evaluated and applicable information assurance requirements are determined.
2	Inform the DAA, certifier, and user representative that the system will require C&A support (register the system).
3	Prepare the environment and threat description. Threats should be assessed against specific business functions based on the specific system description. The threat and subsequent vulnerability assessments, must be used in establishing and selecting the IA policy objectives that will counter the threat.
4	Prepare system architecture description, describe the C&A boundaries, and document relationships with external systems or equipment.
5	Determine the system security requirements. The risk management and vulnerability assessment actions commence.
6	Tailor the C&A tasks, determine the level of effort, and prepare a C&A plan. The C&A team determines the level of effort by evaluating the security requirements and the degree of assurance needed in areas such as confidentiality, integrity, availability, and accountability. The planned level of effort is targeted at addressing the security requirements and fulfilling the mission of the program.
7	Identify organizations involved in the C&A and the resources required.
8	Develop the draft SSAA. Tasks conclude with preparing an initial draft of the SSAA. A draft SSAA will need to be developed during the registration activities to consider the program's system development approach and life-cycle stage, existing documentation and environment, architecture and business functions, and other documentation pertaining to users, data classification, and categorization.

- *System life cycle.* Define the system life cycle and where the system is in relationship to its life cycle.
- *System CONOPS.* Describe the system CONOPS, including functions performed jointly with other systems.

Registration Task 2: Inform the DAA, Certifier, and User Representative That the System Will Require C&A Support (Register the System)

The objective of this task is to identify the individuals (or other agencies) and their responsibilities in the C&A process and notify them of the status of the system.

Because security is the concern of everyone affiliated with an organization, the C&A of the system includes many organizational elements within the agency. When the process includes a wider audience, the organization's management is better able to manage risks based on the agency's mission and not an objective important to only one or two organization elements.

The ISSEP should identify at least four specific roles to participate in the C&A process: (1) program manager, (2) DAA, (3) certifier, and (4) user community representative. Table 8.2 provides a condensed overview of the roles and responsibilities for each C&A phase. These are important ingredients in the quest for C&A, and these roles can play a pivotal role in the success of the process.

Obviously, agencies have the option to add additional roles to increase the integrity and objectivity of the process. However, this core group is responsible for tailoring and scoping the C&A effort specific to the organization's mission, operating environment, system architecture and threats, as well as business concerns such as funding and schedule development of a new system.

Program Manager

The program managers' role is critical because it is intended to represent the interests of the system throughout its life-cycle management. The manager may represent numerous organizations within this life cycle because of the maturation a product goes through. All aspects of coordination throughout this process are the responsibility of the program manager. The program manager is also responsible for schedules, costs and performance, and informing the other team members of status. During the second phase, the program manager assumes an information liaison responsibility by providing details of the system to the DAA, certifier, and user representative. During the final phase, the program manager ensures that appropriate configuration management practices are in place for the certification-ready system.

DAA

The DAA is the principal government official responsible for implementing the system in a favorable security posture. The DAA is an upper-level manager who has the authority and ability to evaluate the mission, business case, and budgetary needs of the system, while also considering the security risks. This is the person who would be responsible for determining a system's acceptable level of residual risk. Upon receipt of the accreditation package, the DAA determines whether the system is to be accredited, given Interim Authority To Operate (IATO), or denied accreditation because the system's risks are not at acceptable levels to proceed to an operational state.

Certifier

The certifier(s) are considered the technical experts of the C&A process and can be an individual or an entire team. The certifiers determine whether a system is ready to undergo certification and then use their expertise to conduct the system certification. The certification is the comprehensive evaluation of both technical and nontechnical security features of the system based on the requirements documented in the SSAA. Once the certification effort concludes, the certifier is responsible for providing the DAA with a certification report and a recommendation for certification options. To ensure an objective opinion or recommendation, the certifier should be an independent party not affiliated with the organization.

User Representative

The final role is the user representative. This group ensures that the operational interests of the system are maintained. The user groups serve as advocates for attributes such as system availability, access, performance, integrity, and functionality. Because users can be found at all levels of an organization, this group is responsible for representing the entire user community and serves as a liaison between the certification process and community.

Table 8.2 Management Responsibilities by C&A Phases

Phase	Management Roles		Security Roles	User Roles
	Program Manager	DAA	Certifier	User Rep.
Phase 1	Initiate security dialogue with DAA, certifier, and user representative. Define system schedule and budget. Support C&A tailoring and level of effort determination. Define system architecture. Prepare life-cycle management plans. Define security architecture.	Define accreditation requirements. Obtain threat assessment. Assign the certifier Support C&A tailoring. Approve the SSAA.	Begin vulnerability and risk assessments. Review threat definition. Lead C&A tailoring. Determine level of certification effort. Describe certification team roles and responsibilities. Draft SSAA.	Support C&A tailoring and level of effort determination. Define operational needs in terms of mission. Identify vulnerabilities to mission. Define operational resource constraints.
Phase 2	Develop system or system modifications. Support certification activities. Review certification results. Revise system as needed. Resolve security discrepancies.	Support certification activities.	Conduct certification activities. Assess vulnerabilities. Report results to the program manager, DAA, and user representative. Determine if system is ready for certification. Update the SSAA.	Prepare security Rules of Behavior (ROB) and Standard Operating Procedures (SOP). Support certification actions.

Phase 3	Support certification activities. Provide IS access for ST&E. Provide system corrections under configuration management. Support certification efforts. Implement and maintain SOP and ROB. Review certification results.	Assess vulnerabilities and residual risk. Decide to accredit, IATO, or terminate system operations.	Conduct certification activities. Evaluate security requirements compliance. Assess vulnerabilities and residual risk. Report results to the program manager, DAA, and user rep. Recommend risk mitigation measures. Prepare final SSAA. Recommend accreditation type.	Assess vulnerabilities and support certification efforts. Implement and maintain SOP and ROB. Review certification results.
Phase 4	Update IS to address Phase 3 reported vulnerabilities and patches under configuration management. Report security-related changes to the IS to the DAA and user representative. Review and update life-cycle management policies and standards. Resolve security discrepancies.	Review the SSAA. Review proposed changes. Oversee compliance validation. Monitor C&A integrity. Decide to reaccredit, accredit, IATO, or, if SSAA is no longer valid, terminate system operations.		Report vulnerability and security incidents. Report threats to mission environment. Review and update system vulnerabilities. Review and change security policy and standards. Initiate SSAA review if changes to threat or system.

Note: Based on NSTISSI No. 1000 (2000) and DoDI 8510.1-M, (2000, p. 138).

Registration Task 3: Prepare the Environment and Threat Description

As defined in DoD 8510.1-M, task 3 is defined as "the environment and threat description task describes the operating environment, system development environment, and potential system threats. The description of the operating environment should address all relevant parts of the system's environment, including descriptions of the physical, administrative, development, and technical areas. The description should also include any known or suspected threats specifically directed at the described environment (p. 43)."

The **operating environment** is defined as "the physical, personnel, communications, emanations, hardware, software, and procedural security features that will be necessary to support site operations. Operating environment security involves the measures designed to prevent unauthorized personnel from gaining physical access to equipment, facilities, material, and documents and to safeguard the assets against espionage, sabotage, damage, and theft (p. 43)."

The **system development environment** is defined as "the system development approach and the environment within which the system will be developed. The system development approach is an information security strategy that incorporates security into each phase of a system's life cycle (p. 44)."

The **potential system threats** are the "potential threats and single points of failure that can affect the confidentiality, integrity, and availability of the system. Clearly state the nature of the threat that is expected and where possible, the expected frequency of occurrence" (p. 45).

Registration Task 4: Prepare System Architecture Description and Describe the C&A Boundary

As defined in DoD 8510.1-M, the system architecture task is defined as "the system hardware, software, firmware, and interfaces. This description contains an overview of the internal system structure including the anticipated hardware configuration, application software, software routines, operating systems, remote devices, communications processors, network, and remote interfaces. The system architecture includes the configuration of any equipment or interconnected system or subsystem of equipment used in the automatic acquisition, storage, manipulation, management, movement, control, display, switching, interchange, transmission, or reception of data or information and includes computers, ancillary equipment, software, firmware, and similar procedures and services, including support services and related resources (p. 50)." Further definitions for this task include (p. 50–51):

- *System hardware.* Describe the target hardware and its function.
- *System software.* Describe the operating system(s), database management system(s), and software applications and how they will be used.
- *System firmware.* Describe the firmware that is stored permanently in a hardware device that allows reading and execution of the software, but not writing or modifying it.
- *System interfaces.* Describe the system's external interfaces, including the purpose of each external interface and the relationship between the interface and the system.
- *Data flows.* Describe the system's internal interfaces and data flows, including the types of data and the general methods for data transmission. Describe the specific transmission media or interfaces to other systems.
- *Accreditation boundary.* Describe the boundary of the system.

Registration Task 5: Determine the System Security Requirements

DoD 8510.1-M defines task 5 as "the National, DoD and data security requirements, governing security requisites, network connection rules, and configuration management requirements. The DAA, Certifier, program manager, and user representative must reach an agreement on the security for the system and certification level based on these requirements and the CRR. The requirements may have significant cost and schedule impacts that need to be resolved in the negotiation activity (p. 46)."

Further task definitions include (DoD 8510.1-M, p. 46–48):

- *Applicable instructions or directives.* Determine the security instructions or directives applicable to the system.
- *Data security requirements.* Determine the type of data processed by the system.
- *Security concept of operations.* Describe the security CONOPS, including system input, system processing, final outputs, security controls and interactions, and connections with external systems. Include diagrams, maps, pictures, and tables in the security CONOPS.
- *Network connection rules.* Identify any additional requirements incurred if the system is to be connected to any other network or system.

■ *Configuration management.* Determine if there are any additional requirements based on the Configuration Management Plan.

■ *Reaccreditation requirements.* Determine if there are unique organizational requirements related to the reaccreditation or reaffirmation of the approval to operate the system.

■ *Requirements Traceability Matrix (RTM).* Analyze the directives and security requisites to determine the system security requirements. Take a section of a directive and parse it into a basic security requirement statement. The security requirements can then be entered into a RTM to support the remainder of the C&A effort.

The RTM is an important element of the ISSE model and C&A process. The more complex the system or sensitive the data, the more comprehensive the requirement's evaluation must be. Because of its importance, a brief description of how to write not only an RTM, but also a security RTM is included.

Security Requirements Traceability Matrix (RTM)

When developing the RTM, the first step is to analyze the policies, directives, and security requisites to determine the system security requirements. For information on how to determine the basic security requirements, refer to DoD Instruction 8500.2, "Information Assurance (IA) Implementation" (February 2003), section E3.4 Elements of a DoD Information System IA Program. Essentially, the requirements are based on the Mission Assurance Category (MAC I, II, or III), information classification or sensitivity, and need to know. These three categories identify security requirements based on how critical the information is to the mission of the organization.

As noted in DoD 8500.2 there are security controls mandatory for each MAC category. For example, DoD information systems with a MAC I rating have 70 total IA controls: 32 for integrity and 38 for availability. An example is shown in Table 8.3.

These types of security controls can be entered into an RTM to support the remainder of the C&A effort. The RTM is used to track the source of the requirement, the requirement statement, any related requirements and a review method. As shown in Table 8.4, from DoDI 8510.1-M, if applicable, the requirements number will show the category, and the requirement column will describe the control from DoD 8500.2. The review method column identifies the review process for each requirement. The review methods are defined as follows:

Table 8.3 MAC I Information Assurance (IA) Control Example

Subject Area	Security Design and Configuration/Availability
Control number, name, and text	DCAR-1 Procedural Review
IA service	An annual IA review is conducted that comprehensively evaluates existing policies and processes to ensure procedural consistency and to ensure that they fully support the goal of uninterrupted operations.

- ■ I: Interview
- ■ D: Document Review
- ■ O: Observation
- ■ T: Test

You may find it helpful to remember the review methods by using the acronym DOIT.

The RTM is used to develop the Certification Test and Evaluation (CT&E) procedures used in Phase 2 and the System Test and Evaluation (ST&E) procedures used in Phase 3. CT&E is conducted during Phase 2. It is usually required for systems, or components of the system within a specific configuration that will be used for multiple deployments of the same configuration or type accreditation activities. ST&E evaluates the correct implementation of the security mechanisms in the final stages of development. The RTM must be satisfied regardless of the certification level of effort.

Registration Task 6: Tailor the C&A Tasks, Determine the C&A Level of Effort, and Prepare a C&A Plan

DoD 8510.1-M defines task 6 as determining the appropriate certification level and adjusting the C&A activities to the program strategy and system life cycle. Tailoring the security activities to system development activities ensures that the security activities are relevant to the process and provide the required degree of analysis. Tailoring permits the C&A to remain responsive to operational requirements and priorities.

Before the C&A plan can be developed, the level of effort required to certify and accredit the system needs to be determined. The level of effort is determined based on the certification level required for the system, particularly because the system could range from a simple stand-alone personal computer, to a large data center running dozens of applications on varied hardware platforms, to a complex distributed multilevel secure system.

Table 8.4 Example of the Security RTM

REQ No.	Requirement	Source	Related Requirement	I	D	O	T	Comments
	1.0 General							
	1.1 Fundamental Computer Security Requirements							
Fundamental 1	Requirement 1 – SECURITY POLICY – There must be an explicit and well-defined security policy enforced by the system.	TCSEC, INTRO p.3 TNI 2.2.1	DOJ 2640.2C-14	X	X	X		See FUND 2–6
Fundamental 2	Requirement 2–Marking Access control labels must be associated with objects...	TCSEC, INTRO p.3	TCSEC 2.2.1.1	X	X	X		See DAC 1–DAC 6
	1.2 General Requirements							
General 1	Agencies must implement and maintain a program to assure that adequate security is provided for all agency information collected, processed, transmitted, stored, or disseminated in general support systems and major applications.	OMB Circular A-130 Appendix III A.3 (referenced)		X	X		X	

(Review Method* columns: I, D, O, T)

Source: From DoDI 8510.1-M, 2000, p. 49.

"To determine the appropriate level of certification, the Certifier must analyze the:

■ System business functions
■ National, departmental (i.e., DoD), and service or agency security requirements
■ Criticality of the system to the organizational mission
■ Software products
■ Computer infrastructure
■ Data processed by the system
■ Types of users" (DoD 8510.1-M, p. 30)

Based on this preliminary information, the Certifier begins to determine the degree of CIA and accountability required for the system.

DITSCAP/NIACAP has four levels of certification to provide the flexibility for appropriate assurance within schedule and budget limitations. The DITSCAP/NIACAP certification tasks must be performed at one of these four levels of certification. Table 8.5 provides more detail on the four Certification Levels (CLs). The CLs are:

■ CL 1 Basic Security Review
■ CL 2 Minimum Analysis
■ CL 3 Detailed Analysis
■ CL 4 Extensive/Comprehensive Analysis

Again, before beginning the C&A process, the first step is to determine the targeted certification level of the system, so that the depth and level of the DITSCAP/NIACAP activities are based on the appropriate level.

Table 8.5   Certification Levels

Certification Levels	Level Certification/Level Description
1 Basic Security Review	Level 1 requires completion of the minimum security checklist. The system user or an independent certifier can complete the checklist.
2 Minimum Analysis	Level 2 requires the completion of the minimum security checklist and independent certification analysis.
3 Detailed Analysis	Level 3 requires the completion of the minimum security checklist and a more in-depth, independent analysis.
4 Extensive Analysis	Level 4 requires the completion of the minimal security checklist and the most extensive independent analysis.

Source: From DoD 8510.1-M, 2000, p. 53.

Table 8.6   Weighted Value Characteristics

	Characteristic	Evaluation Criteria	Weighted Values
1	Interfacing mode	Does the system interact with other systems and to what degree: benign, passive or active?	Weighted 0–6
2	Processing mode	Is the mode of operation dedicated, systems high, multilevel, or multi-lateral?	Weighted 1–8
3	Attribution mode	How complex is the accountability of the system required to identify, verify, and track entities from rudimentary to comprehensive?	Weighted 0–6
4	Mission reliance	Is the mission partially or completely reliable on the system?	Weighted 0–7
5	Availability	How long can the system be down before operations are affected?	Weighted 1–7
6	Integrity	Is the data accuracy approximate or exact?	Weighted 0–6
7	Information categories	Classifications such as Confidential, Secret, Top Secret, or SCI	Weighted 0–8

Source: From DoD 8510.1-M, 2000.

To determine the CL, the C&A team examines seven system characteristic values. These characteristics are shown in Table 8.6. The level is determined by combining the data classification and weighted values.

Points are assigned to the characteristics of the system, with the higher points assigned to the more complex, critical, and severe mission systems and data. The total weights are calculated for the system and the CL is determined based on the total score within the weighted value range. Table 8.7 provides an example of how to complete the weighted analysis.

In our example shown in Table 8.8, a weighted value of 22 would indicate a certification level of 2 or 3. Remember that a CL1 is for weighted values less than 16 and CL4 is for weighted values higher than 38. Thus, for this system, the weighted value would be presented to the DAA and data owner to make the final determination whether the CL would be 2 or 3. The results of the CL analysis help determine which requirements will be evaluated and to what extent.

Although the C&A process will be similar for any type of system, the analysis and level of effort needed will vary. From an ISSE perspective,

Table 8.7   System Characteristics and Weights

Characteristic	Alternatives and Weights	Weight
Interfacing mode	Benign (w = 0), Passive (w = 2), Active (w = 6)	
Processing mode	Dedicated (w = 1), System High (w = 2), Compartmented (w = 5), Multilevel (w = 8)	
Attribution mode	None (w = 0), Rudimentary (w = 1), Selected (w = 3), Comprehensive (w = 6)	
Mission reliance	None (w = 0), Cursory (w = 1), Partial (w = 3), Total (w = 7)	
Availability	Reasonable (w = 1), Soon (w = 2), ASAP (w = 4), Immediate (w = 7)	
Integrity	Not-applicable (w = 0), Approximate (w = 3), Exact (w = 6)	
Information categories	Unclassified (w = 1), Sensitive (w = 2), Confidential (w = 3), Secret (w = 5), Top Secret (w = 6), Compartmented/Special Access Classified (w = 8)	
	Total of all weights	

Source: From DoD 8510.1-M, p. 53.

Table 8.8   Example of CL Determination

Characteristic	Definition	Weighted Value
Interfacing mode	Processing MAC II data in a passive mode	2
Processing mode	System is classified as High	2
Attribution mode	Selected attribution mode	3
Mission reliance	Partial mission reliance	3
Availability	Availability is partial	3
Integrity	Must meet requirements above approximate	4
Information categories	Classified as Secret	5
	Total	22

the analysis should be simplified to ensure that the appropriate level of resources is applied to the C&A effort.

The ISSEP should *not* confuse the C&A certification levels with those of the Common Criteria. The C&A levels are distinguished from Common Criteria security functional requirements in that the former apply to the definition, configuration, operation, interconnection, and disposal of DoD information systems. They form a management framework for the allocation, monitoring, and regulation of IA resources that is consistent with Federal guidance provided in OMB Circular A-130 (2000). In contrast, Common Criteria security functional requirements apply only to IA and IA-enabled IT products that are incorporated into information systems. They form an engineering language and method for specifying the security features of individual IT products and for evaluating the security features of those products in a common way that can be accepted by all.

The last step of task 6 is to document the C&A plan. DoD 8510.1-M (2000, p. 60) defines this as preparing a C&A plan that documents the tailoring and defines the activities required for the C&A process. The tasks, milestones, and schedule must be consistent with the system development or maintenance schedule. The level of effort and roles and responsibilities must also be consistent with the program development process and management plan. The DAA, Certifier, program manager, and user representative must review the SSAA and C&A plan to ensure that the C&A effort is consistent with program schedules. The DAA must receive certification evidence in sufficient time to review the material and make an informed decision regarding the approval to operate the system.

Registration Task 7: Identify Organizations That Will Be Involved in the C&A and Identify Resources Required

This task identifies the appropriate authorities, resource, and training requirements and determines the certification team's roles and responsibilities. The C&A process may involve many organizations spanning a number of roles (DoD 8510.1-M, p. 51).

Task 7 definitions include (DoD 8510.1-M, p. 50–51):

- *Organizations.* Identify the organizations, individuals, and titles of the key authorities in the C&A process.
- *Resources.* Identify the resources required to conduct the C&A. If a contractor is involved or individuals from other government organizations are temporarily detailed to assist in the C&A process, funding requirements must be defined and included in the SSAA.
- *Resources and training requirements.* Describe the training requirements, types of training, who is responsible for preparing and

conducting the training, what equipment is required, and what training devices must be developed to conduct the training. Funding for the training must be identified.

■ *Other supporting organizations.* Identify any other organizations or working groups that are supporting the C&A process.

Registration Task 8: Develop the Draft SSAA

The final step in the registration activities is preparation of the SSAA. DoD 8510.1-M outlines this task as "this task completes the SSAA document. As each Phase 1 task is completed, a section of the SSAA is prepared. These sections must be assembled into the formal SSAA document. The certification team is responsible for the preparing the SSAA. After the document is completed, the draft SSAA is submitted to the DAA, Certifier, program manager, and user representative for their review. The draft SSAA establishes a reference for discussions during negotiation (p. 60)."

The Security System Authorization Agreement (SSAA)

The Security System Authorization Agreement (SSAA) is the cornerstone of DITSCAP/NIACAP and serves as the tracking document for C&A activities. The SSAA consists of multiple sections and appendices that outline the operation and features of the system. It is considered a binding agreement as to the level of security on a system. Also, during development and post accreditation, the SSAA serves as the baseline security configuration document for the system.

The initial SSAA is developed during the registration activity of Phase 1 and updated during each of the remaining phases. It flows with the project throughout the life cycle and is considered a living document. It chronicles the development of the systems from inception to retirement and tracks all the changes and modifications to the system. The SSAA can be written by any number of security personnel, including the ISSO, ISSE, ISSM, or someone from a commercial contracting organization tasked with the C&A responsibilities.

The SSAA should contain the following elements:

■ Organization's missions
■ Security requirements
■ Risk assessment
■ Concept of operations
■ Level of effort
■ Schedule

- Describe the operating environment while identifying the threats that may exist
- Describe the system security architecture
- Documented the C&A boundaries
- Documented formal agreement among role players
- Documented accreditation requirements
- Consolidated documentation requirements
- Documented the C&A process
- Test plans, risk management plans, and certification results

The SSAA preparation must involve all representatives, including the CA, program sponsor, threat specialist, etc. The draft is used as a guide to establish the basis for discussions during the negotiation activities between the C&A representatives (i.e., DAA, the CA, the program manager, and the user representative).

The SSAA is intended to reduce the need for extensive documentation by consolidation of security-related documentation into one document. That eliminates the redundancy and potential confusion as multiple documents describe the system, security policy, system and security architecture, etc. When feasible, the SSAA can be tailored to incorporate other documents, such as appendices, or by reference to the pertinent document.

In accordance with DoD 5200.40 (1997), paragraph E3.3.5.2 specifies that each IT system is required to have an SSAA. The physical characteristics of the SSAA will depend on the system class and level of effort needed for C&A. The SSAA can be as simple as a single coordinated message or as complex as a detailed system security plan. For generic accreditations, a single SSAA can be prepared for the system, but the description of the operating environment will need to reflect each proposed operation location. The goal is to produce an SSAA that will be the basis of agreement throughout the system's life cycle.

Appendices shall be added to include system C&A artifacts. Optional appendices can be added to meet specific needs. Include all documentation that will be relevant to the system's C&A that is acceptable by the DAA during negotiations.

Table 8.9 lists the documents that make up the SSAA and the organization responsible for its development. The system's developer can be the ISSO operations organization, someone from the PM's office, or a government contractor. The SSAA is intended to be a living document that binds the agreement on the level of security of the system. The SSAA is intended to steer and capture the results of C&A and thus is discussed throughout the duration of this chapter.

After completing all the registration tasks, the next activity in Phase 1 is negotiation.

Table 8.9 SSAA Document Guide

	Description	Responsible Organization
Main SSAA	The format and content include: • Mission Description and System • Identification, Environmental Description • Systems Architecture Description • System Security Requirements • Organization and Resources • C&A Workplan	System Dev., PM
Appendix A	Acronym list	System Dev, PM
Appendix B	Definitions	System Dev, PM
Appendix C	References	System Dev, PM
Appendix D	System Concept of Operations	System Dev, PM
Appendix E	Information Systems Security Policy	System Dev, PM
Appendix F	Security requirements and/or Requirements Traceability Matrix (RTM)	System Dev, PM
Appendix G	Certification Test and Evaluation Plan and Procedures	System Dev, PM
Appendix H	Security Test and Evaluation Plan and Procedures	System Dev, PM
Appendix I	Applicable System Development Artifacts or Systems Documentation	System Dev, PM
Appendix J	System rules of behavior	System Dev, PM
Appendix K	Incident Response Plan	System Dev, PM
Appendix L	Contingency plan(s)	System Dev, PM
Appendix M	Personnel controls and technical security controls	System Dev, PM
Appendix N	Memorandums of Agreement (MOAs) for systems interconnect	Between different orgs. or DAAs
Appendix O	Security Education Training and Awareness Plan	System Dev, PM

Table 8.9 (continued)   SSAA Document Guide

	Description	*Responsible Organization*
Appendix P	Test and Evaluation Report	Certifier, System Dev.
Appendix Q	Residual Risk Assessment Results	Certifier
Appendix R	Certification and Accreditation Statement	Certifier

Negotiation Activity

The third activity in Phase 1 is negotiation. The purpose of **negotiation** is to ensure that the SSAA drafted during the registration activity properly and clearly defines the approach and level of effort. During negotiation, all participants develop an understanding of their roles and responsibilities. Essentially, during this activity, all participants involved in the systems development, acquisition, operation, security certification, and accreditation reach agreement on the implementation strategy to satisfy the security requirements identified during system registration.

The participants are the DAA, Certifier, program manager, and user representatives. The DAA conducts a complete review of the draft SSAA to determine that all applicable IA and security requirements are included. The Certifier conducts an evaluation of the technical and nontechnical security features of the IS based on the negotiated certification level of effort. The Certifier is the technical expert that documents trade-offs between security requirements, cost, availability, and schedule to manage security risk. The program manager reviews the SSAA for accuracy, completeness, costs, and schedule considerations. The user representative reviews the SSAA to determine if the system will support the user's mission and that appropriate security operating procedures will be available at system delivery. All participants are responsible for reviewing the proposed certification level and resource requirements to determine that the appropriate assurance is being applied.

The negotiation tasks are:

- Task 1: Conduct the Certification Requirements Review (CRR).
- Task 2: Agree on the security requirements, level of effort, and schedule.
- Task 3: Approve final Phase 1 SSAA.

Negotiation Task 1: Conduct the Certification Requirements Review (CRR)

The CRR task provides an opportunity for the DAA, Certifier, program manager, and user representative to discuss the system functionality, security requirements, level of effort, and planned C&A scheduled. The CRR must result in an agreement regarding the level of effort and the approach that will be taken to implement the security requirements (DoD 8510.1-M).

Before the Phase 1 activities are complete, the primary participants agree on the strategy for implementing security requirements documented in the initial draft of the SSAA. They conduct a CRR to review and approve all information contained in the SSAA, such as mission and system information, operational and security functionality, operational environment, security policy, system security requirements, known security risks, problems, or deficiencies, and other security-relevant information.

Negotiation Task 2: Agree on the Security Requirements, Level of Effort, and Schedule

As part of the negotiation activity, the participants agree to the level of effort and schedule needed to complete the C&A activities. This may also include reviewing the objective and parameters of the program, such as cost, schedule, and accuracy. The final step is to have the DAA make a decision on the Phase 1 SSAA that approves the system functionality, operating environment, development environment, potential threats, security requirements, system architecture, organization and resource requirements, tailoring factors, certification level, and C&A plan.

Negotiation Task 3: Approve Final Phase 1 SSAA

The final step is to have the DAA make a decision on the Phase 1 SSAA, which approves the system functionality, operating environment, development environment, potential threats, security requirements, system architecture, organization and resource requirements, tailoring factors, certification level, and C&A plan (DoD 8510-1M).

The negotiation activity should be used to ensure needs are met while also ensuring the security posture of the system. It is imperative that an agreement is reached during this activity. Otherwise, progress will stall at the negotiation stage until an agreement is reached. Thus, negotiation ends when the responsible organizations adopt the SSAA and concur that those objectives have been reached.

In this section, the three main activities of Phase 1 — preparation, registration, and negotiation — were outlined. The roles and responsibilities of the DAA, Certifier, program manager, and the users were also discussed. The results of Phase 1 activities are documented in the draft SSAA, which will continue to be modified and updated throughout the remaining phases.

One final task that is often overlooked is to get a signed copy of the SSAA. Often, the DAA is reluctant to sign, while the C&A team may be reluctant to push for the signing. However, having a signed copy of the SSAA provides an indication that the C&A team is ready to move to the next phase.

Phase 2: Verification

Phase 2, Verification, is intended to **verify** that the evolution of the system complies with the risk management requirements as detailed in the SSAA. The activities and tasks in this phase document compliance of the system with previously agreed-on security requirements. Oftentimes, this phase is used as an opportunity for the C&A team to conduct an initial C&A assessment of the system.

The Verification phase is used as a performance measure during system development and modification to ensure that security requirements are met. This is done by certification analysis and then an assessment of the certification results. The first two phases heavily depend on each other, considering the verification charter in Phase 2 is contingent on compliance with the agreements, as outlined in the SSAA, and definitions defined in Phase 1.

Verification is conducted using many of the techniques identified in the Validation activity, such as certification analysis. Among the main objectives of this phase are to refine the SSAA and allow for modifications to the system prior to the validation phase. The revisions should be ongoing throughout the phase and should capture all changes and results of the certification analysis.

This section discusses Phase 2 activities. These activities occur between the signing of the initial version of the SSAA and the certification of the system or components (beginning of Phase 3). Phase 2 activities include:

1. SSAA refinement
2. System development and integration
3. Initial certification analysis
4. Analysis of the certification results

Within each activity are tasks that must be completed. After each task is completed, a Task Analysis Summary Report is prepared. The Task Analysis Summary Report activities include (DoD 8510.1-M):

1. Recording the findings
2. Evaluating the vulnerabilities discovered during evaluations
3. Summarizing the analysis level of effort
4. Summarizing the tools used and results obtained
5. Making recommendations (p. 68)

Conducting an initial certification analysis during the initial design stage can verify that the system design has included the SSAA requirements. During the system development phase, performing the certification analysis tasks can help indicate whether the integration phase will meet the security requirements. Essentially, conducting incremental verifications throughout the life cycle is better than waiting until the product is completed and would be costly to change or modify. The activity can be considered a pre-test to ensure that the system is ready to undergo the security test and evaluations activities. Also, the initial assessments can verify the development, modification, and integration efforts will result in high probability of favorable results during Phase 3.

The Verification phase complements the functional testing certification tasks that occur during system validation. The process flow of Phase 2 and its required inputs and activities are detailed in Figure 8.4.

SSAA Refinement Activity

Phase 2 starts with a review of the SSAA and ends with an updated SSAA. As the system development activity progresses and details of the system evolve, the certification effort examines the updated system and its design. All Phase 2 activities are tailored to meet the certification level defined in Phase 1.

DoD 8510.1-M notes that as more details about the hardware and software architecture become available, the design information should be added to the SSAA as justification to support the agreed-on level of certification actions. When completed, the security test plans and procedures are added to the SSAA. Security testing resource estimates should be reviewed and refined as Phase 2 activities continue. Vulnerability Evaluation Reports and Analysis Summary Reports are included as part of the evidence package. Should any changes occur to the security posture proposed in the approved SSAA, these changes must be submitted to the DAA, certifier, program manager, and user representative for approval and inclusion in the revised agreement.

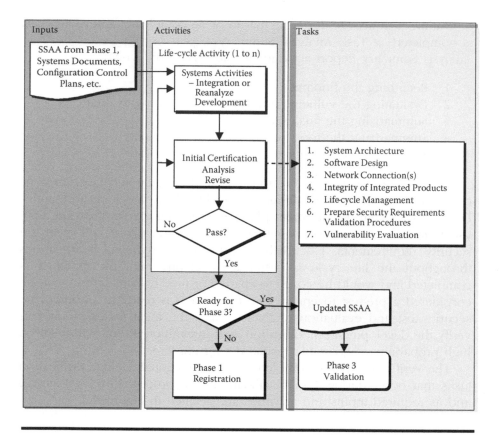

Figure 8.4   Phase 2 overview.

System Development and Integration Activity

System development and integration activities are those activities required for development or integration of the system's components. According to DoD 8510.1-M, the specific activities will vary, depending on the overall program strategy, the life-cycle management process, and the position of the system in the life cycle. During system development and integration, there are corresponding certification analysis tasks. These activities verify the requirements in the SSAA are met in the evolving system before it is integrated into the operating environment.

Initial Certification Analysis (ICA) Activity

The initial certification verifies by analysis, investigation, and comparison methodologies that the system design implements the SSAA requirements. Phase 2 initial analysis tasks complement the functional testing certification tasks that occur during Phase 3. The following tasks are part of the initial certification analysis:

- System architecture analysis
- Software design analysis
- Network connection rule compliance analysis
- Integrity analysis of integrated products
- Life-cycle management analysis
- Security requirements validation procedures preparation
- Vulnerability assessment

The goal of reviewing this information prior to validation is to reduce any known or expected issues before the official test and evaluation is conducted in Phase 3. These specific tasks will be seen again in Phase 3 and are added to the Minimal Security Activity Checklist (MSAC). Certification tasks are tailored to the system development activities to ensure that they are relevant to the process and provide the required degree of analysis to ensure conformance with the SSAA.

Initial Certification Analysis Task 1: System Architectural Analysis

The objective of this task is to compare the system architecture with the architecture description in the SSAA. DoD 8510.1-M defines this task as "reviewing network connections and interfaces, system application specifications and requirements. The system architecture analysis task verifies how well the security requirements defined in the SSAA are integrated into the system security architecture. The security architecture should state clearly which requirements are to be implemented by the system architecture and which requirements will be satisfied within the system's operating environment. Analysis of system level information reveals how effectively the security architecture implements the security policy and requirements. The interfaces between this and other systems must be identified. These interfaces must be evaluated to assess their effectiveness in maintaining the security posture of the infrastructure (p. 68)."

Initial Certification Analysis Task 2: Software, Hardware, and Firmware Design Analysis

This task evaluates how well the software, hardware, and firmware reflect the specified technical security requirements and the security architecture of the system. In addition, the design of the security-critical software, hardware, and firmware is reviewed to identify and evaluate vulnerabilities. To complete this task, a detailed analysis of software, hardware, and firmware specifications and design documentation is conducted. If appropriate, the

Trusted Computing Base (TCB) is identified and analyzed for proper and full implementation of the security requirements. The activities in the task include assessing whether the critical security features (identification and authentication, access controls, auditing, etc.) are implemented correctly and completely.

Initial Certification Analysis Task 3: Network Connection Rule Compliance Analysis

DoD 8510.1-M defines this task as "evaluating the intended connections to other systems and networks to ensure that the system design will enforce specific network security policies and protect the system from adverse confidentiality, integrity, availability, and accountability impacts. The connection of an information system to a network requires that the particular system will not adversely affect the network's security posture. Connection also requires that the network will not adversely affect the information systems own security posture (p. 74)."

Initial Certification Analysis Task 4: Integrity Analysis of Integrated Products

This task evaluates the integration of commercial-off-the-shelf (COTS), government-off-the-shelf (GOTS), and other hardware or software to ensure that the integration complies with the system security architecture while maintaining the integrity of each product. "Oftentimes, the integration of other products can detrimentally affect the security of a system. Integrity analysis of products being integrated into the system must identify the security functionality of each product. The certification team should verify the product security functionality to confirm that the needed security functions are present and properly integrated into the system. This task determines whether or not evaluated products are being used for their intended purpose. Product integrity analyses must include an examination of system and subsystem interfaces, product evaluations by the National Institute of Standards and Technology (NIST) or the National Computer Security Center (NCSC), information flows, and applicable use of selected product features" (DoD 8510.1-M, p. 77).

Initial Certification Analysis Task 5: Life-Cycle Management Analysis

This task verifies that the configuration management and change control practices are in place and sufficient to safeguard the authenticity of the

Table 8.10 System Life-Cycle Management Documentation

1	Life-Cycle Management Plan
2	Configuration Identification Procedures
3	Configuration Control Procedures
4	Configuration Status Accounting Procedures
5	Configuration Audit Procedures and Reports
6	Software Engineering Procedures (development approach and engineering environment)
7	Trusted Distribution Plans

Source: From DoD 8510.1-M, p. 80.

security-related hardware and software. Configuration Management (CM) is an important process for tracking changes to the information system throughout its life cycle.

According to DoD 8510.1-M (2000, p. 80), "in some cases, the security requirements may dictate special needs for the development environment and the development or integration team (cleared facilities or cleared programmers). If this is the case, the development approach, procedures, and environment are assessed during the system development and again at the operational site (p. 80)."

It is also used for version control and to baseline any changes to the SSAA during the systems life-cycle development. This process may require examining the types of documents or procedures shown in System Life-Cycle Management Documentation (Table 8.10).

Initial Certification Analysis Task 6: Security Requirements Validation Procedure Preparation

In this task, the certification team writes the procedures to be used in Phase 3 to validate compliance with all the defined technical security requirements. The security requirements document should identify the type of review required to validate each requirement: test, observation, document review, or interview. Many organizations use an RTM to identify the applicable security requirements and the appropriate method to validate the requirements. At certification Level 1, the test procedures may be a detailed checklist. At certification Levels 2 through 4, a test, observation, document review, or interview should verify compliance with each requirement. If test procedures are prepared (either mandated by policy or at the DAA discretion), they should be added to the SSAA" (DoD 8510.1-M, p. 82).

Initial Certification Analysis Task 7: Vulnerability Assessment

This task evaluates the security susceptibility with regards to confidentiality, integrity, availability, and accountability while recommending appropriate countermeasures. DoD 8510.1-M states that "in Phase 2, the vulnerability assessment concentrates on the sufficiency to the specified technical security requirements to protect and secure the information resources (p. 84)."

During the vulnerability assessment, weaknesses of the system are identified. If appropriate to the size of the system, a vulnerability assessment is conducted to evaluate the system architecture, design, any network interfaces, and integration of components in the operational system. Also, the configuration management practices are analyzed to determine susceptibility to exploitation by any related threat.

Many analysts tend to focus on weaknesses in software applications. The USG has put increasing pressure on software vendors to deliver more security features and not release software unless it has been extensively tested for vulnerabilities, such as buffer overflows. For example, an October 2003 Microsoft press release noted that Chief Executive Officer Steve Ballmer, in a conference speech, highlighted the need for security innovation, pointing out that patches and guidance are only part of the solution and that as exploits become more sophisticated the technology must evolve to become more resilient. Microsoft's approach is to design new safety technologies that will enable customers to more effectively protect their computers from malicious attacks even if patches do not yet exist or have not yet been installed.

Conducting vulnerability assessments can be complex. Many factors can influence the outcome, such as the knowledge of the team conducting the assessment. If the team is very familiar with the operating system, applications, hardware, or other components, they will be able to identify vulnerabilities easier and quicker. One method of beginning the assessment is to create a vulnerability table as shown in Table 8.11. The

Table 8.11 Vulnerability Table

System Data Attributes and Vulnerabilities/Risks			
Data Attribute	Sensitivity	Description	Vulnerability
List of telephone numbers for personnel	FOUO	Data integrity issues	Data field is stored in cleartext. By default, all employees have change access to the application fields.

vulnerability table simply documents the information on the system, key characteristics, and the vulnerability.

Vulnerability assessments can be conducted using techniques such as flaw hypothesis, fault-injection, and threat-vulnerability pairing. Flaw hypothesis includes conducting both a system analysis and penetration test. The system analysis determines the functions of the real or planned system and how it relates to any other system. To conduct the penetration test, the first step is to review the information from the system analysis, such as the system specifications and documentation, and produce a list of hypothetical flaws. For example, using a specific version of a software product might allow a buffer overflow attack to occur; thus, this would be included in the list. This list is then prioritized based on several factors: the estimated probability that the flaw exists, the ease of exploiting it, the potential reward to the exploiter, the related threat, and any residual risk. Determination of the potential rewards to the exploiter should consider the sensitivity of the data and processes, criticality of system operation, time criticality, ability to recreate the data or processes, etc. The prioritized list of weaknesses is used to perform penetration testing of the system. Depending on the agreement for conducting the penetration test, a weakness may try to be exploited to verify whether the vulnerability does indeed exist based on the environment and configuration of the system. Using the flaw hypothesis technique (sometimes referred to as fault-tree) can determine the ability of attackers to exploit the vulnerabilities.

The fault-injection technique involves deliberately adding faults to the system and then analyzing how the system responds. This technique is conducted in the design and development phases and would not be used once the system is operational.

The threat-vulnerability pairing is determined by ranking the evaluated vulnerabilities against threat, ease of exploitation, potential rewards to the exploiter, and a composite of the three areas. All risks must be identified and evaluated. The evaluation should indicate the operational impacts associated with these risks. Appropriate countermeasures must be determined for each of the high-risk vulnerabilities.

When Phase 2 initial certification analysis is completed, several items should have been determined and documented. They include the system security specification, comprehensive test plan and procedures, and written assurance that all network and other interconnection requirements have been determined. When systems are being deployed to multiple locations, their planned interfaces with other components of the operating environment must be verified. All COTS and GOTS products used in the system design must be evaluated to ensure that they have been integrated properly and that their functionality meets the security and operational needs of the system. Life-cycle management plans must be analyzed to verify that sufficient plans and procedures are in place to maintain the security posture. If the system is being type accredited, CT&E plans and procedures are prepared as applicable, or ST&E plans and procedures for Phase 3 if another accreditation is being sought.

Analysis of the Certification Results Activity

Conducting an assessment of the certification analysis results completes the phase. At the conclusion of each development or integration milestone, the certification analysis results are reviewed and assessed. If the results indicate significant deviation from the SSAA, the C&A process should return to Phase 1 to resolve the problems. If the results are acceptable, C&A proceeds to the next task (or on to Phase 3).

The assessment should verify that:

- The system has documented security specifications, comprehensive test procedures, and written assurances that all network and other interconnection requirements have been implemented.
- When systems are being deployed to multiple locations, their planned interfaces with other components of the operating environment are secure.
- COTS and GOTS products used in the system have been integrated properly and their functionality meets the security and operational requirements of the system.
- Life-cycle management plans contain sufficient plans and procedures to maintain the security posture.
- Phase 3 test procedures are prepared as applicable.
- The vulnerability assessment identifies the residual risk.

Because C&A is a success-oriented process, the assessment of the certification analysis should also verify that the development, modification, and integration efforts will result in a higher probability of success for an accreditable information system prior to the Validation phase. The certification analysis results will be reviewed for SSAA compliance at the conclusion of each development or integration milestone. In the event that the initial certification and accreditation analysis indicates significant deviation from the SSAA, the C&A team member should return to the first phase to resolve outstanding issues; otherwise, the process will proceed to the Validation phase. Once all parties have agreed to the changes needed in the SSAA, a review will be conducted and agreement will be reached as defined in Phase 1. DITSCAP/NIACAP provides for a cyclical process and often asks for the process to return to the beginning phase to address concerns prior to proceeding to the next phase, Validation.

Phase 3: Validation

The third phase begins at the completion of system integration. This phase is intended to validate that the preceding efforts have produced a fully integrated information system that, In Its specific environment and con-figuration as specified in the SSAA, operates with an acceptable level of residual risk. The goal is to perform activities that will culminate in the accreditation of the post-integrated information system. Validation culmi-nates in an approval to operate. The process flow of Phase 3 and its required inputs and activities are detailed in Figure 8.5.

Phase 3 includes the following activities:

- SSAA refinement
- Certification evaluation of the integrated system
- Recommendation to DAA
- DAA accreditation decision

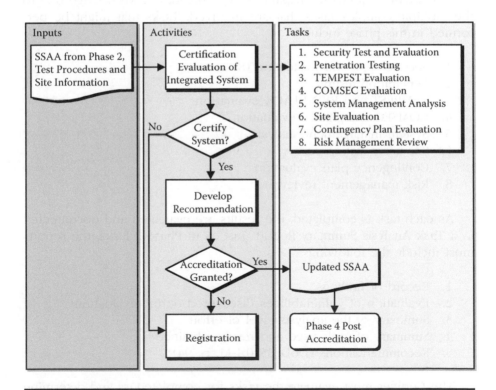

Figure 8.5   Phase 3 overview.

SSAA Refinement Activity

Phase 3 begins with a review of the SSAA to ensure that its requirements and agreements still apply. At each stage of the validation process, details are added to the documents reflecting the current state of the system. The SSAA review continues throughout Phase 3. Required changes must be submitted to the DAA, Certifier, program manager, and user representative so the revised agreement can be approved and implemented.

Certification Evaluation of the Integrated System Activity

This activity certifies that the fully integrated and operational system will comply with the requirements stated in the SSAA and the system will be operated with an acceptable level of residual risk. During this activity, certification tasks are performed to ensure that the system is functionally ready for operation. The certification tasks and the extent of the tasks will depend on the level of certification analysis in the SSAA.

This phase requires participants with a breadth of knowledge due to the multiple complex tasks that are involved. Tasks that might be performed in this phase include:

1. Security Test and Evaluation (ST&E)
2. Penetration testing
3. TEMPEST and RED-BLACK evaluation
4. COMSEC compliance evaluation
5. System management analysis
6. Site accreditation survey
7. Contingency plan evaluation
8. Risk management review

As each task is completed, the results are evaluated and documented in a Task Analysis Summary Report. Just as in Phase 2 tasks, the reports must include the following:

1. Record of findings
2. Evaluation of vulnerabilities discovered during evaluations
3. Summary of the analysis level of effort
4. Summary of tools used and results obtained
5. Recommendations (DoD 8510.1-M, p. 94)

The Certifier must evaluate the tasks for completeness and determine if the activity is consistent with the approach stated in the SSAA. The results of the completed task analysis, once documented, are then added to the SSAA. If problems occur while evaluating the integrated system, the Certifier must notify the program manager. If the problem can be fixed, the Certifier can repeat the task analysis activity. The problem and the solution must be included as part of the findings.

Certification Evaluation Task 1: Security Test and Evaluation (ST&E)

ST&E is geared toward assessing the technical implementation of the security design and to ascertain whether the security software, hardware, and firmware, which affect CIA and accountability, have been implemented according to the SSAA and are performing as intended. The objective of the ST&E is to validate the implementation of:

- Identification and Authentication (I&A)
- Audit capabilities
- Access controls
- Object reuse (resource control)
- Trusted recovery
- Network connection rule compliance

One might remember these categories from the Trusted Computer System Evaluation Criteria (TCSEC), commonly known as the "Orange Book." These categories are still important for conducting the ST&E of the system. Individual tests evaluate system conformance with the requirements, mission, environment, and security architecture.

The ST&E plans and procedures need to address all security requirements and produce sufficient evidence as to the amount of residual risk. This requires the C&A team to schedule and establish an ST&E Plan outlining what kind of tests must be performed and the objective of the tests, which is to validate the proper integration and operation of all security features.

Hands-on testing should focus on Trusted Computing Base (TCB) interfaces, system initialization, shutdown, and aborts to ensure that the system remains in a secure state. Because it is not feasible to include every possible input when testing a system, the tester should select those inputs that exercise every security module or every system security function and place stress on the system. Errors should be introduced to test if the system fails to perform its function when given invalid commands. If network connections are being used, the team should verify that the connection rules are enforced.

ST&E is similar to CT&E except ST&E focuses on the systems as it is installed at the deployed location where CT&E is completed in Phase 2 when type accreditation is being sought. When a system is developed for deployment to multiple locations, a type accreditation may be desirable. In this situation, a CT&E should occur at a central integration and test facility or at one of the intended operating sites, if such a facility is not available. Software and hardware security tests of common system components at multiple sites are not recommended. At the conclusion of the type accreditation CT&E, the test results, certifier's recommendation, and the type accreditation are documented in the SSAA. This SSAA is then sent with the software and hardware suite to each site where the system will be installed. The site will not need to repeat the baseline test conducted by the type accreditation effort. However, the system installation and security configuration should be tested at each operational site in the site ST&E.

Certification Evaluation Task 2: Penetration Testing

Penetration testing is recommended for systems with any criticality or complexity and requires CL 3 and/or CL 4 efforts. This testing is conducted on the system *after* installation and *before* accreditation. The objective of the testing is to assess the system's ability to withstand intentional attempts at circumventing the system's security features. Internal and external attempts will be made to exploit the technical security vulnerabilities. The results of the testing will be included in the Accreditation package.

Certification Evaluation Task 3: TEMPEST and RED-BLACK Verification

TEMPEST and RED-BLACK verification will validate that the physical equipment and site environment meet security requirements. TEMPEST and RED-BLACK evaluations are conducted on systems that process classified information only. Before a determination can be made on whether or not the system or site requires a TEMPEST (EMSEC) evaluation, the organization must complete the TEMPEST Requirements Questionnaire (TRQ). This questionnaire contains information about the physical security of the site, locations of classified processing systems, and percent of classified information being processed on the systems. It also includes how much control is needed and the amount of accessible or inspectable space available to protect the classified signals from emanating or radiating beyond the boundary of the controlled space.

The next step is for the Certified TEMPEST Technical Authority (CTTA) to review the TRQ. The CTTA determines whether TEMPEST countermeasures are needed and provides recommendations on how to control or suppress those signals. This could include no-cost techniques such as red and black separation, grounding, using shielded cables, fiber-optic cable, or a number of other protection controls. For systems that process higher levels of classified information, TEMPEST zoning or TEMPEST testing of the facilities or equipment may be required. The results of the TEMPEST activities are included in the accreditation package for DAA review.

Certification Evaluation Task 4: COMSEC Compliance Evaluation

Validation of Communications Security (COMSEC) Compliance ensures that NSA-approved COMSEC practices and key management procedures are in use. The validation ensures that COMSEC materials and procedures meet the requirements defined in the SSAA. COMSEC Compliance validation ensures that classified processing systems (signals/data) that traverse public spaces use NSA-approved Type 1 encryption or be in a protected distribution system. It also verifies that COMSEC keying material is properly controlled, stored, and handled within a physical environment that is certified to house the material, and that procedures are in place to provide guidance and direction to those personnel involved in the key management and distribution. COMSEC analysis evaluates how well these procedures are defined in the SSAA and how the architecture utilizes COMSEC within its security perimeter. Note that this type of analysis would not be required for CL1 because CL1 is valid for sensitive but unclassified information only.

Certification Evaluation Task 5: System Management Analysis

System management analysis is conducted to ensure that system security management procedures are in place, operational, and effective. During this analysis, the C&A team verifies that configuration management policies and programs consider security implications in all modifications to the accredited system baseline and operational concept. It determines whether the infrastructure adequately supports the maintenance of the environment, mission, and architecture as described in the SSAA. This includes the examination of documentation that may provide insight into the security operations of the site such as security policies, system and security management organizations, system operating procedures, incident response plans and procedures, virus detection procedures, configuration management, and security training and awareness. These components provide insight into security operations at the site.

Certification Evaluation Task 6: Site Accreditation Survey

A Site Accreditation Survey/Evaluation validates that site operations where the information system resides are in accordance with the SSAA. It ensures that the integration and operation of the system pose an acceptable risk to the information being processed. An analysis should be conducted of the site's operational procedures for the information system, personnel security, physical security, and overall environment to identify the existence of unacceptable risks to the information being processed. If the system is not confined to a fixed site (tactical or mobile systems and embedded systems in ships or aircraft), then the system must be examined in representative sites or environments.

Certification Evaluation Task 7: Contingency Plan Evaluation

A Contingency Plan Evaluation ensures that contingency plans are developed and provide reasonable continuity of information system support if events occur that prevent normal operations. The contingency plan analyzes the contingency, backup, and continuity of service plans to ensure the plans are consistent with the requirements of the SSAA. Note that periodic testing of the contingency plan is required by OMB A-130 (Ref. 1) and DoD 8500.1 for critical systems and is encouraged for all other systems.

Certification Evaluation Task 8: Risk Management Review

The risk management review assesses the operation of the system security design and architecture against the concept of operations, operational environment, information security policy requirements, and threats to ensure that risks to the CIA of the information and system are successfully maintained at an acceptable level. This includes the assessment of the system's vulnerabilities with respect to the documented threats, ease of exploitation, potential rewards, and probability of occurrence. The operational procedures and safeguards will be evaluated to gauge effectiveness and ability to offset risks.

The purpose of the risk management review is to determine if countermeasures are adequate to limit the probability of loss or the impact of loss is reduced to an acceptable level. For each residual risk, a statement should be made to indicate the rationale for accepting or rejecting the risk, as well as possible future modifications to resolve the problem. If future solutions are proposed, a tentative implementation schedule should be included. This is the final review before developing the recommendation to the DAA.

Accreditation Recommendations to DAA

This activity begins after completion of all certification tasks and ends with a system accreditation recommendation. The recommendation to the DAA is the consolidation of the findings developed during the certification of the integrated system and culminates with a submission of the certifier's report to the DAA. The certifier has three options to recommend:

1. The first option is when the certifier determines that the integrated system satisfies the SSAA security requirements and issues a *System Certification Statement*. The system certification statement certifies that the IS has complied with the documented security requirements. The certifier can also provide supplemental recommendations to improve the system's security posture to be used as input for future system enhancements and configuration management decisions.
2. In the second option, the certifier identifies deficiencies in the system but determines that the short-term system operations are within the bounds of acceptable risk. Thus, the certifier would recommend an Interim Authority to Operate (IATO), which is contingent upon the correction of the deficiencies in a predetermined period of time specified by the DAA. The recommendation of the certifier and the subsequent action or activities must be documented in the SSAA and an agreement obtained on the conditions under which the system can be operated and the date by when the deficiencies must be remedied.
3. Finally, if the certifier determines that the system does not satisfy the security requirements of the SSAA and that short-term risks place the system or its information in jeopardy, the certifier must recommend that the information system not be accredited.

DAA Accreditation Decision Activity

The final step in the pre-accreditation activities is the accreditation decision of the DAA. Once the DAA has received the certifier's recommendation, the DAA will review the SSAA and make an accreditation determination, which is then added to the SSAA. The SSAA accreditation package includes the certifier's recommendation, including security deficiencies and actions to resolve the deficiencies, as well as any risks to the operation of the system.

If the decision is to accredit, the decision will include security parameters under which the information system is authorized to operate. In some situations, the system may not meet the security requirements stated in the SSAA but mission criticality will mandate that the system become operational. If this occurs, DITSCAP/NIACAP allows for the issuance of an IATO. However, the DAA, Certifier, program manager, and user representative must agree to the proposed solutions, schedule, security actions, milestones, and maximum length of time for the IATO validity.

If the decision is to not accredit, the C&A process reverts to Phase 1, and the role players must reach agreement on the proposed solutions that meet an acceptable level of risk. The DAA must state the specific reasons for denial and, if possible, provide suggested solutions.

In some situations, a common set of software, hardware, and firmware is installed at multiple locations. Because it is difficult to accredit the common systems at all possible locations, the DAA may issue a type accreditation for a typical operating environment. The type accreditation is the official authorization to employ identical copies of a system in a specified environment. The SSAA must be modified to include a statement of residual risk and clearly define the intended operating environment. The SSAA must identify specific uses of the system, operational constraints, and procedures under which the system can operate. In that case, the DAA would include a statement with the accreditation, such as, "This system is supplied with a type accreditation. With the type accreditation, the operators assume the responsibility to monitor the environment for compliance with the environment as described in the accreditation documentation." The program manager, user representative, and ISSO should ensure that the proper security operating procedures, configuration guidance, and training are delivered with the system.

The final SSAA accreditation package will include the certifier's recommendation, the supporting documentation, and the DAA authorization to operate. When the system accreditation has been issued, the responsibility for the SSAA usually moves to the maintenance organization for the IS, such as the ISSO.

Phase 3 culminates with the accreditation of the system. Accreditation is granted to the system's owner when all security requirements are met and the system can operate at an acceptable level of residual risk. All systems have some vulnerability; uncovering and managing those vulnerabilities at an acceptable level is the overall objective of the C&A process. When the certifier recommends to the DAA an Approval/Authority To Operate (ATO), it is time for a modest celebration right after the signing party but before getting back to the business of maintaining the system security posture throughout the three-year accreditation period. Final comment: be sure to get the signature of the DAA on the signature page of the SSAA. Once the system has been accredited, Phase 4 begins. When the system accreditation is issued, it is also important to baseline and version control the SSAA so that any further revisions will be captured in a separate version of the document.

Phase 4: Post Accreditation

True or False? After all the hard work is completed in the first three phases, it is time to relax. Have you ever heard this statement: "If we can just get through C&A this year, then we'll be left in peace for the next three years?" Sometimes, C&A is viewed as a one-time event; however, a good system owner knows that the security of the system must be maintained. Essentially, if all of the phases were followed properly and the system is accredited for operation, the activities in Phase 4 may actually provide the key to realistically managing C&A for the life of the system.

The post-accreditation activities are the foundation of the fourth phase of the C&A process. The Phase 4 activities of maintaining the SSAA, system and security operations, management and compliance validation are required to continue to operate and manage the system so that it will maintain the acceptable level of residual risk. This level of residual risk is to be maintained throughout the life of the system. Keep in mind that Phase 4 is an ongoing activity and requires effort until a major change is planned for the system, a periodic compliance validation is required, or the system is removed from service. When a change is planned or a compliance validation is required, the C&A team would start the C&A process with Phase 1.

The process flow of Phase 4 and its required inputs/activities are detailed in Figure 8.6. Post accreditation activities include:

- System and security operation
- Compliance validation

System and Security Operation Activities

Systems and security operational requirements address the operational activity of the system in the computing environment. The requirements ensure that the information system is operating within the stated parameters of accreditation. The responsibility of the post-accreditation tasks fall within the realm of site operations staff, the user community, and the Information System Security Officer (ISSO). The ISSO is responsible for determining the extent to which a change will affect the security posture of the IS, obtaining approval of security-relevant changes, and documenting the implementation of that change in the SSAA and site operating

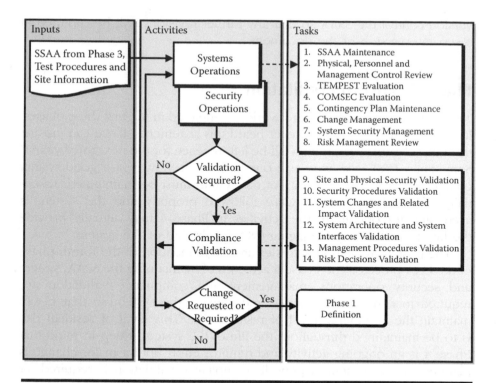

Figure 8.6 Phase 4 overview.

procedures. The users are responsible for operating the system under the security guidelines detailed in the SSAA.

The continuous nature of the secure system management task carries over to the evaluation of risk. Effective risk management requires continuous evaluation of threats that the system is exposed to, determines the capabilities of the system to minimize the risks (countermeasures), and balances additional security measures against cost and system performance. An important element of risk management is determining the acceptable level of risk based on the relationship of mission, environment, and architecture of the information system.

Secure system management is a continuous process that involves the users, ISSOs, acquisition or maintenance organizations, configuration management officials, and the DAA. These individuals are responsible for ensuring the following security tasks during the post-accreditation phase:

1. SSAA maintenance
2. Physical, personnel, and management control review

3. TEMPEST evaluation
4. COMSEC compliance evaluation
5. Contingency plan maintenance
6. Configuration management
7. System security management
8. Risk management review

After each task, a Task Summary Evaluation Report should be completed. The five items in the report are (8510.1-M):

1. Record of findings
2. Evaluation of vulnerabilities discovered during evaluations
3. Summary of the analysis level of effort
4. Summary of tools used and results obtained
5. Recommendations (p. 94)

The definitions for each task are from DoD 8510.1-M, Chapter 6.

System and Security Operation Task 1: SSAA Maintenance

Maintaining and updating the SSAA involves the ongoing review of the SSAA to ensure it remains current. When any changes occur to the system mission, the threat, operating environment, security architecture, or any operating procedures, those changes should be reflected in the SSAA.

System and Security Operation Task 2: Physical, Personnel, and Management Control Review

This review continues to analyze the operational procedures for the information system, environment concerns, operational procedures, personnel security controls, and physical security, which were analyzed in Phase 3. This task is targeted at ensuring none of the aforementioned pose any unacceptable risks to the information.

System and Security Operation Task 3: TEMPEST Evaluation

TEMPEST evaluation is a periodic verification to ensure that the equipment and site meet the TEMPEST and RED-BLACK security requirements. In situations that require this testing, an inspection must be completed to determine if adequate practices are being followed, and the equipment may be subjected to TEMPEST testing.

System and Security Operation Task 4: COMSEC Compliance Evaluation

COMSEC compliance evaluation determines that approved COMSEC key management procedures continue to be used. This task evaluates how well the SSAA-defined COMSEC requirements are integrated into the system architecture and site management procedures.

System and Security Operation Task 5: Contingency Plan Maintenance

Contingency plan maintenance includes the periodic review of the contingency plan and related procedures to ensure they remain current. A contingency plan should prepare for emergency response, incident response, backup operations, and post-disaster recovery.

Typically, the contingency plan and procedures consider natural disasters, enemy actions, or malicious attacks. An important aspect of contingency planning is ensuring that there are adequate resources available to support the continuity of operations in an emergency situation.

System and Security Operation Task 6: Configuration Management

Configuration management is required to maintain an acceptable level of residual risk. The changes to the information system and its operating environment must be controlled after its approval for operation. Although a change may adversely affect the overall security posture of the system and its infrastructure, it is an ongoing activity. System owners will deal with change as they respond to the needs of the user and new technology developments. Also, as the threats become more sophisticated, controls must be strengthened or added to provide adequate protection. Thus, configuration management is required to maintain an acceptable level of residual risk.

The strategy for managing change must be defined in the SSAA. The ISSO and system users must support the system configuration management process. The ISSO must review and approve changes relating to security and document the implementation of a change in the SSAA. Changes that significantly affect the system security posture must be forwarded to the DAA, certifier, user representative, and program manager for approval. In some agencies, a configuration management committee or board is responsible for approving all changes to the system.

System and Security Operation Task 7: System Security Management

System security management frequently examines the system management infrastructure to determine whether it continues to adequately support the maintenance of the environment, mission, and architecture as described in the SSAA.

System and Security Operation Task 8: Risk Management Review

Risk management review continues to assess the overall system security design, architecture, and other SSA requirements against the concept of operations, operational environment, and threats to determine that risk to CIA and accountability is maintained at an acceptable level. Known threats, as well as any new threats, must be analyzed to determine if the system still adequately protects against them.

According to 8510.1-M, possible changes to threats include:

1. A change in the IT mission or user profile
2. A change in the IT architecture, such as the addition of a LAN or WAN connection
3. A change in criticality or sensitivity level that causes a change in the countermeasures required
4. A change in the security policy
5. A change in the threat or system risk
6. A change in the activity that requires a different security mode of operation
7. A breach of security, a breach of system integrity, or an unusual situation that may invalidate the accreditation by revealing a flaw in security design
8. Results of an audit or external assessment (p. 123)

Compliance Validation Activity

All accredited systems are required to undergo a periodic review of the operational system and its computing environment to validate the system's security requirements, current threat assessment, and concept of operations. The compliance validation tasks ensure that the SSAA addresses the functional environment where the system has been placed.

The compliance validation tasks should repeat all the applicable Phase 2 and 3 tasks and, at a minimum, the following tasks should be completed:

1. Site and physical security validation
2. Security procedures validation
3. System changes and related impact validation
4. System architecture and system interfaces validation
5. Management procedures validation
6. Risk decisions validation

Phase 4 begins with the accreditation of the information system. This is what we have been waiting for — an accredited system operating at an acceptable level of residual risk. During this phase, the system is monitored for changes by utilizing periodic reevaluation techniques, such as risk assessments, audits, policy and procedure enforcement, and configuration management. The accreditation will be valid for a period of three years unless significant changes occur to the IS. At that time, the IS and C&A team will begin the C&A process, starting at Phase 1.

Summary

C&A is defined by the Office of Management and Budget (OMB) Circular A-130, Management of Federal Information Resources (Ref. 1), which mandates that all information systems (IS) that operate conduct an assessment of management, operational, and technical controls and also be accredited. Accordingly, the government has developed processes for organizations to use when having their information systems certified and accredited. This guidance includes DITSCAP, NIACAP, and SP 800-37.

This chapter reviewed the four phases of DITSCAP/NIACAP:

Phase 1: Definition
Phase 2: Verification
Phase 3: Validation
Phase 4: Post Accreditation

The process flow of all four phases along with required inputs and activities are detailed in Figure 8.7. Each provides a summary of the phases by providing an overview of the main inputs, activities, and associated tasks of each phase.

The C&A phases span from the initial system concept throughout the system's life cycle. Phase 1 Definition involves the definition of activities, practices, and procedures to certify, accredit, and maintain the security posture of an information system. During Phase 1, the SSAA is started and all members agree to the scope of the C&A process. The second phase, Verification, ensures that the design of the system meets all of the requirements identified in the SSAA. An important activity in the verification phase is to verify that the evolving system's development and integration

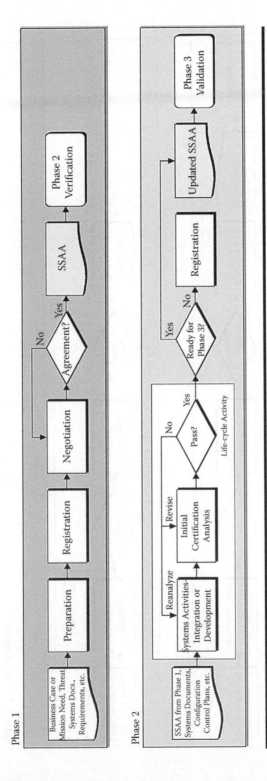

Figure 8.7 Phases summary.

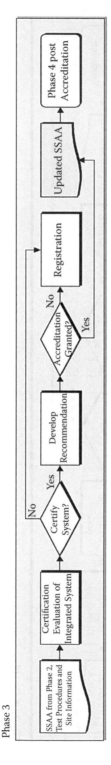

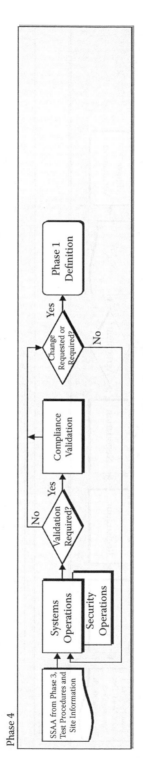

Figure 8.7 **(continued)**

is in compliance with the agreements documented in the first phase. Phase 2 solidifies the SSAA, which serves as a focal point for the C&A process. The third phase, Validation, provides a sanity check through security tests, government acceptance testing, and operational tests and evaluations. Validation begins once the system has been fully integrated. This phase confirms the compliance of the system in accordance with the SSAA. From this phase, the team produces the appropriate documentation to support the DAA in the accreditation decision. The fourth and final phase, Post Accreditation, encompasses the activities needed to ensure that the management, operation, and maintenance of the system adheres to the SSAA and operates at an acceptable level of risk. The final phase continues until reaccreditation, which is required every three years when major changes occur, or until the system is removed from service.

The process was developed for the Department of Defense and U.S. Government agencies, and establishes the minimal standards for certifying and accrediting IT systems with a national security interest. The government's aim was to produce an adaptable process providing standard activities, general tasks, and management structures while maintaining or enhancing the security posture of the system or site.

The ISSEP should have an understanding of the four phases and their individual inputs, activities, tasks, and targeted outputs. The ISSEP should understand the role of the SSAA and the importance of its accuracy. Finally, the ISSEP must be familiar with the roles needed to conduct C&A.

Author's Note: References for this chapter are provided at the end of Chapter 9.

9

C&A NIST SP 800-37

Introduction

The Certification & Accreditation (C&A) process requires a systemic perspective that is attentive to the dependencies of related processes, business activities, and interconnected information systems. Federal information systems are complex in nature; they are often distributed, utilize heterogeneous operating systems and hardware, and have data inputs and outputs between many sources. The C&A challenge for agencies is to determine whether their systems meet a standard, consistent, measurable level of security.

The National Institute of Standards and Technology (NIST) released Special Publication 800-37 (SP 800-37), "Guide for the Security Certification and Accreditation of Federal Information Systems," in May 2004. SP 800-37 guidelines are applicable to all Federal information systems other than those systems designated as national security systems as defined in 44 U.S.C., Section 3542. The guidelines have been broadly developed from a technical perspective so as to be complementary to similar guidelines issued by agencies and offices operating or exercising control over national security systems. This publication is intended to provide guidelines to Federal agencies in lieu of Federal Information Processing Standards (FIPS) Publication 102, "Guidelines for Computer Security Certification and Accreditation" (September 1983), which is being rescinded. State, local, and tribal governments, as well as private-sector organizations comprising the critical infrastructure of the United States, are also encouraged to consider the use of these guidelines, as appropriate.

The purpose of SP 800-37 is to provide guidelines for the accreditation of unclassified or Sensitive but Unclassified (SBU) information systems supporting the executive agencies of the Federal government. According to SP 800-37, the guidelines have been developed to:

■ Enable more consistent, comparable, and repeatable evaluations of security controls applied to federal information systems
■ Promote a better understanding of enterprisewide mission risks resulting from the operation of information systems
■ Create more complete, reliable, and trustworthy information for authorizing officials — facilitating more informed security accreditation decisions
■ Help achieve more secure information systems within the Federal government, including the critical infrastructure of the United States

This chapter outlines the four C&A phases and activities discussed in SP 800-37 (Figure 9.1). Although it is not the same as the DITSCAP/NIACAP phases, the Information Systems Security Engineering Professional (ISSEP) will note similarities between the two frameworks. Table 9.1 shows the

Figure 9.1   Chapter overview.

Table 9.1 C&A Phases for DITSCAP/NIACAP and SP 800-37

Phase	DITSCAP/NIACAP	NIST SP 800-37
1	Definition	Initiation
2	Verification	Security Certification
3	Validation	Security Accreditation
4	Post-Accreditation	Continuous Monitoring

four phases for both the DITSCAP/NIACAP and SP 800-37 phases. Since its release, many Federal agencies processing unclassified systems have chosen to adopt the NIST model for their C&A requirements, primarily because the NIST document is written in clear terms and is easy to follow (not to mention that the OMB is encouraging agencies to implement it for non-national security systems).

The most recent federal requirements for C&A include the Federal Information Security Management Act (FISMA) of 2002, the Information Technology Management Reform Act of 1996, and the Paperwork Reduction Act of 1995. All three specifically focus on policies requiring a risk-based approach for cost-effective security controls. Additionally, FISMA requires each Federal agency to create, document, and deploy enterprise-wide security programs in support of its information systems. Such security programs must include policies and procedures, risk assessments, security awareness training, periodic testing and evaluation, procedures to identify and respond to incidents, and plans and procedures related to continuity of operations.

The process of C&A leads to the delivery of two documents: a **certification package** and an **accreditation package**. The certification package contains the findings of the certification team that conducted the evaluation of the system. These findings include the results of the system test and evaluation, vulnerabilities, security controls for mitigating risks, and the residual risk once such controls are implemented.

The accreditation package contains the documentation necessary for the authorizing official to determine whether the system will be fully accredited to operate, will be granted an interim authorization to operate, or will be denied the authority (approval) to operate. Further, this package also contains the rationale used to justify the decision of the authorizing official and may also include additional supporting documentation. Typically, an interim authorization to operate will only be granted in very limited situations where the information system is critical to supporting an agency's mission or other critical business process.

Roles and Responsibilities

The C&A of an information system may involve many individuals; however, there are only a few key roles. Based upon SP 800-37, the roles relevant to the C&A process include:

- *The authorizing official.* The executive or senior manager authorized to approve the operation of the information system. Through security accreditation, this official assumes accountability and responsibility for the risks of operating the information system within a known environment. (In some agencies, the authorizing official is referred to as the designated approving/accrediting authority [DAA] or the Principal Approving Authority [PAA].)

- *Designated representative of the authorizing official.* The federal agency staff member chosen by the authorizing official to act on his or her behalf to coordinate and carry out the necessary activities required during the security C&A of an information system. The only task that cannot be delegated to this individual is the decision for security accreditation and the signing of the accreditation decision letter.

- *Chief Information Officer (CIO).* The agency official responsible for: (1) designating a senior agency or Chief Information Security Officer (CISO); (2) developing and maintaining information security policies, procedures, and control techniques to address all applicable requirements; (3) training and overseeing personnel with significant responsibilities for information security; (4) assisting senior agency officials concerning their responsibilities; and (5) in coordination with other senior agency officials, reporting annually to the agency head on the effectiveness of the agency's information security program, including progress of remedial actions.

- *Senior Agency Information Security Officer.* The agency official, also referred to as the Chief Information Security Officer (CISO), responsible for (1) carrying out the CIO's FISMA responsibilities; (2) possessing professional qualifications, including training and experience, required to administer the information security program functions; (3) having information security duties as that official's primary duty; and (4) heading an office with the mission and resources to assist in ensuring agency compliance with FISMA.

- *Information system owner.* The person responsible for notifying key officials within the agency of the need for a security C&A of the information system, making resources available, and providing the relevant documents to support the process. This individual represents the concerns of the user community for the system, is responsible for developing a security plan, and ensures that the system operates according to the security plan. The owner also puts together the security certification package and submits it to the authorizing official or designated representative.

- *Information owner.* The agency official with statutory or operational authority for specified information and responsibility for establishing the controls for its generation, collection, processing, dissemination, and disposal.
- *Information System Security Officer (ISSO).* The individual responsible to the authorizing official, information system owner, or the CISO for ensuring that the appropriate operational security posture is maintained for an information system or program. The ISSO may be held responsible for the operational security of the system, which includes physical and personnel security, incident handling, and security awareness training. This person often plays a significant role in the development and maintenance of the security plan and is involved with assessing the risks and impacts caused by changes to the system.
- *Certification agent.* The individual (or team) who conducts the evaluation of security controls, assesses the effectiveness of such controls, identifies vulnerabilities, and makes recommendations to correct them. To ensure a degree of unbiased objectivity, this individual should be independent from the management or operations of the information system. As such, this individual is frequently an outside contractor or consultant.
- *User representative.* The individual who represents the interests of the community.
- *Delegated roles.* According to SP 800-37, agency officials can appoint appropriately qualified persons, to include contractors, to perform the activities associated with a particular security C&A role. However, the role and signature responsibility of the authorizing official cannot be delegated to non-government personnel.

Scope of C&A Activities

One of the first C&A activities is defining the scope of work. This can be difficult due to the interconnected nature of most information systems and the associated fuzziness of where the boundaries of one system end and another begins. The NIST-recommended approach is to delineate boundaries based on the umbrella of management responsibility or the operational environment in which a system resides. Once boundaries are established that identify all the components of the system that must be evaluated for the particular C&A effort, a strategy for conducting the tasks can be developed. For very large systems, a *decomposition* approach should be considered that allows for the compartmentalization of the system, *into high, medium, and low risk subcomponents*. By taking a decomposition approach to large systems, each subcomponent can then be evaluated individually.

Another scenario applies to distributed systems that deploy duplicate units (smaller systems) to many different locations. In this case, the smaller systems can be evaluated and have a *type certification* conducted. A type certification approach allows for the reuse of information because each location would contain the same quantity and configuration of hardware and software. To support this approach, each location would also require a *site certification* that addresses the unique security concerns related to the specific operational environments that contain a node of the larger distributed system. This dual approach facilitates the overall C&A process through the reuse of data for similar system configurations and only requires additional C&A activities related to site-specific operational environment differences.

Another key task that is necessary for understanding the approach that should be undertaken is directly tied to the categorization of an information system that ranks the level of risk to that system. The approach used to define risk categorizations (i.e., High, Medium, Low) is identified in FIPS Publication 199 (February 2004), "Standards for Security Categorization of Federal Information and Information Systems." To address various levels of risk, mitigation techniques and controls are identified in NIST SP 800-53 (February 2005), "Security Controls of Federal Information Systems." Although SP 800-53 is currently a SP, it is scheduled to become a FIPS in December 2005.

To achieve an agency-wide view of the security program, agency officials need to identify *common security controls* that can be applied to one or more agency information systems. SP 800-37 states that common security controls can apply to:

1. [A]ll agency information systems;
2. [A] group of information systems at a specific site (sometimes associated with the terms site certification/accreditation);
3. [C]ommon information systems, subsystems, or applications (i.e., common hardware software, and/or firmware) deployed at multiple operational sites (sometimes associated with the terms type certification/accreditation) (p. 17).

Common security controls have the following properties:

■ The development, implementation, and assessment of common security controls can be assigned to responsible agency officials or organizational elements (other than the information system owners whose systems will implement or use those common security controls).

■ The results from the assessment of the common security controls can be used to support the security certification and accreditation processes of agency information systems where those controls have been applied.

For example, management and operational controls such as contingency planning, incident response, security training and awareness, personnel security, and physical security can be designated as common security controls because all agencies will need these controls on a minimum basic level. The goal is to reduce security costs by centrally managing the development, implementation, and assessment of the common security controls designated by the agency — and subsequently, sharing assessment results with the owners of information systems where those common security controls are applied. If a security control is not designated as a common security control, is it considered a *system-specific control* and is the responsibility of the information system owner. The SSP should clearly identify those security controls designated as either common security controls or system-specific controls.

The C&A Process

The next sections outline the specific phases of the SP 800-37 C&A process. Much of this material is drawn directly from SP 800-37, with additional supporting discussion inserted for clarification purposes.

The SP 800-37 C&A process consists of four distinct phases:

■ Phase 1: Initiation
■ Phase 2: Security Certification
■ Phase 3: Security Accreditation
■ Phase 4: Continuous Monitoring

Each phase consists of a set of well-defined tasks and subtasks that are to be carried out by the authorizing official, authorizing official's designated representative, information system owner, certification agent, and user representative.

The C&A activities can be applied to an information system at appropriate phases in the system development life cycle by selectively tailoring the various tasks and subtasks. Figure 9.2 provides a high-level view of the C&A process, including the tasks associated with each phase in the process.

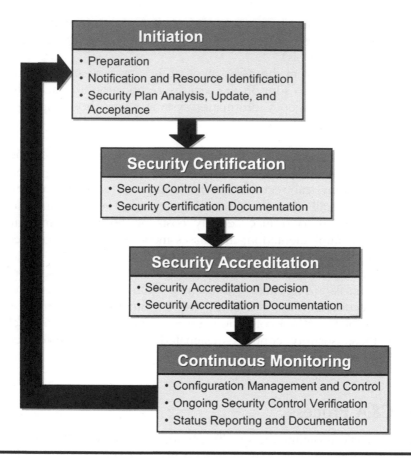

Figure 9.2   SP 800-37 C&A phases.

The assessment of risk and the development of security plans are two important activities in an agency's information security program that directly support the security accreditation process and are required under FISMA and OMB Circular A-130. *Risk assessments,* whether done formally or informally, influence the development of the security requirements and the security controls for information systems and generate much of the information needed for the associated security plans for those systems.

In either case, the assessment of risk is a process that should be incorporated into the system development life cycle, and the process should be reasonable for the agency concerned. At a minimum, documentation should be produced that describes the process employed and describes the results obtained. NIST SP 800-30 (January 2002), "Risk Management Guide for Information Technology Systems," provides recommendations on conducting risk assessments and is appropriate for either situation described above.

Security plans document the security requirements and security controls for information systems and provide essential information for security accreditations. NIST SP 800-18 (December 1998), "Guide for Developing Security Plans for Information Technology Systems," provides guidance and recommendations on the format and content of security plans.

In addition to risk assessments and security plans, security evaluation also plays an important role in the security accreditation process. It is essential that agency officials have the most complete, accurate, and trustworthy information possible on the security status of their information systems in order to make credible, risk-based decisions on whether to authorize operation of those systems. This information and supporting evidence for system authorization is often developed during a detailed security review of the information system, typically referred to as security certification.

System Development Life Cycle

All federal information systems, including operational systems, systems under development, and systems undergoing some form of modification or upgrade, are in some phase of what is commonly referred to as the System Development Life Cycle (SDLC).

There are many activities occurring during the life cycle of an information system dealing with the issues of cost, schedule, and performance. In addition to the functional requirements levied on an information system, security requirements must also be considered. In the end, the information system must be able to meet its functional requirements and do so in a manner that is secure enough to protect the agency's operations (including mission, functions, image, or reputation) and assets. In accordance with the provisions of FISMA, agencies are required to have an information security program that should be effectively integrated into the SDLC. The security C&A process is an important part of the agency's information security program and therefore the activities associated with certifying and accrediting an information system should also be integrated into the agency's SDLC.

The C&A tasks should be appropriately tailored to the life-cycle phase of the information system. For systems under development, the C&A tasks begin early in the life cycle with an opportunity to shape and influence the security capabilities of the system. For operational systems and many legacy systems in the Federal inventory, the C&A tasks may, by necessity, begin later in the life cycle. In either situation, all C&A tasks should be completed to ensure that: the information system has received the necessary attention with regard to security; and, the authorizing official explicitly accepts the residual risk to agency operations, agency assets, or

Table 9.2 Five-Phase System Development Life-Cycle Process

Phase 1 Initiation	Phase 2 Development and Acquisition	Phase 3 Implementation	Phase 4 Operations and Maintenance	Phase 5 Disposal
The need for a system is expressed and the purpose and high-level requirements are documented.	The system is designed, purchased, programmed, developed, or otherwise constructed.	After initial system testing, the system is installed or fielded.	The system performs the work for which it was developed.	The system is disposed of once the transition to a new computer system is complete.

individuals after the implementation of an agreed-upon set of security controls. Using a generalized SDLC, there are typically five phases that represent the life cycle of an information system, as shown in Table 9.2.

The SDLC breaks down the systems development process into phases during which discrete systems products are developed. This approach to systems development leads to well-documented systems that are easier to test and maintain. Additionally, an organization can have confidence that the system's functions will be fulfilled with a minimum of unforeseen problems.

The SP 800-37 C&A methodology is based on a four-phase approach. As depicted in Table 9.3 these four well-defined C&A phases run from the initial concept throughout the system's life cycle.

Table 9.3 SDLC and C&A Phases

Phase 1 Initiation	Phase 2 Development and Acquisition	Phase 3 Implementation	Phase 4 Operations and Maintenance	Phase 5 Disposal
C&A Phase 1: Initiation Phase				
	C&A Phase 2: Security Certification Phase			
		C&A Phase 3: Security Accreditation Phase		
			C&A Phase 4: Continuous Monitoring Phase	

Phase 1: Initiation

The purpose of this phase is to ensure that the authorizing official or designated representative is in agreement with the contents of the security plan for the information system before the certification agent begins the independent testing and evaluation of security controls. The early involvement of the authorizing official or designated representative is paramount to the success of the C&A effort.

The initiation of a system (or project) begins in the SDLC Phase 1 when a business or agency need or opportunity is identified. The primary objective of the SDLC is to ensure that the system is developed in accordance with the stated requirements, is cost effective, works correctly, and is maintainable. The inclusion of security controls and measures during SDLC Phase 1 helps to ensure that safeguards are part of the design and development. An overview of Phase 1 is shown in Table 9.4, which also includes the supporting documentation for each task. Once all the necessary controls are identified, they must be agreed upon before moving to the next phase, SDLC Phase 2.

The Initiation phase consists of three activities:

1. Preparation
2. Notification and resource identification
3. Security plan analysis, update, and acceptance

A significant portion of the information needed during C&A Phase 1 should have been previously generated by the agency during the initial risk assessment and the development of the System Security Plan (SSP). In many cases, risk assessments and SSPs have already been reviewed and approved by agency officials. If so, the subtasks in Task 1, Preparation, should be reviewed to ensure all were completed. If an agency has not completed a risk assessment and an SSP, those activities should be completed prior to proceeding with the security C&A process.

Next we look at the three activities of C&A Phase 1.

Preparation Activity

SP 800-37 defines the objective of the preparation task as "to prepare for security certification and accreditation by reviewing the SSP and confirming that the contents of the plan are consistent with an initial assessment of risk (p. 27)."

The tasks involved in the preparation activity are:

- Information system description
- Security categorization

Table 9.4   C&A Phase 1, Initiation: Tasks and Subtasks

Phase 1 Initiation	Phase 2 Development and Acquisition	Phase 3 Implementation	Phase 4 Operations and Maintenance	Phase 5 Disposal
C&A Phase 1: Initiation Phase				
Preparation Activity • System Description: NIST 800-18, 800-30 • Security Categorization: FIPS 199, NIST 800-18, 800-30 • Threat Identification: NIST 800-18, 800-30 • Security Control Identification: NIST 800-18, 800-30, 800-53 • Vulnerability Identification: NIST 800-18, 800-30 • Residual Risk Determination (Expected): FISMA, OMB Circ. A-130, NIST 800-30 Notification and Resource Identification Activity • Notification: OMB Circ. A-130 • Planning and Resources: OMB Circ. A-130 Security Plan Analysis, Update, and Acceptance Activity • Security Plan Analysis: NIST 800-18 • Security Plan Update: NIST 800-18 • Security Plan Acceptance: NIST 800-30				

- Threat identification
- Vulnerability identification
- Security control identification
- Initial risk determination

Preparation Task 1: Information System Description

SP 800-37 states that the objective of this task is to "confirm that the information system has been fully described and documented in the SSP or an equivalent document (p. 27)," This includes more than 24 items, such as the name of the system; purposes, functions, and capabilities of the system; the boundary; applicable laws, directives, policies, regulations, or standards; users; hardware, software, and system interfaces, and network connections.

Preparation Task 2: Security Categorization

In this task, the goal is to confirm that the security category (i.e., unclassified, SBU) of the information system has been determined and documented in the SSP or an equivalent document. Of special consideration is to make sure it is not a national security system.

Preparation Task 3: Threat Identification

This task confirms that "potential threats that could exploit information system flaws or weaknesses have been identified and documented in the SSP, risk assessment, or an equivalent document" (SP 800-37, p. 29).

Preparation Task 4: Vulnerability Identification

Similar to Task 3, vulnerability identification confirms "that flaws or weaknesses in the information system that could be exploited by potential threat sources have been identified and documented in the SSP, risk assessment, or an equivalent document" (SP 800-37, p. 29).

Preparation Task 5: Security Control Identification

In Task 5, the objective is to "confirm that the security controls (either planned or implemented) for the information system have been identified and documented in the SSP or an equivalent document. Security controls for information systems are listed in NIST SP 800-53. These predefined sets of security controls provide a baseline or starting point for agencies in addressing the necessary safeguards and countermeasures required for their information systems" (SP 800-37, p. 30).

Preparation Task 6: Initial Risk Determination

The final task in the preparation activity, confirms that the risk to agency operations, agency assets, or individuals has been determined and documented in the SSP, risk assessment, or an equivalent document. Of particular importance to this task is the Federal requirement from FISMA and OMB Circular A-130, Appendix III, to conduct risk assessments as part of a risk-based approach to determining adequate, cost-effective security for an information system. Refer to NIST SP 800-30 (discussed in Chapter 14) for more information on risk management and conducting risk assessments.

Notification and Resource Identification Activity

SP 800-37 notes that the objective of the notification and resource identification activity is to:

■ Provide notification to all concerned agency officials as to the impending security certification and accreditation of the information system.
■ Determine the resources needed to carry out the effort.
■ Prepare a plan of execution for the certification and accreditation activities indicating the proposed schedule and key milestones.

The two tasks under the notification and resource identification activity are:

1. Notification
2. Planning and resources

Notification Task 1: Notification

SP 800-37 states that under this task, it is necessary to "inform the senior agency information security officer, authorizing official, certification agent, user representatives, and other interested agency officials that the information system requires security certification and accreditation support (p. 32)."

Notification Task 2: Planning and Resources

During this task, the level of effort is determined, the resources required for the C&A of the information system (including organizations involved) are determined, and a plan of execution is prepared.

Security Plan Analysis, Update, and Acceptance Activity

As noted in SP 800-37, the final activity of Phase 1 is to:

■ Perform an independent review of the FIPS 199 security categorization.
■ Obtain an independent analysis of the SSP.

- Update the SSP as needed based on the results of the independent analysis.
- Obtain acceptance of the SSP by the authorizing official and senior agency information security officer prior to conducting an assessment of the security controls in the information system (p. 33).

The four tasks for this activity are:

1. Security categorization review
2. SSP analysis
3. SSP update
4. SSP acceptance

If comparing the DITSCAP/NIACAP process to SP 800-37, the role of the SSAA and SSP are very similar. Both are carried through the entire C&A process and become the document necessary for completion in evaluating the risk of the system under review.

Security Plan Task 1: Security Categorization Review

In this task, the objective is to "review the FIPS 199 security categorization described in the SSP to determine if the assigned impact values with respect to the potential loss of confidentiality, integrity, and availability are consistent with agency's actual mission requirements" (SP 800-37, p. 33).

Security Plan Task 2: SSP Analysis

If necessary, conduct an independent review of the SSP to determine if the vulnerabilities in the information system and the resulting risk to agency operations, agency assets, or individuals are actually what the plan would produce, if implemented.

Security Plan Task 3: SSP Update

Based on the results from Task 2, the next task is to update the SSP and make recommendations to the certification agent, authorizing official, and senior agency information security officer.

Security Plan Task 4: SSP Acceptance

In this final task, the system owner reviews and accepts the risk to the system as documented in the SSP.

After completing the three Phase 1 activities, the C&A process is ready to move into Phase 2, Security Certification.

Phase 2: Security Certification

Security certification directly supports security accreditation by evaluating the security controls implemented in the information system. The evaluation is conducted to determine the **effectiveness** of those security controls in a particular environment of operation and the vulnerabilities in the information system after the implementation of such controls. Security certification can include a variety of verification techniques and procedures to demonstrate the effectiveness of the security controls. These techniques and procedures can include activities such as observations, interviews, exercises, functional testing, penetration testing, regression testing, system design analysis, and test coverage analysis.

The level of rigor applied during evaluation is based on the robustness of the security controls employed in the information system — where robustness is defined by the strength of the security controls and the assurance that the controls are effective in their operation. Security certification does not include the determination of residual risk to agency operations or agency assets that might result from these information system vulnerabilities. The determination of residual risk to agency operations or agency assets generally requires a broader, more strategic view of the enterprise than can be obtained from the more technically focused, local view of the system that results from security certification. Authorizing officials and their designated representatives are better positioned to make residual risk determinations and decisions on the acceptability of such risk. Authorizing officials or their designated representatives can, when needed, consult certification agents during any phase in the security C&A process to obtain technical advice on the security of the information system. The results of the security certification are used to reassess the risks and update the security plan for the information system — thus providing the factual basis for the authorizing official to render the security accreditation decision.

The purpose of this phase is to ensure that the actual vulnerabilities in the information system are determined through independent evaluation of the security controls and that recommended corrective actions are provided to the information system owner and authorizing official. NIST SP 800-53A (initial draft Spring 2004), "Techniques and Procedures for Verifying the Effectiveness of Security Controls in Federal Information Systems," provides guidelines based upon established methods and tests for validating the effectiveness of standard security controls. Upon successful completion of this phase, the authorizing official will have the information needed from the security certification to determine the actual residual risk to agency operations and assets and thus will be able to render an appropriate security accreditation decision for the information system.

The Security Certification phase consists of two activities:

- Security control assessment
- Security certification documentation

Security Control Assessment Activity

The goal of this activity is to prepare for the assessment of the current security controls, conduct the assessment, and then document the assessment. Within this activity there are four specific tasks:

1. Review documentation and supporting materials.
2. Develop methods and procedures.
3. Conduct security assessment.
4. Create security assessment report.

Security Control Assessment Task 1: Review Documentation and Supporting Materials

Assemble any documentation and supporting materials necessary for the assessment of the security controls in the information system. If these documents include previous assessments of security controls, review the findings, results, and evidence.

Security Control Assessment Task 2: Develop Methods and Procedures

Select, or develop when needed, appropriate methods and procedures to assess the management, operational, and technical security controls of the information system.

Security Control Assessment Task 3: Conduct Security Assessment

Assess the management, operational, and technical security controls of the information system using methods and procedures selected or developed.

Security Control Assessment Task 4: Create Security Assessment Report

Prepare the final security assessment report.

Security Certification Documentation Activity

As stated in SP 800-37, the objective of this task is to "(i) provide the certification findings and recommendations to the information system owner; (ii) update the SSP as needed; (iii) prepare the plan of action and milestones; and (iv) assemble the accreditation package (p. 38)."

The security certification document tasks are to:

1. Present findings and recommendations.
2. Update SSP.
3. Prepare plan of action and milestones.
4. Assemble accreditation package.

Security Certification Document Task 1: Present Findings and Recommendations

In this task the information system owner is provided with the security assessment report. Because the system owner relies on the expertise of the certification agent, it is important that deficiencies in the network are appropriately documented and suggestions made as to what is necessary to improve the security of the system.

Security Certification Document Task 2: Update SSP

If there have been any modifications based on the certification process and recommendations to the system owner, then the SSP can also be updated.

Security Certification Document Task 3: Prepare Plan of Action and Milestones

In this task the Plan of Action and Milestones (POA&M) is prepared. As stated in SP 800-37, the POA&M is "one of three key documents in the security accreditation package; it describes actions taken or planned by the information system owner to correct deficiencies in the security controls and to address remaining vulnerabilities in the information system (i.e., reduce, eliminate, or accept the vulnerabilities). The POA&M document identifies: the tasks needing to be accomplished; the resources required to accomplish the elements of the plan; any milestones in meeting the tasks; and, scheduled completion dates for the milestones (p. 39)."

Security Certification Document Task 4: Assemble Accreditation Package

The final task is for the system owner to assemble and compile the final security accreditation package and submit it to authorizing official. The package must be as complete as possible and contain all the information needed by the authorizing official to make a solid assessment of the status of security on the system. Because the authorizing official will essentially be accepting any residual risk remaining on the system, the remaining risk must be clearly stated.

The *security accreditation package* documents the results of the security certification and provides the authorizing official with the information needed to make a credible, risk-based decision on whether to authorize operation of the information system. The accreditation package contains the following documents:

- Approved SSP (written by the system owner; provides an overview of the security requirements and describes the controls in place to meet the requirements)
- Security assessment report (written by the certification agent and documents that the security controls in place are implemented and operated correctly)
- Plan of Action and Milestones (POA&M) (written by the system owner; describes the measures implemented or planned to correct deficiencies noted in the security assessment and to reduce or eliminate known vulnerabilities)
- The latest copy of the risk assessment

During C&A Phase 2, as shown in Table 9.5, the actual information security controls of the project are developed, evaluated, and tested. Testing is the actual test of the products or processes created within the SDLC Phase 2. The SDLC Phase 3 involves putting the tested and approved products or processes into an operational environment for use by the customer. Documentation includes the creation of written operational manuals, standards, systems outputs, and performance reports that document the requirements and use of the product. All of these components combined provide the basis for SDLC Phase 2 and SDLC Phase 3. Upon

Table 9.5 SDLC and C&A Phase 2, Security Certification: Tasks and Subtasks

Phase 1 Initiation	Phase 2 Development and Acquisition	Phase 3 Implementation	Phase 4 Operations and Maintenance	Phase 5 Disposal
C&A Phase 1: Initiation Phase				
	C&A Phase 2: Security Certification Phase			
	4 Security Control Verification			
	4.1 Documentation and Supporting Materials			
	4.2 Reuse of Evaluation Results			
	4.3 Techniques and Procedures: NIST 800-53A			
	4.4 Security Evaluation			
	4.5 Security Test & Evaluation Report; NIST 800-53A			
	5 Security Certification			
	Documentation Certification Agent Findings and Recommendations: NIST 800-53A			
	5.1 Security Plan Update: NIST 800-18			
	5.2 Security Certification Package Assembly: OMB Circ. A-130			

completion of the test and evaluation portion, an extensive review of all documentation is performed and the findings are documented in the System Security Plan.

Phase 3: Security Accreditation

The purpose of this phase is to ensure that the actual residual risk to agency operations (including mission, functions, image, or reputation) or agency assets is acceptable to the authorizing official and that the acceptability of that risk forms the basis of the security accreditation decision. Upon successful completion of this phase, the information system owner will either have full authorization to operate the information system, an interim approval to operate the information system under specific terms and conditions, or denial of authorization to operate the information system.

The Security Accreditation phase consists of two tasks:

1. Security accreditation decision
2. Security accreditation package documentation

The objective of the C&A Phase 3, as depicted in Table 9.6, is to validate that the preceding work has produced an information system that operates in a specified computing environment with an acceptable level of residual risk. The C&A Phase 3 consists of process activities in SDLC Phase 3 that occur after the system is integrated and culminates in the accreditation of the IT system, such as a review of the agreement, or an evaluation of the integrated IT system, certification, and accreditation. Upon completion of the C&A Phase 3, the Security Plan is updated and the system is placed into full operation and maintenance, which is SDLC Phase 4.

Table 9.6   C&A Phase 3, Security Accreditation: Tasks and Subtasks

Phase 1 Initiation	Phase 2 Development and Acquisition	Phase 3 Implementation	Phase 4 Operations and Maintenance	Phase 5 Disposal
C&A Phase 1: Initiation Phase				
	C&A Phase 2: Security Certification Phase			
		C&A Phase 3: Security Accreditation Phase		
		6 Security Accreditation Decision		
		6.1 Final Risk Determination: NIST 800-30		
		6.2 Residual Risk Acceptability: OMB Circ. A-130		
		7 Security Accreditation Documentation		
		7.1 Security Accreditation Package Transmission: OMB Circ. A-130		
		7.2 Security Plan Update: NIST 800-18		

Security Accreditation Decision Activity

SP 800-37 notes the objective is to determine the risk to agency operations, agency assets, or individuals; and also determine if the agency-level risk is acceptable. There are two tasks in this activity that relate to the final analysis of risk and acceptance of residual risk:

1. Final risk determination
2. Residual risk acceptability

Security Accreditation Decision Activity Task 1: Final Risk Determination

Based on the information in the accreditation package, the authorizing official makes a determination of the risk to agency operations or agency assets. Of key importance for the authorizing official is understanding the importance and sensitivity of the information that is being reviewed. This determination is made by reviewing the vulnerabilities identified in the SSP, the current controls, and any planned corrective actions that will eliminate or reduce the vulnerabilities.

Security Accreditation Decision Activity Task 2: Residual Risk Acceptability

In this task the authorizing official makes the decision to accept the system's residual risk and allow the system to operate. The authorizing official must balance the security considerations with those of operational needs. Although it is easily written, it is not so easy to achieve. Many factors will influence the authorizing official's decision and may involve careful guidance from other security professionals, including the ISSEP, on what risk is acceptable and what cannot be accepted. If the risk is not acceptable, additional controls must be added to reduce the vulnerabilities.

Security Accreditation Package Documentation Activity

The objective of the security accreditation documentation activity is to transmit the final security accreditation package and update the SSP. The two tasks in this activity reflect these two objectives:

1. Security accreditation package transmission
2. SSP update

Security Accreditation Package Task 1: Security Accreditation Package Transmission

The authorizing official responds to the security accreditation package by transmitting a *security accreditation decision letter* (also called the accreditation package) to the system owner. The decision letter indicates the:

- *Accreditation decision*. Indicates whether the system is fully authorized to operate, has interim authority to operate, or is not authorized to operate
- *Supporting rationale for the decision*. Justification of the decision by the authorizing official
- *Terms and conditions for the authorization*. Describes any limitations or restrictions placed on the operation of the system that must be adhered to by the system owner

The security accreditation decision letter is attached to the original security accreditation package and returned to the information system owner. The information system owner keeps the original security accreditation decision letter and accreditation package on file. The authorizing official also retains copies of the decision letter and accreditation package.

Security Accreditation Package Task 2: SSP Update

The final task in accreditation is to update the SSP based on the final determination of risk to agency operations, agency assets, or individuals.

Security accreditation should not be viewed as a static process. An information system is authorized for operation at a specific point in time reflecting the current security state of the system. However, the inevitable changes to the hardware, firmware, and software in the information system and the potential impact those changes may have on the security of that system require a more dynamic process — a process capable of monitoring the ongoing effectiveness of the security controls in the information system. Thus, the initial security accreditation of the information system must be supplemented and reinforced by a structured and disciplined process involving (1) the continuous monitoring of the security controls in the system and (2) the continuous reporting of the security state of the system to appropriate agency officials.

This authorization, given by a senior agency official, is applicable to a particular environment of operation, and explicitly accepts the risk to agency operations (including mission, functions, image, or reputation), agency assets, or individuals remaining after the implementation of an agreed-upon set of security controls. By accrediting an information system, the agency official is not only responsible for the security of the system, but is also accountable for adverse impacts on the agency if a breach of security occurs. Security accreditation required under OMB Circular A-130, provides a form of quality control and challenges managers and technical staff at all levels to implement the most effective security controls and techniques, while taking into account the mission requirements and the technical constraints, operational constraints, and cost and schedule constraints.

Phase 4: Continuous Monitoring

The purpose of this phase is to provide oversight and monitoring of the security controls in the information system on an ongoing basis and to inform the authorizing official or designated representative when changes occur that may impact the security of the system. The activities in C&A Phase 4 continue until the need for reaccreditations occurs, either because of specific changes to the information system (event driven) or because of federal or agency policies requiring reauthorization of the system within a specified timeframe.

The Continuous Monitoring phase consists of the following activities:

■ Configuration management and control
■ Ongoing security control verification
■ Status reporting and documentation

The C&A Phase 4, as depicted in Table 9.7, can also involve the disposition of information, hardware, and software. Activities might include moving, archiving, discarding, or destroying information and sanitizing the hardware and software that occur in SDLC Phase 5. Risk management activities are performed for system components that will be disposed of or replaced to ensure that the hardware and software are properly disposed of, that residual data is appropriately handled, and that system migration is conducted in a secure and systematic manner.

Configuration Management and Control Activity

SP 800-37 states that the objective of this activity is to first document the proposed or actual changes to the information system and then determine the impact of proposed or actual changes on the security of the system. These are also the two tasks for this activity:

1. Documentation of information system changes
2. Security impact analysis

Table 9.7 SDLC and C&A Phase 4, Continuous Monitoring: Tasks and Subtasks

Phase 1 Initiation	Phase 2 Development and Acquisition	Phase 3 Implementation	Phase 4 Operations and Maintenance	Phase 5 Disposal
C&A Phase 1: Initiation Phase				
	C&A Phase 2: Security Certification Phase			
		C&A Phase 3: Security Accreditation Phase		
			C&A Phase 4: Continuous Monitoring Phase	
			8 Configuration Management and Control	
			8.1 Documentation of Information System Changes	
			8.2 Security Impact Analysis: NIST 800-30	
			9 Ongoing Security Control Verification	
			9.1 Security Control Selection: FISMA, OMB Circ. A-130, NIST 800-53	
			9.2 Security Control Monitoring: FISMA, OMB Circ. A-130, NIST 800-53, NIST 800-26	
			10 Status Reporting and Documentation	
			10.1 Security Plan Update: NIST 800-18	
			10.2 Status Reporting: FISMA, OMB Circ. A-130	

Configuration Management Task 1: Documentation of Information System Changes

In this task the agency must establish configuration management and control procedures that will document proposed or actual changes to the information system (including hardware, software, firmware, and surrounding environment).

Configuration Management Task 2: Security Impact Analysis

The next task is to analyze any proposed or actual changes to the information system to determine the security impact of such changes.

Ongoing Security Control Verification Activity

The purpose of having continuous monitoring of security controls is to identify potential security-related problems that are not identified during the security impact analysis conducted as part of the configuration management and control process. The first task is to select which controls should be monitored, and the second task is to actually assess the controls using verifiable test methods.

Ongoing Security Control Verification Task 1: Security Control Selection

Simply stated, the security controls to be monitored on a continuous basis are selected.

Ongoing Security Control Verification Task 2: Selected Security Control Assessment

Once the organization has selected the security controls, the next task is to assess the extent to which the controls are implemented correctly, operating as intended, and producing the desired outcome with respect to meeting the security requirements for the system.

Status Reporting and Documentation Activity

SP 800-37 states the objective of the status reporting and documentation activity is to "update the SSP to reflect the proposed or actual changes to the information system and the identified or potential security impacts associated with those proposed or actual changes; and report the proposed or actual changes and identified or potential security impacts to the authorizing official and senior agency information security officer (p. 37)." These two objectives are also related to the two tasks for this activity;

1. SSP update
2. Status reporting

Status Reporting and Documentation Task 1: SSP Update

The SSP should be updated based on the documented changes to the information system and the results of the continuous monitoring process.

Status Reporting and Documentation Task 2: Status Reporting

As appropriate, the authorizing official and senior agency information security officer should be updated on the continuous monitoring activities and status of the POA&M. The time interval at which reports should be generated is based on each agency's needs.

Summary

The NIST approach to C&A has matured into a comprehensive and integrated set of processes and methodologies. It draws upon best practices of the software/system life cycle and has identified clear guidance for each stage of the required C&A activities. This guidance is contained in specific NIST Special Publications for each task area:

- NIST SP 800-18 for SSPs
  - NIST SP 800-26 a Security Self-Assessment Guide
  - NIST SP 800-30 for risk management
  - NIST SP 800-53 for selection of security controls
  - NIST SP 800-53A for verification of security controls
  - NIST SP 800-37 for overall C&A guidance that identifies how each document addresses each task area

The key point to remember is that the SP 800-37 approach to C&A consists of four phases with specific tasks and activities integrated into the SDLC processes for the information system. These phases include Initiation, Security Certification, Security Accreditation, and Continuous Monitoring. The personnel involved with C&A activities for all phases include the authorizing official, designated representative of the authorizing official, information system owner, information systems security officer, certification agent, and user representative. Additionally, qualified individuals may be contracted to conduct the activities for specific C&A roles. However, the role and signature responsibility of the authorizing official cannot be delegated to non-government personnel.

Domain 2 References

44 United States Code (USC), Chapter 35 Coordination of Federal Information Policy (1995, Amended 1996, 1997, 2000, and 2002). "Paperwork Reduction Act." Available at http://uscode.house.gov/.

DoD Directive 5000.1 (May 2003). The Defense Acquisition System. DoD 5000 Series Resource Center: http://dod5000.dau.mil/.

DoD Instruction 8510.1-M (July 2000). DoD Information Technology Security Certification and Accreditation Process (DITSCAP) — Application Manual. Available at http://www.dtic.mil/whs/directives/index.html.

DoD Instruction 5200.40 (December 1997). DoD Information Technology Security Certification and Accreditation Process (DITSCAP). Available at http://www.dtic.mil/whs/directives/index.html.

DoD Directive No. 5220.22 (December 1980). DoD Industrial Security Program. Available at http://www.dtic.mil/whs/directives/index.html.

DoD Directive No. 8500.1 (October 24, 2002 — certified current as of November 21, 2003). Information Assurance (IA). Available at http://www.dtic.mil/whs/directives/index.html.

DoD Instruction 8500.2 (February 2003). Information Assurance (IA) Implementation. Available at: http://www.dtic.mil/whs/directives/index.html.

FIPS-199 (February 2004). Standards for Security Categorization of Information and Information Systems. NIST Publications: Gaithersburg, MD. Available at http://csrc.nist.gov/publications/fips/index.html.

HR 145 Public Law 100-235 (June 1987). Computer Security Act of 1987. The act can be downloaded from http://csrc.nist.gov/secplcy/csa_87.txt.

HR 2458 Public Law 107-30 (November 2002). E-government Act of 2002. Title III — Information Security Section 301, Information Security. Federal Information Security Management Act of 2002. Available at http://csrc.nist.gov/policies/FISMA-final.pdf.

Information System Security Engineer Professional (ISSEP) Study Guide (May 2003). International Information System Security Certification Consortium (ISC)². Available for download from http://www.isc2.org.

NIST SP 800-18 (December 1998). *Guide for Developing Security Plans for Information Technology Systems.* Available at the NIST Web site: http://csrc.nist.gov/publications/nistpubs/index.html.

NIST SP 800-26 (April 2005). *System Questionnaire with NIST SP 800-53 References and Associated Control Mappings.* Available at the NIST Web site: http://csrc.nist.gov/ publications/nistpubs/index.html.

NIST SP 800-30 (January 2002). Risk Management Guide for Information Technology Systems. Available at the NIST Web site: http://csrc.nist.gov/publications/nistpubs/index.html.

NIST SP 800-30A DRAFT (2004). Revision to Risk Management Guide for Information Technology System, NIST Publications: Gaithersburg, MD. Available at http://csrc.nist.gov/publications/nistpubs/index.html.

NIST SP 800-37 (May 2004). Guide for the Security Certification and Accreditation of Federal Information Systems. NIST Publications: Gaithersburg, MD. Available at: http://csrc.nist.gov/publications/nistpubs/index.html.

NIST SP 800-53 (February 2005). Recommended Security Controls for Federal Information Systems. NIST Publications: Gaithersburg, MD. Available at http://csrc.nist.gov/publications/nistpubs/index. html.

NIST SP 800-53A DRAFT (Spring 2004). Techniques and Procedures for Verifying the Effectiveness of Security Controls in Federal Information Systems. Available at http://csrc.nist.gov/publications/nistpubs/index.html.

NSTISSP No. 6 (April 1994). National Policy on Certification and Accreditation of National Security Telecommunications and Information Systems. Available at http://www.nstissc.gov/Assets/pdf/NSTISSP_6.pdf.

NSTISSI No. 1000 (April 2000). National Information Assurance Certification and Accreditation Process (NIACAP). Available at http://www.nstissc.gov/html/library.html.

OMB Circular No. A-130, (last revised November 2000). Management of Federal Information Resources. Available at http://www.whitehouse.gov/omb/circulars/index.html.

Title 40, Code of Federal Regulations (CFR), Chapter 113 (1996). Information Technology Management Reform Act of 1996, later renamed: Clinger-Cohen Act. Available at http://ecfr.gpoaccess.gov/.

Web Sites

http://iase.disa.mil/ditscap/
http://niap.nist.gov
http://www.nstissc.gov

Acronyms

The list of acronyms below is used throughout this domain. They are from DITSCAP Manual 8510.1-M.

ATO: Authority (approval) to operate
CA: Certification agent
C&A: Certification and Accreditation
CCB: Change Control Board
CIA: Confidentiality, integrity, and availability

CL: Certification Level
CM: Configuration management
COMSEC: Communications security
CONOPS: Concept of operations
COTS: Commercial-off-the-shelf
CRR: Certification Requirements Review
CT&E: Certification Test and Evaluation
DAA: Designated approving (accrediting) authority
DII: Defense information infrastructure
DISSP: Defense Wide Information Systems Security Program
DITSCAP: Department of Defense Information Technology Security Certification and Accreditation Process
DoD: Department of Defense
DoDD: Department of Defense Directive
DoDI: Department of Defense Instruction
DODIIS: Department of Defense Intelligence Information System
FCA: Functional configuration audit
FIPS: Federal Information Protection Standards
FISMA: Federal Information Security Management Act
GOTS: Government-off-the-shelf
IA: Information assurance
IAW: In accordance with
IATO: Interim authority (approval) to operate
IS: Information system
ISSE: Information Systems Security Engineering
ISSM: Information Systems Security Manager
ISSO: Information Systems Security Officer
ISSEP: Information Systems Security Engineering Professional
IT: Information technology
LAN: Local area network
MAC: Mission assurance category
MSAC: Minimum Security Activity Checklist
MILDEP: Military department
MOA: Memorandum of Agreement
NIACAP: National Information Assurance Certification Accreditation Program
NIST: National Institute of Standards and Technology
NSTISSI: National Security Telecommunications and Information Systems Security Instruction
OMB: Office of Management and Budget
PCA: Physical configuration audit
PM: Program management (manager)
RTM: Requirements Traceability Matrix

ROB: Rules of behavior
SCI: Sensitive compartmented information
SDLC: System development life cycle
SFUG: Security features users guide
SOP: Standard operating procedure
SP: Special Publication
SSAA: Systems Security Authorization Agreement
ST&E: Systems Test and Evaluation
TEMPEST: Not an acronym, but an unclassified short title referring to the investigation and study of compromising emanations
TCSEC: Telecommunications security
TFM: Trusted facility manual
USG: United States Government
VLAN: Virtual local area network
VPN: Virtual private network
WAN: Wide area network

ISSE Domain 3

TECHNICAL

MANAGEMENT

In the previous sections of this book, the overall Information Systems Security Engineering (ISSE) phases were explained. The Information Assurance Technical Framework (IATF) describes the ISSE as the art and science of implementing systems with economy and elegance to safely resist the forces to which they may be subjected. This is referred to as good, practical design for the real world. However, the ISSE process will not provide good design unless the principles are actually followed. This section moves away from "what" it is, to "how to make it happen." Essentially, how do you manage this process to make it work?

Note to ISSEP candidates: Most of the material in this chapter is for reference and provides the essential management skills necessary to manage technical projects. The (ISC)² ISSEP® exam typically covers the documentation requirements of technical management, such as the System Engineering Management Plan, PERT charts, etc.

Contributors and Reviewers

Susan Hansche contributed, edited, and finalized the material in this domain. She would like to thank the following individuals for their contributions:

Bruce Matthews, CISSP, contributed the initial research, draft, and reviews of the material for Domain 3. He is currently the Division Chief for the Security Engineering and Computer Division of the Bureau of Diplomatic Security, U.S. Department of State in Washington, D.C.

Larry L. Buickel, CISSP, reviewed and edited Chapter 10. He is an enterprise security consultant with Graphic Example Technologies, Inc.

10

Technical Management

Introduction

There are nearly as many definitions of technical management as there are books and courses on the subject. Most variations are simply tweaks in the semantics; a different selection of words to be precise or as vague as needed, depending upon the level of detail presented. Rather than adding yet another definition to the fray, let us explore what can be inferred from the name.

Management means to direct resources. Resources, also referred to as assets, are comprised of people, money, time, and tangible things. A manager must ensure that all the resources combine in concert with one another to reach specified goals. In effect, the manager is a conductor of an orchestra in which each instrument has a unique role, yet depends upon the others to create the desired sound. Individual instruments enter the composition at different times, or play different notes or rhythms. Each has a job to do, and coordination and timing are essential. If an instrument plays at the wrong moment, the entire audience knows it and finds it detracting, although it could be reasoned as statistically inconsequential (hey, the other 8000 notes were played correctly). Likewise, if the users of a completed information system cannot open their documents, there is no sympathy for the level of complexity or demonstrated technical marvel. A seemingly small oversight can completely derail success. But, if done correctly, the orchestra bows to a standing ovation.

Unfortunately, the successful management of a project rarely ends in joyous, emotional applause, particularly if security is the key function being managed. Instead, there may be an endless number of critics stating how it could have been done just a bit better. Although every user is not an expert, it is the comments from all that ensure progress is never ending and improvements are continually made. If you want to be a technical manager for fame and public recognition, you may want to rethink your future. Public recognition of technical managers usually stems from major problems of a project or when security has failed. How many have seen the faces of NASA engineers behind the countless success stories of American space exploration? Yet compare that with how many times we saw the NASA managers explaining themselves on television after the shuttle disasters. That is the risk of technical management and the challenge before you as Information Systems Security Engineering Professionals (ISSEPs) — getting it right when the definition of "right" is very illusive.

A conductor follows a prewritten score, often composed and arranged by others. The conductor assures everyone knows his or her part, each instrument is in tune, and every note is played on time. This perfection is achieved largely through rehearsal — endless repetition until the performance is just right. Unfortunately, this analogy does not translate well to the technical manager. By this time, the technical manager would be replaced and the luxury of rehearsal (that is, doing the project over again to get it right) is rarely possible. There are no dress rehearsals as such. If an IT project is poorly managed, it will be evident at show time.

In contrast to an orchestra, one of the issues with security engineering is that the results of a poor performance may not be revealed at show time. It may take months or years before the consequences of poor security design are known. Lacking a crystal ball to the future, we must rely on a sensible, systematic approach to identify and address the risks. The Information Systems Security Engineering (ISSE) process is rigorous and thorough, and making it a reality can be a challenge, but without it, security becomes a "best-guess" endeavor.

People, money, time, and tangible assets are all requisite ingredients but they serve different purposes. Money and time are consumed by people who work with, or use, tangible assets. Directing these resources includes predicting what resources are required, planning how to make the best use of them, ensuring they are used as planned, and redirecting them when plans change or results differ from expectations. In essence, the manager plans, directs, and controls the resources. The methods in which they do this are called processes. A model is basically a recommended set of processes or methods — it becomes the roadmap of how to get to a destination. This chapter unfolds the maps and shows what is involved in getting to a project's destination.

Elements of Technical Management

A technical effort can be defined as any activity that has an effect on defining, designing, building, or executing a task, requirement, or procedure. All the activities required to design, implement, and execute the systems engineering process are technical efforts. Technical management of those activities is required to progress efficiently and effectively from a business need to the deployment and operation of the system.

A project is defined as a planned, temporary (it has a beginning and an end) undertaking to create a unique product or service. Project management can be defined as applying knowledge, skills, tools, and techniques to a broad range of activities to meet project requirements. You may have heard of the "big three" of project management:

1. Time (schedule)
2. Cost (budgeted versus actual)
3. Quality (performance)

The challenge for those managing projects, and in system engineering the technical efforts, is to provide a quality product, within budget and on time. Adding scope and risk to the three attributes would make it the "big five." Another important project management attribute is to understand and meet the customer's needs and requirements.

The question is: can it be done? Do you have the right skills to provide this type of support to your customers? Before answering, first think about this question: Does the ISSEP® need to have project management skills? In this domain, we explain some basic management elements that every ISSEP should know when supporting a project. Although you may not write the PERT chart, you still need to know what it is and how it is used in the project. Thus, the ISSEP should have some basic understanding of managing a technical project.

The systems engineering management involves two major activities. The first is planning the effort. The second is managing the effort, which includes organizing tasks, directing activities, monitoring progress, and reporting status as appropriate. In this chapter, we focus on the primary systems engineering activities involved in planning and managing the project, the technical roles and responsibilities, the types of technical documentation needed, and technical management tools available to help manage the project.

This chapter is separated into five primary sections:

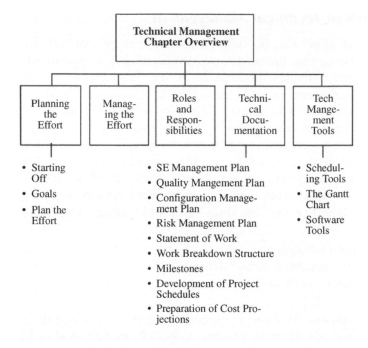

Figure 10.1 Chapter overview.

1. Planning the Effort
2. Managing the Effort
3. Technical Roles and Responsibilities
4. Technical Documentation
5. Technical Management Tools

Figure 10.1 provides an overview of the chapter, with major topics indicated. In the first section, "Planning the Effort," several key project-planning issues are outlined, such as defining the project's goal, scope, and resource requirements. "Managing the Effort" involves directing and monitoring the various activities and tasks, and reporting the project status. The "Technical Roles and Responsibilities" section defines the key players and their roles in managing the project. In the fourth section, we explain a very important document, the Systems Engineering Management Plan (SEMP), as well as the Statement of Work and Work Breakdown Structure. The final section, "Technical Management Tools," briefly introduces the Gantt chart and the PERT chart.

Planning the Effort

Starting Off

Like a story, every project has a beginning, middle, and end. Although it may seem obvious, the tendency is to dig right in ... straight to the middle. Before long, the project, which once seemed so clear, is suddenly unfamiliar and too complex. Little problems occur, there are no more personnel to delegate the problem to, and the software has not actually been released (it is still in beta testing). At this point, it may be necessary to halt or delay the project due to security concerns.

To prevent this disaster from happening, it is important to fight the tendency to jump right in; instead, one should jump right into planning. Understand that the planning discussed here is not that of planning the actual security design; it is planning the effort to make and implement the security design. During the planning stage of managing a technical project, one will, in general:

- Review the goals and scope of a project.
- Define the management structure.
- Determine the requisite resources.
- Develop schedules and dependencies.
- Quantify the results.

These are very broad categories and do not represent a particular management process or model, although they are present in some form in nearly all management models. What is important here is that these are not static tasks. The parameters these tasks represent will change continually during the course of a project. Project management essentially becomes a constant planning exercise. Because of this, planning the technical effort and managing the technical effort were given separate activity and task numbers within the IATF because they occur at all stages of the ISSE process. Appendix J of the IATF states: "Planning the technical effort occurs throughout the ISSE process. The information systems security engineer must review each of the following areas to scope support to the customer in conjunction with the other activities. This set of tasks is recognized separately because it is applied similarly across all of the other activities, requires a unique skill set, and is likely to be assigned to senior-level personnel."

IEEE Standard 1220-1998, "Systems Engineering Process," combines together the planning and management principles under a single heading of "Control." Again, this gives recognition that planning and management are inseparable dynamic activities. Words such as "dynamic" and "continually" should alert you to a key point: Plans must be flexible! Ever hear of Plan B? Well, before you are done with a project, you should plan for multiple changes, each one a small revision of the previous plan. Some parameters may not be flexible, such as the available budget or the lead time for procurement, but proper planning will identify and incorporate the fixed parameters with an eye toward minimizing the impact when other parameters change.

Goals

When starting a project, among the first questions asked are what is the technical effort trying to achieve and what is the security effort trying to achieve. Any impending technical effort will have been proposed for a reason (or perhaps several reasons). The greater the understanding of those reasons, the better direction the manager will have. The principal security engineering goals should be outlined in documents such as the Information Protection Policy.

Initially, the goals may be poorly defined or incomplete ideas. During the initial phases of a project, Systems Engineers (SEs) will assist customer in formulating the information management needs in relation to the reasons given by the customer for needing the project or effort. The ISSEP must also be engaged in this process to assist in deriving the information protection needs. In the ISSE model, this activity is referred to as "Discovering Information Protection Needs." These needs are the basis for the technical security manager's goals. Therefore, it is up to technical security managers to ensure that a representative of their staff is involved as early as possible.

Whomever the manager assigns to the "discovery" process should have enough knowledge and experience in the field to recognize the consequences of the established goals. The employee will be, in effect, signing up the ISSEPs to binding commitments, and this may be the only chance the ISSEP has to help steer the defined goals into a realistic direction. If potential problem areas are not flagged during the discovery process, then security could be held responsible for needlessly delaying a project during later stages of design or implementation, and subsequently overruled or bypassed.

Initial goals are typically too ill-defined for a detailed evaluation, so the assigned ISSEP will have to rely on experience to negotiate potential problem areas. The ISSEP should have sufficient knowledge to not merely consider the technical feasibility of proposed goals, but also view them from the perspective of time, budget, and resource constraints. For example, if the solution would require security expertise of a large software application not currently used by the organization, development of a security configuration policy may take longer than the organization business managers would assume is possible. Not knowing this could result in goals with unrealistic implementation dates. Theoretically, this would not be of great consequence because the final time frame for deploying a solution should not be determined until after the technical requirements and critical path timelines are generated. In the real world, however, senior executives have a habit of making the deadline part of the stated goals, such as, "Every employee will have desktop Internet connectivity by next summer." This may be considered quite feasible by the SE because it requires only a simple add-on to the existing network; however, it could represent a significant shift in vulnerability. The ISSEP must be capable of explaining the consequences to the overall project effort (in high-level, general terms) and be prepared to offer realistic alternatives.

An essential skill for the manager is to choose individuals who will admit to their own limitations and, when needed, seek additional input. In most cases, it is better for the ISSEP to seek advice rather than commit to an unattainable goal. Another decision for the manager is to decide whether anyone will have the authority to commit to the established goals on the manager's behalf. In short, if possible, assign a senior ISSEP to work with project goals and the discovery process.

Goals also affect quality. The more detailed and specific the goal, the easier it is to evaluate the potential information protection needs and subsequent design requirements. There is a balance, however. If the goals are too specific, design alternatives may be unintentionally eliminated. The goals should provide clear direction of outcome, not implementation. This is a key point highlighted in Principle 2 of the ISSE process. Principle 2 states, in part, "... Often customers talk to engineers in terms of technology and their notion of solutions to their problems, rather than in terms of the problem. Systems engineers and information systems security engineers must set these notions aside and discover the customer's underlying problem. ..."

The point in this section is not how to define the goals, but that if the goals have been properly addressed with this principle in mind, then they represent the problem to be solved by the technical effort. The manager should ensure that the subsequent steps do not stray from the goals.

As the technical effort progresses, secondary or lower-level goals will be defined. The manager should ensure that each level of effort and task is linked to a clear goal. As a summary, the key learning points for goals include:

■ Assigning senior people to work with goals
■ Getting senior people involved early
■ Ensuring that the technical effort does not stray from the goals

Plan the Effort

Let us now take a closer look at what comprises planning a technical effort. The IATF, Appendix J states that "the information systems security engineer must review each of the following areas to scope support to the customer in conjunction with the other activities. This set of tasks is recognized separately because it is applied similarly across all the other activities, requires a unique skill set, and is likely to be assigned to senior-level personnel. Bear in mind that at the beginning of a technical effort, you may have only general information about each of the tasks, but this will evolve in detail as the effort proceeds. The tasks are:

- *Task 1:* Estimate project scope
- *Task 2:* Identify resources and availability
- *Task 3:* Identify roles and responsibilities
- *Task 4:* Estimate project costs
- *Task 5:* Develop project schedule
- *Task 6:* Identify technical activities
- *Task 7:* Identify deliverables
- *Task 8:* Define management interfaces
- *Task 9:* Prepare technical management plan
- *Task 10:* Review project plan
- *Task 11:* Obtain customer agreement (p. J-5)"

Task 1: Estimate Project Scope

The project scope is a concise and accurate description of the deliverables expected from the project. It describes the processes required to ensure that the project includes all the work required, and only the work required, to complete the project successfully. The scope of work is the extent of work required to produce the project's deliverables (or end product). It is not the goal of the project, but the type and degree of work needed to meet the goal of the project. Project scope management consists of initiation, scope planning, scope definition, scope verification, and scope change control in an effort to ensure the project has all of the necessary work required.

Table 10.1 is adapted from the DoE Project Plan and provides some guidelines on project sizing. Note that the effort required represents all project activities, including those of functional areas. Also, there may be other factors unique to a particular project or situation that will influence project size.

Table 10.1   Estimating Project Scope

Complexity: - Key Attributes	Effort Required (In Person-Months)		
	1–8	9–24	25–X

Low:
  Existing or known technology
  Simple interfaces
  Requirements well known
  Skilled project team
	Small	Small	Medium

Medium:
  Some new technology
  Multiple interfaces
  Requirements not well known
  Skills not readily available
	Small	Medium	Large

High:
  New technology
  Numerous complex interfaces
  Numerous resources required
  Skills must be acquired
	Medium	Large	Large

Task 2: Identify Resources and Availability

To complete and maintain a project, the organization must ensure that it has the proper people, skills, and other resources. The resources required depend on factors such as specific skills needed, staff available, time, and whether development and maintenance will be performed in-house or using outside personnel (contractors).

Task 3: Identify Roles and Responsibilities

Specify the numbers and types of personnel required to conduct the project. Required skill levels, start times, duration of need, and methods for obtaining, training, retaining, and phasing out personnel will be specified.

Task 4: Estimate Project Costs

Cost estimating involves developing an approximation of the costs of the resources needed to complete the project activities and tasks. Typical resources to estimate costs might include a Work Breakdown Structure (WBS), resource requirements, resource rates (i.e., personnel hourly rates or cost per unit), activity and task duration estimates, and risks that might affect costs.

Task 5: Develop Project Schedule

Developing a schedule means determining start and finish dates for project activities and tasks. For these dates to be as realistic as possible, previous experience can be useful in determining how long and how many resources it will take to complete the activity or task.

Task 6: Identify Technical Activities

Activity definition involves identifying and documenting the specific activities that must be performed to produce the deliverables. These activities are sequenced and linked, if necessary, in a WBS. The WBS also provides a framework for assigning responsibilities. The scope of work is a major source for activity definition because it contains the project justification and objectives.

The activity and task descriptions are considered the main component of the project scope because they clearly define the exact steps needed to complete each task. Tasks should describe a logical, sequential description of the work. Itemize specific tasks to be performed in successive order from planning through completion (i.e., a logical, sequential description of the proposed work). It is helpful to start each activity or task with an action word (e.g., *create* a design document). Identify methods and materials that will be used in performing the work.

Task 7: Identify Deliverables

As part of the planning effort, the technical activities and tasks are defined and documented. This involves describing the actions (tasks), products (deliverables), and success criteria of the work to be performed. Identify deliverables resulting from each task. Identify one or more success criteria for each specific project activity and how it can be measured.

Task 8: Define Management Interfaces

Identify the necessary interfaces needed between all parties. These include the interfaces required for monitoring, supervising, and reviewing all work performed; coordinating, budgeting, and scheduling to ensure that the project is completed within budget and schedule; and completion of all project tasks in accordance with approved procedures and applicable laws and regulations.

Communications management involves methods for communicating and receiving information about the project to and from the project customer, stakeholders, and other participants. The methods to disseminate information are varied. One method is the monthly Technical Status Report. Additional performance reporting requirements can include, but are not limited to, special project manager's progress reports, quarterly project reports, weekly or monthly status briefings to the stakeholders and management, and project status review presentations.

More formal and frequent communications management may be required for projects with critical importance to program objectives and are large in size, complex, or highly visible, thus requiring a high degree of oversight. All project communications requirements should be identified in the detailed management plan.

Task 9: Prepare Technical Management Plan

The enterprise manages the tasks and activities of the System Engineering Management Plan (SEMP) to control data generated, configuration of the design solutions, interfaces, risks, and technical progress. The enterprise needs to maintain the correct staffing, facilities, equipment, and tools; manage costs and schedules; plan development activities, as required; coordinate technical interactions with customers; assure proper training of technical personnel and team members; measure technical progress; and coordinate the activities among the technical and business specialties needed to accomplish the systems engineering tasks.

An initial Technical Management Plan (TMP) is developed for a new task or project. The TMP is included in the Project Management Plan (PMP) that occurs as a result of the project manager planning the scope of a project, specific project deliverable activities, staffing, activity sequencing, activity duration estimating, schedule development, resource planning, cost estimation, and cost budgeting. The PMP is a consistent, coherent, dynamic document used to guide both project execution and project control.

The PMP contains the project goals, objectives, scope, and product overview. It is used to guide project execution; document project planning assumptions and decisions regarding alternatives chosen; facilitate communications among stakeholders; define key management reviews as to content, extent, and timing; and, provide a baseline for progress measurement and project control. The PMP is reviewed and revised as needed, typically at the end of stages, phases, or any logical checkpoint within a project. Critical project decisions made can also result in the PMP being revised (DoE Project Management Guidelines, 1998).

The SEMP will be prepared and updated throughout the system life cycle to guide and control the technical efforts of the project. It should reflect an integrated technical effort responsible for product development, which addresses all factors associated with meeting system life-cycle requirements.

Task 10: Review Project Management Plan

The SEMP must be continually reviewed and updated to maintain the integrity of the product and project. All approved changes must be reflected in the plan. For example, changes to the product scope (i.e., features and functions) must be reflected in the definition of the project scope. The plans for producing both scheduled and unscheduled updates to the project plan and dissemination of information methods should be specified. Part of the review process is placing the initial version of the plan under configuration management control to manage changes.

Task 11: Obtain Customer Agreement

Project planning activities are reviewed with senior management on a periodic basis.

IEEE 1220-1998 states that planning the technical effort is a process whereby the enterprise shall prepare and implement the technical plans and schedules necessary to guide the project toward accomplishment of its objectives and proper conclusion. Given the project's authorization and objectives, the enterprise should establish an engineering plan, a master schedule, and a detail schedule. The engineering plan should be the main planning document for all technical efforts and describe the tailored application of IEEE 1220. The master schedule (an event-based schedule) and the detail schedule (a calendar-based schedule derived from the master schedule) should address the development activities for the product, as well as support life-cycle processes. The master schedule and detail schedule can be combined into a single engineering schedule.

The U.S. Department of Energy's Systems Engineering Office has a checklist that can be helpful. It can be downloaded from the DoE Web site (see references for http address).

IEEE 1220 states "The Project Planning Checklist is intended to provide system owners, project managers, and other information system development and maintenance professionals with guidance in identifying and preparing project planning activities. The checklist reflects recognized project planning activities to be performed throughout the information systems project life cycle.

Project planning is generally characterized as a process for selecting the strategies, policies, programs, and procedures for achieving the objectives and goals of the project.

The objectives of project planning for information systems projects are summarized as the following:

- User's environment is analyzed.
- Project objectives and scope are defined.
- High-level functional requirements are estimated.
- Feasibility of the project is determined.
- The project plan is developed and approved" (p. 2).

Managing the Effort

According to IATF, managing the technical effort occurs throughout the ISSE process. The ISSEP must review all technical activities and documentation to ensure quality in conjunction with the other activities. This set of tasks is recognized separately because it is applied similarly across all the other activities, requires a unique skill set, and is likely to be assigned to senior-level personnel. The tasks are:

- *Task 1:* Direct technical effort
- *Task 2:* Track project resources
- *Task 3:* Track technical parameters
- *Task 4:* Monitor progress of technical activities
- *Task 5:* Ensure quality of deliverables
- *Task 6:* Manage configuration elements
- *Task 7:* Review project performance
- *Task 8:* Report project status

The following material is based on information from IEEE 1220, p. 61.

Task 1: Direct Technical Effort

Typically, the project manager (PM) has responsibility for the overall project and focuses on the schedule, cost, and technical performance of the system. The project manager may also have a Chief Systems Engineer (CSE) as the key manager for all the engineering work on the project and assume responsibility for the technical performance of the system. The CSE would be responsible for both contributing technical guidance as well as managing activities or personnel. The CSE would spend the majority of time in finding the correct technical solution for the customer and managing the engineering team.

Task 2: Track Project Resources

Define the reporting mechanisms, report formats, information flows, review and audit mechanisms, and other tools and techniques to be used in tracking and overseeing adherence to the various project plans. Project tracking will occur at the level of work packages, completion of deliverables, and logical checkpoints in the project. The relationship of tracking and oversight mechanisms to the project support functions will also need to be outlined.

Task 3: Track Technical Parameters

The enterprise should collect, analyze, and track product and process metrics to:

- Determine technical areas requiring project management attention
- Determine the degree of customer satisfaction and public acceptance
- Provide cost and schedule estimates for new products and provide faster response to customers

Task 4: Monitor Progress of Technical Activities

The enterprise measures, evaluates, and tracks the progress of technical efforts with the help of the master schedule, Technical Performance Measures (TPMs), cost and schedule performance measurements, and technical reviews. The activities associated with these measurements are described as follows:

- The master schedule identifies tasks and activities, with associated success criteria, of an element of the System Breakdown Structure (SBS) that should be accomplished to pass a defined technical event. A master schedule provides top-level process control and progress measurements that:
    - Ensure completion of required technical tasks
    - Demonstrate progressive achievements and maturity
    - Ensure that integrated, interdisciplinary information is available for decisions and events
    - Demonstrate control of cost, schedule, and performance risks in satisfying technical tasks, requirements, and objectives

TPMs, when appropriately selected, are key to progressively assessing technical progress. Each critical technical parameter should be tracked relative to time, with dates established as to when progress will be checked and when full conformance will be met. Key technical parameters are measured relative to lower-level elements of the SBS by estimate, analysis, or test, and values are rolled up to the system level. The TPMs are also used to:

■ Assess conformance to requirements
■ Assess conformance to levels of technical risk
■ Trigger development of recovery plans for identified deficiencies
■ Examine marginal cost benefits of performance in excess of requirements

The enterprise reports out-of-tolerance measurements to the project manager so that needed corrective actions may be taken.

Task 5: Ensure Quality of Deliverables

Metrics are collected, tracked, and reported at preestablished control points during each stage of development to enable the:

■ Establishment of a quality system and achievement of efficient use of resources
■ Overall system quality and productivity evaluation
■ Comparison to planned goals and targets
■ Early detection of problems
■ Benchmarking of the SEP

Task 6: Manage Configuration Elements

The enterprise updates specifications and configuration baselines to reflect all changes approved by the configuration control board. The original configuration baseline, with approved changes, provides the basis for continuing technical efforts.

Task 7: Review Project Performance

The enterprise collects and sorts data reflecting plan activities and tracks progress against engineering and technical plans to determine deviations from plans and needed changes, and to document changes, decisions, and accomplishments.

Task 8: Report Project Status

Cost and schedule performance measurements assess progress based on actual cost of the work performed, the planned cost of the work performed, and the planned cost of the work scheduled. Calculated cost and/schedule variances quantify the effect of problems being experienced. Cost and schedule performance measurements are integrated with TPMs to provide current cost, schedule, and performance impacts, and to provide an integrated corrective action to variances identified.

Technical reviews are conducted at the completion of an application of the SEP or end of a stage of development to assure that all master schedule criteria have been met; assess development maturity to date and the product's ability to satisfy requirements; assure traceability of requirements and validity of decisions; and assess risks related to investment needed for, and preparation for, the next stage of the life cycle.

Technical Roles and Responsibilities

Throughout this book, the technical roles and responsibilities have been mentioned and outlined. However, in this section, a composite of the various roles and responsibilities is provided in Table 10.2. The checkpoint function indicates the type of decisions made throughout a project's life cycle.

Projects have logical checkpoints (stages or phases) that are delineated in the project management plan. Project evaluations are conducted at these checkpoints and may involve an approval process by various members of the project team. For example, stakeholders will take these opportunities to validate that the project is meeting requirements; that requirements are still worthwhile; note how and if requirements have changed; and, make decisions regarding continuing with or terminating the project.

As defined by the Departmental Information Systems Engineering Guidance, Volume 2 (2002), the key roles for the project management processes are the Federal Program Manager, the Federal Technical Manager, and the PM (typically a contractor but may be a Federal employee).

The *Federal Program Manager* is generally assigned to a Federal employee who is responsible for the oversight of a program that is supported by a team of people that may include, or be exclusively comprised of contractors. The Federal Program Manager also ensures that performance indicators are established, met, and an appropriate transition to operations and maintenance occurs.

Table 10.2   Roles and Responsibilities

Role	Project Development Responsibility	Checkpoint Function
System Owner	Verifies developers' understanding of the application purpose and design. Has overall responsibility and accountability for system and data. Helps resolve conflict.	Approve
User Point of Contact (POC)	In representing the user community, acts as the single point of contact for approving project deliverables and changes. Resolves conflicts.	Approve
Client Representative	Reviews project deliverables. Represents the field's interests and ensures that the organization's information needs are met.	Approve
Quality Assurance Manager	Reviews and approves project deliverables from QA perspective. Reviews plans and deliverables for compliance with applicable standards. Provides guidance and assistance on process matters.	Approve
Project Manager	Responsible for daily planning and control of the project. Coordinates resolution of issues. Manages and coordinates technical effort. Performs adequate and timely staffing. Provides regular and timely communications.	Conduct
Project Planner	Prepares and administers project plans. Tracks and reports progress.	Support
Project Manager's Manager	Provides support and guidance to the project manager and team. Ensures project staffing. Resolves conflict across organizations. Facilitates communications.	Approve

Table 10.2 (continued)   Roles and Responsibilities

Role	Project Development Responsibility	Checkpoint Function
Senior Analyst	Reviews data model and assists in interviewing. Acts as primary author of design document.	Support
Senior Programmer 1	Designs user interface for the application. Writes or delegates the writing of all programs related to the application.	Support
Senior Programmer 2	Designs user interface for the application. Acts as primary author of design document. Writes or delegates the writing of all programs related to the application.	Support
Programmer	Assists the designer/programmer in writing programs.	Support
Configuration Manager	Prepares the Configuration Management Plan. Handles configuration management activities.	Support
Independent Tester	Conducts testing of the application at all stages of development.	Support
Acceptance Tester	Evaluates the application for overall operability and ease of user interface at acceptance.	Support
Documentation Specialist	Writes the user and programmer manuals.	Support
Trainer	Assists in the development of the Training Plan. Trains users.	Support
LAN Engineer	Provides internal consulting, testing, and support.	Support
Information System Security Engineer (ISSE)	Provides guidance in the design and development of the application and system security plan and related documentation.	Approve/ Support

Source: Adapted from *DoE Management Guide* (1998).

The Federal Program Manager responsibilities include:

- Ensure justification of expenditures and investment in systems engineering activities.
- Coordinate activities to obtain funding.
- Review and approve project plans.
- Review and approve deliverables throughout the project life cycle.
- Ensure processes are applied that will foster delivery of quality products and services.
- Coordinate issue resolution and escalation to higher management.
- Ensure acceptance testing and acceptance by the customer or system owner.

The *Federal Technical Monitor* (TM) is typically the Federal project manager who administers funded contractor task assignments. A TM must be involved in all funded contractor projects. TM project-related responsibilities include the following:

- Serve as the project manager for special, integrated, organizational, and agencywide projects as assigned by a program manager.
- Develop a clear and definitive Statement Of Work (SOW) for contractor task assignments, and provide independent government estimates for manpower and funding resources.
- Ensure plans and reports for managing and monitoring the task or project are identified and that they support effective management and satisfy technical and financial reporting requirements. Review, analyze, evaluate, and act on information provided through the plans and reports.
- Ensure coordination with all Federal and contractor project participants at project inception.
- Provide technical direction, planning, funding, and monitoring of contractor resources, including the approval of related travel and training.
- Closely monitor cost control, quality of technical performance, and timely milestone and schedule accomplishment through trend analysis and other means.
- Provide written evaluation of resource workplans, technical schedules, cost, and project management performance.
- Promptly review and approve management and project plans, and draft deliverables.
- Initiate written modifications to tasks upon change in scope or the period of performance.

Table 10.3 Example of Project Team

Project Team		
Development Team	Service and Support	Approvers
Project Manager	Independent tester	User point of contact
Senior Analyst	Documentation specialist	Client representative
Project Planner	Trainer	Quality assurance
Senior Programmer 1	ISSEP	Project manager's manager
Senior Programmer 2	LAN engineer	System owner
Programmer	Acceptance tester	
Configuration Manager		

Source: Adapted from DoE Project Plan Example (2001).

- Advise customers on the appropriate telecommunications and computer technology and their capabilities and limitations.
- Periodically evaluate contractor performance and provide comments and grades.

The *Federal* or *Contractor Project Manager* is the person responsible for daily planning, tracking, reporting, and coordination of project activities. These activities include the performance or oversight of configuration management, requirements management, risk management, and quality management. The PM is also typically responsible for personnel actions and issue resolution. Other common titles for the PM's role include project coordinator, project leader, project officer, and systems integrator.

The PM's role may be full or part-time. The PM may be a federal or contractor employee. It may be common for a contract PM to report to a contractor manager from an organizational perspective, but receive functional direction from the Federal program manager or TM.

An example of a project team and the roles is shown in Table 10.3. It defines the project team for a specific information system project.

Technical Documentation

The systems engineering plan is a living document that is structured to allow for ease of updating to reflect changes and progress throughout the ISSE model phases. Because there is a lot of information that must be included, the project manager should be careful not to duplicate the same information in multiple sections. In some projects, the plan that encompasses all the documentation may need to have a simple cross-reference table to help readers know where to find specific information.

Some of the typical documentation needed for an information systems engineering project includes:

- System Engineering Management Plan
- Quality Management Plan
- Configuration Management Plan
- Risk Management Plan
- Statement of Work
- Work Breakdown Structure
- Milestones
- Development of Project Schedules
- Preparation of Cost Projections

System Engineering Management Plan (SEMP)

The System Engineering Management Plan (SEMP) is an integrated plan that brings together many of the independent plans involved in systems design. It prevents redundancies and inconsistencies in objectives, schedules, and requirements. Essentially, the SEMP is a "master" document that references and explains who, what, where, when, and how the project will be managed.

- Who is doing what?
- Who is in charge of what?
- Who is responsible for whom?
- What are the management processes?
- When will things be done?
- How will they be done?
- How will all of this be organized?
- Where is documentation kept?
- Where is work to be accomplished?

The SEMP basically tells how project management is to be implemented. Because the plan is a living document, it should be flexible and accessible enough to incorporate change. The project manager will use the SEMP as a guide and reference throughout the systems security engineering process.

There are several standardized templates available, although each project will need to tailor the templates according to the management needs of any given project. There is some commonality between the SEMP outlines in various standards and handbooks. They generally include sections that describe:

- The systems engineering processes to be used
- The management processes to be used
- The documentation and associated processes to be used
- Systems engineering integration efforts to be applied
- Additional system engineering activities not covered elsewhere

For years, the U.S. DoD relied on MIL-STD-499, which described the requirements for drafting systems engineering management plans. It was cancelled without replacement in 1995 (although AFSCM 375-25 could serve as a *de facto* replacement). However, in 1998, the DoD adopted IEEE 1220 as the guiding document for management of the systems engineering process. Annex B of IEEE 1220 is a template for a SEMP (see fig. 1). For examination purposes, the reader should also be familiar with a modified MIL-STD-499 that was published (see fig. 2). It includes additional information regarding specialty skill areas and production management information.

Modern systems engineering processes, such as the IEEE 1220 SEP, incorporate those skill requirements throughout the process, making it redundant and unnecessary in current SEMPs. However, other MIL standards and handbooks still use terms and information contained within the MIL-STD-499, such as Contract Work Breakdown Structures (CWBS), that are not specifically identified in the IEEE 1220 SEMP template. In this chapter, we focus on the template offered by IEEE 1220-1998, supplemented with information from the other documents.

When looking at the outline in Table 10.4 (based on the IEEE 1220 SEMP Sample Table of Contents), the SEMP may appear to be very daunting or even contain information that is already documented elsewhere, such as the configuration management plan or the customer needs analysis. The purpose of the SEMP is not to repeat the information, but rather to ensure that there are processes in place to conduct those functions. The SEMP documents how those processes will be implemented and by whom. It should state where management information resides, such as where the QM plan resides, who is in charge of maintaining it, how it will be controlled, etc. Despite this, large and complex projects may still end up with a fairly daunting SEMP.

The SEMP template is intended for guidance only. The exact contents will vary by project and the structure should be flexible to accommodate frequent changes during the life of the project.

Referring to Table 10.4 and skipping over the self-evident Title Page and Table of Contents, we begin with Section 1.0 — Scope. This section should provide a summary of the project (or system) purpose, a summary of the SEMP, and a configuration management plan for keeping the SEMP up-to-date.

Table 10.4   Sample SEMP Template

I   Scope
II   Applicable Documents
III   Systems Engineering Process (SEP) Application
  • Systems Engineering Process Planning
    o   Major Deliverable and Results
    o   Integrated Database
    o   Specification Baselines
    o   Process Inputs
    o   Technical Objectives
    o   System Breakdown Structure (SBS)
    o   Training
    o   Standards and Procedures
    o   Resource Allocation
    o   Constraints
    o   Work Authorization
    o   Requirements Analysis
  • Requirements Baseline Validation
  • Functional Analysis
  • Functional Verification
  • Synthesis
  • Design Verification
  • Systems Analysis
    o   Trade-off Analysis
    o   System/Cost-Effectiveness Analysis
    o   Risk Management

  • Control
    o   Design Capture
    o   Interface Management
    o   Data Management
    o   Systems Engineering Master Schedule
    o   Technical Performance Measurement
    o   Technical Reviews
    o   Supplier Control
    o   Requirements Traceability
IV   Transitioning Critical Technologies
V   Integration of Systems Engineering Effort
  • Organizational Structure
  • Required Systems Engineering Integration Tasks
VI   Additional Systems Engineering Activities
  • Long-lead Items
  • Design to Cost
  • Value Engineering
  • Systems Integration Design
  • Interface with Other Life-cycle Support Functions
  • Safety Plan
  • Other Plans and Controls
VII   Notes
  • General Background Information
  • Acronyms and Abbreviations
  • Glossary
Appendices

■ ***Section 2.0 — Applicable Documents.*** This section should list all required project documentation. The list would include any standards (MIL, ISO, IEEE, etc.), references, guidance, corporate policy, etc.

■ ***Section 3.0 — Systems Engineering Process (SEP) Application.*** This section describes the plan as it pertains to the technical effort. Remember that this is a management plan — meaning that the description should describe how the SE tasks will be implemented. Are there SE steps modified or omitted? How are the processes applied within the enterprise? Who is responsible for what processes? List which offices or individuals have the organizational authorities for the SE activities. Significant project milestones and scheduling information should be noted, along with narratives, graphs, and charts that demonstrate the processes of the SE.

■ *Section 3.1 — Systems Engineering Process Planning.* This section summarizes the key project technical objectives, project deliverables, required process inputs and outputs, and product Work Breakdown Structure development.

  – *Section 3.1.1 — Major Deliverable and Results.* This section provides a detailed description of the technical deliverables.

    ■ *Section 3.1.1.1 — Integrated Database.* The integrated database is the central repository for all data collected as part of the SE process. This section describes how the database is created and maintained.

    ■ *Section 3.1.1.2 — Specification Baselines.* This section describes how specifications and baselines will be created, documented, and controlled.

  – *Section 3.1.2 — Process Inputs.* This section identifies the level of information needed for the SE plan and how that information will be collected.

  – *Section 3.1.3 — Technical Objectives.* This section provides a detailed narration of the technical objectives to be achieved by the SE plan and project. It also covers system products and their life-cycle processes.

  – *Section 3.1.4 — System Breakdown Structure (SBS).* The SBS section should describe how the SBS elements are developed and their relationship to the specification tree and the drawing tree. How the element work packages are planned and managed should also be included.

  – *Section 3.1.5 — Training.* This section should identify both internal and external training, and include analyses that link performance to training.

  – *Section 3.1.6 — Standards and Procedures.* This is where required standards and procedures are identified.

- *Section 3.1.7* — *Resource Allocation.* The methods of resource allocation for the technical tasks should be fully described here, including procedures for determining resource requirements, control, and reallocation.
- *Section 3.1.8* — *Constraints.* Describe the project constraints, to include constraints on funding, personnel, facilities, manufacturing capability and capacity, critical resources, and other constraints. Also identify what the project will and will not do.
- *Section 3.1.9* — *Work Authorization.* Describe the work authorization procedures as well as change management approval processes.

■ *Section 3.2* — *Requirements Analysis.* This section details the methods whereby system requirements are to be determined. Methods to define both functional as well as performance requirements should also be detailed, along with how they relate to specified quality factors. As we will see in the Quality Management section, the suitability of a solution relies heavily upon understanding the problem in terms of needs. Needs are expressed in terms of requirements. Thus, the methods used to determine requirements will have a direct impact upon how successful the engineering effort will be. Documenting them allows for reviews to identify potential flaws in methodology or amendments if the nature of the requirements changes during the development effort.

■ *Section 3.3* — *Requirements Baseline Validation.* This section describes the methods and approach to validate the requirements baseline established during requirements analysis. Section 3.2 establishes the methods used to determine requirements. Section 3.3 details the reasoning behind why and how those methods were selected.

■ *Section 3.4* — *Functional Analysis.* This section describes the methods for determining lower-level functions and their requirements, interfaces, and architecture.

■ *Section 3.5* — *Functional Verification.* This section describes the methods to ensure that the functional architecture is properly derived from a validated requirements baseline.

■ *Section 3.6* — *Synthesis.* This section describes how the functional architecture will be realized into a detailed system design solution (hardware, software, and human). This section also explains how design trade-offs are selected and how system requirements will be translated into design specifications.

■ *Section 3.7* — *Design Verification.* This section describes how the detailed system design will be validated against the functional requirements and the validated specification baseline.

■ *Section 3.8 — Systems Analysis.* One cannot have everything. One might want everything, but systems engineering is about compromise and balancing performance, risks, and costs. This section of the SEMP details the methods and reasoning planned to make the requisite trade-offs between functionality, performance, cost, and risk.

■ *Section 3.9 — Control.* Project management requires the control of resources, time, and efforts. This section of the SEMP explains how configuration control will be implemented. It includes descriptions, data management, scheduling, technical reviews, performance measures, and supplier control. Requirements traceability should also be included.

■ **Section 4.0 — Transitioning Critical Technologies.** This section describes how the project will handle the incorporation of critical technologies. It should include methods of identifying the key critical technologies, the risks associated with them, and how they will be assessed. Evolution of those technologies as well as alternatives should also be described.

■ **Section 5.0 — Integration of Systems Engineering Effort.** This section details the organizational aspects of the engineering effort. It should include the planned structure, reporting chain, and how the various disciplines will be integrated. Personnel requirements are also addressed in this section.

■ **Section 6.0 — Additional Systems Engineering Activities.** This section provides the catchall for activities that do not fit neatly into previous sections. This section could include activities relating to handling long-lead items, design to cost analysis, value engineering, systems integration design, safety plans, and systems integration design. Special or unique tools to be used on the project development could be identified here. This section should basically cover any remaining plans and controls not included elsewhere.

■ **Section 7.0 — Notes.** This section includes general background information, acronyms and abbreviations, the glossary, and other information pertinent to understanding how the development effort will be managed.

■ **Appendices:** No elaboration needed.

Quality Management Plan

The Concept of Quality

"They just don't make them like they used to" is an old phrase repeated through the years. You may have heard it as a child when a parent was desperately trying to assemble a new toy and Tab A simply refused to align with Slot B. With a little pressure here and a bit of twisting there, the toy would eventually fit together. Either that, or it snapped off with a sharp crack, in which case an unprintable exclamation was usually followed with a comment that if it broke, it needed replacing anyway. Replacement meant an untimely trip to the store with a grumpy claim that your parent did not break it, it just came that way. It was obviously a defective product.

These days, you ponder why your bicycle tire is flat when you pumped it up only a week ago, or why the light bulb is blown and you are sure you just installed a new one last month. Events such as these cause you to question where the quality has gone. Is the world doomed to a slow decay of increasingly poor quality? Well, probably not. It is quite likely that folks from your parent's generation heard a phrase similar to "they don't make them like they used to" from their parents, and you will probably continue the tradition by muttering it yourself, if you have not already done so. The fact is, needs and requirements change. Quality is not just about how long a product lasts or how much is costs; it is about how suitable a product is for your needs.

Baguley (2001) notes that Joseph Juran, considered by many as the father of quality, claimed that "quality is fitness for purpose or use." Philip Crosby, a leading quality guru, has stated that "quality has to be defined as conformance to requirements, not as goodness" (Baguley, 2001, p. 93). Fitness and conformance equate to performance, whereas documented purpose and requirements can be viewed as specifications. Based on these concepts, detailed specifications and needs analysis became very important to ensuring quality. If specifications and requirements are properly documented with sufficient detail and clarity, then the ability to conform to the specifications should result in a product or service that meets the needs — hence quality.

People assume quality costs, but cost can be viewed in a couple different ways. First, cost relates to "value" and is treated separately from quality. To illustrate value, a high quality for a low cost will yield better value than high quality at a high cost. Second, it can be inherent in the requirements. If the end user has a fixed amount of capital to spend, then performance is not achieved if the product cost exceeds the financial ceiling. So in the first case, cost is not a factor of quality but instead is used with quality to equate value. In the second case, it is an inherent factor in *achieving* quality.

Ever hear the phrase, "the customer is always right"? In the earlier example, you wanted your bicycle tire to hold air for more than a week, but if it stays inflated during your ride, then it has met your basic need. So if the tire met the basic need, or requirement, why are you still not happy if it does not hold air for more than a week? Because we expect it to; and if it does not, we are not satisfied. Satisfaction is directly related to customer expectations. Putting this together, quality is the composite of relevant attributes, which include the performance features and characteristics of a product or service to satisfy a customer's need. The quality of products or services can therefore be measured as the degree to which they meet (or exceed) requirements and satisfy the customer, at an affordable cost (DoD/DS/SE *Quality Homepage*).

The key point here is customer satisfaction. According to Lock (1989), this is the ultimate goal of quality: to attain customer satisfaction with the proper consideration for costs. The customer is the end judge of "satisfaction," but true quality must include consideration of factors that may not be immediately evident or measurable in terms of performance. This is particularly important with security. A poorly designed software program or network configuration may have exploitable security holes that are not noticed until an adversary takes advantage of them. Or worse, the holes are not discovered until months or years after the adversary has exploited them.

Quality Management Plan

Quality management should be applied to all activities of project management, which include (but are not limited to) planning, organizing, monitoring, controlling, reporting, and taking corrective actions. How it is implemented will vary from organization to organization and even from project to project, and should be detailed in a quality management plan. The plan answers who, what, when, and how by specifying the procedures and resources to be used. For example, the plan might specify types of performance data to be collected prior to passing the product to the next phase of design.

Quality Control

Traditional methods of tracking quality involve statistical data. In the 1950s, the U.S. military controlled quality with stringent specifications. Essentially, any product that failed to meet the military specifications was rejected.

Software developers have several methods for measuring quality, but a common measure includes the following metrics: correctness, maintainability, integrity, and usability (Pressman, 1994, p. 801). Correctness is usually measured in terms of defects per 1000 lines of code (KLOC) and represents how well the code conforms to requirements. Maintainability is considered the mean time to correct errors once they are found. Integrity refers to the software's resiliency to attack — which is a key security concern. Usability is characterized by four attributes:

1. Physical and/or intellectual skills required
2. The time it takes to become reasonably proficient in using the software
3. The productivity gains through using the software
4. User attitudes toward the product

All these metrics are "after-the-fact" quantities. Essentially, they quantify how well the software performs once it is deployed. For example, the correctness parameter is often determined statistically over an entire year after the product has been released. Considering the size and popularity of Internet security advisory lists, a lot of damage can be invoked over the course of a year due to software holes and bugs. Many of these bugs are found only through rigorous and continuous hostile inspection of the programs or systems by people other than the design team. It can literally take years to uncover some of the more sophisticated flaws.

Considering that customer satisfaction is the primary quality goal and is theoretically reached through meeting detailed performance criteria, it would seem that more care is needed in defining measurable requirements. Unfortunately, the complexity of modern code and integrated systems makes it very difficult — if not impossible — to create a "mil-spec" for software code prior to actual development. It is not practical to ensure quality by trying to predict all measurable requirements for each system component to a level necessary to ensure system integrity (we could still be waiting for the release of Windows 95). The abundance of security flaws is perhaps more a measure of complexity rather than indifference to quality concerns.

To improve upon the pass/fail metrics, the source of errors rather than the error itself must be addressed. This requires an understanding of the processes involved in production, development, deployment, and end use. Proper data collection can help find errors in design methods, tolerance control techniques, and aid in conducting quality inspections. Selecting what data to measure and how to collect it depends on what purpose the data will serve and how it will be analyzed. Suppose a firewall malfunctions. We use the word "malfunction" to mean that an attack gets through when, by design, it should not have. The malfunction could be the result of a poor user interface that made it easy to select an incorrect setting or miss a menu. It could have been caused by poor operator training, in which it was not made clear what settings to use. Or a flaw in the software algorithms could be the culprit. Data of successful attacks might highlight the problem, but not the source. Recording the number of times test subjects configured the firewall correctly may point to training or interface problems. Further data may underscore the lack of timely feedback from initial beta testers to interface coders, or even the lack of ergonomic training and awareness for the interface designers.

Statistical process control (SPC) is used primarily in manufacturing but has application in software development. It uses a variety of statistical data analysis tools to determine the source of problems and improve the associated processes. In general, SPC involves:

- Defining data to be collected
- Collecting actual data
- Processing collected data
- Analyzing results using statistical methods

Although the choice of data analysis tools used in SPC may not be entirely relevant to non-manufacturing efforts, the general steps are relevant. Understand the data to be collected and why it is needed. Collect it in a meaningful way, and then process and analyze.

Total Quality Management

While it will probably not be on the ISSEP Exam, Total Quality Management (TQM) makes a nice lead into the concept of quality process. TQM professes that quality of all the processes within an organization contribute to the quality of the product. Those processes, whether administrative, engineering, human resource, or even social, should be continually refined for improvement until those functions are done right — the first time and every time. If all the processes contributing to product development are continually improved, and the refinement cycle is extended to the product itself, then the best quality will be achieved. According to Imai (1986, p. 259), the three main activities in TQM are:

1. Maintenance of quality
2. Quality improvements
3. Quality renewal

Maintenance, improvements, and renewal are all continuous activities. They imply repetitive dynamic processes as opposed to one-time checks for quality. Thus, the collection of data and quality metrics outlined in the previous sections is an ongoing endeavor. After the data is analyzed, corrective steps to improve the process must be decided upon and taken. The data is again collected and analyzed, and again subsequent adjustments are made.

Quality Management

Ensuring quality can be viewed as an evolving series of corrective measures on a process. In this context, a process is the development effort, either taken as a whole or as a subprocess within it. If the development effort is ill-defined or poorly structured, then the quality metrics fed back will be of minimal value. For this reason, quality is increasingly based on how well an effort is managed. The development models and strategies used must include provisions for the collection of quality-related data and the means to make use of that data for improvement, all on a continual basis. This reinforces the need for understanding and using accepted development models and the ISSE model. For example, IEEE Std 1220-1998, Sec 4.13, entitled "Quality Management" states that "The enterprise shall monitor product and process quality factors and shall continuously improve products and processes throughout the system life cycle."

The USG is increasingly following the lead of international standards by requiring contractors to comply with formal development and quality processes with the assumption that, if followed, a quality product will result. This is a dramatic departure from the traditional approach of conformance to specification requirements. In DoD 5000.2-R (April 2002), the DoD highlighted this strategic shift by stating that "...product quality is now viewed as an attribute that is controlled by the engineering/design and business processes, as well as the maturation of the associated manufacturing/production process." Further, for the DoD to achieve quality products and services, one must focus on *conformance to requirements, fitness for use, cost,* and *quality of design.* The first three attributes embody the basic description of quality, customer expectations, and value, whereas the fourth (quality of design) adds the principle of "process." The term "quality of design" is defined as the effectiveness of the design process in capturing the performance, manufacturing, and operational support requirements, and translating them into robust requirements that can be manufactured, coded, and supported in a consistent manner.

Quality Management in a Project — ISO 10006

The leading international reference for quality management practices is the ISO 9000 series of standards. The U.S. adopted version, the ANSI/ASQC Q9000 series, basically requires processes like those explained in the ISSE model. A related document, ISO 10006, entitled "Quality Management Systems — Guidelines for Quality Management in Projects," draws upon principles in the ISO 9000 series and relates them to project management. Aside from preliminaries such as scope and definitions, the ISO 10006 divides project management into four sections:

1. Management responsibility
2. Resource management
3. Product realization
4. Measurement, analysis, and improvement

Management Responsibility

One of the elements of management responsibility is *commitment*. Top management must be committed to the quality process. ISO 10006 points out that there are two key areas for quality management in projects: the process and the end product. Both of these areas must be addressed to avoid a significant impact on the product quality goals. Effectively addressing both areas means senior management must instill the commitment to quality goals at all levels within the organization and accept overall responsibility. However, each level of project management remains responsible for the quality of their respective products and processes.

- *Strategic process.* Because it must address both the organizational processes as well as end product, choosing to implement a quality management system is a strategic decision within an organization. Its implementation will affect all aspects of a development cycle. The eight ISO guiding principles for quality management are discussed in Domain 1, Chapter Seven. They are repeated here for clarity.
  - Customer focus
  - Leadership
  - Involvement of people
  - Process approach
  - System approach to management
  - Continual improvement
  - Factual approach to decision making
  - Mutually beneficial supplier relationships
- *Management reviews.* Remember the concept of continual improvement? It also applies to the quality management system. At planned intervals, the quality management system should be examined to ensure that it is still applicable and effective.
- *Progress evaluations.* Regular evaluations on project achievements indicate how well a project is progressing. Although not strictly a performance evaluation, progress evaluations do reflect performance attributes and can provide valuable information to performance and management reviews.

Resource Management

Resources are comprised of people, money, and things. *Things* include documents, software, test equipment, office supplies, etc. A contracted service could be viewed as an outside resource of *people* and *things*. If there are insufficient resources, quality will suffer. Resources must be planned for and controlled. Resource planning is critical to identify the requisite personnel, funding, and tangible assets and ensure they are available when needed. The following parameters should be considered:

- Supplier lead times
- Supplier reliability
- Source of resources
- Procedures for distributing or allocating resources
- Limitations of resources
- Contingency planning or alternate resource

Once resources are planned and acquired, their use must be monitored and, if needed, adjusted to prevent shortages and delays. A delay in one part of a project could have a domino effect on other project activities. The project management plan should specify resource-reporting requirements.

In terms of human resources, quality is derived from ensuring the right skill sets are in place and the people with those skills can function effectively within the organizational structure. The administrative environment should be conducive to improved productivity with a proper balance between substantive work and bureaucratic overhead. Employees drowning in paperwork could mean that there are not enough workers, or that the level of reporting requirements is not on par with the practical benefits. The ISO standards committee demonstrated a sterling example of this when it revised the ISO 9000 series in 2000. The ISO modified some of the original documentation requirements to meet compliance in response to criticism by smaller companies that found the amount of documentation impractical for the value it achieved in their business processes. In essence, smaller companies simply did not have the staff, so attempting to comply did more to detract from quality rather than enhance it.

If organizational processes are not well defined or easily engaged, productivity declines. For example, if a review process engages more people or offices than necessary, then obtaining a timely consensus might prove extremely difficult. In the security world, if people do not receive timely answers, they tend to move on without it. On the other hand, if a review process does not include the appropriate expertise, serious flaws might pass unnoticed to the next stage of development and even find their way into the final product.

Teamwork is an essential ingredient in creating and sustaining a productive workforce. When a person lacks the requisite skills, the effect on product quality is fairly self-evident. Adjustments to personnel staffing and training are obvious solutions, but teamwork can also play a major role. Collaboration with team members can be a quick way to bridge a skill gap, draw upon a wider base of experience, or facilitate minor adjustments to the staffing workload. However, being too qualified can be as detrimental as being under-qualified, in which case understanding and embracing teamwork takes on even greater importance. Team members should be made aware of the importance of their contribution and the effect they have on product quality. Wider experience complements the team balance, and the source of that experience should take pride in imparting those skills to others. Teamwork training will help cultivate the personnel processes within the team.

Product Realization

Product realization consists of seven project management process groupings:

1. Interdependency-related processes
2. Scope-related processes
3. Time-related processes
4. Cost-related processes
5. Communication-related processes
6. Risk-related processes
7. Purchasing-related processes

Interdependency-related processes. This refers to managing the links and communications between the project tasks and is the responsibility of the project manager. Examples of interdependency-related processes are project initiation, the project management plan, interaction management, change management, and process and project closure.

Scope-related processes. These processes define and characterize the project's product and how conformance is to be quantified and measured. Scope establishes the project boundaries in accordance with project goals, and the project manager should ensure that all work is kept within those boundaries. Examples of scope-related processes are concept development, scope development and control, definition of activities, and control of activities.

Time-related processes. These processes describe the links and time dependencies between project activities to ensure a timely completion of the project. Examination of these processes will allow a project manager to calculate the required timing of project resources as well as the impact if the timing should slip or change. Examples of time-related processes include planning of activity dependencies, estimation of duration, schedule development, and schedule control.

Cost-related processes. Controlling costs is central to every project. The cost-related processes seek to predict and control the project costs to ensure that they are within budget constraints. The cost-related processes include cost estimation, budgeting, and cost control.

Communication-related processes. Because of the interdependencies between various project activities as well as with organizational processes, efficient communication is essential. Establishing and maintaining good communication requires communication planning, information management, and communication control.

Risk-related processes. Risk, covered in a separate section of the book, is a measure of uncertainty — both good and bad. Risk-related processes are essential to minimize any negative impact due to uncertainty, yet capitalize on opportunities for improvement. Risk-related processes are risk identification, risk assessment, risk treatment, and risk control. With any project, risks are always present, and "risk treatment" refers to the plans to mitigate the risks.

Purchasing-related processes. Most projects involve the purchasing of goods or services to realize project objectives. Purchasing, particularly from within a government organization, can be fraught with uncertainties (such as delivery date slippage due to a snag in the procurement administrative process). This does not imply that the procurement sections are unresponsive; rather, it is a statement of how complex a government procurement process can be. It is probably one of the most hazardous areas affecting schedule control for a new or inexperienced project manager. Purchasing-related processes include purchasing planning and control, documentation of purchasing requirements, supplier evaluation, and contract control. Various government or organizational regulations and policies already specify much of the purchasing-related processes. The project manager, having little hope of changing any of these regulations, must work within the procedures already established. Therefore, purchasing planning is vital step in preventing a project from being derailed.

Measurement, Analysis, and Improvement

Improvement requires knowledge of "what is" so it can be compared with "what is desired." Determining "what is" involves the collection of data that characterizes the relevant process performances with respect to the desired metric of improvement. Improvement is questionable at best, unless the measurement data is reliable and accurate. The collection process itself should be efficient and detract or interfere as little as possible with the development effort.

Typical performance measurements include audits, evaluation of individual tasks, product evaluations, evaluations of supplier performance, resource usage compared to resource estimates, work progress, and customer satisfaction. Nonconformities to project requirements or specifications should be documented and examined for potential corrective action. Because not all nonconformities are significant enough to necessarily warrant documentation or corrective action, the project organization should confer with the customer as to which nonconformities will be addressed.

Other sources of information include project logs, claims, and project reviews. The data should be examined carefully to ensure relevance and accuracy. According to AFSCM 375-5, typical project reviews conducted for the DoD can include:

■ System requirements review
■ System design review
■ Preliminary design review
■ Critical design review
■ First article configuration inspection
■ Acceptance test
■ Technical approval demonstration

To facilitate continuous improvement, the organization must define the information necessary to gauge the performance, as well as the appropriate collection methods and manner of storage and retrieval. The information collected and subsequent lessons learned should be shared, when relevant, with other projects within the organization. This ensures that quality improvement is not limited to a single effort, but becomes an institutional benefit.

It is the responsibility of the project organization to ensure that the project management system can accommodate data collection and process improvement, and that improvements are indeed implemented (see Table 10.5).

Configuration Management Plan

Consider the first mantra for anti-virus software: always update the virus list. For security, change is a staple ingredient. Software and hardware products continually change; thus, threats and attack techniques are moving targets. Each new batch of programming code or system configuration brings an opportunity for security flaws. In this respect, a system security development process must stay on top of current security issues and adjust accordingly. However, the adjustments must be made with care. A tweak in one aspect of design may very well tear a security hole in another aspect, possibly in a later stage. Configuration management brings into play a process for due consideration of potential consequences.

Configuration Management (CM) allows potential changes to a project to be identified, evaluated, implemented, tracked, and controlled throughout the system engineering and product life cycle. CM is largely a consequence

Table 10.5   Quality Management (QM) Key Learning Points

- A quality product or service is one that meets customer needs and expectations
- Quality management focuses on conformance to requirements, fitness for use, quality of design, and cost
- Expectations are expressed as requirements
- Requirements include relevant product features, characteristics, measurable performance levels, and cost
- Requirements can also be called specifications
- Quality management is an evolving series of corrective measures on a process
- QM ensures processes are in place to deliver a quality product or service
- A QM plan answers who, what, when and how by specifying procedures and resources to be used
- Quality management addresses the source of errors, not just the resulting error
- Development processes must include provision to collect quality-related performance data on a continual basis
- Quality-related performance data must be relevant to finding the source of error
- Four areas of project management quality responsibility include:
  - management responsibility
  - resource management
  - product realization
  - measurement, analysis, and improvement
- Management provides quality commitment
- Resources must be sufficient and available
- Engineering, production, and service delivery processes must be controlled in terms of time, costs, communication, scope, and interdependencies
- Collection of quality performance data must be reliable, accurate and interfere as little as possible
- Performance measures can include audits, evaluations, supplier performance, resource usage, work progress, and customer satisfaction

of quality management systems and of systems engineering development models. Remember that quality management involves a constant evaluation of the development processes and products, and compares them against performance data. Improvement is sought by recommending (or mandating) subsequent changes. If this is a continuous process, then change is constant. To prevent the chaos of constant change, CM systems instill order and discipline. CM provides a methodical and logical approach to managing change to ensure the correct version (typically the latest version), of the product or process is in use.

The implementation of CM will vary from organization to organization and from project to project. Factors such as technical complexity, size of effort, and source of funding influence how the CM system is structured. Organizations such as government offices often have specific CM rules and policies for the implementation framework. Others may cite guidelines to follow such as the ISO 10007. The U.S. DoD falls somewhere in between by citing a very detailed and extensive handbook for guidance, MIL-HDBK-61A, which in turn embraces industry practice. Descriptions will also vary; but regardless of the specified reference or forms to fill out, the basic principles are fairly consistent. The following list nicely sums up the commonly understood benefits of CM and is consistent with DoD guidelines and international standards. Burke (2003) suggests that CM offers:

- A process that formally documents procedures for changing official project documents
- A listing of the people with authority to make the changes in requirements
- An up-to-date description of the product
- Baseline configuration history and traceability
- Record and audit trails of approved changes
- A framework to monitor, evaluate, and update the baseline with respect to changes in scope or requirements
- Automatic approval for emergency situations

By way of contrast, when there is a lack of CM, there may be:

- Equipment failures due to incorrect part installation or replacement
- Schedule delays and increased cost due to unanticipated changes
- Operational delays due to mismatches with support assets
- Maintenance problems, downtimes, and increased maintenance costs due to inconsistencies between equipment and its maintenance instructions
- Numerous other circumstances that decrease the operational effectiveness and add costs

There are numerous circumstances that could decrease the operational effectiveness of the security requirements, and the consequences could be severe.

Reasons for Change

It is a rare project that does not need adjustment or refinement during its lifetime. There are many reasons for requiring change. When an error is found, it usually needs to be corrected. What is the first thing we do after purchasing a brand new piece of software? We download the latest patch. Then we check back again later, often when something goes wrong, find and download another patch. An error in terms of CM is generally an item that does not meet the measurable specifications or defined requirements.

Change may not be due to error, but a change in project scope or user requirements. Suppose there was a requirement for an eight-hour battery backup. Then, part way through the development process, staffing at the implementation site moved to a 24-hour schedule. As a result, the customer decides to draw back to a one-hour battery backup.

Change could also be due to resource or product availability. Suppose there was a requirement that the system software and hardware had to be compatible with the Mt. Waddle, Inc., High-Top Data Security and Pro Backup package. This outstanding package fulfills several project requirements and is off-the-shelf. No additional project engineering is needed — a perfect project solution. Then nearing the final development phase, Mt. Waddle goes bust. Facing that dilemma, a change will certainly be needed.

Not all change is due to negative factors. New technology can invoke change. Initially, a security project may have called for separate telephone, CCTV, and LAN cabling to another building. But as the project evolved, it became evident that cost savings could be realized using new LAN-based telephone and CCTV devices in a single cable run.

Other reasons for change include available funding, contractual partnerships, compatibility of items and processes, concerns for future availability, and service or support. Table 10.6 provides a summary of the typical reasons for change.

Implementation of Changes

There are three basic categories or, more specifically, implementations of change:

1. Change to product or service specifications
2. Change to processes
3. Change to documentation

These three categories refer to the actual CM actions and are different than the causes. For example, a change in project scope would be considered the cause, whereas the change is implemented by making the

Table 10.6   Reasons for Change in a Project

- An item does not meet the measurable specifications or defined requirements
- Change in project scope or user requirements
- Resource or product availability
- New technology available
- Changes in available funding
- Changes in contractual partnerships
- Compatibility of items
- Compatibility of processes
- Concerns for future availability, service or support

appropriate modifications in either the specifications or the processes. Perhaps a security-scanning tool was originally intended to be operated only by the security officers at the corporate headquarters. After a few presentations to senior management, they become enthusiastic and decide tremendous cost savings could be realized if the tool was used throughout all corporate facilities. A nice idea, but current staffing levels do not permit deployment of such a labor-intensive tool in every facility. Thus, this change in project scope results in a new requirement for the tools to be used across the network. This requirement is implemented by the CM system as changes to the product specifications.

Product specifications may not be the only change. There will be changes to the development process as well. The composition of project groups may change. In the example above, a network programmer might be added, or maybe the design approval hierarchy would now include the network management section head.

Some improvements require only changes in documentation. For example, as the security scanning tool is going through initial testing, it is decided that the workstation user should be logged off before running the tool. Thus, the documentation is changed to incorporate the new operational procedures.

Evolution of Change

A change in scope or requirements will usually result in a combination of all three change implementations at some level. However, the relative distribution will tend to shift as the project progresses through its life cycle. Early on in a project, people are still trying to come to grips with scope and purpose, or nailing down the basic requirements. Information is gathered and various options are considered. Most changes during this period will be to the product or service specifications.

When the project is well into the detailed design or coding stages, constraints, incompatibilities, and limitations become more apparent, Corrections at this point tend to affect the ongoing development processes. Toward the end, when a considerable amount of documentation exists, any tweaks or adjustments in the product may have a ripple effect on an increasing number of project documents.

The DoD Configuration Management System

The MIL-HDBK-61A (2001) describes *configuration management* as knowing the correct current configuration of defense assets and the relationship of those assets to associated documents. The CM process efficiently manages necessary changes, ensuring that all impacts to operation and support are addressed.

A key word in this definition is *impact*. Changing any defined element — called a Configuration Item (CI) — could significantly impact other configurable items or development processes. This could include serious consequences on contracts, agreements, budgets, and timelines. Thus, the CM activity is integral to the system engineering management process and should be viewed as a collection of processes. As shown in Figure 10.2, there are five basic processes that comprise CM:

1. Management and planning
2. Configuration identification
3. Configuration control
4. Configuration status accounting
5. Configuration verification and audit

Although all of these CM processes happen continuously during the project life cycle, the bulk of management and planning occurs during the project initiation phase when the requirements or specification analysis (scope definition) occurs. Configuration identification goes hand in hand with functional analysis and allocation. Configuration control gets its heaviest workout during the detailed design, fabrication, and implementation processes.

CM Management and Planning

The CM system should be fully documented in a PMP and approved by the customer and the project manager. The PMP should identify who has authorities and responsibilities for approving and implementing change.

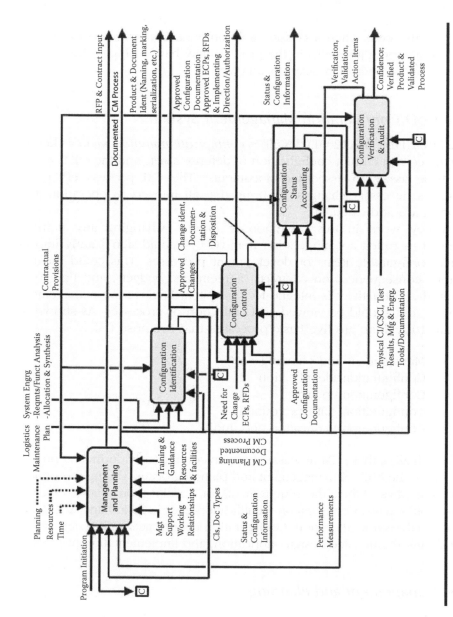

Figure 10.2 Top-level configuration management activity model. (*Source:* From MIL-HDBK-61A, 2001.)

ISO 10007 (2003) notes that the level of authority granted will be governed by several factors, such as:

- Complexity and nature of the product
- Needs of the different product life-cycle stages
- Interfaces inside the organization and to outside parties

The plan should consider who would have the authority for verifying change and for dispositioning authority. The dispositioning authority verifies that change is necessary, the consequences would be acceptable, the change is documented, and the implementation plans are satisfactory.

The PMP should document the CM procedures to be used, as well as draw from successful procedures in existing or previous plans when possible. The plan should also identify required and referenced standards, policy documents, etc.

Change management relies on good communication. Without an organized communication structure, people may end up incorporating an outdated item or faulty process. Common quality management communication structures are sequential, parallel (sometimes called spoke or star), or group. Sequential means that change requests, evaluations, and approvals are passed sequentially from one person to another. This has the advantage that each person in the chain has the benefit of seeing the comments and judgments collected along the way. On the downside, overall progress is slower and tracking the progress can be difficult or time consuming.

Parallel is when the documentation goes to several people simultaneously. The obvious benefits here are rapid dissemination and return to a single point. Tracking progress is relatively easy (although getting people to act on it might not be). The downside is the potential for uninformed decisions. It may be critical for someone to know another office's perspective before passing judgment. The project manager should weigh these options carefully and apply them as best suited, depending on the items, type of changes required, or size of potential impact.

Group sessions can be difficult if not administered well. The most common is a *Configuration Control Board* (CCB). The idea is that all interested parties come together for discussions and decisions. The problem is there is usually a tremendous amount of the former, but very little of the latter. Discussions can lead on forever, demonstrating President Lincoln's principle that you cannot please everyone all of the time. Lengthy discussions are typically the result of not enough valid information. The less information, the more opinion weighs in. A proper balance of data and opinion must be struck. Opinion should not be ignored, as it is often the voice of valuable experience. It is the edge between experience and speculation upon which the value of opinion balances. Finally, whether it is by vote or single authority, a method of determining by whom and when the outcome will be decided is important.

On the plus side, a group such as a CCB is an excellent method of getting information disseminated quickly, hearing feedback quickly (sometimes too quickly), and tracking progress real-time. Everyone has the benefit of knowing the collective judgments. The CCB has the advantages of both parallel and sequential communication structures.

Communication with CM, regardless of the method (or combination of methods) used, requires an active involvement to be successful. Teamwork and personal relations can make or break an effective CM system.

Configuration Identification

The *configuration identification* process defines which items will be configuration managed, how they are to be identified, and how they are to be documented. The configuration identification model might include:

- Evaluating the product structure
- Determining configurable items
- Defining the configuration documentation
- Approving and releasing of baseline documentation

Product Structure

The items that merit being tracked are called Configuration Items (CIs) and are usually based on a certain level of design detail of the specifications. The product structure is evaluated to determine the level at which component documentation and implementation of requirements can be effectively controlled.

When planning a project, the system specifications are broken down into subordinate levels of increasing detail. This usually takes the form of a Work Breakdown Structure (WBS). It would not be feasible to document and track every change to every item in a project. One would spend more time documenting than developing. At some point, the specifications describe the physical, functional, and performance attributes of system components in sufficient detail to characterize them as having a single primary function. Each can then be tagged as a CI.

Configuration Items

The actual selection of CIs is based on several mitigating factors. CIs should be far enough down the specification tree to be considered as

Table 10.7   Considerations for Identifying Configurable Items

- Configuration Items should have a single function, or a collection of like functions

- High enough on the specification tree to be manageable

- Low enough of a specification level to avoid being too vague

- High risk or critical components.

- Availability of suppliers

- Procurement conditions

- Future servicing needs

- Use of a new technology, method of fabrication, or new type of programming

having a single function, or a collection of like functions. Too far down the tree and the number of interfaces with other items or system components becomes unmanageable. Too high a specification level and the interface may be too complex (or vague) to appropriately characterize. High-risk or critical components should be identified and tracked, even if they do not conform to the standard level of detail. Availability of suppliers, procurement conditions, such as COTS products or government GSA schedules, or future servicing needs all affect the choice of CI. If a component makes use of a new technology, method of fabrication, or new type of programming, it may warrant a CI label due to uncertainties. Table 10.7 summarizes the considerations.

CIs can be comprised of both software and hardware. Because software is usually integral to controlling system functionality, it is almost always a configurable item. Hardware CIs are designated as HWCI and software is similarly labeled as SWCI.

Configuration Baseline and Documentation

Configuration documentation defines a CI's performance, and functional and physical attributes, including internal and external interfaces. The documentation can include source specifications, materials, processes, performance data, physical diagrams, standards, etc. Once approved for release, these documents essentially become the baseline configuration for the item, which is then protected from unmanaged change.

There are four categories of configuration baselines.

1. *Functional baseline.* This baseline is the approved set of documents that describes the overall system specifications. It is the top-level CI and is produced during the initial phases of a technical effort. It should include system performance specifications (functional, interoperability, and interface characteristics) as well as requirements for verifying that the produced system has met those specifications. In terms of the ISSE process, the functional baseline is a product of the Define System Requirements activity.
2. *Allocated baseline.* This baseline describes the performance specifications of the lower-level CI. It is intended to reflect the criteria for design, not the actual component design solution. Similar to a functional baseline but applied to the system components, it should also include performance verification requirements. These documents are produced during the ISSE Define System Requirements, and possibly Design System Architecture, activities.
3. *Development configuration.* This is a baseline that documents the evolving CI design solution. The development configuration includes all approved technical documentation for the software and hardware design. This is accomplished during the ISSE Develop Detailed Design activity. With the USG's current emphasis on performance criteria, creating the Development Configuration is primarily a contractor task.
4. *Product baseline.* Accomplished during the ISSE Implement System activity, the product baseline is the approved technical documentation for a CI during production, deployment, and operational support phases of its life cycle. The documentation should fully describe the CI in terms of physical form, fit, and function. It should also include all testing requirements to verify performance and acceptance.

Configuration Control

The procedures for controlling configuration vary but generally begin with a document that initiates the change, a review process to evaluate the requested change, and an implementation process (Figure 10.3).

In a typical government–contractor relationship, the government is usually responsible for initiating the change documentation, although it may be at the request of the contractor. The contractor is typically responsible for evaluating and implementing the change. The government then tracks the change control process. Figure 10.4 shows the overall configuration control process outlined in MIL-HDBK-61A.

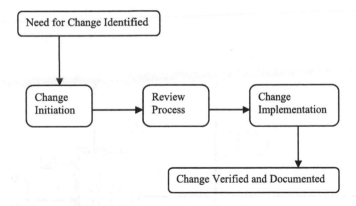

Figure 10.3 Basic configuration control process.

Change Initiation

The document that initiates the change, generically called a *change proposal*, should include:

■ Who initiated the change request
■ CI tracking details (such as revision number, etc.)
■ Description of requested change
■ Reason for request (justification or need)
■ Impact on configuration items or interfaces
■ Categorization of change (in terms of product complexity and impact to resources and scheduling)

Each organization or project will have its own forms for change proposals, but the forms are commonly referred to as Engineering Change Proposals (ECPs) and Requests for Deviation (RFDs). Engineering Change Proposals can be initiated for a variety of reasons, such as performance improvements, corrections to out-of-spec CIs, security, process improvements, and technology improvements. However, non-performance change requests may be due to issues such as safety or availability.

In a situation where a CI will not meet the specified baseline requirements, yet the cost or effort to invoke an ECP or bring the CI into conformance exceeds the realistic impact, an RFD may be issued; that is, it may be easier and more cost effective to just live with the nonconformity than correct it. The ECP would change the baseline configuration data, whereas the RFD just notes the noncompliance and calls it a "deviation." The deviation is not necessarily intended to be a permanent change. It may be for a specified period of time or number of units produced.

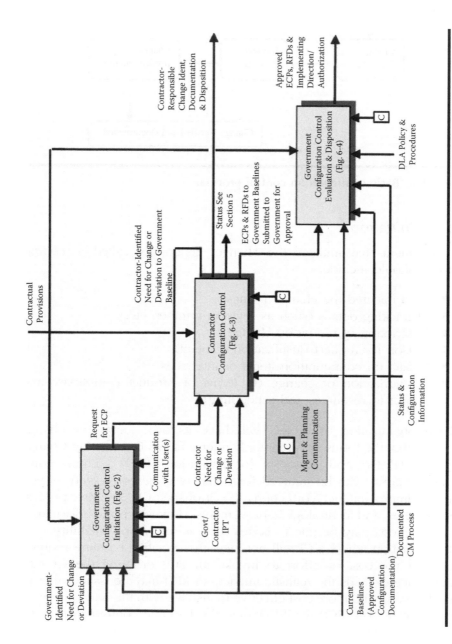

Figure 10.4 DoD configuration control process. (*Source:* From MIL-HDBK-61A, 2001.)

RFDs may not require a deviation but instead seek a waiver, exception, or a concession. A waiver provides acceptance of a nonconformity after the fact, usually when a CI has failed some aspect of the acceptance criteria. For example, the computer chassis and rack are beige when they were specified as black. The cost and time of converting them is not comparable to the detriment to aesthetics they cause. Perhaps the menu of a CI application has the user first name appearing after the last name when the specification called for last name to be listed first. Again, a simple waiver may be appropriate.

The ECP or RFD Review Process

The review process examines the what, why, how, alternatives, and impacts. During the review of a change request, the following aspects should be evaluated:

- Reaffirm the need or justification
- Technical merits and risks
- Appropriateness of categorization of change
- Potential resource impact (financial and scheduling)
- Regulatory and legal impacts
- Contract impacts
- Impact of interchangeability and interfaces
- Manufacturing, test methods, and support

The review process can be lengthy, so lead time should be considered when preparing an ECP or RFD. The review may be through a series of offices or considered by a Configuration Control Board.

Figure 10.5 illustrates the DoD version of Change Initiation in a typical USG–contractor relationship. Figure 10.6 illustrates the contractor role within the Configuration Control Process.

Configuration Status and Accounting

Configuration status and accounting is the process of keeping track of the changes so the latest acceptable configuration specifications are readily available. MIL-HDBK-61A defines it as "the process of creating and organizing the knowledge base necessary for the performance of configuration management." In general, the status and accounting process involves:

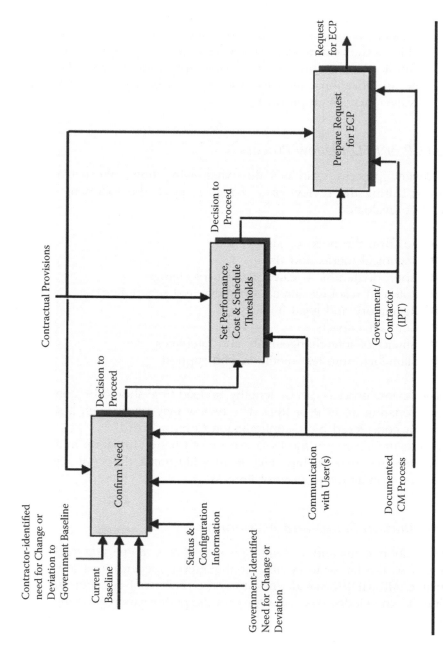

Figure 10.5 DoD change initiation process. (*Source:* From MIL-HDBK-61A, 2001.)

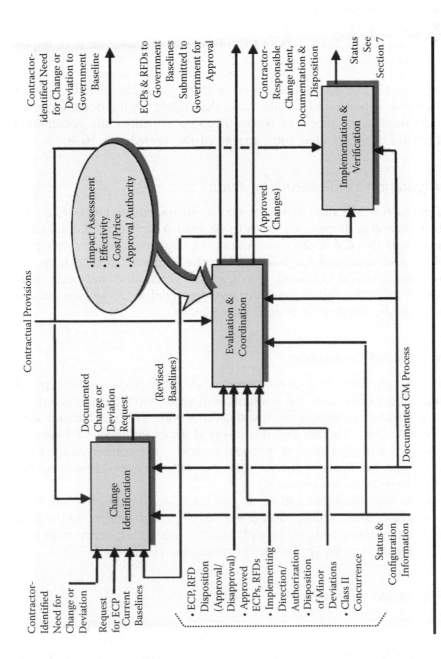

Figure 10.6 Contractor role in configuration control process. (*Source:* From MIL-HDBK-61A, 2001.)

- Keeping records of CI identification and details (part number, revision number, effective dates, change history)
- Cross-referencing
- Data storage and retrieval
- Compiling reports: lists of CI, histories of change, status of implementation

For a given CI, these activities can occur throughout the CI's life cycle or perhaps only a portion of the life cycle, depending on the documentation and CM needs. The extent of record keeping is realistically constrained by the level of automation and capacity of the knowledge base.

Configuration Verification and Audit

Configuration verification is where quality management meets CM. The verification and audit processes seek to establish a high level of confidence in how well the CM activity is working. A high degree of confidence provides assurance that CIs not meeting the required specifications are being identified and corrected. Configuration verification and audits may be conducted at the end of the ISSE Develop Detailed Design activities or throughout the Implement System activity.

Configuration Verification

Nearly all processes in a development cycle incorporate some type of configuration verification. The configuration verification process compares the documented configuration specifications with the performance data collected. It also confirms that the physical attributes meet CI baselines through physical examination, process control, or a combination of the two. Change verification checks that any subsequent changes to the baseline have been incorporated.

Due to the reiterative nature of processes, configuration verification may take place several times during the development process. In the case of complex systems, particularly with many CI interfaces, verification may take a long time or be spread out in staged increments.

Configuration Audits

Configuration audits validate the verification process. It is an accounting that all the CI documentation exists, is current, and is accessible. Performance specifications baselined by the customer usually become a contractual commitment; therefore, a configuration audit tells the customer whether or not those contractual requirements have been met. Configuration audits are divided into two categories: a Functional Configuration Audit (FCA) and a physical configuration audit (PCA). The FCA examines the performance-related documentation, whereas the PCA, as the name implies, examines the configuration documentation related to the actual or tangible attributes of the CIs. The FCA identifies deficiencies in performance and the PCA identifies deficiencies of operational capability.

The audits are specified in the Statement of Work (SOW) and are usually required before final acceptance of a CI or complete system. They do not replace the requirements of validation checks or other inspections, but may use those results as part of the audit. Audits may be carried out more than once, such as when a CI has failed to meet the requirements, when a system has been shut down for a length of time, or when the system production contract for a CI has been handed over to a different vendor.

Conducting Configuration and Verification Audits

As the U.S. Government evolves into using more performance-based contracts, which is now required by the DoD, the task of conducting configuration verification falls primarily to the contractors. Because of their connection to contractual acceptance of CIs and systems, audits are normally conducted by the USG. Depending on factors such as size, quantity, complexity, availability, commonality, and cost, the USG may elect not to conduct a PCA but rely upon the contractor's internal audit process instead.

The audit process is conducted in three stages. The first stage is the audit preparation. Logistical details, scope of audit, attendees, agenda, method of examination, etc. are all worked out during the preparation stage. The second stage is the audit itself, verifying documentation and examining the CI and performance data. The final stage is the follow-up of any issues identified by the audit process.

Risk Management Plan

Risk management is discussed in various chapters and in detail in Chapter 14. A brief overview is provided in this chapter to provide a reference to it as an important technical management process. Thus, some of the material is similar to what has already been discussed.

To have a successful information system security program, an effective risk management process must be included. The goal of risk management is to not only protect the IT assets, but also to protect the organization and its ability to perform its mission. Because of this importance, the risk management process should be treated as an essential management function of the organization, not as a technical function carried out by the IT experts who operate and manage the IT system (NIST SP 800-30, 2001).

The risk management plan is the document that defines how risk management is to be implemented in the context of a particular project. It is used to describe:

- The process that will identify, analyze, and manage risks throughout the project's life cycle
- How often risks will be reviewed, who will be the reviewers, and the process for the review
- Those individuals responsible for the various aspects of risk management
- The type of reports or status documents for the project and who will approve the documentation
- The risk baseline and planned controls to reduce the likelihood of those risks occurring and who will be responsible for implementing the controls

NIST SP 800-30 (2001) defines risk as "a function of the **likelihood** of a given **threat-source's** exercising a particular potential **vulnerability**, and the resulting **impact** of that adverse event on the organization." To determine the likelihood of a future adverse event, threats to an IT system must be analyzed in conjunction with the potential vulnerabilities and the controls in place for the IT system. Impact refers to the magnitude of harm that could be caused by a threat's exercise of vulnerabilities. The level of impact is governed by the potential mission impacts and, in turn, produces a relative value for the IT assets and resources affected (e.g., the criticality and sensitivity of the IT system components and data) (NIST SP 800-30, p. 8).

The first process in risk management is *risk assessment*. A risk assessment determines the extent of the potential threat and the risk associated with an IT system throughout its system development life cycle (SDLC). The results of this process can help identify the appropriate security controls for reducing or eliminating risk during the risk mitigation process.

The second activity of risk management is *risk mitigation*. Risk mitigation involves prioritizing, evaluating, and implementing the appropriate risk-reducing controls based on the results and recommendations from the risk assessment process.

Because the elimination of all risk is usually impractical or close to impossible, it is the responsibility of senior management and functional and business managers to use the *least-cost approach* and implement the *most appropriate controls* to decrease mission risk to an acceptable level, with *minimal adverse impact* on the organization's resources and mission (NIST SP 800-30, 2001, p. 27).

Residual risk is the risk that remains after the implementation of new or enhanced controls. Residual risk must be closely managed by senior managers to ensure that changes to the environment, system, etc. do not affect the impact of the residual risk.

This ties in with the Certification and Accreditation (C&A) requirements mandated by OMB Circular A-130. Whether following DITSCAP, NIACAP, or NIST processes, C&A requires an organization's approving authority (i.e., senior management) to authorize the IT system to begin or continue to operate. At a minimum, this authorization (or accreditation) must occur at least every three years or whenever major changes are made to the system. The intent of C&A is to identify risks that are not fully addressed and to determine whether additional controls are needed to mitigate the risks identified in the system. After the appropriate controls have been implemented for the identified risks, the approving authority signs a statement accepting any residual risk and authorizing the operation of the IT system.

More information on NIST SP 800-30 and risk management is provided in Chapter 14.

Statement of Work (SOW)

The Statement of Work (SOW) is a document that details all of the deliverable products, services, and associated work required for a project. Generally used to identify contractual obligations of a supplier, the SOW is a principal document to measure contract delivery compliance.

Because the SOW is used by a variety of people, including accountants, contracting officers, and project managers, it must be written clearly and concisely. The wording of an SOW should be precise and unambiguous. While it should use language that is understandable and avoid overly technical details, it should also avoid simplicity that falls short of the deliverable requirements. The SOW is often no more than a few pages, although it should be complete enough to be used for legal purposes if needed.

The Work Breakdown Structure (WBS) provides a good starting point for drafting the SOW. Although the WBS details only products, it serves as a guide to structure the SOW and can be used as a checklist to ensure that all the elements of the program are addressed. The SOW goes hand-in-hand with the WBS to define a complete list of project specifications known as the *specification tree* (see Figure 10.7).

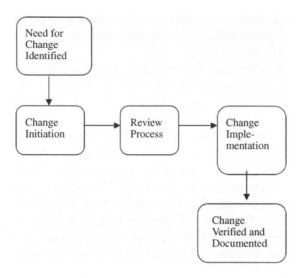

Figure 10.7   Relationship between SOW, WBS, and specifications. (*Source:* From MIL-HDBK-245, 1996, p. 17.)

Specifications can be referenced within an SOW but should not be described in actual detail. For example, if a referenced document specifies a method of measuring performance, the SOW should require the contractor to implement a program to ensure the performance is met in accordance to the reference. It should not repeat the actual performance requirements already contained in the referenced document. In terms of project management, the SOW should state requirements in terms of the results needed and not make an attempt to dictate the actual management procedures for the contractor to follow.

For inclusion into a Systems Engineering Management Plan (SEMP), the SOW should contain the following (Blanchard, 1998, p. 239):

- A summary statement of the tasks accomplished.
- Identification of the input requirements for other tasks, including results from other tasks accomplished within the project.
- References to specifications, standards, procedures, and related documentation as necessary to complete the scope of work. These references should be identified as key requirements of the project documentation set.
- A description of the specific results to be achieved, including deliverable equipment, software, design data, reports, and related documentation. The proposed schedule of delivery should also be included.

Format

A statement of work can be organized into the following sections:

1. Scope
2. Applicable Documents
3. Requirements

Section 1: Scope

This section defines the boundaries for the work to be accomplished under the contract. It should begin with a brief statement of the products and services to be delivered and the associated work required to make it happen. Background material should be included here if warranted, and then only to the extent needed to understand the requirements.

Scope should *not* include specifications of data requirements, directions on performing work tasks, and descriptions of deliverable products (MIL-HDBK-245D, 1996, p. 7).

Section 2: Applicable Documents

All references to specifications, guidance, handbooks, written policy, etc. should be cited here. The reference should include specific versions and dates, as well as the applicable sections. This last point is somewhat critical. Unless specific sections, paragraphs, or pages are cited, the entire document becomes contractually applicable, which could have enormous financial (and time) consequences. This has been a historical problem in USG acquisitions whereby compliance to sections, which have no relevance to the projects, resulted in huge cost overruns (MIL-HDBK-245D, 1996, p. 8).

Although "Applicable Documents" is the second section, it should actually be drafted after the completion of Section 3: Requirements. This is because all the documents cited in Section 2 must be justified within the Requirements section; and conversely, all documents referred to or specified in Section 3 should be listed in Section 2.

Section 3: Requirements

The SOW requirements are the actual work tasks to be conducted by the contractor. All deliverables must be listed, along with clear descriptions, if needed, to ensure a common, unambiguous understanding of what is expected by the contractor. The SOW should also be examined for potential misinterpretations from a legal standpoint. As stated above, all specification documents justified and referenced here should be cited in Section 2.

Required delivery times and methods should be listed. For example, if a product deliverable is a software program, the type of media may be important. It would be problematic (although not necessarily catastrophic) if the software was delivered on a DVD and your classified system only had a normal CD-ROM drive (it is not appropriate to specify the DVD to justify an upgrade to the system — you will need to justify the upgrade on its own merits).

The Requirements section should be sufficiently detailed to estimate the resources that will be required to fulfill the tasks. These estimates will be used by both the contractor and the client. Initially, the contractor will use them for calculating costs and preparing bid packages, and the client will use them to judge appropriateness of the received proposals and bids. Language used within the SOW should allow the reader to easily distinguish between what is background material, guidance, or suggestions, and what is actually required to fulfill minimum needs of the client. There should be no disparity of expectation between the client and the contractor.

MIL-HDBK-245D (1996) offers the following guidance when drafting an SOW:

- DOs:
    - Select a competent team with an experienced team leader.
    - Exclude "how-to" requirements because the offeror should be tasked to provide the deliverables under the contract in the most cost-effective manner.
    - Use the program WBS to help outline the required work effort.
    - Explicitly define the tailored limitations of all standards and specifications cited.
    - Exclude design control or hardware performance parameters because these requirements should be covered a specification.
    - Educate personnel with respect to acquisition streamlining (DFARS 211.002-70 Contract Clause).
    - Give priority to commercial items over specification items when the former satisfies the requirements.
    - Give priority to commercial practices (as opposed to government practices) as a means of acquisition (DFARS 212 Acquisition of Commercial Items — General).

- DON'Ts:
  - Do not specify technical proposal criteria or evaluation factors.
  - Do not establish a delivery schedule. (May include significant milestones for clarity.) (Note that there is a fair amount of disagreement on this point within various reference materials. Suffice it to say, it will be probably be dictated by the cognizant acquisition office; but if you work for the DoD, follow the above.)
  - Do not specify design control parameters or the performance of hardware because these items should be covered in the specification.
  - Do not impose on the contractor a government format when a contractor format is acceptable.
  - Do not over-specify. Specify only what is required and let the contractor establish the best method to fulfill the requirement.
  - Do not invoke in-house management instructions.
  - Do not use the SOW to establish or amend a specification.

Work Breakdown Structure (WBS)

A Work Breakdown Structure (WBS) is a hierarchical product-oriented description of the items to be developed by a systems engineering effort. A tree diagram can visually represent the WBS, where the top block of the tree describes the primary product and the lower branches describe the items that make up the primary product in ever-increasing detail (see Figure 10.8). Each item is referred to as an *element* and is the basic building block of the WBS. Elements can be comprised of hardware,

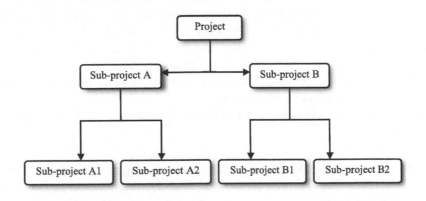

Figure 10.8   Generic WBS tree diagram.

software, documents, services, data, and facilities. Each layer in the tree is called a "level." For example, the top block is called a Level 1 element, and items in the next layer are called Level 2 elements. The WBS can be expanded to any number of layers; however, three layers are typically sufficient for project management. If a particular element is costly or deemed to have a high risk, then lower levels of detail may be required.

As a product family tree, the WBS displays the product elements and shows the work relationships between elements. It is important to remember that the WBS is product oriented, not task oriented. The elements describe the items to be produced, not the processes to create them. For example, "create firewall rule set" is a process and would not be listed as an element in a WBS. However, the item "firewall rule set" would be included in the WBS. The process to create the firewall rule set is an associated task of the firewall rule set element.

WBS and the ISSE Model

The WBS is a linking document central to the ISSE Model. It provides a connecting point for system requirements, configuration management, quality management, scheduling, resource planning, and communication. During the Discover Needs and Define System Requirements activities, the product is described essentially in terms of performance. During the Design System Architecture activity, the products needed to realize the system requirements begin to emerge. At this point, preliminary WBSs are drafted that display the breakdown of the principal product into elementary products. The elementary products can then be examined to determine the resource and scheduling requirements. Performance measures can be assigned to each element and configuration data generated (see Figure 10.9). The WBSs are further refined during the Develop Detailed Design activity. Once approved, the WBSs are used throughout the Implement System activity for specifying and managing contracts, managing in-house work, providing a reporting framework, and supporting the configuration and quality management processes.

In terms of benefits during the life of a program, a WBS (MIL-HDBK-881, 1998):

- Separates the product into its component parts, making the relationship between the parts clear and the relationship between the tasks clearer
- Significantly assists planning and the assignment of management and technical responsibilities

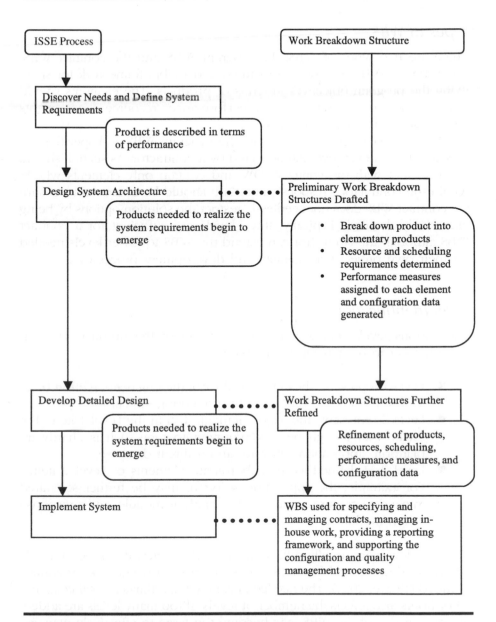

Figure 10.9   Relationship between WBS and the SSEP.

- Assists in resource allocations, cost estimates, expenditures, cost and technical performance, and tracking the status of engineering efforts
- Helps managers of lower level components relate their work, data, and progress to the higher-level products

Types of WBS

There are two types of WBS: the program WBS and the contract WBS. The program WBS provides a structured and visible framework for specifying the program objectives in terms of products. The elements should reflect logical points for assessing performance, resource requirements and usage, and progress in schedules.

The contract WBS is derived from the program WBS and specifies the products to be developed and delivered by a contractor. As such, it should be consistent with the contract SOW and contain only elements wholly within the contractor's responsibility. Care should be exercised to ensure the contract WBS does not needlessly restrict the solution options by being excessively detailed. Typically, three levels are sufficient for a contract WBS although the contractor can extend the WBS to lower levels needed for their own project management and development processes.

Level Identification

The various levels represent increasing detail of the product. The top three levels can be generalized as follows:

- Level 1 represents the entire product of the engineering effort (e.g., a firewall or a network security monitoring system).
- Level 2 represents the major elements within the Level 1 item. For the firewall, it might be broken down into items such as a hardware platform, application software, and a threat database.
- Level 3 is defined as the subordinate elements of Level 2 items. For example, the application software may be further separated into a data capture module, a data analysis module, and a response action module.

Three levels are usually sufficient, although the actual number of levels will depend on several factors, such as the level of detail, risk, or control required (Burke, 2003). The needed accuracy for estimates, total cost, and labor hours also affects the number of levels. If too many levels are added, the overall size of the WBS may become too large to effectively manage. In those cases, the overall project may be broken down into sub-projects, each with its own WBS. This is an effective way for a prime contractor to delegate required work to a subcontractor. Sub-project managers each have responsibility for their own WBS.

Elements within each level should be assigned some sort of alphanumeric indexing, referenced to their level. This allows for easy tabulation

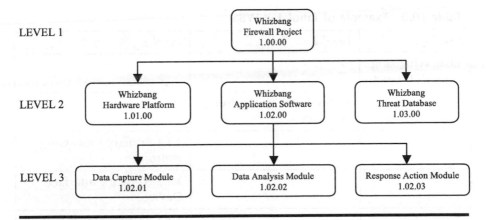

Figure 10.10 Example WBS numbering system.

by databases, spreadsheets, and project management software. For example, the Level 1 element representing the firewall could be assigned an element number of 01.00.00 (see Figure 10.10). The first field represents Level 1, the second field would represent an element on Level 2, and the third set of digits would represent an element on Level 3. An element number of 01.03.12 would indicate that it is a Level 3 item because the third field is non-zero. Further, it is a subset of the third element on Level 2. The scheme could have a mixture of letters and numbers. For example, Level 1 might be alphabetic and Levels 2 and 3 numeric, yielding A.03.12 for the example above.

The same WBS information can be represented in a tabular or spreadsheet format as well as illustrated in Table 10.8.

Selecting WBS Elements

Because the WBS represents the translation of project goals into products, the WBS elements should be logical points where the product specifications can be measured and progress assessed.

Once the program WBS has been defined, the contract WBS can be established. It may look quite similar to the program WBS but will include only those items for which the contractor is responsible. Because the contract WBS is used extensively during production, it should assist in contract management and maintenance but not be too constraining. The level of detail should be such that any major modifications should not result in a change to the WBS. Tracking modifications is a responsibility of the change management process. Figure 10.11 compares a sample program WBS with the contract WBS matrix.

Table 10.8   Example of Tabulated WBS

Level 1	Level 2	Level 3
1.0.0 Whizbang Firewall Project		
	1.1.0 Whizbang Hardware Platform	
		1.1.1 Primary Processing Platform
		1.1.2 Network Interface Device
		1.1.3 Backup Power System
	1.2.0 Whizbang Application Software	
		1.2.1 Data Capture Module
		1.2.2 Data Analysis Module
		1.2.3 Response Action Module
	1.3.0 Whizbang Threat Database	
		1.3.1 External attacks
		1.3.2 Trojans and spyware
		1.3.3 Viruses and worms

WBS Dictionary

As the Program WBS evolves, the program manager should also develop a WBS dictionary. The dictionary should define all the elements within the WBS by describing the element, the resources and processes required to produce the element, and a link to its detailed definitions and specifications. The dictionary should also incorporate any changes to the element that occur during a systems engineering process.

What a WBS Is Not

When drafting a WBS, items that represent processes, costing, or management functions should not be included as an element in the WBS. The

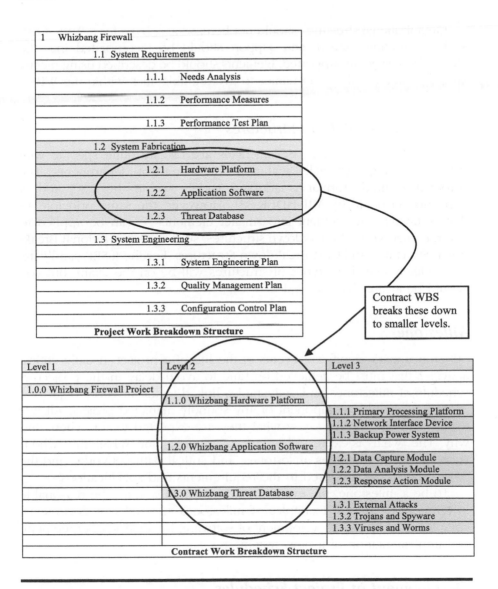

Figure 10.11   Relationship between project WBS and contract WBS.

WBS is strictly for identifying products and deliverables. The WBS should *not* include the following elements:

- Elements that are not products
- Program phases or activities
- Rework retesting or refurbishing
- Quality or performance testing

Organizational structures should not be used as a basis for a WBS. Costs such as meetings, travel, and support should be incorporated into the element that is being supported. Elements should be described using precise language and actual system names to avoid ambiguities within the WBS.

Other Work Breakdown Structures

The U.S. DoD and other USG agencies are usually quite specific with WBS formatting, especially within the procurement departments. The "product-oriented" format is adopted widely within the USG and is explained in detail by MIL-HDBK-881. However, the same principle — that of dividing an element into smaller elements — can be applied to several other types of breakdown structures, such as Organizational Breakdown Structures and Cost Breakdown Structures. For the ISSEP candidate, it is unlikely that these types of structures will be on the exam, but you should be aware that they exist.

Milestones

Milestones mark significant events in the life of a project, usually critical activities that must be achieved on time to avoid delay in the project. A schedule of milestones and deliverables linked to the project's objectives is an indispensable component of any soundly managed project. All key team members need to know what they are expected to do, when, and why. The "what" is expressed in task assignments and WBSs; the "when" is contained in schedules, milestones, and critical path networks; and the "why" should be answered in the requirements and specifications.

To be a milestone, the event should be significant and be reasonable in terms of deadlines. Examples of milestones are drafts of documents, completion of phases, development of software, installation of equipment, and implementation of a new system.

Development of Project Schedules

Project scheduling includes various tools that help managers direct the activities needed during the development of a project. Scheduling occurs before the project begins and involves:

- Identifying the activities/tasks for the project
- Estimating how much time is needed to complete the activity or task
- Allocating personnel resources or financial resources
- Scheduling when the activity or task will begin and when it is expected to finish

An important role of the project manager is to ensure that the plan throughout the project phases continues to represent the best prediction of what will occur in the future. If necessary, the manager will revise the plan to reflect the current design and development processes.

Preparation of Cost Projections

There are several approaches to estimating system costs. The top-down cost estimating begins at the system level and adds detail by sequentially dividing the system into smaller and smaller parts. The bottom-up cost estimating begins at the finest level of detail in a system and aggregates cost upward from that point.

A few factors that affect cost projections are cost learning, which is the reduction in costs that occur from previous experience in designing, developing, and operating a similar system. Essentially, the process of continually improving production so that it results in cost reductions is referred to as cost learning. Cost spreading is the process of estimating how costs spread over time. If a project is estimated to take several years to complete, an estimate of the total cost may not be sufficient. Thus, estimates must take into account the various costs that will occur during each year.

Another cost estimating approach is to base costs on the life-cycle phases. When this is done, the phase must be outlined, each phase must be estimated, and then costs are combined across all phases to obtain the total life-cycle cost.

When estimating costs, managers take into account the labor and materials required for a particular project. This would include how many hours a task would take and which employee is needed to complete the task. Direct labor costs can be developed from assigning people to the various activities (tasks) of the schedule. This could involve constructing a task responsibility matrix assigning categories of personnel to the various project tasks in order to develop the project budget. Tracking costs as a function of time can be done by creating cost budgets by week or by month.

In addition to direct labor costs, each project must absorb a portion of the cost of running the business. The rent payments, electric and telephone bills, and receptionist's time are all necessary to operate the business, but these types of costs cannot be allocated to a specific project. Instead, they are allocated across all projects and are usually referred to as indirect costs. Indirect costs are any costs that cannot be reasonably attributed to a particular project. Indirect costs can sometimes be seen as fringe costs (e.g., vacations, holidays, training), and overhead costs (e.g., personnel to check security clearances). Other direct costs include purchase of software and hardware, and general and administrative costs (e.g., general management and administration of the business).

For government contracts, these costs are submitted and approved by the government as allowable expenses to the government. For example, the Defense Contract Audit Agency (DCAA), under the authority, direction, and control of the Under Secretary of Defense, is responsible for performing all contract audits for the Department of Defense. The DCAA provides accounting and financial advisory services regarding contracts and subcontracts to all DoD components responsible for procurement and contract administration. These services are provided in connection with negotiation, administration, and settlement of contracts and subcontracts. The DCAA also provides contract audit services to some other government agencies.

The next section discusses the tools available for managing technical projects.

Technical Management Tools

Time management is a key concern for any manager. Throughout the development cycle, work is defined and established by such documents as WBSs and SOWs. Schedules are necessary to control when the work is actually conducted to ensure a successful project completion on time. The difficult part is determining what "on time" should mean. The end date could be calculated by logically sequencing and adding up the time required to complete all the tasks defined within the project WBSs and SOWs, and projecting that forward from the start date. However, it is more common in the real world to be handed a deadline first. Then the challenge becomes sorting out just how realistic the stated time objectives are, and then how to make it work. Having too much time is a rare complaint and one likely to be kept quiet by the project manager. McConnell (1996) notes that there are several causes for the project manager having overly optimistic schedules and not enough time to complete the tasks:

- External deadlines imposed
- Senior managers or customers refuse to accept range of dates
- Managers and developers deliberately underestimate because they like working under pressure
- Project length deliberately underestimated to secure a winning bid
- Developers underestimate an interesting project to get funding
- Beliefs that developers will work harder if schedule is ambitious
- Top management, marketing, or external customers want particular deadlines
- Added features make realistic schedule unrealistic
- Project is simply estimated poorly

When time is short and deadlines are in danger of being overrun, security is often the first place corners are cut. The timely deployment of an IT system can be afforded a far greater importance by stakeholders than the security necessary to go with it. If a deployment date was originally based upon unrealistic assumptions or invalid data, then the ultimate reliability, and hence the security, of the system is tenuous unless corrections are made during the development stages. Corrections may be relatively easy for small or minor systems, but strong and forthright leadership is required to change course for a major system or deployment. Unless the project manager can make a compelling case with specific reasons for delay, senior stakeholders will have trouble reconciling the need to delay with the apparent benefits of staying the course.

Fortunately, there are several indispensable tools for establishing realistic schedules and weeding out the invalid assumptions. These include Gantt charts, PERT charts, Requirements Traceability Matrix (RTM), and spreadsheets. All of these tools begin with the basic building block of a schedule, the timeline.

Scheduling Tools

A timeline is a diagram of tasks and activities represented along an axis that represents time. It becomes a schedule when it is organized into a plan detailing the order in which tasks must be done. Two main methods of describing a schedule are in use today: the Gantt chart and the PERT chart.

The size of a project, the complexity, previous experience, and the type of available data are factors that will help determine which methods are most appropriate for a project. Once a project is underway, the schedules are used to determine the ongoing progress and facilitate adjustments as necessary.

The Gantt Chart

Named after Henry L. Gantt, an American engineer and social scientist who used it as a production control tool in 1917, the Gantt chart expresses the project tasks as a collection of horizontal bar graphs (Figure 10.12). It continues to be one of the most popular tools in use today, with approximately 80 percent of Microsoft Project users preferring the bar chart for planning projects (Burke, 2003). The work tasks are listed in a vertical column on the left side, and the time increments horizontally along the top. The increments may be in appropriate units such as days, weeks, months, or even years. They might be listed in absolute dates, or relative

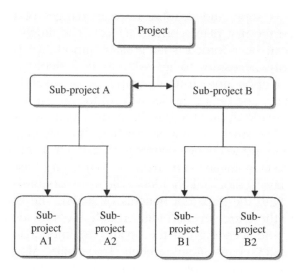

Figure 10.12   Example Gantt chart.

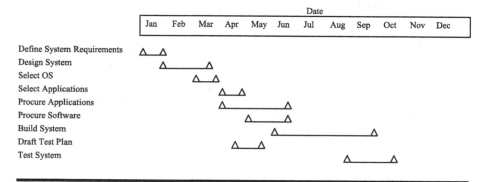

Figure 10.13   Milestone example.

to an event such as the start of project or contract award. The durations of the tasks are scheduled as horizontal lines across the chart, depicting the planned start and end times. The charts are usually enhanced with a second line (or change in color of the first line) indicating actual progress.

The Gantt charts are often used to display project milestones (Blanchard, 1998). Milestones represent significant events within a project. They could represent when tasks change hands from one group to another, percentages of overall project completion, or completion of major assemblies (Figure 10.13).

They are helpful for displaying, at a glance, the relative time relationships between major work tasks. However, the Gantt charts lack information regarding the dependencies between tasks, or more details about the tasks themselves. For example, if a task is delayed, a Gantt chart does not give any indication of the impact on other tasks. For this kind of information, the PERT chart is more appropriate.

The PERT Chart

The Program Evaluation and Review Technique (PERT), also known as the Critical Path Method (CPM), plots the logical flow of the tasks against their interdependencies. Although the origins of PERT and CPM differ, the terms are now used interchangeably (Burke, 2003).

The PERT chart is developed by first listing all the key events of a project, such as the milestones, then creating a network diagram that shows the flow of work from one event to the next. The flow is defined in terms of time required to reach the next event. Calculating the total project time is a matter of adding up the time along the paths through the network diagram. As one can guess, there will be several available paths through the work network diagram, although the project cannot finish any sooner than the longest path, known as the "critical path."

There are several advantages to using PERT. First, actual dates are not needed to create the chart, only relative times; thus, one can use it in the early stages of project planning when actual dates are not pinned down. In fact, a key purpose of this method is to assist in establishing realistic dates. Second, the impact of slippage or early completion is readily incorporated. The "domino effect" of any delay in work becomes readily apparent in the network diagram. Third, it provides a well-organized and structured view of complex projects.

PERT Example

The following sections work through an example of how to apply the PERT. In this example, we will build a security appliance, the new revolutionary BX-5000. Although what it actually does will remain a mystery, we will use the following basic steps to apply the technique:

1. List the key events and activities.
2. Define the logical relationships between the events.
3. Assign duration values for the activities.
4. Analyze the paths.

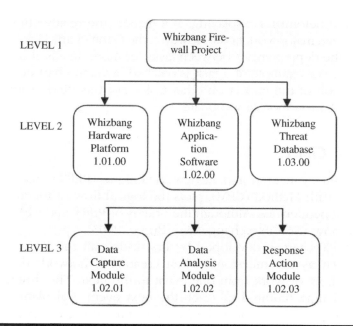

Figure 10.14   Relationship between events and activities.

Key Events and Activities

The completion of an *activity*, such as a work task, results in *events* such as project milestones (Figure 10.14). An activity is any work, task, operation, or process that must take place to complete the project or reach the event. For example, a milestone (event) might be Firewall Rules Established, and the activity to realize that might be Research Threats and Attacks. Events and activities are separate components and, in the purest sense, labeled differently. However, the labels for events and activities can be nearly one and the same: that is, the above activity could have been labeled as Establish Firewall Rules and the event as Firewall Rules Completed. Regardless of how one labels it, one must be able to assign "durations" to activities, which will then result in events.

Although PERT can be applied to virtually any level of detail, the WBS is a good place to start developing the list of activities. The WBS already divides the project into sets of practical work tasks or work packages. These can be further broken down as needed to determine realistic time estimates. As mentioned, the Milestone list or chart may serve as a good source for identifying the appropriate events. For ease of tabulation, each activity and event is assigned an alphanumeric label. Often, the labels correspond to those used in the WBS. Table 10.9 provides a list of possible tasks to create the BX-5000 and Table 10.10 provides the associated events.

Defining Logical Relationships

For simplicity of presentation, the list of tasks for the BX-5000 has been distilled into less detail in Table 10.11. This is not entirely unrealistic. Until a project becomes more defined, the available task and time estimates may be very high level. As the project development process moves forward, more detail and accuracy can be incorporated.

Using the events and activities from Table 10.11, a graphical network diagram can be produced by placing the activities in a logical, sequential order (Figure 10.15). Activities can take place in series or in parallel. If one event depends on a previous event being completed, then the associated activities will be in series. If an event is independent of a previous activity, then it may occur simultaneously or in parallel. For example, Building the System (Task A90) cannot take place until the parts are procured (Tasks A70 and A80). Whereas, Drafting the Test Plan (A100) has virtually no dependency on procurement, but will be highly dependent upon the established performance measures (A20) or possibly what hardware is chosen (Task A70). A network diagram can only have one beginning point, and a single end point, but as many paths as needed in between. Sometimes it is easier to work backward when developing the network diagram, starting with the end events and breaking those down into the component events required to realize them. It is almost the same process as constructing the WBS — start large and work down to detail.

Assigning Durations

Once the logical flow and dependencies have been established, values for duration should be determined. Three values of primary interest will be eventually assigned for each activity:

1. Planned duration
2. Early finish
3. Late finish

Other values such as Late Start and Early Start may also be calculated; however, the above times will yield the potential range of time deviation for the project. The estimated (planned) durations (in days) are listed in Table 10.12 along with the early finishes (TE) and late finishes (TL).

Table 10.9 BX5000 Tasks

Description	Activity	Description	Activity
Management Documentation		**System Fabrication**	
Prepare Project Management Plan	M10	Test Hardware	F10
Security Engineering Management Plan	M20	Test Software	F20
Quality Management Plan	M30	System Assembly	F30
Statement of Work	M40	Test Configuration	F40
Prepare Work Breakdown Structure	M50		
Project Milestones	M60	**Installation**	
Configuration Management Plan	M70	Site Requirements	N10
		Site Selections	N20
Resources		Site Preparation	N30
Estimate Budget	R10	Prepare Hardware for Shipment	N40
Submit Budget Request	R20	Ship Hardware	N50
Estimate Personnel Requirements	R30	System Delivery	N60
Submit Personnel Requests	R40	System Installation	N70
Review Applicants	R50	System Test	N80
Select Applicants	R60	Operator Training	N90
		System Acceptance	N100
System Design		System Certification	N110

Prepare Requirements Doc	S10
Design Concept	S20
Draft Preliminary Design	S30
Review Design Proposals	S40
Select Design Proposal	S50
Research Hardware Options	S60
Research Software Options	S70
Selection of OS	S80
Selection of Applications	S90
Selection of Collaboration Software	S100
Draft Final Design	S110

Procurement

Submit Request for Design Proposals	P10
Submit Request for Bid	P20
Review Bids	P30
Select Bids	P40
Award Contract	P50
Prepare Equipment Lists	P60
Prepare Software Lists	P70
Submit Request for Quotes Software	P80
Submit Request for Quotes Hardware	P90
Order Hardware	P100
Order Software	P110
Contract Completion	P120

System Documentation

Prepare Configuration Test Plan	D10
Submit Configuration Test Plan	D20
Site Environmental Requirements	D30
Site Security Requirements	D40
Site Acceptance Plan	D50
Prepare System Acceptance Test Plan	D60
Submit System Acceptance Test Plan	D70
Prepare SOPs	D80
Prepare Operator Manuals	D90
Prepare Security Procedures	D100
Prepare Certification Documentation	D110
Submit Certification Documentation	D120

Table 10.10 BX-5000 Milestone Events

1   Project Start
2   System Requirements Defined
3   Performance Measures Established
4   System Design Complete
5   Operating Systems Selected
6   Applications Selected
7   Hardware Selected
8   Components Delivered
9   System Complete
10 Project Complete

Table 10.11   Modified Activities and Events

Milestones	Tasks	Activity	Associated Milestone
1 Project Start	Define system requirements	A10	2
2 Systems Requirements Defined	Establish performance measures	A20	3
3 Performance Measures Established	Design system	A30	4
4 System Design Complete	Select OS	A40	5
5 Operating Systems Selected	Select applications	A50	6
6 Applications Selected	Select hardware	A60	7
7 Hardware Selected	Procure hardware	A70	8
8 Components Delivered	Procure software	A80	8
9 System Complete	Build system	A90	9
10 Project Complete	Draft test plan	A100	9
	Test system	A110	10

The duration of any activity will be constrained by several factors, such as available resources, shipping schedules, and other team commitments. TE represents the shortest time a task could be completed in a best-case, yet realistic scenario. It represents the optimistic viewpoint. TL represents the worst-case, yet realistic scenario and is considered the pessimistic viewpoint. Planned Duration, or just Duration in Table 10.12, is the target or most likely scenario to occur. These times are now transferred from the table to the network diagram (Figure 10.16).

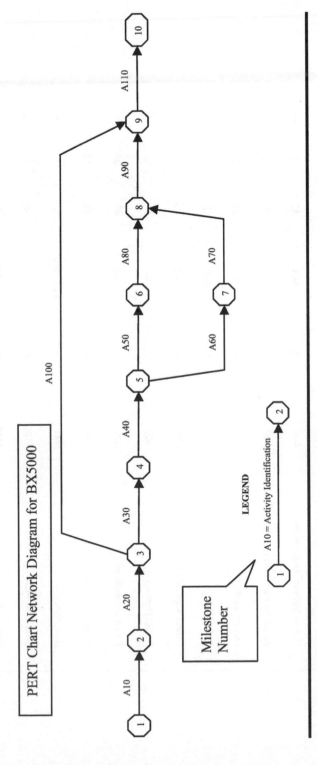

Figure 10.15   PERT chart network diagram for BX-5000.

Table 10.12 Estimated Activity Duration

Activity Description	Label	Associated Milestone	Preceding Activity	Duration	TE	TL
Define System Requirements	A10	2	N/A	10	7	15
Establish Performance Measures	A20	3	A10	5	3	8
Design System	A30	4	A20	30	25	40
Select OS	A40	5	A30	2	1	3
Select Applications	A50	6	A40	10	5	15
Select Hardware	A60	7	A40	10	5	15
Procure Hardware	A70	8	A60	40	35	45
Procure Software	A80	8	A50	15	10	20
Build System	A90	9	A70, A80	10	5	15
Draft Test Plan	A100	9	A20	10	5	15
Test System	A110	10	A90, A100	5	4	8

Duration in Days, TE = Time Early Finish, TL = Time Late Finish

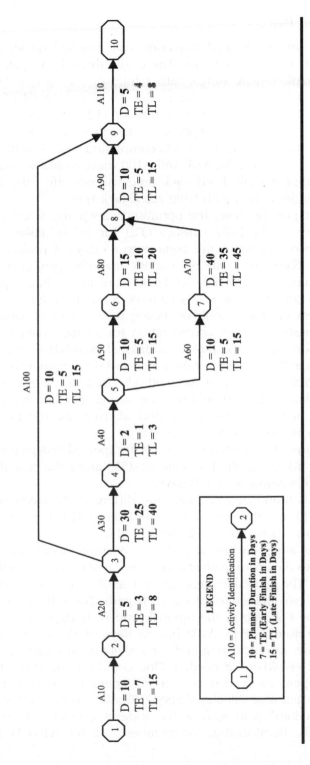

Figure 10.16 PERT chart network diagram with durations added for BX-5000.

Analyzing the Paths

Working with just the Planned Durations, one can add up all the times associated with the various paths. There are three basic paths in this simplified example (Figure 10.16). Path A follows 1-2-3-9-10 for a total of 30 days. Path B follows events 1-2-3-4-5-6-8-9-10 for a total of 87 days. Path C follows 1-2-3-4-5-7-8-9-10 for a total of 112 days. Path C therefore represents the "critical path." Slippage of activities that are components of the critical path will affect the project completion date. Activities outside the critical path, such as A50, A80, and A100, have available "slack time" and delays within the calculated slack time will not affect the end date. Activities along the critical path have zero slack time.

The earliest possible date, the optimistic viewpoint, is calculated by adding together all the Early Finishes (TE) for all the tasks along the critical path. In our example, this equates to 85 days. A project schedule that imposes a completion date prior to 85 days after project start would be considered unachievable. If the end date were an absolute requirement, tasks along the critical path would need to be reexamined for possible time savings. Theoretically, there should not be any time savings available because the chart is constructed with consideration for all the available options, although as more detail is explored, additional possibilities may surface. Bear in mind that the accuracy of the times and dates within the schedule are depend on the accuracy of the methods used to calculate the times of each individual activity. Should no time savings become apparent after reviewing the activities, estimations, and alternatives, the final option would be to scale back the project scope.

Moving in the other direction, the latest expected completion date is determined by adding all the Late Finishes (TL) along the critical path. In the example, this amounts to 149 days.

Slack time is found by calculating the difference between latest estimated time (TL) and the earliest estimated time (TE). For activities not along the critical path, the slack time is the difference between the common points along the critical path. For example, looking at the path to A100, it leaves the critical path at Milestone 3 and rejoins it at Milestone 9 (Figure 10.16). The allowable slack time for A100 is the difference in time between these two milestones along each path. For Path A, the optimal time is 10 days. For Path C, the optimal time is 92 days (30 + 2 + 10 + 40 + 10). Therefore, activity A100 has 82 days of slack time. With that much slack time, resources required for activity A100 might be available for other work elsewhere, if needed. One could end up short, however, if the critical path proceeded at a more optimistic pace. For realistic planning, the slack time calculated above should use the earliest possible time for the critical path against the longest estimated time for the noncritical path. Recalculating the numbers, TL for A100 is 15 days, whereas TE for the critical path between Milestones 3 and 9 is 71 days. A much more conservative number of 56 days is the result.

Impact of Change

The layout of a PERT chart allows for quick visual interpretation of the consequences if scheduling data changes. For example, what if during the project one realizes that Task A50 "Select Applications" in Figure 10.13 is going to take 18 days to complete? That is 3 days longer than the most pessimistic planned timeframe of 15 days for A50. At a glance, one can readily see that it will have a direct consequence on Task A80. People involved in A80 will require a "heads-up" that their start date will be delayed. One can also see that A50 and A80 have at least an estimated five-day slack time over A60 and A70. This is found by adding the TL of A50 and A80 (15 + 20) and subtracting that from the sum of TE of A60 and A70 (5 + 35), which works out to 5 (40 − 35). In this case, the three-day overrun does not exceed the estimated slack time of five days. Therefore, if A60 and A70 move at the most optimistic pace, and A80 moves at its most pessimistic pace, the overall project completion date should not be impacted, and Task A90 will commence within the planning time window.

Suppose a problem occurs and A50 will actually take 22 days to complete. This is seven (7) days over the most pessimistic schedule of A50 and it exceeds the most conservative slack time estimation by 2 (the slack time calculated above minus 7). This means if Tasks A60 and A70 are completed at the most optimistic pace, then Task A90 may have to wait an additional two days before commencing for Tasks A50 and A80 to catch up (although they are not in the critical path). Fortunately, a two-day delay is still well within the allowable project schedule because it does not exceed the total estimated TL for Tasks A60 and A70. The schedule allows for a pessimistic TL of 60 days (15 + 45) for A60 and A70, which yields a slack time of 22 days over A50 (18 actual) and A80 (TL of 20). This means that even with A50 exceeding the most pessimistic time by 2 days, an additional 22 days could be tolerated before the planned project completion time of 149 days (total critical path TL) would be in jeopardy.

Table 10.13 provides a summary of the keypoints for both Gantt and PERT charts.

Software Tools

The number-intensive nature of the PERT chart makes it well suited for software tools and spreadsheets. As the planned numbers are updated with refined or actual values, the impact can be automatically calculated

Table 10.13 Key Points for Gantt and PERT Charting

KEY POINTS for GANTT CHARTING

- Easier to plot than PERT
- Displays duration of tasks
- Does not indicate interdependencies between tasks
- Impact of slippage not as easily determined

KEY POINTS for PERT CHARTING

- PERT chart tabulates activities and events (milestones)
- Displays dependencies between activities
- Impact of slippage easily determined
- More difficult to create than GANTT

throughout the downstream portion of the chart. Potential problem areas will be highlighted almost immediately. Gantt charts can be easily mapped in a spreadsheet. Spreadsheets are also handy for listing milestones and tables of activities. A recent study of project managers showed that there are dozens of project management software tools in use (Spence, 1998).

In addition, there are several software tools available through the Internet for implementing PERT and Gantt charts such as SmartDraw (www.smartdraw.com) or ILOG (www.ilog.fr). Other software packages, such as Microsoft Project, Primavera Project, and Visibility's Project Workbench, are popular for managing all aspects of project resources. The study concluded that the choice of tool depended on project duration and size. General-purpose tools such as spreadsheets tended to be more popular with projects of less than six-months' duration, and project management software was more popular on projects lasting more than six months.

Summary

This chapter was devoted to the management of systems engineering projects from a technical management perspective. In the first section, Planning the Effort, several key project-planning issues were outlined, such as defining the project's goal, scope, and resource requirements. The eleven IATF planning tasks were outlined to ensure that project scope is clearly delineated and understood, resources, roles and responsibilities are outlined, project costs can be estimated, project schedules can be developed, technical activities and deliverables are identified, and the technical management plan and project plan have been prepared and approved by the customer.

Managing the Effort involves directing and monitoring the various activities and tasks, and reporting the project status. According to IATF, managing the technical effort occurs throughout the ISSE process. The ISSEP must review all technical activities and documentation to ensure quality in conjunction with the other activities. The eight management tasks included directing the technical effort, tracking project resources and technical parameters, monitoring progress of technical activities, ensuring the quality of deliverables, managing configuration elements, reviewing project performance, and reporting project status.

The Technical Roles and Responsibilities section defined the key players and the roles they play in managing the project. The roles include system owner, user point of contact, client representative, quality assurance manager, project manager, project planner, analysts, programmers, configuration managers, testers, documentation specialist, trainers, users, and the ISSEPs.

In the fourth section, a very important document, the Systems Engineering Management Plan (SEMP) as well as the Statement of Work (SOW) and Work Breakdown Structure (WBS) were explained. In addition, the Quality Management Plan, Risk Management Plan, and Configuration Management Plan were explained in light of managing a technical project.

The final section, Technical Management Tools, briefly introduced the two primary scheduling tools available — the Gantt chart and the PERT chart. Both are used to map the tasks or activities of the project along a timeline. The primary difference between the two is that the PERT chart is used to place tasks along a longest path, which is known as the critical path.

References

AFSCM 375-5 (1966). Systems Engineering Management Procedures. U.S. Air Force Systems Command: USA. Available at http://www.incose.org/stc/afscm375.htm.

Baguley, Phil (2001). *Successful Performance Management in a Week.* Hodder & Stoughton: London.

Blanchard, Benjamin S. (1998). *Systems Engineering Management, 2nd edition.* Wiley: New York, NY.

Burke, Rory (2003). *Project Management: Planning and Control Techniques. 4th edition.* John Wiley & Sons: New York, NY.

DoD 5000.2-R (April 2002). Mandatory Procedures for Major Defense Acquisition Programs (MDAPS) and Major Automated Information System (MAIS) Acquisition Programs. Available at http://www.acq.osd.mil/ap/50002-R_Final_April_5_2002.doc.

DoE Software Engineering Methodology, (SEM) Project Plan Example, Revised: August, 2001: Available at http://cio.doe.gov/ITReform/sqse/download/ projplnx.doc.

DoE Information Management Project Management Guide, September 1998. Available at http://cio.doe.gov/ITReform/sqse/download/prjmgde.doc.

DoE Departmental Information Systems Engineering Guidance, Volume 2, (2002). Managing DOE IT Projects (March 26, 2002). Developed by the Software Quality and Systems Engineering Program, Office of the Chief Information Officer. Available at http://cio.doe.gov/ITReform/sqse/download/DI-V2-D20-122702.doc.

DoE Project Planning Checklist (not dated). Available at http://cio.doe.gov/ITReform/ sqse/download/planning.doc.

Imai, Masaaki (1986). *Kaizen: The Key to Japan's Competitive Success*. McGraw-Hill: New York, NY.

Institute of Electrical and Electronics Engineers, Inc., IEEE Std 1220-1998, IEEE Standard for Application and Management of the Systems Engineering Process, 1998. IEEE Inc., 345 East 47th Street, New York, NY.

ISO 10007 (2003). International Standards Organization, ISO, Case Postale 56 CH-1211 Geneva 20.

Lock. Dennis. (1989). *Handbook of Engineering Management*. Butterworth/Heinemann: Woburn, MA.

McConnell, Steve (1996). *Rapid Development: Taming Wild Software Schedules*. Microsoft Press.

MIL-HDBK-245D (April 1996). U.S. DoD Handbook for Preparation of Statement of Work (SOW). (Superseding MIL-HDBK-245C 10 September 1991). Available by download at http://acc.dau.mil/.

MIL-HDBK-61A (SE) (February 2001). Military Handbook Configuration Management Guidance. (Superseding MIL-HDBK-61 30 Sep 1997.) Available at http://www.acq.osd.mil/io/se/cm&dm/pdf_files/MIL-HDBK-61A.pdf.

MIL-HDBK-881 (January 1998). U.S. DoD, Work Breakdown Structure. Available by download at http://www.acq.osd.mil/pm/newpolicy/wbs/mil_hdbk_881/ mil_hdbk_881.htm.

NIST SP 800-30 (October 2001). Risk Management Guide for Information Technology Systems. NIST Publications: Gaithersburg, MD. Available at http://csrc.nist.gov/publications/nistpubs/index.html.

NIST SP 800-30A DRAFT (2004). Revision to Risk Management Guide for Information Technology System. NIST Publications: Gaithersburg, MD. Available at http://csrc.nist.gov/publications/nistpubs/index.html.

Pressman Roger, S. and D. Ince (1994). *Software Engineering: A Practitioner's Approach, 3rd edition*. McGraw-Hill: London.

Spence, T.L.F.J.W., (1998). Tools of the Trade: A Survey of Project Management Tools. *Project Management Journal*, Volume 29(3).

USAF, MIL-STD-499A Notice of Cancellation, Notice 1, 27 February 1995.

Web Sites

http://www.acq.osd.mil/io/se/quality/index.htm for information on DoD Systems Engineering Quality.

http://www.projectmanagement.tas.gov.au/f_sheets/riskmanplan_fsv1.0.htm for information on risk management.

http://www.SearchCIO.com for definition of Gantt chart.

ISSEP® Domain 4

INTRODUCTION TO UNITED STATES GOVERNMENT INFORMATION ASSURANCE REGULATIONS

This domain is separated into five chapters in an attempt to logically group the United States Government (USG) information assurance (IA) regulations. Chapter 11 provides an outline of the various Federal agencies and departments involved in setting security policies, regulations, and policies. Included in Chapter 11 are a few of the most pertinent Federal IA laws. Chapter 12 focuses on policies distributed by the Department of Defense (DoD) and includes the 8500 series of DoD Directives and Instructions. Chapter 13 outlines the policies, advisory memoranda, directives, and instructions released by the Committee National Security Systems

(CNSS), formerly called the National Security Telecommunications Information Systems Security Committee (NSTISSC). Chapter 14 provides information on policies (Federal Information Processing Standards — FIPS) and Special Publications distributed by the National Institute of Standards and Technology (NIST). Chapter 15 is dedicated to the National Information Assurance Partnership (NIAP) and Common Criteria standard.

Contributors and Reviewers

Susan Hansche contributed, reviewed, edited, and finalized the material in this domain. She would like to thank the following individuals for also contributing and reviewing some or all of the material in this domain:

> **Robert B. Batie Jr.**, CISSP, ISSAP, ISSEP, CISM, contributed to the initial research, and provided review of this domain. He is a Security Engineering Manager for Raytheon NCS, St. Petersburg, Florida.
>
> **Benjamin Bergersen**, CISSP, CISA, IAM, reviewed several of the chapters in this domain. He is a Security & Privacy Senior in the Washington Federal Practice at PricewaterhouseCoopers.
>
> **Larry L. Buickel**, CISSP, provided review and edits. He is an enterprise security consultant with Graphic Example Technologies, Inc.
>
> **H. Skip Chapman**, CISSP, NSA-IAM, provided technical review and edits. He is President of Globalwatch Technologies, McLean, Virginia.

11

Information Assurance Organizations, Public Laws, and Public Policies

Introduction

Federal laws, regulations, policies, standards, baselines, and guidelines are key elements in ensuring that federal agencies, personnel, and contractors understand how to handle specific responsibilities and job tasks. **Laws** are federally mandated policies that organizations and individuals must follow. Federal regulations and policies are mandatory requirements. Federal **standards** are mandatory activities, actions, rules, or regulations designed to provide policies with the support structure and specific direction required to be meaningful and effective. A standard is defined as a specific product or mechanism that is selected for universal use throughout the government to support the policy. **Baselines** are descriptions of how to implement security packages to ensure that implementations result in a consistent level of security throughout the organization. Different systems (platforms) have different methods of handling security issues. Baselines are created to inform user groups about how to set up the security for each platform so that the desired level of security is achieved consistently. **Guidelines** are more general statements designed to achieve the policy's objectives by providing a framework within which to implement controls not covered by procedures. While standards are mandatory, guidelines are discretionary recommendations.

The first section of this chapter provides brief overviews of the federal agencies and organizations responsible for releasing Information Assurance (IA) policies, procedures, directives, and guidelines. The second section discusses some of the pertinent federal laws and policies applicable to all Federal entities and individuals. Note that this material is not intended as a comprehensive tutorial or manual on the broad topic of USG information systems security policy, but is simply an aid to assist the security practitioner in understanding the content of policies and how they might affect integrating mission needs, mission threats, and system-specific security needs when designing, developing, validating, certifying, and accrediting information systems. The information system security policy serves as a key part of early consideration and acts as a useful tool throughout a system's life cycle.

Section 1: Federal Agencies and Organizations

As shown in Figure 11.1, this section provides background information related to eight Federal agencies and security organizations. A brief overview of each is provided so that a baseline is established regarding the role of the various policy and regulation makers.

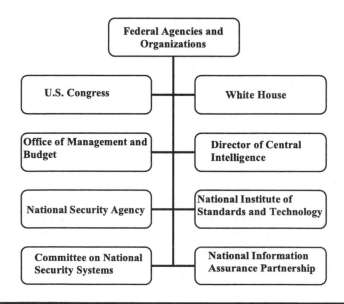

Figure 11.1   Section 1 overview.

U.S. Congress

The U.S. Congress, comprised of the House of Representatives and the Senate, has the chief function of making laws. The Office of the Law Revision Counsel prepares and publishes the United States Code (USC), which is a consolidation and codification by subject matter of the general and permanent laws of the United States.

Pertinent public laws related to security are described in Section 2 of this chapter.

The USC (e.g., public laws) can be searched and viewed at http://uscode.house.gov and public laws can be researched at http://thomas.loc.gov.

White House

The President of the United States has the statutory authority to issue presidential directives establishing new policy, decreeing the commencement or cessation of some action, or ordaining that notice be given to some declaration. The instruments used by Presidents are known by various names, and some have prescribed forms and purposes. Executive Orders and Proclamations are two of the best-known types, largely because of their long-standing use and publication in the *Federal Register* and the *Code of Federal Regulations*.

Presidential Decision Directives (PDDs) are also released for specific purposes. For example, in 1998, President Clinton signed PDD-63, "Protecting America's Critical Infrastructures," which outlined a national effort to assure the security of the United States critical interconnected infrastructures, such as telecommunications, banking and finance, energy, transportation, and essential government services. In 2001, President Bush signed Executive Order (EO) 13231 on "Critical Infrastructure Protection." EO 13231 authorized a protection program to secure information systems for critical infrastructure, including emergency preparedness communications, and the physical assets that support such systems. EO 13231 is described in more detail in Section 2 of this chapter.

Following the September 11, 2001, attacks on the United States, President Bush issued the first instrument (on October 29, 2001) in a new series denominated as Homeland Security Presidential Directives (HSPDs). HSPDs record and communicate presidential decisions about the homeland security policies of the United States.

Executive Orders signed by President Bush can be viewed at http://www.whitehouse.gov/news/orders. Executive Orders signed by President Clinton can be viewed at http://www.archives.gov/federal_register/executive_orders/clinton.html.

Office of Management and Budget (OMB)

The predominant mission of the OMB is to assist the President in over-seeing the preparation of the Federal budget and to supervise its administration in Executive Branch agencies. In helping to formulate the President's spending plans, the OMB evaluates the effectiveness of agency programs, policies, and procedures; assesses competing funding demands among agencies; and sets funding priorities. The OMB ensures that agency reports, rules, testimony, and proposed legislation are consistent with the President's Budget and with Administration policies.

In addition, the OMB oversees and coordinates the Administration's procurement, financial management, information, and regulatory policies. In each of these areas, the OMB's role is to help improve administrative management, to develop better performance measures and coordinating mechanisms, and to reduce any unnecessary burdens on the public.

OMB policies and guidance can be found in Section 2 of this chapter.

The OMB distributes Circulars and Memoranda. OMB information can be viewed at http://www.whitehouse.gov/omb.

Director of Central Intelligence/Director of National Intelligence

According to the National Security Act of 1947 (as amended by executive orders and other statutes and directives), the Director of Central Intelligence (DCI) was the U.S. Director of Intelligence. The security responsibilities of the DCI included the protection of intelligence sources and methods from unauthorized disclosure. The DCI was also assigned the responsibility of ensuring that programs are developed to protect intelligence sources, methods, and analytical procedures. The DCI established directives (DCID) and these directives serve as the principal means by which the DCI provided guidance, policy, and direction to the U.S. Intelligence Community. (The U.S. Intelligence Community is a group of 15 government agencies and organizations that carry out the intelligence activities of the USG.)

Prior to 2005, the DCI oversaw the Intelligence Community and served as the principal intelligence adviser to the president, in addition to serving as head of the Central Intelligence Agency. Since the creation of the Director of National Intelligence, the DCI's title has become the Director of the Central Intelligence Agency (DCIA) and that post serves only as head of the CIA.

In December 2004, the Intelligence Reform Act was passed to reform the coordination and management of U.S. intelligence information. The Act was based on recommendations from the 9/11 Commission that was responsible for investigating the September 11 attacks. One of the initiatives of this Act was to establish a Director of National Intelligence (DNI) and the Office of Director of National Intelligence (ODNI). The DNI is a cabinet-level position responsible for coordinating and managing the national intelligence effort and also serve as the principal intelligence adviser to the president. The Act also placed the budgets and most assets of the intelligence agencies under the DNI. In April 2005, John D. Negroponte was sworn in as the first Director of National Intelligence.

National Security Agency (NSA)

The National Security Agency/Central Security Service is America's crypto-logic organization. It coordinates, directs, and performs highly specialized activities to protect U.S. information systems and produce foreign intelligence information.

According to the NSA Web site, NSA employs the country's premier cryptologists and is said to be the largest employer of mathematicians in the United States. Its mathematicians contribute directly to the two missions of the Agency: designing cipher systems that will protect the integrity of U.S. information systems and searching for weaknesses in adversaries' systems and codes.

The second mission involves protecting all classified and sensitive information that is stored or sent through U.S. Government equipment. Further information can be found at http://www.nsa.gov/.

NSA initiatives in enhancing software security cover both proprietary and open source software. The NSA has used both proprietary and open source models in its research activities. For example, the NSA has developed and distributed security configuration guidance for a wide variety of software, from open source to proprietary software. The objective of the configuration guidance program is to provide NSA customers with the best possible security options in the most widely used products. The security configuration guides include those from Microsoft, Oracle, Solaris, and Cisco products. Security configuration guides can be found at http://www.nsa.gov/snac/index.cfm.

Note to (ISC)² ISSEP® candidates: Specific security configuration guides are not included on the to (ISC)² ISSEP exam; however, these configuration guidelines provide good information on how to best "harden" the standard or default release of operating systems, applications, databases, Web servers, etc.

NSA Information Assurance Directorate (IAD)

The NSA provides IA support for the U.S. National Security Information Infrastructure through the NSA IAD organization. The NSA/IAD Web site defines IAD's mission as detecting, reporting, and responding to cyber-threats; making encryption codes to securely pass information between systems; and embedding IA measures directly into the emerging Global Information Grid. It includes building secure audio and video communications equipment, making tamper resistant products, and providing trusted microelectronics solutions. It entails testing the security of customers' systems, providing OPSEC assistance, and evaluating commercial software and hardware against nationally set standards.

To better meet the nation's IA needs, there are IAD teams across government, industry, and academia. The cyber-defense National InfoSec Education and Training Program (NIETP) directly supports the Committee on National Security Systems (CNSS) and plays a major role in ensuring personnel in all Federal departments and agencies with national security systems are trained to safeguard information resources. More information can be found at http://www.nsa.gov/ia/.

National Institute of Standards and Technology (NIST)

The National Institute of Standards and Technology (NIST) is a nonregulatory Federal agency within the U.S. Commerce Department's Technology Administration. According to the NIST Web site, its mission is "to develop and promote measurement, standards, and technology to enhance productivity, facilitate trade, and improve the quality of life" (www.nist.gov).

Various Federal laws have charged NIST with responsibility for computer security and information assurance. For example, under the Computer Security Act of 1987 (P.L. 100-235), the Computer Security Division of the Information Technology Laboratory (ITL) was tasked with developing computer security prototypes, tests, standards, and procedures to protect sensitive information from unauthorized access or modification. Focus areas included cryptographic technology and applications, advanced authentication, public key infrastructure, internetworking security, criteria and assurance, and security management and support. Also, under the 2002 Federal Information Security Management Act (FISMA), NIST was given the responsibility to write the standards and guidelines Federal agencies would need to follow to meet the law's requirements. NIST publications present the results of specialized studies, investigations, and research on information technology security issues.

NIST publications are issued as Special Publications (SPs), NISTIRs (Internal Reports), and ITL (formerly CSL) Bulletins. Special Publications include the 500 series (Information Technology) and the 800 series (Computer Security). Computer security-related Federal Information Processing Standards (FIPS) are also included.

NIST policies (FIPS) and guidance (Special Publications) can be found in Chapter 14.

The NIST Web site is www.nist.gov, and publications can be found at http://csrc.nist.gov/publications/index.html.

Committee on National Security Systems (CNSS)

The CNSS (formerly known as the National Security Telecommunications and Information Systems Security Committee) provides a forum for the discussion of policy issues; sets national policy; and promulgates direction, operational procedures, and guidance for the security of national security systems through the CNSS Issuance System.

More information on CNSS and NSTISSC is provided in Chapter 13.

The Web site for CNSS is www.cnss.gov.

National Information Assurance Partnership (NIAP)

The National Information Assurance Partnership (NIAP) is a USG initiative designed to meet the security testing, evaluation, and assessment needs of both information technology (IT) producers and consumers. NIAP is a partnership between NIST and NSA.

More information on NIAP and Common Criteria appears in Chapter 15.

More information on NIAP can be found at http://www.niap.nist.gov/.

Section 2: Federal Laws, Executive Directives and Orders, and OMB Directives

U.S. Congress: Federal Laws

In this section, a few of the most pertinent federal laws (as shown in Table 11.1) relating to information assurance are discussed. It begins with one of the most well-known law, the Computer Security Act of 1987.

Table 11.1   Federal Laws

U.S. Congress: Federal Laws
Computer Security Act of 1987
Government Information Security Reform Act
Federal Information Security Management Act
10 USC 2315 Defense Services
Privacy Act of 1974
Computer Fraud and Abuse Act

H.R.145 Public Law: 100-235 (01/08/1988)

P.L. 100-235 is most commonly known as the Computer Security Act of 1987. The purpose of the law is defined as "the Congress declares that improving the security and privacy of sensitive information in Federal computer systems is in the public interest, and hereby creates a means for establishing minimum acceptable security practices for such systems, without limiting the scope of security measures already planned or in use" (Sec. 2 (a)).

Important elements of the Computer Security Act are:

- To assign to the National Bureau of Standards (now NIST) responsibility for developing standards and guidelines for federal computer systems, including responsibility for developing standards and guidelines needed to assure the cost-effective security and privacy of sensitive information in federal computer systems, drawing on the technical advice and assistance (including work products) of the National Security Agency, where appropriate
- To require establishment of security plans by all operators of federal computer systems that contain sensitive information
- To require mandatory periodic training for all persons involved in management, use, or operation of federal computer systems that contain sensitive information

P.L. 100-235 is available from http://csrc.nist.gov/secplcy/csa_87.txt and can be researched from: http://thomas.loc.gov/cgi-bin/bdquery/z?d100: HR00145:|TOM:/bss/d100query.html|.

Chapter 35 of Title 44, United States Code

Government Information Security Reform Act (GISRA) (replaced by FISMA)

The Government Information Security Reform Act of 2000 (GISRA, Security Act) amended the Paperwork Reduction Act of 1995 (PRA) by adding a new subchapter on information security. The Security Act reinforced and built upon the Computer Security Act of 1987 and the Information Technology Reform Act of 1996 (Clinger–Cohen Act). Similar to the PRA and Clinger–Cohen Acts, GISRA required Federal agencies to tie their information security programs and practices with their overall information technology program management, capital planning, and budget. Essentially, security for information systems had to be included in all information technology plans.

GISRA generally addressed the program management and evaluation aspects of information security. It established roles and responsibilities for information security, risk management, testing, training and authorizes NIST and NSA to provide guidance for security planning and implementation. It covers unclassified and national security systems and creates the management framework for each of the following:

- Agencywide program practiced throughout the system life cycle
- Incident response capability
- Annual program review
- Reporting significant deficiencies
- Annual agency performance plan

The GISRA divided security programs into three basic components: management, implementation, and evaluation.

1. For *management*, it recognized that while security has a technical component, it is at its core, an essential management function.
2. For *implementation*, it essentially codified the OMB's security policies and recognized that program officials (not security officers or CIOs) are primarily responsible for ensuring that security is integrated and funded within their programs and tied to the program goals. GISRA did not introduce new technical or procedural security requirements that result in greatly increased funding needs.
   - The Security Act highlights the reality that when security funding and implementation are separated from operational programs, program officials and users begin to ignore it. Separation sends the incorrect signal that it is not a program responsibility.
   - CIOs also have a significant role. They must take an agencywide strategic view of implementation and ensure that the security of each program is appropriately consistent with and integrated into the agency's overall program and enterprise architecture. Security officials are also essential but they cannot do it all.
3. For *evaluation*, the Security Act requires program officials and CIOs to conduct annual security reviews of all programs and systems. Inspectors General are to perform independent evaluations of an agency's security program and an appropriate subset of an agency's systems and report their findings to the OMB.

To review a GISRA report from the OMB to the White House, refer to the Web site at http://www.whitehouse.gov/omb/infor eg/ fy01securityactreport.pdf. This law can be searched at http://uscode.house. gov/usc.htm.

OMB M-01-08, "Guidance on Implementing the Government Information Security Reform Act," is covered in the Office of Management and Budget topic of this section.

H.R. 2458-48, Chapter 35 of Title 44, United States Code
TITLE III — Information Security §301 Information Security

Federal Information Security Management Act (FISMA)

As of November 2002, the Government Information Security Reform Act (GISRA) expired. The Federal Information Security Management Act (FISMA) of 2002, which was passed as TITLE X of The Homeland Security Act (signed into law on November 27, 2002) and TITLE III of the E-Government Act of 2002 (signed into law on December 17, 2002).

The purposes of FISMA are to (FISMA, Sec. 3541):

1. Provide a comprehensive framework for ensuring the effectiveness of information security controls over information resources that support federal operations and assets.
2. Recognize the highly networked nature of the current federal computing environment and provide effective governmentwide management and oversight of the related information security risks, including coordination of information security efforts throughout the civilian, national security, and law enforcement communities.
3. Provide for development and maintenance of minimum controls required to protect federal information and information systems.
4. Provide a mechanism for improved oversight of Federal agency information security programs.
5. Acknowledge that commercially developed information security products offer advanced, dynamic, robust, and effective information security solutions, reflecting market solutions for the protection of critical information infrastructures important to the national defense and economic security of the nation that are designed, built, and operated by the private sector.
6. Recognize that the selection of specific technical hardware and software information security solutions should be left to individual agencies from among commercially developed products.

The FISMA grants more responsibility to NIST to develop and maintain standards for minimum information security controls. Compliance with the standards outlined in FISMA is compulsory. FISMA grants authorities, assigns responsibilities, and provides for appropriations of funding to ensure compliance with this act across all Federal organizations. The authorities of the Director shall be delegated to the Secretary of Defense for DoD collateral information systems and Director of Central Intelligence for information systems that process intelligence information.

FISMA Annual Independent Evaluation (Agency Reporting)

FISMA directs Federal agencies to conduct annual IT security reviews and Inspectors General (IGs) to perform annual independent evaluations of agency programs and systems and report their results to OMB and Congress. Even prior to FISMA, there was OMB policy requiring agencies to incorporate IT security in the development of both new and existing IT investments and demonstrate that action in their IT budget materials. More recently, OMB has released guidance on the specific security implementations that the agencies have undertaken. This includes:

■ Report security costs for their IT investments
■ Document in their business cases that adequate security controls have been incorporated into the life cycle planning of each IT investment
■ Reflect the agency's security priorities as reported in their Plan of Actions and Milestones (POA&Ms)
■ Tie their POA&Ms for an IT investment directly to the business case for that investment.

The 2003 FISMA report from OBM to Congress is available online at: http://www.whitehouse.gov/omb/inforeg/fy03_fisma_report.pdf.

FISMA Federal Information Security Incident Center

The Director shall ensure the operation of a central Federal information security incident center and provide timely technical assistance to operators of agency information systems regarding security incidents.

To meet this requirement, the US-CERT was established to protect the nation's infrastructure by coordinating defense against and response to cyber attacks. US-CERT created the National Cyber Alert System, which is a national cyber security system for identifying, analyzing, and prioritizing emerging vulnerabilities and threats. According to the US-CERT website, the system relays computer security update and warning information to all users. It provides all citizens — from computer security professionals to home computer users with basic skills — with free, timely, actionable information to better secure their computer systems. You can subscribe to the following free email lists through the US-CERT web site:

- *Cyber Security Bulletins:* Written for technical audiences, Cyber Security Bulletins provide weekly summaries of security issues, new vulnerabilities, potential impact, patches and workarounds, as well as actions recommended to mitigate risk.
- *Technical Cyber Security Alerts:* Written for technical audiences, Cyber Security Alerts provide timely information about current security issues, vulnerabilities, and exploits.
- *Cyber Security Alerts:* Written for non-technical home and corporate computer users, Cyber Security Alerts provide timely information about security issues, vulnerabilities, and exploits currently occurring.
- *Cyber Security Tips:* Written for non-technical home and corporate computer users, the bi-weekly Cyber Security Tips provide information on computer security best practices.

The US-CERT website is www.us-cert.gov.

Responsibilities for Federal Information Systems Standards

Federal agencies are authorized to prescribe and make mandatory, standards and guidelines for information systems within their purview. The FISMA grants the authority to the President to disapprove or modify the standards and guidelines referred to in specific subsections if the President determines that such action is in the public interest. NIST shall submit standards developed pursuant to specific subsections and assist the private sector, upon request, in using and applying the results. The FISMA also authorized the appropriation to the Secretary of Commerce $20,000,000 for each of fiscal years 2003, 2004, 2005, 2006, and 2007 to enable NIST to carry out the provisions of this section.

Information Technology Security Training Program

Each Federal agency shall provide for mandatory periodic training in computer security awareness and accepted computer security practice of all employees who are involved with the management, use, or operation of each federal computer system within or under the supervision of the agency.

The full text of the FISMA can be found at the Department of Homeland Security's Web site at http://www.fedcirc.gov/library/legislation/FISMA.html.

10 USC 2315 Defense Program

The 10 USC 2315 Defense Program requires that all Department of Defense (DoD) telecommunications products must be certified as secure prior to purchase. Specifically, it states that "(A) a certification by the Secretary that the telecommunications procurement known as FTS-2000 or the other telecommunications procurement will provide assured, secure telecommunications support (including associated telecommunications services) for Department of Defense activities; and (B) a description of how the procurement will be implemented and managed to meet defense information infrastructure requirements, including requirements to support deployed forces and intelligence activities" (Title 10 — Armed Forces Subtitle A — General Military Law, Part IV — Service, Supply, and Procurement, Chapter 137 — Procurement Generally).

More information is available at http://www.access.gpo.gov/.

5 USC § 552a, PL 93-579: The U.S. Federal Privacy Act of 1974

This is not listed in the (ISC)² ISSEP exam requirements, but it is important to the field.

According to the Department of Justice "Overview of the Privacy Act of 1974," the law has been in effect since September 27, 1975, and can generally be characterized as an omnibus "code of fair information practices" that attempts to regulate the collection, maintenance, use, and dissemination of personal information by Federal executive branch agencies. However, the Act's imprecise language, limited legislative history, and somewhat outdated regulatory guidelines have rendered it a difficult statute to decipher and apply. Moreover, even after more than 25 years of administrative and judicial analysis, numerous Privacy Act issues remain unresolved or unexplored. Adding to these interpretational difficulties is the fact that many Privacy Act cases are unpublished district court decisions.

Broadly stated, the purpose of the Privacy Act is to balance the government's need to maintain information about individuals, with the rights of individuals to be protected against unwarranted invasions of their privacy stemming from Federal agencies' collection, maintenance, use, and disclosure of personal information about them. The historical context of the Act is important in terms of understanding its remedial purposes: In 1974, Congress was concerned with curbing the illegal surveillance and investigation of individuals by Federal agencies that had been exposed during the Watergate scandal; it was also concerned with potential abuses presented by the government's increasing use of computers to store and retrieve personal data by means of a universal identifier — such as an individual's social security number. The Act focuses on four basic policy objectives (U.S. DoJ Overview from Web site):

1. To restrict *disclosure* of personally identifiable records maintained by agencies
2. To grant individuals increased rights of *access* to agency records maintained on themselves.

3. To grant individuals the right to seek *amendment* of agency records maintained on themselves upon a showing that the records are not accurate, relevant, timely, or complete
4. To establish a code of *fair information practices* that requires agencies to comply with statutory norms for collection, maintenance, and dissemination of records

This Act was amended in 1980. The complete USC can be searched at http://uscode.house.gov/usc.htm, and the DoJ overview can be found at http://www.usdoj.gov/04foia/04_7_1.html.

Fraud and Related Activity in Connection with Computers

This is not listed in the (ISC)² ISSEP exam requirements, but it is important to the field.

This April 1999 example of computer crime is available on the DoJ Web site and provides a good example of one type of computer crime. Depending on your perspective, it also provides a reason for why there is a need for laws to prosecute such offenders.

> On April 7, 1999, visitors to an online financial news message board operated by Yahoo!, Inc. got a scoop on PairGain, a telecommunications company based in Tustin, California. An e-mail posted on the message board under the subject line "Buyout News" said that PairGain was being taken over by an Israeli company. The e-mail also provided a link to what appeared to be a website of Bloomberg News Service, containing a detailed story on the takeover. As news of the takeover spread, the company's publicly traded stock shot up more than 30 percent, and the trading volume grew to nearly seven times its norm. There was only one problem: the story was false, and the website on which it appeared was not Bloomberg's site, but a counterfeit site. When news of the hoax spread, the price of the stock dropped sharply, causing significant financial losses to many investors who purchased the stock at artificially inflated prices.
>
> Within a week after this hoax appeared, the Federal Bureau of Investigation arrested a Raleigh, North Carolina man for what was believed to be the first stock manipulation scheme perpetrated by a fraudulent Internet site. The perpetrator was traced through an Internet Protocol address that he used, and he was charged with securities fraud for disseminating false information

about a publicly traded stock. The Securities and Exchange Commission also brought a parallel civil enforcement action against him. In August, he was sentenced to five years of probation, five months of home detention, and over $93,000 in restitution to the victims of his fraud.

—http://www.usdoj.gov/criminal/cybercrime/unlawful.htm

The use of new technology to commit traditional crimes, such as securities fraud, is not new. Advances in technology have always given wrongdoers new means for engaging in unlawful conduct. The Internet is no different: it is simply a new medium through which traditional crimes can now be committed, albeit through the use of inexpensive and widely available computer and telecommunications systems, and with unprecedented speed and on a far-reaching scale. At the same time, as exemplified by the PairGain case, the tools and capabilities associated with new technologies can in many instances help law enforcement agencies solve such crimes.

18 USC § 1030. P.L. 99-474: The Computer Fraud and Abuse Act of 1984, Amended in 1994 and 1996, Broadened in 2001

This is not listed in the (ISC)² ISSEP exam requirements, but it is important to the field.

The Computer Fraud and Abuse Act (CFAA) was originally enacted to provide a clear statement of proscribed activity concerning computers to the law enforcement community, those who own and operate computers, and those tempted to commit crimes by unauthorized access to computers. Instead of trying to add computer crime to the multitude of other relevant USC, it was decided to establish the Computer Fraud and Abuse statute, 18 USC 1030, as a single statute for computer-related offenses. This first Federal computer crime statute was designed to protect computer data from theft. For example, CFAA made it a felony to access classified information in a computer without authorization and a misdemeanor to access financial records or credit histories in financial institutions or trespass into a government computer. [http://www.usdoj.gov/criminal/cybercrime/s982.htm#I]

Essentially, unauthorized access or access in excess of authorization became a felony on classified information and a misdemeanor for financial information. It also became a misdemeanor to access a government computer with or without authorization should the government's use of the computer be affected.

In subsequent years, the statute has been amended and broadened. The CFAA generally prohibits the following:

- Obtaining information from a computer through unauthorized access (unauthorized use of computers to obtain U.S. agency information, private financial record information, or information from any protected computer if the conduct involved an interstate or foreign communication).
- Trespassing in Federal government computers. In October 2001, Congress expanded CFAA to include any computer located outside the United States that is used in a manner that affects interstate or foreign commerce or communication in the United States.
- Committing fraud (knowingly and with intent to defraud, accesses a protected computer without authorization, or exceeds authorized access, and by means of such conduct furthers the intended fraud and obtains anything of value, unless the object of the fraud and the thing obtained consists only of the use of the computer and the value of such use is not more than $5,000 in any 1-year period).
- Transmitting harmful computer viruses (the law states "knowingly causes the transmission of a program, information, code, or command, and as a result of such conduct, intentionally causes damage without authorization, to a protected computer" [Sec. 5a]).
- Trafficking in computer access passwords.
- Damaging computer data.

The CFAA is one of the most frequently used laws by the Federal Bureau of Investigations (FBI) to investigate computer-related crimes. The FBI investigates computer crimes when a violation of the Federal criminal code has occurred within the jurisdiction of the FBI.

This law can be searched at http://uscode.house.gov/usc.htm, and analysis can be found at http://www.usdoj.gov/criminal/cybercrime/s982.htm#I.

For more information about Federal legal codes related to cyber-crime, visit http://www.usdoj.gov/criminal/cybercrime/fedcode.htm.

Executive Orders

Executive Order (EO) 13231: Critical Infrastructure Protection in the Information Age (October 18, 2001)

EO 13231 is the United States policy to protect against disruption of the operation of information systems for critical infrastructure. It provides protection for the people, economy, essential human and government services, and national security of the Untied States. It ensures that any disruptions that occur are infrequent, minimal, manageable, and cause the least amount of damage possible.

EO 13231 Section 1 *Policy* states:

■ (a) The information technology revolution has changed the way business is transacted, government operates, and national defense is conducted. Those three functions now depend on an interdependent network of critical information infrastructures. The protection program authorized by this order shall consist of continuous efforts to secure information systems for critical infrastructure, including emergency preparedness communications, and the physical assets that support such systems. Protection of these systems is essential to the telecommunications, energy, financial services, manufacturing, water, transportation, health care, and emergency services sectors.
■ (b) It is the policy of the United States to protect against disruption of the operation of information systems for critical infrastructure and thereby help to protect the people, economy, essential human and government services, and national security of the United States, and to ensure that any disruptions that occur are infrequent, of minimal duration, and manageable, and cause the least damage possible. The implementation of this policy shall include a voluntary public-private partnership, involving corporate and nongovernmental organizations.

This document can be downloaded from http://www.archives.gov/federal_register/executive_orders/disposition_tables.html.

Office of Management and Budget (OMB) Circulars and Memoranda

This topic outlines OMB Circular A-130, which is an important document for information systems security (see Table 11.2). Also, several information systems security OMB memoranda are included.

Office of Management and Budget (OMB) Circular A-130

The Office and Management and Budget (OMB) Instructions or information issued by the OMB to federal agencies are expected to have a continuing effect of two years or more. Circular No. A-130 provides uniform government-wide information resources management policies as required by the

Table 11.2   OMB Circular and Memoranda

Office of Management and Budget (OMB)
Circular A-130
OMB M-99-18
OMB M-00-13
OMB M-00-07
OMB M-01-08
OMB M-03-19

Paperwork Reduction Act of 1980 and as amended by the Paperwork Reduction Act of 1995, 44 USC Chapter 35.

The policies in Circular No. A-130 apply to the information activities of all agencies of the executive branch of the federal government. It requires all agency information systems to provide a level of security commensurate with the sensitivity of the information, the risk of its unauthorized access, and the harm that could result from improper use. It also requires all agencies to establish security programs to safeguard the sensitive information they process.

History

Circular No. A-130 was first legislated in 1985 to provide a policy framework for the management of federal information resources. It has been revised in 1993, 1996, and 2000. As of publication date, the last revision to Circular No. A-130 came in 2000 to bring the regulation in line with the Clinger–Cohen Act of 1996, which set IT management policy and created the position of Chief Information Officer for agencies. The November 2000 update included procedural and analytic guidelines for implementing specific aspects of these policies as appendices to include:

- Focusing information resources planning to support their strategic missions
- Implementing a capital planning and investment control process that links to budget formulation and execution
- Rethinking and restructuring the way agencies do their work before investing in information systems

The 1996 revisions focused on Appendix III, which established a minimum set of controls to be included in federal automated information security programs, assigned federal agency responsibilities for the security of automated information, and required agency automated information security programs and agency management control systems to be established in accordance with OMB Circular No. A-123.

In the 1993 revisions, the focus was on bringing the Federal government into the information age. It was a major step toward realizing the vision of a government that uses technology better to communicate with the American people. The goal was to use information technology to make government information available to the public in a timely and equitable manner, via a diverse array of sources, both public and private. Along with this was the goal of ensuring that privacy and security interests are protected.

In December 2003, the OMB released information stating that it plans massive updates to the rules overseeing Federal information technology management. In addition to standing policies, OMB officials have introduced new guidance in a number of areas — including security and privacy — under new mandates from the E-Government Act of 2002. Those directions will be the basis for a major rewrite of OMB Circular A-130.

Policy: The Importance of Appendix III

OMB Circular No. A-130 establishes policy for the management of Federal information resources. The OMB includes procedural and analytic guidelines for implementing specific aspects of these policies as appendices. They include:

- Appendix I: Federal Agency Responsibilities for Maintaining Records about Individuals
- Appendix II: Implementation of the Government Paperwork Elimination Act
- Appendix III: Security of Federal Automated Information Resources
- Appendix IV: Analysis of Key Sections

Because Appendix III is directly related to security, a few points are mentioned. First is the definition of what is considered "adequate security" for Federal systems. "Adequate Security means security commensurate with the risk and magnitude of the harm resulting from the loss, misuse, or unauthorized access to or modification of information. This includes assuring that systems and applications used by the agency operate effectively and provide appropriate confidentiality, integrity, and availability, through the use of cost-effective management, personnel, operational, and technical controls" (A130, Appendix III, Section 2, Definitions).

Appendix III also provides definitions for General Support Systems (GSS) and Major Applications (MA), and policies are sometimes divided into these two categories. A GSS means an interconnected set of information resources under the same direct management control that shares common functionality. MA means an application that requires special attention to security due to the risk and magnitude of the harm resulting from the loss, misuse, or unauthorized access to or modification of the information in the application.

Some key security responsibilities are: agencies shall implement and maintain a program to assure that adequate security is provided for all agency information collected, processed, transmitted, stored, or disseminated in general support systems and major applications. The program must include: assign responsibility for security, a system security plan (an important new requirement for a security plan is the establishment of a set of rules of behavior for individual users of each GSS), review of security controls, and authorize processing (C&A). Additional responsibilities include:

- *Correction of deficiencies.* Agencies shall correct deficiencies identified through the reviews of security for systems and major applications. Agencies shall include a summary of their system security plans and major application plans in the strategic plan required by the Paperwork Reduction Act (44 USC 3506).
- *Incident response capability.* When faced with a security incident, an agency should be able to respond in a manner that both protects its own information and helps to protect the information of others who might be affected by the incident. To address this concern, agencies should establish formal incident response mechanisms.
- *Continuity of support.* Inevitably, there will be service interruptions. Agency plans should ensure an ability to recover and provide service sufficient to meet the minimal needs of system users. Manual procedures are generally *not* a viable backup option.
- *Technical security.* Agencies should ensure that each system appropriately uses effective security products and techniques, consistent with standards and guidance from NIST.
- *System interconnection.* For a community to effectively manage risk, it must control access to and from other systems. The degree of such control should be established in the rules of the system, and all participants should be made aware of any limitations on outside access. Technical controls to accomplish this should be put in place in accordance with guidance issued by NIST.
- *Review of security controls.* The security of a system will degrade over time, as the technology evolves and as people and procedures change. Reviews should ensure that management, operational, personnel, and technical controls are functioning effectively. Security controls can be reviewed by an independent audit or a self-review.

The type and rigor of review or audit should be commensurate with the acceptable level of risk established in the rules for the system and the likelihood of learning useful information to improve security. Technical tools such as virus scanners, vulnerability assessment products (which look for known security problems, configuration errors, and the installation of the latest patches), and penetration testing can assist in the ongoing review. However, these tools are no substitute for a formal management review at least every three years. Indeed, for some high-risk systems with rapidly changing technology, three years will be too long of a time interval.

■ *Authorize processing.* The authorization of a system to process information, granted by a management official, provides an important quality control (this is also referred to as accreditation). By authorizing processing in a system, a senior-level manager accepts the risk associated with it. Authorization is not a decision that should be made by the security staff.

■ *Information sharing (major applications only).* Ensure that information shared with federal organizations, state and local governments, and the private sector is appropriately protected, comparable to the protection provided when the information is within the application. Controls on the information may stay the same or vary when the information is shared with another entity.

■ *Public access controls.* Permitting public access to a federal application is an important method of improving information exchange with the public. At the same time, it introduces risks to the federal application. To mitigate these risks, additional controls should be in place as appropriate. These controls are in addition to controls such as firewalls that are put in place for the security of the general support system.

■ *Assignment of responsibilities.* Appendix III assigns governmentwide responsibilities to agencies, responsibilities that are consistent with their missions and the Computer Security Act. The Circular clarifies that information classified for national security purposes should also be handled in accordance with appropriate national security directives. Where classified information is required to be protected by more stringent security requirements, those requirements should be followed rather than the requirements of Appendix III.

■ *Reports.* Appendix III requires agencies to provide two reports to the OMB. The first is a requirement that agencies report security deficiencies and material weaknesses within their reporting mechanisms as defined by OMB Circular No. A-123, "Management Accountability and Control," and take corrective actions in accordance with that directive. The second, defined by the Computer

Security Act, requires that a summary of agency security plans be included in the information resources management plan required by the Paperwork Reduction Act.

Appendix III no longer requires the preparation of formal risk analyses. In the past, substantial resources were expended doing complex analyses of specific risks to systems, with limited tangible benefit in terms of improved security for the systems. Rather than continue to try to precisely measure risk, security efforts are better served by generally assessing risks and taking actions to manage them. While formal risk analyses need not be performed, the need to determine adequate security will require that a risk-based approach be used. This risk assessment approach should include a consideration of the major factors in risk management: the value of the system or application, threats, vulnerabilities, and the effectiveness of current or proposed safeguards. Additional guidance on effective risk assessment is available in NIST SP 800-12, "An Introduction to Computer Security: The NIST Handbook" (March 16, 1995).

Circular No. A-130, Revised, Transmittal Memorandum No. 4 (November 2000)

In November 2000, the OMB released Transmittal Memorandum No. 4 with guidance on how to implement OMB Circular No. A-130. The first section answers the questions of how agencies must conduct information management planning, followed by how agencies should manage information systems and information technology. Section 2 describes how agencies must document and submit their initial enterprise architecture to the OMB.

Of more importance to the ISSEP is Section 3, which defines how agencies must ensure that security is an integral aspect of information systems. The policy states that agencies must incorporate security into the architecture of their information and systems to ensure that security supports agency business operations and that plans to fund and manage security are built into life-cycle budgets for information systems. Specifically, Transmittal Memorandum No. 4 states the following:

- "(a) To support more effective agency implementation of both agency computer security and critical infrastructure protection programs, agencies must implement the following:
  - (i) Prioritize key systems (including those that are most critical to agency operations);
  - (ii) Apply OMB policies and, for non-national security applications, NIST guidance to achieve adequate security commensurate with the level of risk and magnitude of harm;

- ■ (b) Agencies must make security's role explicit in information technology investments and capital programming. Investments in the development of new or the continued operation of existing information systems, both general support systems and major applications must:
  - (i) Demonstrate that the security controls for components, applications, and systems are consistent with, and an integral part of, the Enterprise Architecture (EA) of the agency;
  - (ii) Demonstrate that the costs of security controls are understood and are explicitly incorporated into the life-cycle planning of the overall system in a manner consistent with OMB guidance for capital programming;
  - (iii) Incorporate a security plan that complies with Appendix III of OMB A-130 and in a manner that is consistent with NIST guidance on security planning;
  - (iv) Demonstrate specific methods used to ensure that risks and the potential for loss are understood and continually assessed, that steps are taken to maintain risk at an acceptable level, and that procedures are in place to ensure that controls are implemented effectively and remain effective over time;
  - (v) Demonstrate specific methods used to ensure that security controls are commensurate with the risk and magnitude of harm that may result from the loss, misuse, or unauthorized access to or modification of the system itself or the information it manages;
  - (vi) Identify additional security controls that are necessary to minimize risk to and potential loss from those systems that promote or permit public access, other externally accessible systems, and those systems that are interconnected with systems over which program officials have little or no control;
  - (vii) Deploy effective security controls and authentication tools consistent with the protection of privacy, such as public-key based digital signatures, for those systems that promote or permit public access;
  - (viii) Ensure that the handling of personal information is consistent with relevant government-wide and agency policies;
  - (ix) Describe each occasion the agency decides to employ standards and guidance that are more stringent than those promulgated by NIST to ensure the use of risk-based cost-effective security controls for non-national security applications;
- ■ (c) OMB will consider for new or continued funding only those system investments that satisfy these criteria. New information technology investments must demonstrate that existing agency systems also meet these criteria in order to qualify for funding."

The Transmittal Memorandum and can be downloaded from http://www.whitehouse.gov/omb/circulars/a130/a130trans4.html.

OMB M-99-18: Privacy Policies and Data Collection on Federal Web Sites (June 1999)

This is a memorandum for the heads of executive departments and agencies. It is the predecessor of OMB M-00-13, which is listed in the (ISC)² ISSEP study guide.

This memorandum directed Federal departments and agencies to post clear privacy policies on World Wide Web (WWW) sites and provided guidance on how to post privacy policies. The policy dictates that agencies must clearly and concisely inform visitors accessing their Web sites what information the agency collects about individuals, why the agency collects it, and how the agency will use it. Also, privacy policies must be clearly labeled and easily accessed when someone visits a Web site.

With the memorandum is an attachment that provides guidance and model language on privacy statements. Agencies could use this guidance and model language to help identify the issues that privacy policies must cover, draft the language, and get it approved. It was intended to help agencies post privacy and usage policies expeditiously.

The memorandum can be downloaded from http://www.whitehouse. gov/omb/memoranda/m99-18.html.

OMB M-00-13: Privacy Policies and Data Collection on Federal Web Sites (June 2000)

Continuing from OMB M-99-18, the purpose of OMB M-00-13 was to remind Federal agencies that it is required by law and policy to establish clear privacy policies for Web activities and to comply with those policies. Agency contractors should also comply with those policies when operating Web sites on behalf of agencies. The main privacy policies are:

- Agencies are to post clear privacy policies on agency principal Web sites, as well as at any other known, major entry points to sites, and at any Web page where substantial amounts of personal information are posted.
- Privacy policies must be clearly labeled and easily accessed when someone visits a Web site.
- Particular privacy concerns may be raised when uses of Web technology can track the activities of users over time and across different Web sites. These concerns are especially great where

individuals who have come to government Web sites do not have clear and conspicuous notice of any such tracking activities. "Cookies" — small bits of software that are placed on a Web user's hard drive — are a principal example of current Web technology that can be used in this way. Because of the unique laws and traditions about government access to citizens' personal information, the presumption should be that "cookies" will not be used at Federal Web sites. In accord with the Memorandum, federal Web sites should not use persistent cookies unless four conditions are met:

- The site gives clear and conspicuous notice.
- There is a compelling need to gather the data on the site.
- Appropriate and publicly disclosed privacy safeguards exist for handling any information derived from the cookies.
- The agency head gives personal approval for the use.

■ All federal Web sites and contractors, when operating on behalf of agencies, shall comply with the standards set forth in the Children's Online Privacy Protection Act of 1998 with respect to the collection of personal information online at Web sites directed to children.

The memorandum can be downloaded from http://www.whitehouse. gov/omb/memoranda/m00-13.html.

OMB M-00-07: Incorporating and Funding Security in Information Systems Investments (February 2000)

This is not listed in the (ISC)² ISSEP exam requirements, but it is one of my favorites, so it is included.

OMB M-00-07 notes that security should be built into and funded as part of the system architecture. It is the responsibility of each agency to make security's role explicit in IT investments and capital programming. The memorandum states:

Accordingly, investments in the development of new or the continued operation of existing information systems, both general support systems and major applications, proposed for funding in the President's budget must:

1. Be tied to the agency's information architecture.
   Proposals should demonstrate that the security controls for components, applications, and systems are consistent with and an

integral part of the information technology architecture of the agency.

2. Be well-planned, by:

Demonstrating that the costs of security controls are understood and are explicitly incorporated in the life-cycle planning of the overall system in a manner consistent with OMB guidance for capital programming. Incorporating a security plan that discusses:

1. The rules of behavior for the system and the consequences for violating those rules;
2. Personnel and technical controls for the system;
3. Methods for identifying, appropriately limiting, and controlling interconnections with other systems and specific ways such limits will be monitored and managed;
4. Procedures for the on-going training of individuals that are permitted access to the system;
5. Procedures for the on-going monitoring of the effectiveness of security controls;
6. Procedures for reporting and sharing with appropriate agency and government authorities indications of attempted and successful intrusions into agency systems;
7. Provisions for the continuity of support in the event of system disruption or failure.

3. Manage risks by:

a) Demonstrating specific methods used to ensure that risks and the potential for loss are understood and continually assessed, that steps are taken to maintain risk at an acceptable level, and that procedures are in place to ensure that controls are implemented effectively and remain effective over time.

b) Demonstrating specific methods used to ensure that the security controls are commensurate with the risk and magnitude of harm that may result from the loss, misuse, or unauthorized access to or modification of the system itself or the information it manages.

c) Identifying additional security controls that are necessary to minimize risks to and potential loss from those systems that promote or permit public access, other externally accessible systems, and those systems that are interconnected with systems over which program officials have little or no control

4. Protect privacy and confidentiality, by:

a) Deploying effective security controls and authentication tools consistent with the protection of privacy, such as public-key based digital signatures, for those systems that promote or permit public access.

b) Ensuring that the handling of personal information is consistent with relevant government-wide and agency policies, such as privacy statements on the agency's web sites.

5. Account for departures from NIST Guidance. For non-national security applications, to ensure the use of risk-based cost-effective security controls, describe each occasion when employing standards and guidance that are more stringent than those promulgated by the National Institute for Standards and Technology.

The key to this memorandum is that, in general, the OMB will consider new or continued funding only for those system investments that satisfy these criteria and will consider funding IT investments only upon demonstration that existing agency systems meet these criteria.

The memorandum can be downloaded from http://www.whitehouse.gov/omb/memoranda/m00-07.html.

OMB M-01-08: Guidance on Implementing the Government Information Security Reform Act (January 2001)

This is a memorandum for the heads of executive departments and agencies and provides guidance to agencies on carrying out the Act. The guidance focuses on unclassified Federal systems and addresses only those areas of the legislation that introduce new or modified requirements. The Act requires for both unclassified and national security programs: (1) annual agency program reviews; (2) annual Inspector General (IG) evaluations; (3) agency reporting to the OMB the results of IG evaluations for unclassified systems and audits of IG evaluations for national security programs; and (4) an annual OMB report to Congress summarizing the materials received from agencies. Agencies will submit this information beginning in 2001 as part of the budget process.

Specifically, it answers the following questions:

■ Part 1: General Overview
  – A. How does the Security Act affect existing security policy and authorities?
  – B. Does the Security Act pertain to existing agency systems?
  – C. Does the Security Act pertain to contractor systems?
  – D. How does the Security Act's new definition of "mission-critical system" affect agency security responsibilities?
  – E. What is the relationship between the new Security Act and PDD-63, Critical Infrastructure Protection?
  – F. What are the relationships between the agencywide security program and agencywide security plan? Who is responsible for these and do individual systems still require security plans?

■ Part 2: Agency Responsibilities
- A. What new agency responsibilities are found in the Security Act?
- B. What are the responsibilities of the agency head?
- C. What are the responsibilities of program officials?
- D. What are the responsibilities of the agency Chief Information Officer?

■ Part 3: Inspector General Responsibilities
- A. What are the responsibilities of the agency Inspector General?

■ Part 4: OMB Responsibilities
- A. What are OMB's responsibilities under the Security Act?
- B. Will OMB be revising its security policies?

■ Part 5: Reporting Requirements
- A. What does the Security Act require agencies to report?
- B. What does the Security Act require OMB to report?

■ Part 6: Additional Responsibilities of Certain Agencies
- A. Department of Commerce
- B. Department of Defense and the Intelligence Community
- C. Department of Justice
- D. General Services Administration
- E. Office of Personnel Management

The memorandum can be downloaded from http://www.whitehouse. gov/omb/memoranda/m01-08.pdf.

OMB M-03-19: Reporting Instructions for the Federal Information Security Management Act and Updated Guidance on Quarterly IT Security Reporting (August 6, 2003)

This memorandum is for the heads of executive departments and agencies.

This is not listed on the (ISC)² ISSEP exam requirements; however, because the GISRA was replaced by FISMA, it is my belief that this memorandum will soon replace the requirement to know OMB M-01-08.

This guidance provides direction to agencies on implementing FISMA and consists of four attachments:

■ *Attachment A.* The information in this attachment is new and highlights the more substantive changes introduced by FISMA from previous IT security legislation.
■ *Attachment B.* This attachment contains the FY03 FISMA reporting instructions for agencies and Inspectors General.
■ *Attachment C.* This attachment contains directions for agencies on quarterly reporting on IT security efforts. It includes both the

continued quarterly plan of action and milestone updates and performance measure updates.

■ *Attachment D.* This attachment contains definitions in law and policy referenced in the guidance.

The memorandum can be downloaded from http://www.whitehouse. gov/omb/memoranda/m03-19.pdf.

Director of Central Intelligence Directive DCID 6/3

Note to ISSEP candidates: This is not listed on the (ISC)² ISSEP exam requirements; but if you work within the intelligence community, this may be appropriate to know.

DCID 6/3 provides policy and procedures for handling classified intelligence information under the purview of the Director of Central Intelligence (DCI). Although this Directive is not tested as part of the ISSEP examination, ISSEPs who are tasked with certification and accreditation of intelligence information systems should and will become very familiar with its content. The entire document is labeled For Official Use Only (FOUO).

There are several implementations of the document in that different agencies within the Intelligence Community (IC) have a slightly different implementation and language in identifying various roles and responsibilities. It also establishes the security policy and procedures for storing, processing, and communicating classified intelligence information in information systems (ISs). For purposes of this Directive, intelligence information refers to Sensitive Compartmented Information and special access programs for intelligence under the purview of the DCI. An information system is any telecommunications or computer related equipment or interconnected system or subsystems of equipment that is used in the acquisition, storage, manipulation, management, movement, control, display, switching, interchange, transmission, or reception of voice and/or data (digital or analog); it includes software, firmware, and hardware.

"Intelligence information shall be appropriately safeguarded at all times, including when used in information systems. The information systems shall be protected. Safeguards shall be applied such that:

1. Individuals are held accountable for their actions;
2. Information is accessed only by authorized individuals with the appropriate clearance, formal access approvals, and need-to-know and processes;

3. Information is used only for its authorized purpose(s);
4. Information retains its content integrity;
5. Information is available to satisfy mission requirements; and
6. Information is appropriately marked and labeled.

Intelligence information constitutes an asset vital to the effective performance of our national security roles. It is essential that this information be properly managed, and that its confidentiality, integrity, and availability be ensured. Therefore, this policy and its implementation manual:

a. Provide policy and procedures for the security and protection of systems that create, process, store, and transmit intelligence information.
b. Provide administrative and system security requirements, including those for interconnected systems.
c. Define and mandate the use of a risk management process.
d. Define and mandate the use of a certification and accreditation process.
e. Promote the use of efficient procedures and cost-effective, computer-based security features and assurances.
f. Describe the roles and responsibilities of the individuals who constitute the decision-making segment of the IS security community and its system users.
g. Require a life-cycle management approach to implementing system security requirements.
h. Introduce the concepts Levels-of-Concern and Protection Level of information."

More information on DCID is available at http://www.fas.org/irp/offdocs/DCID_6-3_20Manual.htm.

Summary

This chapter provided an introduction to the federal agencies and organizations responsible for IA policies, procedures, directives, and guidelines. Eight federal agencies and security organizations were outlined in the first section. The second section looked at several policies or directives released from U.S. Congress as federal laws, executive orders from the White House, Office of Management and Budget Circulars and Memoranda, and a directive from the Director of Central Intelligence.

The remaining chapters in this domain review the policies and procedures released by the National Security Agency, Department of Defense, National Institute of Standards and Technology, and the National Information Assurance Partnership, which specifically covers the Common Criteria.

As mentioned, this material is not intended as a comprehensive tutorial or manual on the broad topic of U.S. Government information systems security policy. It simply provides an overview of some key policies that can help the security practitioner understand the content of policies and, most importantly, how they might affect integrating mission needs, mission threats, and system-specific security needs when designing, developing, validating, certifying, and accrediting information systems.

References

5 U.SC § 552a, PL 93-579. The U.S. Federal Privacy Act of 1974.

18 U.SC § 1030, PL 99-474. The Computer Fraud and Abuse Act of 1986, Amended in 1996.

44 U.SC Section 3506 (1975). Paperwork Reduction Act Section 3506 Coordination of Federal Information Policy. Available at http://www.archives.gov/federal_register/public_laws/paperwork_reduction_act/3506.html.

Analysis of Federal Information Security Management Act (FISMA), 4 March 2003, Center for Medicare and Medicaid Service. Available at http://cms.hhs.gov/it/security/docs/FISMA_Analysis.pdf.

DCI Directive 1/1 (November 1998). The Authorities and Responsibilities of the Director of Central Intelligence as Head of the U.S. Intelligence Community. Available at http://www.fas.org/irp/offdocs/dcid1-1.htm.

DCID 6/3 (June 1999). Protecting Sensitive Compartmented Information within Information Systems, Director of Central Intelligence Directive. Available at http://www.fas.org/irp/offdocs/DCID_6-3_20Policy.htm.

Executive Order (EO) 13231 (October 18, 2001). Critical Infrastructure Protection in the Information Age. Presidential Documents, *Federal Register,* Vol. 66, No. 202, Thursday, October 18, 2001.

HR 145 Public Law 100-235 (June 1987). Computer Security Act of 1987. The act can be downloaded from http://csrc.nist.gov/secplcy/csa_87.txt.

H.R. 2458-48, Chapter 35 of Title 44, United States Code TITLE-III — Information Security §301 Information Security (December 2002). Federal Information Systems Management Act (FISMA).

OMB Circular No. A-123 (June 1995). Management Accountability and Control. Available at http://www.whitehouse.gov/omb/circulars/a123/a123.html.

OMB A-130, Management of Federal Information Resources (last revised November 2000). Available at http://www.whitehouse.gov/omb/circulars/index.html.

OMB Circular No. A-130, Revised, Transmittal Memorandum No. 4 (November 2000). Available at http://www.whitehouse.gov/omb/.

OMB M-99-18 (June 1999). Privacy Policies and Data Collection on Federal Web Sites. Available at http://www.whitehouse.gov/omb/.

OMB M-00-13 (June 2000). Privacy Policies and Data Collection on Federal Web Sites. Available at http://www.whitehouse.gov/omb/.

OMB M-01-08 (January 2001). Guidance on Implementing the Government Information Security Reform Act. Available at http://www.whitehouse.gov/omb/.

OMB M-03-19 (August 2003). Reporting Instructions for the Federal Information Security Management Act and Updated Guidance on Quarterly IT Security Reporting. Available at http://www.whitehouse.gov/omb/.

NIST SP 800-12 (March 1995). An Introduction to Computer Security: The NIST Handbook. Available at http://csrc.nist.gov/publications/nistpubs/index.html.

Presidential Decision Directive 63 (PDD-63) (May 1998). Protecting America's Critical Infrastructures. Available at http://www.usdoj.gov/criminal/cybercrime/factsh.htm.

Public Law 106-398, Title X, Subtitle G (Chapter 35 of Title 44) (October 30, 2000). Government Information Security Reform Act (GISRA). Available at http://uscode.house.gov/usc.htm.

The Electronic Frontier: The Challenge of Unlawful Conduct Involving the Use of the Internet: A Report of the President's Working Group on Unlawful Conduct on the Internet (March 2000). Available at http://www.usdoj.gov/criminal/cybercrime/unlawful.htm.

The National Information Infrastructure Protection Act of 1995 (August 27, 1996). Information available at http://www.usdoj.gov/criminal/cybercrime/s982.htm#I.

Web Sites

http://uscode.house.gov for information on public laws.

http://thomas.loc.gov for information on public laws.

http://www.whitehouse.gov/news/orders/ for information on Presidential Executive Orders.

http://www.whitehouse.gov/omb/ for information on OMB.

http://www.cia.gov/ for information on the Director of Central Intelligence.

http://www.whitehouse.gov/news/orders/ for information on Homeland Security Presidential Directives (HSPDs).

http://www.state.gov/r/pa/ho/time/cwr/17603.htm for information on National Security Act of 1947.

http://www.nsa.gov/snac/index.cfm for NSA security configuration guides.

http://www.nsa.gov for information on NSA.

http://www.nsa.gov/ia/ for the information assurance directorate at NSA.

http://www.nist.gov for information on NIST.

http://csrc.nist.gov/publications/index.html for NIST publications.

http://www.nstissc.gov for information on CNSS (the Web site for CNSS is still under the previous acronym).

http://www.niap.nist.gov for information on NIAP.

http://www.fedcirc.gov/library/legislation/FISMA.html for information on FISMA.

http://www4.law.cornell.edu/uscode/10/2315.notes.html for information 20 U.SC
Section 2315.

http://uscode.house.gov/usc.htm for information on the Computer Fraud and
Abuse Act. http://www.usdoj.gov/criminal/cybercrime/s982.htm#I for information on the Computer Fraud and Abuse Act.

http://www.usdoj.gov/criminal/cybercrime/unlawful.htm for information on the
Computer Fraud and Abuse Act.

http://www.panix.com/~eck/computer-fraud-act.html.

http://www.fas.org/irp/offdocs/DCID_6-3_20Manual.htm.

12

Department of Defense (DoD) Information Assurance Organizations and Policies

Introduction

In 1949, the Department of Defense (DoD) was designated an executive department with a single cabinet-level secretary for the Army, Navy, Marine Corps, Coast Guard, and Air Force. According to the DoD Web site, the DoD is the nation's largest employer, with 1.4 million men and women on active duty; 654,000 civilians; and another 1.2 million volunteers serving in the Guard and Reserve. The DoD also supports 2.0 million retirees and families that are receiving benefits (http://www.dod.mil/home/about-dod.html; April 2002).

Imagine trying to provide security for 600,000 individual buildings and structures located at more than 6,000 different locations or sites in over 146 countries. Not only must these locations be operational, but they must also provide information services with a high degree of Confidentiality, Integrity, and Availability (CIA). Because of this enormous task, the DoD must create and implement policies and procedures that will guide the operational capabilities in a secure manner.

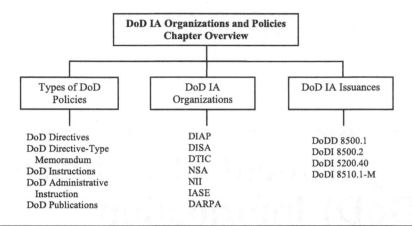

Figure 12.1   Chapter overview.

This chapter begins with an overview of DoD policies and explains the types of DoD issuances (see Figure 12.1). The second section briefly explains the major DoD agencies and departments with Information Assurance (IA) responsibilities. The final section provides details of several specific DoD issuances related to IA. Before beginning the chapter, those not familiar with the DoD environment should read the background information, which provides information on the DoD vision of implementing a net-centric data strategy.

Background Information

Note to the ISSEP candidate: For the (ISC)² ISSEP® exam, this information is not necessarily included, although there might be some terms used. For those working in the DoD environment, it is important to know the vision and goals of the DoD net-centric data strategy.

There are many adjectives that can be used to describe the DoD network environment — complex, intriguing, fascinating, and revolutionary. Although it is a large governmental department with a single mission, it has distinct and separate organizations that have operated in a stovepipe fashion. Due to the changing needs of the military, there is a need for a centralized approach that allows communications to occur between all entities, regardless of which organization they belong. In addition, technology advances have changed the way the DoD operates and it is expected that more technical changes will occur during the coming decades. To meet these changing needs, the DoD Chief Information Officer (CIO) in 2003 released a memorandum and strategy that outlined a net-centric approach.

According to the DoD CIO, DoD systems are in transition based upon a new concept of net-centricity. **Net-centricity** is the realization of a networked environment, including infrastructure, systems, processes, and people, that enables a completely different approach to warfighting and business operations. The goal is to securely interconnect people and systems independent of time or location. The foundation for net-centricity is the DoD Global Information Grid (GIG). The GIG is defined as a globally interconnected, end-to-end set of information capabilities, associated processes, and personnel for collecting, processing, storing, disseminating, and managing information on demand to warfighters, defense policymakers, and support personnel.

The DoD CIO believes that implementing a net-centricity approach will:

- Support a substantially improved military situational awareness.
- Provide better access to business information.
- Decrease decision cycles.
- Empower users to better protect assets and more effectively exploit information.
- Provide more efficient use of resources.
- Create extended, collaborative communities to focus on the mission.

The DoD not only recognizes the importance of technology in implementing the GIG, but also takes into account the importance of people. The DoD Net-Centric Data Strategy (2003) states that the approach to implementing the GIG is to use "communications, computing, and applications technologies but also recognizes that the cultural barriers against trust and data sharing must be addressed (p. 1)." To achieve an integrated approach, the DoD is combining the overall net-centric data strategy and an IA strategy with the implementation of GIG layers as shown in Figure 12.2.

The DoD data vision is based upon using the data effectively. The DoD Net-Centric Data Strategy states:

> The core of the net-centric environment is the data that enables effective decisions. In this context, data implies all data assets such as system files, databases, documents, official electronic records, images, audio files, web sites, and data access services. One of the CIO goals, as confirmed by the Deputy Secretary of Defense in Management Initiative Decision 905, is to populate the network with all data (intelligence, nonintelligence, raw, and processed). The DoD CIO also wants to change the paradigm from "process, exploit, and disseminate" to "post before processing." All data is advertised and available for users and

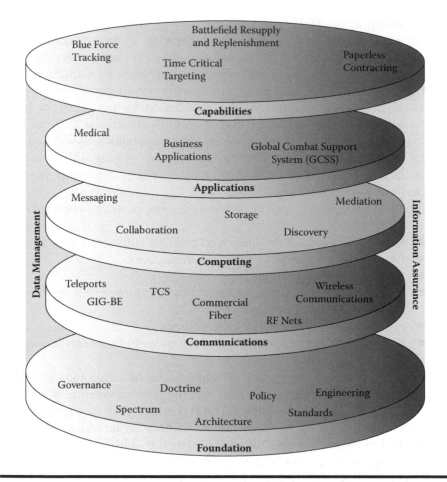

Figure 12.2 Integrated approach for delivering a net-centric environment. (*Source:* From DoD Net-Centric Data Strategy, 2003, p. 1.)

applications when and where they need it. In this environment, users and applications search for and pull data as needed. Alternatively, users receive alerts when data to which they have subscribed is updated or changed (i.e., publish/subscribe). Authorized users and applications have immediate access to data posted to the network without processing, exploitation, and dissemination delays. Users and applications "tag" data assets with metadata, or data about data, to enable discovery of data. Users and applications post all data assets to "shared" space for use by the Enterprise. Tagging, posting, and sharing of data are encouraged through the use of incentives and metrics (p. 3).

Three key elements of the data vision are:

1. *Communities of Interest.* Address organization and maintenance of data.
2. *Metadata.* Provides a way to describe data assets and the use of registries, catalogs, and shared spaces, which are mechanisms to store data and information about data.
3. *GIG Enterprise Services (GES).* Enable data tagging, sharing, searching, and retrieving.

Communities of Interest

The Communities of Interest (COIs) are a cornerstone of the net-centric approach. Each community is a collaborative group of users who must exchange information to obtain their shared goals, interests, missions, or business processes. The COI will provide an organizational framework for data so that data goals can be realized. The objective is to move the responsibility for managing data elements from many individual levels to a shared, coordinated community level.

Communities will form in a variety of ways and can be composed of members from one or more functions and organizations as needed to develop a shared mission vocabulary. The COI will support users across the enterprise by promoting data posting, establishing shared space, and creating metadata catalogs. Data within a COI can be exposed within the COI or across the enterprise by having users and applications "advertise" their data assets by cataloging the associated metadata. These catalogs, which describe the data assets that are available, are made visible and accessible for users and applications to search and pull data as needed (DoD Net Centric Data Strategy).

Metadata

Another important concept is metadata. Metadata can be employed in a variety of ways to enhance the value and usability of data assets. The traditional DoD data administration approach used metadata to define data structures and relationships (e.g., data models) to support the development of databases and software applications. This "structural" metadata defines how data assets are physically composed and can include information that describes the relationship between specific parts of the data asset and what elements, or fields, are used in its definition.

There are many other types of metadata, including vocabularies, taxonomic structures used for organizing data assets, interface specifications, and mapping tables. GIG Enterprise Services (GES) capabilities use metadata, in its various forms, to support data asset discovery and interoperability and to provide a richer semantic understanding of all data and metadata.

Various mechanisms are used to store and process the different types of metadata and data. Three mechanisms are used to store data and information about data to enable discovery, support interoperability, and enhance data asset understanding:

1. *Metadata registries.* Contain information describing the structure, format, and definitions of data.
2. *Metadata catalogs.* Contain the instances of metadata associated with individual data assets.
3. *Shared spaces.* Provide storage of and access to data for users within a bounded network space.

GIG Enterprise Services (GES)

GES enables the data goals by providing basic computing capabilities to the enterprise. For example, GES must provide reliable identification and authorization services to ensure the security of the data. In addition, users and applications will need easy-to-use search tools and software agents to allow them to search metadata catalogs and pull data from across the various communities and the enterprise.

These three elements, establishing communities of interest, using metadata to share information across the enterprise, and basic computing capabilities managed and supported at an enterprise level, when combined with bandwidth enhancements and fusion capabilities are critical to realizing a net-centric environment.

Net-Centric Data Strategy

The strategy lays the foundation for realizing the benefits of net-centricity by identifying data goals and approaches for achieving those goals. To realize the vision for net-centric data, two primary objectives must be emphasized: increasing the data that is available to communities or the enterprise; and, ensuring that data is usable by both anticipated and unanticipated users and applications. Table 12.1 describes the data goals in the context of these two objectives. These goals pertain to all DoD legacy and new data assets.

Two additional data properties are frequently considered: data quality and data accuracy. The net-centric strategy views data quality and accuracy as integrated within the other goals. Quality and accuracy do not need to be separate items as each will improve as a result of achieving the identified data goals. For example, if data is made more visible and usable across the enterprise, it will create an incentive to produce quality and accurate data.

The next section provides an overview of how DoD policies are issued.

Overview of DoD Policies

The top of the DoD chain of command is the National Command Authority, which is the term used to collectively describe the President of the United States (Commander-in-Chief and ultimate authority) and the Secretary of Defense. The Office of the Secretary of Defense (OSD) carries out the Secretary of Defense policies by tasking the:

- Military departments (trains and equips the forces)
- Chairman of Joint Chiefs of Staffs (plans and coordinates deployments and operations)
- Unified commands (conducts operations)

The Secretary has four key Undersecretaries who help in the critical areas of Policy, Finance, Force Readiness, and Purchasing. This chapter focuses on the Undersecretary for Policy, who is responsible for (1) formulating national security and defense policy, (2) integrating and overseeing DoD policy, and (3) making and integrating plans to achieve national security objectives.

The Assistant Secretary of Defense Networks and Information Integration (ASD NII) is the principal OSD staff assistant responsible for the development, oversight, and integration of DoD policies and programs relating to the strategy of managing information for the DoD. ASD NII functions include information policy and information management, command and control, communications, counterintelligence, security, information assurance, information operations, space systems and space policy, intelligence, surveillance and reconnaissance, and intelligence-related activities conducted by the Department. In addition, the ASD NII serves as the CIO of the DoD.

Table 12.1   Net-Centric Data Strategy Goals

Goal	Description
Goals to Increase Enterprise and Community Data over Private User and System Data	
Visible	Users and applications can discover the existence of data assets through catalogs, registries, and other search services. All data assets (intelligence, non-intelligence, raw, and processed) are advertised or "made-visible" by providing metadata, which describes the assets.
Accessible	Users and applications post data to a "shared space." Posting data implies that (1) descriptive information about the asset (metadata) has been provided to a catalog that is visible to the Enterprise and (2) the data is stored such that users and applications in the Enterprise can access it. Data assets are made available to any user or application except when limited by policy, regulation, or security.
Institutionalize	Data approaches are incorporated into Department processes and practices. The benefits of Enterprise and community data are recognized throughout the Department.
Goals to Increase Use of Enterprise and Community Data	
Understandable	Users and applications can comprehend the data, both structurally and semantically, and readily determine how the data may be used for their specific needs.
Trusted	Users and applications can determine and assess the authority of the source because the pedigree, security level, and access control level of each data asset is known and available.
Interoperable	Many-to-many exchanges of data occur between systems, through interfaces that are sometimes predefined or sometimes unanticipated. Metadata is available to allow mediation or translation of data between interfaces, as needed.
Responsive to user needs	Perspectives of users, whether data consumers or data producers, are incorporated into data approaches via continual feedback to ensure satisfaction.

Source: From DoD Net Centric Data Strategy, 2003, p. 10.

The ASD NII releases IA issuances in several different forms, such as directives, instructions, and memoranda. These are defined as (modified from http://www.dtic.mil/whs/directives/general.html):

- *DoD Directives (DoDDs)*. Broad policy documents containing what is required by legislation, the President, or the Secretary of Defense to initiate, govern, or regulate actions or conduct by the DoD Components within their specific areas of responsibilities. DoD Directives establish or describe policy, programs, and organizations; define missions; provide authority; and assign responsibilities. One-time tasking and assignments are not appropriate in DoD Directives.
- *DoD Directive-Type Memoranda*. Memoranda issued by the Secretary of Defense, Deputy Secretary of Defense, or Office of the Secretary of Defense (OSD) Principal Staff Assistants (PSAs) that, because of time constraints, cannot be published in the DoD Directives System. Directive-type memoranda signed by PSAs are procedural in nature. They implement policy documents, such as DoD Directives, Federal laws, and Executive Orders. Directive-type memoranda signed by the Secretary or Deputy Secretary of Defense are policy-making documents. A directive-type memorandum shall be converted into a DoD Directive or DoD Instruction within 180 days, unless the subject is classified with limited distribution or is material of limited or temporary relevance. A copy of the signed memorandum shall be forwarded to the Director, Executive Services and Communications Directorate, Washington Headquarters Services (WHS).
- *DoD Instructions (DoDIs)*. DoD issuances that implement the policy, or prescribe the manner or a specific plan or action for carrying out the policy, operating a program or activity, and assigning responsibilities.
- *DoD Administrative Instruction (DoD AI)*. An instrument that supplements DoD Directives and DoD Instructions that apply to the OSD/WHS Components and the DoD Field Activities. They also disseminate policy, procedures, and continuing informational guidance to the DoD Components in the National Capital Region serviced by Washington Headquarters Services.
- *DoD Publication (DoDP)*. A DoD issuance that implements or supplements a DoD Directive or a DoD Instruction by providing uniform procedures for management or operational systems and disseminating administrative information. DoD Publications include Catalogs, Directories, Guides, Handbooks, Indexes, Inventories, Lists, Manuals, Modules, Pamphlets, Plans, Regulations, and Standards.

DoD Information Assurance (IA) Organizations and Departments

There are several organizations that are important to the DoD's IA mission. The list that follows does not include all; instead, it contains entities that provide direct support to meeting the IA goals.

Note to (ISC)² ISSEP candidates: many of these are not included on the exam requirements; but if you are performing IA work for DoD, they are important to know.

Defensewide Information Assurance Program (DIAP)

The DIAP was established in January 1998 and formalized in 1999 under the National Defense Authorization Act for Fiscal Year (FY) 2000 (codified at 10 USC 2224). Section 2224 states that the Secretary of Defense shall carry out a program, to be known as the "Defense Information Assurance Program (DIAP)," to protect and defend DoD information, information systems, and information networks that are critical to the Department and the armed forces during day-to-day operations and operations in times of crisis.

Therefore, the DIAP is the Office of the Secretary of Defense (OSD) mechanism to plan, monitor, coordinate, and integrate IA activities. The DIAP Web site defines DIAP's role as acting as a facilitator for program execution by the combatant commanders, Military Services, and Defense Agencies. The DIAP staff combines functional and programmatic skills for a comprehensive Defensewide approach to IA. The staff's continuous development and analysis of IA programs and functions will provide an overall picture of the DoD's IA posture that identifies redundancies, incompatibilities, and general shortfalls in IA investments, and deficiencies in resources, functional and operational capabilities.

The DIAP defines its mission as ensuring that the DoD's vital information resources are secured and protected by unifying/integrating IA activities to achieve secure net-centric GIG operations enablement and information superiority by applying a Defense-in-Depth methodology that integrates the capabilities of people, operations, and technology to establish a multi-layer, multidimension protection.

More information on the DIAP is available at http://www.defenselink.mil/nii/org/sio/ia/diap/.

Defense Information Systems Agency (DISA)

The Defense Information Systems Agency (DISA) is a DoD agency that is responsible for planning, engineering, acquiring, fielding, and supporting global net-centric solutions and operating the GIG to serve the needs of the President, Vice President, the Secretary of Defense, the Joint Chiefs of Staff, the Combatant Commanders, and other DoD components under all conditions of peace and war (www.disa.mil).

DISA also provides the following services:

- Information Assurance Support Environment (IASE): a Web-based clearinghouse for DoD IA.
- IASE Info Desk: info place in support of DoD organizations for IA-related questions.
- Global Directory Service (GDS) provides an enterprisewide service for identification and other pertinent information about people, objects and resources, and makes it accessible from any place at any time. The GDS can replicate data from multiple data sources and make it available to DoD users through a central site. It is only available through PKI-enabled DoD users.
- DISA provides management and oversight of DoD long-haul telecommunications circuit and infrastructure for both Secret IP Routing Network (SIPRNET) and the Non-classified IP Routing Network (NIPRNET). DISA established the DoD Security Accreditation Working Group (DSAWG) to manage the certification and accreditation of both the SIPRNET and NIPRNET.

More information on DISA is available at http://www.disa.mil/.

Defense Technical Information Center (DTIC®)

According to the DTIC Web site, the Defense Technical Information Center (DTIC®) is "the central facility for the collection and dissemination of scientific and technical information for the Department of Defense (DoD). The DTIC mission is to serve as a vital link in the transfer of information among DoD personnel, DoD contractors, and potential contractors and other U.S. Government agency personnel and their contractors" (www.dtic.mil). DTIC reports to the Director, Defense, Research & Engineering (DDR&E).

The DTIC has 11 Information Analysis Centers (IACs) that assist in locating, analyzing, and using scientific and technical information. In addition, they collect, maintain, and develop analytical tools and techniques, including databases, models, and simulations. One of the IACs focuses on IA — the Information Assurance Technology Analysis Center (IATAC). The IATAC Web site states its mission as "serving as a central authoritative source for IA vulnerability data, information, methodologies, models, and analyses of emerging technologies relating to the survivability, authenticity, and continuity of operation of information systems critical to the nation's defense in support of the agencies' front line missions" (http://iac.dtic.mil/iatac/). The IATAC publishes a semi-weekly news summary for IA professionals. The *IA Digest* is transmitted in an HTML formatted e-mail and provides hot links to articles and news summaries across a spectrum of IA topics.

The DTIC, under the Washington Headquarters Services, Directives and Records Division, Directives Section, administers and operates the *DoD Directives System*. The DoD Directives System provides a single, uniform system of DoD issuances and directive-type memoranda used to convey DoD policies, responsibilities, and procedures. This includes the orderly processing, approval, publication, distribution, internal review, and records management of DoD Directives, DoD Instructions, and DoD Publications. To find DoD issuances, refer to Web site at http://www.dtic.mil/whs/directives/index.html.

National Security Agency (NSA) Information Assurance Directorate (IAD)

According to its Web site, the mission of the NSA IAD involves detecting, reporting, and responding to cyber-threats, making encryption codes to securely pass information between systems, and embedding IA measures directly into the emerging GIG. It includes building secure audio and video communications equipment, making tamper protection products, and providing trusted microelectronics solutions. It entails testing the security of customers' systems, providing Operational Security (OPSEC) assistance, and evaluating commercial software and hardware against nationally set standards. To better meet our nation's IA needs, IAD teams span government, industry, and academia. More information on the NSA IAD is available at http://www.nsa.gov/ia.

Networks and Information Integration (NII)

According to the NII Web site, the Assistant Secretary of Defense for Networks and Information Integration (ASD NII)) is the principal OSD staff assistant for the development, oversight, and integration of DoD policies and programs relating to the strategy of information superiority for the DoD. The mission of ASD NII is to provide capabilities that enable the military forces of the United States to generate, use, and share the information necessary to survive and succeed on every mission. More information on NII is available at http://www.dod.mil/nii/.

Information Assurance Support Environment (IASE)

The IASE Web site serves as an IA portal or clearinghouse for IA professionals within the government and the commercial world. It houses current DoD policies and processes used for IA purposes.

According to the DoD IA Portal, the mission of the *DoD IA Portal* is to be "a customized, personalized, ever-changing mix of news, resources and tools/applications that will be the desktop destination for everyone in the DoD IA Community — and the primary vehicle by which people do their work. It will provide a trusted, "one-stop" source for the latest IA information" (http://iase.disa.mil/iaportal.html).

One of the IASE subject matter areas is the DoD Computer Network Defense (CND). According to the CND Web site, the mission of CND is to:

> [D]escribes the actions taken, within the Department of Defense (DoD), to protect, monitor, analyze, detect, and respond to unauthorized activity within DoD information systems and computer networks. CND protection activity employs information assurance principals and includes deliberate actions taken to modify an assurance configuration or condition in response to a CND alert or threat information. http://iase.disa.mil/cnd

Information on IASE and the various subject matter areas is available at the IA portal Web site: http://iase.disa.mil/. Some of the information on the IA portal is restricted to hosts in the .mil and .gov domains.

Defense Advanced Research Projects Agency (DARPA)

According to the DARPA Web site, it is the "central research and development organization for the Department of Defense. It manages and directs selected basic and applied research and development projects for DoD. Its other responsibility is to pursue research and technology with high risk and where success may dramatically advance traditional military roles and missions" (http://darpa.mil).

A relevant IA DARPA research program is the Organically Assured and Survivable Information Systems (OASIS). The OASIS goal is to "to provide defense capabilities against sophisticated adversaries to allow sustained operation of mission critical functions in the face of known and future cyber attacks against information systems" (http://www.darpa.mil/ipto/ Programs/oasis/index.htm.). The technical goals for the OASIS program are listed on the DARPA OASIS Web site and provide insight into how SE methodologies will be used to develop the next generation of information systems. Of specific importance is the statement that the OASIS program "follows a systems requirements-driven research and development approach" — the cornerstone of the IATF Information Systems Security Engineering (ISSE) model.

Information on DARPA and its programs is available at Web site: http://www.darpa.mil/.

The next section provides an overview of several DoD issuances.

DoD Issuances

There are many DoD issuances related to computer security, information security, network security, and IA. For a full listing of DoD IA policies, refer to http://iase.disa.mil/policy.html.

Keep in mind that an *information system security policy* is the set of security objectives that guide how a designated mission's sensitive or critical assets (including information) are managed, protected, and distributed. The DoD 8500 policy series (shown in Table 12.2) represent the Department's information assurance strategy. The primary purpose of the DoD 8500 series is to establish baseline controls so users can keep requirements in mind as they design networks, acquire products, and implement life-cycle decisions. It outlines five broad goals:

1. Protecting information
2. Defending systems
3. Providing command and control and situational awareness
4. Making sure information assurance is integrated into processes
5. Increasing security awareness throughout the DoD's workforce

Table 12.2   DoD Emerging Policy Series

DoD Policy Series	Policy Subject Area
8500	General
8510	IA Certification and Accreditation
8520	Security Management
8530	Computer Network Defense
8540	Interconnectivity
8550	Network and Web
8560	IA Monitoring
8570	IA Education, Training, and Awareness
8580	Other (Integration)

Table 12.3 Superseded DoD Policies and Replacement

New Policies	Superseded Policies	Date Superseded
DoD 8500.1 Information Assurance (IA)	DoD 5200.28	Oct. 2002
	DoD 5200. 28 –M	Feb. 2003
DoD 8500.2 IA Implementation	DoD 5200.28 -STD	
DoD 8510.1 (8510.1b currently in draft) (DITSCAP update)	DoD 5200.40	Pending
DoDI 8510.1-M	DoDI 5200.40-M	July 2000

This chapter only highlights the few DoD documents that have been listed in the (ISC)² ISSEP study guide. As with all policies, one of the challenges is to keep track of what is current; what has been superseded; and if it has been superseded; and, which sections are still relevant. Table 12.3 lists the DoD policies, instructions, and directives that have been superseded. It includes the replacement policies and the date the policies were no longer in effect.

DoD 8500.1 Information Assurance (IA) (October 2002/November 2003)

DoD 8500.1, Information Assurance (October 24, 2002; Certified Current as of November 21, 2003), establishes policy and assigns responsibilities to achieve DoD IA through a defense-in-depth approach that integrates the capabilities of personnel, operations, and technology, and supports the evolution to network-centric warfare. It supersedes DoD Directive 5200.28, DoD 5200.28-M, DoD 5200.28-STD, and DoD Chief Information Officer (CIO) Memorandum 6-8510.

The Directive applies to all DoD-owned or -controlled information systems that receive, process, store, display, or transmit DoD information, regardless of mission assurance category, classification or sensitivity, including but not limited to:

- DoD information systems that support special environments (e.g., Special Access Programs [SAP] and Special Access Requirements [SAR]), as supplemented by the special needs of the program
- Platform IT interconnections (e.g., weapons systems, sensors, medical technologies, or utility distribution systems) to external networks
- Information systems under contract to the Department of Defense
- Outsourced information-based processes such as those supporting E-business or E-commerce processes
- Information systems of Non-appropriated Fund Instrumentalities

- Stand-alone information systems
- Mobile computing devices such as laptops, hand-held devices, and personal digital assistants operating in either wired or wireless mode, or other information technologies as may be developed

Note to the ISSEP candidate: The (ISC)² ISSEP candidate does not need to know all the specific requirements set forth in DoD 8500.1. However it is the foundation for all DoD IA policies, procedures, guidelines, thus it is beneficial to have some knowledge and understanding. DoD 8500.1 is listed here in abbreviated form. Refer to pages 3 through 8 in DoD 8500 for more information.

4.1 Information assurance requirements shall be identified and included in the design, acquisition, installation, operation, upgrade, or replacement of all DoD information systems.

4.2 All DoD information systems shall maintain an appropriate level of confidentiality, integrity, authentication, non-repudiation, and availability that reflect a balance among the importance and sensitivity of the information and information assets; documented threats and vulnerabilities; the trustworthiness of users and interconnecting systems; the impact of impairment or destruction to the DoD information system; and, cost effectiveness. For IA purposes all DoD information systems shall be organized and managed in the four categories: Automated Information System (AIS) applications, enclaves (which include networks), outsourced IT-based processes, and platform IT interconnections.

4.3 IA shall be a visible element of all investment portfolios incorporating DoD-owned or controlled information systems, to include outsourced business processes supported by private sector information systems and outsourced information technologies; and, shall be reviewed and managed relative to contributions to mission outcomes and strategic goals and objectives.

4.4 Interoperability and integration of IA solutions within or supporting the DoD shall be achieved through adherence to an architecture that will enable the evolution to network-centric warfare by remaining consistent with the command, control, communications, computers, intelligence, surveillance, reconnaissance architecture framework, and a defense-in-depth approach.

4.5 The DoD shall organize, plan, assess, train for, and conduct the defense of DoD computer networks as integrated Computer Network Defense (CND) operations that are coordinated across multiple disciplines.

<u>4.6</u>   IA readiness shall be monitored, reported, and evaluated as a distinguishable element of mission readiness throughout all the DoD Components and validated by the DoD CIO.

<u>4.7</u>   All DoD information systems shall be assigned a mission assurance category that is directly associated with the importance of the information they contain relative to the achievement of DoD goals and objectives, particularly the warfighters' combat mission.

<u>4.8</u>   Access to all DoD information systems shall be based on a demonstrated need-to-know and granted in accordance with applicable laws and DoD 5200.2-R for background investigations, special access, and IT position designations and requirements.

<u>4.9</u>   Foreign exchange personnel and representatives of foreign nations, coalitions or international organizations may be authorized access to DoD information systems containing classified or sensitive information only if all of the following conditions are met:
  – Access is authorized only by the DoD Component Head.
  – Mechanisms are in place to strictly limit access to information that has been cleared for release to the represented foreign nation, coalition or international organization, for classified information, and other policy guidance for unclassified information.

<u>4.10</u> Authorized users who are contractors, DoD direct or indirect hire foreign national employees, or foreign representatives as described in paragraph 4.9, shall always have their affiliation displayed as part of their e-mail addresses.

<u>4.11</u> Access to DoD-owned, -operated, or -outsourced Web sites shall be strictly controlled by the Web site owner using technical, operational, and procedural measures appropriate to the Web site audience and information classification or sensitivity.

<u>4.12</u> DoD information systems shall regulate remote access and access to the Internet by employing positive technical controls such as proxy services and screened subnets, also called Demilitarized Zones (DMZs), or through systems that are isolated from all other DoD information systems through physical means.

<u>4.13</u> All DoD information systems shall be certified and accredited in accordance with DoD Instructions.

<u>4.14</u> All interconnections of DoD information systems shall be managed to continuously minimize community risk by ensuring that the assurance of one system is not undermined by vulnerabilities of interconnected systems.

<u>4.15</u> All DoD information systems shall comply with DoD ports and protocols guidance and management processes, as established.

4.16 The conduct of all DoD communications security activities, including the acquisition of COMSEC products, shall be in accordance with DoD Directives.

4.17 All IA or IA-enabled IT hardware, firmware, and software components or products incorporated into DoD information systems must comply with the evaluation and validation requirements of National Security Telecommunications and Information Systems Security Policy Number 11.

4.18 All IA and IA-enabled IT products incorporated into DoD information systems shall be configured in accordance with DoD-approved security configuration guidelines.

4.19 Public domain software products, and other software products with limited or no warranty, such as those commonly known as freeware or shareware, shall only be used in DoD information systems to meet compelling operational requirements. Such products shall be thoroughly assessed for risk and accepted for use by the responsible Designated Approving Authority (DAA).

4.20 DoD information systems shall be monitored based on the assigned mission assurance category and assessed risk in order to detect, isolate, and react to intrusions, disruption of services, or other incidents that threaten the IA of DoD operations or IT resources, including internal misuse.

4.21 Identified DoD information system vulnerabilities shall be evaluated for DoD impact, and tracked and mitigated in accordance with DoD-directed solutions, e.g., Information Assurance Vulnerability Alerts (IAVAs).

4.22 All personnel authorized access to DoD information systems shall be adequately trained in accordance with DoD and Component policies and requirements and certified as required in order to perform the tasks associated with their IA responsibilities.

4.23 Individuals shall be notified of their privacy rights and security responsibilities in accordance with DoD Component General Counsel-approved processes when attempting access to DoD information systems.

4.24 Mobile code technologies shall be categorized and controlled to reduce their threat to DoD information systems in accordance with DoD and Component policy and guidance.

4.25 A DAA shall be appointed for each DoD information system operating within or on behalf of the Department of Defense, to include outsourced business processes supported by private sector information systems and outsourced information technologies. The DAA shall be a U.S. citizen, a DoD employee, and have a level of authority commensurate with accepting, in writing, the risk of operating DoD information systems under his or her purview.

4.26 All military voice radio systems, to include cellular and commercial services, shall be protected consistent with the classification or sensitivity of the information transmitted on the system.

DoD 8500.1 also outlines the roles and responsibilities for those individuals responsible for carrying out the IA policies.

DoD 8500.2 Information Assurance Implementation (February 2003)

DoD 8500.2 follows 8500.1 and provides guidance on how to implement policy, assign responsibilities, and prescribe procedures for applying integrated, layered protection of the DoD information systems and networks. It begins with a definition of why an IA program is critical to the DoD: "The Department of Defense has a crucial responsibility to protect and defend its information and supporting information technology. DoD information is shared across a Global Information Grid that is inherently vulnerable to exploitation and denial of service. Factors that contribute to its vulnerability include: increased reliance on commercial information technology and services; increased complexity and risk propagation through interconnection; the extremely rapid pace of technological change; a distributed and non-standard management structure; and the relatively low cost of entry for adversaries" (DoD 8500.2, Section E3.1-1).

DoD Instruction 8500.2 assigns responsibilities and prescribes procedures for applying integrated layered protection of the DOD information systems and networks in accordance with the DoD 8500.1 policy. It provides specific guidelines on how to implement an IA program.

The DoD IA program is predicated upon five essential competencies that are the hallmark of any successful risk management program. They include:

1. The ability to assess security needs and capabilities
2. The ability to develop a purposeful security design or configuration that adheres to a common architecture and maximizes the use of common services
3. The ability to implement required controls or safeguards
4. The ability to test and verify
5. The ability to manage changes to an established baseline in a secure manner

It establishes IA controls for information systems according to the Mission Assurance Categories (MAC) and confidentiality levels. There are three MAC levels:

■ MAC I: systems are high availability and high integrity
■ MAC II: high integrity and medium availability
■ MAC III: basic integrity and availability

Robustness Levels

An important concept in defining IA controls is the robustness level of the controls. Robustness is defined as the strength and level of confidence required of each IA solution. It is a function of the value of what is being protected (e.g., the mission assurance category or confidentiality level of the information being supported by the DoD information system) and the threat. To ensure that each component of an IA solution is correctly implementing its intended security services and is protecting its information from the identified threat, each component within the network system needs to provide an appropriate level of robustness.

The more robust a particular component, the greater the level of confidence in the protection provided to the security services it supports. The three levels of robustness are (DoD 8500.2, Section E2.1.47.1-3):

1. *Basic.* Security services and mechanism that equate to best commercial practices
2. *Medium.* Security services and mechanisms that provide for layering of additional safeguards above good commercial practices
3. *High.* Security services and mechanisms that provide the most stringent protection and rigorous security countermeasures

Although robustness is an abstract concept and can therefore be difficult to describe, there are two distinguishing characteristics that determine the robustness for a product. The first is the value of the resources, and the second is the authorization of entities with means to access the resources. Thus, the level of robustness needed is determined by first knowing the value of the resource and then determining who needs access and what level of authorization they need, such as security clearance or the ability to read/write/make changes to the resource. The robustness can be applied to the data itself, the product that protects the data (e.g., firewall), or the product itself (e.g., Web server).

Basic robustness security services and mechanisms are usually represented by good commercial practice. Basic robustness technical solutions require, at a minimum, authenticated access control, NIST-approved key management algorithms, NIST FIPS validated cryptography, and the assurance properties specified in NSA-endorsed basic robustness protection profiles or the Protection Profile Consistency Guidance for Basic Robustness (DoD 8500.2, Section E3.2.4.3.4).

Note to ISSEP candidates: (ISC)² ISSEP candidates should note that this level of detail is not covered in the exam requirements, but it does help to explain the concept of robustness.

Ken Elliott, of The Aerospace Corporation, in his "Robustness in DoD Protection Profiles" presentation to the IATF, compared robustness levels to the Common Criteria (CC) Evaluation Levels (EALs) (Elliott, 2004).

Elliott's comments were that *basic robustness* provides assurance by an analysis of the Target of Evaluation (TOE) security functions using guidance documentation, functional specification, high-level design, and interface specification. For a CC EAL 2, the augmented portions would require:

- Accuracy of system documentation
- Tracking of correction of system flaws
- Flaw reporting procedures
- Examination of guidance

Medium robustness security services and mechanisms provide for additional safeguards above *Basic*. *Medium* robustness technical solutions require, at a minimum, strong (e.g., crypto-based) authenticated access control, NSA-approved key management, NIST FIPS-validated cryptography, and the assurance properties as specified in NSA-endorsed Medium Robustness Protection Profiles or the Protection Profile Consistency Guidance for Medium Robustness (DoD 8500.2, Section E3.2.4.3.3).

Elliott defines *medium robustness* as providing assurance by an analysis of the TOE security functions using:

- Architectural design documents
- Low-level design of the TOE
- Implementation representation of the entire TSF. Simply stated, that TSF is the hardware, software, and firmware only, while the TOE, includes guidance documentation.
- Complete interface specifications
- Systematic cryptographic module covert channel
- Informal TOE security policy model
- Modular TOE design

Under the Medium robustness level, only complete TOEs (i.e., hardware, operating system and application software) are required. It requires the use of remote administration, separate roles, and the use of encryption. Medium robustness includes components that are equivalent to an EAL 4 that is augmented with:

- Implementation of the TSF
- Testing — low-level design
- Flaw reporting procedures
- Moderately resistant
- Functional specification
- Security enforcing high-level design
- Security enforcing low-level design
- Architectural design with justification
- Modular decomposition
- Systematic cryptographic module covert channel analysis

High robustness security services and mechanisms provide, through rigorous analysis, the most confidence in those security mechanisms. Generally, High robustness technical solutions require NSA-certified high robustness solutions for cryptography, access control and key management, and high assurance security design as specified in NSA-endorsed high robustness protection profiles, where available (DoD 8500.2, Section E3.2.4.3.2).

Elliott added that the High robustness level builds upon the Medium robustness requirements and is currently being targeted at an EAL 6 level. The exact assurance requirements are still being developed. More information on CC and EAL is provided in Domain 4, Chapter 15, "IA Regulations and Common Criteria."

One of the problems with defining robustness and the CC level occurs when the product or component is evaluated at a specific level but will be implemented with other components having a different CC EAL. This is sometimes referred to as the *composition problem* — that is, how to combine various products into a system that meets a required level of assurance and security features and functions.

DoD IA Policies and DITSCAP

The new paradigm in IA policies, procedures, and standards is fundamental to the DoD 8500 policy series. DoD Directive 8500.1 and DoD Instruction 8500.2 are the "capstone" policy documents that lay the foundation for the framework. The change in policies will transition away from the traditional IA and C&A models that were system centric, to one that is network-centric. It will also transition from the current DITSCAP to DoD Information Assurance Certification and Accreditation Process (DIACAP).

DoDI 5200.40 DITSCAP (December 1997) is still in effect, pending approval of DoDI 8510.1. DoDI 8510.1-M (discussed earlier in Domain 3, DITSCAP) has already replaced the DITSCAP Manual but not the DITSCAP policy.

DoDI 5200.40 implements policy, assigns responsibilities, and prescribes procedures under reference for Certification and Accreditation (C&A) of information technology (IT). The DoD 5200.40 Policy does the following:

- Implements policy, assigns responsibilities, and prescribes procedures for C&A of IT, including automated information systems, networks, and sites in the Department of Defense
- Creates DITSCAP for security C&A of unclassified and classified IT systems
- Stresses the importance of a life-cycle management approach to the C&A and reaccreditation of DoD IT

The C&A policy applies to any DoD system that collects, stores, transmits, or processes unclassified or classified information. It applies to any IT or information system life cycle, including the development of new IT systems, the incorporation of IT systems into an infrastructure, the incorporation of IT systems outside the infrastructure, the development of prototype IT systems, the reconfiguration or upgrade of existing systems, and legacy systems.

DoDI 5200.40 defines the activities leading to security C&A. These activities are grouped together in a logical sequence and present the objectives, activities, and management of the DITSCAP process.

The objective of DITSCAP is to establish a DoD standard infrastructure-centric approach that protects and secures the entities comprising the Defense Information Infrastructure (DII). The set of activities presented in the DITSCAP standardize the C&A process for single IT entities leading to more secure system operations and a more secure DII. The process considers the system mission, environment, and architecture while assessing the impact of the operation of that system on the DII.

The DITSCAP manual defines a process that standardizes all activities leading to a successful accreditation. The principal purpose of that process is to protect and secure the entities comprising the DII. Standardizing the process will minimize risks associated with nonstandard security implementations across shared infrastructure and end systems. The DoD Information Assurance Support Environment (IASE) has been developed as the mechanism to support the implementation of DITSCAP activities. It also establishes a requirement for a Requirements Traceability Matrix (RTM).

The DITSCAP process consists of four phases, which were discussed in detail in Chapter 8 and are briefly listed here.

DITSCAP Phases

Phase 1: Definition

The Definition phase shall include activities to document the system mission, environment, and architecture; identify the threat; define the levels of effort; identify the Certification Authority (CA) and the DAA; and document the necessary security requirements for C&A. Phase 1 shall culminate with a documented agreement, between the program manager, the DAA, the CA, and the user representative of the approach and the results of the Phase 1 activities.

Phase 2: Verification

The Verification phase shall include activities to verify compliance of the system with previously agreed security requirements. For each life-cycle development activity there is a corresponding set of security activities that shall verify compliance with the security requirements and evaluate vulnerabilities.

Phase 3: Validation

The Validation phase shall include activities to evaluate the fully integrated system to validate system operation in a specified computing environment with an acceptable level of residual risk. Validation shall culminate in an approval to operate.

Phase 4: Post Accreditation

The Post Accreditation phase includes activities to monitor system management and operation to ensure an acceptable level of residual risk is preserved. Security management, change management, and periodic compliance validation reviews are conducted.

DoDI 5200.40 also provides instructions and directions for completing the Systems Security Authorization Agreement (SSAA) and can be found at http://www.dtic.mil/whs/directives/.

DoD 8510.1-M DITSCAP (July 2000)

This manual supports DITSCAP by presenting a detailed approach to the activities comprising the C&A process. It provides standardized activities leading to accreditation and establishes a process and management baseline. C&A assistance can be obtained from the DoD IASE. The IASE provides both self-help and assisted help in implementing uniform C&A practices and describes in detail how to execute the C&A activities. This manual was discussed in detail in Domain 3.

DoD 8510.xx DIACAP

DoDI 5200.40 may be termed the beginning process of meeting C&A requirements. It served the community well by being the first document to define the C&A process and helped users to make sense of the Federal requirement to accredit systems. However, now that it has been used for a few years, there are several identified weaknesses in the process that should be revised. The next policy, DoD 8510.xx, will define the C&A roles, responsibilities, and processes. It is currently in the approval phase. In the new C&A processes, more attention is given to sustainment of network services.

Important changes between DoD 5200.40 DITSCAP and the newer DoD 8510.xx DIACAP include:

1. Modifying the language and focus from "information technology" (IT) to "information assurance" (IA)
2. Less focus on documentation
3. More attention given to "system definition"
4. Built around a standard set of security controls

Summary

This chapter began with a brief background of the DoD net-centric data strategy and how these goals will allow the DoD to move into the next century of protecting information, defending its systems and networks, integrating and approving the IA processes, and creating an IA-empowered workforce to meet those needs. The GIG transformation is designed so that IA capabilities and services will be expressed in an architectural format. The capabilities of the GIG will be delivered by the enterprise to meet the needs of all communities of users.

The primary topics addressed the organizations responsible for implementing the DoD net-centric strategy and briefly explained two of the documents from the new DoD 8500 policy series. DoDI 8500.1 establishes policy and assigns responsibilities to achieve DoD IA goals through a defense-in-depth approach. The objective of the IA policy is to integrate the capabilities of personnel, operations, and technology to support the evolution to network-centric warfare. DoD 8500.2 follows DoD 8500.1 and provides guidance on how to implement policy, assign responsibilities, and prescribe procedures for applying integrated, layered protection of the DoD information systems and networks.

References

10 USC 2224 (2000). National Defense Authorization Act for FY2000. Available at http://www.defenselink.mil/nii/org/sio/ia/diap/accessible/usc-a.html.

DoD 101: An Introductory Overview of the Department of Defense (2002). Available at http://www.dod.mil/pubs/dod101/.

DoD Chief Information Officer Annual Information Assurance Report Fiscal Year 2000. Available at http://www.defenselink.mil/nii/org/sio/ia/diap/documents/DIAP2000.pdf.

DoD Chief Information Officer Memorandum Regarding the DoD Net-Centric Data Strategy (May 9, 2003). Available at http://www.afei.org/pdf/ncow/DoD_data_strategy.pdf.

DoD Chief Information Officer (2003). Department of Defense Net-Centric Data Strategy. Available at http://www.afei.org/pdf/ncow/DoD_data_strategy.pdf.

DoD Directive No. 8500.1 (October 24, 2002 — Certified Current as of November 21, 2003). Information Assurance (IA). Available at http://www.dtic.mil/whs/directives/index.html.

DoD Instruction 8500.2 (February 2003). Information Assurance (IA) Implementation. Available at http://www.dtic.mil/whs/directives/index.html.

DoD Instruction 5200.40 (December 1997). DoD Information Technology Security Certification and Accreditation Process (DITSCAP). Available at http://www.dtic.mil/whs/directives/index.html.

DoD Instruction 8510.1-M (July 2000). DoD Information Technology Security Certification and Accreditation Process (DITSCAP) — Application Manual. Available at http://www.dtic.mil/whs/directives/index.html.

Elliott, Ken (2004). Robustness in DoD Protection Profiles. Presentation at the IATF Seminar, March 26, 2004. Contact: elliott@aero.org.

Web Sites

DIAP: http://www.defenselink.mil/nii/org/sio/ia/diap/
DISA: http://www.disa.mil/
DTIC: http://www.dtic.mil
NSA: http://www.nsa.gov/
NII: http://www.dod.mil/nii/
IASE: http://iase.disa.mil/
DARPA: http://www.darpa.mil/
http://www.nsa.gov/ia/index.cfm for information on NSA IAD.
http://www.dtic.mil/whs/directives/index.html for DoD issuances.
http://iase.disa.mil/cnd/ for information on CND.

13

Committee on National Security Systems*

Introduction

The National Security Telecommunications and Information Systems Security Committee (NSTISSC) was established in July 1990 by President George H. Bush under National Security Directive 42 (NSD 42), "National Policy for the Security of National Security Telecommunications and Information Systems." NSD 42(a) establishes the NSTISSC to consider technical matters and develop operating policies, procedures, guidelines, instructions, and standards as necessary to implement provisions of NSD 42. Due to a Freedom of Information Act (FOIA) request, a partial version of NSD 42 is available on the Web at http://www.fas.org/irp/offdocs/nsd/nsd_42.htm.

For clarity, NSD 42 provides the following definition for telecommunications and information security: "protection afforded to telecommunications and information systems in order to prevent exploitation through interception, unauthorized electronic access, or related technical intelligence threats, and to ensure authenticity. Such protection results from the application of security measures (including crypto security, transmission security, emission security, and computer security) to systems which generate, store process transfer, or communicate information of use to an

---

* Formerly known as the National Security Telecommunications Information Systems Security Committee

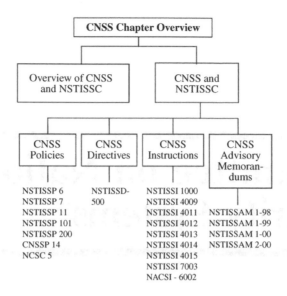

Figure 13.1   CNSS chapter overview.

adversary, and also includes the physical protection of technical security material and technical security information (Section 11C)."

In October 2001, under Executive Order 13231, "Critical Infrastructure Protection in the Information Age," President Bush redesignated the National Security Telecommunications and Information Systems Security Committee (NSTISSC) as the Committee on National Security Systems (CNSS). The Department of Defense continues to chair the committee under the authorities established by NSD 42. As a standing committee of the President's Critical Infrastructure Protection Board, the CNSS reports fully and regularly on its activities to the Board (http://www.ncs.gov/library.html).

This chapter begins by describing the mission and goals of CNSS (and previously NSTISSC). The second section provides a brief introduction to the various CNSS (since 2001) and the previous NSTISSC policies. Figure 13.1 provides an overview of the sections and CNSS issuances shown in this chapter. The CNSS releases four primary types of issuances:

1. *Policies.* Assign responsibilities and establish criteria (National Security Telecommunications and Information Systems Security Policy (NSTISSP) or Committee of National Security Systems Policy (CNSSP).
2. *Directives.* Establish or describe policy, programs, provide authority, or assign responsibilities (National Security Telecommunications and Information Systems Security Directive [NSTISSD]).

3. *Instructions.* Describe how to implement the policy or prescribe the manner of a policy (National Security Telecommunications and Information Systems Security Instruction [NSTISSI]).
4. *Advisory memoranda.* Provide guidance on policy and may direct policy (National Security Telecommunications and Information Systems Security Advisory Memorandum [NSTISSAM]).

Overview of CNSS and NSTISSC

Executive Order 13231 directs the protection of information systems for critical infrastructure, including emergency preparedness communications and the physical assets that support such systems. The Secretary of Defense and the Director of Central Intelligence (DCI) are responsible for developing and overseeing the implementation of governmentwide policies, principles, standards, and guidelines for the security of systems with national security information.

The CNSS (and previously the NSTISSC) provides a forum for the discussion of policy issues, sets national policy, and promulgates direction, operational procedures, and guidance for the security of national security systems through the CNSS Issuance System. As a reference, national security systems are described as containing classified information or involving:

- Intelligence activities
- Cryptographic activities related to national security
- Command and control of military forces
- Equipment that is an integral part of a weapon or weapons system(s)
- Critical military or intelligence missions (not including routine administrative and business applications)

The CNSS accomplishes its tasks through a combination of subcommittees, issue groups, and working groups. The Committee has two Subcommittees: (1) a Subcommittee on Telecommunications Security (STS) and (2) a Subcommittee on Information Systems Security (SISS). The Subcommittees share information and coordinate recommendations concerning implementation of protective measures. The Subcommittees are comprised of representatives from the organizations represented on the Committee.

Matters under the cognizance of the Subcommittees shall include the following (NSTISSD No. 900, April 2000):

- Telecommunication technology
- Secure voice systems
- Secure record and data systems
- Space and satellite telecommunications systems
- Command and control telecommunications systems

- Compromising emanations
- Electronic key management/key management infrastructures
- Operations security (OPSEC) aspects of telecommunications security
- Information systems security and related topics
- Computer security aspects of telecommunications and network security
- Information Assurance (IA)
- Insider threat
- Other related subjects as appropriate

All of these groups, as well as the day-to-day activities of the CNSS, are supported by a Secretariat. The CNSS has voting members who review, approve, and exercise their vote on directions, policies, and instructions involving national security information issues. The CNSS voting members are listed in Table 13.1.

An important responsibility of the CNSS and its subcommittees is ensuring the development of an annual assessment on the status of national security systems. These assessments will contain information on threats and evidence of exploitation of such systems. The reports generated by subcommittees are submitted to the NSTISSC Chair, who subsequently submits them to the National Security Council and the President.

The Web site for CNSS is www.cnss.gov.

Table 13.1   CNSS Voting Members

CNSS Voting Members	
Department of State	Department of Defense
Department of Treasury	U.S. Army
Department of Justice	U.S. Navy
Department of Commerce	U.S. Air Force
Department of Transportation	U.S. Marine Corps
Department of Energy	National Security Agency
Office of Management and Budget	Defense Intelligence Agency
Central Intelligence Agency	Joint Chiefs of Staff
Federal Bureau of Investigation	Assistant to the President for National Security Affairs
Federal Emergency Management Agency	General Services Administration
National Communications System	

National Communication Security Committee (NCSC)

The National Communication Security Committee (NCSC) developed the *Orange Book,* a subset of the *Rainbow Series,* which is a series of information security guidelines and best practices used in the development of secure information system. This series of documents is still needed for reference, but is no longer required. Publications from the NCSC can be found on the CNSS (previously NSTISSC) Web site at www.cnss. gov.

CNSS and NSTISSC Issuances

The CNSS is responsible for the establishment and maintenance of a national system for promulgating operating policies, directives, instructions, and advisory information. CNSS releases an Index of National Security System Issuances that is updated periodically. In the January 2005 release, the CNSS lists the following issuances:

- 15 policies
- 9 directives
- 55 instructions
- 27 advisory memoranda

The 21 issuances highlighted in this chapter are either listed as (ISC)² ISSEP® exam requirements or are specific to Information Systems Security Engineering (ISSE) job functions.

CNSS Policies

The CNSS policies discussed include:

- NSTISSP No. 6, National Policy on Certification and Accreditation of National Security Telecommunications and Information Systems (April 1994)
- NSTISSP No. 7, National Policy on Secure Electronic Messaging Service (February 1995)
- NSTISSP No. 11, National Policy Governing the Acquisition of Information Assurance (IA) and IA-Enabled Information Technology (IT) Products (Revision July 2003)
- NSTISSP No. 101, National Policy on Securing Voice Communications (September 1999)
- NSTISSP No. 200, National Policy on Controlled Access Protection (July 1987)

- CNSSP No. 14, National Policy Governing the Release of Information Assurance Products and Services to Authorized U.S. Persons or Activities that Are Not a Part of the Federal Government Superseded (November 2002)
- NCSC No. 5, National Policy on Use of Cryptomaterial by Activities Operating in High Risk Environments (January 1981)

NSTISSP No. 6, National Policy on Certification and Accreditation of National Security Telecommunications and Information Systems (April 1994)

NSTISSP No. 6 established a mandatory requirement that all Federal agencies operating national security systems must establish and implement Certification and Accreditation (C&A) programs. The purpose of the C&A programs were to ensure that information processed, stored, or transmitted by national security systems is adequately protected with respect to requirements for confidentiality, integrity, and availability.

NSTISSI No. 1000, National Information Assurance Certification and Accreditation Process (NIACAP) (April 2000), provides guidance on how to implement NSTISSP No. 6. NSTISSI No. 1000 is discussed under CNSS Instructions.

NSTISSP No. 7, National Policy on Secure Electronic Messaging Service (February 1995)

Electronic messaging services are those that, in addition to providing interpersonal messaging capability, meet specified functional, management, and technical requirements and, taken together, yield a business-quality electronic mail service suitable for conducting official government business.

The policy states that:

1. Federal government departments and agencies shall establish and implement a program for secure government-wide interoperable electronic messaging services for the protection of information contained on national security systems.
2. This policy is implemented to assure rapid progress in achieving this goal. Specifically, that plans and programs are designed to achieve substantial implementation by the year 2000.
3. The policy shall be implemented by appropriate NSTISSC issuances that establish common standards and procedures necessary to achieve these goals

NSTISSP No. 11, National Policy Governing the Acquisition of Information Assurance (IA) and IA-Enabled Information Technology (IT) Products (Revision July 2003)

NSTISSP No. 11 establishes the policy that IA shall be achieved through the acquisition and appropriate implementation of evaluated or validated Government-Off-The-Shelf (GOTS) or Commercial-Off-The-Shelf (COTS) IA and IA-enabled IT products. Thus, to meet the IA requirements for national security systems, all products must be evaluated according to the guidelines set forth by the Common Criteria Evaluation Levels.

For assurance purposes, it is important that COTS products acquired by U.S. government (USG) departments and agencies be subject to a standardized evaluation process that will provide some assurances that these products perform as advertised. Accordingly, NSTISSP No. 11 was developed as a means of addressing this problem for those products acquired for national security applications. NSTISSP No. 11 also rightfully points out that the protection of systems encompasses more than just acquiring the right product. Once acquired, these products must be integrated properly and subject to an accreditation process, which will ensure total integrity of the information and systems to be protected.

The document begins by explaining the need for the policy: "The technological advances and threats of the past decade have drastically changed the ways we think about protecting our communications and communications systems" (NSTISSP No. 11, Revision 2003, p. 1). Three factors in NSTISSP No. 11 are of particular significance:

- The need for protection encompasses more than just confidentiality
- COTS security and security-enabled IA products are readily available as alternatives to traditional NSA-developed and produced communications security equipment (i.e., GOTS products).
- An increased and continuing recognition that the need for IA transcends more than just the traditional national security applications of the past (p. 1).

The policy states that IA shall be considered a requirement for all systems used to enter, process, store, display, or transmit national security information. IA shall be achieved through the acquisition and appropriate implementation of evaluated or validated GOTS or COTS IA and IA-enabled IT products. These products should ensure the confidentiality and integrity of information, provide for the availability of the systems, and ensure the authentication and non-repudiation of parties in electronic transactions.

Further, NSTISSP No 11 states that, effective January 2001, preference shall be given to the acquisition of COTS IA and IA-enabled IT products (to be used on systems entering, processing, storing, displaying, or transmitting national security information) evaluated and validated, as appropriate, in accordance with:

■ The International Common Criteria for Information Security Technology Evaluation Mutual Recognition Arrangement
■ The National Security Agency (NSA)/National Institute of Standards and Technology (NIST) National Information Assurance Partnership (NIAP) Evaluation and Validation Program
■ NIST Federal Information Processing Standard (FIPS) validation program.

The evaluation and/or validation of COTS IA and IA-enabled IT products will be conducted by accredited commercial laboratories or NIST. Since July 2002, DoD IT acquisitions (if following the guidelines) are limited to products that have been evaluated.

The International Common Criteria is for COTS IA and IA enabling products that will be evaluated for Evaluation Assurance Levels (EAL) 1-4. That is, if the USG wanted to use a product that was evaluated in a British laboratory (or other CC Partners) and received an EAL 4 rating, the product would be acceptable to use in a USG system requiring an EAL 4. However, if a USG organization would like an EAL 5-7 product, then the product must be evaluated under the direct coordination of the NIAP and not an international partner's laboratory.

The NIST Cryptographic Module Validation Program (CMVP) encompasses validation testing for cryptographic modules and algorithms. The CC and CMVP FIPS 140-2 evaluations are different in the abstractness and focus of tests. The CMVP website states that "FIPS 140-2 testing is against a defined cryptographic module and provides a suite of conformance tests to four security levels. FIPS 140-2 describes the requirements for cryptographic modules and includes such areas as physical security, key management, self tests, roles, and services, etc. The standard was initially developed in 1994 — prior to the development of the CC. CC is an evaluation against a created protection profile (PP) or security target (ST). Typically, a PP covers a broad range of products. A CC evaluation does not supersede or replace a validation to either FIPS 140-1 or FIPS 140-2. The four security levels in FIPS 140-1 and FIPS 140-2 do not map directly to specific CC EALs or to CC functional requirements. A CC certificate cannot be a substitute for a FIPS 140-1 or FIPS 140-2 certificate.

The only allowed exceptions to NSTISSP No 11 are:

■ COTS or GOTS IA and IA-enabled IT products acquired prior to the effective dates of the policy.
■ Rapid technologic changes and the amount of time it takes to successfully complete a product evaluation also affect compliance

with NSTISSP No. 11. Therefore, full and immediate compliance with NSTISSP No. 11 may not be possible for all acquisitions.

- No blanket or open-ended waivers to NSTISSP No. 11 will be authorized, but a Deferred Compliance Authorization (DCA) may be granted on a case-by-case basis.

NSTISSP No. 101, National Policy on Securing Voice Communications (September 1999)

This policy was originally issued as NCSC 8, which was a classified document. In 1999, it was downgraded to unclassified and reissued as the present NSTISSP No. 101. The intent of this policy is to improve U.S. communications security and to reduce the vulnerability of governmental voice communications to exploitation.

NSTISSP No. 101 establishes national policy that requires that:

- All military voice radio systems are secured.
- Civil government voice systems that carry traffic of significant intelligence value are secured.
- There is implementation of this policy in each department or agency.
- Departments establish priorities based on an assessment of threat to specific voice systems, dispositions, or operations.

NSTISSP No. 200, National Policy on Controlled Access Protection (July 1987)

The National Policy on Controlled Access Protection (NSTISSP No. 200) states that all Automated Information Systems (AIS) that are accessed by more than one user, when those users do not have the same authorization to use all of the classified or sensitive unclassified information processed or maintained by the AIS, shall provide automated controlled access protection for all classified and sensitive unclassified information.

This policy defines AIS, controlled access protection, and the Trusted Computer System Evaluation Criteria (TCSEC). These are standard definitions that can be found in the CNSS 4009 Glossary. The main point of NSTISSP No. 200 is that the policy applies to all government agencies and government contractors whose information systems process sensitive or classified information. Essentially, these entities must meet the minimum controlled access protection (C2) as described in the TCSEC.

NSTISSP states that the major characteristics of controlled access protection include:

- Individual accountability through identification and authentication of each individual automated information system user
- Maintenance of audit trails of security-relevant events
- An ability to control a user's access to information according to the authorization the user has
- Preventing one user from obtaining another user's residual data (p. 3)

Based on a system risk assessment, additional protections may be required. Other exceptions include solutions that are prohibitively costly, technically unsound, or may have an adverse impact on timely operational needs. A provision of this policy allows the Approving Authority to make exceptions in writing.

ISSEPs need to recognize that this policy was released in 1987 and it stated that the "minimum level of protection shall be provided within five years of the promulgation of this policy" (NSTISSP No. 200, Revision 1987, p. 3). Thus, all systems processing classified or sensitive information must already be C2 compliant at this time. Also note that the TCSEC standard has been replaced by the Common Criteria (CC) standard; therefore, systems must meet the C2 equivalency in the CC (not always, but typically referred to as EAL 4).

CNSS Policy No. 14, National Policy Governing the Release of Information Assurance Products and Services to Authorized U.S. Persons or Activities That Are Not a Part of the Federal Government (November 2002), Superseded NCSC-2 (1983)

This policy assigns responsibilities and establishes the criteria to be applied when USG activities provide IA products and services to other U.S. persons or activities that are not a part of the Federal government. This policy supersedes NCSC 2, National Policy on Release of Communications Security Information to U.S. Contractors and Other U.S. Nongovernmental Sources dated July 7, 1983.

CNSS Policy No. 14 states: "U.S. Government activities are responsible for protecting U.S. Government classified and sensitive unclassified information. However, there may be certain circumstances when U.S. entities may also have a legitimate need to protect U.S. Government classified and sensitive unclassified information. In such situations, the U.S. Government may release IA products to these U.S. entities in accordance with the limitations set forth as follows:

5. Security policies and procedures applicable to any IA product that is released outside the Federal government shall, in all cases, be

consistent with established national IA doctrine and the specific requirements of this policy. In particular:

a. All individuals who are granted access to U.S. Government IA products must be U.S. citizens. Such access shall be controlled on a strict need-to-know basis and shall be granted only in conformance with procedures established for the particular type of IA products involved. Requests for release of IA products and services to U.S. individuals who are not U.S. citizens shall be processed as an exception to this policy.

b. Contracting for design, development, modification, production, or developmental testing of cryptographic equipment shall require prior approval of the Director, National Security Agency (NSA).

c. As a prior condition of release, IA products provided to U.S. entities shall be subsequently controlled in such a manner to prevent further dissemination outside the Federal government. The same controls shall be in place to preclude the unauthorized transfer of technology contained therein.

d. Individuals who require access to U.S. classified cryptographic information must comply with applicable cryptographic access policies.

6. U.S. Government IA products may be released outside of the Federal government provided the following criteria can be satisfied:

a. A valid need must exist for the individual or activity to:

1) Install, maintain, or operate secure network or telecommunications equipment for the U.S. Government;

2) Participate in the design, planning, production, training, installation, maintenance, operation, logistical support, integration, modification, testing, or study of IA products or techniques; or

3) Communicate U.S. Government classified or sensitive unclassified information using secure network or telecommunication systems.

b. Individuals who are granted access to classified IA products must hold a final U.S. Government security clearance appropriate to the level of the classified material involved. Access to TOP SECRET material shall only be granted to individuals whose clearance is predicated on a favorable background investigation. Individuals who are granted an interim TOP SECRET clearance may not be granted access to IA products classified higher than SECRET.

c. All individuals who are granted access to IA products must receive a briefing regarding the unique nature of this material and must be made aware of their security responsibilities to properly safeguard and control any classified IA product.

d. All individuals who perform maintenance on hardware components of U.S. Government secure network or telecommunications equipment must receive formal NSA-approved training for the equipment or equipment family involved (p. 2-3)."

NCSC-5, National Policy on Use of Cryptomaterial by Activities Operating in High Risk Environments (U) (January 1981)

This policy provides guidance on the selection and protection of machine cryptosystems for use in high-risk environments by the Heads of Federal Departments and Agencies, the Joint Chiefs of Staff, the Commanders of the Unified and Specified Commands, and Military Commanders.

The NCSC-5 policy states that:

a. The selection of machine cryptosystems for use in high risk environments shall be a deliberate decision taking into consideration the factors promulgated by the Director, NSA. High risk environments for machine cryptosystems shall be identified in accordance with standardized criteria.

b. In all cases where machine cryptosystems will be used in high risk environments a workable plan will be developed and implemented to protect, evacuate, or destroy COMSEC equipment and other COMSEC materials which may be jeopardized.

c. Only the minimum amount of mission essential COMSEC material may be located at high risk environments.

d. Point-to-point keying material, rather than netted or common user keying material, will be used for secure communications to high risk areas (p. 1).

CNSS Directive

NSTISSD-500, Information Systems Security (INFOSEC) Education, Training, and Awareness (February 1993)

This directive establishes the requirement for federal departments and agencies to develop and implement information systems security (INFOSEC) education, training, and awareness programs for national security systems.

Education, training, and awareness are countermeasures that effectively reduce exposure to a variety of known risks. To achieve this end, it is essential to have a Federal workforce that is aware of and educated about the problems of INFOSEC. This directive is issued in response to the national policy and establishes the requirement for Federal departments and agencies to develop and implement INFOSEC education, training, and awareness programs. This directive supersedes NSTISS Directive No. 500 (June 1987), "Telecommunications and Automated Information Systems Security Education, Training, and Awareness."

The directive states that INFOSEC education, training, and awareness activities are required for all employees and must meet the levels of knowledge, experience, and responsibilities of employees, as well as the specific needs of individual departments and agencies. It is applicable to all departments and agencies of the U.S. Government, their employees, and contractors who develop, acquire, manage, or use information systems operated by or on behalf of the Federal government to store, use, process, transmit, or communicate national security information.

Directive 500 outlines the specific messages that need to be conveyed as:

a. "Organizations critically rely on information and information systems' resources.
b. The organization, through its management, commits to protect information and information systems' resources.
c. There are threats, vulnerabilities, and related risks associated with the organization's information systems.
d. There are consequences from the lack of adequate protection of the organization's information systems' resources.
e. The employee is the essential element of a successful protection program (p. 2)."

It further states that "every INFOSEC education, training, and awareness program will contain three types of activities:

- Initial orientation
- More advanced education and training commensurate with duties and responsibilities
- Reinforcement activities

All training activities shall be conducted by individuals who are knowledgeable of INFOSEC principles and concepts, as well as their application (p. 2)."

CNSS Instructions

The CNSS instructions discussed include:

- NSTISSI No. 1000, National Information Assurance Certification and Accreditation Process (NIACAP) (April 2000)
- CNSS No. 4009, National Information Assurance Glossary (May 2003)

■ NSTISSI No. 4011, National Training Standard for INFOSEC Professionals (June 1994)
■ CNSSI No. 4012, National Information Assurance Training Standard for Senior System Managers (June 2004)
■ CNSSI No. 4013, National Information Assurance Training Standard for System Administrators (April 2004)
■ CNSSI No. 4014, National Information Assurance Training Standard for Information Systems Security Officers (ISSO) (April 2004)
■ NSTISSI No. 4015, National Training Standard for System Certifiers (December 2000)
■ NSTISSI No. 7003, Protected Distribution Systems (December 1996)
■ NACSI--6002, National ComSec Instruction — Protection of Government Contractor Telecommunications (June 1984)

NSTISSI No. 1000, National Information Assurance Certification and Accreditation Process (NIACAP) (April 2000)

NSTISSI No. 1000 establishes the minimum national standards for certifying and accrediting national security systems. It provides guidance on how to implement NSTISSP No. 6, National Policy on Certification and Accreditation of National Security Telecommunications and Information Systems (April 1994). The NIACAP process provides a standard set of activities, general tasks, and a management structure to certify and accredit systems that will maintain the IA and security posture of a system or site. This process focuses on an enterprisewide view of the information system (IS) in relation to the organization's mission and the IS business case.

NIACAP is designed to certify that the IS meets documented accreditation requirements and will continue to maintain the accredited security posture throughout the system life cycle. NIACAP was discussed in detail in Chapter 8.

CNSS No. 4009, National Information Assurance Glossary (May 2003)

CNSS No. 4009 provides definitions for terminology used in National and DoD directives. Section I of the document contains a glossary of IA terms, while Section II provides a list of common acronyms.

CNSS (NSTISSI) Training Standards

NSTISS Directive No. 501 (1992) established the requirement for Federal departments and agencies to implement training programs for "INFOSEC professionals." An INFOSEC professional was defined as the individual responsible for the security oversight or management of national security systems during all life cycle phases. Although the USG no longer uses the term INFOSEC professional, the requirement for training those responsible for security systems still remains. In 2002, the Federal Information Security Management Act (FISMA) established requirements for Federal departments and agencies to implement training programs for IA professionals.

This series of CNSS instructions (NSTISSI) establish and outline the national training standards for IA professionals responsible or national security systems. Three of the documents (4012, 4013, and 4014) were updated in 2004 and released as CNSS Instructions (CNSSI). These instructions establish the minimum training standards for IA professionals. CNSS training issuances include:

- NSTISSI No. 4011, National Training Standards for Information Systems Security (INFOSEC) Professionals (June 1994)
- CNSSI No. 4012 (June 2004), National Information Assurance Training Standard for Senior System Managers, supersedes NSTISSI No. 4012 (August 1997), National Training Standard for Designated Approving Authority (DAA)
- CNSSI No. 4013 (April 2004), National Information Assurance Training Standard for System Administrators, supersedes NSTISSI No. 4013 (August 1997), National Information Assurance Training Standard for System Administrators (SA)
- CNSSI No. 4014 (April 2004), National Information Assurance Training Standard for Information Systems Security Officers (ISSO), supersedes NSTISSI No. 4014 (August 1997), National Training Standard for Information Systems Security Officers (ISSO)
- NSTISSI No. 4015 (December 2000), National Training Standard for Systems Certifiers

Note to ISSEP candidates: The (ISC)² ISSEP® exam requirements list each of the NSTISSI training standards as study items. The detail provided here is more than sufficient for the exam.

NSTISSI No. 4011, National Training Standard for INFOSEC Professionals (June 1994)

This instruction provides the minimum course content for the training of information systems security (INFOSEC) professionals in the disciplines of telecommunications security and AIS security.

NSTISSI No. 4011 provides a recommended course curriculum for the minimum training required for the IT professional. A course outline would be structured to provide instructional content, behavioral outcome, and topical content for the following high-level topic items:

- Communications basics (awareness level)
- AIS basics (awareness level)
- Security basics (awareness level)
- NSTISS basics (awareness level)
- System operating environment (awareness level)
- NSTISS planning and management (performance level)
- NSTISS policies and procedures (performance level)

Table 13.2 is based on the guidance in NSTISSI No. 4011 and provides an overview of the training requirements based on either an awareness or performance level. Essentially, the No. 4011 states that the curriculum should be designed to provide two levels of knowledge:

a. "Awareness Level. Creates sensitivity to the threats and vulnerabilities of national security information systems, and recognition of the need to protect data, information and the means of processing them; and builds a working knowledge of principles and practices in INFOSEC.
b. Performance Level. Provides the employee with the skill or ability to design, execute, or evaluate agency INFOSEC security procedures and practices. This level of understanding will ensure that employees are able to apply security concepts while performing their tasks (p. 5)."

Note to ISSEP candidates: It is not necessary to know the elements of Table 13.2. It is provided as a reference for understanding the basics of how the NSTISS training standards are represented.

CNSSI No. 4012 (June 2004), National Information Assurance Training Standard for Senior System Managers, Supersedes NSTISSI No. 4012, National Training Standard for Designated Approving Authority (DAA) (August 1997)

CNSSI No. 4012 establishes the minimum standard for the development and implementation of IA training for senior systems managers (SSMs), such as the Chief Information Officer (CIO), Designated Approving Authority (DAA), Chief Technology Officer (CTO), etc.

Table 13.2   Security Education and Training Plan

Instructional Content	Behavioral Outcomes	Topical Content
Communications Basics (Awareness Level)		
Introduce the evolution of modern communications systems Describe vehicles of transmission	Outline chronology of communications systems and development	Historical versus current methodology Capabilities and limitations of various communications systems
Automated Information Systems (AIS) Basics (Awareness Level)		
Provide AIS language Describe an AIS environment Provide an overview of hardware, software	Define terms in an AIS Define functions performed Describe interrelations among AIS components	Historical versus current methodology HW, SW, memory, media, and networks
Security Basics (Awareness Level)		
Introduce a comprehensive model of information systems security that addresses: Critical characteristics of information information states, and security measures	The student will: List and describe the elements of AIS security Summarize security disciplines used in protecting government automated information systems Give examples of determinants of critical information	INFOSEC overview INFOSEC policies Operational security (OPSEC) INFOSEC
NSTISS Basics (Awareness Level)		
Describe components (with examples to include: national policy, threats and vulnerabilities, countermeasures, risk management, systems life-cycle management, trust, modes of operation, roles of organizational units, and facets of NSTISS)	Outline national NSTISS policies Cite examples of threats and vulnerabilities of AIS Give examples of Agency implementation of NSTISS policy, practices, and procedures	National policy and guidance Threats and vulnerabilities of systems Legal elements Countermeasures Concepts of risk management, life-cycle management. and trust

Table 13.2 (continued)   Security Education and Training Plan

Instructional Content	Behavioral Outcomes	Topical Content
		Roles of operational personnel Modes of operations Facets of NSTISS
System Operating Environment (Awareness Level)		
Outline Agency-specific AIS and telecommunications systems Describe Agency "control points" for purchase and maintenance of Agency AIS and telecommunications systems Review Agency AIS and telecommunications security policies	Summarize Agency AIS and telecommunications systems in operation Give examples of current Agency AIS/telecommunications systems and configurations List Agency-level contact points for AIS and telecommunications systems and maintenance Cite appropriate policy and guidance	AIS-HW, SW, and FW Telecommunications systems HW, SW Agency-specific security policy Agency-specific AIS and telecommunications policies
NSTISS Planning and Management (Performance Level)		
Discuss practical performance measures employed in designing security measures and programs Introduce generic security planning guidelines/documents	Build a security plan that encompasses NSTISS components in designing protection/security for an instructor-supplied description of an AIS/telecommunications system	Security planning Risk management Life-cycle management Contingency planning
NSTISS Policies and Procedures (Performance Level)		
Describe specific technological, policy, and educational solutions for NSTISS Elements of vulnerability and threat that exist in an AIS/telecommunications system with corresponding protection measures	Playing the role of system penetrator or system protector, the student will discover points of exploitation and apply appropriate countermeasures in an instructor-supplied description of an Agency AIS/telecommunications system	Physical security measures Personnel security policies and procedures Software security Network security Administrative security procedural controls Auditing and monitoring

Table 13.2 (continued)   Security Education and Training Plan

Instructional Content	Behavioral Outcomes	Topical Content
		Crypto security
		Key management
		Transmission security
		TEMPEST (EMSEC)

Note: Based on NSTISSI No. 4011 (1994).

The objective of CNSSI No. 4012 is "when given a final report requesting approval to operate an information system at a specified level of trust, the SSM will analyze and judge the information for validity and reliability to ensure the system will operate at the proposed level of trust. This judgment will be predicated on an understanding of system architecture, system security measures, system operations policy, system security management plan, legal and ethical considerations, and provisions for system operator and end user training" (p. A-1).

CNSSI No. 4012 outlines the ten primary functions of an SSM as:

1. *Grant final approval to operate (ATO).* Granting final approval to operate an IS or network in a specified security mode.
2. *Review accreditation.* Reviewing the accreditation documentation to confirm that the residual risk is within acceptable limits for each network and/or information system (IS).
3. *Verify compliance.* Verifying that each information system complies with the IA requirements.
4. *Ensure establishment of security controls.* Ensuring the establishment, administration, and coordination of security for systems that agency, service, or command personnel or contractors operate.
5. *Ensure program managers define security in acquisitions.* Ensuring that the program manager/official defines the system security requirements for acquisitions.
6. *Assign responsibilities.* Assigning IA responsibilities to the individuals reporting directly to the SSM.
7. *Define criticality and sensitivity.* Defining the criticality and classification and sensitivity levels of each IS and approving the classification level required for the applications implemented on them.
8. *Allocate resources.* Allocating resources to achieve an acceptable level of security and to remedy security deficiencies.
9. *Multiple and joint accreditation.* Resolving issues regarding those systems requiring multiple or joint accreditation. This may require

documentation of conditions or agreements in Memoranda of Agreement (MOA).

10. *Assess network security.* Ensuring that when classified and sensitive information is exchanged between IS or networks (internal or external), the content of this communication is protected from unauthorized observation, manipulation, or denial.

The remainder of CNSSI No. 4012 outlines the specific training topics and subtopics for each of the ten functional responsibilities.

CNSSI No. 4013 (April 2004), National Information Assurance Training Standard for System Administrators Supersedes NSTISSI No. 4013 National Training Standard for System Administrators (August 1997)

This instruction establishes the minimum course content or standard for the development and implementation of IA training for System Administrators (SAs) for national security systems. It also may offer guidelines for administrators of unclassified systems.

CNSSI No. 4013 states that the IA functions of a system administrator are:

1. *Secure use.* Working closely with the Information Systems Security Officer (ISSO) to ensure the information system (IS) or network is used securely.
2. *Incidents.* Participating in the information systems security incident reporting program.
3. *Configuration.* Assisting the ISSO in maintaining configuration control of the systems and applications software.
4. *Anomalies and integrity.* Advising the ISSO of security anomalies or integrity loopholes.
5. *Administration.* Administering, when applicable, user identification or authentication mechanism(s) of the IS or network.

The instructions outline objectives for three different levels of study:

■ *"Entry level.* Given various scenarios and typical situations containing information systems security issues, the SA will be able to describe and apply the appropriate actions to manage and administer an IS in a secure manner. To be acceptable, the description and application must be in accordance with applicable IA regulations, policies, and guidelines.

- *Intermediate level.* Given various scenarios and typical situations containing information systems security issues, the SA will be able to explain and implement the appropriate actions to manage and administer an IS in a secure manner. To be acceptable, the explanation and implementation must be in accordance with applicable IA regulations, policies, and guidelines.
- *Advanced level.* Given various scenarios and typical situations containing information systems security issues, the SA will be able to verify that the appropriate actions are implemented to manage and administer an IS in a secure manner. To be acceptable, verification must be in accordance with applicable IA regulations, policies, and guidelines" (CNSSI 4013, 2004, p. A-1).

The remainder of CNSSI No. 4013 outlines specific training topic and subtopics.

CNSSI No. 4014 (April 2004), National Information Assurance Training Standard for Information Systems Security Officers (ISSO), Supersedes NSTISSI No. 4014, National Training Requirements for Information System Security Officers (August 1997)

CNSSI No. 4014 establishes the minimum training standard for the development and implementation of training for Information Systems Security Officers (ISSOs) in the disciplines of telecommunications and information system (IS) security.

The ISSO job functions were identified using competencies in DoDD 8500.2, Information Assurance Implementation Common Criteria for Information Technology Security Evaluation, and DCID 6/3, Protecting Sensitive Compartmented Information Within Information Systems. CNSSI No. 4014 identifies the following ISSO functions:

1. *Develop certification and accreditation posture.* Maintain a plan for site security improvements and progress toward meeting the accreditation.
2. *Implement site security policy.* Ensure that the IS is operated, used, maintained, and disposed of in accordance with security policies and practices.
3. *Support certification and accreditation.* Ensure that the IS is accredited and certified.
4. *Enforce and verify site security policy.* Ensure that users and system support personnel have required security clearances, authorization

and need-to-know, are indoctrinated, and are familiar with internal security practices before access to the IS granted.

5. *Enforce security policies and safeguards.*
6. *Ensure audit trails are reviewed periodically* (e.g., weekly, daily) and *audit records are archived for future reference, if required.*
7. *Initiate protective or corrective measures.*
8. *Report on site security status.* Report security incidents in accordance with agency-specific policy to the senior system manager (SSM) when the IS is compromised.
9. *Report the security status of the IS,* as required by the SSM.
10. *Evaluate known vulnerabilities* to ascertain if additional safeguards are needed.

The policy states that ISSO training should be established at three different levels of experience: entry level, intermediate level, and advance levels of expertise. No. 4014 defines these levels as:

■ *"Entry level.* Given a series of system security breaches, the ISSO will identify system vulnerabilities and recommend security solutions required to return systems to operational level of assurance.
■ *Intermediate level.* Given a proposed new system architecture requirement, the ISSO will investigate and document system security technology, policy, and training requirements to assure system operation at a specified level of assurance.
■ *Advanced level.* Given a proposed IS accreditation action, the ISSO will analyze and evaluate the system security technology, policy, and training requirements in support of the SSM approval to operate the system at a specified level of assurance. This analysis will include a description of the management/technology team required to successfully complete the accreditation process (p. A-2)."

The remainder of CNSSI No. 4014 outlines specific ISSO training topics and subtopics.

NSTISSI No. 4015, National Training Standard for System Certifiers (December 2000)

NSTISSI No. 4015 establishes the minimum course content or standard for the development and implementation of education and training for *system certifier* professionals in the disciplines of telecommunications security and information systems (IS) security.

The introduction to NSTISSI No. 4015 provides an overview of the system certifier role and outlines the importance and necessary qualifications in order to adequately perform the functions of certifying an information system. It states the following:

"The System Certifier is an individual or a member of a team who performs the comprehensive multi-disciplined assessment of the technical and non-technical security features and other safeguards of an information system in an operational configuration, made in support of the accreditation process. The Certifier identifies the assurance levels achieved in meeting all applicable security policies, standards, and requirements for the DAA, who in turn determines whether or not an information system and/or network is operating within the bounds of specified requirements and at an acceptable level of risk.

The designated Certification Authority (sometimes referred to as "certification agent," as defined in CNSS No. 4009) is ultimately responsible for determining the correct skill sets required to adequately certify the system, and for identifying personnel to accomplish the comprehensive evaluation of the technical and non-technical security features of the system. The scope and the complexity of the information system determine whether the Certifier will be an individual or a member of a team performing the certification. The Certifiers' responsibilities evolve as the system progresses through the life-cycle process. Because an in-depth understanding and application of the C&A process is required of the System Certifiers, these professional operate at the highest level of the Information Technology Security Learning Continuum model referenced in the NIST SP 800-16. According to this model, learning starts with awareness, builds to training, and evolves into education, the highest level. Overall the performance items contained in this training standard are at that advanced level.

To be a qualified System Certifier, one must first be formally trained in the fundamentals of INFOSEC, and have field experience. It is recommended that System Certifiers have system administrator and/or basic ISSO experience, and be familiar with the Knowledge, Skills and Abilities (KSAs) required of the DAA. Throughout the complex information systems certification process, the Certifiers exercise a considerable amount of INFOSEC-specific as well as non-INFOSEC-specific KSAs (p. 2)."

NSTISSI No. 4015 states that the INFOSEC functions for a systems certifier are performed during various phases of the certification process. These include:

1. *"Documenting mission need.* The System Certifiers need to develop a comprehensive understanding of the mission and the functional responsibilities in order to ensure the success of the C&A processes. Certifiers must possess a global understanding of the C&A process, the system, and the mission it supports.

2. *Conducting registration.* Registration involves the collection of information needed to address the certification process in a repeatable, understandable, and effective manner. These tasks involve gathering information to determine the security requirements and the level of effort necessary to accomplish C&A. The level of effort is influenced by the degree of assurance needed in the areas of confidentiality, integrity, accountability, and availability. Certifiers must consider the mission, environments, system life cycle, existing documentation, risk, architecture, users, data classifications, external interfaces, etc.

3. *Performing negotiation.* Negotiation is involved in every facet of the C&A process. Given the potentially large numbers of people and functional organizations involved, Certifiers must draw upon many sub-disciplines and roles to accomplish this mission. To this end, Certifiers must possess broad, well-developed negotiation skills. Negotiation skills are especially important for determining methodologies, defining the scope of the certification process, and acquiring the resources necessary to support the mission. Effective written and oral communication skills, flexibility, creativity, political acumen, and objectivity all contribute to effective negotiation activities.

4. *Preparing the System Security Authorization Agreement (SSAA).* Certifiers are part of a team composed of the Certification Authority, the program sponsor, a threat specialist, and others. This team prepares the SSAA, a document that describes the planned operating condition of the system being certified and the expected residual risk in operating the system. The Designated Approving Authority (DAA) approves the SSAA and the system is then implemented with the security requirements that have been determined for it. It is important to note that the SSAA is a living document, and as such will require periodic maintenance throughout the life-cycle management of the system.

5. *Supporting systems development.* During the systems development phase of a system certification, the Certifiers are responsible for

evaluating the design of the system and ensuring that the security requirements are being properly addressed and satisfied. The specific activities are a function of the overall program strategy, the life-cycle management process, and the position of the information system in the life cycle. As in the Certification Analysis phase, the system development activities ensure that the requirements of the SSAA are followed during each life-cycle phase of the development and modification of the information system.

6. *Performing certification analysis.* Certification analysis is the process of interacting with the system developer or owner/operator, and reviewing the documentation to carefully assess the functionality of the developing system, ensuring that it meets the security requirements as defined for its users, environment, connectivity, and other technical and non-technical factors in the SSAA.

7. *Certification evaluation.* Security certification evaluation is the process whereby the Certifiers verify and validate through formal security testing and evaluation (ST&E), that the implementation of the IS complies with the technical and non-technical security requirements stated in the SSAA, and that any observed deficiencies are fully documented and presented to the DAA for consideration in the accreditation decision.

8. *Developing recommendation to the DAA.* The Certifiers prepare appropriate documentation regarding all findings resulting from the ST&E, and recommends to the DAA the degree to which the evaluated system satisfies all the defined security requirements. In addition, this documentation offers the Certifier's opinion concerning any identified residual risk that may preclude accreditation of the system for operation.

9. *Compliance validation.* The Certifier's focus during this phase is the audit of the accredited IS, which is operating under the approval of the DAA, who has accepted any identified residual risk. Therefore, the Certifiers audit operations to ensure they remain consistent with the DAA accepted level of risk.

10. *Maintenance of the SSAA.* The Maintenance of the SSAA function involves determining whether or not any IS implementation changes that dictate a need to re-certify the implementation of the IS will require an update of the SSAA. If changes occur that dictate a need for a re-certification effort, then the Certifier functions as defined in the C&A process are again performed for these changes, or for the entire IS as necessary. Additionally, Certifiers must ensure that the re-certification effort is reported to the DAA for continued approval to operate (p. A-1–A-3)."

The NSTISSI training objective states that "[g]iven an information system, the System Certifiers will explain and apply a recognized methodology leading to the security certification of that system in accordance with a prescribed set of criteria (i.e., the Mission Assurance Categories I, II, or III or Protection Levels 1–5), and provide an accreditation recommendation to the DAA for consideration in the accreditation decision. To be acceptable, the certification must be performed in accordance with applicable INFOSEC regulations, policies, and guidelines (p. A-3)."

The remainder of NSTISSI No. 4015 outlines specific training topic and subtopics.

NSTISSI No. 7003, Protected Distribution Systems (December 1996)

NSTISSI No. 7003 (1996) stipulates approval authority, standards, and guidance for the design, installation, and maintenance of Protected Distribution Systems (PDSs). The PDS can be either a wire-line or fiber-optic distribution system that is used to transmit unencrypted classified National Security Information (NSI) through an area of lesser classification or control. The policy states that "inasmuch as the classified NSI is unencrypted, the PDS must provide adequate electrical, electromagnetic, and physical safeguards to deter exploitation (p. 4)."

NSTISSI No. 7003 provides an overview of when and how PDS can be used and also when a PDS cannot be used, such as high-risk environments. Some specific comments include:

> "The instruction incorporates a philosophy of 'risk management' in lieu of the "risk avoidance" philosophy employed in previous documents. Absent specific facts, unique to each facility, suggesting greater or lesser risks, these standards shall be applied. However, sensible risk management practice dictates each facility must be evaluated on its own risks and vulnerabilities based on factors such as location, physical security, environment, access controls, and personnel security requirements, etc. The overall security afforded by PDS is the result of a layered approach incorporating various protection techniques. The emphasis is placed on "detection" of attempted penetration in lieu of "prevention" of penetration. Criteria called out are based on threat or risk analysis relative to the location of the PDS. This generally results in reduced requirements and cost savings during installation and maintenance of PDS.

This instruction applies to U.S. Government departments and agencies and their contractors and vendors who use, or are contemplating the use of a PDS to protect the transmission of unencrypted classified NSI. This instruction describes the requirements for PDS installed within the U.S. (including its territories and possessions) and within LOW and MEDIUM threat locations outside of the United States. The threat within the U.S. is low. The use of PDS within a HIGH or CRITICAL threat location is not recommended. If PDS are used in these locations, protection techniques are determined on a case-by-case basis by the Approval Authority (p. 3)."

Annex B of NSTISSI No. 7003 provides specific requirements for installing a PDS.

NACSI-6002, Protection of Government Contractor Telecommunications (June 1984)

National COMSEC Instruction (NACSI) No. 6002 implements three key policies as they pertain to the telecommunications of government contractors. Significantly, this NACSI "establishes a policy of allowing government contractors to charge their communications security or protection costs back to the government in the same manner as they would charge other contract security costs" (Foreword).

NACSI-6002 states that to increase the protection given to information transmitted between and among the government and its contractors, action must be taken to implement the provisions of national policy, as follows:

a. "Contract-related telecommunications which require communications security or protection must be identified during the contracting process and specific implementation provisions made for such communications security or protection.

b. Contractors' communications security or protection costs must be allowable in the same manner as they would charge other contract security costs. For applications involving government-provided equipment, this will extend to the associated operating and administrative costs. For applications involving contractor-owned equipment, it will also include associated investment costs.

c. Identify mechanisms by which communications security equipment or approved protection measures can be made directly available to qualified Government contractors in support of national policy and the provisions of this Instruction (p. 2)."

CNSS Advisory Memoranda

The NSTISSAM are advisory memoranda developed by CNSS (NSTISSC) for USG agencies and departments. They cover a variety of topics involving information assurance, telecommunications security, and network security. They are periodically revised and updated to reflect changes in technology implementation and national policy.

The following CNSS Advisory Memoranda are discussed:

- NSTISSAM COMPUSEC 1-98, The Role of Firewalls and Guards in Enclave Boundary Protection (December 1998)
- NSTISSAM COMPUSEC 1-99, Advisory Memorandum on the Transition from Trusted Computer System Evaluation Criteria (TCSEC) to the International Common Criteria (CC) for Information Security Technology Evaluation (March 1999)
- NSTISSAM INFOSEC/1-00, Advisory Memorandum for the Use of FIPS 140 Validated Cryptographic Modules in Protecting Unclassified National Security Systems (February 2000)
- NSTISSAM INFOSEC 2-00, Advisory Memorandum for the Strategy for Using National Information Assurance Partnership (NIAP) for the Evaluation of Commercial Off-the-Shelf (COTS) Security Enabled Information Technology Products (February 2000)
- CNSSAM 1-04, Advisory Memorandum for Information Assurance (IA) — Security through Product Diversity (July 2004)

NSTISSAM COMPUSEC 1-98, The Role of Firewalls and Guards in Enclave Boundary Protection (December 1998)

NSTISSAM 1-98 establishes the basic information related to guards and firewalls. It is based on the understanding of the defense-in-depth strategy of several systems, the computing environment, enclave boundaries, networks and infrastructure, and supporting infrastructures. This policy is based on the concept of a protecting an information system's enclave boundary. The required protections include a combination of security configuration elements, such as firewalls and guards, as well as authenticators, encryption devices, and virus and intrusion detectors.

An *enclave boundary* is a collection of local computing devices, regardless of physical location, that are interconnected via local area networks (LANs) and governed by a single security policy. Enclaves typically contain multiple LANs with computing resource components such as servers; client workstations; networks, applications, and communication servers; printers; and local routing/switching devices. It is defined as an environment under the control of a single authority with personnel and physical security measures. Refer to Chapter 3 for more information on an enclave boundary.

NSTISSAM 1-98 states that "firewalls and guards are enclave boundary protection devices located between a local area network, that the enterprise system has a requirement to protect, and a wide area network, which is outside the control of the enterprise system. Their primary purpose is to control access to the local area network from the outside wide area network, and to control access from the local area network to the wide area network. In many instances, they are also used within local area networks to provide a level of access control between different sub-networks within the local area network (p. 3)."

Because the technical information provided in NSTISSAM was written in 1998, it does not include many of the new options for firewalls and guards. However, the content remains important for understanding the use of firewalls and guards to protect the system's boundary.

The policy states there are three general types of firewalls:

1. Packet (or traffic) filtering
2. Application filtering (proxy)
3. Hybrid of both packet and application filtering

NSTISSAM 1-98 provides the following definitions for each firewall type:

> *"Packet (or traffic)* filtering devices as "typically filter (inspect) the source and destination address headers and/or service type (e.g., FTP, Telnet) on individual data packets flowing across the device. Packet filtering devices are simple and fast. However, they make access control decisions based on a very limited amount of information.

> *Application filtering,* also known as proxy servers, generally provide more security, but they are extremely complex and can be slower than packet filtering devices. Application filtering firewalls serve as proxies for outside users, intercepting packets and forwarding them to the appropriate application on the inside. Thus, outside users never have a direct connection to anything beyond the firewall. The fact that the firewall looks at the application information means that it can distinguish between different services such as Telnet, FTP, or SMTP traffic. Since application firewalls operate at the application layer of the OSI model they have more flexibility to perform detailed analysis on transiting packets.

> *Hybrid firewalls* usually employ some combination of security characteristics of both packet filtering and application filtering products (p. 3)."

Currently on the market are more complex and comprehensive firewalls, such as those that employ stateful inspection. Stateful-inspection firewalls are advanced packet filter firewalls that employ TCP conversation information above the standard source and destination of a packet filtering firewall. For example, Check Point Firewall-1 and Cisco PIX both have stateful-inspection packet filtering for high-speed traffic and proxy firewall services to provide application layer security.

In addition to firewalls, guards also provide boundary protections. Guards are distinguished from firewalls in three major ways:

1. "Guards have an application filtering capability that is much stronger than a typical application filtering firewall. Guards use a reclassifier application to control what data is passed from one enclave to another. The reclassifier application uses a collection of filters to review application data content.
2. Guard software is generally developed to meet higher assurance requirements.
3. Guards undergo a much more extensive test and evaluation (e.g., source code analysis, unconstrained penetration testing, and design documentation review) to provide a significantly higher level of confidence that they will operate correctly (NSTISSAM I-98, p. 4)."

The National Security Agency (NSA), in conjunction with other members of the IA community and written in accordance with the Common Criteria standards, is specifying the security functions needed from firewalls and guards. These specifications are documented in Protection Profiles. More information on Protection Profiles is provided in Chapter 15.

NSTISSAM 1-98 provides the following guidelines for using firewalls and guards:

- Guards should only be specified for use in security configurations bridging and protecting local networks with classified information from unclassified networks.
- Only firewalls meeting published Protection Profiles should be specified for use in security configurations protecting local networks containing administrative information (e.g., payroll, medical, or logistics records), or sensitive but unclassified information, or for providing sub-network protection within classified network environments.
- Firewalls should not be used to protect connections between classified systems and unclassified systems.
- Firewalls with an application filtering capability provide more granular access control and a higher degree of security and, therefore, are preferred from a security perspective in many environments.

NSTISSAM COMPUSEC 1-99, Advisory Memorandum on the Transition from Trusted Computer System Evaluation Criteria (TCSEC) to the International Common Criteria (CC) for Information Security Technology Evaluation (March 1999)

NSTISSAM 1-99 provides guidance regarding the transition from the TCSEC to the CC evaluation system. It is intended to introduce the new criteria and provide an opportunity to evaluate its applicability to USG IA operating environments and requirements.

The rationale for adopting the CC standards is stated as:

> "[W]ithin the last several years, IA has evolved at a pace whereby it has become increasingly clear that the TCSEC is too rigid and limited in scope for many of today's security-enabled products and user application environments. As the state of the art for IA continues to evolve worldwide, it has become increasingly clear that updated criteria are required. Additionally, information security vendors have been pleading for internationally accepted criteria instead of individual nationally based criteria which required their products be evaluated against a multitude of different standards depending on the region of the world where sales were being targeted (NSTISSAM, p. 3)."

Specific information related to Common Criteria can be found in Chapter 15.

NSTISSAM INFOSEC/1-00, Advisory Memorandum for the Use of FIPS 140 Validated Cryptographic Modules in Protecting Unclassified National Security Systems (February 2000)

NSTISSAM INFOSEC/1-00, dated 8 February 2000, is the Advisory Memorandum for the Use of FIPS 140 Validated Cryptographic Modules in Protecting Unclassified National Security Systems. Essentially, the policy states that for applications or devices that include cryptography, USG agencies are required to use a cryptographic product that has been FIPS 140 validated or Common Criteria (CC) validated.

The guidance on an acquisition approach for products containing noncryptographic IA or IA-enabled features is:

1. Choose a product from the NIAP CCEVS Validated Products List that is compliant with the requirements of a government sponsored

protection profile for the desired technology (e.g., firewalls). In the absence of any products that are compliant with a government sponsored protection profile, or where there is no government sponsored protection profile for that particular technology, the consumer should choose from the CCEVS Validated Products List an evaluated product from the desired technology that has met its security target requirements. Finally, where no evaluated or validated product is on the CCEVS Validated Products List, the consumer should check the CCEVS Products and Protection Profiles Evaluation List for a potential product.

2. All proposed contracts for acquisition of IA or IA-enabled IT products should contain language that very specifically documents the requirement for NSTISSP No. 11 validated products. This can be accomplished in two ways:

   a. Where a government-sponsored protection profile exists, the acquisition or contract language should state that the product must be valuated/validated as compliant with the requirements of the protection profile; or

   b. In the absence of a protection profile, the acquisition or contract language should call for the product to have been evaluated against a consumer-defined set of functions at a given EAL.

   Where no product exists for a particular technology on the Validated Products List, the acquisition should require, as a condition of purchase, that a vendor submits the product for evaluation/validation and ensure completion of the evaluation in accordance with the requirements of NSTISSP No. 11.

3. When a U.S. Government protection profile is developed and released, products of that particular type that are still in development should target their final product to be conformant to the new protection profile (Source: CNSS FAQ, March 2005).

More information on the FIPS 140 standard is provided in Chapter 14.

NSTISSAM INFOSEC 2-00, Advisory Memorandum for the Strategy for Using National Information Assurance Partnership (NIAP) for the Evaluation of Commercial Off-the-Shelf (COTS) Security Enabled Information Technology Products (February 2000)

NSTISSAM INFOSEC 2-00 is an advisory memorandum on the strategy for using the NIAP partnership for evaluating COTS IA and IA enabling products. It establishes the use of commercial facilities for certification of products according to the International Common Criteria National Volunteer Laboratory Accreditation Program (NVLAP).

Laboratories will evaluate products against the security target (ST) provided by the vendor's functionality claims and the desired level of evaluation. If the product meets the ST criteria, it issues a report to NIAP documenting the results. The NIAP reviews the lab report to determine if the product evaluation is consistent with the Common Criteria (CC) requirements. Most companies that have certified labs conduct CC evaluations up through Evaluated Assurance Level (EAL) 4. EAL 5-7 requires that code examination and a more rigorous testing and evaluations. If the evaluation is satisfactory, the NIAP issues a certificate to the vendor or sponsor of the evaluation validating the product's claim.

These products are not NSA, NIST, or USG endorsements or certifications. The evaluation process only validates that the product met the security claims consistent with the level of analysis and the CC Evaluation Methodology requirements.

There have been cases where the evaluation of a product met the ST as stated by the vendor but did not provide adequate protection. To provide customer guidance on recommended minimum essential security robustness requirements for security and security-enabled COTS IT products, the NSA is issuing a series of technology-based CC Protection Profiles (PPs). The Information Assurance Technology Framework (IATF) assists with the development of the PPs in further cooperation with the user community and security vendors. PPs are also being developed for levels of robustness designated as Basic, Medium, and High. If a PP does not exist, a USG agency may request that NSA review and evaluate a product's security target to ensure that the product will meet the security requirements. More information on CC is provided in Chapter 15.

CNSSAM 1-04, Advisory Memorandum for Information Assurance (IA) — Security through Product Diversity (July 2004)

CNSSAM 1-04 advises USG departments and agencies to emphasize a multi-layered and multi-vendor approach to security when architecting information systems. It provides further clarification on NSTISSP No. 11, which limits the selection of IA products to those evaluated or validated by criteria specified in the policy. However, NSTISSP No. 11 does not provide guidance on how to compose compliant products into secure systems.

The CNSSAM emphasizes that protecting systems encompasses more than just acquiring compliant products. It states that "security of information systems is best achieved through a multi-layered security approach that employs sound information system security engineering, integrated security solutions, and good IA practices" (p. 1).

The CNSSAM 1-04 recommendation is for USG agencies and departments to use a multi-layer approach to security when developing and deploying security solutions. An example of a multi-layer approach is a defense-in-depth solution. When possible, compliant products should also be acquired from a diverse group of vendors because inadvertent or deliberate vulnerabilities present in one vendor's products may be offset by security afforded by products acquired from other vendors. When agencies combine product layers and diversity for both software and hardware, the overall security of the systems will be enhanced.

Summary

The CNSS provides a forum for the discussion of policy issues, sets national policy, and promulgates direction, operational procedures, and guidance for the security of national security systems through the CNSS Issuance System.

This chapter described the mission and goals of CNSS (and previously NSTISSC) and, most importantly, provided an overview of several major CNSS and NSTISSC guidances. This included seven primary policies, one directive, nine instructions, and four advisory memoranda. This is by no means the complete listing of national security system issuances related to information systems. For information regarding all CNSS issuances, refer to the "Index of National Security Systems Issuances" (June 2004). With one exception (NSTISSAM 1-00), all CNSS issuances highlighted in this chapter are available from a public domain source.

References

CNSS Policy No. 14 (November 2002). National Policy Governing the Release of Information Assurance Products and Services to Authorized U.S. Persons or Activities that Are Not a Part of the Federal Government Superseded NCSC-2 (1983). Available at http://www.nstissc.gov/Assets/pdf/cnss_policy_14.pdf.

CNSS FAQ (March 2005). Committee on National Security Systems, Frequently Asked Questions: National Policy Regarding the Evaluation of Commercial Products. Available at: http://niap.nist.gov/cc-scheme/nstissp-faqs.html#Question_I_1

CNSSI No. 4009 (May 2003). National Information Assurance Glossary, supersedes NSTISSI No. 4009 (May 2003), National Information System Security Glossary. Available at http://www.cnss.gov/issuances.html

CNSSI No. 4012 (June 2004). National Information Assurance Training Standard for Senior System Managers, supersedes NSTISSI No. 4012 (August 1997), National Training Standard for Designated Approving Authority (DAA). Available at http://www.cnss.gov/issuances.html

CNSSI No. 4013 (March 2004). National Information Assurance Training Standard for System Administrators, supersedes NSTISSI No. 4013 (August 1997), National Information Assurance Training Standard For System Administrators (SA). Available at http://www.cnss.gov/issuances.html

CNSSI No. 4014 (April 2004). National Information Assurance Training Standard for Information Systems Security Officers (ISSO), supersedes NSTISSI No. 4014 (August 1997), National Training Standard for Information Systems Security Officers (ISSO). Available at http://www.cnss.gov/issuances.html

Executive Order (EO) 13231 (October 18, 2001). Critical Infrastructure Protection in the Information Age. Presidential Documents, *Federal Register,* Vol. 66, No. 202, Thursday, October 18, 2001.

Index of National Security Systems Issuances (June 2004). Some issuances are available from the CNSS Web site. Other issuances can be obtained through USG representatives of the CNSS from: CNSS Secretariat, NSA, Fort Meade, MD. U.S. Government contractors should contact their Contracting Officer Representative regarding distribution of these documents. Available at http://www.nstissc.gov/Assets/pdf/cnss_index_jun_04.pdf.

NACSI-6002 (June 1984). Protection of Government Contractor Telecommunications. Available at http://www.nstissc.gov/Assets/pdf/NACSI_6002.pdf.

NCSC-5 (January 1981). National Policy on Use of Cryptomaterial by Activities Operating in High Risk Environments (U). Available at http://www.nstissc.gov/Assets/pdf/NCSC-5.pdf.

NIAP Frequently Asked Questions, Version 2.1 (January 2002). National Policy Regarding the Evaluation of Commercial Products. Available at http://niap.nist.gov/cc-scheme/nstissp_11.pdf.

NSTISSD 501 (1993). National Training Program for Information Systems Security (INFOSEC) Professional. Available at http://www.nstissc.gov/Assets/pdf/nstissd_501.pdf.

NSTISSD No. 900 (April 2000). Governing Procedures of the National Security Telecommunications and Information Systems Security Committee (NSTISSC). Available at http://www.nstissc.gov/Assets/pdf/nstissd_900.pdf.

NSTISSP No. 6 (April 1994). National Policy on Certification and Accreditation of National Security Telecommunications and Information Systems. http://www.nstissc.gov/Assets/pdf/NSTISSP_6.pdf.

NSTISSP No. 7 (February 1995). National Policy on Secure Electronic Messaging Service. Available at http://www.nstissc.gov/Assets/pdf/NSTISSP_7.pdf.

NSTISSP No. 11 (Revision June 2003). National Policy Governing the Acquisition of Information Assurance (IA) and IA-Enabled Information Technology (IT) Products. Available at http://www.nstissc.gov/Assets/pdf/NSTISSP_11_revised_fst.pdf.

NSTISSP No. 101 (September 1999). National Policy on Securing Voice Communications. Available at http://www.nstissc.gov/Assets/pdf/NSTISSP%20_101.pdf.

NSTISSP No. 200 (July 1987). National Policy on Controlled Access Protection. Available at http://www.nstissc.gov/Assets/pdf/NTISSP_200.pdf.

NSTISSD-500 (February 1993). Information Systems Security (INFOSEC) Education, Training, and Awareness. Available at http://www.nstissc.gov/Assets/pdf/ nstissd_500.pdf.

NSTISSI No. 1000 (April 2000). National Information Assurance Certification and Accreditation Process (NIACAP). Available at http://www.nstissc.gov/ Assets/pdf/nstissi_1000.pdf.

NSTISSI No. 4009 (Revised May 2003). National Information System Security (INFOSEC) Glossary. Available at http://www.nstissc.gov/Assets/pdf/ 4009.pdf.

NSTISSI No. 4011(June 1994). National Training Standard for INFOSEC Professionals. Available at http://www.nstissc.gov/Assets/pdf/4011.pdf.

NSTISSI No. 4012 (August 1997). National Training Standard for Designated Approving Authority (DAA). Available at http://www.nstissc.gov/Assets/ pdf/4012.pdf.

NSTISSI No. 4013 (March 2004). National Information Assurance Training Standard for System Administrators (SA). Available at http://www.nstissc.gov/Assets/ pdf/4013.pdf.

NSTISSI No. 4014 (August 1997). National Training Standard for Information System Security Officers. Available at http://www.nstissc.gov/Assets/pdf/4014.pdf.

NSTISSI No. 4015 (December 2000). National Training Standard for System Certifiers Available at http://www.nstissc.gov/Assets/pdf/nstissi_4015.pdf.

NSTISSI No. 7003 Protected Distribution Systems (December 1996). Available at http://www.nstissc.gov/Assets/pdf/nstissi_7003.pdf.

NSTISSAM COMPUSEC 1-98 (December 1998). The Role of Firewalls and Guards in Enclave Boundary Protection. Available at http://www.nstissc.gov/ Assets/pdf/NSTISSAM%20COMPUSEC1-98.pdf.

NSTISSAM COMPUSEC 1-99 (March 1999). Advisory Memorandum on the Transition from Trusted Computer System Evaluation Criteria to Evaluation Criteria (TCSEC) to the International Common Criteria (CC) for Information Security Technology Evaluation. Available at http://www.nstissc.gov/ Assets/pdf/nstissam_compusec_1-99.pdf.

NSTISSAM INFOSEC/1-00 (February 2000). Advisory Memorandum for the Use of FIPS 140 Validated Cryptographic Modules in Protecting Unclassified National Security Systems. Was not available for download from the Web. Contact the CNSS Secretariat, NSA, Fort Meade, MD.

NSTISSAM INFOSEC 2-00 (February 2000). Advisory Memorandum for the Strategy for Using National Information Assurance Partnership (NIAP) for the Evaluation of Commercial Off-the-Shelf (COTS) Security Enabled Information Technology Products. Available at http://www.nstissc.gov/Assets/pdf/ nstissam_infosec_2-00.pdf.

TIPS for FIPS 140: Selling Applications with Cryptography to Federal Agencies. © 2003 RSA Security. Available at http://www.rsasecurity.com/products/ bsafe/whitepapers/FIPS_WP_0603.pdf.

Web Sites

http://www.fas.org/irp/offdocs/nsd/nsd_42.htm for FOIA request of NSD 42.
http://www.rsasecurity.com/products/bsafe/whitepapers/FIPS_WP_0603.pdf.

Web Sites

14

National Institute of Standards and Technology (NIST) Publications

Introduction

The National Institute of Standards and Technology (NIST) is a nonregulatory federal agency within the U.S. Commerce Department's Technology Administration. The NIST Web site (http://www.nist.gov/) states the core purpose of NIST as "enabling a better future." The primary mission is "to develop and promote measurement, standards, and technology to enhance productivity, facilitate trade, and improve the quality of life."

NIST carries out its mission in four cooperative programs:

1. *NIST Laboratories.* The laboratories conduct research to advance the nation's technology infrastructure.
2. *Baldrige National Quality Program.* Promotes performance excellence among U.S. manufacturers, service companies, educational institutions, and healthcare providers. It also manages the annual Malcolm Baldrige National Quality Award that recognizes performance excellence and quality achievement.
3. *Manufacturing Extension Partnership.* A nationwide network of local centers offering technical and business assistance to small manufacturers.

4. *Advanced Technology Program.* Accelerates the development of innovative technologies for broad, national benefit by co-funding research and development partnerships with the private sector.

Of particular importance to Information Systems Security Engineering Professionals (ISSEPs) and the field of Information Assurance (IA) is the Computer Security Division (CSD), one of the eight divisions under the Information Technology Laboratory, which is part of the NIST Laboratories Program. The mission of NIST's CSD is to improve information systems security by:

- "Raising awareness of IT risks, vulnerabilities and protection requirements, particularly for new and emerging technologies
- Researching, studying, and advising agencies of IT vulnerabilities and devising techniques for the cost-effective security and privacy of sensitive Federal systems
- Developing standards, metrics, tests and validation programs:
  - To promote, measure, and validate security in systems and services
  - To educate consumers and
  - To establish minimum security requirements for Federal systems
- Developing guidance to increase secure IT planning, implementation, management and operation (http://csrc.nist.gov/mission.html)."

Note to ISSEP candidates: The following NIST CSD information is not listed as an (ISC)² ISSEP® exam requirement. However, it provides a good overview of the role of NIST and the various programs it supports, of which the majority of these programs are relevant to the various Information Systems Security Engineering (ISSE) model activities and in protecting U.S. Government (USG) information systems.

The CSD is grouped into five major categories:

- *Cryptographic standards and applications.* "Focus is on developing cryptographic methods for protecting the integrity, confidentiality, and authenticity of information resources; and addresses such technical areas as: secret and public key cryptographic techniques, advanced authentication systems; cryptographic protocols and interfaces; public key certificate management, smart tokens; cryptographic key escrowing; and, security architectures. Helps enable widespread implementation of cryptographic services in applications and the national infrastructure" (http://csrc.nist.gov/focus_areas. html). The Cryptographic Standards and Applications group responsibilities include the following programs:

- *Advanced Encryption Standard (AES).* Released FIPS 197 standard indicating approval for the Rijndael encryption algorithm as a FIPS approved symmetric encryption algorithm. As FIPS approved standard it may be used by USG organizations to protect sensitive information.
- *Public Key Infrastructure (PKI) and S/MIME.* Responsibility for development of a Federal Public Key Infrastructure that supports digital signatures and other public key-enabled security services. The Secure Mail program recently merged into the PKI program.
- *Cryptographic Standards Toolkit.* The Cryptographic Technology Standards and Guidance (CTSG) group is responsible for the development, maintenance, and promotion of a number of standards and guidance covering cryptographic technology. Their goal is to provide a cryptographic toolkit of standards (not applications or implementations) that Federal agencies can use to select cryptographic components.
- *Encryption Key Recovery.* This project was developed to support emergency access to encrypted data where required to support federal agencies' needs. Its current mission is work with the PKI group to establish Federal PKI standards that would include encryption key recovery.
■ *Security testing and metrics.* "Focus is on working with government and industry to establish more secure systems and networks by:
  - Developing, managing, and promoting security assessment tools, techniques, services
  - Supporting programs for testing, evaluation and validation that address such areas as development and maintenance of security metrics, security evaluation criteria and evaluation methodologies, tests and test methods
  - Evaluating security-specific criteria for laboratory accreditation
  - Providing guidance on the use of evaluated and tested products
  - Conducting research to address assurance methods and system-wide security and assessment methodologies
  - Conducting security protocol validation activities
  - Participating in the appropriate coordination with assessment-related activities of voluntary industry standards bodies and other assessment regimes" (http://csrc.nist.gov/focus_areas. html). The Security Testing and Metrics Group primary responsibilities include:
    ■ *Cryptographic Module Validation Program (CMVP).* The CMVP encompasses validation testing for cryptographic modules and algorithms. This includes validating vendor algorithms to meet cryptographic standards such as FIPS

140-2 (Security Requirements for Cryptographic Modules), FIPS 197 (AES), FIPS 46-3 (DES), FIPS 186-2 (Digital Signature), FIPS 180-1 (Secure Hash Standard), and FIPS 185 (Escrowed Encryption Standard).

■ *National Information Assurance Partnership (NIAP).* This is a USG initiative to meet the security testing needs of information technology consumers and producers. It is a collaboration between NIST and NSA. More information on NIAP is provided in Chapter 15.

■ *Security research and emerging technologies.* "Focus is on research necessary to understand and enhance the security utility of new technologies while also working to identify and mitigate vulnerabilities. Addresses such technical areas as: advanced countermeasures such as intrusion detection, firewalls, and scanning tools; security testbeds, vulnerability analysis/mitigation, access control, incident response, active code, and Internet security" (http://csrc.nist.gov/focus_areas.html). This group is responsible for the following programs:

– *Authorization Management and Advanced Access Control Models (AM&AACM).* This program is responsible for the explaining the benefits, costs, and economic impacts of the Role Based Access Controls (RBAC) standards. Of pride to the RBAC group is a 2002 benefit study conducted by the Research Triangle Institute (RTI). The RTI estimates that by 2006, between 30 and 50 percent of employees in the service sector, and between 10 and 25 percent of employees in the non-service sectors, will be managed by RBAC systems. The RTI also estimates that this degree of market penetration will result in economic benefits to the U.S. economy through 2006 of approximately $671 million in net present value terms (NIST Planning Report 02-1, February 2002).

– *IPSec.* This project is concerned with providing authentication, integrity, and confidentiality security services at the Internet (IP) layer, for both the current IP (IPv4) and the next-generation IP (IPv6).

– *Mobile Agent Intrusion Detection and Security (MAIDS).* This project has two primary research areas. The first area is evaluating existing mobile agent security mechanisms and developing new countermeasures for mobile agent security threats. The second research focus evaluates the applicability and benefits of using mobile agents for intrusion detection in large-scale enterprise applications, high-speed networks, high-volume data management requirements, and highly distributed and heterogeneous environments.

- *Critical Infrastructure Grants Program.* This program funds research leading to commercial solutions to information technology security problems central to critical infrastructure protection.
- *Smart card security and research.* This group works with industry and other government agencies to provide organizations with interoperability specifications and guidelines for an open and standard method for using smart cards.
- *Wireless security.* Provides an outreach program to both industry and USG regarding the use of the IEEE 802.11 standard for wireless LAN security. This is a new program that hopes to play a productive role in the development of wireless security standards.

■ *Security management and guidance.* "Focus is on developing security management guidance, addressing such areas as: risk management, security program management, training and awareness, contingency planning, personnel security, administrative measures, and procurement, and in facilitating security and the implementation of such guidance in Federal agencies via management and operation of the Computer Security Expert Assist Team" (http://csrc.nist. gov/focus_areas.html). This group's responsibilities include:

- *Computer security guidance.* Responsible for the NIST publications issued as Special Publications (SP), NISTIRs (Internal Reports), and ITL Bulletins. Special Publications series include the SP 500 series (Information Technology) and the SP 800 series (Computer Security). Computer security-related Federal Information Processing Standards (FIPS) are also included.
- *Program Review for Information Security Management Assistance (PRISMA).* PRISMA provides an independent review (not an audit or inspection) of the maturity of an agency's IT security program. Agencies request this review from the PRISMA office (formerly known as the Computer Security Expert Assistance Team [CSEAT]).

■ *Outreach, awareness, and education.* "Focus is on activities to support wider awareness of the importance and need for IT security, promoting the understanding of IT security vulnerabilities and corrective measures, and in facilitating greater awareness of the Division's programs and projects" (http://csrc.nist.gov/focus_areas. html). Other programs are involved with and support this initiative. The primary activities include:

- *Computer Security Resource Center (CSRC).* Provides information related to information assurance through various media, including the CSRC Web site.
- *Small business computer security workshops.* NIST, in co-sponsorship with the Small Business Administration (SBA) and the Federal

Bureau of Investigation (FBI), conducts workshops on information security threats and solutions. The workshops are designed for small businesses and not-for-profit organizations.

- *Information Security and Privacy Advisory Board (ISPAB).* The objectives of the ISPAB are to identify emerging managerial, technical, administrative, and physical safeguard issues relative to information security and privacy; advise on information security and privacy issues pertaining to Federal government information systems; and to annually report its findings.
- *Federal Computer Security Program Managers' Forum.* NIST sponsors an informal group to promote the sharing of computer security information among federal agencies. The Forum hosts the Federal Agency Security Practices Web site, maintains an extensive e-mail list, and holds bimonthly meetings to discuss current issues and developments of interest to those responsible for protecting sensitive (unclassified) federal systems.
- *Federal Information Systems Security Educators' Association (FISSEA).* The FISSEA is an organization run by and for Federal information systems security professionals. It assists Federal agencies in meeting their computer security training responsibilities.

Brief descriptions of current NIST projects are also available from the "Guide to NIST" at www.nist.gov/guide.

As shown in Figure 14.1, this chapter is divided into two sections representing information on two types of NIST issuances: (1) Federal Information Processing Standards (FIPS) and (2) Special Publications (SPs).

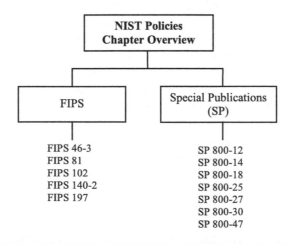

Figure 14.1   NIST Chapter overview.

One key item to remember is that FIPS are mandatory and SPs are recommended guidelines. Also, after a predetermined period of time, some SPs may become FIPS and thus become mandatory standards. FIPS and SPs are defined as:

- FIPS focus on design, implementation, and approval of cryptographic algorithms. The chapter includes high-level descriptions on FIPS Pub. 46-3, FIPS Pub. 81, FIPS Pub. 102, FIPS Pub. 140-2, and FIPS Pub. 197.
- SPs are recommended guidelines for engineering, managing, processing, protecting, and controlling national security and sensitive but unclassified information. The SPs are *not* national policy. The NIST SPs discussed in this chapter include SP 800-12, SP 800-14, SP 800-18, SP 800-25, SP 800-27, SP 800-30, and SP 800-47. Note that SP 800-55 and SP 800-26 are discussed in Chapter 7.

Note to ISSEP candidates: The ISSEP should understand the difference in encryption standards and policies to assist in the design of networks where such security features may be implemented. In addition, the ISSEP should be familiar with the NIST principles and guidelines and be able to use this information in the design, development, and operation of government information systems.

Federal Information Processing Standards (FIPS)

FIPS are issued by NIST after approval by the Secretary of Commerce pursuant to Section 5131 of the Information Technology Management Reform Act of 1996 and the Computer Security Act of 1987, Public Law 104-106. The five issuances highlighted in this chapter are either listed as ISSEP (ISC)[2] exam requirements or are pertinent to ISSEP job functions related to cryptography.

Each FIPS provides applicability sections noting how it must be used in Federal information systems. FIPS do not apply to national security systems, which must follow policies from the Committee of National Security Systems (CNSS).

The five FIPS discussed in this section are:

1. FIPS 46-3, "Data Encryption Standard (DES)" (October 1999)
2. FIPS 81, "DES Mode of Operation" (December 1980)
3. FIPS 102, "Guidelines for Computer Security Certification and Accreditation" (September 1983) (FIPS 102 is an outdated policy but it is listed on the ISSEP (ISC)[2] exam requirements.)

4. FIPS 140-2, "Security Requirement for Cryptographic Modules" (May 2001) (FIPS 140-2 supersedes FIPS 140-1 published in January 1994.)
5. FIPS 197, "Advance Encryption Standard" (November 2001)

Note that FIPS 199 is discussed in detail in Chapter 2. FIPS 201 (February 2005) "Personal Identity Verification (PIN) for Federal Employees and Contractors" is a recent FIPS that specifies the architecture and technical requirements for a common identification standard for federal employees and contractors. The goal is to verify the claimed identity of those seeking physical access to federally controlled government facilities.

Note: The issuances can be found in Adobe® PDF format in the library section of the NIST Web site (http://www.csrc.nist.gov/publications/fips/index.html). Some are not available online but can be ordered through the NIST FIPS Web site.

The FIPS in this section discuss cryptography. As an ISSEP, you may hear the terminology of Type I or Type II encryption devices. The following definitions from FIPS 185 (February 1994) are provided as a reference:

■ *Type I cryptography.* A cryptographic algorithm or device approved by the National Security Agency for protecting classified information.
■ *Type II cryptography.* A cryptographic algorithm or device approved by the National Security Agency for protecting sensitive unclassified information in systems as specified in Section 2315 of Title 10 United States Code, or Section 3502(2) of Title 44, United States Code.
■ *Type III cryptography.* A cryptographic algorithm or device approved as a Federal Information Processing Standard.
■ *Type III (E) cryptography.* A Type III algorithm or device that is approved for export from the United States.

FIPS 46-3, Data Encryption Standard (DES) (Reaffirmed October 1999)

The first version of FIPS 46 became effective July 1977 and was reaffirmed in 1983, 1988, 1993, and 1999. It explains the necessity of using cryptography to provide adequate security to USG information. The latest release, FIPS 46-3, specifies two cryptographic algorithms that can be used by Federal organizations to protect sensitive data: the Data Encryption Standard (DES) and the Triple Data Encryption Algorithm (TDEA). The standard must be reviewed every five years. Currently, it is due for update, especially because DES is only for legacy systems. Triple DES and the Advanced Encryption Standard (AES) are the common algorithms.

FIPS 46-3 acknowledges that specific utilization of encryption and the implementation of the DES and TDEA are based on many factors particular to the computer system and its associated components. However, it does provide the following: "cryptography is used to protect data while it is being communicated between two points or while it is stored in a medium vulnerable to physical theft. Communication security provides protection to data by enciphering it at the transmitting point and deciphering it at the receiving point. File security provides protection to data by enciphering it when it is recorded on a storage medium and deciphering it when it is read back from the storage medium. In the first case, the key must be available at the transmitter and receiver simultaneously during communication. In the second case, the key must be maintained and accessible for the duration of the storage period" (p. 3).

Most importantly, the FIPS 46-3 standard states the following:

1. "Triple DES (i.e., TDEA), as specified in ANSI X9.52 will be recognized as a FIPS approved algorithm. (Note: When used in conjunction with American National Standards Institute (ANSI) X9.52 standard, FIPS 46-3 provides a complete description of the mathematical algorithms for encrypting and decrypting binary coded information.)
2. Triple DES will be the FIPS approved symmetric encryption algorithm of choice.
3. Single DES (i.e., DES) will be permitted for legacy systems only. New procurements to support legacy systems should, where feasible, use Triple DES products running in the single DES configuration.
4. Government organizations with legacy DES systems are encouraged to transition to Triple DES based on a prudent strategy that matches the strength of the protective measures against the associated risk (p. 4-5)."

Note to ISSEP candidates: The following DES background information is for reference only.

DES Background Information

This information is based on material from the "Official (ISC)² Guide to the CISSP Exam" (2004, p. 408–409 and p. 412).

Computer cryptography began in the 1960s, primarily because organizations needed secure ways to transmit information across the ever-expanding telecommunications links. Because there was no standard, financial institutions wanted a standard encryption method that they could have confidence in and could use for secure data exchange. Based on this identified need, in 1972, NIST assisted in the development of a secure cryptographic algorithm for sensitive, not government classified information. In 1974 it settled on DES, a method submitted by IBM. Despite some controversy, in 1977, DES was finally adopted as the federal standard (FIPS 46) for unclassified documents and has the most widely used cryptographic method in history.

NIST made the DES design public, and the proliferation of computer technology permitted faster processing, making software implementations of DES feasible. The 1977 FIPS 46 standard mandated a review every five years. In 1983, DES was approved for a further five years. In 1987, DES was approved for another five years, with the provision that it would expire before 1992. In 1993, DES was again approved for another five years. In 1997, NIST solicited candidates for a new symmetric key cryptography standard called the Advanced Encryption Standard (AES).

DES is a symmetric key cryptography algorithm that uses a key of 56 bits and 16 rounds of transposition and substitution to encrypt each group of eight (64-bit) plaintext letters. The original IBM design proposed a key length of 128 bits, but the NSA shortened it to 56 bits. In 1977, a 56-bit key was considered an excellent defense.

The best attack on DES is brute force — to try each possible key. A cryptanalyst without the key would need to try all 56 combinations of 0's and 1's (72 quadrillion possibilities) to find the correct key. Working at one million keys per second, this would take an attacker 1000 years to try them all. In the late 1970s, the computer could try half of the DES keys in about 100,000 days (300 years). With the advent of faster computer chips, this requirement has been greatly reduced. Computers have become about 100,000 times more powerful and the original 56-bit DES key is not considered adequate. This led to the development of Double and Triple DES.

Increasing the key length is an effective defense against a brute-force (trying every key) attack. Double and Triple DES improved the DES algorithm's resistance to a brute-force attack by effectively increasing the key. This is accomplished by using multiple 56-bit DES keys.

Double DES refers to the use of two DES encryptions with two separate keys. This seemed an improvement; however, there is an attack on Double DES that reduces its effective number of keys to about the same number as in DES. This attack is known as the "meet-in-the-middle" attack and it reduces the strength of Double DES to almost the same as DES, which doesn't make it practical for use.

Triple DES is more secure, so much so that although attacks on it have been proposed, the data requirements have made them impractical. With Triple DES uses three DES encryptions with either two or three different and separate keys. The various ways of using Triple DES include:

- DES-EEE3: three DES encryptions with three different keys.
- DES-EDE3: three DES operations in the sequence encrypt-decrypt-encrypt with three different keys.
- DES-EEE2 and DES-EDE2: same as the previous formats except that the first and third operations use the same key.

FIPS 81, DES Mode of Operation (December 1980)

FIPS 81 provides information related to the original FIPS 46 standard released in 1977. While FIPS 46-3 specified that DES and now Triple DES cryptographic algorithms must be used for the cryptographic protection of Sensitive but Unclassified (SBU) computer data, FIPS 81 explains the four modes for DES operation. FIPS 81 also includes a May 1996 Change Notice that provided editorial changes, updated references, a correction to Figure 3, and updated guidance to Federal agencies regarding the 64-bit Output Feedback Mode.

An important element of U.S. cryptographic standards is the regulations pertaining to export of the cryptographic algorithms. Devices implementing the FIPS 81 standard and technical data must also comply with the Federal Regulations in Title 22, Code of Federal Regulations, Parts 121–128.

The FIPS 81 standard provides specifications of the recommended modes of operation but does not specify the necessary and sufficient conditions for their secure implementation in a particular application. FIPS 81specifies the numbering of data bits, how the bits are encrypted and decrypted, and the data paths and the data processing necessary for encrypting and decrypting data or messages.

The four DES modes of operation specify how data will be encrypted (cryptographically protected) and decrypted (returned to original form). FIPS specifies these four modes because of their capability to provide acceptable levels of protection for all anticipated unclassified Federal information system encryption applications. The modes are:

- Electronic Codebook (ECB) mode
- Cipher Block Chaining (CBC) mode
- Cipher Feedback (CFB) mode
- Output Feedback (OFB) mode

ECB and CBC are considered block ciphers, while CFB and OFB are considered stream ciphers. Stream modes are usually implemented in hardware, whereas the block modes are usually implemented in software.

A brief overview of these four modes is provided. This discussion will be high level. The detailed mathematical explanations are not discussed here but are reserved for the FIPS 81 document. The content of this section is, for the most part, direct quotes from the FIPS 81. *The ISSEP does not need to know the exact details of these algorithms; it is provided simply as reference material.*

As background, the following provides the basics terms and conditions for cryptography based on FIPS 81 information:

> Binary data may be cryptographically protected (encrypted) using devices implementing the algorithm specified in the Data Encryption Standard (DES) (FIPS PUB 46) in conjunction with a cryptographic key. The cryptographic key controls the encryption process and the identical key must also be used in the decryption process to obtain the original data. Since the DES is publicly defined, **cryptographic security depends on the secrecy of the cryptographic key.** (FIPS 81, Section 1: Introduction)

> Unencrypted data is called plaintext. Encryption (also called enciphering) is the process of transforming plaintext into ciphertext. Decryption (also called deciphering) is the inverse transformation. The encryption and decryption processes are performed according to a set of rules, called an algorithm that is typically based on a parameter called a key. The key is usually the only parameter that must be provided to or by the users of a cryptographic system and must be kept secret. The period of time over which a particular key is used to encrypt or decrypt data is called its crypto period. (FIPS 81, Appendix A)

> Two categories of methods for incorporating the DES in a cryptographic system are **block methods** and **stream methods**. In a block method, the DES input block is (or is a simple function of) the plaintext to be encrypted and the DES output block is the ciphertext. A stream method is based on generating a pseudo-random binary stream of bits, and then using the exclusive-OR binary operation to combine this pseudo-random sequence with the plaintext to produce the ciphertext. Since the exclusive-OR operator is its own binary inverse, the same pseudo-random binary stream is used for both the encryption of plaintext, P, and the decryption of ciphertext, C. If 0 is the pseudo-random binary stream, then $C = P \wedge 0$ and inversely, $P = C \wedge 0$. (FIPS 81, Appendix A)

Electronic Codebook (ECB) Mode

With a block cipher, to process more than 64 bits of data (for example, an e-mail message of several thousand bytes), the simplest approach is to start at the beginning of the plaintext file and process 64-bit blocks one block at a time, until you reach the end of the file. Decrypting would begin at the start of the ciphertext file, and process 64-bit blocks one block at a time until you reach the end of the file. This ECB approach is simple and fast to implement but has the following problems:

- Each 64-bit chunk of ciphertext is a separately attackable problem, using exactly the same key. In many files, the first few bytes may be known or guessable, possibly allowing a known plaintext attack, and the recovered key could then be used to decrypt the remaining blocks.
- A given 64-bit value in the plaintext will always produce the same ciphertext.
- A given message and key will always produce the same ciphertext.

FIPS 81 defines ECB as:

The Electronic Codebook (ECB) mode is a basic, block, cryptographic method, which transforms 64 bits of input to 64 bits of output as specified in FIPS PUB 46. The analogy to a codebook arises because the same plaintext block always produces the same ciphertext block for a given cryptographic key. Thus a list (or codebook) of plaintext blocks and corresponding ciphertext blocks theoretically could be constructed for any given key. In electronic implementation the codebook entries are calculated each time for the plaintext to be encrypted and, inversely, for the ciphertext to be decrypted.

Since each bit of an ECB output block is a complex function of all 64 bits of the input block and all 56 independent (non-parity) bits of the cryptographic key, a single bit error in either a ciphertext block or the non-parity key bits used for decryption will cause the decrypted plaintext block to have an average error rate of fifty percent. However, an error in one ECB ciphertext block will not affect the decryption of other blocks, i.e., there is no error extension between ECB blocks.

If block boundaries are lost between encryption and decryption (e.g., a bit slip), then synchronization between the encryption and decryption operations will be lost until correct block boundaries are reestablished. The results of all decryption operations will be incorrect until this occurs.

Since the ECB mode is a 64-bit block cipher, an ECB device must encrypt data in integral multiples of sixty-four bits. If a user has less than sixty-four bits to encrypt, then the least significant bits of the unused portion of the input data block must be padded, e.g., filled with random or pseudo-random bits, prior to ECB encryption. The corresponding decrypting device must then discard these padding bits after decryption of the ciphertext block.

The same input block always produces the same output block under a fixed key in ECB mode. If this is undesirable in a particular application, the CBC, CFB or OFB modes should be used (Appendix B).

Cipher Block Chaining (CBC) Mode

A simple modification to ECB mode that adds encryptive feedback across the blocks effectively solves the problems associated with ECB. This also makes the file or message encryption much stronger. The basic idea is to generate a block of 64 randomly chosen bits, with the key word being "randomly." This is called an Initialization Vector, or IV. The IV itself is encrypted with DES in ECB mode and sent as the first block of ciphertext. You then exclusive OR (XOR) this IV with the first 64-bit block of plaintext, then encrypt the resulting value with DES to produce the second block of ciphertext. The next block of plaintext is XORed not with the IV, but with the ciphertext from the previous block, then encrypted with DES to make the next block of ciphertext. This is repeated until the end of the file.

To decrypt the file, you recover the original IV by decrypting the first 64-bit block of ciphertext with the key. You then decrypt the second block of ciphertext with DES and XOR the result with the IV to recover the first block of plaintext. You decrypt the third block of ciphertext and XOR the result with the previous block of ciphertext to recover the next block of plaintext. This is repeated until the end of the file, and then the recovered IV can be discarded. The advantages of CBC over ECB include:

- Even if the plaintext is simple ASCII text, decrypting any block does not produce any recognizable pattern.
- The encryptive feedback (chaining) between blocks destroys any long running pattern — even a file of all zeros would produce no repeating 64-bit groups in the ciphertext.
- If the IV is chosen differently each time, even the exact same file will produce different ciphertext each time it is sent.

FIPS 81 defines CBC as:

CBC is a block cipher system in which the first plaintext data block is exclusive-ORed with a block of pseudo-random data prior to being processed through the DES. The resulting ciphertext block is then exclusive-ORed with the next plaintext data block to form the next input block to the DES, thus chaining together blocks of ciphertext. The chaining of ciphertext blocks provides an error extension characteristic which is valuable in protecting against fraudulent data alteration. A CBC authentication technique is described in Appendix F of FIPS 81.

The CBC mode produces the same ciphertext whenever the same plaintext is encrypted using the same key and Initialization Vector (IV). Users who are concerned about this characteristic should incorporate a unique identifier (e.g., a one-up counter) at the beginning of each CBC message within a cryptographic period in order to insure unique ciphertext. If the key and the IV are the same and no identifier precedes each message, messages that have the same beginning will have the same ciphertext when encrypted in the CBC mode until the blocks that differ in the two messages are encrypted.

Since the CBC mode is a block method of encryption, it must operate on 64-bit data blocks. Partial data blocks (blocks of less than 64 bits) require special handling. One method of encrypting a final partial data block of a message is described below. Others may be defined for special applications.

The following method may be used for applications where the length of the ciphertext can be greater than the length of the plaintext. In this case the final partial data block of a message is padded in the least significant bits positions with '0's, '1's or pseudo-random bits. The decryptor will have to know when and to what extent padding has occurred. This can be accomplished explicitly, e.g., using a padding indicator, or implicitly, e.g., using constant length transactions.

The padding indicator will depend on the data being encrypted. If the data is pure binary, then the partial data block should be left justified in the input block and the unused bits of the block set to the complement of the last data bit, i.e., if the last data bit of the message is '0' then '1's are used as padding bits and if the last data bit is '1' then '0's are used. The input block is then encrypted (Appendix C).

Cipher Feedback (CFB) Mode

Cipher Feedback mode (CFB) emulates a stream cipher. In this mode, the ciphertext is fed back into the key-generating device to create the next key stream. Each encryption depends on previous ciphertext. CFB is best for encrypting a stream of data one character at a time (e.g., between a terminal and a host). With 8-bit CFB, encryption is able to start and operate on each 8-bit character. Sometimes it is desirable to use a block cipher in a mode that approximates a stream cipher — where the receiver or transmitter can begin to play with the block, before its transmission is complete. This is exactly what CFB does. With CFB, a block-sized buffer is viewed as a shift register composed of *units*. After filling this register for the first time with a seed, it is encoded using an encryption function. The left-most byte of the output is considered to be "live." That is, it is the key to encrypt the next unit of plaintext. That unit of plaintext is then pushed into the right side of the register, shifting the register left. That process is repeated to encode the next unit of plaintext.

CFB requires a unique IV for each message to avoid being vulnerable to replay attacks. An IV is defined as a non-secret binary vector used as the initializing input algorithm for the encryption of a plaintext block sequence. It increases security by introducing additional cryptographic variance and by synchronizing cryptographic equipment.

Errors in this mode of DES will propagate. For example, 8-bit CFB will produce 9 bytes of garbled plaintext from the point of error if a 1-bit error has occurred in the ciphertext.

FIPS 81 (1980, Appendix D) defines CFB as:

> The CFB mode is a stream method of encryption in which the DES is used to generate pseudo-random bits, which are exclusive-ORed with binary plaintext to form ciphertext. The ciphertext is fed back to form the next DES input block. Identical messages that are encrypted using the CFB mode and different IVs will have different ciphertexts. IVs that are shorter than 64 bits should be put in the least significant bits of the first DES input block and the unused, most significant, bits initialized to '0's.

> In the CFB mode, errors in any K-bit unit of ciphertext will affect the decryption of the garbled ciphertext and also the decryption of succeeding ciphertext until the bits in error have been shifted out of the CFB input block. The first affected K-bit unit of plaintext will be garbled in exactly those places where the ciphertext is in error. Succeeding decrypted plaintext will have an average error rate of fifty percent until all errors have

been shifted out of the DES input block. Assuming no additional errors are encountered during this time, the correct plaintext will then be obtained.

If K-bit boundaries are lost during decryption, then cryptographic synchronization will be lost until cryptographic initialization is performed or until 64 bits after the K-bit boundaries have been reestablished.

The encryption and decryption processes in the CFB mode both use the encrypt state of the DES. Examples of 1-, 8-, and 64-bit CFB mode are given in Tables D1, D2, and D3, respectively of the FIPS 81.

The 7-bit CFB alternative mode is defined in the standard in order to encipher and decipher 7-bit codes and still use an 8-bit feedback path. Most commercial implementations of the DES are designed to efficiently handle 8-bit bytes of data and key. Most computer and communication systems of recent architecture are also designed to efficiently handle full 8-bit bytes. However, some systems use the most significant bit as a parity bit. These systems often generate the parity bit during transmission and check its validity during reception (Appendix D).

Output Feedback (OFB) Mode

Output Feedback mode (OFB) is another DES mode that emulates a stream cipher in which errors in the ciphertext are not extended to cause additional errors in the decrypted plaintext. The key stream that is XORed with the message stream is constantly changing because of the feedback process used to generate the key stream. OFB is best for error-prone environments. It is used for handling asynchronous data streams (keyboard input) because most of the "cipher" is performed based on prior input and is ready when the last n-bit character is typed in. OFB requires an initialization vector. This prevents codebook collection problems, but OFB remains susceptible to block replay attacks. Errors do not propagate or extend. However, several analyses have shown that unless the n-bit feedback size is the same as the block size, the algorithm strength will be significantly reduced.

FIPS 81 defines OFB as:

> The Output Feedback (OFB) mode is an additive stream cipher in which errors in the ciphertext are not extended to cause additional errors in the decrypted plaintext. One bit in error in

the ciphertext causes only one bit to be in error in the decrypted plaintext. Therefore, this mode cannot be used for data authentication but is useful in applications where a few errors in the decrypted plaintext are acceptable.

In the OFB mode, the same K bits of the DES output block that are used to encrypt a K-bit unit of plaintext are fed back for the next input block. This feedback is completely independent of all plaintext and all ciphertext. As a result, there is no error extension in OFB mode. If cryptographic synchronization is lost in the OFB mode, then cryptographic initialization must be performed. The OFB mode is not a self-synchronizing cryptographic mode (Appendix E).

FIPS 102, Guidelines for Computer Security Certification and Accreditation (September 1983)

FIPS 102 (1983) was a guideline for establishing a comprehensive program and a technical process for certifying and accrediting sensitive computer applications. NIST SP 800-37 (May 2004), "Guide for the Security Certification and Accreditation of Federal Information Systems," is intended to provide guidelines to Federal agencies in lieu of FIPS 102, which is being rescinded. For more information on NIST SP 800-37, refer to Chapter 9.

FIPS 140-2, Security Requirement for Cryptographic Modules (May 2001; Supersedes FIPS 140-1, January 1994)

FIPS 140-2 (2001) specifies the security requirements that will be satisfied by a cryptographic module utilized within a security system protecting sensitive but unclassified information. A cryptographic module is defined as "a set of hardware, software, firmware, or some combination thereof that implements cryptographic functions or processes, including cryptographic algorithms and, optionally, key generation, and is contained within a defined cryptographic boundary" (FIPS 140-2, p. 13).

Note to the ISSEP candidate: The information provided for FIPS 140-2 is extensive. The ISSEP should have an overall grasp of the security levels and when they would be used. Table 14.1 provides a good reference for this information. I did not find it necessary to memorize every detail of the four security levels and eleven security requirements, but it is provided so that the ISSEP can review the intention of the standard. For example,

Table 14.1 Summary of Security Requirements

	Security Level 1	Security Level 2	Security Level 3	Security Level 4
Cryptographic Module Specification	Specification of cryptographic module, cryptographic boundary, Approved algorithms, and Approved modes of operation. Description of cryptographic module, including all hardware, software, and firmware components. Statement of module security policy.			
Cryptographic Module Ports and Interfaces	Required and optional interfaces. Specification of all interfaces and of all input and output data paths.		Data ports for unprotected critical security parameters logically separated from other data ports.	
Roles, Services, and Authentication	Logical separation of required and optional roles and services.	Role-based or identity-based operator authentication.	Identity-based operator authentication.	
Finite State Model	Specification of finite state model. Required states and optional states. State transition diagram and specification of state transitions.			
Physical Security	Production grade equipment.	Locks or tamper evidence.	Tamper detection and response for covers and doors.	Tamper detection and response envelope. EFP and EFT.
Operational Environment	Single operator. Executable code. Approved integrity techniques.	Referenced PPs evaluated at EAL2 with specified discretionary access control mechanisms and auditing.	Referenced PPs plus trusted path evaluated at EAL3 plus security policy modeling.	Referenced PPs plus trusted path evaluated at EAL4.

Table 14.1 (continued) Summary of Security Requirements

	Security Level 1	Security Level 2	Security Level 3	Security Level 4
Cryptographic Key Management	Key management mechanisms: random number and key generation, key establishment, key distribution, key entry/output, key storage, and CSP zeroization.			
	Secret and private keys established using manual methods may be entered or output in plaintext form.		Secret and private keys established using manual methods shall be entered or output encrypted or with split knowledge procedures.	
EMI/EMC	47 CFR FCC Part 15. Subpart B, Class A (Business use). Applicable FCC requirements for radio signals.		47 CFR FCC Part 15. Subpart B, Class B (Home use).	
Self-Tests	Power-up tests: cryptographic algorithm tests, software/firmware integrity tests, critical functions tests. Conditional tests.		Statistical RNG tests — callable on demand.	Statistical RNG tests — performed at power-up.
Design Assurance	Configuration management (CM). Secure installation and generation. Design and policy correspondence. Guidance documents.	CM system. Secure distribution. Functional specification.	High-level language implementation.	Formal model. Detailed explanations (informal proofs). Preconditions and post-conditions.
Mitigation of Other Attacks	Specification of mitigation of attacks for which no testable requirements are currently available.			

Source: From FIPS 140-2, 2001, p. 12.

a question might read: Which FIPS 140-2 security level requires an operator to identify him/herself using an identity based authentication mechanism?

The FIPS 140-2 security requirements are derived from the following high-level functional security objectives for a cryptographic module:

- To employ and correctly implement the Approved security functions for the protection of sensitive information.
- To protect a cryptographic module from unauthorized operation or use.
- To prevent the unauthorized disclosure of the contents of the cryptographic module, including plaintext cryptographic keys and Critical Security Parameters (CSPs).
- To prevent the unauthorized and undetected modification of the cryptographic module and cryptographic algorithms, including the unauthorized modification, substitution, insertion, and deletion of cryptographic keys and CSPs.
- To provide indications of the operational state of the cryptographic module.
- To ensure that the cryptographic module performs properly when operating in an Approved mode of operation.
- To detect errors in the operation of the cryptographic module and to prevent the compromise of sensitive data and CSPs resulting from these errors (p. 11).

The cryptographic module receives a security level rating based on a scale of 1 to 4 that has increasing, qualitative levels of security. The four security levels are specified for each of eleven requirement areas. Each security level offers an increase in security over the preceding level, with Level 1 providing a minimal level of security and Level 4 providing the highest level of security.

The working group for FIPS 140 identified requirements for the four security levels to provide for a wide spectrum of data sensitivity (e.g., low value administrative data, million-dollar fund transfers, and life protecting data) and a diversity of application environments (e.g., a guarded facility, an office, and a completely unprotected location).

Brief descriptions of the four security levels are:

- *Security Level 1.* Provides the lowest level of security. It specifies basic security requirements for a cryptographic module.
- *Security Level 2.* Improves the physical security of a Security Level 1 cryptographic module by adding the requirement for tamper-evident coatings or seals, or for pick-resistant locks.

- *Security Level 3*. Requires enhanced physical security, attempting to prevent the intruder from gaining access to critical security parameters held within the module.
- *Security Level 4*. Provides the highest level of security. Level 4 physical security provides an envelope of protection around the cryptographic module to detect a penetration of the device from any direction.

The actual security level definitions from FIPS 140-2 are:

Security Level 1

Security Level 1 provides the lowest level of security. Basic security requirements are specified for a cryptographic module (e.g., at least one Approved algorithm or Approved security function shall be used). No specific physical security mechanisms are required in a Security Level 1 cryptographic module beyond the basic requirement for production-grade components. An example of a Security Level 1 cryptographic module is a Personal Computer (PC) encryption board.

Security Level 1 allows the software and firmware components of a cryptographic module to be executed on a general purpose computing system using an unevaluated operating system. Such implementations may be appropriate for some low-level security applications when other controls, such as physical security, network security, and administrative procedures are limited or nonexistent. The implementation of cryptographic software may be more cost-effective than corresponding hardware-based mechanisms, enabling organizations to select from alternative cryptographic solutions to meet lower-level security requirements (p. 12).

Security Level 2

Security Level 2 enhances the physical security mechanisms of a Security Level 1 cryptographic module by adding the requirement for tamper-evidence, which includes the use of tamper-evident coatings or seals or for pick-resistant locks on removable covers or doors of the module. Tamper-evident coatings or seals are placed on a cryptographic module so that the coating or seal must be broken to attain physical access to the plaintext cryptographic keys and Critical Security Parameters (CSPs) within the module. Tamper-evident seals or pick-resistant locks are placed on covers or doors to protect against unauthorized physical access.

Security Level 2 requires, at a minimum, role-based authentication in which a cryptographic module authenticates the authorization of an operator to assume a specific role and perform a corresponding set of services.

Security Level 2 allows the software and firmware components of a cryptographic module to be executed on a general purpose computing system using an operating system that:

- Meets the functional requirements specified in the Common Criteria (CC) Protection Profiles (PPs) listed in Annex B; and
- Is evaluated at the CC Evaluation Assurance Level (EAL) 2 (or higher).

An equivalent evaluated trusted operating system may be used. A trusted operating system provides a level of trust so that cryptographic modules executing on general purpose computing platforms are comparable to cryptographic modules implemented using dedicated hardware systems (p. 1-2).

Security Level 3

In addition to the tamper-evident physical security mechanisms required at Security Level 2, Security Level 3 attempts to prevent the intruder from gaining access to CSPs held within the cryptographic module. Physical security mechanisms required at Security Level 3 are intended to have a high probability of detecting and responding to attempts at physical access, use or modification of the cryptographic module. The physical security mechanisms may include the use of strong enclosures and tamper detection/response circuitry that zeroizes all plaintext CSPs when the removable covers/doors of the cryptographic module are opened.

Security Level 3 requires identity-based authentication mechanisms, enhancing the security provided by the role-based authentication mechanisms specified for Security Level 2. A cryptographic module authenticates the identity of an operator and verifies that the identified operator is authorized to assume a specific role and perform a corresponding set of services.

Security Level 3 requires the entry or output of plaintext CSPs (including the entry or output of plaintext CSPs using split knowledge procedures) be performed using ports that are physically separated from other ports, or interfaces that are logically separated using a trusted path from other interfaces. Plaintext CSPs may be entered into or output from the cryptographic module in encrypted form (in which case they may travel through enclosing or intervening systems).

Security Level 3 allows the software and firmware components of a cryptographic module to be executed on a general purpose computing system using an operating system that

- Meets the functional requirements specified in the PPs listed in Annex B with the additional functional requirement of a Trusted Path (FTP_TRP.1), and
- Is evaluated at the CC evaluation assurance level EAL 3 (or higher) with the additional assurance requirement of an Informal Target of Evaluation (TOE) Security Policy Model (ADV_SPM.1).

An equivalent evaluated trusted operating system may be used. The implementation of a trusted path protects plaintext CSPs and the software and firmware components of the cryptographic module from other untrusted software or firmware that may be executing on the system (p. 2-3).

Security Level 4

Security Level 4 provides the highest level of security defined in this standard. At this security level, the physical security mechanisms provide a complete envelope of protection around the cryptographic module with the intent of detecting and responding to all unauthorized attempts at physical access. Penetration of the cryptographic module enclosure from any direction has a very high probability of being detected; resulting in the immediate zeroization of all plaintext CSPs. Security Level 4 cryptographic modules are useful for operation in physically unprotected environments.

Security Level 4 also protects a cryptographic module against a security compromise due to environmental conditions or fluctuations outside of the module's normal operating ranges for voltage and temperature. Intentional excursions beyond the normal operating ranges may be used by an attacker to thwart a cryptographic module's defenses. A cryptographic module is required to either include special environmental protection features designed to detect fluctuations and zeroize CSPs, or to undergo rigorous environmental failure testing to provide a reasonable assurance that the module will not be affected by fluctuations outside of the normal operating range in a manner that can compromise the security of the module.

Security Level 4 allows the software and firmware components of a cryptographic module to be executed on a general purpose computing system using an operating system that:

- Meets the functional requirements specified for Security Level 3, and
- Is evaluated at the CC evaluation assurance level EAL 4 (or higher).

An equivalent evaluated trusted operating system may be used (p. 3).

The 11 security requirement areas identified in FIPS 140 relate to the secure design, implementation, and self-tests of cryptographic modules. These areas are:

- *Cryptographic module specification.* A cryptographic module shall implement at least one Approved security function used in an Approved mode of operation.
- *Cryptographic module ports and interfaces.* A cryptographic module shall restrict all information flow and physical access points to physical ports and logical interfaces that define all entry and exit points to and from the module.
- *Roles, services, and authentication.* A cryptographic module shall support authorized roles for operators and corresponding services within each role. *Services* shall refer to all of the services, operations, or functions that can be performed by a cryptographic module, such as show status or perform self-test. *Authentication* mechanisms may be required within a cryptographic module to authenticate an operator accessing the module and to verify that the operator is authorized to assume the requested role and perform services within that role.

■ *Finite state model.* The operation of a cryptographic module shall be specified using a finite state model (or equivalent) represented by a state transition diagram and/or a state transition table. The state transition diagram and/or state transition table includes:
   – All operational and error states of a cryptographic module
   – The corresponding transitions from one state to another
   – The input events that cause transitions from one state to another
   – The output events resulting from transitions from one state to another

■ *Physical security.* A cryptographic module shall employ physical security mechanisms to restrict unauthorized physical access to the contents of the module and to deter unauthorized use or modification of the module (including substitution of the entire module) when installed. Physical security requirements are specified for three defined physical embodiments of a cryptographic module:
   – *Single-chip cryptographic modules* are physical embodiments in which a single integrated circuit (IC) chip may be used as a stand-alone device or may be embedded within an enclosure or a product that may not be physically protected. Examples of single-chip cryptographic modules include single IC chips or smart cards with a single IC chip.
   – *Multiple-chip embedded cryptographic modules* are physical embodiments in which two or more IC chips are interconnected and are embedded within an enclosure or a product that may not be physically protected. Examples of multiple-chip embedded cryptographic modules include adapters and expansion boards.
   – *Multiple-chip standalone cryptographic modules* are physical embodiments in which two or more IC chips are interconnected and the entire enclosure is physically protected. Examples of multiple-chip, stand-alone cryptographic modules include encrypting routers or secure radios.

■ *Operational environment.* This refers to the management of the software, firmware, and/or hardware components required for the module to operate. The operational environment can be non-modifiable or modifiable, but it must be documented according to the security level requirements.

■ *Cryptographic key management.* The security requirements for cryptographic key management encompass the entire life cycle of cryptographic keys, cryptographic key components, and CSPs employed by the cryptographic module. Key management includes random number and key generation, key establishment, key distribution, key entry/output, key storage, and key zeroization.

- *Electromagnetic interference/electromagnetic compatibility (EMI/ EMC).* Cryptographic modules must meet specific requirements for EMI/EMC based on the security level. Documentation shall include proof of conformance to EMI/EMC requirements.
- *Self-tests.* A cryptographic module shall perform power-up self-tests and conditional self-tests to ensure that the module is functioning properly.
- *Design assurance.* This refers to the use of best practices by the vendor of a cryptographic module during the design, deployment, and operation of a cryptographic module, providing assurance that the module is properly tested, configured, delivered, installed, and developed, and that the proper operator guidance documentation is provided.
- *Mitigation of other attacks.* Cryptographic modules may be susceptible to other attacks for which testable security requirements were not available at the time this version of the standard was issued (e.g., power analysis, timing analysis, and/or fault induction) or the attacks were outside of the scope of the standard (e.g., TEMPEST). If a cryptographic module is designed to mitigate one or more specific attacks, then the module's security policy shall specify the security mechanisms employed by the module to mitigate the attack(s). (Definitions for each from FIPS 140-2, 2001, pp. 13–39.)

Table 14.1 summarizes the security requirements for the four security levels and the eleven categories. The requirements for each security level are in the applicable cell of the table. For example, "Cryptographic Module Specification" applies to each level, while "Roles, Services, and Authentication" has a different requirement for security Levels 1 and 2 but the same requirement for security Levels 3 and 4.

To be FIPS 140-2 compliant, the cryptographic module must be tested against the requirements of each of the 11 areas and be independently rated in each area. The RSA Security Web site states that the "review is a complex process and excellence in creating solid cryptographic algorithms and modules is difficult to achieve." From an interview conducted with NIST, the RSA ("Tips for FIPS 140" © 2003 RSA Security, p. 1) notes the following statistics from a NIST survey of accredited laboratories:

Of the 162 cryptographic modules surveyed, during testing the labs found:
- 48.8% (80) included security flaws
- 96.3% (158) included FIPS interpretation and documentation errors

Of the 332 DES, 3DES, DSA and SHA-1 algorithm validations surveyed, during testing the labs found:

– 26.5% (88) included security flaws
– 65.1% (216) included FIPS interpretation and documentation errors

The FIPS 140 standard is reexamined and reaffirmed every five years. A document posted on the NIST Web site at http://csrc.nist.gov/publications/nistpubs/800-29/sp800-29.pdf gives an overview of the differences between FIPS 140-1 and FIPS 140-2.

The DES Challenge

One of the weaknesses of cryptographic algorithms is brute-force attacks, which are also referred to as exhaustive search attacks. This technique involves trying every possible combination (key) until the correct one is identified. Advances in technology and computing performance have made brute-force attacks increasingly practical against keys of a fixed length, such as the DES algorithm. For example, when DES was designed, it was considered secure against brute-force attacks. Over the years, this type of attack has become increasingly attractive to attackers because the cost and time involved in finding a DES key has been reduced dramatically.

In 1997, RSA Security started the "DES Challenge." The purpose of the DES challenge was to quantify the security of the DES cipher. Essentially, RSA offers prize money to the first organization (or person) that successfully cracks one fixed-key size, 56-bit DES cipher. To show the complexity of the possible 72 quadrillion DES combinations, RSA (RSA Security, 2004, Cryptographic Challenges) gives the following statistics:

> Solving a DES challenge requires finding one key in 72 quadrillion. Finding a DES key amongst 72 quadrillion keys seems an unfathomable, incomprehensible task. We decided to convert this notion of 72 quadrillion into some interesting real-world equivalents.
>
> ■ 72 quadrillion golf balls would massively overfill the entire San Francisco Bay and then some, with over 5 times as many pouring out into the Pacific Ocean. (based on assumptions that a standard 1.7 inch diameter golf ball, packed approximately 404 balls/per cubic foot in volume (using hexagonal close packing) would yield a volume of 1.78×10^{14} cubic feet, and that the San Francisco Bay runs 90 miles long, 30 miles wide, and 500 feet deep. Yielding a volume of 3.76×10^{13} cubic feet.)

- 72 quadrillion people would weigh, (assuming 150 lbs each) 1.08×10^{19} lbs. (Which is surprisingly still only one millionth the weight of the Earth, at a whopping 1.3×10^{25} lbs. However, if 72 quadrillion people could stand 4 per square meter, and could stand on every square meter of the earth's surface (including the ocean floors), they would need 350,000 earths for a modest amount of elbow room.
- If you didn't have a computer, but could somehow check one DES key per second in your head, it would still take over 9 billion years to test the DES key space. This is comparable or possibly longer than the time the universe has existed (estimates on the existence of the universe vary from 7 to 20 billion years; talk about your margins of error!).
- 72 quadrillion inches, a little over 1.82×10^{12} kilometers, is still a little shy of the distance light travels in one year, 9.5×10^{12} km, but if you decided to travel it in the Earth's orbit around the sun instead (1.49×108 km) you could go around the sun more than 10,000 times.

The first DES Challenge was cracked by a group of Internet users in a distributed brute-force attack. The attack began on March 13, 1997, and 90 days later it was successfully completed on June 17th. The DES Challenge II consisted of two contests; the first was January 1998 and was cracked by a distributed effort in 39 days. In less than a year, the time it took to crack the first cipher was reduced by 50 percent. The second contest in July 1998 was solved in less than three days (RSA Security, 2004). The rules for DES Challenge III were listed on the RSA Security Web site as:

> The previous best exhaustive search time for a DES key was considered to be 56 hours. The prize structure for this challenge is shown in Table 14.2. There is no prize for times greater than 56 hours (http://www.rsasecurity.com/rsalabs/).

Table 14.2   DES Challenge III

Time for Solution	Prize
Less than or equal to 24 hours	$10,000
Greater than 24 hours but less than or equal to 48 hours	$5,000
Greater than 48 hours but less than or equal to 56 hours	$1,000

Source: http://www.rsasecurity.com/rsalabs/.

You can see that with today's technology, DES only offers a few hours of protection from brute-force attacks. An exhaustive search of DES's 56-bit key space would still take tens or hundreds of years on the fastest general-purpose computer available today, but the growth of the Internet has made it possible to utilize thousands of machines in a distributed search by splitting the key space and allocating those key spaces to each computer. DES was clearly in need of a replacement.

In 1997, NIST held an international competition involving some of the world's leading cryptographers to develop the Advanced Encryption Standard (AES) as a replacement for DES. In 2000, NIST announced the winner was Rijndael, a block cipher designed by Belgian cryptographers Vincent Rijmen and Joan Daemen. It was adopted as a Federal standard in 2001.

FIPS 197, Advance Encryption Standard (AES) (November 2001)

FIPS 197 (2001) announced the Rijndael algorithm as a FIPS approved standard that Federal agencies could use to protect electronic data. Rijndael's key length was designed to be variable, meaning that it can be set to be 128, 192, or 256 bits. It must be one of these three lengths, and not anything arbitrary. It also has a variable block size of 128, 192, or 256 bits. All nine combinations of key length and block size are possible; however, they are not adopted in the FIPS 197 standard. The official AES block size is 128. The number of rounds, or iterations of the main algorithm, can vary from 10 to 14 and depends on the block size and key length. The low number of rounds has been one of the main criticisms of Rijndael; but if this ever becomes a problem, the number of rounds can easily be increased at little extra cost.

It is not mandatory for Federal agencies to use AES; other FIPS-approved cryptographic algorithms may be used in addition to, or in lieu of AES. Also, AES can be adopted and used by non-Federal government organizations, such as financial institutions or other commercial and private organizations that need to provide a desired level of security.

The FIPS 197 approved AES algorithm can be implemented in software, firmware, hardware, or any combination thereof. The specific implementation may depend on several factors, such as the application, the environment, the technology used, etc. Implementations of the algorithm that are tested by an accredited laboratory and validated will be considered as complying with this standard. Because cryptographic security depends on many factors in addition to the correct implementation of an encryption algorithm, Federal government employees, and others, should also refer to NIST SP 800-21 (November 1999), "Guideline for Implementing Cryptography in the Federal Government," for additional information and guidance.

FIPS 197 and CNSS Policy No. 15

FIPS 197 approved the AES algorithm for use in protecting Sensitive (unclassified) Federal information; however, it did not state whether AES could also be employed in the protection of Classified Federal information. To address this question, the National Security Agency (NSA) conducted a review and analysis of AES and its applicability to the protection of national security systems and information. The policy guidance resulting from the analysis was issued by the Committee of National Security (CNSS) in June 2003 as CNSS Policy Number 15, Fact Sheet No. 1, "National Policy on the Use of the Advanced Encryption Standard (AES) to Protect National Security Systems and National Security Information."

CNSSP No. 15 describes under what conditions AES can be implemented to protect classified information and at what classification levels. The policy states:

> NSA-approved cryptography is required to protect (i.e., to provide confidentiality, authentication, non-repudiation, integrity, or to ensure system availability) national security systems and national security information at all classification levels.

> The design and strength of all key lengths of the AES algorithm (i.e., 128, 192 and 256) are sufficient to protect classified information up to the SECRET level. TOP SECRET information will require use of either the 192 or 256 key lengths. The implementation of AES in products intended to protect national security systems and/or information must be reviewed and certified by NSA prior to their acquisition and use.

> Subject to the policy and guidance for non-national security systems and information (e.g., FIPS 140-2), U.S. Government Departments and Agencies may wish to consider the use of security products that implement AES for IA applications where the protection of systems or information, although not classified, nevertheless, may be critical to the conduct of organizational missions. This would include critical infrastructure protection and homeland security activities as addressed in Executive Order 13231, Subject: Critical Infrastructure Protection in the Information Age (dated 16 October 2001), and Executive Order 13228, Subject: Homeland Security (dated 8 October 2001), respectively. Evaluations of products employing AES for these types of applications are subject to review and approval by the National Institute of Standards and Technology (NIST) in accordance with the requirements of Federal Information Processing Standard (FIPS) 140-2 (p. 2).

The next section of this chapter discusses several NIST SPs pertinent to the role and responsibilities of the ISSE.

NIST Special Publications

NIST Special Publications (SPs) are recommended guidelines for engineering, managing, processing protecting and controlling National Security and Sensitive but Unclassified (SBU) information. There are more than 50 draft and final released SPs currently listed on the NIST publications Web site. Included in this chapter are:

- NIST SP 800-12, An Introduction to Computer Security: The NIST Handbook (October 1995)
- NIST SP 800-14, Generally Accepted Principles and Practices for Securing Information Technology Systems (September 1996)
- NIST SP 800-18, Guide for Developing Security Plans for Information Technology Systems (December 1998)
- NIST SP 800-25, Federal Agency Use of Public Key Technology for Digital Signatures and Authentication (October 2000)
- NIST SP 800-27, Engineering Principles for Information Technology Security (A Baseline for Achieving Security) (June 2001)
- NIST SP 800-30, Risk Management Guide for Information Technology Systems (January 2002)
- NIST SP 800-47, Security Guide for Interconnecting Information Technology Systems (September 2002)

NIST SP 800-12, An Introduction to Computer Security: The NIST Handbook (October 1995)

NIST SP 800-12 contains more than 200 pages of assistance in securing computer-based resources. It provides explanations of important concepts, cost considerations, and interrelationships of security controls so that readers can gain an understanding of the benefits of computer security controls. It provides an introduction to computer security and is an excellent primer for anyone who needs to learn the basic of computer security or wants a broad overview of the subject.

SP 800-12 is separated into several sections. The first section contains background and overview material, briefly discusses threats, and explains the roles and responsibilities of individuals and organizations involved in computer security. It also explains the executive principles of computer security. For example, one important principle that is repeatedly stressed is that only security measures that are cost-effective should be implemented. A familiarity with the principles is fundamental to understanding the handbook's philosophical approach to the issue of security (NIST SP 800-12, p. 4).

The three control sections discuss the security controls based on the following categories:

1. *Management controls.* These controls focus on the management of the computer security program and the management of risk within the organization.
2. *Operational controls.* The focus is on controls that are implemented and executed by people (as opposed to systems).
3. *Technical controls.* These security controls are executed by the computer system. However, operational and management controls are necessary to make sure they are implemented correctly and managed appropriately.

Within each of the sections the material is divided into subtopics that define the control; explain how it can be implemented; cost considerations in selecting, implementing, and using the control; and, selected interdependencies that may exist with other controls.

The SP 800-12 principles of computer security are:

1. Computer security should support the mission of the organization.
2. Computer security is an integral element of sound management.
3. Computer security should be cost-effective.
4. Computer security responsibilities and accountability should be made explicit.
5. System owners have computer security responsibilities outside their own organizations.
6. Computer security requires a comprehensive and integrated approach.
7. Computer security should be periodically reassessed.
8. Computer security is constrained by societal factors (p. 9).

The eight principles are based on the Organization for Economic Cooperation and Development's (OECD) 1992 "Guidelines for the Security of Information Systems" (subsequently replaced by the OECD May 2004 "Guidelines for the Security of Information Systems and Networks: Towards a Culture of Security"). The OECD Guidelines were developed by a group of international experts to provide a foundation from which governments and the private sector could construct a framework for securing IT systems. A brief description of the current OECD principles is provided in Table 14.3.

Table 14.3 Guidelines for Security of Information Systems

Principle	Description
Awareness	Participants should be aware of the need for security of information systems and networks and what they can do to enhance security.
Responsibility	All participants are responsible for the security of information systems and networks.
Response	Participants should act in a timely and cooperative manner to prevent, detect, and respond to security incidents.
Risk assessment	Participants should conduct risk assessments.
Ethics	Participants should respect the legitimate interests of others.
Security design and implementation	Participants should incorporate security as an essential element of information systems and networks.
Security management	Participants should adopt a comprehensive approach to security management.
Reassessment	Participants should review and reassess the security of information systems and networks, and make appropriate modifications to security policies, practices, measures, and procedures.
Democracy	The security of information systems and networks should be compatible with the essential values of a democratic society.

When developing the eight principles, NIST drew upon the OECD Guidelines, added material, and combined some principles and rewrote others.

The principles added by NIST are in keeping with the OECD principles but not directly stated. For example, NIST added the principle that "computer security supports the mission of the organization." Prior to developing these principles, NIST thoroughly reviewed what is currently being accomplished in the IT Security principles area. With much consideration, a determination was made that the U.S. Government would benefit from its own set of principles. The eight principles provide an anchor on which the Federal community should base its IT security programs. These principles are intended to guide agency personnel when creating new systems, practices, or policies. They are not designed to produce specific answers. The principles should be applied as a whole, pragmatically, and reasonably.

In the early development of NIST SP 800-12, NIST considered obtaining a copyright release for a good practices document that originated in the United Kingdom. Although the copyright was not obtainable, British Standard 7799 (2002), "A Code of Practice for Information Security Management," was referenced while preparing this material. BS 7799 is a code of practice for information security management and a specification for an information security management system (ISMS). An ISMS is defined as a method by which senior management monitors and controls their security, minimizing the residual business risk and ensuring that security continues to fulfill corporate, customer, and legal requirements. BS 7799 was the basis for an international standard initially released in 2000, "ISO/IEC 17799:2000 Code of Practice for Information Security Management." ISO 17799 is a comprehensive set of controls comprising best practices in information security. Since its initial release, it has become an internationally recognized generic information security standard.

NIST SP 800-14, Generally Accepted Principles and Practices for Securing Information Technology Systems (September 1996)

NIST SP 800-14 describes the eight principles from SP 800-12 and adds fourteen practices. This guidance is intended to add best practices of how organizations can achieve the principles.

SP 800-14 provides a bit of an explanation for each of the eight principles:

1. *Computer security supports the mission of the organization.* The explanation for this principle is: "The purpose of computer security is to protect an organization's valuable resources, such as information, hardware, and software. Through the selection and application of appropriate safeguards, security helps the organization's mission by protecting its physical and financial resources, reputation, legal position, employees, and other tangible and intangible assets" (p. 5).

2. *Computer security is an integral element of sound management.* The explanation for this principle is: "As with other resources, the management of information and computers may transcend organizational boundaries. When an organization's information and IT systems are linked with external systems, management's responsibilities extend beyond the organization. This requires that management (1) know what general level or type of security is employed on the external system(s) or (2) seek assurance that the external

system provides adequate security for their organization's needs" (p. 6).

3. *Computer security should be cost-effective.* This principle is defined as "The costs and benefits of security should be carefully examined in both monetary and non-monetary terms to ensure that the cost of controls does not exceed expected benefits. Security should be appropriate and proportionate to the value of and degree of reliance on the IT systems and to the severity, probability, and extent of potential harm. Requirements for security vary, depending upon the particular IT system" (p. 6).

4. *Systems owners have security responsibilities outside their own organizations.* The explanation for this principle is that: "If a system has external users, its owners have a responsibility to share appropriate knowledge about the existence and general extent of security measures so that other users can be confident that the system is adequately secure. This does not imply that all systems must meet any minimum level of security, but does imply that system owners should inform their clients or users about the nature of the security" (p. 7).

5. *Computer security responsibilities and accountability should be made explicit.* This principle is defined as: "The responsibility and accountability of owners, providers, and users of IT systems and other parties concerned with the security of IT systems should be explicit. The assignment of responsibilities may be internal to an organization or may extend across organizational boundaries" (p. 8).

6. *Computer security requires a comprehensive and integrated approach.* This principle is explained as: "Providing effective computer security requires a comprehensive approach that considers a variety of areas both within and outside of the computer security field. This comprehensive approach extends throughout the entire information life cycle" (p. 9).

7. *Computer security should be periodically reassessed.* This principle is defined as: "Computers and the environments in which they operate are dynamic. System technology and users, data and information in the systems, risks associated with the system, and security requirements are ever-changing. Many types of changes affect system security: technological developments (whether adopted by the system owner or available for use by others); connection to external networks; a change in the value or use of information; or the emergence of a new threat" (p. 9).

8. *Computer security is constrained by societal factors.* This final principle is defined as: "The ability of security to support the mission of an organization may be limited by various factors, such as social

issues. For example, security and workplace privacy can conflict. Commonly, security is implemented on an IT system by identifying users and tracking their actions. However, expectations of privacy vary and can be violated by some security measures. (In some cases, privacy may be mandated by law.) Although privacy is an extremely important societal issue, it is not the only one. The flow of information, especially between a government and its citizens, is another situation where security may need to be modified to support a societal goal. In addition, some authentication measures may be considered invasive in some environments and cultures" (p. 10).

The 14 best practices from SP 800-14 are:

1. *Policy.* The practices for this principle are that organizations should have three different types of computer security policy to support the mission:
   - *Program policies* should (a) create and define a computer security program; (b) set organizational strategic directions; (c) assign responsibilities; and (d) address compliance issues.
   - *Issue-specific policies* should (a) address specific areas; (b) be updated frequently; and (c) contain an issue statement.
   - *System-specific policies* should (a) focus on decisions; (b) be made by management officials; (c) vary from system to system; and (d) be expressed as rules.
2. *Program management.* The practices for this principle can be based on having at least two levels of computer security management; the *central* level and the *system* level. Each of these would contain the following:
   - "*Central level security program* should provide distinct types of benefits, such as increased efficiency and economy of security throughout the organization and the ability to provide centralized enforcement and oversight.
   - While the central program addresses the entire spectrum of computer security for an organization, *system-level computer security programs* ensure appropriate and cost-effective security for each system. System-level computer security programs may address, for example, the computing resources within an operational element, a major application, or a group of similar systems (either technologically or functionally)" (p. 16, 17).
3. *Risk management.* This practice is based on the concept of risk management which consists of two primary and one underlying activity; risk assessment and risk mitigation are the primary activities

and uncertainty analysis is the underlying one. More on risk management is discussed in SP 800-30.

4. *Life-cycle planning.* The practices include managing security based on a plan to include it throughout the IT system life cycle. A security plan should be initiated to ensure that security is included during all phases of the life cycle. There are many models for the IT system life cycle, which are explained in Chapter 1.

5. *Personnel/user issues.* The practices revolve around personnel and user issues, such as users, designers, implementers, and managers. A broad range of security issues, such as determining staffing requirements, position sensitivities, and friendly and unfriendly terminations relate to how these individuals interact with computers and the access and authorities they need to do their job.

6. *Preparing for contingencies and disasters.* The practices for this principle are based on contingency and disaster recovery planning. Contingency planning directly supports an organization's goal of continued operations and to be effective it must be tested through practice to make sure it is relevant and makes business sense.

7. *Computer security incident handling.* The practices for this principle are the requirements for developing an incident handling capability to address computer security incidents. The incident handling capability should be able to (a) provide ability to respond quickly and effectively; (b) contain and repair damage from incidents; and (c) prevent future damage.

8. *Awareness and training.* An effective computer security awareness and training program requires proper planning, implementation, maintenance, and periodic evaluation.

9. *Security considerations in computer support and operations.* Computer support and operations refers to system administration and tasks external to the system that support its operation (e.g., maintaining documentation).

10. *Physical and environmental security.* Physical and environmental security controls are implemented to protect the facility housing system resources, the system resources themselves, and the facilities used to support their operation.

11. *Identification and authentication.* Identification is the means by which a user *provides* a claimed identity to the system. Authentication is the means of establishing the *validity* of this claim.

12. *Logical access control.* Logical access controls are the system-based means to explicitly enable or restrict access in some way. They can prescribe not only who or what is to have access to a specific system resource but also the type of access that is permitted.

13. *Audit Trails.* Audit trails maintain a record of system activity by system or application processes and by user activity. In conjunction with appropriate tools and procedures, audit trails can provide a means to help accomplish *several* security-related objectives, including individual accountability, reconstruction of events, intrusion detection, and problem identification.

14. *Cryptography.* Cryptography is traditionally associated only with keeping data secret. However, modern cryptography can be used to provide many security services, such as electronic signatures and ensuring that data has not been modified.

The best practices covered in SP 800-14 are the basis for computer security policies and procedures as well as certification and accreditation requirements that are levied on information systems processing various levels of sensitive information. These practices are broad in that they look across the entire spectrum of defense-in-depth and suggest protective measures that are designed to preserve the availability, integrity, and confidentiality of the information system.

NIST SP 800-18, Guide for Developing Security Plans for Information Technology Systems (December 1998)

The first thing to say about System Security Plans (SSPs) is that they are a requirement stated in Office of Management and Budget (OMB) Circular A-130, "Management of Federal Information Resources," Appendix III, "Security of Federal Automated Information Resources" and Public Law 100-235, "Computer Security Act of 1987." The goal of SSPs is to improve protection of IT resources by documenting the protection in the SSP. In SP 800-18, the generic term "system" is used to mean either a major application or a general support system. Also, OMB A-130 requires a summary of the security plan to be incorporated into the strategic IRM plan required by the Paperwork Reduction Act (44 U.S.C. Chapter 35, 1995).

As with many of the NIST SPs, the original documents were intended to be released as part of a grouping. NIST SP 800-12 (1995 — provides an overview of general security principles), SP 800-14 (1996 — provides practices relevant to the general principles), and SP 800-18 (1998 — builds on the practices and expands the relevancy) together provide a NIST trilogy of IT security program-level guidance. Currently, NIST is developing another seven-part guidance series to reflect the current trends in IA. Although SP 800-18 was released a few years ago, the principles and concepts remain pertinent for current SSP developments. At time of publication it was being updated to reflect changes brought on by FISMA, FIPS 199, and SP 800-53.

SP 800-18 defines the purpose of SSPs as to:

■ Provide an overview of the security requirements of the system and describe the controls in place or planned for meeting those requirements.
■ Delineate responsibilities and expected behavior of all individuals who access the system (p. 3).

The security plan should be viewed as documentation of the structured process of planning adequate, cost-effective security protection for a system. The system owner is the person ultimately responsible for ensuring that the system has a SSP. However, the SSP should include input from managers with system responsibilities, including information owners, system administrators or operators, and the Information System Security Officer (ISSO).

An important element of SP 800-18 and SSPs is the tie-in to the Certification and Accreditation (C&A) process outlined in NIST SP 800-37 (May 2004). The assessment of risk (NIST SP 800-30, July 2002) and the development of security plans are two important activities in an agency's information security program that directly support the security accreditation process and are required under FISMA and OMB Circular A-130. During Phase 1 of the SP 800-37 C&A process, the three tasks are:

1. Preparation
2. Notification and resource identification
3. **Security plan analysis, update, and acceptance**

Developing an SSP

The first step taken to develop an SSP is to determine which type of plan is required for the system. This includes system analysis to determine the boundaries and type of the system. NIST SP 800-18 defines a system as "it can be identified by constructing logical boundaries around a set of processes, communications, storage, and related resources. The elements within these boundaries constitute a single system requiring a security plan. Each element of the system must:

■ Be under the **same** direct management control
■ Have the **same** function or mission objective

- Have essentially the **same** operating characteristics and security needs
- Reside in the **same** general operating environment" (p. 5)

The next step is to categorize each system as either a "major application" or as a "general support system." SP 800-18 (1998, p. 7) defines these as:

- "Major Applications (MAs) are federal applications that have value and require some level of protection. Certain applications, because of the information they contain, process, or transmit or because of their criticality to the organization's missions, require special management oversight.
- A General Support System (GSS) is interconnected information resources under the same direct management control, which shares common functionality. A GSS normally includes hardware, software, information, data, applications, communications, facilities, and people and provides support for a variety of users and/or applications. For example, a LAN, backbone, or communications systems." (p. 7)

The remaining steps of developing the SSP are based on a format specified in SP 800-18. The guidelines note that there are several formats or frameworks that will meet the OMB A-130 requirement. However, a standardized approach should be developed for each agency so that an SSP for a GSS is similar in format to that of an MA. The level of detail necessary for the SSP should be consistent with the criticality and value of the system to the organization's mission. Of key importance is that the SSP identify and describe the controls currently in place or planned for the system.

The topic areas along with a short description of details that should be included in the security plans are shown in Table 14.4. This information is based on the SP 800-18 guidance.

As shown in Table 14.4, the SSP contains an extensive list of subject areas that must be identified as in place or planned for. The SSP is not something that can be accomplished in a short period of time or by one person. For most organizations, developing the SSP takes thought processes and coordination from many individuals within the organization. However, once a central template is defined, it is easier for other GSS or MA owners to document their SSPs. Also, not all topics are required for each plan; but if it is not covered, it should be noted as not applicable to that system. Finally, the depth of the material in the SSP is based on the mission criticality, complexity, and sensitivity of the information and its system.

Table 14.4 System Security Plan Outline

Topic	Description
Plan Controls	The plan should be marked, handled and controlled based on the level of sensitivity determined by organizational policy.
System Identification	General description of the system, including system name, responsible organization, contact information, and individuals responsible for system security.
Operational Status	Indicate whether the system is operational, under development, or undergoing a major upgrade.
General Description and Purpose	A brief description about the function and purpose of the system.
System Environment	Description of the technical system and operating environment, including factors that raise special security concerns, such as connections to the Internet, locations in a harsh or overseas environment.
System Interconnection and Information Sharing	Provide information concerning the authorization for the connection to other systems or the sharing of information, such as a list of interconnected systems (including Internet); unique system identifiers, name of system(s); or organization owning the other system(s).
Sensitivity of Information Handled	Defines the types of information handled by the system and an analysis of the criticality of the information. It is important that the degree of sensitivity be assessed by considering the requirements for the confidentiality, integrity, and availability (CIA) of the information. Also list any applicable laws, policies, and directives that are required to preserve the AIC of the system.
Management Controls	Describe the management control measures (in place or planned) that are intended to meet the protection requirements of the major application or general support system.
Risk Management	OMB Circular A-130 requires an assessment of risk as part of a risk-based approach to determining adequate, cost-effective security for a system.
Review of Security Controls	Systems should be reviewed at least every three years or as major changes/upgrades occur. The SSP should describe the type of review and findings conducted on the GSS or MA in the previous three years.

Table 14.4 (continued) System Security Plan Outline

Topic	Description
Rules of Behavior	The rules of behavior should clearly delineate responsibilities and expected behavior of all individuals with access to the system, and should be included as an appendix to the SSP and referenced in this area.
Planning for Security in the Life-Cycle	Documents which phase(s) of the life cycle the system, or parts of the system, are in Identifies how security has been handled during the applicable life-cycle phases
Authorized Processing	In this section, include the date of authorization, name, and title of management official. If not authorized, provide the name and title of manager requesting approval to operate and date of request.
Operational Controls	This is where the information contained in the SSP may differ based on whether it is for a GSS or MA. The operational controls address security methods that focus on mechanisms that primarily are implemented and executed by people.
Personnel Controls	This section includes detailed information about personnel security measures, such as background checks or security clearances.
Physical and Environmental Protection	Briefly describe the physical and environmental controls in place, such as physical access controls, fire safety, supporting utilities, mobile or portable systems, and server room (data center) controls.
Production, Input/Output Controls	Provide a synopsis of the procedures in place that support the operations of the application, such as procedures for ensuring that only authorized users pick up, receive, or deliver input and output information and media.
Contingency Planning	Procedures that would be followed to ensure the GSS and MA are always available.
Software Maintenance Controls	For MAs, describe the controls in place to monitor the installation of, and updates to, application software. Controls may include a software configuration policy that grants managerial approval (re-authorize processing) to modifications and requires that changes be documented.

Table 14.4 (continued)   System Security Plan Outline

Topic	Description
Hardware and System Software Maintenance Controls	For a GSS, provide information on the hardware and system software maintenance controls in place or planned; this would also include configuration management controls.
Data Integrity and Validation Controls	Describe any controls that provide assurance to users that the information has not been altered and that the system functions as expected. This may include virus protections, intrusion detection tools, message authentication, or digital signatures.
Documentation	List the documentation maintained for the application (examples include vendor-supplied documentation of hardware or software, application requirements, application security plan, testing procedures and results, standard operating procedures, emergency procedures, or contingency plans).
Security Awareness and Training	Include information about the plans and procedures for awareness and training for using and maintaining the system.
Incident Response	Description of plans and procedures for handling computer-related incidents such as viruses or malicious activities
Technical Controls	Describe the technical control measures (in place or planned) that are intended to meet the protection requirements.
Identification and Authentication	Describe procedures and mechanisms to identify and authenticate users to the system and its information.
Logical Access (Authorization/ Access) Controls	Discuss the controls in place to authorize or restrict the activities of users and system personnel within the MA or GSS (this would also include the use of a warning banner).
Public Access Controls	If the public accesses the MA or GSS, describe the additional controls in place.
Audit Trails	Describe the audit trail mechanisms in place.

NIST SP 800-25, Federal Agency Use of Public Key Technology for Digital Signatures and Authentication (October 2000)

NIST SP 800-25 encourages the thoughtful use of public key technology by Federal agencies to eliminate paperwork and move processes to ones that are technology based. The Government Paperwork Elimination Act (GPEA) (Public Law 105-277; Federal Register Notice, Volume 65, Number 85, 1998) requires Federal agencies to allow individuals or entities that deal with an agency the option to submit information or perform transactions with an agency electronically, when practicable, and to maintain records electronically, when practicable. The GPEA states that electronic records and their related electronic signatures are not to be denied legal effect, validity, or enforceability merely because they are in electronic form, and encourages Federal government use of a range of electronic signature alternatives. An example of the use of public key technologies has been the ability to electronically file Federal (or State) income taxes.

One of the options available for Federal agencies is to implement public key technology to provide the necessary protections for electronic transactions. NIST SP 800-25 discusses several issues specifically related to digital signatures and authentication over an open network. The issues are focused on "evaluating the potential applications of public key technology involving digital signatures or authentication, considering whether the application warrants such use as set forth in the OMB GPEA guidance; and implementing those applications selected. The questions and issues address technical, business, policy, and legal aspects, and they are fashioned to inform all agency elements who play a part in evaluating how public key technology may be applied to agency operations" (NIST SP 800-25, 2000, p. 1).

When Federal agencies are deciding on the use of secure electronic transactions for use by the public or with other Federal agencies, they should have reasonable assurance that:

1. "The information sender and recipient both will be identified uniquely so the parties know where the information is coming from and where it is going (identification and authentication);
2. The transmitted information was not altered deliberately or inadvertently (data integrity);
3. There is a way to establish that the sender's identity is inextricably bound to the information (technical non-repudiation); and
4. The information will be protected from unauthorized access (confidentiality or privacy). This functionality is included for completeness since public key technology and a Public Key Infrastructure provide it; however, confidentiality and privacy concerns are not covered in detail in this guidance" (NIST SP 800-25, p. 2)

An example of the type of questions and discussion in SP 800-25 is:

"Question: What are the risks associated with the use of public key technology for this application?

Discussion: (1) Three areas of risks associated with the use of public key technology are (a) fraud; (b) failure of the system to fulfill its purpose (service failure or shortfall); and (c) liability. Agencies considering each area should evaluate risk in two separate contexts. First, does the use of public key technology create "new" risk? If so, what is its "absolute" level, that is, the greatest monetary or intangible loss the agency can suffer? Second, how does that level of risk compare to the risk already experienced using existing systems that supply the same service to the public or other entities today? In other words, what is the relative risk?" (p. 18)

When considering any type of new information system, one of the most important elements for organizations to ask is whether the business case for public key technologies is linked to its mission and goals.

NIST SP 800-27 Rev. A, Engineering Principles for Information Technology Security: A Baseline for Achieving Security, Revision A (June 2004)

NIST SP 800-27 provides a list of system-level security principles to be considered in the design, development, and operation of an information system. The 33 engineering principles are intended to provide a foundation for designing, developing, and implementing IA capabilities. They do not replace the Information Assurance Technical Framework (IATF) activities or phases, but rather provide generally accepted best practices for implementing security when using a systems engineering approach.

SP 800-27 is also tied into SP 800-12 and SP 800-14. The engineering principles are derived primarily from concepts found in the eight principles and fourteen practices identified in SP 800-12 and SP 800-14. The difference is that SP 800-27 principles provide a system-level (versus organizational-level) perspective for IA.

SP 800-27 states that the principles do not apply to all systems at all times. However, "each principle should be carefully considered throughout the life-cycle of every system. Moreover, because of the constantly changing information system security environment, the principles identified are not considered to be an inclusive list. Instead, SP 800-27 is an attempt to present in a logical fashion, fundamental security principles that can be used in today's operational environments. As technology improves and security techniques are refined, additions, deletions, and refinement of these security principles will be required" (NIST SP 800-27, 2004, p. 5).

SP 800-27 lists the engineering principles in a table-type format that indicates where the principle should be applied during the system's life cycle. It also provides an explanation that further defines the principle. The engineering principles are applied to a generic life-cycle model that outlines the following five phases:

1. Initiation phase
2. Development/acquisition phase
3. Implementation phase
4. Operation/maintenance phase
5. Disposal phase

Following the SP 800-27, Rev. A format, Table 14.5 identifies each engineering principle and the life-cycle phases. An "asterisk" is used to indicate if the principle should be considered or applied during the specified phase. One asterisk "*" signifies the principle can be used to support the life-cycle phase, and two asterisks "**" signify the principle is key to successful completion of the life-cycle phase. The absence of an asterisk indicates the principle does not affect that particular phase of the life cycle. Refer to SP 800-27, Rev. A, for discussion and clarification of each principle.

A key point of many of the NIST documents is, if security is done with proper planning, it can become an enabler for the organization, an element that helps the organization achieve its mission. SP 800-27 is intended to provide a starting point, with the hope that the principles will contribute to improved IT security in any organization.

Table 14.5 Engineering Principles and Life-Cycle Phases Based on NIST SP 800-27

	Initiation	Development/ Acquisition	Implement	Operate/ Maintain	Disposal
Security Foundation: Principles 1–4					
Principle 1	Establish a sound security policy as the "foundation" for design				
Applicability	**	*	*	*	*
Principle 2	Treat security as an integral part of the overall system design				
Applicability	**	**	**	**	*

Table 14.5 (continued)   Engineering Principles and Life-Cycle Phases Based on NIST SP 800-27

	Initiation	Development/ Acquisition	Implement	Operate/ Maintain	Disposal
Principle 3	Clearly delineate the physical and logical security boundaries governed by associated security policies				
Applicability	**	**	*	*	
Principle 4	Ensure that developers are trained in how to develop secure software				
Applicability	**	**	*		
Risk-Based: Principles 5–11					
Principle 5	Reduce risk to an acceptable level				
Applicability	**	**	**	**	**
Principle 6	Assume that external systems are insecure				
Applicability	**	**	**	**	*
Principle 7	Identify potential trade-offs between reducing risk and increased costs and decrease in other aspects of operational effectiveness				
Applicability	**	**		**	
Principle 8	Implement tailored system security measures to meet organizational security goals				
Applicability	*	**	*	**	*
Principle 9	Protect information while being processed, in transit, and in storage				
Applicability	*	**	*	**	*
Principle 10	Consider custom products to achieve adequate security				
Applicability	*	**	*	*	
Principle 11	Protect against all likely classes of "attacks"				
Applicability	*	**	**	*	*
Ease of Use: Principles 12–15					
Principle 12	Where possible, base security on open standards for portability and interoperability				
Applicability	*	**	*		

Table 14.5 (continued) Engineering Principles and Life-Cycle Phases Based on NIST SP 800-27

	Initiation	Development/ Acquisition	Implement	Operate/ Maintain	Disposal
Principle 13	Use common language in developing security requirements				
Applicability	**	*		**	
Principle 14	Design security to allow for regular adoption of new technology, including a secure and logical technology upgrade process				
Applicability		**	*	**	
Principle 15	Strive for operational ease of use				
Applicability	*	**	*	**	
Increase Resilience: Principles 16–23					
Principle 16	Implement layered security (Ensure no single point of vulnerability)				
Applicability	*	**	*	**	*
Principle 17	Design and operate an IT system to limit vulnerability and to be resilient in response				
Applicability	*	**		**	
Principle 18	Provide assurance that the system is, and continues to be, resilient in the face of expected threats				
Applicability	*	**	*	**	*
Principle 19	Limit or contain vulnerabilities				
Applicability		**	*	*	
Principle 20	Isolate public access systems from mission-critical resources (e.g., data, processes, etc.)				
Applicability	*	**	*	*	
Principle 21	Use boundary mechanisms to separate computing systems and network infrastructures				
Applicability		**	*	**	
Principle 22	Design and implement audit mechanisms to detect unauthorized use and to support incident investigations				
Applicability	*	**	**	*	

Table 14.5 (continued)   Engineering Principles and Life-Cycle Phases Based on NIST SP 800-27

	Initiation	Development/ Acquisition	Implement	Operate/ Maintain	Disposal
Principle 23	Develop and exercise contingency or disaster recovery procedures to ensure appropriate availability				
Applicability	*	*	*	**	
Reduce Vulnerability: Principles 24–29					
Principle 24	Strive for simplicity				
Applicability	*	**	*	**	
Principle 25	Minimize the system elements to be trusted				
Applicability	*	**	*	**	
Principle 26	Implement least privilege				
Applicability	*	*	*	**	
Principle 27	Do not implement unnecessary security mechanisms				
Applicability	*	**	**	*	*
Principle 28	Ensure proper security in the shutdown or disposal of a system				
Applicability		*		*	**
Principle 29	Identify and prevent common errors and vulnerabilities				
Applicability		**	**		
Design with Network in Mind: Principles 30–33					
Principle 30	Implement security through a combination of measures distributed physically and logically				
Applicability		**	*	*	*
Principle 31	Formulate security measures to address multiple overlapping information domains				
Applicability	*	**	*	*	
Principle 32	Authenticate users and processes to ensure appropriate access control decisions both within and across domains				
Applicability	*	*	*	**	
Principle 33	Use unique identities to ensure accountability				
Applicability	*	*	*	**	

NIST SP 800-30, Risk Management Guide for Information Technology Systems (January 2002)

NIST SP 800-30 was developed by NIST to provide a foundation for the development of an effective risk management program. The document contains definitions and practical guidance for assessing and mitigating risks identified within IT systems. It states that the ultimate goal of SP 800-30 "is to help organizations to better manage IT-related mission risks." NIST SP 800-30A, Revision to Risk Management Guide for Information Technology Systems, is currently in Draft form. The Revision is intended to update SP 800-30 to reflect the FISMA requirements.

SP 800-30 is based on the general guidance and principles from NIST SP 800-14 and SP 800-25. It is consistent with the FIPS-199, "Standards for Security Categorization of Information and Information Systems" (2004); NIST SP 800-37 (2004), "Guide for the Security Certification and Accreditation of Federal Information Systems" (2004); and NIST SP 800-53, "Recommended Security Controls for Federal Information Systems" (2005). Again, readers of NIST documents can begin to see that NIST is striving to tie in various documents that will form a continuum of IA policies and recommendations for Federal agencies.

To begin, the document establishes several objectives for why organizations should perform risk management to accomplish its mission(s). SP 800-30 states that risk management helps organizations by:

- "Better securing the IT systems that store, process, or transmit organizational information
- Enabling management to make well-informed risk management decisions to justify the expenditures that are part of an IT budget
- Assisting management in authorizing (or accrediting) the IT systems on the basis of the supporting documentation resulting from the performance of risk management" (p. 2)

SP 800-30 discusses and describes the following:

- An overview of risk management, how it fits into each phase of the system's life cycle, and the roles of individuals who support and use this process
- The risk assessment methodology and the nine primary steps in conducting a risk assessment of an IT system
- The risk mitigation process, including risk mitigation options and strategy, approach for control implementation, control categories, cost-benefit analysis, and residual risk
- The good practice and need for an ongoing risk evaluation and assessment and the factors that will lead to a successful risk management program

Additional information, including sample interview questions, outlines, references, glossary, and table of safeguards, can be found in the six appendices.

Overview of Risk Management

Risk management is defined as the process that allows managers to balance the operational and economic costs of protective measures and achieve gains in mission capability by protecting the IT systems and data that support their organizations' missions. Risk management encompasses three processes: risk assessment, risk mitigation, and evaluation and assessment. The results of the *risk management* process are provided to the authorizing official, who is responsible for determining whether the remaining risk is at an acceptable level. (Acceptable level is defined in OMB Circular A-130, Appendix III, and is quoted in Chapter 11.) If it is not, then the authorizing official must make plans for additional security controls to be implemented that will reduce or eliminate the residual risk.

Part of the overall view of risk management is an explanation of how the risk management methodology fits into each phase of the systems life cycle. The life-cycle phases, phase characteristics, and risk management activities are shown in Table 14.6. Support for risk management activities occurs in each of the five phases. Chapter 1 contains a similar table that also includes the ISSE phases.

Table 14.6   Life-Cycle Phases and Risk Management

SDLC Phases	Phase Characteristics	Support from Risk Management Activities
Phase 1, Initiation	The need for an IT system is expressed and the purpose and scope of the IT system is documented.	Identified risks are used to support the development of the system requirements, including security requirements, and a security concept of operations (strategy).
Phase 2, Development and Acquisition	The IT system is designed, purchased, programmed, developed, or otherwise constructed.	The risks identified during this phase can be used to support the security analyses of the IT system that may lead to architecture and design trade-offs during system development.

Table 14.6 (continued)   Life-Cycle Phases and Risk Management

SDLC Phases	Phase Characteristics	Support from Risk Management Activities
Phase 3, Implementation	The system security features should be configured, enabled, tested, and verified.	The risk management process supports the assessment of the system implementation against its requirements and within its modeled operational environment. Decisions regarding risks identified must be made prior to system operation.
Phase 4, Operation or Maintenance	The system performs its functions. Typically, the system is being modified on an ongoing basis through the addition of hardware and software and by changes to organizational processes, policies, and procedures.	Risk management activities are performed for periodic system reauthorization (or reaccreditation) or whenever major changes are made to an IT system in its operational or production environment (e.g., new system interfaces).
Phase 5, Disposal	This phase may involve the disposition of information, hardware, and software. Activities may include moving, archiving, discarding, or destroying information and sanitizing the hardware and software.	Risk management activities are performed for system components that will be disposed of or replaced to ensure that the hardware and software are properly disposed of, that residual data is appropriately handled, and that system migration is conducted in a secure and systematic manner.

Source: From NIST SP 800-30, Rev. A, p. 7.

NIST SP 800-30 provides a common foundation for experienced and inexperienced, and technical and nontechnical personnel who support or use the risk management process for their IT systems. These personnel are listed in Table 14.7.

Table 14.7 Key Roles of Risk Management

Personnel	Interest in Security Risk Management
Senior Management	Decision makers about the IT security budget and have ultimate responsibility for the security of the system.
Federal Chief Information Officers	Responsible for the agency's IT planning, budgeting, and performance, including its information security components
Approving Authority	Responsible for the final decision on whether to allow operation of an IT system
Information System Security Officers (ISSO)	Responsible for their organizations' security programs, including risk management ISSOs play a leading role in introducing an appropriate, structured methodology to help identify, evaluate, and minimize risks to the IT systems that support their organizations' missions
IT System and Information Owners	Responsible for ensuring that proper controls are in place to address integrity, confidentiality, and availability of the IT systems and data they own
Business or Functional Managers	These managers are the individuals with the authority and responsibility for making the trade-off decisions essential to mission accomplishment.
IT Security Practitioners	Responsible for proper implementation of security requirements in their IT systems To include network, system, application, and database administrators; computer specialists; security analysts; and security consultants
Security Awareness Trainers (Security/Subject Matter Professionals)	IT security trainers or security/subject matter professionals must understand the risk management process so that they can develop appropriate training materials and incorporate risk assessment into training programs to educate the end users.

Note: Based on NIST SP 800-30, Rev. A, p. 8–9.

Next we discuss the risk assessment methodologies.

Risk Assessment

Risk assessment is the first process in the risk management process. NIST SP 800-30 offers a risk assessment method that is comprised of nine primary steps:

Step 1: System characterization
Step 2: Vulnerability identification
Step 3: Threat identification
Step 4: Control analysis
Step 5: Likelihood determination
Step 6: Impact analysis
Step 7: Risk determination
Step 8: Control recommendations
Step 9: Results documentation

Figure 14.2 depicts these steps and the inputs to and outputs from each. Steps 2, 3, and 4 can be conducted in parallel after Step 1 has been completed. It is important that the ISSEP understand risk management and the role risk assessment plays in the system design and implementation. Note that Step 2 and Step 3 have been reversed in NIST SP 800-37 Rev. A; the change is noted as "Reversed order of vulnerability analysis and threat analysis. Threat is threat source/vulnerability pair; so although threat-source and vulnerability can be analyzed in parallel, threat analysis cannot be performed until after vulnerability analysis has been conducted (p. v)."

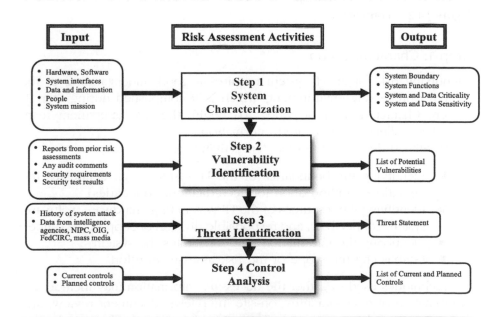

Figure 14.2   Risk assessment methodology.

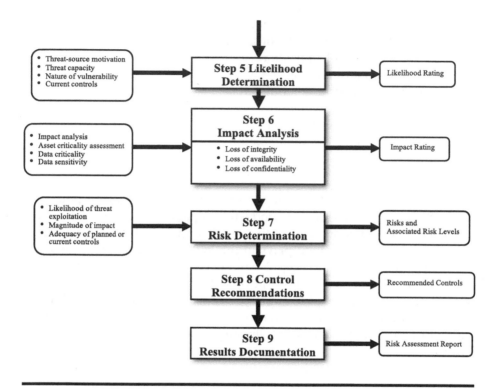

Figure 14.2 (continued)

Step 1: Characterization

Identifying risk for an IT system requires a good understanding of the system's processing environment, which is accomplished during Step 1, System Characterization, activities. To begin, the risk assessment team must first collect system-related information.

SP 800-30 describes the first step activities as:

■ Identifying the boundaries of the IT system (e.g., delineates the operational authorization [or accreditation] boundaries)
■ Identifying the resources of the IT system (e.g., hardware, software, system connectivity, and responsible division or support personnel)
■ Identifying the information that constitutes the system
■ Establishing the scope of the risk assessment effort

Techniques used to gather the necessary information may include any combination of questionnaires, on-site interviews, document review, and use of automated scanning tools. The output from *Step 1: Characterization* should present a good picture of the IT system environment, the information processed on the system, and delineation of system boundary.

Step 2: Vulnerability Identification

The goal of the Vulnerability Identification step is to develop a list of system vulnerabilities (flaws or weaknesses) that could be exploited by the potential threat-sources. Vulnerability indicates a weakness that can be accidentally triggered or intentionally exploited.

Recommended methods for identifying system vulnerabilities include:

- *Vulnerability sources.* Include both technical and nontechnical vulnerabilities associated with an IT system's processing environment. Sources include previous risk assessments, audit reports, security review reports, vendor advisories, and commercial or government security advisories.
- *System security testing.* Depending on the resources available, test methods could include automated vulnerability scanning tools, Security Test and Evaluations (ST&E), and penetration testing.
- *Development of a security requirements checklist.* This would include questions that discuss the security criteria and security areas listed in Table 14.8.

The output from Step 2, vulnerability identification, is a list of system vulnerabilities that could be exercised by the potential threat-sources.

Step 3: Threat Identification

NIST SP 800-30 defines threat as "the potential for a particular threat-source to successfully exercise a particular vulnerability. A threat-source does not present a risk when there is no vulnerability that can be exercised. In determining the likelihood of a threat, one must consider threat-sources, potential vulnerabilities, and existing controls (p. 10)." The goal of this step is to identify the potential threat-sources and compile a threat statement listing potential threat-sources that are applicable to the IT system being evaluated.

In Chapter 1, there is a listing of many types of threats based on information from the IATF for ISSE. SP 800-30 also provides a listing of possible threats. A unique feature of the listing from SP 800-30 is it includes a motivation for human threats. Table 14.9 shows the human threat-source, motivation, and threat actions. SP 800-30 also provides information regarding

Table 14.8 Security Criteria

Security Area	Security Criteria
Management Security	Assignment of responsibilities
	Continuity of support
	Incident response capability
	Periodic review of security controls
	Personnel clearance and background investigations
	Risk assessment
	Security and technical training
	Separation of duties
	System authorization and reauthorization
	System or application security plan
Operational Security	Control of air-borne contaminants (smoke, dust, chemicals)
	Controls to ensure the quality of electrical power supply
	Data media access and disposal
	External data distribution and labeling
	Facility protection (e.g., computer room, data center, office)
	Humidity/temperature control
	Workstations, laptops, and stand-alone computers
Technical Security	Communications (e.g., dial-in, system interconnection, routers)
	Cryptography
	Discretionary access control
	Identification and authentication
	Intrusion detection
	Object reuse
	System audit

Source: From NIST SP 800-30, 2002, pp. 18–19.

threats from natural disasters (e.g., hurricanes, earthquakes) and the environment (e.g., power failures, chemical spills).

An aspect of evaluating the threats to a system is identifying the vulnerabilities associated with the system environment. Table 14.10 from NIST SP 800-30 provides examples of vulnerability/threat pairs.

The output from Step 3, threat identification, is a threat statement containing a list of threat-sources that could exploit system vulnerabilities.

Table 14.9   Human Threat-Sources, Motivation, and Threat Actions

Threat-Sources	Motivation	Threat Actions
Hacker, cracker	Ego Challenge Rebellion	Hacking Social engineering Intrusions and break-ins Unauthorized access
Computer criminal	Destruction of information Monetary gain Illegal disclosure Unauthorized data alteration	Computer crime Fraudulent act Information bribery Spoofing System intrusion
Terrorist	Blackmail Destruction Exploitation Revenge	Bomb/terrorism Information warfare System attack (e.g. distributed denial of Service attack) System penetration System tampering
Industrial espionage (foreign government, companies, etc.)	Competitive advantage Economic espionage	Economic exploitation Social engineering System penetration Unauthorized access to classified, proprietary, or high-tech related information Intrusions on personal privacy
Insiders (poorly trained, disgruntled, terminated, malicious, etc.)	Curiosity Monetary gain Revenge Intelligence Unintentional errors or omissions (data entry or programming errors	Assault on employees Fraud and theft Blackmail Browsing proprietary data Computer abuse False input or corrupted data Information bribery Interception Malicious code Sale of personal information Systems bugs, intrusion, and sabotage Unauthorized system/data access

Source: From NIST SP 800-30, 2002, p. 14.

Table 14.10 Vulnerabilities/Threat Pairs

Vulnerabilities	Threat-Sources	Threat Actions
Terminated employees system identifiers (ID) are not removed from the system	Terminated employees	Remotely accessing the company's network and accessing company proprietary data
Company firewall allows inbound telnet, and *guest* ID is enabled on XYZ server	Unauthorized users (e.g., hackers, terminated employees, computer criminals, terrorists)	Using telnet to XYZ server and browsing system files with the *guest* ID
The vendor has identified flaws in the security design of the system; however, new patches have not been applied to the system	Unauthorized users (e.g., hackers, disgruntled employees, computer criminals, terrorists)	Obtaining unauthorized access to sensitive system files based on known system vulnerabilities
Data center uses water sprinklers to suppress fire; tarpaulins to protect hardware and equipment from water damage are not in place	Fire, negligent persons	Water sprinklers being turned on in the data center

Source: From NIST SP 800-30, 2002, pp. 15–16.

Step 4: Control Analysis

The goal of analyzing controls that have been implemented or planned for implementation is to minimize or eliminate the likelihood (or probability) of threats exercising the system's vulnerabilities. This involves analyzing control methods, control categories, and control analysis technique.

NIST SP 800-30 defines controls methods, categories, and analysis techniques as:

"**Control Methods.** Security controls encompass the use of technical and non-technical methods. Technical controls are safeguards that are incorporated into computer hardware, software, or firmware (e.g., access control mechanisms, identification and authentication mechanisms, encryption methods, intrusion detection software). Non-technical controls are management and operational controls, such as security policies; operational procedures; and personnel, physical, and environmental security.

Control Categories. The control categories for both technical and non-technical control methods can be further classified as either preventive or detective. Preventive controls inhibit attempts to violate security policy and include such controls as access control enforcement, encryption, and authentication. Detective controls warn of violations or attempted violations of security policy and include such controls as audit trails, intrusion detection methods, and checksums.

Control Analysis Technique. The development or use of a security requirements checklist will be helpful in analyzing controls in an efficient and systematic manner. The security requirements checklist can be used to validate security non-compliance as well as compliance. Therefore, it is essential to keep the checklists updated with the organization's latest environmental controls (e.g., changes in security policies, methods, and requirements) to ensure the checklist's validity (p. 20)."

The output from Step 4, control analysis, is a list of current or planned controls used for the IT system that will mitigate the likelihood of vulnerability's being exercised and reduce the impact of such an adverse event.

Step 5: Likelihood Determination

In this step, the goal is to determine the likelihood of the threat attacking the vulnerability. NIST SP 800-30 identifies several factors that can be used to determine this likelihood. The factors include the:

- Threat-source motivation and capability
- Nature of the vulnerability
- Existence and effectiveness of current controls

NIST SP 800-30 explains that the likelihood that a potential vulnerability could be exercised by a given threat-source can be described on a scale of high, medium, or low. Table 14.11 defines the three likelihood levels.

The output from Step 5, likelihood determination, for whether a threat-source will attack vulnerabilities is based on a scale of high, medium, or low.

Table 14.11 Likelihood Definitions

Likelihood Level	Likelihood Definition ,
High	The threat-source is highly motivated and sufficiently capable, and controls to prevent the vulnerability from being exercised are ineffective.
Medium	The threat-source is motivated and capable, but controls are in place that may impede successful exercise of the vulnerability.
Low	The threat-source lacks motivation or capability, or controls are in place to prevent, or at least significantly impede, the vulnerability from being exercised.

Source: From NIST SP 800-30, 2002, p. 21.

Step 6: Impact Analysis

The next step, *impact analysis,* determines the adverse impact that would result from a successful threat exercising vulnerabilities. The adverse impact of a security event can be described in terms of loss or degradation of any, or a combination of any, of the three primary security goals: integrity, availability, and confidentiality.

As noted in NIST SP 800-30, "some tangible impacts can be measured quantitatively in lost revenue, the cost of repairing the system, or the level of effort required to correct problems caused by a successful threat action. Other impacts (e.g., loss of public confidence, loss of credibility, damage to an organization's interest) cannot be measured in specific units but can be qualified or described in terms of high, medium, and low impacts (p. 22)."

Because SP-800-30 is written in a generic nature, it designates and describes only qualitative categories for impact of high, medium, and low. Table 14.12 provides a definition of these categories.

The output from Step 6, impact analysis, explains the magnitude or impact to the organization of a threat attacking vulnerabilities based on a scale high, medium, or low.

Step 7: Risk Determination

The purpose of this step is to assess the level of risk to the system. NIST SP 800-30 states that the "determination of risk for a particular threat/vulnerability pair can be expressed as a function of:

Table 14.12 Magnitude of Impact Definitions

Magnitude of Impact	Impact Definition
High	Exercise of the vulnerability (1) may result in the highly costly loss of major tangible assets or resources; (2) may significantly violate, harm, or impede an organization's mission, reputation, or interest; or (3) may result in human death or serious injury.
Medium	Exercise of the vulnerability (1) may result in the costly loss of tangible assets or resources; (2) may violate, harm, or impede an organization's mission, reputation, or interest; or (3) may result in human injury.
Low	Exercise of the vulnerability (1) may result in the loss of some tangible assets or resources or (2) may noticeably affect an organization's mission, reputation, or interest.

Source: From NIST SP 800-30, 2002, p. 23.

■ The likelihood of a given threat-source's attempting to exercise a given vulnerability
■ The magnitude of the impact should a threat-source successfully exercise the vulnerability
■ The adequacy of planned or existing security controls for reducing or eliminating risk (p. 24)"

As this point, the results from the previous steps are combined to determine risk. In this method, risk is derived by multiplying the ratings from Step 5 where the *threat likelihood* was determined and the data from Step 6, which outlined the *impact of the threat* on the organization's mission.

Table 14.13 is an example of a threat matrix from NIST SP 800-30 that shows how the overall risk ratings might be determined based on inputs from the threat likelihood and threat impact categories. The matrix is a 3 × 3 matrix of threat likelihood (High, Medium, and Low) and threat impact (High, Medium, and Low). Depending on the site's requirements and the granularity of risk assessment desired, some sites may use a 4 × 4 or 5 × 5 matrix. The latter can include a Very Low/Very High threat likelihood impact, which would generate a Very Low/Very High risk level. A Very High risk level may require possible system shutdown or stopping of all IT system integration and testing efforts (NIST SP 800-30).

Table 14.13   Risk-Level Matrix

Threat Likelihood	Impact		
	Low (10)	Medium (50)	High (100)
High (1.0)	Low $10 \times 1.0 = 10$	Medium $50 \times 1.0 = 50$	High $100 \times 1.0 = 100$
Medium (0.5)	Low $10 \times 0.5 = 5$	Medium $50 \times 0.5 = 25$	Medium $100 \times 0.5 = 50$
Low (0.1)	Low $10 \times 0.1 = 1$	Low $50 \times 0.1 = 5$	Low $100 \times 0.1 = 10$

Note: Risk Scale: High (>50 to 100); Medium (>10 to 50); and Low (1 to 10).

Source: From NIST SP 800-30, 2002, p. 25.

"The sample matrix shows how the overall risk levels of High, Medium, and Low are derived. The determination of these risk levels or ratings may be subjective. The rationale for this justification can be explained in terms of the probability assigned for each threat likelihood level and a value assigned for each impact level. For example, the probability assigned for each threat likelihood level is 1.0 for High, 0.5 for Medium, 0.1 for Low. The value assigned for each impact level is 100 for High, 50 for Medium, and 10 for Low" (NIST SP 800-30, p. 25).

Thus, to measure risk, the organization must develop a risk scale that can be applied to a risk-level matrix. NIST SP 800-30 defines a standard risk scale and how it could be utilized in a risk matrix. Table 14.14 describes a generic risk scale that can be used. As noted in NIST SP 800-30, "this risk scale, with its ratings of High, Medium, and Low, represents the degree or level of risk to which an IT system, facility, or procedure might be exposed if a given vulnerability were exercised. The risk scale also presents actions that senior management, the mission owners, must take for each risk level (p. 25)."

The output from Step 7, determining risk, is a risk matrix and a risk scale based on a scale of High, Medium, or Low.

Step 8: Control Recommendations

In this step, recommendations are made regarding additional controls that could mitigate or eliminate the identified risks. NIST SP 800-30 states that "the goal of the recommended controls is to reduce the level of risk to the IT system and its data to an acceptable level. Factors that should be

Table 14.14   Risk Scale and Necessary Actions

Risk Level	*Risk Description and Necessary Actions*
High	If an observation or finding is evaluated as a high risk, there is a strong need for corrective measures. An existing system may continue to operate, but a corrective action plan must be put in place as soon as possible.
Medium	If an observation is rated as medium risk, corrective actions are needed and a plan must be developed to incorporate these actions within a reasonable period of time.
Low	If an observation is described as low risk, the system's DAA must determine whether corrective actions are still required or decide to accept the risk.

Source: From NIST SP 800-30, 2002, p. 25.

considered in recommending controls and alternative solutions to minimize or eliminate identified risks include:

- Effectiveness of recommended options (e.g., system compatibility)
- Legislation and regulation
- Organizational policy
- Operational impact
- Safety and reliability (p. 26)"

An important item to note is that not all possible recommended controls can be implemented to reduce loss. To determine which ones are required and appropriate for a specific organization, a cost-benefit analysis should be conducted for the proposed recommended controls. This analysis demonstrates that the costs of implementing the controls can be justified by the reduction in the level of risk. In addition, the operational impact (e.g., effect on system performance) and feasibility (e.g., technical requirements, user acceptance) of introducing the recommended option should be evaluated carefully during the risk mitigation process (NIST SP 800-30). The output from Step 8, control recommendations, is a list of recommendations of control(s) and alternative solutions that will mitigate the identified risk.

Step 9: Results Documentation

The final step in the risk assessment is to make sure the results from the assessment (threat-sources and vulnerabilities identified, risks assessed, and recommended controls provided) have been documented in an official report or briefing.

NIST SP 800-30 states that a "risk assessment report is a management report that helps senior management, the mission owners, make decisions on policy, procedural, budget, and system operational and management changes. Unlike an audit or investigation report, which looks for wrong-doing, a risk assessment report should not be presented in an accusatory manner but as a systematic and analytical approach to assessing risk so that senior management will understand the risks and allocate resources to reduce and correct potential losses. For this reason, some people prefer to address the threat/vulnerability pairs as observations instead of findings in the risk assessment report (p. 27)."

The output from Step 9, results documentation, is a risk assessment report that describes the threats and vulnerabilities, measures the risk, and provides recommendations for control implementation.

The next step in the risk management process is risk mitigation.

Risk Mitigation

Risk mitigation involves prioritizing, evaluating, and implementing the appropriate risk-reducing controls recommended from the risk assessment process. Because the elimination of all risk is usually impractical or close to impossible, the guidance provided in SP 800-30 is that senior manage-ment and functional and business managers should "use the **least-cost approach** and implement the **most appropriate controls** to decrease mission risk to an acceptable level, with **minimal adverse impact** on the organization's resources and mission" (NIST SP 800-30, 2002, p. 27).

Risk mitigation can be achieved through any of the following risk mitigation options:

- *Risk assumption.* To accept the potential risk and continue oper-ating the IT system or to implement controls to lower the risk to an acceptable level
- *Risk avoidance.* To avoid the risk by eliminating the risk cause or consequence (e.g., forego certain functions of the system or shut down the system when risks are identified)
- *Risk limitation.* To limit the risk by implementing controls that minimize the adverse impact of a threat's exercising a vulnerability (e.g., use of supporting, preventive, detective controls)
- *Risk planning.* To manage risk by developing a risk mitigation plan that prioritizes, implements, and maintains controls
- *Research and acknowledgment.* To lower the risk of loss by acknowledging the vulnerability or flaw and researching controls to correct the vulnerability
- *Risk transference.* To transfer the risk by using other options to compensate for the loss, such as purchasing insurance

When selecting a risk mitigation strategy, it is important to consider the goals and mission of an organization. Because it may not be practical to deal with all identified risks, priority should be given to the threats and vulnerabilities that have the potential to cause significant mission impact or harm. Usually, the best approach is to use appropriate technologies from various vendor security products, along with the appropriate risk mitigation options and nontechnical, administrative measures (NIST SP 800-30).

The ISSEP should understand risk mitigation process. Most times, they are not directly responsible for the risk management but they are required to provide support, advice, and assistance to the systems engineers, security architects, and C&A personnel in identifying and mitigating risk.

The next topic describes risk mitigation options, risk mitigation strategy, an approach for control implementation, control categories, cost-benefit analysis used to justify the implementation of the recommended controls, and residual risk.

NIST SP 800-30 provides a flowchart with action points that can help senior management answer the questions of when to take actions, which controls to implement, and when they should be implemented. In addition to the flowchart in Figure 14.3, the following guidance is provided:

1. *"When vulnerability (or flaw, weakness) exists* — implement assurance techniques to reduce the likelihood of a vulnerability being exercised.
2. *When vulnerabilities can be exercised* — apply layered protections, architectural designs, and administrative controls to minimize the risk of or prevent this occurrence.
3. *When the attacker's cost is less than the potential gain* — apply protections to decrease an attacker's motivation by increasing the attacker's cost (e.g., use of system controls such as limiting what a system user can access and do, which can significantly reduce an attacker's gain).
4. *When loss is too great* — apply design principles, architectural designs, and technical and non-technical protections to limit the extent of the attack, thereby reducing the potential for loss." (p. 28)

When control actions must be taken, the ISSEP should address the "greatest risks and strive for sufficient risk mitigation at the lowest cost, with minimal impact on other mission capabilities" (NIST SP 800-30, p. 29). Figure 14.4 describes the approach to control implementation. It begins with a review of the risk assessment report to prioritize actions and develop a ranking of High, Medium, or Low. The remaining five steps are relatively self-explanatory (see NIST 800-30 for complete details). The results of

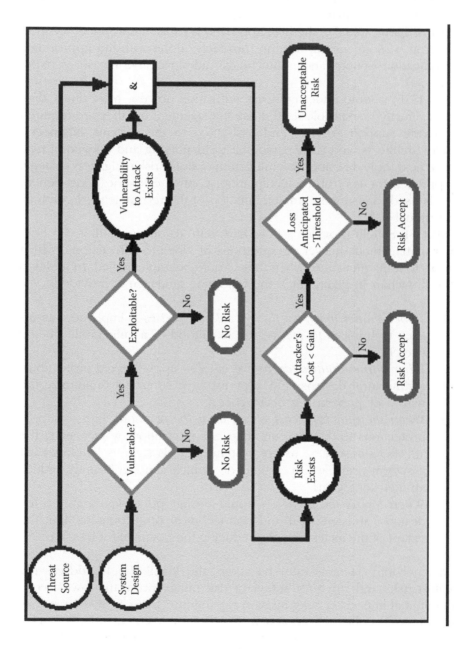

Figure 14.3 Risk mitigation action points. (*Source:* From NIST SP 800-30, 2002, p. 28.)

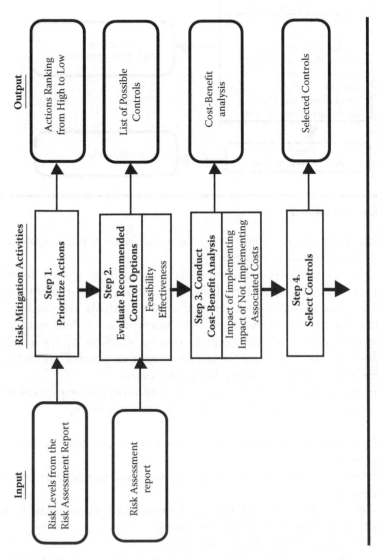

Figure 14.4 **Risk mitigation activities. (*Source:* From NIST SP 800-30, 2002, p. 31.)**

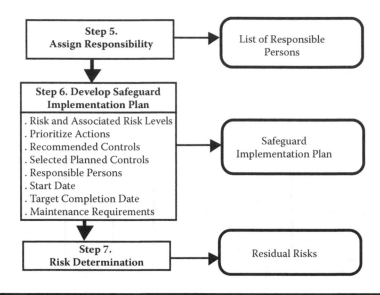

Figure 14.4 (continued)

completing these steps should determine the risks for the system and produce a residual risk statement.

After identifying all possible controls and evaluating their feasibility and effectiveness, the organization should conduct a cost-benefit analysis for each proposed control to determine which controls are required and appropriate for their circumstances. The purpose is to demonstrate that the costs of implementing the controls can be justified by the reduction in the level of risk. The cost of implementing a control should never exceed the value of the property being protected.

According to NIST SP 800-30, a cost-benefit analysis for proposed new controls or enhanced controls encompasses the following:

■ "Determining the impact of implementing the new or enhanced controls
■ Determining the impact of not implementing the new or enhanced controls
■ Estimating the costs of the implementation. These may include, but are not limited to, the following:
    − Hardware and software purchases
    − Reduced operational effectiveness if system performance or functionality is reduced for increased security
    − Cost of implementing additional policies and procedures
    − Cost of hiring additional personnel to implement proposed policies, procedures, or services

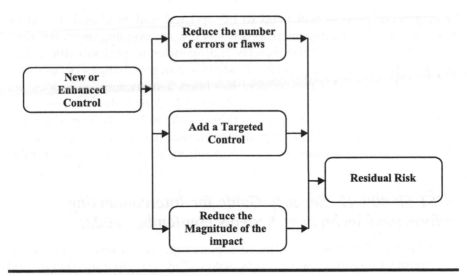

Figure 14.5   Residual risk. (*Source:* From NIST SP 800-30, 2002, p. 40.)

- Training costs
- Maintenance costs
■ Assessing the implementation costs and benefits against system and data criticality to determine the importance to the organization of implementing the new controls, given their costs and relative impact (p. 38)"

The final aspect of risk mitigation is the concept of residual risk. The risk that remains after implementing the controls is called residual risk. The relationship between control implementation and residual risk is graphically presented in Figure 14.5. All systems will have some level of residual risk that will be acceptable. A key point for the ISSEP is to make sure that the approving authority clearly and completely understands the level of risk that remains.

The final step in the risk management process is evaluation and assessment.

Evaluation and Assessment

No system remains static. Based on new mission needs or requirements, the information system will continually be expanded and updated, its components changed, and its software applications replaced or updated with newer versions. Other change factors include personnel changes, security policy changes, new threats, or newly identified vulnerabilities. Because of these changes, new risks will become a concern, and the risk management process will need to be updated and modified. It can be said that the risk management process is always ongoing and evolving.

OMB Circular A-130 requires Federal agencies to perform risk assessments at least every three years, or whenever major changes occur to the system. However, this requirement has been a misnomer — it does not mean that Federal agencies forget about risk during those three years. Federal agencies must continually address risk; to be effective, risk management must be an ongoing commitment that has the backing of senior management with awareness and cooperation from the user community.

NIST SP 800-47, Security Guide for Interconnecting Information Technology Systems (September 2002)

NIST SP 800-47 provides guidance for planning, establishing, maintaining, and terminating interconnections between IT systems that are owned and operated by different organizations. A system interconnection is defined as the direct connection of two or more IT systems for the purpose of sharing data and other information resources. Keep in mind that NIST guidelines are intended for unclassified networks; thus, SP 800-47 does not address classified systems or data, and it should not be used for guidance on securing or interconnecting such systems.

The first section of SP 800-47 describes various benefits of interconnecting IT systems, identifies the basic components of an interconnection, identifies methods and levels of interconnectivity, and discusses potential security risks associated with an interconnection. The remaining sections present an interconnection life-cycle management approach that focuses on security. The four phases of the interconnection life cycle are (NIST SP 800-47, 2002, ES-1):

1. *Planning the interconnection.* "The participating organizations perform preliminary activities; examine all relevant technical, security, and administrative issues; and form an agreement governing the management, operation, and use of the interconnection."
2. *Establishing the interconnection.* "The organizations develop and execute a plan for establishing the interconnection, including implementing or configuring appropriate security controls."
3. *Maintaining the interconnection.* "The organizations actively maintain the interconnection after it is established to ensure that it operates properly and securely."
4. *Disconnecting the interconnection.* "One or both organizations may choose to terminate the interconnection. The termination should be

conducted in a planned manner to avoid disrupting the other party's system. In response to an emergency, however, one or both organizations may decide to terminate the interconnection immediately."

SP 800-47 also contains guides for developing an Interconnection Security Agreement (ISA) and templates for a Memorandum of Understanding/Agreement (MOU/A). The ISA specifies the technical and security requirements of the interconnection, and the MOU/A defines the responsibilities of the participating organizations. The publication also contains a guide for developing a System Interconnection Implementation Plan, which defines the process for establishing the interconnection, including scheduling and costs.

NIST acknowledges that there are many methods for interconnecting systems. SP 800-47 is intended only as guidance and it should not be construed as defining the only approach possible. The framework it provides can be most helpful to organizations that have not previously interconnected IT systems or to enhance the security of existing interconnections.

SP 800-47 explains that a system interconnection has three basic components as shown in Figure 14.6. The components are the two IT systems (System A and System B) and the mechanism by which they are joined (the "Pipe" through which data is made available, exchanged, or passed one way only). It is assumed that System A and System B are owned and operated by different organizations. The connecting pipe can be a dedicated line that is owned or leased by one of the organizations, such as a high-speed terrestrial or satellite link. Another alternative is to connect systems using a Virtual Private Network (VPN) over a public network such as the Internet.

SP 800-47 notes that regardless of the interconnection advantages, interconnecting IT systems can expose the participating organizations to risk. It states that "if the interconnection is not properly designed, security failures could compromise the connected systems and the data that they store, process, or transmit. Similarly, if one of the connected systems is

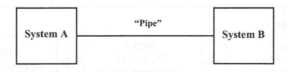

Figure 14.6 System interconnection components. (*Source:* From NIST SP 800-47, 2002, p. 2-1.)

compromised, the interconnection could be used as a conduit to compromise the other system and its data. The potential for compromise is underscored by the fact that, in most cases, the participating organizations have little or no control over the operation and management of the other party's system" (p. 2-2).

Because of the risks to each organization, it is important that both parties understand what risks are associated with the planned or current interconnection and also the security controls that can be implemented to mitigate those risks. Part of this process would be for each organization to review each other's System Security Plans (SSPs) that identify the controls currently in place for that system. OMB Circular A-130 mandates that agencies obtain written management authorization before connecting their IT systems to other systems, based on an acceptable level of risk. The written authorization should define the rules of behavior and controls that must be maintained for the system interconnection. These authorizations would then be included in each organization's SSPs.

Next is an overview of the four life-cycle management steps in developing an interconnection agreement.

Step 1: Planning the Interconnection

The first step in creating a system interconnection between two organizations is to complete an interconnection plan. As part of the planning, each organization performs preliminary activities and examines all relevant technical, security, and administrative issues. The objective of taking time to plan for the interconnection is to ensure that the interconnection will operate as efficiently and securely as possible. Figure 14.7 presents the recommended steps for planning a system interconnection.

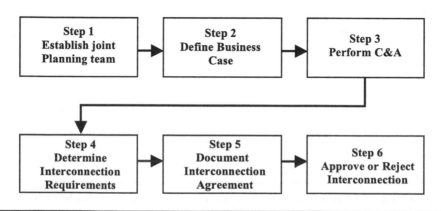

Figure 14.7   Steps to plan a system interconnection. (*Source:* From NIST SP 800-47, 2002, p. 3-1.)

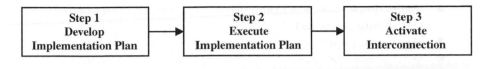

Figure 14.8 Implementing interconnections. (*Source:* From NIST SP 800-47, 2002, p. 4-1.)

Step 2: Establishing the Interconnection

Following approval of the interconnection plan, the next step is to implement the plan and activate the interconnection. As shown in Figure 14.8, establishing the interconnection can be accomplished in three steps. In most cases, it is helpful to develop an implementation plan that both organizations agree to and follow. The plan would be agreed to by senior management of both organizations, and the ISSEPs should review the plans to make sure the security requirements are identified and will be implemented during the establishment of the interconnection.

SP 800-47 provides a list of recommended tasks for establishing an interconnection. These are identified as:

- Implementing or configuring security controls, including firewalls, IDS, audit, identification and authentication, logical access controls, virus scanning, encryption, and physical and environmental controls
- Installing or configuring hardware and software such as VPNs, routers, hubs, servers, and workstations
- Integrating applications such as word processing, database applications, e-mail, Web browsers, application servers, authentication servers, and domain servers
- Conducting operational and security testing to ensure that the equipment operates properly and there are no obvious ways to circumvent the security controls
- Conducting security training and awareness
- Updating the security plans to include the new functionality
- Reaccrediting the system

Once the implementation plans tasks are completed, the interconnection can be activated and maintained.

Step 3: Maintaining the Interconnection

Maintaining the interconnection includes the day-to-day and periodic operations required to ensure that the interconnection maintains adequate security and functions properly. SP 800-47 identifies some of the tasks included as:

- ■ "Maintain clear lines of communication between both organizations with frequent contact
- ■ Maintain equipment
- ■ Manage user profiles
- ■ Conduct security reviews
- ■ Analyze audit logs
- ■ Report and respond to security incidents
- ■ Coordinate contingency planning activities
- ■ Perform change management
- ■ Maintain system security plans (p. 5-1)"

Step 4: Disconnecting the Interconnection

The process for terminating the system interconnection should, if possible, be accomplished in a methodical manner to avoid disrupting the other party's IT system. NIST SP 800-47 provides the following guidelines: "The decision to terminate the interconnection should be made by the system owner with the advice of appropriate managerial and technical staff. Before terminating the interconnection, the initiating party should notify the other party in writing, and it should receive an acknowledgment in return. The notification should describe the reason(s) for the disconnection, provide the proposed timeline for the disconnection, and identify technical and management staff who will conduct the disconnection (p. 6-1)."

In addition, once the disconnection occurs, each organization should update its system security plan and related documents to reflect the changed security environment in which its respective system operates (NIST SP 800-47, p. 6-2).

SP 800-47 does allow for an emergency disconnection, whereby one or both organizations detect an attack, intrusion attempt, or other contingency that exploits or jeopardizes the connected systems or their data. This would require one of the organizations to abruptly terminate the interconnection without providing written notice to the other party. It is noted that this measure should be taken only in extreme circumstances and only after consultation with appropriate technical staff and senior management (NIST SP 800-47, p. 6-2).

Summary

The NIST documents provide both requirements and recommendations for Federal agencies to use in implementing an IA program. The specific FIPS and Special Publications discussed in this chapter are just a few of the documents that can be helpful. Since FISMA was passed, NIST has received funding to update and provide new issuances that will directly impact the way Federal agencies will implement security on its information systems.

The introduction provided an overview of NIST and many of the programs it sponsors that are related to information assurance. The next section reviewed several FIPS related to the cryptographic standards. ISSEPs need to know the basic elements of the FIPS and how they might impact the design and development of information systems. FIPS 46-3 explained the first USG-announced encryption standard — DES. In addition to the FIPS document, the chapter outlined some of the background and history of DES and its importance in the beginning phases of distributed information systems. The next standard discussed was FIPS 81, which outlined the four modes of the DES algorithm. These modes are Electronic Codebook (ECB) mode, Cipher Block Chaining (CBC) mode, Cipher Feedback (CFB) mode, and the Output Feedback (OFB) mode.

FIPS 140-2, an updated version of FIPS 140-1, identified the requirements for four cryptographic module security levels. The four security levels have eleven requirement areas, with each security level increasing in security over the preceding level. These four increasing levels of security allow for cost-effective solutions that are appropriate for different degrees of data sensitivity and different application environments.

The final mandatory standard discussed was FIPS 197, which announced the Advanced Encryption Standard (AES) as a replacement for the DES algorithm. AES is based on the Rijndael algorithm, which won an international competition. FIPS 197 is applicable to unclassified or SBU information. Also mentioned was CNSSP No. 15, which stated that AES could also be used for classified information up to the Secret level.

The second section of the chapter focused on the guidance found in several NIST Special Publications. These are recommendations and guidelines that Federal agencies can use to implement IA. NIST SP 800-12 provided an overview of information system security and introduced eight IA principles. SP 800-14 built upon and further defined the eight principles. SP 800-14 also added fourteen practices that can be utilized to achieve the eight principles. SP 800-18 is a guideline for developing System Security Plans (SSPs), which are fundamental to all ISSE activities and also a key component of the C&A process.

The chapter also explained with a fair amount on SP 800-30 and risk management. Throughout the ISSE process, risk management is an integral and necessary element. In addition, FISMA states that Federal agencies must use a risk-based approach to address security for information systems. Although SP 800-30 has a draft revision, the current draft does not change the nine fundamental steps of the risk management process.

The final SP, SP 800-47, focused on a life-cycle approach to interconnection agreements between two organizations. OMB Circular A-130 mandates that interconnections have an Interconnection Agreement, and also provides guidelines that can be used to plan for, establish, maintain, and evaluate the interconnections.

As a final note to this chapter, ISSEPs responsible for Federal agencies are encouraged to review the many NIST issuances and keep current on what is released as both FIPS and Spec. Pubs. (SPs). With the advent of FISMA, it is necessary to document and report on how the systems are meeting these standards and guidelines.

References

44 United States Code (U.S.C.), Chapter 35 Coordination of Federal Information Policy (1995, Amended 1996, 1997, 2000, and 2002). "Paperwork Reduction Act." Available at http://uscode.house.gov/.

British Standard (BS) 7799 (2002). "A Code of Practice for Information Security Management." Published by the British Standards Institution: London, U.K. It can be purchased at http://www.bspsl.co.uk/17799/.

CNSS Policy No. 15, Fact Sheet No. 1 (June 2003). "National Policy on the Use of the Advanced Encryption Standard (AES) to Protect National Security Systems and National Security Infor mation." Available at http://www.nstissc.gov/html/library.html.

FIPS 46-3 (October 1999). "Data Encryption Standard (DES)." NIST Publications, Computer Security Division, NIST: Gaithersburg, MD. Available at http://csrc.nist.gov/publications/fips/index.html.

FIPS 81 (December 1980). "DES Mode of Operation." NIST Publications, Computer Security Division, NIST: Gaithersburg, MD. Available at http://csrc.nist.gov/publications/fips/index.html.

FIPS 102 (September 1983). "Guidelines for Computer Security Certification and Accreditation," NIST Publications, Computer Security Division, NIST: Gaithersburg, MD. Available at http://csrc.nist.gov/publications/fips/index.html.

FIPS 140-2 (May 2001). "Security Requirement for Cryptographic Modules." NIST Publications, Computer Security Division, NIST: Gaithersburg, MD. Available at http://csrc.nist.gov/publications/fips/index.html.

FIPS 185 (February 1994). "Escrowed Encryption Standard." NIST Publications, Computer Security Division, NIST: Gaithersburg, MD. Available at http://csrc.nist.gov/publications/fips/index.html.

FIPS 197 (November 2001). "Advance Encryption Standard." NIST Publications, Computer Security Division, NIST: Gaithersburg, MD. Available at http://csrc.nist.gov/publications/fips/index.html.

FIPS-199 (February 2004). "Standards for Security Categorization of Information and Information Systems." NIST Publications, Computer Security Division, NIST: Gaithersburg, MD. Available at http://csrc.nist.gov/publications/fips/index.html.

Hansche, Susan, John Berti, and Chris Hare (2004). "Official (ISC)² Guide to the CISSP Exam." CRC Press/Auerbach: Boca Raton, FL.

HR 145 Public Law 100-235 (June 1987). "Computer Security Act of 1987." The act can be downloaded from: http://csrc.nist.gov/secplcy/csa_87.txt.

HR 2458 Public Law 107-30 (November 2002). E-government Act of 2002. Title III — Information Security Section 301, Information Security. "Federal Information Security Management Act of 2002." Available at http://csrc.nist. gov/policies/FISMA-final.pdf.

H.R. 4328, Public Law 105-277, Federal Register Notice, Volume 65, Number 85 (October 1998). "Government Paperwork Elimination Act (GPEA)." Available at http://www.cio.noaa.gov/itmanagement/pea.pdf.

IEEE 802.11 (1999–2004), Series of Specifications for wireless local networks. Available at www.ieee.org

Information Assurance Technical Framework (IATF), Version 3.1 (September 2002). National Security Agency, Information Assurance Solutions, Technical Directors. Fort Meade, MD.

ISO/IEC 17799 (2000). "Code of Practice for Information Security Management." It can be purchased through the ISO Web site at http://www.iso.ch/iso/en/ ISOOnline.frontpage.

NIST Planning Report 02-1 (February 2002). "Economic Impact Assessment of NIST's Role-Based Access Control (RBAC) Program." NIST Publications: Gaithersburg, MD. Available at http://csrc.nist.gov/rbac/rbac-impact-summary.doc.

NIST SP 800-12 (March 1995). An Introduction to Computer Security: The NIST Handbook. NIST Publications, Computer Security Division, NIST: Gaithersburg, MD. Available at http://csrc.nist.gov/publications/nistpubs/index.html.

NIST SP 800-14 (September 1996). "Generally Accepted Principles and Practices for Securing Information Technology Systems." NIST Publications, Computer Security Division, NIST: Gaithersburg, MD. Available at http://csrc. nist.gov/publications/nistpubs/index.html.

NIST SP 800-18 (December 1998). "Guide for Developing Security Plans for Information Technology Systems." NIST Publications, Computer Security Division, NIST: Gaithersburg, MD. Available at http://csrc.nist.gov/publications/ nistpubs/index.html.

NIST SP 800-21 (November 1999). "Guideline for Implementing Cryptography in the Federal Government." NIST Publications, Computer Security Division, NIST: Gaithersburg, MD. Available at http://csrc.nist.gov/publications/ nistpubs/index.html.

NIST SP 800-25 (October 2000). "Federal Agency Use of Public Key Technology for Digital Signatures and Authentication." NIST Publications, Computer Security Division, NIST: Gaithersburg, MD. Available at http://csrc.nist. gov/publications/nistpubs/index.html.

NIST SP 800-27, Rev. A (June 2004). "Engineering Principles for Information Technology Security (A Baseline for Achieving Security), Revision A." NIST Publications, Computer Security Division, NIST: Gaithersburg, MD. Available at http://csrc.nist.gov/publications/nistpubs/index.html.

NIST SP 800-30 (October 2001). "Risk Management Guide for Information Technology Systems." NIST Publications, Computer Security Division, NIST: Gaithersburg, MD. Available at http://csrc.nist.gov/publications/nistpubs/ index.html.

NIST SP 800-30A DRAFT (2004). Revision to Risk Management Guide for Information Technology System. NIST Publications, Computer Security Division, NIST: Gaithersburg, MD. Available at http://csrc.nist.gov/publications/ nistpubs/index.html.

NIST SP 800-37 (May 2004). "Guide for the Security Certification and Accreditation of Federal Information Systems." NIST Publications, Computer Security Division, NIST: Gaithersburg, MD. Available at http://csrc.nist.gov/publications/ nistpubs/index.html.

NIST SP 800-47 (September 2002). "Security Guide for Interconnecting Information Technology Systems." NIST Publications, Computer Security Division, NIST: Gaithersburg, MD. Available at http://csrc.nist.gov/publications/nistpubs/ index.html.

NIST SP 800-53 DRAFT (October 2003 released for comments). "Recommended Security Controls for Federal Information Systems." NIST Publications, Computer Security Division, NIST: Gaithersburg, MD. Available at http://csrc.nist.gov/publications/nistpubs/index.html.

OECD (May 2004). "Guidelines for the Security of Information Systems and Networks: Towards a Culture of Security." OECD Publications, 2, rue André-Pascal, 75775 Paris Cedex 16, France.

OMB Circular No. A-130, (last revised November 2000). "Management of Federal Information Resources." Available at http://www.whitehouse.gov/omb/ circulars/index.html.

RSA Security (2003). "Tips for FIPS 140." © 2003, RSA Security. Available at www.rsasecurity.com.

Title 22, Code of Federal Regulations (CFR), Foreign Relations, Chapter 1 Department of State, Section 121-128. Available at http://ecfr.gpoaccess.gov/.

Title 47, Code of Federal Regulations (CFR) codifies Federal Communications Commission (FCC) rules and regulations. Part 15 Radio Frequency Devices. Available at http://www.access.gpo.gov/nara/cfr/waisidx_03/47cfr15_03.html.

Web Sites

www.nist.gov
www.csrc.nist.gov
http://www.rsasecurity.com/rsalabs/node.asp?id=2112 for DES Challenge

15

National Information Assurance Partnership (NIAP) and Common Criteria (CC)

Introduction

Is this product secure? How do I know it is secure? For the past 30 years, the U.S. Government (USG) has sought answers to these questions when acquiring products for information systems. Regardless of whether the product is an operating system, application, hardware product, or the system itself, how does the USG determine what security services it provides, what level (i.e., high, medium, low) of security is provided, and how can the USG be sure the product does what it claims? Because it is important for the USG to be assured the products it uses provide the necessary security requirements, evaluation methods have been developed to provide this assurance.

The available methods used for evaluating products or systems include:

- Trusting the advertisements from the manufacturer/vendor
- Performing system tests internally within the organization
- Trusting an impartial, independent assessment authority

Because it is difficult for general users to perform security tests, the preferred method is to trust an independent assessment authority. Throughout the world there are various assessment authorities that perform evaluations based on a previously designed set of criteria. The assessment authorities then rate the product or system according to the defined criteria. The manufacturers and vendors subsequently use the established rating in the marketing and advertisement of their products.

When looking at evaluation methods, it is necessary to first identify what is to be evaluated — a product or a system. An example of a *product* is a specific operating system that will be used in any number of applications, or a specific application that will be operated in a set of defined conditions. Typically, a *system* is a collection of products that together meet the specific requirements of a given application. The differences between the two are helpful in understanding the various security evaluation criteria.

Some questions or factors involved in selecting products include:

- Security:
  - How secure is the system?
  - What access control and privilege management is available?
  - How secure is the encryption algorithm and process, if used?
  - Has any rigorous, formal testing been conducted?
  - Can it connect to an existing security infrastructure?
  - Does privilege management to maintain a segregation of duties exist?
- Cost:
  - Are volume discounts, pricing alternatives, or site licensing available?
  - What other costs impact the product selection? Hardware, maintenance, upgrades, etc. all contribute considerably to the cost.
- Flexibility considerations:
  - Length of company commitment
  - Ease of change to alternative product
  - Interface with other security products
- Environmental considerations:
  - Ability to accommodate hardware and operating system evolution
  - Ability to accommodate changes in user procedures
- User interface considerations:
  - User ease of operation
  - Number of rules to understand and follow
- System administration:
  - Initial effort and ongoing administration
  - Ability to centrally recover from user error

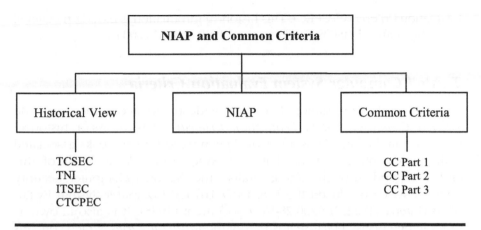

Figure 15.1   Chapter overview.

- – Specialized skills and training for the administrators
- – Integration with other applications
- ■ Future developments of a product:
  - – What and when planned?
  - – Will it be easier for the user? Will it reduce administrative workload?
- ■ Process:
  - – What processes exist to provide ongoing operation as defined in the previous controls? Failing to provide processes to maintain the system operation provides a significant security risk.

This chapter begins with a section that discusses the historical evaluation criteria, such as the Trusted Computer System Evaluation Criteria.

The second section provides a quick introduction to the National Information Assurance Partnership (NIAP) and explains the role it plays in Common Criteria Evaluation. The final section is an overview of Common Criteria (CC). Figure 15.1 is an overview of this chapter.

Historical View of IT Security Evaluations

Note to ISSEP candidates: This material was also covered in the CISSP® material; thus, it should be familiar. It is not listed in the (ISC)² study guide, but it does provide reference to understanding the Common Criteria evaluation scheme. ISSEPs are expected to know Common Criteria.

This section provides background information on legacy evaluation schemes including the Trusted Computer System Evaluation Criteria (TCSEC), the Trusted Network Interpretation (TNI), the Information Technology Security Evaluation Criteria (ITSEC), and the Canadian Trusted Computer Product

Evaluation Criteria (CTCPEC). This historical information is based on material from the "Official (ISC)² Guide to the CISSP Exam" (2004).

Trusted Computer System Evaluation Criteria

The first evaluation standard to gain widespread acceptance was the *Trusted Computer System Evaluation Criteria (TCSEC)*. As a historical reference, in the late 1960s, the DoD began to address the risks associated with implementing systems that were not secure. As a result of this endeavor (and through various drafts), the National Computer Security Center (NCSC) produced the U.S. DoD Trusted Computer System Evaluation Criteria (TCSEC) 5200.28-STD document (1985). It is also known as the "Orange Book" because it is part of the *Rainbow Series,* which contains several color-bound reference documents about computer and information system security. The criteria were broken down into four divisions: A, B, C, and D. Products rated in meeting the A division provided the most comprehensive security functionality and those rated for the D division provided essentially none. The NCSC evaluated products against the criteria under the Trusted Product Evaluation Criteria. Although the "Orange Book" only addressed confidentiality, it provided guidelines for the evaluation of security products, such as hardware and operating systems.

According to TCSEC, the criteria were developed with three objectives in mind:

1. To provide users with a yardstick with which to assess the degree of trust that can be placed in computer systems for the secure processing of classified or other sensitive information
2. To provide guidance to manufacturers as to what to build into their new, widely available trusted commercial products to satisfy trust requirements for sensitive applications
3. To provide a basis for specifying security requirements in acquisition specifications

The TCSEC defined evaluation as assessing whether a product has the security properties claimed for it. Typically, an evaluation tried to give assurance that a product or system was secure based on three principles:

1. *Functionality.* The security features of the system, such as authentication and auditing.
2. *Effectiveness.* The mechanisms used are appropriate to the stated security requirements.
3. *Assurance.* The completeness of the evaluation identifying to what level the functionality can be trusted to perform.

The four evaluation classes of the "Orange Book" were based on several elements from the following:

- *Security policy*. Mandatory or discretionary access control policies
- *Marking of objects*. Labels indicating the sensitivity of objects
- *Identification of subjects*. Subjects must identified and authenticated
- *Accountability*. Security-related events must be contained in audit logs
- *Assurance*. Refers to operational assurance, such as system architecture, protected execution domain, system integrity; and life-cycle assurance, such as design methodology, security testing, and configuration management
- *Documentation*. Users and system administrators need to know how to install and use the security features of a secure system, and evaluators need documentation for testing
- *Continuous protection*. Guarantees that security mechanisms cannot be tampered with or modified

Based on these criteria, four security divisions and seven security classes were used as ratings. They are shown in Table 15.1.

Although TCSEC was replaced by the Common Criteria, the A-B-C-D levels are still referred to by information system security practitioners when discussing evaluation categories. They are also used to create a reference (or comparison) level for the Common Criteria levels.

According to NSTISSAM COMPUSEC I-99, the Common Criteria differ from the TCSEC with respect to the standardization approach. The TCSEC defined the specific security functionalities that must exist and the specific testing that must be performed to verify that the security functionalities were implemented correctly (i.e., assurance) in predefined classes such as C2, B1, etc. Conversely, the Common Criteria represent more of a lexicon or language that provide a standardized and comprehensive list of security functionalities and analysis techniques that may be performed to verify proper implementation, as well as a common evaluation methodology to perform the tests. The greater the degree of analysis, the higher the assurance that the product performs as advertised. It is up to the customer to select from these lists the security functionalities required in a specific product or application, as well as the degree of evaluation to be performed. This is documented in a "Protection Profile." Thus, the TCSEC C2 class, for example, can be specified in a Protection Profile using the language of the Common Criteria by choosing the appropriate security functionalities and level of assurance from the Common Criteria lists. Similarly, product vendors can specify the security functionalities existing in their product, as well as the tests performed to verify proper implementation in a "Security Target."

Table 15.1   TCSEC Levels

Security Division	Explanation
A—Verified Protection	A1 is equivalent to B3; however, it achieves the highest assurance level through the use of formal methods. A system security administrator is supported. Very few products have been evaluated to class A1.
B—Mandatory Protection, includes B1, B2, and B3	The B class is intended for products that handle classified data and enforce the mandatory Bell-LaPadula access control policies.
	To achieve the B1 (Labeled Security Protection) rating, an informal or formal model of the security policy, data labeling, and mandatory access control over named subjects and objects is required. The capability must exist for accurately labeling exported information. Testing and documentation must be more thorough, and any flaws identified by testing must be removed. The design document, source code, and object code must be analyzed. It is intended for system high environments with compartments.
	B2 (Structured Protection) increases assurance by adding requirements to the design of the system. A formal model of the security policy and a descriptive top-level specification of the system are required. A covert channel analysis needs to be conducted. Authentication mechanisms are strengthened, trusted facility management is provided in the form of support for system administrator and operator functions, and stringent configuration management controls are imposed.
	B3 (Security Domains) is graded as highly resistant to penetration. The new elements in B3 are related to security management, involving security administrator support and audit capabilities supporting automatic notification of suspicious activities. Trusted recovery after a system failure must be included.
C—Discretionary Protection, includes C1 and C2	C1 (Discretionary Security Protection) systems are intended for an environment where cooperating users process data at the same level of sensitivity. Users are able to protect information and keep other users from accidentally reading or destroying their data.

Table 15.1 (continued)   TCSEC Levels

Security Division	Explanation
	C2 (Controlled Access Protection) systems make users individually accountable for their actions through log-in procedures, auditing of security-relevant events, and resource isolation. DACs are enforced at the granularity of single users. Although C2 systems are considered weak, they are regarded as the most reasonable class for commercial applications.
D—Minimal Protection	In this class, products were submitted for evaluation but did not meet the requirements of any higher TCSEC class.

The Trusted Network Interpretation (TNI)

The *Trusted Network Interpretation (TNI)*, also called the "Red Book," was published in 1987 (NCSC-TG-005). With the "Orange Book" as its basis, the "Red Book" addressed security for networks and telecommunications. The purpose was to evaluate vendor products for use in trusted (secure) networks and let users know the level of trust they could expect from these products. The A, B, C, and D levels of trust described in the "Orange Book" are used.

According to TNI, it was prepared for the following purposes:

- To provide a standard to manufacturers regarding the security features and assurance levels to build into their new and planned commercial network products to provide widely available systems that satisfy trust requirements for sensitive applications
- To provide a metric by which to evaluate the degree of trust that can be placed in a given network system for processing sensitive information
- To provide a basis for specifying security requirements in acquisition specifications

Some key features of the "Red Book" include:

- *Integrity.* The Biba model for integrity is suggested as a formal integrity model. Information transfer integrity refers to the correctness of message transmission, including the authentication of source and destination of a message. Cryptography is introduced as protection against the modification of data.

■ *Labels.* To guarantee mandatory access controls, which include mandatory integrity policies, *integrity labels* are introduced. An example of an integrity label is one that would indicate whether or not an object has ever been transmitted.

■ *Other security services.* These include several types of security services grouped into three main categories:

  – *Communication integrity,* including authentication, communication field integrity, and non-repudiation

  – *Denial of service,* including continuity of operation, protocol-based protection, and network management

  – *Compromise protection,* including data confidentiality and traffic confidentiality

For each of these factors, the functionality, strength, and assurance must be specified.

One of the issues with TNI, and many of the "product" evaluation schemes, is how to combine a product evaluation method into evaluating a system that includes multiple products. For example, having one TCSEC C2 evaluated product in a system does not make the entire system equal to a C2 level. Schell (2001) notes the problem as well. He acknowledges that TCSEC was a system evaluation criterion and the "Red Book" or TNI criterion imposed the context of a "network security architecture" that permitted components of systems to be individually evaluated in a way that would ensure the eventual composition of the overall system to be secure. Schell also acknowledges that the Common Criteria (CC), on the other hand, provide a framework for evaluation that does not necessarily answer the question of whether the system is secure. He states that the CC evaluations need not provide a system context. So, again, even using the CC evaluation, it is only evaluating a product or component and not the entire system. Regardless of the evaluation criteria employed, the issue of "composition" is an ongoing challenge for evaluating the security of the entire system.

Information Technology Security Evaluation Criteria (ITSEC)

Following the release of the "Orange Book," several European countries issued their own criteria. The European *Information Technology Security Evaluation Criteria (ITSEC)* was first drafted in 1990 and became endorsed by the Council of the European Union in 1995. It was the result of Dutch, English, French, and German activities to define and harmonize a European national security evaluation criterion. Although ITSEC includes concepts from the TCSEC, the "Orange Book" was thought to be too rigid. Thus, ITSEC attempted to provide a more flexible framework for security evaluation. One major difference between the two is ITSEC's inclusion of integrity and availability as security goals in addition to confidentiality.

The ITSEC recognizes that the security of an IT system can often be achieved through nontechnical measures, such as organizational and administrative controls. Technical security measures are used to counter remaining threats. The ITSEC ratings are based on *effectiveness* and *correctness*. Effectiveness describes how well a system is suited for countering the predicted threats. Correctness involves assurance aspects related to the development and operation of a system. The ITSEC criterion makes a distinction between products and systems. A product can be a hardware or software package bought off the shelf and used in a variety of operational environments. A system is deployed in a specific real-world environment and designed and built for the needs of a specific user. Both products and systems are comprised of components. To cover both options, ITSEC uses the term *Target of Evaluation (TOE)*.

The sponsor of the evaluation determines the operational requirements and threats. The *security objectives* for the TOE depend on legal or other regulations. The security objectives establish the required security functionality and evaluation level. The *security target* specifies all aspects of the TOE that are relevant for evaluation.

The security target may contain the following:

- Security objectives
- Statements about the system environment
- Assumptions about the TOE environment
- Security functions
- Rationale for security functions
- Required security mechanisms
- Required evaluation level
- Claimed rating of the minimal strength of mechanisms

The *security functionality* is described as being able to answer the following:

- *Security objectives:* why is the functionality wanted?
- *Security functions:* what is actually done?
- Security mechanisms: how is it done?

The types of security functions include identification and authentication, access control, accountability, audit, object reuse, accuracy, reliability, and data exchange.

ITSEC ratings come in pairs: *Function (F)* shown in Table 15.2 and *Assurance (E)* shown in Table 15.3. The ratings are hierarchical; each class

Table 15.2 ITSEC Functionality Levels

Functionality (F)	Class Characteristics
F1–F5	Mirror the functionality aspects of the Orange Book classes
F6	For systems with high integrity requirements for data and programs (e.g., databases)
F7	Sets requirements for the high availability of a complete system or special functions of a system
F8	Sets high requirements for data integrity during communications
F9	Addresses systems with high demands on data confidentiality during communications
F10	It is intended for networks with high demands on data confidentiality and integrity during communications

adds to the one above. The testing is done at the Assurance (E) level. The functionality of a TOE can be specified individually or by reference to one of the predefined functionality classes.

Assurance of correctness is expressed using seven evaluation fields, E0 through E6, each representing ascending levels of confidence. They refer to the construction and to the operation of the TOE, specify the list of documents that need to be provided by the sponsor, and the actions to be performed by the evaluator.

Currently, E3 is the most popular evaluation level for commercial security products. Secure operating systems or database management systems typically try for the combination of F2+E3.

Canadian Trusted Computer Product Evaluation Criteria (CTCPEC)

The CTCPEC is a computer security standard comparable to the TCSEC but considered more advanced. Its intent was to be applied to any kind of computer product that processed sensitive information. It deals with monolithic systems, multi-processor systems, databases, subsystems, distributed systems, networked systems, and others. In comparison to TCSEC and ITSEC, which have a hierarchical specification of security, the CTCPEC addressed an object-oriented approach to security. It has been superseded by the international Common Criteria standard.

Table 15.3   ITSEC Assurance Levels

Assurance (E)	Class Characteristics
E0	Inadequate assurance; assigned to those that fail to meet E1
E1	There shall be a security target and an informal description of the TOE Functional testing must satisfy its security target
E2	Adds an informal description of detailed design, testing evidence is evaluated Requires configuration control and controlled distribution process
E3	Source code/drawings are evaluated Testing evidence of security mechanisms evaluated
E4	Formal model of security policy Semiformal specification of security enforcing functions Architectural design and detailed design
E5	Close correspondence between detailed design and source code/drawings must be established The vulnerability analysis uses the source code
E6	Formal specifications of the security architecture of the TOE (enforcing functions and architectural design) that are consistent with the formal model of the security policy It must be possible to relate portions of the executable form of the TOE to the source code

During the early 1990s, the United States began to update the TCSEC. However, the update was stopped in favor of combining efforts with the Europeans and Canadians to develop the Common Criteria (CC). The CC evaluates software systems based on both functionality and assurance in terms of integrity, confidentiality, and availability.

National Information Assurance Partnership (NIAP)

The National Information Assurance Partnership (NIAP) is a USG initiative designed to meet the security testing, evaluation, and assessment needs of both IT producers and consumers. The NIAP is a collaboration between NIST and NSA to fulfill their respective responsibilities under both the

Computer Security Act of 1987 and, most recently, FISMA. The partnership, originated in 1997, combines the extensive security experience of both agencies to promote the development of technically sound security requirements for IT products and systems and appropriate metrics for evaluating those products and systems. The long-term goal of the NIAP is to help increase the level of trust consumers have in their information systems and networks through the use of cost-effective security testing, evaluation, and assessment programs.

As stated on the NIAP Web site (http://niap.nist.gov/), the NIAP objectives are:

- "Promote the development and use of evaluated IT products and systems.
- Champion the development and use of national and international standards for IT security.
- Foster development of IT security requirements, test methods, tools, techniques, and assurance metrics.
- Support a framework for international recognition and acceptance of IT security evaluation results.
- Facilitate the development and growth of a commercial IT security testing industry within the U.S."

This organization continues to build important relationships with government agencies and industry in a variety of areas to help meet current and future IT security challenges affecting the nation's critical information infrastructure. The NIAP Web site (http://niap.nist.gov/) lists all the approved hardware and software products that have completed or are currently under CC evaluation.

More information on NIAP can be found at www.niap.nist.gov.

The Common Criteria

The Common Criteria (CC) provides a means to define, assess, and measure the security aspects of IT products. The CC supports understanding "**what security does the product have**" (security functionality) and "**how sure you are of that security**" (security assurance). It is now an ISO standard — ISO/IEC 15408 (2000) — which provides an open standard for IT security evaluations.

Until the CC there was no testing standard that was accepted worldwide. The question of how to interpret another country's evaluation was challenging for consumers and developers. To resolve these issues and the duplication of similar IT security evaluation criteria by the United States (TCSEC), Canada (CTCPEC), and several European nations (ITSEC), the effort to harmonize existing evaluation criteria into a common criterion began. This eventually led to the creation of the standard: "Common Criteria (CC) for Information Technology Security Evaluation." The CC is the internationally accepted and standards based method to evaluate trust in IT products.

The United States (U.S.) began to update TCSEC into a Federal Criteria. The CC is based in part on the U.S. Federal Criteria, but it also expanded on the ITSEC. The Federal Criteria kept the linkage between function and assurance in the evaluation classes and tried to overcome the rigid structure of the TCSEC by adding Protection Profiles. The CC leaves the flexibility of ITSEC and follows the Federal Criteria by using protection profiles and predefined security classes. Thus, it can be said that the CC merged the best ideas from various predecessors.

In 1993, Canada, the United Kingdom (U.K.), and the United States began a joint activity to align their separate criteria into a single set of IT security criteria. Four years later, the three countries entered into the CC Interim Agreement. In March of 1998, the second interim agreement included the initial three countries plus France, Germany, and the Netherlands. The Full Interim in October 1998 added Australia and New Zealand to the group. In May 2000, the Harmonized Agreement added Finland, Greece, Italy, Norway, and Spain. This was significant because it merged the members of two prior arrangements: members of the CC Mutual Recognition Arrangement (October 1998) with members of the ITSEC arrangement that existed in Europe. In November 2000, Israel joined; and in February 2002, Sweden joined. Japan, Turkey, and Hungary have also joined the arrangement. In 1999, the sponsoring countries (Canada, France, Germany, Netherlands, the United Kingdom, and the United States) granted non-exclusive license to the ISO/IEC to use CC version 2.1 in the continued development/maintenance of the ISO/IEC 15408 international standard.

According to the NIAP Web site (http://niap.nist.gov/cc-scheme/ccra-participants.html), of the participating nations, Australia/New Zealand (combined), Canada, France, Germany, Japan, the United States, and the United Kingdom have programs in place to evaluate COTS IA and IA-enabled IT products against the CC. The remaining nations do not have evaluation programs but have agreed to accept the certificates produced by those nations that do have evaluation programs.

Tinto (2004) noted some interesting business changes in the United States from the TCSEC evaluation program (Trusted Product Evaluation Program [TPEP]) to the CC evaluation program (Common Criteria Evaluation and Validation Scheme [CCEVS]). The first is who bears the financial cost for the evaluation and also a change in the evaluation workforce. Under the TCSEC model, the financial costs to evaluate IT products were paid for by the USG. In addition, the employees who conducted the evaluations were direct-hire employees of the USG who worked in the evaluation labs for many years. Thus, employees had a strong technical focus and a solid understanding of the requirements.

The CC model is vendor-fee based; that is, vendors pay for the evaluation of their IT product. Also, individuals responsible for conducting the evaluations are not necessarily direct-hire USG employees. Thus, evaluators are more likely to be contractors who have been certified by the USG. Although contractors provide for greater scalability, they also introduce a relatively volatile workforce that may have a reduced technical focus and understanding of requirements.

That said, there are certainly advantages and disadvantages to both models. For example, under the CC model, the financial burden is not on the USG; however, high employee turnover rates at contractors may lower the expertise level of those conducting the evaluations. Because it is still a relatively new program, it is understood that more time is needed to work through the intial growing pains.

The CC requirements specification framework is based on five factors:

1. *Process independence.* The CC specification framework can be integrated into existing processes for acquiring, specifying, designing, developing, integrating, evaluating, and certifying products or systems. The CC does not replace existing processes — it augments those processes to deliver added value.
2. *The CC specification constructs: protection profiles and security targets.* These can be applied to networked and distributed systems and used for purposes other than formal evaluation.
3. *Technology independence.* The CC can be used to specify security requirements implemented by combinations of hardware, firmware, and software. The CC is scalable and can be used to specify security requirements for information technology implementations ranging from discrete embedded components to a system comprised of networked and distributed components.
4. *Functionality independence.* The CC includes a catalog of functional requirements that serve as security capability building blocks from which one can develop specifications for security applications and services as required to support the business case, mission need, or application domain.
5. *Goal independence.* The CC was developed to provide support for formal evaluation. However, the CC framework is now being effectively utilized to address the concerns of organizations with other end-goals, such as Acquisition Support, Certification & Accreditation, Operational Test & Evaluation, and baselining the "as-built" requirements to design tomorrow's solutions.

Next we delve into the particulars of the CC evaluation scheme. Following the introduction and general model (Part 1), the CC document is separated along the functional requirements (Part 2) and the assurance requirements (Part 3). This next section follows a similar separation of the three parts of the CC.

CC Part 1: Introduction and General Model

To begin, it is important to establish the definition of a few key CC terms.

Protection Profile (PP)

An implementation-independent set of security requirements for a category of Target of Evaluations (TOEs) that meet specific consumer needs. It contains a set of security requirements, which should include an Evaluation Assurance Level (EAL). It is intended to be reusable and to define TOE requirements known to be useful and effective in meeting the identified objectives, both for functions and assurance. Also, a PP contains the rationale for security objectives and security requirements.

A PP can be developed by consumers (i.e., user communities), developers (i.e., IT product vendors), or other parties interested in defining a common set of requirements. The goal of the PP is to give consumers a tool to refer to a specific set of security needs and to facilitate future evaluations against those needs.

The USG has developed PPs for certain types of IA-enabling products. These PPs can assist vendors (and customers) in developing Security Targets that will meet the requirements for full compliance with USG policies. If an approved PP exists, the vendor must agree to have the product evaluated. If no profile exists, and the acquiring organization chooses not to acquire products that have been evaluated, the acquiring organization must require, prior to purchase, that vendors provide a Security Target of their products, and submit their products for evaluation and validation at a DAA-approved EAL.

Security Target (ST)

A combination of the TOE security threats, objectives, requirements, and summary specifications of security functions and assurance measures is used as the basis for evaluation. An ST is the basis for agreement between all parties as to what security the TOE offers.

The security requirements contained in a ST can be determined based on a PP, directly referenced to CC functional or assurance components, or stated explicitly. The ST provides an expression of the security requirements for a specific TOE, which will be shown by evaluation, to be useful and effective in meeting the identified objectives. It also contains the TOE summary specification, together with the security requirements and objectives, and the rationale for each.

Target of Evaluation (TOE)

A TOE is an IT product or system and its associated administrator and user guidance documentation that is the subject of an evaluation.

Evaluation

This is the assessment of a PP, an ST, or a TOE against defined criteria, that is, the inputs to the evaluation are the documented security requirements (PP), a documented definition of the security functions needed to meet the security requirements (ST), and the IT product and related documentation (the TOE).

- A review of the PP is performed to demonstrate that the PP is complete, consistent, and technically sound and suitable for use as a TOE statement of requirements.
- An ST evaluation for the TOE is performed against the CC ST evaluation criteria. The objective is to demonstrate that the ST is complete, consistent, and technically sound and hence suitable for use as the basis for the corresponding TOE evaluation. Also, in the case where an ST claims conformance to a PP, a review is conducted to demonstrate that the ST properly meets the requirements of the PP.
- A TOE evaluation is performed against the CC TOE evaluation criteria using an evaluated ST as the basis. The purpose is to demonstrate that the TOE meets the security requirements contained in the ST.

Evaluation Assurance Level (EAL)

EALs are predefined assurance packages. They constitute a baseline set of assurance requirements for evaluation. Individually, EALs define a consistent set of assurance requirements. Together, the EALs form an ordered set that is the predefined assurance scale of the CC. The various EALs and a short description are provided in CC Part 3.

The CC involves three distinct audiences:

1. *Consumers.* Those who purchase the product and thus will create the security requirements. They want to be sure which security aspects of the product were tested, how these aspects were tested, and how they can trust the testing facility. Consumers could use each part of the CC as follows:
   - Introduction and General Model: use for background information and reference purposes. Structure guidance for PPs.
   - Part 2, Security Functional Requirements: use for guidance and reference when formulating statements of requirements for security functions.
   - Part 3, Security Assurance Requirements: use for guidance when determining required levels of assurance.
2. *Developers.* Those who design and develop the product to meet the security requirements of the consumers. Developers want to know how to design their product so that it can pass an evaluation and obtain assurance that their customers will trust the testing facility. Developers could use each part of the CC as follows:
   - Introduction and General Model: use for background information and reference for the development of requirements and formulating security specifications for TOEs.
   - Part 2, Security Functional Requirements: use for reference when interpreting statements of functional requirements and formulating functional specifications of TOEs.
   - Part 3, Security Assurance Requirements: use for reference when interpreting statements of assurance requirements and determining assurance approaches of TOEs.
3. *Evaluators.* Those who evaluate whether the developer's products meet the stated security requirements of the consumers. They want to meet the CC guidelines for properly assessing a product. Evaluators could use each part of the CC as follows:
   - Introduction and General Model: use for background information and reference. Structure guidance for PPs and STs.
   - Part 2, Security Functional Requirements: use as mandatory statement of evaluation criteria when determining whether a TOE effectively meets claimed security functions.
   - Part 3, Security Assurance Requirements: use as mandatory statement of evaluation criteria when determining the assurance of TOEs and when evaluating PPs and STs.

Along with these three audiences are two distinct categories:

1. *Functional requirements* define the desired security requirements. This is used by the consumer group to define what security

requirements are wanted or needed from a product. Examples of functional requirements include requirements for identification, authentication, security audit, and non-repudiation of origin.

2. *Assurance requirements* define the basis for gaining confidence that the claimed security measures are effective and implemented correctly. This is used by the evaluators to determine how well the developer's product meets the desired security requirements. Examples of assurance requirements include constraints on the rigor of the development process and requirements to search for and analyze the impact of potential security vulnerabilities.

ISO/IEC 15408 states that the CC is applicable when IT is being used and there is concern about the ability of the IT element to safeguard assets. To show that the assets are secure, the security concerns must be addressed at all levels — from the most abstract to the final IT implementation in its operational environment. To do this, the CC discusses security using a hierarchical set of security concepts and terminology. Figure 15.2 outlines these concepts. To effectively use the CC, it is necessary to have an understanding of these basic security concepts.

The CC layers the different levels of representation. It begins with identifying the TOE physical environment, the assets needing protection, and the purpose of the TOE. This information is needed to establish the security environment (the first layer). The security environment looks at

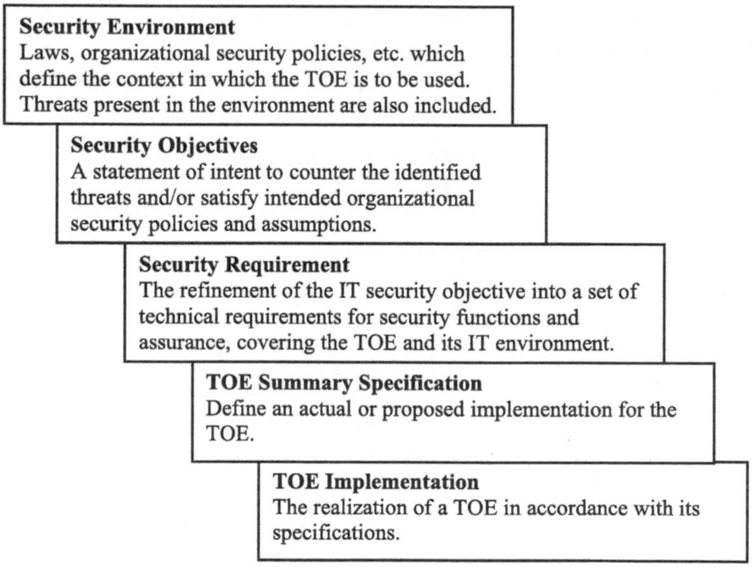

Security Environment
Laws, organizational security policies, etc. which define the context in which the TOE is to be used. Threats present in the environment are also included.

Security Objectives
A statement of intent to counter the identified threats and/or satisfy intended organizational security policies and assumptions.

Security Requirement
The refinement of the IT security objective into a set of technical requirements for security functions and assurance, covering the TOE and its IT environment.

TOE Summary Specification
Define an actual or proposed implementation for the TOE.

TOE Implementation
The realization of a TOE in accordance with its specifications.

Figure 15.2 Security concepts.

the threats to the environment or information, any organizational security policies, and any assumptions related to the environment. From this information, the security objectives are established (the second layer). The security requirements are derived from the security objectives. When defining the security requirements, it is also necessary to define the assurance objectives, which establish criteria for knowing the security objectives were met (the third layer). This information, along with TOE functional requirements, is fed into the TOE summary specification (layer four security specification material). The fifth layer is the implementation of the TOE.

Figure 15.3 illustrates the means by which the security requirements and specifications might be derived when developing a PP or ST. All TOE security requirements ultimately arise from consideration of the purpose and context of the TOE. This chart, taken from CC Part 1, is not intended to constrain the means by which PPs and STs are developed, but rather to illustrate how the results of some analytic approaches relate to the content of PPs and STs.

Security Environment

Defining the security environment is an important element. To establish the security environment, the writer of the PP or ST must take into account:

1. "The TOE physical environment which identifies all aspects of the TOE operating environment relevant to TOE security, including known physical and personnel security arrangements;
2. The assets requiring protection by the element of the TOE to which security requirements or policies will apply; this may include assets that are directly referred to, such as files and databases, as well as assets that are indirectly subject to security requirements, such as authorization credentials and the IT implementation itself;
3. The TOE purpose, which would address the product type and the intended usage of the TOE (CC Part 1, p. 22)."

It continues explaining the security environment as "[I]nvestigation of the security policies, threats and risks should permit the following security specific statements to be made about the TOE:

1. A statement of assumptions which are to be met by the environment of the TOE in order for the TOE to be considered secure. This statement can be accepted as axiomatic for the TOE evaluation.
2. A statement of threats to security of the assets would identify all the threats perceived by the security analysis as relevant to the

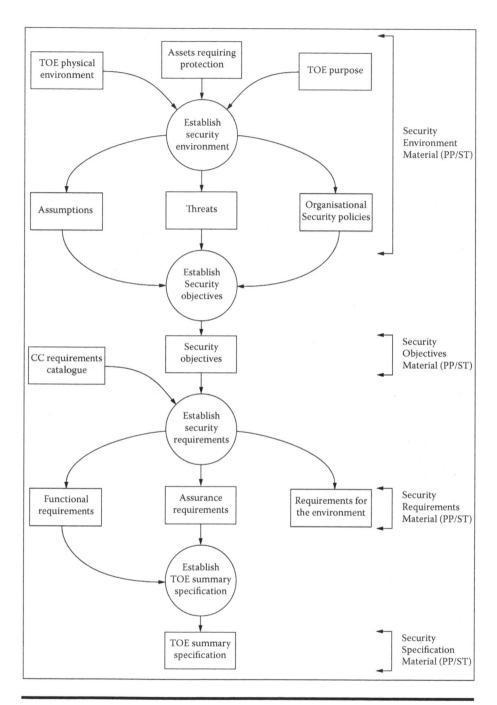

Figure 15.3   Requirements and specifications derivations. (*Source:* From CC Part 1, p. 20.)

TOE. The CC characterizes a threat in terms of a threat agent, a presumed attack method, any vulnerabilities that are the foundation for the attack, and identification of the asset under attack. An assessment of risks to security would qualify each threat with an assessment of the likelihood of such a threat developing into an actual attack, the likelihood of such an attack proving successful, and the consequences of any damage that may result.

3. A statement of applicable organizational security policies would identify relevant policies and rules. For an IT system, such policies may be explicitly referenced, whereas for a general purpose IT product or product class, working assumptions about organizational security policy may need to be made" (CC Part 1, p. 22).

Security Objectives

Based on the results of the security environment, the next step is to state the security objectives that counter the identified threats and, if appropriate, any organizational security policies and assumptions. When determining security objectives, the goal is to address all the security concerns and to declare and document which security aspects are either addressed directly by the TOE or by its environment. The process of determining this is based on incorporating engineering judgment about the system, security policies already established, current or future economic factors, and management's risk acceptance decisions.

Security Requirements

The security requirements reflect two items: (1) a fine-tuning of the security objectives into a set of security requirements for the TOE; and (2) a set of security requirements for the environment that, if met, will ensure that the TOE can meet its security objectives. Remember that the CC defines security requirements into two categories: functional requirements and assurance requirements.

Security requirements usually include two requirements: the desired behavior and the absence of undesired behavior. In most situations, it is possible to demonstrate the presence of the desired behavior either by use or testing. The challenge is to perform a conclusive demonstration of the absence of undesired behavior. To reduce the risk that the undesired behavior is included, it is necessary to perform testing, design review, and implementation reviews. Also, rationale statements provide further support to the claim that such undesired behavior is absent (CC Part 1, p. 24).

The CC security requirements are organized into a hierarchy of class → family → component. These are defined in CC Part 1 (p. 25–26) as:

- *Class.* At the top level is a "class" of security requirements used for the most general grouping of security requirements. All the members of a class share a common focus while differing in coverage of security objectives.
- *Family.* The members of a class are "families," which share security objectives but may differ in emphasis or rigor.
- *Components.* The members of a family are termed "components." A component describes a specific set of security requirements and is the smallest selectable set of security requirements defined in the CC. The set of components within a family can be ordered to represent increasing strength or capability of security requirements that share a common purpose. In some instances, there is only one component in a family, so ordering is not applicable.
  - *Package.* A combination of components is called a package. A package indicates a set of functional or assurance requirements that meet an identifiable subset of security objectives. It is designed to be reusable and to define requirements that are known to be useful and effective in meeting the identified objectives. A package can be used in the construction of larger packages, PPs, and STs.

Security requirements are represented in two categories: functional requirements (CC Part 2) and evaluation assurance requirements (CC Part 3). Both are discussed a little later in this topic.

CC does acknowledge that dependencies may exist between components. A dependency occurs when a component is not self-sufficient and relies upon the presence of another component. Dependencies can exist between functional components, between assurance components, and between functional and assurance components.

CC components can be used exactly as defined in the CC, or they can be tailored through the use of permitted operations to meet a specific security policy or counter a specific threat. These four operations are described as follows:

1. "*Iteration* permits the use of a component more than once with varying operations;
2. *Assignment* permits the specification of a parameter to be filled in when the component is used;
3. *Selection* permits the specification of items that are to be selected from a list given in the component;
4. *Refinement* permits the addition of extra detail when the component is used (CC Part 1, p. 26)."

Some required operations may be completed (in whole or part) in the PP or left for completion in the ST. Nevertheless, all operations must be completed in the ST (CC Part 1, p. 26).

TOE Summary Specification

The TOE summary specification provided in the ST defines the instantiation of the security requirements for the TOE. It provides a high-level definition of the security functions claimed to meet the functional requirements and assurance measures taken to meet the assurance requirements (CC Part 1, p. 24).

TOE Implementation

The TOE implementation is the realization of the TOE based on its security functional requirements and the TOE summary specification contained in the ST. TOE implementation is accomplished using a process of applying security and IT engineering skills and knowledge. The TOE will meet the security objectives if it correctly and effectively implements all the security requirements contained in the ST (CC Part 1, p. 24).

Protection Profile and Security Target Contents

Appendices B and C of CC Part 1 outline the contents of PPs and STs. To provide clarity, an outline of what is contained in each appendix follows.

Protection Profile Contents

Figure 15.4 from CC Part 1, Appendix B, provides on overview of the elements contained in a PP. The descriptions are taken from CC Part 1, Appendix B.

- *PP introduction.* The introduction contains document management and overview information necessary to operate a PP registry.
- *TOE description.* This describes the TOE as an aid to the understanding of its security requirements and shall address the product type and the general IT features of the TOE.
- *TOE security environment.* This statement describes the security aspects of the environment in which the TOE is intended to be used and the manner in which it is expected to be employed.

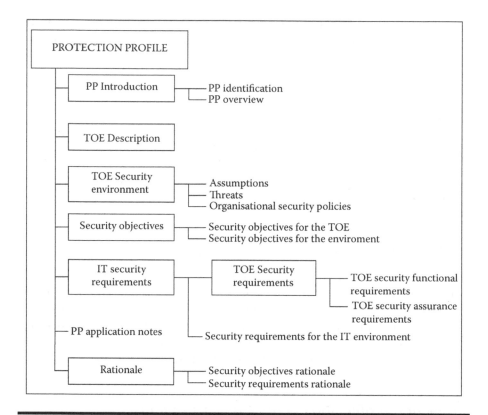

Figure 15.4 Protection profile contents. (*Source:* From CC Part 1, Appendix, p. 39.)

- *Security objectives.* This statement defines the security objectives for the TOE and its environment. The security objectives address the identified security environment aspects. The security objectives reflect the stated intent and shall be suitable to counter all identified threats and cover all identified organizational security policies and assumptions.
- *IT security requirements.* This part defines the detailed IT security requirements that shall be satisfied by the TOE or its environment.
- *Application notes.* This optional part may contain additional supporting information considered relevant or useful for the construction, evaluation, or use of the TOE.
- *Rationale.* This part presents the evidence used in the PP evaluation. This evidence supports the claims that the PP is a complete and cohesive set of requirements and that a conformant TOE would provide an effective set of IT security countermeasures within the security environment.

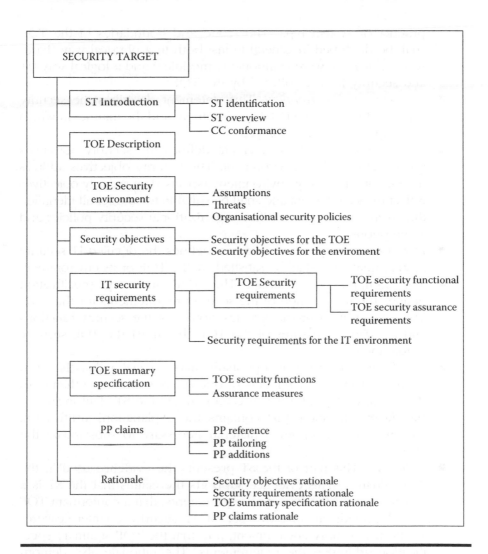

Figure 15.5 Security target contents. (*Source:* From CC Part 1, Appendix C, p. 46.)

Security Target Contents

Figure 15.5 provides on overview of the elements contained in a ST. The descriptions are taken from CC Part 1, Appendix C.

- *ST introduction.* The ST introduction shall contain document management and overview information.
- *TOE description.* This part describes the TOE as an aid to the understanding of its security requirements and shall address the

product or system type. The scope and boundaries of the TOE shall be described in general terms: both in a physical way (hardware and/or software components/modules) and a logical way (IT and security features offered by the TOE).

■ *TOE security environment.* This statement describes the security aspects of the intended TOE environment and the manner in which it is expected to be employed.

■ *Security objectives.* This statement defines the security objectives for the TOE and its environment. The security objectives address the identified security environment aspects. The security objectives reflect the stated intent and shall be suitable to counter all identified threats and cover all identified organizational security policies and assumptions.

■ *IT security requirements.* This part defines the detailed IT security requirements that shall be satisfied by the TOE or its environment.

■ *TOE summary specification.* The TOE summary specification defines the instantiation of the security requirements for the TOE. This specification provides a description of the security functions and assurance measures of the TOE that meet the TOE security requirements.

■ *PP claims.* The ST may optionally make a claim that the TOE conforms to the requirements of one (or possibly more than one) PP. For any PP conformance claims made, the ST shall include a **PP claims** statement that contains the explanation, justification, and any other supporting material necessary to substantiate the claims.

■ *Rationale.* This part of the ST presents the evidence used in the ST evaluation. This evidence supports the claims that the ST is a complete and cohesive set of requirements, that a conformant TOE would provide an effective set of IT security countermeasures within the security environment, and that the TOE summary specification addresses the requirements. The rationale also demonstrates that any PP conformance claims are valid.

The next two topics cover Part 2 of the CC (Security Functional Requirements) and Part 3 (Security Assurance Requirements).

CC Part 2: Security Functional Requirements

CC Part 2 begins by explaining the security functional components as the basis for the IT product's security functional requirements expressed in a PP or an ST. It states that "these security requirements describe the desired security behavior expected of a TOE and are intended to meet the security objectives as stated in a PP or an ST. These requirements describe security properties that users can detect by direct interaction with the TOE, such as inputs or outputs, or by the product's response to stimulus" (CC Part 2, p. 1).

The security functional components are intended to "state the security requirements intended to counter threats in the defined operating environment of the product and/or cover any identified organizational security policies and assumptions" (CC Part 2, p.1). Table 15.4 lists the primary classes of the security functional requirements. Note that the abbreviations for the classes for the security functions begin with an "F" — this denotes its reference to the functional requirements. (Assurance class acronyms begin with "A.") This can be helpful if you just see the acronym, such as FPR. Drop the F, and PR makes sense as an acronym for privacy. A summarized list of the security functional requirements grouped by class and family from CC Part 2 is contained in Appendix D of this book.

CC Part 3: Security Assurance Requirements

The CC philosophy is to provide assurance based upon an evaluation (active investigation) of the IT product or system that is to be trusted. The CC proposes measuring the validity of the documentation and of the resulting IT product or system by expert evaluators with increasing emphasis on scope, depth, and rigor.

Part 3 of the CC covers three different evaluation areas:

1. *Protection profile and security target evaluation criteria.* There are two classes containing assurance requirements for evaluation PPs and STs.
2. *Assurance classes, families, and components.* The evaluation assurance classes contain seven classes from which the evaluation assurance requirements can be chosen.
3. *Assurance maintenance paradigm.* The final evaluation class is an assurance maintenance class that provides requirements that should be applied after the TOE has been certified against the CC.

More on each assurance evaluation is discussed later in the section. Before these definitions, it may be helpful to review some background information on what assurance means to the CC model. A summarized list of the security assurance requirements for each class and family from CC Part 3 is contained in Appendix B.

Although information in this section is taken directly from CC Part 3, it does provide a good introduction and explanation of why the CC assurance evaluations are needed. CC Part 3 states that "IT security

Table 15.4 Security Function Requirement Classes

Security Function Class (Fxx)	Description
Audit (FAU)	Security auditing involves recognizing, recording, storing, and analyzing information related to security activities
	The class includes families that define requirements for the selection of auditable events, the analysis of audit records, their protection, and their storage
Communications (FCO)	Provides two families concerned with assuring the identity of a party participating in data exchange
	The families are concerned with non-repudiation by the originator and the recipient of data
Cryptographic Support (FCS)	Used when the TOE implements cryptographic functions
	The two families cover the operational use and management of cryptographic keys
User Data Protection (FDP)	The class contains families specifying requirements relating to the protection of user data
	These families address user data within the TOE during import, export, and storage
	Also covers security attributes related to user data
Identification and Authentication (FIA)	The requirements for I&A ensure the unambiguous identification of authorized users and the correct association of security attributes with users and subjects
	Families in this class deal with determining and verifying user identity, determining their authority to interact with the TOE, and with the correct association of security attributes with the authorized user
Security Management (FMT)	The class is used to specify the management of the product's security functions' attributes, data, and functions (e.g., different management roles and their interaction, such as separation of duties)
	The class is also used to cover the management aspects of other functional classes

Table 15.4 (continued)   Security Function Requirement Classes

Security Function Class (Fxx)	Description
Privacy (FPR)	Privacy requirements provide a user with protection against discovery and misuses of identity by other users The families in this class are concerned with anonymity, pseudonymity, unlinkability, and unobservability
Protection of the TOE Security Functions (FPT)	The class is focused on protection of TOE security functions data rather than user data The class relates to the integrity and management of the TOE security function mechanisms and data
Resource Utilization (TRU)	Resource utilization provides three families that support the availability of required resources, such as processing capability and storage capacity The families detail requirements for fault tolerance, priority of service, and resource allocation
TOE Access (FTA)	The class specifies functional requirements, in addition to those specified for I&A, for controlling the establishment of a user's session The requirements for TOE access govern such controls as limiting the number and scope of user sessions, displaying the access history, and the modification of access parameters
Trusted Path/Channels (FTP)	The class is concerned with trusted communications paths between the users and the TOE security functions, and between TOE security functions Trusted paths are constructed from trusted channels. They exist for inter-trusted security function communications providing a means for users to perform functions through a direct interaction with the trusted security function The user of trusted security function can initiate the exchange, which is guaranteed to be protected from modification by untrusted applications

breaches arise through the intentional exploitation or the unintentional triggering of vulnerabilities in the application of IT within business concerns. Steps should be taken to prevent vulnerabilities arising in IT products and systems. To the extent feasible, vulnerabilities should be:

1. *Eliminated* — that is, active steps should be taken to expose, and remove or neutralize, all exercisable vulnerabilities;
2. *Minimized* — that is, active steps should be taken to reduce, to an acceptable residual level, the potential impact of any exercise of a vulnerability;
3. *Monitored* — that is, active steps should be taken to ensure that any attempt to exercise a residual vulnerability will be detected so that steps can be taken to limit the damage (p. 2)."

"Vulnerabilities can arise through failures in:

1. *Requirements* — that is, an IT product or system may possess all the functions and features required of it and still contain vulnerabilities that render it unsuitable or ineffective with respect to security;
2. *Construction* — that is, an IT product or system does not meet its specifications and/or vulnerabilities have been introduced as a result of poor constructional standards or incorrect design choices;
3. *Operation* — that is, an IT product or system has been constructed correctly to a correct specification but vulnerabilities have been introduced as a result of inadequate controls upon the operation" (p. 3).

"Assurance is grounds for confidence that an IT product or system meets its security objectives. Assurance can be derived from reference to sources such as unsubstantiated assertions, prior relevant experience, or specific experience. However, the CC provides assurance through active investigation. Active investigation is an evaluation of the IT product or system in order to determine its security properties" (p. 3).

"Evaluation has been the traditional means of gaining assurance, and is the basis of the CC approach. Evaluation techniques can include, but are not limited to:

1. Analysis and checking of process(es) and procedure(s);
2. Checking that process(es) and procedure(s) are being applied;
3. Analysis of the correspondence between TOE design representations;
4. Analysis of the TOE design representation against the requirements;
5. Verification of proofs;
6. Analysis of guidance documents;

7. Analysis of functional tests developed and the results provided;
8. Independent functional testing;
9. Analysis for vulnerabilities (including flaw hypothesis);
10. Penetration testing" (p. 3).

"The CC philosophy asserts that greater assurance results from the application of greater evaluation effort, and that the goal is to apply the minimum effort required to provide the necessary level of assurance. The increasing level of effort is based upon:

1. *Scope* — that is, the effort is greater because a larger portion of the IT product or system is included;
2. *Depth* — that is, the effort is greater because it is deployed to a finer level of design and implementation detail;
3. *Rigor* — that is, the effort is greater because it is applied in a more structured, formal manner" (p. 4).

The next three topic areas focus on the specific evaluation classes.

Protection Profile (PP) and Security Target (ST) Evaluation Criteria

Also included in CC Part 3 is information regarding the two evaluation classes for PPs and STs. The first evaluation class is for the evaluation of PPs (Class APE) and the second is for the evaluation of STs (ASE). All of the requirements in the relevant class should be applied for a PP or ST evaluation. The criteria should be applied in order to find out whether the PP or ST is a meaningful basis for a TEO evaluation.

Table 15.5 provides a description of the PP and ST classes. A summarized list of the PP and ST evaluation class and families from CC Part 3 is contained in Appendix B.

Assurance Classes, Families, and Components

The seven evaluation assurance classes and families are:

1. Class ACM: Configuration Management
   - CM automation ACM_AUT
   - CM capabilities ACM_CAP
   - CM scope ACM_SCP
2. Class ADO: Delivery and Operation
   - Delivery ADO_DEL
   - Installation, generation, and start-up ADO_IGS

Table 15.5 Assurance Requirements Classes

Evaluation of PPs and STs	Description
Protection Profile Evaluation (APE)	The goal is to demonstrate that the PP is complete, consistent, and technically sound The PP should be a statement of the requirements for a TOE that can be evaluated The families in this class are concerned with the TOE Description, Security Environment, Security Objectives, and TOE Security Requirements
Security Target Evaluation (STE)	The goal is to demonstrate that the ST is complete, consistent, technically sound, and is a suitable basis for the TOE evaluation The requirements for the families of this class are concerned with the TOE Description, Security Environment, Security Objectives, any PP claims, TOE Security Requirements, and the TOE Summary Specifications
Evaluation Assurance Class (Axx)	The Assurance Maintenance (AMA) class provides requirements that are intended to be applied after a TOE has been certified against the CC
Configuration Management (ACM)	Configuration Management (CM) requires that the integrity of the TOE be adequately preserved. Specifically, CM provides confidence that the product and documentation used for evaluation are the ones prepared for distribution The families in this class are concerned with the capabilities of the CM, its scope, and its automation
Delivery and Operations (DO)	This class provides families concerned with the measures, procedures, and standards for secure delivery, installation, and operational use of the TOE (this ensures that the security protection offered by the TOE is not compromised during these events)
Development (ADV)	The families of this class are concerned with the refinement of the TOE security functions from the specification defined in the ST to the implementation, and a mapping from the security requirements to the lowest level representation
Guidance Documents (AGD)	Guidance documents are concerned with the security operational use of the TOE by the users and administrators

Table 15.5 (continued) Assurance Requirements Classes

Evaluation of PPs and STs	Description
Life-Cycle Support (ALC)	The requirements of the families concerns with the life cycle of the TOE include life-cycle definition, tools and techniques, security of the development environment, and the remediation of flaws found by TOE consumers
Tests (ATE)	This class is concerned with demonstrating that the TOE meets its functional requirements The families address coverage and depth of developer testing and requirements for independent testing
Vulnerability Assessment (AVA)	This class defines requirements directed at the identification of exploitable vulnerabilities introduced by construction, operation, misuse, or incorrect configuration of the TOE The families identified here are concerned with identifying vulnerabilities through covert channel analysis, analysis of the configuration of the TOE, examining the strength of mechanisms of the security function, and identifying laws introduced during development of the TOE
Assurance Maintenance Class	Assurance class AMA is aimed at maintaining the level of assurance that the TOE will continue to meet its security target as changes are made to the TOE or its environment

Source: Based on information from CC Part 3.

3. Class ADV: Development
   - Functional specification ADV_FSP
   - High-level design ADV_HLD
   - Implementation representation ADV_IMP
   - TSF internals ADV_INT
   - Low-level design ADV_LLD
   - Representation correspondence ADV_RCR
   - Security policy modeling ADV_SPM
4. Class AGD: Guidance Documents
   - Administrator guidance AGD_ADM
   - User guidance AGD_USR
5. Class ALC: Life-Cycle Support
   - Development security ALC_DVS
   - Flaw remediation ALC_FLR

      – Life-cycle definition ALC_LCD
      – Tools and techniques ALC_TAT
  6. Class ATE: Tests
      – Coverage ATE_COV
      – Depth ATE_DPT
      – Functional tests ATE_FUN
      – Independent testing ATE_IND
  7. Class AVA: Vulnerability Assessment
      – Covert channel analysis AVA_CCA
      – Misuse AVA_MSU
      – Strength of TOE security functions AVA_SOF
      – Vulnerability analysis AVA_VLA

Table 15.5 provides an overview of the evaluation assurance classes. A summarized list of the assurance classes and families is contained in Appendix B. The acronym for the evaluation assurance classes begin with the letter "A." Just like in the functional security requirement classes, if you drop the A, the next two letters will be an acronym for the class. Take, for example, ADO; drop the A and DO represents Delivery and Operation.

Assurance Maintenance Class

The one class for this evaluation is Maintenance of Assurance (AMA). The four families for AMA are:

  1. Assurance maintenance plan AMA_AMP
  2. TOE component categorization report AMA_CAT
  3. Evidence of assurance maintenance AMA_EVD
  4. Security impact analysis AMA_SIA

The AMA class provides requirements that are intended to be applied after a TOE has been certified against the CC. A brief overview of the AMA class is in Table 15.5. The AMA requirements focus on assuring the TOE will continue to meet its security target as changes are made to the TOE or its environment. The class contains families that cover the content of the assurance maintenance plan, the security categorization of TOE components, and the analysis of changes for security impact, and the provision of evidence that procedures are being followed. The objective of this class is to provide building blocks for the establishment of assurance maintenance schemes.

A key feature of this class is the development of an assurance maintenance plan that identifies the plans and procedures the developer will implement to ensure that the assurance that was established in the certified

TOE is maintained as changes are made to the TOE or its environment. The Assurance Maintenance Plan should include four types of procedures. The first are configuration management procedures that control and record changes in the product and any supporting documentation. The second set of procedures consists of those that maintain assurance evidence, such as functional testing of the security functions of the TOE. The third are the procedures governing the security impact of changes affecting the TOE, such as new threat or attack methods. The final set of procedures relates to flaw remediation procedures that cover the tracking and correction of reported security flaws. Refer to Appendix B for a summary of the AMA families.

Evaluation Assurance Levels

The CC contains a set of predefined evaluation assurance levels (EALs) constructed using components from the assurance families. These levels provide backward compatibility to source criteria and also provide internally consistent general-purpose assurance packages. Other groupings of components are not excluded. To meet specific objectives, an assurance level can be "augmented" by one or more additional components.

Assurance levels are defined using an increasingly hierarchical scale for measuring the criteria for the evaluation of PPs and STs. *EALs are constructed from the assurance components.* Each of the seven evaluation assurance classes contributes to the assurance that a TOE meets its security claims. The EALs scale balances the level of assurance obtained with the cost and feasibility of acquiring that degree of assurance.

The increase in assurance from one level to the next is accomplished by substituting hierarchically higher assurance components from the same assurance family, such as increasing rigor, scope, or depth. It is also accomplished by the addition of assurance components from other assurance families, such as adding new requirements.

A brief description of the seven EALs is shown in Table 15.6, with EAL 1 as the lowest level and EAL 7 as the highest level.

Table 15.7 (from CC Part 3) expresses the EALs with the evaluation assurance classes.

Note to ISSEP candidates: Although it is highly unlikely that this will be on the exam, it does provide an understanding of how the evaluation levels and evaluation assurance classes fit together.

The columns in Table 15.7 represent a hierarchically ordered set of EALs, while the rows represent assurance families. Each number in the resulting matrix identifies a specific assurance component where applicable.

Table 15.6 Evaluated Assurance Levels

EAL	Description
EAL 1 Functionally Tested	Provides an evaluation of the TOE as it is made available to the customer
EAL 2 Structurally Tested	Adds requirements for TOE configuration list, delivery and high-level design documentation, developer functional testing, vulnerability analysis, and more independent testing
EAL 3 Methodically Tested and Checked	Adds requirements for development environment controls of TOE, Configuration Management, high-level design documentation, more complete developer functional testing, and analysis of guidance documents
EAL 4 Methodically Designed, Tested and Reviewed	The highest level likely for retrofit of an existing product Additional requirements for CM system automation, complete interface specs, low-level design documentation, analysis of a subset of the TSF implementation, life-cycle definition, and informal security policy model
EAL 5 Semi-Formally Designed and Tested	Comprehensive CM, semiformal functional specification and high-level design, formal security policy model, analysis based on the entire implementation, covert channel analysis, and modular TOE design
EAL 6 Semi-Formally Verified Design and Tested	Layered TOE design, semi-formal low-level design, documents, complete CM structured development environment
EAL 7 Formally Verified Design and Tested	Formal methods are documented, including functional specifications, high-level design, evidence of complete developer testing, and independent confirmation

Refer to Appendix B for a description of the assurance class families and their acronyms.

What does this all mean? To gain some perspective, take a look at sections of the evaluation documentation and material for the operating system Microsoft Windows 2000 Professional Server and Advanced Server with SP3 and Q326886 Hotfix. This software was evaluated as EAL4. For

Table 15.7   Evaluation Assurance Level Summary

Assurance Class	Assurance Family	Assurance Components by Evaluation Assurance Level						
		EAL 1	*EAL 2*	*EAL 3*	*EAL 4*	*EAL 5*	*EAL 6*	*EAL 7*
Class ACM: Configuration Management	ACM_AUT				1	1	2	2
	ACM_CAP	1	2	3	4	4	5	5
	ACM_SCP			1	2	3	3	3
Class ADO: Delivery and Operation	ADO_DEL		1	1	2	2	2	3
	ADO_IGS	1	1	1	1	1	1	1
Class ADV: Development	ADV_FSP	1	1	1	2	3	3	4
	ADV_HLD		1	2	2	3	4	5
	ADV_IMP				1	2	3	3
	ADV_INT					1	2	3
	ADV_LLD				1	1	2	2
	ADV_RCR	1	1	1	1	2	2	3
	ADV_SPM				1	3	3	3
Class AGD: Guidance Documents	AGD_ADM	1	1	1	1	1	1	1
	AGD_USR	1	1	1	1	1	1	1
Class ALC: Life Cycle Support	ALC_DVS			1	1	1	2	2
	ALC_FLR							
	ALC_LCD				1	2	2	3
	ALC_TAT				1	2	3	3
Class ATE: Tests	ATE_COV		1	2	2	2	3	3
	ATE_DPT			1	1	2	2	3
	ATE_FUN		1	1	1	1	2	2
	ATE_IND	1	2	2	2	2	2	3
Class AVA: Vulnerability Assessment	AVA_CCA					1	2	2
	AVA_MSU			1	2	2	3	3
	AVA_SOF		1	1	1	1	1	1
	AVA_VLA		1	1	2	3	4	4

Source: From CC Part 3, p. 54.

Table 15.8 CC Part 3 Assurance Class and Components

Assurance Class	Assurance Components
Class ACM: Configuration Management	ACM_AUT.1 Partial CM automation
	ACM_CAP.4 Generation support and acceptance procedures
	ACM_SCP.2 Problem tracking CM coverage

brevity, we focus only on the Assurance Class ACM: Configuration Management. However, the complete information is available on the NIAP Web site.

CC Part 3 (p. 60) defines the EAL4 as "providing assurance by an analysis of the security functions, using a functional and complete interface specification, guidance documentation, the high-level and low-level design of the TOE, and a subset of the implementation, to understand the security behavior. Assurance is additionally gained through an informal model of the TOE security policy." Table 15.8 defines the CC requirements for EAL ACM.

The evaluation of the product was based on the Windows 2000 Security Target, Version 2.0. The security target was written for Microsoft by SAIC. SAIC may have used the PP already documented for "Single Use Operating Systems in Environments Requiring Medium Robustness" (May 23, 2001). This PP specifies security requirements for COTS general-purpose operating systems in networked environments containing sensitive information. It uses DoD IA guidance and policy as a basis to establish the requirements necessary to achieve the security objectives of the TOE and its environment. This previously documented PP for Single-Use Operating Systems in Environments Requiring Medium Robustness has also been validated (May 2001).

The configuration management assurance requirements needed to meet EAL4 are shown in Table 15.9. Note that these requirements are taken from the Windows 2000 Security Target, but they are the exact same requirements from the May 2001 PP for Single Use Operating Systems in Environments Requiring Medium Robustness.

This product type (TOE) was an operating system, vendor Microsoft Corporation was evaluated by the Validation Team (Aerospace Corporation) at the Validation Laboratory (SAIC) in October 2002. The evaluation report *"Common Criteria Evaluation and Validation Scheme Validation Report, Microsoft Corporation, Windows 2000, Report Number: CCEVS-VR-02-0025, Dated: 25 October 2002, Version: 2.0"* stated that "The evaluation determined the product to be Part 2 conformant, Part 3 conformant, and to meet the requirements of EAL 4, augmented with ALC_FLR.3. Additionally, the product is conformant to the *Controlled Access Protection Profile*

Table 15.9   Windows 2000 Security Target

Partial CM automation (ACM_AUT.1)			
ACM_AUT.1.1D	The developer shall use a CM system.	ACM_AUT.1.3C	The CM plan shall describe the automated tools used in the CM system.
ACM_AUT.1.2D	The developer shall provide a CM plan.	ACM_AUT.1.4C	The CM plan shall describe how the automated tools are used in the CM system.
ACM_AUT.1.1C	The CM system shall provide an automated means by which only authorized changes are made to the TOE implementation representation.	ACM_AUT.1.1E	The evaluator shall confirm that the information provided meets all requirements for content and presentation of evidence.
ACM_AUT.1.2C	CM system shall provide an automated means to support the generation of the TOE.		
Generation Support and Acceptance Procedures (ACM_CAP.4)			
ACM_CAP.4.1D	The developer shall provide a reference for the TOE.	ACM_CAP.4.6C	The CM system shall uniquely identify all configuration items.
ACM_CAP.4.2D	The developer shall use a CM system.	ACM_CAP.4.7C	The CM plan shall describe how the CM system is used.
ACM_CAP.4.3D	The developer shall provide CM documentation.	ACM_CAP.4.8C	The evidence shall demonstrate that the CM system is operating in accordance with the CM plan.

Table 15.9 (continued) Windows 2000 Security Target

ACM_CAP.4.1C	The reference for the TOE shall be unique to each version of the TOE.	ACM_CAP.4.9C	The CM documentation shall provide evidence that all configuration items have been and are being effectively maintained under the CM system.
ACM_CAP.4.2C	The TOE shall be labeled with its reference.	ACM_CAP.4.10C	The CM system shall provide measures such that only authorized changes are made to the configuration items.
ACM_CAP.4.3C	The CM documentation shall include a configuration list, a CM plan, and an acceptance plan.	ACM_CAP.4.11C	The CM system shall support the generation of the TOE.
ACM_CAP.4.4C	The configuration list shall describe the configuration items that comprise the TOE.	ACM_CAP.4.12C	The acceptance plan shall describe the procedures used to accept modified or newly created configuration items as part of the TOE.
ACM_CAP.4.5C	The CM documentation shall describe the method used to uniquely identify the configuration items.	ACM_CAP.4.1E	The evaluator shall confirm that the information provided meets all requirements for content and presentation of evidence.
Problem tracking CM coverage (ACM_SCP.2)			
ACM_SCP.2.1D	The developer shall provide CM documentation.	ACM_SCP.2.2C	The CM documentation shall describe how configuration items are tracked by the CM system.

Table 15.9 (continued)   Windows 2000 Security Target

ACM_SCP.2.1C	The CM documentation shall show that the CM system, as a minimum, tracks the following: the TOE implementation representation, design documentation, test documentation, user documentation, administrator documentation, CM documentation, and security flaws.	ACM_SCP.2.1E	The evaluator shall confirm that the information provided meets all requirements for content and presentation of evidence.

Source: From p. 35–37.

(CAPP), Version 1.d, 8 October 1999. This implies that the product satisfies the security technical requirements specified in *Windows 2000 Security Target, Version 2.0*, 18 October 2002" (p. 11).

A complete listing of the requirements for EAL 1 through EAL 7 is available in CC Part 3, which is available on the NIAP Web site.

Before ending this section, it is important to note the role of the Common Criteria Evaluation and Validation Scheme (CCEVS). The CCEVS is an activity jointly managed by NIST and the NSA, and is staffed by personnel from each agency.

According to the CCEVS Web site, the focus of the CCEVS is to establish a national program for the evaluation of IT products for conformance to the International Common Criteria for Information Technology Security Evaluation. The CCEVS approves participation of security testing laboratories in the scheme in accordance with its established policies and procedures. During the course of an evaluation, the CCEVS provides technical guidance to those testing laboratories, validates the results of IT security evaluations for conformance to the Common Criteria, and serves as an interface to other nations for the recognition of such evaluations.

IT security evaluations are conducted by commercial testing laboratories accredited by the NIST National Voluntary Laboratory Accreditation Program (NVLAP) and approved by the CCEVS. These approved testing laboratories are called Common Criteria Testing Laboratories (CCTLs). NVLAP accreditation is one of the requirements for becoming a CCTL. The purpose of the NVLAP accreditation is to ensure that laboratories meet the requirements of ISO/IEC Guide 25, General Requirement for the

Competence of Calibration and Testing Laboratories and the specific scheme requirements for IT security evaluation. Other requirements for CCTL approval are CCEVS specific and are outlined in scheme policies and scheme publications.

The CCEVS assesses the results of a security evaluation conducted by a CCTL within the scheme and, when appropriate, issues a Common Criteria certificate. The certificate, together with its associated validation report, confirms that an IT product or protection profile has been evaluated at an accredited laboratory using the Common Evaluation Methodology for conformance to the Common Criteria. The certificate also confirms that the IT security evaluation has been conducted in accordance with the provisions of the scheme and that the conclusions of the testing laboratory are consistent with the evidence presented during the evaluation.

The next topic is an example of how the CC process can be combined with the ISSE model.

CC Scenario

To provide some perspective on the CC process, the following is an example of how the CC could be used within the ISSE model. (Remember that the ISSE model is also part of this process.)

Phase 1: Mission/Business Need

The U.S. Department of Defense has just signed an agreement with Kuwait and designated Kuwait a major non-NATO ally of America. As part of this agreement, the DoD agrees to grant Kuwait access to certain DoD computer networks. They have asked the ISSE team to design the architecture for this connection.

Phase 2: Identify Security Requirements

In phase 2 of the ISSE model, the ISSEPs decides one of the security functions needed is a firewall. This firewall will be the TOE. As part of this process, the ISSEPs develop a protection profile (PP) outlining the specific security requirements the firewall would need.

Because this is a clever ISSEP team, they know that there is already a protection profile developed for their needs. They quickly download the "U.S. Government Firewall Protection Profile (PP) for Medium Robustness Environments" from the IATF Web site.

This firewall PP specifies the minimum security requirements for network boundary devices that provide controlled connectivity between two or more network environments used by the DoD in Medium Robustness Environments. This specific PP defines:

- "Assumptions about the security aspects of the environment in which the TOE will be used;
- Threats that are to be addressed by the TOE;
- Security objectives of the TOE and its environment;
- Functional and assurance requirements to meet those security objectives; and
- Rationale demonstrating how the requirements meet the security objectives, and how the security objectives address the threats (p. 2)."

Phase 3: Identify Security Architecture

In this phase, the ISSEPs identify the security functions needed to meet the security requirements outlined in the PP. This is documented in the Security Target (ST). Good luck is with these ISSEPs as an ST has already been written for several products. On the NIAP Web site, the ISSE team notes a specific item to review, the *Cisco Secure PIX Firewall Software Version 6.2(2) ST*.

Phase 4: Develop Detailed Security Design

During this phase, the ISSEPs team review additional products that have been evaluated against the previously established PPs and STs. The ISSEPs download the evaluation results for Cisco PIX Firewall Software.

The Cisco PIX Firewall Software Certification Results (2002) state that "[a]fter due consideration of the ETR [i], produced by the Evaluators, and the conduct of the evaluation, as witnessed by the Certifier, the Certification Body has determined that Cisco Secure PIX Firewall Version 6.2(2) meets the Common Criteria Part 3 conformant requirements of Evaluation Assurance Level EAL4, augmented with ALC_FLR.1, for the specified Common Criteria Part 2 conformant functionality, extended by FAU_AUD.1, in the specified environment when running on the PIX 501, 506, 506E, 515, 515E, 520, 525 and 535 hardware platforms as specified in Annex A." (A copy of the Security Target and Evaluation Results can be obtained from the NIAP Web site.)

In this phase, the ISSEPs compare the evaluation documentation against the protection profile that outlined the security requirements needed for a firewall component. If this specific product will meet the security requirements, it is approved for implementation into the system.

Phase 5: Implement System Security

As part of this phase, the ISSE will work with the Certification and Accreditation team to ensure that the components as implemented will meet the overall security requirements. This includes submitting documentation gained from the CC evaluation, such as the PP, ST, and Evaluation Report.

Phase 6: Assess Security Effectiveness

During the final phase, the ISSEPs will assess the degree to which the implemented firewall meets the designed security requirements. Although this may be an ongoing process throughout the design and development of the system, the final step is to look at the processes used for the system and review whether they met the security needs.

Summary

This chapter provided a review of various evaluation criteria, such as the TCSEC, ITSEC, and CTCPEC. NIAP is the collaboration between NIST and NSA to provide a framework and organization to promote the development of technically sound security requirements for IT products and systems and appropriate measures for evaluating those products and systems. We reviewed the three parts of the CC and outlined some of the key terms and processes in developing protection profiles, security targets, and evaluations, especially evaluation assurance levels.

As something to consider, security evaluation criteria have been criticized as an expensive process required by governments. The European Computer Manufacturer's Association (ECMA) has published a report that insists a balance between cost, productivity, and security has too many competing factors. The ECMA warns that the high requirements for security are creating negligence for operational effectiveness. They state that the cost of evaluation (which is between 10 and 40 percent of the development cost) and the time delays in getting the evaluation completed are areas of concern.

In addition to government-sponsored documents, private industry has developed criteria and processes for achieving information security. The ECMA, which is now a worldwide association with members from Europe, the United States, and Japan, has produced the Commercial Oriented

Functionality Class (COFC). The COFC specifies a baseline security standard that is intended to reflect the minimum set of security functionality needed for the commercial market. The objective is to reduce the complexity of the government documents to allow cost- and time-effective applications and also keep standards open for extension and adaptability to any future requirements.

The International Computer Security Association (ICSA) initiated a program for certifying information technology products and operating environments against a set of *de facto* industry standards. Because most organizations purchase commercial off-the-shelf (COTS) products, their approach is based on the principle of "secure enough." Their goal is to develop criteria for at least 80 percent of the products and at least 80 percent of customers and individuals who would rely on the certification. The criteria are based on threats that occur most frequently versus threats that might happen based on an abstract theory. The ICSA has established several certification programs for Web sites, cryptography products, firewalls, anti-virus software, and biometric products.

As mentioned in Chapter 13, NSTISSP No. 11 (2002) states that all IA and IA-enabling products for DoD and national security systems must be evaluated under the Common Criteria evaluation levels. That is, any product with a security component — from an operating system to a firewall — must be assessed by an independent evaluator.

Finally, the question can be asked: "Is the CC effective?" In 2003, the DoD began to conduct a review of the effectiveness of CC for the USG. Frank (2003) notes that, unofficially, DoD experts have found that not enough products have gone through the evaluation. This is complicated by the fact that many agency officials do not understand how CC tests fit in with a complete security strategy. On a positive note, they have found that including the requirements in a larger IA policy helps push security to the development end of a system's life cycle so that less patching is necessary. Frank's article (2003) states that the CC evaluation trend would move even faster if civilian agencies joined in the demand because it would be easier for vendors to justify going through the long and expensive evaluation process.

References

CCIMB-99-031. Common Criteria Information Technology Security Evaluation, Part 1 Introduction and General Model, Version 2.1 (August 1999). Available at http://csrc.nist.gov/cc/CC-v2.1.html.

CCIMB-99-032. Common Criteria Information Technology Security Evaluation, Part 2 Security Functional Requirements, Version 2.1 (August 1999). Available at http://csrc.nist.gov/cc/CC-v2.1.html.

CCIMB-99-033. Common Criteria Information Technology Security Evaluation, Part 3 Security Assurance Requirements, Version 2.1 (August 1999). Available at http://csrc.nist.gov/cc/CC-v2.1.html.

CSC-STD-004-85. "Technical Rational behind SCS-STD-003-85: Computer Security Requirements. Guidance for Applying the Department of Defense Trusted Computer System Evaluation Criteria in Specific Environments." The Rainbow Series: National Institute of Standards and Technology: Gaithersburg, MD.

"The Canadian Trusted Computer Product Evaluation Criteria, Version 3.0e." (1993). Canadian System Security Center.

Common Criteria Evaluation and Validation Scheme Validation Report, Microsoft Corporation, Windows 2000, Report Number CCEVS-VR-02-0025, dated: 25 October 2002, Version: 2.0. Available at http://niap.nist.gov/cc-scheme/CCEVS_VID402-VR.pdf.

Common Criteria Evaluation and Validation Scheme Validation Report, Protection Profile for Single-Level Operating Systems in Environments Requiring Medium Robustness, Version 1.22, dated 23 May 2001. Report Number CCEVS-VR-01-0002 Dated: June 30, 2001, Version: 1.1. Available at http://niap.nist.gov/cc-scheme/PP_VID203-VR.pdf.

Common Criteria Certification Report No. P180, Cisco Secure PIX Firewall Version 6.2(2) (December 2002) © Crown Copyright 2002. UK IT Security Evaluation and Certification Scheme, Certification Body, P.O. Box 152, Cheltenham, Glos GL52 5UF, United Kingdom. Available at http://www.cesg.gov.uk/site/iacs/itsec/media/certreps/CRP180.pdf.

DoD 5200.28-STD (December 1985). Department of Defense Trusted Computer System Evaluation Criteria (TCSEC). Available at http://www.radium.ncsc.mil/tpep/library/rainbow/5200.28-STD.html.

DoD Direction No. 8500.1 (October 24, 2002 — Certified Current as of November 21, 2003). Information Assurance (IA). Available at http://www.dtic.mil/whs/directives/index.html.

Frank, Diane (September 29, 2003). Common Criteria: Ready for prime time? Experts question if security requirements should be mandated across government. Government Computer News. Available at http://www.fcw.com/fcw/articles/2003/0929/pol-security-09-29-03.asp.

Hansche, Susan, John Berti, and Chris Hare (2004). *Official (ISC)² Guide to the CISSP Exam*. CRC Press/Auerbach: Boca Raton, FL.

HR 145 Public Law 100-235 (June 1987). Computer Security Act of 1987. The act can be downloaded from http://csrc.nist.gov/secplcy/csa_87.txt.

HR 2458 Public Law 107-30 (November 2002). E-Government Act of 2002. Title III — Information Security Section 301, Information Security. "Federal Information Security Management Act of 2002." Available at http://csrc.nist.gov/policies/FISMA-final.pdf.

"Information Technology Security Evaluation Criteria (ITSEC), Version 1.2" (1991, updated 1990 version). Commission of the European Communities. Available at http://www.iwar.org.uk/comsec/resources/standards/itsec.htm.

ISO/IEC 15408 (2000). "The Common Criteria." It can be purchased through the ISO Web site at http://www.iso.ch/iso/en/ISOOnline.frontpage.

NCSC-TG-005 Library No. S228,526 Version 1. Trusted Network Interpretation (TNI). Available at http://www.radium.ncsc.mil/tpep/library/rainbow/NCSC-TG-005.html.

NSTISSAM COMPUSEC 1-99 (March 1999). Advisory Memorandum on the Transition from Trusted Computer System Evaluation Criteria to Evaluation Criteria (TCSEC) to the International Common Criteria (CC) for Information Security Technology Evaluation. Available at http://www.nstissc.gov/Assets/pdf/nstissam_compusec_1-99.pdf.

Protection Profile for Single-Level Operating Systems in Environments Requiring Medium Robustness, Version 1.22 (May 23, 2001). NSA Information Assurance Directorate. Available at http://niap.nist.gov/cc-scheme/PP_SLOSPP-MR_V1.22.pdf.

Schell, Roger D. (2001). "Information Security: Science, Pseudoscience, and Flying Pigs." Aesec Corporation. Available at http://www.acsac.org/invited-essay/essays/2001-schell.pdf.

SLOSPP-MR_V1.22. Protection Profile for Single-Level Operating Systems in Environments Requiring Medium Robustness (May 23, 2001). Available at http://niap.nist.gov/cc-scheme/PP_SLOSPP-MR_V1.22.html.

Tinto, Mario (2004). Presentation at the Information Assurance Technical Framework (IATF) Forum, March 25, 2004.

U.S. Government Firewall Protection Profile (PP) for Medium Robustness Environments, Version 1.0 (October 2003). NSA Information Assurance Directorate. Available at http://www.iatf.net/protection_profiles/instructions.cfm.

Windows 2000 Security Target, ST Version 2.0, 18 October 2002. Prepared for Microsoft Corporation. Prepared by Science Applications International Corporation. Available at http://niap.nist.gov/cc-scheme/CCEVS_VID402-ST.pdf.

Web Sites

http://niap.nist.gov/cc-scheme/defining-ccevs.html for information on CCEVS.

Appendix A

Linking ISSE Phases to SE Phases

(Reference to Chapter 1)

DoD 5000.2-R, "Mandatory Procedures for Major Defense Acquisition Programs (MDAP) and Major Automated Information System (MAIS) Acquisition Programs," describes the Systems Engineering Process (SEP) as a comprehensive, iterative, and recursive problem-solving process, applied sequentially, top down. Table A.1 summarizes the DoD 5000.2-R SEP and maps it to similar ISSE tasks.

Table A.2 maps the ISSE phases to the IEEE Standard for Application and Management of the Systems Engineering Process (IEEE Std 1220-1998).

References

DoD 5000.2-R (June 2001). Mandatory Procedures for Major Defense Acquisition Programs (MDAP) and Major Automated Information System (MAIS) Acquisition Programs. Available at http://acc.dau.mil.

Information Assurance Technical Framework (IATF), Version 3.1 (September 2002). National Security Agency, Information Assurance Solutions, Technical Directors; Fort Meade, MD.

IEEE Std 1220-1998 (December 1998, copyrighted January 1999). IEEE Standard for Application and Management of the Systems Engineering Process. IEEE: New York, NY. (Revision of IEEE Std 1220-1994.)

Table A.1   Linkage of DoD 5000.2-R and ISSE Phases

DoD 5000.2-R Systems Engineering Process	ISSE Process

Systems Engineering Process Inputs
 	
■ Customer needs/objectives/ requirements
  – Missions
  – Measures of effectiveness
  – Environments
  – Constraints
■ Technology base
■ Output requirements from prior development effort
■ Program decision requirements
■ Requirements applied through specifications and standards
	Discover Information Protection Needs
	
	■ Analyze organization's mission
	■ Determine relationship and importance of information to mission
	■ Identify legal and regulatory requirements
	■ Identify classes of threats
	■ Determine impacts
	■ Identify security services
	■ Document the information protection needs
	■ Document security management roles and responsibilities
	■ Identify design constraints

Requirements Analysis
 	
■ Analyze missions and environments
■ Identify functional requirements
■ Define or refine performance and design constraint requirements
	Define System Security Requirements
	
	■ Develop system security context
	  – Define system boundaries and interfaces with SE
	  – Document security allocations to target system and external systems
	  – Identify data flows between the target system and external systems and the protection needs associated with those flows
	■ Develop security CONOPS
	■ Develop system security requirements baseline
	  – Define system security requirements
	  – Define system security modes of operation
	  – Define system security performance measures
	■ Review design constraints

Table A.1 (continued)   Linkage of DoD 5000.2-R and ISSE Phases

DoD 5000.2-R Systems Engineering Process	*ISSE Process*
Functional Analysis/Allocation ■ Decompose to lower-level functions ■ Allocate performance and other limiting requirements to all functional levels ■ Define or refine functional interfaces (internal and external) ■ Define/refine/integrate functional architecture	**Design System Security Architecture** ■ Analyze candidate systems architectures ■ Allocate security services to architecture ■ Select mechanism types ■ Submit security architecture(s) for evaluation ■ Revise security architecture(s) ■ Select security architecture

Requirements Loop
■ Reconsider requirements Analysis to establish traceability of functions to requirements
	Assess Information Protection Effectiveness
	■ Provide/present documented information protection needs to the customer
	■ Identify the processes, information, users, threats, and security services that are important to the mission or business
	■ Explain security services, strengths, and priorities
	■ Provide/present security context, security CONOPS, and system security requirements to the customer
	  – Explain allocations to the target and external systems
	  – Ensure that the security mechanisms of the system meet the mission security needs
	  – Obtain concurrence the customer
	Support System C&A
	■ Identify DAA/Accreditor
	■ Identify Certification Authority/Certifier

Table A.1 (continued) Linkage of DoD 5000.2-R and ISSE Phases

DoD 5000.2-R Systems Engineering Process	*ISSE Process*
	■ Identify C&A and acquisition processes to be applied
	■ Ensure Accreditors and Certifiers concurrence
	– System Security Context
	– Security CONOPS
	– System Security Requirements
Synthesis	**Develop Detailed Security Design**
■ Transform architectures (functional to physical)	■ Ensure compliance with security architecture
■ Define alternative system concepts, configuration items, and system elements	■ Perform trade-off studies
	■ Define system security design elements
■ Select preferred product and process solutions	– Allocate security mechanisms to system security design elements
■ Define or refine physical interfaces (internal and external)	– Identify candidate COTS/GOTS security products
	– Identify custom security products
	– Qualify element and system interfaces (internal and external)
	■ Develop specifications
Design Loop	**Assess Information Protection Effectiveness**
■ Revisiting the functional architecture to verify that the physical design synthesized the required functions at the required level of performance	■ Conduct design risk analysis
	■ Ensure that the selected security design provides the required security services
	■ Explain to the customer how the security design meets the security requirements
	■ Explain to the customer, and document, any residual risks of the design
	■ Obtain concurrence from the customer in the detailed security design

Table A.1 (continued) Linkage of DoD 5000.2-R and ISSE Phases

DoD 5000.2-R Systems Engineering Process	*ISSE Process*
	Support System C&A ■ Prepare and submit detailed design documentation for risk analysis ■ Coordinate results of the risk analysis with Accreditor and Certifier
Process Output ■ Development Level Dependent – Decision database – System and configuration item architecture – Specifications and baselines	**Implement System Security** ■ Support security implementation and integration – Participate in implementation planning – Verify interoperability of security tools and mechanisms – Verify implementation against security design – Verify that the security components have been evaluated against the selected evaluation criteria (CCEP, NIAP, FIPS, or other NSA and NIST evaluation criteria) – Assist in the integration of the components to ensure that their integration meets the system security specifications and does not alter the component specifications – Assist in the configuration of the components to ensure that the security features are enabled and the security parameters are correctly set to provide the required security services ■ Support test and evaluation – Build test and evaluation strategy (includes demonstration, observation, analysis, and testing)

Table A.1 (continued) Linkage of DoD 5000.2-R and ISSE Phases

DoD 5000.2-R Systems Engineering Process	ISSE Process
	– Assess available test and evaluation data for applicability (e.g., CCEP, NIAP, internal) – Support development of test and evaluation procedures – Support test and evaluation activities
Verification ■ Comparison of the solution to the requirements	**Assess Information Protection Effectiveness** ■ Monitor to ensure that the security design is implemented correctly ■ Conduct or update risk analysis ■ Define the risks and possible mission impacts and advise the customer and the customer's Certifiers and Accreditors **Support System C&A** ■ Ensure the completeness of the required C&A documentation with the customer and the customer's Certifiers and Accreditors ■ Provide documentation and analysis as required for the C&A process

Source: From IATF, 2002, Appendix J, p. J-1 to J-3.

Table A.2   Linkage of IEEE 1220 and ISSE Phases

IEEE Std 1220-1998 *Systems Engineering Process*	*ISSE Process*
Requirements Analysis ■ Define customer expectations ■ Define project and enterprise constraints ■ Define external constraints ■ Define operational scenarios ■ Define measures of effectiveness ■ Define system boundaries ■ Define interfaces ■ Define utilization environments ■ Define life-cycle process concepts ■ Define functional requirements ■ Define performance requirements ■ Define modes of operations ■ Define technical performance measures ■ Define design characteristics ■ Define human factors ■ Establish requirements baseline	**Discover Information Protection Needs** ■ Analyze organization's mission ■ Determine relationship and importance of information to mission ■ Identify legal and regulatory requirements ■ Identify classes of threats ■ Determine impacts ■ Identify security services ■ Document the information protection needs ■ Document security management roles and responsibilities ■ Identify design constraints

	Define System Security Requirements
	■ Develop system security context
	  – Define system boundaries and interfaces with SE
	  – Document security allocations to target system and external systems
	  – Identify data flows between the target system and external systems and protection needs associated with those flows
	■ Develop security CONOPS
	■ Develop system security requirements baseline
	  – Define system security requirements
	  – Define system security modes of operation
	  – Define system security performance measures
	■ Review design constraints

Table A.2 (continued)   Linkage of IEEE 1220 and ISSE Phases

IEEE Std 1220-1998 Systems Engineering Process	*ISSE Process*

Requirements Verification and Validation
 	
■ Compare to customer expectations
■ Compare to enterprise and project constraints
■ Compare to external constraints
■ Identify variances and conflicts
■ Establish validated requirements baseline
	Assess Information Protection Effectiveness
	
	■ Provide and present documented information protection needs to the customer
	■ Explain security services, strengths, and priorities
	■ Provide and present security context, security CONOPS, and system security requirements to the customer
	■ Obtain concurrence from the customer
	
	Support System C&A
	
	■ Identify DAA/Accreditor
	■ Identify Certification Authority/Certifier
	■ Identify C&A and acquisition processes to be applied
	■ Ensure Accreditor's and Certifier's concurrence
	   – System security context
	   – Security CONOPS
	   – System security requirements

Functional Analysis
 	
■ Functional context analysis
   – Analyze functional behaviors
   – Define functional interfaces
   – Allocate performance requirements
■ Functional decomposition
   – Define subfunctions
   – Define subfunction states and modes
   – Define functional timelines
   – Define data and control flows
	Design System Security Architecture
	
	■ Perform functional analysis and allocation
	   – Analyze candidate systems architectures
	   – Allocate security services to architecture
	   – Select mechanism types
	   – Submit security architecture(s) for evaluation
	   – Revise security architecture(s)
	   – Select security architecture

Table A.2 (continued)   Linkage of IEEE 1220 and ISSE Phases

IEEE Std 1220-1998 *Systems Engineering Process*	*ISSE Process*
– Define functional failure modes and effects – Define safety monitoring functions ■ Establish functional architecture	
Functional Verification ■ Define verification procedures ■ Conduct verification evaluation – Verify architecture completeness – Verify functional and performance measures – Verify satisfaction of constraints ■ Identify variances and conflicts ■ Verified functional architecture	**Assess Information Protection Effectiveness** ■ Ensure that the selected security mechanisms provide the required security services ■ Explain to the customer how the security architecture meets the security requirements ■ Perform risk analysis ■ Obtain concurrence from the customer in the security architecture **Support System C&A** ■ Prepare and submit final architecture documentation for risk analysis ■ Coordinate results with Accreditor and Certifier
Synthesis ■ Group and allocate functions ■ Identify design solution alternatives ■ Assess safety and environmental hazards ■ Assess life-cycle quality factors ■ Assess technology requirements ■ Define design and performance characteristics ■ Define physical interfaces ■ Identify standardization opportunities	**Develop Detailed Security Design** ■ Ensure compliance with security architecture ■ Perform trade-off studies ■ Define system security design elements – Allocate security mechanisms to system security design elements – Identify candidate COTS/GOTS security products – Identify custom security products

Table A.2 (continued)   Linkage of IEEE 1220 and ISSE Phases

IEEE Std 1220-1998 Systems Engineering Process	ISSE Process
▪ Identify off-the-shelf availability ▪ Identify make or buy alternatives ▪ Develop models and fabricate prototypes ▪ Assess failure modes, effects, and criticality ▪ Assess testability needs ▪ Assess design capacity to evolve ▪ Final design ▪ Initiate evolutionary development ▪ Produce integrated data package ▪ Establish design architecture	− Qualify element and system interfaces (internal and external) − Develop specifications
Design Verification ▪ Select verification approach − Define inspection, analysis, demonstration, or test requirements − Define verification procedures − Establish verification environment − Conduct verification evaluation − Verity architecture completeness − Verify functional and performance measures − Verify satisfaction of constraints ▪ Identify variance and conflicts ▪ Verified design architecture ▪ Verified design architectures of life-cycle processes ▪ Verified system architecture ▪ Establish specifications and configuration baselines ▪ Develop product breakdown structures	**Assess Information Protection Effectiveness** ▪ Conduct design risk analysis ▪ Ensure that the selected security design provides the required security services ▪ Explain to the customer how the security design meets the security requirements ▪ Explain to the customer, and document, any residual risks of the design ▪ Obtain concurrence from the customer in the detailed security design **Support System C&A** ▪ Prepare and submit detailed design documentation for risk analysis ▪ Coordinate results with Accreditor and Certifier

Table A.2 (continued)   Linkage of IEEE 1220 and ISSE Phases

IEEE Std 1220-1998 *Systems Engineering Process*	*ISSE Process*

System Analysis
■ Assess requirement conflicts
■ Assess functional alternatives
■ Assess design alternatives
■ Identify risk factors
■ Define trade study scope
  – Select methodology and success criteria
  – Identify alternatives
  – Establish trade study environment
■ Conduct trade study
■ Analyze life-cycle costs
■ Analyze system and cost-effectiveness
■ Analyze environmental impacts
■ Quantify risk factors
■ Select risk handling options
■ Select alternative recommendations
■ Design effectiveness assessment
■ Trade-offs and impacts
	■ System analysis is part of the risk assessment process, which also is part of the analysis performed in each activity. Therefore, the specific tasks are cited in the relative SEP subprocesses.

■ The IEEE standard defines systems engineering as the total development effort and does not address implementation that would be addressed by manufacturing and test processes.	**Implement System Security**
	■ Support security implementation and integration
	  – Participate in implementation planning
	  – Verify interoperability of security tools and mechanisms
	  – Verify implementation against security design
	  – Verify that the security components have been evaluated against the selected evaluation criteria (CCEP, NIAP, FIPS, or other NSA and NIST evaluation criteria)

Table A.2 (continued) Linkage of IEEE 1220 and ISSE Phases

IEEE Std 1220-1998 Systems Engineering Process	ISSE Process
	– Assist in the integration of the components to ensure that their integration meets the system security specifications and does not alter the component specifications – Assist in the configuration of the components to ensure that the security features are enabled and the security parameters are correctly set to provide the required security services ■ Support test and evaluation – Build test and evaluation strategy (includes demonstration, observation, analysis, and testing) – Assess available test and evaluation data for applicability (e.g., CCEP, NIAP, internal) – Support development of test and evaluation procedures – Support test and evaluation activities ■ Support security training **Assess Information Protection Effectiveness** ■ Monitor to ensure that the security design is implemented correctly ■ Conduct or update risk analysis ■ Define the risks and possible mission impacts and advise the customer and the customer's Certifiers and Accreditors

Table A.2 (continued)   Linkage of IEEE 1220 and ISSE Phases

IEEE Std 1220-1998 *Systems Engineering Process*	*ISSE Process*
Control ■ Technical management – Data management – Configuration management – Interface management – Risk management – Performance-based progress measurements ■ Track system analysis, and verification and test data ■ Track requirements and design changes ■ Track performance against project plans ■ Track performance against technical plans ■ Track product and process metrics	**Support C&A** ■ Ensure the completeness of the required C&A documentation with the customer and the customer's Certifiers and Accreditors ■ Provide documentation and analysis as required for the C&A process ■ Plan technical effort ■ Estimate project scope ■ Identify resources and availability ■ Identify roles and responsibilities ■ Estimate project costs ■ Develop project schedule ■ Identify technical activities ■ Identify deliverables ■ Define management interfaces ■ Prepare technical management plan ■ Review project plan ■ Obtain customer agreement ■ Manage technical effort ■ Direct technical effort ■ Track project resources
■ Update specifications and configuration baselines ■ Update requirement views and architectures ■ Update engineering plans ■ Update technical plans ■ Integrated database	■ Track technical parameters ■ Monitor progress of technical activities ■ Ensure quality of deliverables ■ Manage configuration elements ■ Review project performance ■ Report project status

Source: From IATF, 2002, Appendix J, p. J-4 to J-9.

Appendix B

Enterprise Architecture

For those working in Federal agencies, note that the Clinger-Cohen Act requires agencies to develop enterprise architectures as a tool to provide greater E-government collaboration. ISSEs working within a Federal agency should be aware of the efforts of their agencies in creating an enterprise architecture, including the business needs that have been identified and especially the external interface capabilities planned for the future.

Enterprise Architecture

There has been a recent understanding within the IT industry that when current information systems are being designed and developed, they lack some type of design framework or an architect who designs the system. In fact, some have viewed this insight as the next evolution within the information system field — the need for an architectural framework or engineer.

Although the concept of enterprise architecture may seem recent, it is actually a few decades old. In the 1980s, the concept of architecture to describe an enterprise first emerged. Since then, various frameworks for defining enterprise architecture have been published. An enterprise can be defined as any purposeful activity, while the architecture can be characterized as the structure of any activity. An *enterprise architecture* can then be viewed as systematically derived and captured structural descriptions (such as useful models, diagrams, and narratives) of the mode of operation for any given enterprise.

In its simplest definition, it is an attempt to provide to people of all organizational levels an explicit, common, and meaningful structural frame of reference that allows an understanding of (1) what the enterprise does; (2) when, where, how, and why it does it; and (3) what it uses to do it. It provides a clear and comprehensive picture of the structure of an entity, whether an organization or a functional or mission area. It is an essential tool for effectively and efficiently engineering business processes and for implementing and evolving supporting systems (GAO-03-584G, April 2003).

In the mid-1980s, John Zachman, widely recognized as a leader in the field of enterprise architecture, identified the need to use an architecture for defining and controlling the integration of systems and their components. Accordingly, Zachman developed a framework for defining and capturing an architecture, now known simply as the "Zachman framework." His framework identified the kinds of work products needed for people to understand and thus build a given system or entity.

The Zachman framework provides for six perspectives (or windows) from which to view the enterprise or how a given entity operates. Zachman also proposed six abstractions or models associated with each of these perspectives.

Six Perspectives	Six Models
Strategic planner	How the Entity Operates
System user	What the Entity Uses to Operate
System designer	Where the Entity Operates
System developer	Who Operates the Entity
Subcontractor	When Entity Operations Occur
System itself	Why the Entity Operates

The Zachman framework provides a way to identify and describe an entity's existing and planned component parts and the parts' relationships before one begins the costly and time-consuming efforts associated with developing or transforming the entity. Since Zachman introduced his framework, a number of other frameworks have been proposed.

The emergence of Federal frameworks and guidance over the past five years is largely due to the U.S. Congress passing the Clinger-Cohen Act in 1996. This act requires CIOs for major departments and agencies to develop, maintain, and facilitate the implementation of architectures as a means of integrating business processes and agency goals with IT. In September 1999, the U.S. federal CIO Council published the Federal

Enterprise Architecture Framework (FEAF), which describes an entity's business, the data necessary to conduct the business, applications to manage the data, and the technology to support the applications. More recently, the U.S. Office of Management and Budget (OMB) established the Federal Enterprise Architecture Program Management Office to develop the federated enterprise architecture according to a collection of five reference models that are intended to facilitate a governmentwide improvement of IT systems. The five models are (GAO-03-584G, April 2003):

1. The *Business Reference Model* is intended to describe the business operations of the federal government independent of the agencies that perform them, including defining the services provided to state and local governments.
2. The *Performance Reference Model* is intended to provide a common set of general performance outputs and measures for agencies to use to achieve business goals and objectives.
3. The *Data and Information Reference Model* is intended to describe, at an aggregate level, the type of data and information that support program and business line operations, and the relationships among these types.
4. The *Service Component Reference Model* is intended to identify and classify IT service (i.e., application) components that support Federal agencies and promote the reuse of components across agencies.
5. The *Technical Reference Model* is intended to describe how technology is supporting the delivery of service components, including relevant standards for implementing the technology.

Although post-Zachman frameworks differ in their approach, they consistently provide for defining an enterprise's operations in both *logical terms*, such as interrelated business processes and business rules, information needs and flows, and work locations and users; and *technical terms*, such as hardware, software, data, communications, and security attributes and performance standards. The frameworks also provide for defining these perspectives both for the enterprise's current (or as-is) environment and for its target (or to-be) environment, as well as a transition plan for moving from the current to the target environment.

If managed appropriately and effectively, an enterprise architecture can clarify and help optimize the interdependencies and relationships among an organization's business operations and the underlying IT infrastructure and applications that support these operations. Employed in concert with other important management controls, enterprise architectures can greatly increase the chances that organizations' operational and IT environments will be configured so as to optimize mission performance.

Appendix C

Combining NIST SP 800-55 and SP 800-26

(Reference to Chapter 7)

NIST SP 800-55, Appendix A, provides examples of how the security topics and questions in 800-26 can be combined into a security matrix. If you are working with Federal agencies providing IA services, the FISMA reporting requirements shown in Table C.1 will be familiar. They are included here to provide a reference for how SP 800-55 and SP 800-26 are combined to show a metric. An example of the security metric for FISMA Requirement 1.1 is shown in Table C.2 and FISMA Requirement 5.2 in Table C.3.

> Note that OMB FISMA metrics require both numbers and percentages for some or just numbers for other metrics. While Table 7.4 lists all metrics as percentages, the raw number answers to the OMB FISMA metrics are contained in numerators and denominators of formulas. The table specifically points out those metrics for which OMB required raw numbers without percentages and states in a few cases whether numerator or denominator of the metric should be used for response (SP 800-55, p. A-1).

Table C.1   FISMA Metric and OMB Guidance Reference

Critical Element	Metric	OMB Guidance Reference
1.1	Percentage of systems that had formal risk assessments performed and documented	I.C.1.c
2.1	Percentage of total systems for which security controls have been tested and evaluated in the past year	I.C.1.g
3.1	Percentage of total systems that have the costs of their security controls integrated into the life cycle of the system	I.C.1.f
4.1	Percentage of total systems that have been authorized for processing following certification and accreditation	I.C.1.e
5.2	Percentage of current security plans	I.C.1.d
9.2	Percentage of systems that have a contingency plan	I.C.1.h
9.3	Percentage of systems for which contingency plans have been tested in the past year	I.C.1.i
13.1	Percentage of employees with significant security responsibilities who have received specialized training	I.C.3.c (denominator) and I.C.3.d (numerator)
14.1	Percentage of agency components with incident handling and response capability	I.B.8.c (numerator)
14.2	Number of incidents reported externally to FedCIRC or law enforcement	I.B.9.c

A.1 Risk Management

Percentage of systems that had formal risk assessments performed and documented (see Table C.2)

Comments

A number of additional metrics can be created to ascertain the number of systems that have undergone risk assessments after a major change,

Table C.2   Risk Assessment Metrics

Critical Element	1.1 Is risk periodically assessed?
Subordinate Question	1.1.2 Are risk assessments performed and documented on a regular basis or whenever the system, facilities or other conditions change?
Metric	Percentage of systems that had formal risk assessments performed and documented.
Purpose	To quantify the number of risk assessments completed in relation to the organization's requirements.
Implementation Evidence	1. Does your agency maintain a current inventory of IT systems? __ Yes __ No 2. If yes, how many systems are there in your agency (or agency component, as applicable)? _____ 3. Of the systems in your current inventory, how many systems have had risk assessments performed and documented in the following time frames? (Select the nearest time frame for each system; do not count the same system in more than one time frame.) Within past 12 months_____ Within past 2 years_____ Within past 3 years_____ 4. For any system that underwent a risk assessment, list the number of systems after the reason(s) that apply: Scheduled risk assessment_____ Major change in system environment_____ Major change in facilities_____ Change in other conditions (specify) _____ 5. For any system that has not undergone a risk assessment in the past 3 years, list the number of systems after the reason(s) that apply: No policy _____ No resources_____ System tier level does not require _____ System previously not defined____ New system _____ Other (specify) _____
Frequency	Semiannually, annually
Formula	At agency level: Sum of risk assessments on file for each time frame (Question 3) / IT systems in inventory (inventory database) (Question 2)5
Data Source	Inventory of IT systems that includes all major applications and general support systems; risk assessment repository

Table C.2 (continued)   Risk Assessment Metrics

Indicators	This metric computes the percentage of systems that have undergone risk assessments over the last three years (which is normally the required maximum time interval for conducting risk assessments). To establish the distribution of time for risk assessment completion, the number of systems listed for each time frame is computed. The total within three years should equal 100 percent of all required systems. Systems that are not receiving regular risk assessments are likely to be exposed to threats. Question 4 is used to validate the reasons for conducting risk assessments and to ensure that all systems are accounted. Question 5 is included to determine the reason risk assessments were not performed. Defining the cause will direct management attention to the appropriate corrective actions. By documenting and tracking these factors, changes can be made to improve performance by updating the security policy, directing resources, or ensuring that new systems are assessed for risk as required.

Source: From SP 800-55, p. A-4–5.

the number of systems that have undergone risk assessments during the past year, the number of systems that have undergone risk assessments during the past year after a major change, and others. This information can be tracked separately to ensure that this requirement is met and that system changes are monitored and responded to appropriately in a timely manner. A system may have had a risk assessment within the past two years; but if a major change has occurred since then, an additional risk assessment is required to ensure that information about the system's vulnerabilities and exposure to risk is updated and the risk managed (SP 800-55, p. A-4).

A.4 Authorize Processing

Percentage of total systems that have been authorized for processing following certification and accreditation (see Table C.3).

Comments

The implementation evidence for this metric must be extracted by surveying the record custodians for system inventories and C&A documents or by direct query if these inventories and documents are stored in

Table C.3 Certification and Accreditation Metrics

Critical Element	4.1 Has the system been certified/recertified and authorized to process (accredited)?
Subordinate Question	4.1.8 Has management authorized interconnections to all systems including systems owned and operated by another program, agency, organization, or contractor?
Metric	Percentage of total systems that have been authorized for processing following certification and accreditation
Purpose	To determine the percentage of systems that are certified and accredited
Implementation Evidence	1. Does your agency (or agency component, as applicable) maintain a complete and up-to-date inventory of systems? __ Yes __ No 2. Is there a formal C&A process within your agency? __ Yes __ No 3. Is the answer to Question 2 is yes, does the C&A process require management to authorize interconnections to all systems? __ Yes __ No 4. Are interconnections to systems documented? __ Yes __ No 5. How many systems are registered in the system inventory? _____ How many systems have received full C&A? _____
Frequency	Quarterly, semiannually, annually
Formula	Number of systems that have been certified and accredited (Question 6) / Total number of systems (Question 5)
Data Source	System inventory; C&A records
Indicators	This metric measures the existence of, and compliance with, a C&A process. An upward trend for this metric is desirable; the goal is to have 100 percent of systems certified and accredited. C&A shows that the system has been thoroughly assessed for risk, and that an agency official accepts full responsibility for the security of a system.

Source: From SP 800-55, p. A-14.

databases. Questions 3 and 4 are included because it is imperative that the C&A process review the system's interconnections with other systems if the full scope of the system's potential impact on other systems within the agency is to be assessed. Interconnections should be documented to ensure the traceability and accountability of the information used to evaluate systems for C&A. A negative answer to either of these questions makes this metric invalid (SP 800-55, p. A-14–15).

References

NIST SP 800-26 (November 2001). "Security Self-Assessment Guide for Information Technology Systems." NIST Publications, Computer Security Division, NIST: Gaithersburg, MD. Available at the NIST Web site: www.nist.gov.

NIST SP 800-55 DRAFT (July 2003) "Security Metrics Guide for Information Technology Systems." Published by: Computer Security Division, NIST, Gaithersburg, MD 20899-8930. Available at the NIST Web site: www.nist.gov.

H.R. 2458–48, Chapter 35 of Title 44, United States Code TITLE-III — Information Security §301 Information Security (December 2002). Federal Information Systems Management Act (FISMA).

Appendix D

Common Criteria Security Assurance Requirements

This appendix provides a brief overview of the requirements, presented in alphabetical order, of each of the assurance components, grouped by class and family. This information is taken from Common Criteria Information Technology Security Evaluation, Part 3: Security Assurance Requirements (August 1999).

Evaluation Assurance Classes

Class	Class Description
Configuration Management (ACM)	Configuration management (CM) is one method or means for establishing that the functional requirements and specifications are realized in the implementation of the TOE. CM meets these objectives by requiring discipline and control in the processes of refinement and modification of the TOE and the related information. CM systems are put in place to ensure the integrity of the portions of the TOE that they control, by providing a method of tracking any changes, and by ensuring that all changes are authorized.
	Family Name	**Family Description**
	CM automation (ACM_AUT)	The objective of introducing automated CM tools is to increase the effectiveness of the CM system. While both automated and manual CM systems can be bypassed, ignored, or prove insufficient to prevent unauthorized modification, automated systems are less susceptible to human error or negligence.
	CM capabilities (ACM_CAP)	The capabilities of the CM system address the likelihood that accidental or unauthorized modifications of the configuration items will occur. The CM system should ensure the integrity of the TOE from the early design stages through all subsequent maintenance efforts.
	CM scope (ACM_SCP)	The objective of this family is to ensure that all necessary TOE configuration items are tracked by the CM system. This helps to ensure that the integrity of these configuration items is protected through the capabilities of the CM system.

Evaluation Assurance Classes (continued)

Class	Class Description	
Delivery and operation (ADO)	Delivery and operation provides requirements for correct delivery, installation, generation, and start-up of the TOE.	
	Family Name	**Family Description**
	Delivery (ADO_DEL)	The requirements for delivery call for system control and distribution facilities and procedures that provide assurance that the recipient receives the TOE that the sender intended to send, without any modifications. For a valid delivery, what is received must correspond precisely to the TOE master copy, thus avoiding any tampering with the actual version, or substitution of a false version.
	Installation, generation and start-up (ADO_IGS)	Installation, generation, and start-up procedures are useful for ensuring that the TOE has been installed, generated, and started up in a secure manner as intended by the developer. The requirements for installation, generation and start-up call for a secure transition from the TOE's implementation representation being under configuration control to its initial operation in the user environment.
Development (ADV)		
	Family Name	**Family Description**
	Functional specification (ADV_FSP)	The functional specification is a high-level description of the user-visible interface and behavior of the TSF. It is an instantiation of the TOE security functional requirements. The functional specification has to show that all the TOE security functional requirements are addressed.

Evaluation Assurance Classes (continued)

Class	Class Description	
	High-level design (ADV_HLD)	The high-level design of a TOE provides a description of the TSF in terms of major structural units (i.e. subsystems) and relates these units to the functions that they provide. The high-level design requirements are intended to provide assurance that the TOE provides an architecture appropriate to implement the TOE security functional requirements.
	Implementation representation (ADV_IMP)	The description of the implementation representation in the form of source code, firmware, hardware drawings, etc. captures the detailed internal workings of the TSF in support of analysis.
	TSF internals (ADV_INT)	This family addresses the internal structure of the TSF. Requirements are presented for modularity, layering (to separate levels of abstraction and minimize circular dependencies), minimization of the complexity of policy enforcement mechanisms, and the minimization of the amount of non-TSP-enforcing functionality within the TSF—thus resulting in a TSF that is simple enough to be analyzed.
	Low-level design (ADV_LLD)	The low-level design of a TOE provides a description of the internal workings of the TSF in terms of modules and their interrelationships and dependencies. The low-level design provides assurance that the TSF subsystems have been correctly and effectively refined.
	Representation correspondence (ADV_RCR)	The correspondence between the various TSF representations (i.e. TOE summary specification, functional

Evaluation Assurance Classes (continued)

Class	Class Description	
		specification, high-level design, low-level design, and implementation representation) addresses the correct and complete instantiation of the requirements to the least abstract TSF representation provided. This conclusion is achieved by step-wise refinement and the cumulative results of correspondence determinations between all adjacent abstractions of representation.
	Security policy modeling (ADV_SPM)	It is the objective of this family to provide additional assurance that the security functions in the functional specification enforce the policies in the TSP. This is accomplished via the development of a security policy model that is based on a subset of the policies of the TSP, and establishing a correspondence between the functional specification, the security policy model, and these policies of the TSP.
Guidance documents (AGD)	The guidance documents class provides the requirements for user and administrator guidance documentation. For the secure administration and use of the TOE it is necessary to describe all relevant aspects for the secure application of the TOE.	
	Family Name	**Family Description**
	Administrator guidance (AGD_ADM)	Administrator guidance refers to written material that is intended to be used by those persons responsible for configuring, maintaining, and administering the TOE in a correct manner for maximum security. Because the secure operation of the TOE is dependent upon the correct performance of the TSF, persons responsible for performing these

Evaluation Assurance Classes (continued)

Class	Class Description	
		functions are trusted by the TSF. Administrator guidance is intended to help administrators understand the security functions provided by the TOE, including both those functions that require the administrator to perform security-critical actions and those functions that provide security-critical information.
	User guidance (AGD_USR)	User guidance refers to material that is intended to be used by non-administrative human users of the TOE, and by others (e.g. programmers) using the TOE's external interfaces. User guidance describes the security functions provided by the TSF and provides instructions and guidelines, including warnings, for its secure use.
Life-cycle support (ALC)	Life-cycle support is an aspect of establishing discipline and control in the processes of refinement of the TOE during its development and maintenance. Confidence in the correspondence between the TOE security requirements and the TOE is greater if security analysis and the production of the evidence are done on a regular basis as an integral part of the development and maintenance activities.	
	Family Name	**Family Description**
	Development security (ALC_DVS)	Development security is concerned with physical, procedural, personnel, and other security measures that may be used in the development environment to protect the TOE. It includes the physical security of the development location and any procedures used to select development staff.

Evaluation Assurance Classes (continued)

Class	Class Description	
	Flaw remediation (ALC_FLR)	Flaw remediation requires that discovered security flaws be tracked and corrected by the developer. Although future compliance with flaw remediation procedures cannot be determined at the time of the TOE evaluation, it is possible to evaluate the policies and procedures that a developer has in place to track and correct flaws, and to distribute the flaw information and corrections.
	Life-cycle definition (ALC_LCD)	Poorly controlled development and maintenance of the TOE can result in a flawed implementation of a TOE (or a TOE that does not meet all of its security requirements). This, in turn, results in security violations. Therefore, it is important that a model for the development and maintenance of a TOE be established as early as possible in the TOE's life cycle.
	Tools and techniques (ALC_TAT)	Tools and techniques is an aspect of selecting tools that are used to develop, analyze and implement the TOE. It includes requirements to prevent ill-defined, inconsistent or incorrect development tools from being used to develop the TOE. This includes, but is not limited to, programming languages, documentation, implementation standards, and other parts of the TOE such as supporting runtime libraries.
Tests (ATE)	The class "Tests" encompasses four families: coverage (ATE_COV), depth (ATE_DPT), independent testing (e.g. functional testing performed by evaluators) (ATE_IND), and functional tests (ATE_FUN). Testing helps to establish that the TOE security functional requirements are met. Testing provides assurance that the TOE satisfies at least the TOE security functional requirements; although it	

Evaluation Assurance Classes (continued)

Class	Class Description
	cannot establish that the TOE does no more than what was specified. Testing may also be directed toward the internal structure of the TSF, such as the testing of subsystems and modules against their specifications.

	Family Name	**Family Description**
	Coverage (ATE_COV)	This family addresses those aspects of testing that deal with completeness of test coverage. That is, it addresses the extent to which the TSF is tested, and whether or not the testing is sufficiently extensive to demonstrate that the TSF operates as specified.
	Depth (ATE_DPT)	The components in this family deal with the level of detail to which the TSF is tested. Testing of security functions is based upon increasing depth of information derived from analysis of the representations.
	Functional tests (ATE_FUN)	Functional testing performed by the developer establishes that the TSF exhibits the properties necessary to satisfy the functional requirements of its PP/ST. Such functional testing provides assurance that the TSF satisfies at least the security functional requirements; although it cannot establish that the TSF does no more than what was specified. The family "Functional tests" is focused on the type and amount of documentation or support tools required, and what is to be demonstrated through developer testing. Functional testing is not limited to positive confirmation that the required security functions are provided, but may also include negative testing to check for the absence of particular undesired

Evaluation Assurance Classes (continued)

Class	Class Description	
		behavior (often based on the inversion of functional requirements).
	Independent testing (ATE_IND)	One objective is to demonstrate that the security functions perform as specified. An additional objective is to counter the risk of an incorrect assessment of the test outcomes on the part of the developer that results in the incorrect implementation of the specifications, or overlooks code that is non-compliant with the specifications.
Vulnerability assessment (AVA)	The class addresses the existence of exploitable covert channels, the possibility of misuse or incorrect configuration of the TOE, the possibility to defeat probabilistic or permutational mechanisms, and the possibility of exploitable vulnerabilities introduced in the development or the operation of the TOE.	
	Family Name	**Family Description**
	Covert channel analysis (AVA_CCA)	Covert channel analysis is carried out to determine the existence and potential capacity of unintended signaling channels (i.e., illicit information flows) that may be exploited.
	Misuse (AVA_MSU)	Misuse investigates whether the TOE can be configured or used in a manner that is insecure but that an administrator or user of the TOE would reasonably believe to be secure.
	Strength of TOE security functions (AVA_SOF)	Even if a TOE security function cannot be bypassed, deactivated, or corrupted, it may still be possible to defeat it because there is a vulnerability in the concept of its underlying security mechanisms. For those functions a qualification of

Evaluation Assurance Classes (continued)

Class	Class Description	
		their security behavior can be made using the results of a quantitative or statistical analysis of the security behavior of these mechanisms and the effort required to overcome them. The qualification is made in the form of a strength of TOE security function claim.
	Vulnerability analysis (AVA_VLA)	Vulnerability analysis is an assessment to determine whether vulnerabilities identified, during the evaluation of the construction and anticipated operation of the TOE or by other methods (e.g. by flaw hypotheses), could allow users to violate the TSP.

Evaluation of PPs and STs

Class	Class Description
Protection Profile Evaluation (APE)	The goal of a PP evaluation is to demonstrate that the PP Is complete, consistent, and technically sound. An evaluated PP is suitable for use as the basis for the development of STs. Such a PP is eligible for inclusion in a registry.

	Family Name	**Family Description**
	TOE description (APE_DES)	The TOE description is an aid to the understanding of the TOE's security requirements. Evaluation of the TOE description is required to show that it is coherent, internally consistent, and consistent with all other parts of the PP.
	Security environment (APE_ENV)	To determine whether the IT security requirements in the PP are sufficient, it is important that the security problem to be solved is clearly understood by all parties to the evaluation.
	PP introduction (APE_INT)	The PP introduction contains document management and overview information necessary to operate a PP registry. Evaluation of the PP introduction is required to demonstrate that the PP is correctly identified and that it is consistent with all other parts of the PP.
	Security objectives (APE_OBJ)	The security objectives are a concise statement of the intended response to the security problem. Evaluation of the security objectives is required to demonstrate that the stated objectives adequately address the security problem. The security objectives are categorized as security objectives for the TOE and as security objectives for the environment. The security objectives for both the TOE and the environment must be shown to be traced back to the identified threats to be countered and/or policies and assumptions to be met by each.

Evaluation of PPs and STs (continued)

Class	Class Description	
	IT security requirements (APE_REQ)	The IT security requirements chosen for a TOE and presented or cited in a PP need to be evaluated in order to confirm that they are internally consistent and lead to the development of a TOE that will meet its security objectives.
	Explicitly stated IT security requirements (APE_SRE)	This family presents evaluation requirements that permit the evaluator to determine that the explicitly stated requirements are clearly and unambiguously expressed. The evaluation of requirements taken from the CC in conjunction with valid explicitly stated security requirements is addressed by the APE_REQ family.
Security Target Evaluation (ASE)	The goal of a PP evaluation is to demonstrate that the PP is complete, consistent and technically sound. An evaluated PP is suitable for use as the basis for the development of STs. Such a PP is eligible for inclusion in a registry.	
	Family Name	**Family Description**
	TOE description (ASE_DES)	The TOE description is an aid to the understanding of the TOE's security requirements. Evaluation of the TOE description is required to show that it is coherent, internally consistent and consistent with all other parts of the ST.
	Security environment (ASE_ENV)	In order to determine whether the IT security requirements in the ST are sufficient, it is important that the security problem to be solved is clearly understood by all parties to the evaluation.
	ST introduction (ASE_INT)	The ST introduction contains identification and indexing material. Evaluation of the ST introduction is required to demonstrate that the ST is correctly identified and that it is consistent with all other parts of the ST.

Evaluation of PPs and STs (continued)

Class	Class Description	
	Security objectives (ASE_OBJ)	The security objectives are a concise statement of the intended response to the security problem. Evaluation of the security objectives is required to demonstrate that the stated objectives adequately address the security problem. The security objectives are categorized as security objectives for the TOE and as security objectives for the environment. The security objectives for both the TOE and the environment must be shown to be traced back to the identified threats to be countered and/or policies and assumptions to be met by each.
	PP claims (ASE_PPC)	The goal of the evaluation of the Security Target PP claims is to determine whether the ST is a correct instantiation of the PP.
	IT security requirements (ASE_REQ)	The IT security requirements chosen for a TOE and presented or cited in an ST need to be evaluated in order to confirm that they are internally consistent and lead to the development of a TOE that will meet its security objectives.
	Explicitly stated IT security requirements (ASE_SRE)	This family presents evaluation requirements that permit the evaluator to determine that the explicitly stated requirements are clearly and unambiguously expressed. The evaluation of requirements taken from the CC in conjunction with valid explicitly stated security requirements is addressed by the ASE_REQ family.
	TOE summary specification (ASE_TSS)	The TOE summary specification provides a high-level definition of the security functions claimed to meet the functional requirements and of the assurance measures taken to meet the assurance requirements.

Assurance Maintenance Class

Class	Class Description
Maintenance of Assurance (AMA)	The maintenance of assurance class provides requirements that are intended to be applied after a TOE has been certified against the CC. These requirements are aimed at assuring that the TOE will continue to meet its security target as changes are made to the TOE or its environment. Such changes include the discovery of new threats or vulnerabilities, changes in user requirements, and the correction of bugs found in the certified TOE.

	Family Name	Family Description
	Assurance maintenance plan (AMA_AMP)	The Assurance Maintenance Plan (AM Plan) identifies the plans and procedures a developer must implement to ensure that the assurance that was established in the certified TOE is maintained as changes are made to the TOE or its environment. The AM Plan is specific to the TOE, and is tailored to the developer's own practices and procedures.
	TOE component categorization report (AMA_CAT)	The aim of the TOE component categorization report is to complement the AM Plan by providing a categorization of the components of a TOE (e.g., TSF subsystems) according to their relevance to security. This categorization acts as a focus for the developer's security impact analysis, and also for the subsequent re-evaluation of the TOE.
	Evidence of assurance maintenance (AMA_EVD)	The aim of this family of requirements is to establish confidence that the assurance in the TOE is being maintained by the developer, in accordance with the AM Plan. This is achieved through the provision of evidence which demonstrates that the assurance in the TOE has been maintained, which is independently checked by an evaluator. This check, termed an 'AM audit,' is periodically applied during the lifetime of the AM Plan.

Assurance Maintenance Class

Class	Class Description	
	Security impact analysis (AMA_SIA)	The aim of the security impact analysis is to provide confidence that assurance has been maintained in the TOE, through an analysis performed by the developer of the security impact of all changes affecting the TOE since it was certified.

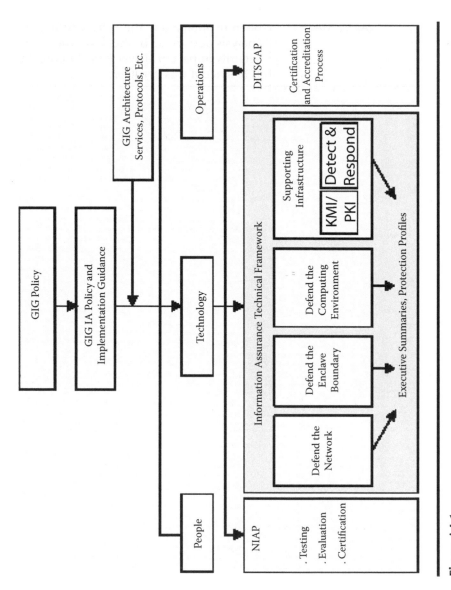

Figure A4.1

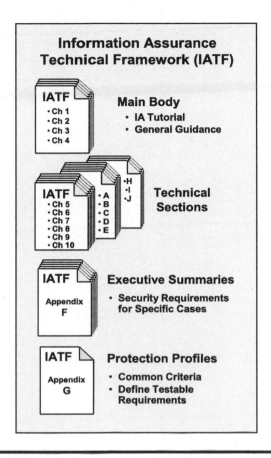

Figure A4.2

Appendix E

ISSEP Sample Questions

ISSEP Sample Questions: Chapter 1

Question 1	A primary focus of the ISSE process is to _____.
A	Identify the information protection needs
B	Educate systems engineers on availability, integrity, and confidentiality
C	Ensure information systems are designed and developed with functional relevance
D	Design information systems that will meet the certification and accreditation documentation
Answer	A
Rationale	The focus of the process is to first identify the information protection needs and then to use a process-oriented approach to identify security risks and subsequently to minimize or contain those risks.

Question 2	What term is used to describe the measures that protect and defend information and information systems by ensuring their availability, integrity, authentication, confidentiality, and non-repudiation?

A	Risk management (RM)
B	Certification and accreditation (C&A)
C	Information assurance (IA)
D	Information systems security engineering (ISSE)
Answer	C
Chapter	1 (NSTISSI No. 4009, p. 32)
Rationale	Direct quote from NSTISSI No. 4009, p. 32. Risk management is a set of processes that ensures a risk-based approach is used to determine adequate, cost-effective security for a system. C&A is a set of processes that culminate in an agreement between key players that a system in its current configuration and operation provides adequate protection controls. ISSE is a set of processes and solutions used during all phases of a system's life cycle to meet the system's information protection needs.

Question 3	Which of the following best describes the Information Systems Security Engineering (ISSE) model?
A	A set of processes that ensures a risk-based approach is used to determine adequate, cost-effective security for a system.
B	A set of processes used during all phases of a system's life cycle to meet the system's information protection needs.
C	A set of processes that culminate in an agreement between key players that a system in its current configuration and operation provides adequate protection controls.
D	A set of processes that provide systems engineers with quality management controls.
Answer	B
Rationale	Answer A is the definition for risk management, C is the definition for C&A, and D is just a distracter.

Question 4	During which phase of the ISSE model are the security functions initially defined?
A	Discover information protection needs
B	Define system security requirements

C	Define system security architecture
D	Develop detailed security design
Answer	C
Rationale	Discover information protection needs: the ISSEP ascertains why the system should be built and what information should be protected. Define system security requirements: the ISSEP defines the system in terms of what security is needed. Define system security architecture: the ISSEP defines the security functions needed to meet the specific security requirements. Develop detailed security design: the ISSEP designs the security functions and features for the system.

Question **5**	During which phase of the ISSE model is the system defined in terms of what security is needed?
A	Discover information protection needs
B	Define system security requirements
C	Define system security architecture
D	Develop detailed security design
Answer	B
Rationale	Discover information protection needs: the ISSEP ascertains why the system should be built and what information should be protected. Define system security requirements: the ISSEP defines the system in terms of what security is needed. Define system security architecture: the ISSEP defines the security functions needed to meet the specific security requirements. Develop detailed security design: the ISSEP designs the security functions and features for the system.

Question **6**	During which phase of the ISSE model are the information management model and protections defined?
A	Discover information protection needs
B	Define system security requirements
C	Define system security architecture
D	Develop detailed security design
Answer	A

Rationale	Discover information protection needs: the ISSEP ascertains why the system should be built and what information should be protected. Define system security requirements: the ISSEP defines the system in terms of what security is needed. Define system security architecture: the ISSEP defines the security functions needed to meet the specific security requirements. Develop detailed security design: the ISSEP designs the security functions and features for the system.

Question 7	During which phase of the ISSE model are the security functions and features further defined?
A	Discover information protection needs
B	Define system security requirements
C	Define system security architecture
D	Develop detailed security design
Answer	D
Rationale	Discover information protection needs: the ISSEP ascertains why the system should be built and what information should be protected. Define system security requirements: the ISSEP defines the system in terms of what security is needed. Define system security architecture: the ISSEP defines the security functions needed to meet the specific security requirements. Develop detailed security design: the ISSEP designs the security functions and features for the system.

Question 8	Who is responsible for defining the information protection needs?
A	Systems engineer
B	Customer
C	Information systems security engineer
D	Certifying agent
Answer	B
Rationale	The ISSEP helps the customer understand the information protection needs that will support the mission or business.

Question 9	Who is responsible for defining the "problem space"?
A	Customer
B	Approving authority
C	Systems engineer
D	Information systems security engineer
Answer	A
Rationale	This is the third principle related to the problem and solution space; "the solution is defined by the systems engineer and the problem is defined by the customer. The customer is the expert on the problem, and the engineer is the expert on the solution."

Question 10	Who is responsible for defining the "solution space"?
A	Customer
B	Certifying agent
C	Approving authority
D	Systems engineer or information systems security engineer
Answer	D
Rationale	This is the third principle related to the problem and solution space: "the solution is defined by the systems engineer and the problem is defined by the customer. The customer is the expert on the problem, and the engineer is the expert on the solution."

Question 11	If the problem is defined as "customer would like to exchange data securely between a remote site and headquarters," which of the following would be considered a constraint?
A	Secure Socket Layer (SSL) protocol
B	Bandwidth costs
C	High-assurance software guard
D	Secure HTTP
Answer	B
Rationale	SSL, software guards, and S-HTTP would be considered solutions, while bandwidth costs would be considered a constraint.

Question 12	If the system is in Phase 2 or the System Development Life Cycle, which of the following would be the role of the information systems security engineer?
A	Define system security requirements
B	Develop detailed security design
C	Configure the security functions
D	Test the security functions
Answer	B
Rationale	Phase 2 of the SDLC is development or acquisition; thus, B, develop the security design, would be the appropriate ISSE activity. Defining the security requirements would be done during SDLC, Phase 1, and configuring and testing the security functions would be done during SDLC, Phase 3, implementation.

Question 13	What is the focus of the operations perspective for the defense-*in*-depth approach?
A	Getting a commitment from senior-level management to establish a culture that values information assurance
B	Assigning roles and responsibilities for ensuring information assurance
C	Establishing effective policies for acquisition of the right security products
D	Implementing effective key management
Answer	D
Rationale	The three perspectives of the defense-in-depth approach are people, technology, and operations. Answers A and B are the focus of the people perspective, C is the focus of the technology perspective, and D is an operations perspective.

Question 14	When implementing a defense-in-depth approach, which of the following is most important for the information systems security engineer to consider?
A	Controls for patch management
B	Additional protection controls behind the firewall
C	Deploying protection controls in multiple places

D	Using the National Security Agency's security configuration guides
Answer	C
Rationale	The first principle of defense-in-depth is providing defense in multiple places. Although the others are important, they are not one of the most important principles.

Question **15**	If an attacker breaks through the first protection control and faces another control, what type of defense has the attacker found?
A	Layered defense
B	Defense in multiple places
C	Availability defense
D	Close-in defense
Answer	A
Rationale	A layered defense is when an organization employs multiple layers of defense. Defense in multiple places is when an organization deploys protection controls in multiple places, not necessarily as a "layer." Availability and close-in defense are distracters.

ISSEP Questions: Chapter 2

Question **1**	What does the information system security engineer (ISSE) use the Information Management Plan (IMP) to determine?
A	Information management model
B	Information protection needs
C	System security requirements
D	C&A roles and responsibilities
Answer	C
Rationale	The information management model and information protection needs are included in the IMP. The IMP is used in Phase 2 of the ISSE model to determine the security requirements for the system. Answer D is a distracter.

Question 2	Which of the following is done while creating the information management model?
A	Identifying users of the information
B	Conducting a threat analysis
C	Defining the impact of a threat exercised
D	Identifying security services needed to protect the information
Answer	A
Rationale	The three tasks of creating the information management model are to identify the information being processed, identify the processes used to access the information, and identify the users of the information and the processes. Conducting a threat analysis, defining the impact of the threat if exercised, and identifying security services are tasks of defining the information protection policy.

Question 3	Which of the following is contained within the Information Management Plan?
A	Information protection policy
B	Quality management plan
C	Configuration control policy
D	Test and evaluation plan
Answer	A
Rationale	The IMP contains three items: the mission/business need, the information management model, and the information protection policy.

Question 4	When the information system security engineer (ISSE) asks the customer to define the deficiencies of a current system, the ISSE is performing which task?
A	Defining the information protection policy
B	Determining the security requirements
C	Defining the system architecture
D	Defining the mission need
Answer	D

Rationale	While defining the mission need, the ISSE asks several types of questions about the current system, such as identifying the deficiencies. This is not considered a specific task that must be achieved while defining the information protection policy, security requirements, or system architecture.

Question 5	If the information system security engineer (ISSE) takes time to learn the customer's mission and business, which of the following is the most important benefit the ISSE has gained?
A	An inside track to the approving authority
B	Respect and confidence of the customer
C	Where the boundaries for the network need to be outlined
D	The ability to meet the contract deliverables on time
Answer	B
Rationale	This should have been an easy one. If the ISSE understands the customer's mission, the customer will feel confident that the ISSE is an important member of the system's life-cycle team.

Question 6	What is the method of describing how information is created, acquired, processed, stored, transferred, or deleted?
A	Document Management Model
B	Development Life Cycle for Information Model
C	Information Management Model
D	Information Monitoring Model
Answer	C
Rationale	A document management model describes how information will be stored. Answers B and D are distracters.

Question 7	If the information system security engineer (ISSE) was asked to follow FIPS 199, what security categories should be used?
A	People, Technology, Operations
B	Confidentiality, Integrity, Availability
C	Users, Information, Process
D	Local, Enclave, Supporting Infrastructure

Answer	B
Rationale	FIPS 199 is a method of defining the impact to information if it was disclosed (confidentiality), unauthorized modification (integrity), or unavailable (availability). People, technology, and operations are three perspectives for defense—in-depth; users, information, and process define an information management model; and local, enclave, and supporting infrastructure are associated with defining boundaries.

Question 8	Which of the following best describes the risk impact?
A	The likelihood of a threat being able to exercise or attack and cause harm to the system's confidentiality, integrity, and availability
B	The ability of an attacker to exercise or attack and cause harm to the system's confidentiality, integrity, and availability
C	The potential magnitude of harm that the loss of confidentiality, integrity, and availability would have on the agency's ability to accomplish its mission
D	The costs of mitigating the loss of confidentiality, integrity, and availability so the agency can accomplish its mission
Answer	C
Chapter	2 (FIPS 199).
Rationale	Answers A and B are both considered definition of threat likelihood, and answer D is the definition of risk mitigation.

Question 9	To establish the appropriate security category of an information type, it is necessary to determine the _____ for each security objective.
A	Potential impact
B	Cost/benefit ratio
C	Potential vulnerability and threat
D	Acceptable value
Answer	A
Rationale	FIPS 199 provides a method for determining the risk level of an information type based on the potential impact to the organization should there be a loss of confidentiality, integrity, and availability.

Question 10	When using FIPS 199 to identify a customer's information domain called "investigation archives," the information system security engineer (ISSE) determines that the potential impact to confidentiality is severe, the potential impact to integrity is serious, and the potential impact to disruption of access is serious. In this scenario, how would the ISSE list the overall potential impact for the investigation archive information domain?
A	None
B	Low
C	Moderate
D	High
Answer	D
Rationale	Low is limited damage, Moderate is serious damage, and High is severe damage. Because there is a "severe or high" potential impact, the highest value must be used for each and each of the security services must be listed.

Question 11	What is the level of impact if the information is labeled "Low?"
A	No adverse effect on the organization's mission
B	Limited adverse effect on the organization's mission
C	Serious adverse effect on the organization's mission
D	Severe adverse effect on the organization's mission
Answer	B
Rationale	This is based on FIPS 199 potential impact definitions.

Question 12	What is the level of impact if the information is labeled "Moderate"?
A	No adverse effect on the organization's mission
B	Limited adverse effect on the organization's mission
C	Serious adverse effect on the organization's mission
D	Severe adverse effect on the organization's mission
Answer	C
Rationale	This is based on FIPS 199 potential impact definitions.

Question 13	What is the level of impact if the information is labeled "High"?
A	No adverse effect on the organization's mission
B	Limited adverse effect on the organization's mission
C	Serious adverse effect on the organization's mission
D	Severe adverse effect on the organization's mission
Answer	D
Rationale	This is based on FIPS 199 potential impact definitions.

Question 14	At a minimum, which information label would be appropriate for an information system containing information on intelligence activities?
A	Unclassified system
B	Unclassified but sensitive system
C	National security system
D	Proprietary system
Answer	C
Rationale	NIST SP 800-59 states that "national security system means any information system used or operated by an agency that involves intelligence activities."

Question 15	Which category is appropriate to describe information on a DoD system that is vital to mission effectiveness and loss would result in immediate loss to mission effectiveness?
A	Mission Assurance Category I
B	Mission Assurance Category II
C	Mission Assurance Category III
D	Mission Assurance Category IV
Answer	A
Rationale	The definition for MAC I is "Vital to mission effectiveness or operational readiness of deployed or contingency forces and the Loss or degradation results in immediate and sustained loss of mission effectiveness." There is no MAC IV category.

Question 16	Which category is appropriate to describe information on a DoD system that is important to support deployed forces and loss of availability would be difficult to manage and only tolerable in the short term?
A	Mission Assurance Category I
B	Mission Assurance Category II
C	Mission Assurance Category III
D	Mission Assurance Category IV
Answer	B
Rationale	The definition for MAC II is "Important to support of deployed or contingency forces and the loss of availability difficult to manage; only tolerable for short term." There is no MAC IV category.

Question 17	Which category is appropriate to describe information on a DoD system that is needed for day-to-day business, but does not support deployed forces in the short term?
A	Mission Assurance Category I
B	Mission Assurance Category II
C	Mission Assurance Category III
D	Mission Assurance Category IV
Answer	C
Rationale	The definition for MAC III is "needed for day-to-day business, but does not support deployed or contingency forces in the short term." There is no MAC IV category.

Question 18	Which category is appropriate to describe information on a DoD system that requires protective measures commensurate with commercial best practices?
A	Mission Assurance Category I
B	Mission Assurance Category II
C	Mission Assurance Category III
D	Mission Assurance Category IV
Answer	C

Rationale	MAC I requires the most stringent protection measures; MAC II requires additional safeguards beyond best practices. There is no MAC IV category.

Question 19	What is a collection of information objects that share the same security policy for privileges and access?
A	Information domain
B	Active Directory domain
C	Enclave domain
D	Automated Information System
Answer	A
Rationale	An Active Directory domain is a Microsoft Windows architecture term; an Enclave is a collection of computing environments connected by one or more internal networks under the control of a single authority and security policy; and an Automated Information System is a combination of hardware, software, and firmware configured to handle and operate (e.g., process, store) information.

Question 20	Which of the following best defines an information domain security policy?
A	A statement containing the users, processes, and information type, and the controls needed for each
B	A statement containing the users, information, and the privileges and rules that apply to the users in managing the information
C	A statement of the privileges allowed within an information domain
D	A statement of the criteria for membership in an information domain
Answer	B
Rationale	The answer A does not include the rules for accessing or operating the information; the answer C does not include the users or information, and answer D does not include the privileges or rules for the users. An information security domain contains the users or members of the information domain, the objects being managed, including processes, and the rules, privileges, roles, and responsibilities that apply to the users in managing all the information.

Question 21	The customer has asked that users be granted access to information only if it is required to accomplish their job duties. Based on this requirement, which of the following should be included in the information management model?
A	Separation of duties
B	Discretionary access controls (DACs)
C	Rule-based access
D	Least privilege
Answer	D
Rationale	Separation of duties: designing a process so that separate steps must be performed by different people; DACs are an access control policy that restricts access to files and other system resources based on the identity and assignment of the user and/or the groups the user belongs to; rule-based access is based on a list of rules that determine if authorization should be granted; and least privilege is when users are allowed access to only those processes and information required to do their jobs.

Question 22	Which one of the following is NOT an activity conducted to define the information protection policy?
A	Determine threat potential
B	Determine security products to reduce threat potential
C	Determine likelihood of threat to exercise
D	Determine level of harm if threat should exercise
Answer	B
Rationale	The information protection policy does not include identifying security products. This would occur in Phase 4 of the ISSE model.

Question 23	Of the following, who is the best source for determining whether a threat is realistic?
A	Customer
B	System owner
C	Information systems security engineer (ISSE)
D	Systems engineer
Answer	C

Rationale	The customer is the best source for knowledge of potential threats, and the ISSE is the best source for deciding whether the threat is realistic.

Question 24	What task is the information systems security engineer (ISSE) performing when assessing the degree of an attacker's motivation and the potential for natural disasters?
A	Determining the potential harmful events
B	Determining the harm to information
C	Conducting a risk assessment
D	Identifying the business and mission needs
Answer	A
Rationale	Determining the harm to information identifies the impact if a threat were to exercise and conducting a risk assessment involves many more steps. Identifying the business and mission needs does not involve identifying threats to the system.

Question 25	What type of attack involves traffic analysis?
A	Active
B	Passive
C	Close-in
D	Distribution
Answer	B
Rationale	An active attack includes attempts to circumvent or break protection features, introduce malicious code, or steal or modify information. A passive attack includes traffic analysis, monitoring of unprotected communications, decrypting weakly encrypted traffic, and capturing authentication information (e.g., passwords). Close-in attack is where an unauthorized individual is in physical close proximity to networks, systems, or facilities for the purpose of modifying, gathering, or denying access to information. Distribution attacks focus on the malicious modification of hardware or software at the factory or during distribution.

Question 26	If John modifies Bob's banking data while the data is in transit, what type of attack would it be?
A	Active
B	Passive
C	Close-in
D	Distribution
Answer	A
Rationale	An active attack includes attempts to circumvent or break protection features, introduce malicious code, or steal or modify information. A passive attack includes traffic analysis, monitoring of unprotected communications, decrypting weakly encrypted traffic, and capturing authentication information (e.g., passwords). Close-in attack is where an unauthorized individual is in close physical proximity to networks, systems, or facilities for the purpose of modifying, gathering, or denying access to information. Distribution attacks focus on the malicious modification of hardware or software at the factory or during distribution.

Question 27	If Sally exploits a well-known vulnerability in an operating system, what type of attack would it be?
A	Active
B	Passive
C	Close-in
D	Insider
Answer	A
Rationale	An active attack includes attempts to circumvent or break protection features, introduce malicious code, or steal or modify information. A passive attack includes traffic analysis, monitoring of unprotected communications, decrypting weakly encrypted traffic, and capturing authentication information (e.g., passwords). Close-in attack is where an unauthorized individual is in close physical proximity to networks, systems, or facilities for the purpose of modifying, gathering, or denying access to information. Malicious insiders have the intent to eavesdrop, steal or damage information, use information in a fraudulent manner, or deny access to other authorized users.

Question 28	If a maintenance worker gains access to information by installing a keystroke capture device, what type of attack would it be?
A	Active
B	Passive
C	Close-in
D	Insider
Answer	C
Rationale	An active attack includes attempts to circumvent or break protection features, introduce malicious code, or steal or modify information. A passive attack includes traffic analysis, monitoring of unprotected communications, decrypting weakly encrypted traffic, and capturing authentication information (e.g., passwords). Close-in attack is where an unauthorized individual is in close physical proximity to networks, systems, or facilities for the purpose of modifying, gathering, or denying access to information. Malicious insiders have the intent to eavesdrop, steal or damage information, use information in a fraudulent manner, or deny access to other authorized users.

Question 29	If an employee accidentally discovers access to unauthorized information on a classified network and transfers it to a lower-sensitivity network, what type of attack would it be?
A	Active
B	Passive
C	Close-in
D	Insider
Answer	D
Rationale	An active attack includes attempts to circumvent or break protection features, introduce malicious code, or steal or modify information. A passive attack includes traffic analysis, monitoring of unprotected communications, decrypting weakly encrypted traffic, and capturing authentication information (e.g., passwords). Close-in attack is where an unauthorized individual is in physical close proximity to networks, systems, or facilities for the purpose of modifying, gathering, or denying access to information. Malicious insiders have the intent to eavesdrop, steal or damage information, use information in a fraudulent manner, or deny access to other authorized users.

Question 30	If during development, a programmer installs Trojan horse code into the software configuration, what type of attack would it be?
A	Active
B	Passive
C	Close-in
D	Distribution
Answer	D
Rationale	An active attack includes attempts to circumvent or break protection features, introduce malicious code, or steal or modify information. A passive attack includes traffic analysis, monitoring of unprotected communications, decrypting weakly encrypted traffic, and capturing authentication information (e.g., passwords). Close-in attack is where an unauthorized individual is in close physical proximity to networks, systems, or facilities for the purpose of modifying, gathering, or denying access to information. Distribution attacks focus on the malicious modification of hardware or software at the factory or during distribution.

Question 31	Which of the following should the information systems security engineer NOT do when presenting the results of the information protection analysis to the customer?
A	Summarize the results
B	Present any unresolved issues
C	Avoid discussing abnormalities
D	Express priorities or highest needs
Answer	C
Rationale	The ISSE should summarize the results to make it easier for the customer to understand; present any unresolved issues so the customer can provide feedback; discuss abnormalities with the customer so the customer can provide feedback; and express priorities so the customers will know where to focus their resources.

Question 32	What is the difference between a security service and a security control?
A	A security service is provided and maintained by a specific vendor; a security control is a technology implemented to meet a protection need.

B	A security service is a policy implemented to meet the protection need; a security control is a technology implemented to meet a protection need.
C	A security service is both an internal policy combined with an external vendor to meet the protection need; a security control is a technology and policy to meet a protection need.
D	A security service is a high-level security need; a security control is a technology and policy to meet the security service.
Answer	D
Rationale	Security services should not be confused with security controls or countermeasures. Security services are high-level security needs, while security controls are the technologies or procedures implemented to meet the security services.

ISSEP Questions: Chapter 3

Question 1	A narrative discussion of how a system is intended to operate is a _____.
A	Information Management Plan (IMP)
B	System Configuration Guidebook
C	CONOPS
D	Security Configuration Guidebook
Answer	C
Rationale	An IMP contains the mission need, information management model, and the information protection policy. A CONOPS captures all aspects of the system operation. Answers "b" and "d" are distracters.

Question 2	When defining the security requirements, the information systems security engineer (ISSE) should define the _____.
A	Relationship between the security controls and security components
B	Responsibilities of the system owner in acquiring security components
C	Responsibilities of the security components

D	Relationships between target and external systems
Answer	D
Rationale	The major focus of defining security requirements is to define what security will be required for the entire system, including what security functions the target system needs to perform and whether it will need to interact with other systems in the solution set. Thus, the ISSE must identify the relationships between the target and external system to adequately define the security requirements needed for the entire system.

Question 3	When defining the system requirements, which of the following would NOT be considered an operational requirement for the system?
A	Number of customer sites where the system will be used
B	Hardware disposal procedures
C	Capacity output necessary for the system functions
D	Anticipated time duration the system will be needed
Answer	B
Rationale	A procedure for disposing of hardware would not be considered a factor in determining the operational requirement. Although it might be done during the operational phase of the life cycle, it is unlikely it would dictate an operational requirement.

Question 4	Delivery time frames, national and international laws, and product capabilities are considered _____.
A	Constraints
B	Resources
C	Compliance factors
D	Qualifiers
Answer	A
Rationale	Constraints is the best choice. Resources would include personnel and financial abilities and not national and international laws. Compliance factors would also be considered a constraint and would not include delivery time frames. Qualifiers is a distracter.

Question 5	What is an operational scenario?
A	An anticipated use of the system
B	An estimate of how many operational personnel will be needed
C	An anticipated operational test of the security functions
D	An anticipated schematic layout of the operational center
Answer	A
Rationale	An operational scenario is an anticipated use of the system and its components; it should depict the full range of circumstances in which the system may be expected to operate.

Question 6	Which of the following defines a measure of effectiveness (MOE)?
A	It is the defined basis for testing the products during system integration
B	The level of bandwidth that must be distributed between the boundary enclaves
C	The defined level of satisfaction by the customer after the first testing of products
D	The defined metric the customer can use to measure satisfaction with products of the acquisition phase
Answer	D
Rationale	Answers A, B, and C are not related. To define MOEs, the customer identifies measures of system effectiveness that will reflect overall expectations and satisfaction, such as performance, safety, operability, usability, reliability, maintainability, ease of use, cost to train, workload, etc.

Question 7	Which of the following is used to indicate the range of anticipated uses of system products?
A	Functional baselines
B	System specifications
C	Operational scenarios
D	Interface specifications
Answer	C

Rationale	The customer identifies and defines the operational scenarios to indicate the range of anticipated uses of system products. Functional baselines, system specifications, and interface specifications are documents the systems engineers will use as build-to requirements.

Question 8	The _____ identify the different functions that the system will need to perform to meet the documented mission/business needs.
A	Performance requirements
B	Modes of operations
C	Functional requirements
D	Technical performance measures
Answer	C
Rationale	Performance requirements are the agreed-upon terms of how well the system functions. The modes of operation define the mode, such as training mode, pre-production mode, etc. Technical performance measures are key indicators of system performance such as key critical measures of effectiveness that will put the project at risk.

Question 9	A System CONOPS is written for the _____, while the System Specifications are written for the _____.
A	Systems engineers, information systems security engineers
B	Developers, information systems security engineers
C	Systems engineers, users
D	Users, developers
Answer	D
Rationale	A CONOPS is a user-oriented document that describes system characteristics for a proposed system from the users' viewpoint. The CONOPS is different from the system specifications, which is a formal statement of what the system must do <u>and</u> is written for the developers.

Question 10	What does the system security context define?
A	System boundaries and interfaces with other systems
B	Functional requirements

C	Functions matched to requirements
D	Functions to testing requirements
Answer	A
Rationale	The system security context defines the boundaries and interfaces with other systems and any data flows between the target and external systems.

Question 11	What do the system security requirements specify?
A	Security components needed to meet the security services
B	Security components as defined by the security architecture
C	Security functional baseline
D	Security functions a system must perform at a high level
Answer	D
Rationale	The system security requirements specify what security a system must perform, without specifying its design or implementation.

Question 12	Which of the following is NOT included in a Preliminary System Security CONOPS?
A	Information management functions the system will need to perform
B	Step-by-step procedures for system security functions
C	Information protection functions the system will need to perform
D	Interface with other systems and services they provide to the system
Answer	B
Rationale	The PRELIMINARY System Security CONOPS does not include step-by-step procedures. Although the final System Security CONOPS might contain this information, during Phase 2 of the ISSE model when the Preliminary Security CONOPS is developed, the step-by-step procedures would not be known.

Question 13	What is the purpose of a preliminary system security CONOPS?

A	To document the system's characteristic for the developers to use during the implementation phase
B	To help the developers understand the user's perspective and bridge a gap between the developers and the users
C	To document the security step-by-step procedures
D	To document the security requirements and security architecture
Answer	B
Rationale	The initial system security CONOPS will be used by the systems engineers in the architecture and design phase to help understand the operational community. It does not define the step-by-step procedures. Because it is done in the requirements phase, it is too early to define the security architecture. The final system security CONOPS may include the architecture, but not the preliminary system security CONOPS.

ISSEP Questions: Chapter 4

Question *1*	What is a framework of hardware, software, and interfaces that is used to develop computer systems?
A	Functional flow block diagram
B	Systems Requirements
C	Systems Baseline
D	Systems Architecture
Answer	D
Rationale	A functional flow block diagram is a method of decomposing system functions. System requirements are a high-level view of what the system must do. A system baseline is the design of a system established at a beginning point in time that captures both the structure and details of a configuration.

Question *2*	Which of the following is NOT a fundamental step in defining the system architecture?
A	Determine the intended use of the architecture
B	Determine the roles and responsibilities

C	Determine characteristics to be captured
D	Determine views and products to be build
Answer	B
Rationale	According to the DoD Architectural Framework, determining roles and responsibilities is not one of the six fundamental steps in defining the system architecture.

Question 3	What is the Federal Enterprise Architecture Framework?
A	A tool to collect and store common federal architecture information
B	A mandatory process that all federal agencies must use to define their enterprise architectures
C	A Congressional oversight program for ensuring that federal agencies are following the federal Enterprise Architecture requirements
D	A framework federal agencies can use to evaluate the interface connections between all federal agencies
Answer	A
Rationale	According to the Federal Enterprise Architecture Framework (FEAF) Program Management Office, the FEAF is a collaboration tool to collect common architecture information and build a repository for storing this information. Answers B, C, and D are nonexistent distracters.

Question 4	What is the goal of conducting a functional analysis?
A	Determine the system requirements
B	Provide the customer with a prototype design
C	Translate system requirements into detailed function criteria
D	Match the system requirements to the mission or business need
Answer	C
Rationale	Functional analysis is the process of translating system requirements into detailed function criteria. The functions generally include the actions and sequence of actions necessary to meet each system requirement.

Question 5	What is the process of breaking down higher-level functions into lower-level functions?
A	Functional analysis
B	Functional allocation
C	Functional baselining
D	Functional composing
Answer	a
Rationale	Functional allocation is the process of allocating performance and design requirements to each function. Function baselining and composing are distracters.

Question 6	What would the Information Systems Security Engineer use to review the major system level functions that must be performed by the system?
A	System Context Document
B	Functional Flow Block Diagram
C	PERT Chart
D	Information Management Model
Answer	B
Rationale	The system context is used to define the target and interfaces to external systems. The PERT chart is used for managing technical programs. The IMM is a tool that helps break down user roles, processes, and information until ambiguity is reduced to a satisfactory degree.

Question 7	During the architecture design phase, what is the goal of conducting a functional allocation?
A	Translate system requirements into detailed function criteria
B	Match the system requirements to the mission or business need
C	Allocate information protection needs to high-level functions
D	Allocate performance and design requirements to each system function and sub-function
Answer	D

Rationale	Functional analysis is the process of translating system requirements into detailed function criteria. Matching system requirements to mission needs does not occur during the architecture design phase. Allocating information protection needs are matched to requirements, which are matched to functions. Thus, answer D is the best answer.

Question 8	On Monday, the customer asked the Information Systems Security Engineer (ISSE) to perform a traceability matrix. What does the ISSE give to the customer?
A	An outline of the functions decomposed into sub-functions
B	An outline of the functions decomposed into sub-function and components
C	An outline that links the system requirements to the systems specifications
D	An outline that links the system requirements and interface requirements -
Answer	C
Rationale	Answers A and B are both functional analysis tasks. Answer D is a distracter. Traceability, a key concept in SE, is the process of ensuring that system requirements have been addressed in the system design. Forward traceability is derived from the system requirements to the system specification. Backward traceability is from the system specification to the system design

Question 9	What is used to describe how the security functions in the system will follow the security requirements?
A	National Security System Identification Checklist
B	System security baseline
C	Security architecture
D	System Engineering Management Plan
Answer	C
Rationale	The National Security System Identification Checklist is one method of determining whether a system is a national security system. A system security baseline is the design established at a beginning point in time that captures both the structure and details of a security configuration. The SEMP is a technical management planning document and tool.

Question 10	Which of the following is NOT done during the security architecture design phase?
A	Define the specific brand for a component
B	Define the security component needed for a security function
C	Define the security function needed for a security requirement
D	Define the performance of a security function
Answer	A
Rationale	Defining the exact brand name for a component is not completed during the architecture phase.

Question 11	The Information Assurance Technical Framework (IATF) divides the information system into four reasonable areas. Which of the following is one of those four areas?
A	Local Computing Environment
B	Heating, Ventilation, and Air Conditioning
C	Wide Area Network
D	Global Area Network
Answer	A
Rationale	The four areas defined by the IATF are Local Computing Environment, Enclave Boundaries, Networks and Infrastructures, and Supporting Infrastructures.

Question 12	Of the four information systems areas defined by the IATF, which is the collection of local computing devices, regardless of physical location, that are interconnected via local area networks and governed by a single security policy?
A	Local Computing Environment
B	Enclave Boundary
C	Network and Infrastructure
D	Supporting Infrastructure
Answer	B

Rationale	The local computing environment contains servers, client workstations, operating system, and applications. The enclave boundary is the collection of local computing devices, regardless of physical location, interconnected via local area networks and governed by a single security policy. The network and infrastructure provides the network connectivity between enclaves. The supporting infrastructure provides the foundation upon which security service mechanisms are used in the network, enclave, and computing environments.

Question 13	Of the four information systems areas defined by the IATF, where would the intrusion detection control be placed?
A	Local Computing Environment
B	Enclave Boundary
C	Network and Infrastructure
D	Supporting Infrastructure
Answer	D
Rationale	The IATF states that the supporting infrastructure provides the foundation upon which security service mechanisms are used in the network, enclave, and computing environments. The two areas addressed in the IATF are Key Management Infrastructure (KMI), which provides a unified process for the secure creation, distribution, and management of public key certificates, and Detect and Respond Infrastructures, which provide the ability to detect and respond to intrusions.

Question 14	How does the information systems security engineer (ISSE) determine whether one security function could meet several security requirements?
A	Conduct a security functional analysis and allocation.
B	Conduct a system design review (SDR).
C	Conduct a security trade-off analysis.
D	Conduct a component item (CI) review.
Answer	A

Rationale	The SDR verifies the conceptual design against activities conducted in the preliminary and detailed system design. A security trade-off analysis determines distinguishing characteristics of the solutions and notes the strengths and weaknesses. A CI review is a distracter.

Question 15	Which security function would provide a mechanism for allowing or disallowing connections based on identification?
A	Application program interface (API)
B	Application layer guard
C	Packet filter guard
D	Secure Socket Layer (SSL) protocol
Answer	B
Rationale	APIs provide standard interfaces so that multiple vendors can provide interoperable solutions. Packet filtering firewalls commonly operate at the network layer and check the IP and protocol headers against a set of predefined rules. SSL exists just above the transport layer and provides data encryption, server authentication, message integrity, and optional client authentication for a TCP/IP connection.

Question 16	Which of the following is NOT provided by a file encryptor?
A	Confidentiality and integrity for individual files
B	A means of authenticating a file's source
C	A means of exchanging encrypted files between computers
D	A connection point between a client and a server
Answer	D
Rationale	A circuit gateway or proxy provides a connection point in a session between a client and a server.

Question 17	Which security function would provide network layer protection for confidentiality?
A	IPSec
B	Hardware tokens

C	S/MIME
D	SOCKS Protocol
Answer	A
Rationale	A hardware token is an access control device. S/MIME is a specification for adding security for e-mail in Multipurpose Internet Mail Extensions (MIME) format, supporting binary attachments as well as text. The SOCKS Protocol supports application-layer firewall traversal for both reliable TCP and User Datagram Protocol (UDP) transport services by creating a shim-layer between the application and the transport layers. IPSec is the security framework standardized by the Internet Engineering Task Force (IETF) as the primary network-layer protection mechanism.

Question 18	Which of the following best describes a security Requirements Traceability Matrix (RTM)?
A	Ability to match a security requirement to a mission need
B	Ability to evaluate software systems based on both functionality and assurance in terms of integrity, confidentiality, and availability
C	Ability to trace a security requirement, both forwards and backwards, throughout the life cycle
D	Ability to identify the procedure for identifying, recording, and tracking test results to closure, including any change control procedures
Answer	C
Rationale	Answer A is not the best definition of an RTM, B is related to Common Criteria evaluations, and D defines a control for a system security testing plan

Question 19	Which of the following are review methods in completing a Requirements Traceability Matrix (RTM)?
A	Documentation review, test, observation, independent verification and validation
B	Interview, verify, validate, test
C	Interview, documentation review, observation, validation
D	Interview, documentation review, test, observation

Answer	D
Rationale	DITCAP states that the review process for each requirement, where I = Interview, D = Documentation review, T = Test the scientific instrumented evaluation, and O = Observation (or demonstration of the security function).

Question 20	Interconnections among DoD information systems with different security domains shall be employed under what circumstances?
A	Operational convenience
B	Compelling operational requirements
C	Approved certification of connected systems
D	International agreements dictating such connections
Answer	B
Rationale	According to DoDD 8500.1, "Interconnections among DoD information systems of different security domains or with other U.S. Government systems of different security domains shall be employed only to meet compelling operational requirements, not operational convenience." This question addresses when interconnections can be made. Once made, they must follow DoD IA policies such as C&A and any international agreements.

Question 21	What is conducted during the architecture phase to analyze alternatives and choose the most appropriate solution?
A	Conduct a security functional analysis and allocation
B	Conduct a system design review (SDR)
C	Conduct a security trade-off analysis
D	Conduct a component item (CI) review
Answer	C
Rationale	The security functional analysis and allocation decomposes the security functions and sub-functions and allocates performance to the functions. The SDR verifies the conceptual design against activities conducted in the preliminary and detailed system design. A security trade-off analysis determines distinguishing characteristics of the solutions and notes the strengths and weaknesses. A CI review is a distracter.

ISSEP Questions: Chapter 5

Question 1	What occurs during the synthesis phase?
A	A baseline configuration is developed to demonstrate the design concepts
B	System functions are allocated to the target system
C	System functions are allocated to the target system and external systems
D	Initial Security CONOPS is developed for user comments
Answer	A
Rationale	Answers B, C, and D all occur during the architecture phase. The synthesis (design) phase follows the architecture phase and defines the build-to specifications.

Question 2	If the information systems security engineer (ISSE) is asked to review the systems specification document, what is the ISSE looking for?
A	Whether the system is vulnerable to predetermined threats
B	Whether the previously defined requirements are met
C	Whether it is written from a user perspective and captures all aspects of the system operations
D	Whether the test plans will indicate the components' reliability
Answer	B
Rationale	Vulnerabilities and threats are not usually included in the systems specification document; C is the definition of System CONOPS; and D is a distracter.

Question 3	What is the most key design document?
A	System requirements
B	Quality assurance requirements
C	System specifications
D	Information management plan
Answer	C

Rationale	The system specifications become the source for all of the subordinate specifications produced at later stages through the design and development process. If the system specification is firm, an effective foundation is formed for the remainder of the design and development effort.

Question 4	If the client asks the information systems security engineer (ISSE) to create a System Breakdown Structure, what is wanted?
A	A graphical depiction of the functional requirements
B	A graphical depiction of the functions matched to the requirements
C	A depiction of the specifications based on development specifications, product specifications, and material specifications
D	A depiction of the hierarchy of products and processes that comprise the system architecture
Answer	D
Rationale	IEEE 1220 notes that a System Breakdown Structure (SBS) depicts the hierarchy of products and processes that comprise the system architecture. The SBS should be used by the organization for development and control of planning packages and their conversion to work packages, sizing of work packages, configuration management, resource allocation, traceability of requirement changes, interface control, cost reporting, and event-based scheduling.

Question 5	Which of the following would include system interface specifications and the system specifications?
A	System baseline
B	Functional baseline
C	Allocated baseline
D	Product baseline
Answer	A

Rationale	IEEE 1220 states that "the system baselines should include the system interface specifications, the product interface specifications, the system specifications, the product specifications, and the integrated database that captures the design, data, models, metrics, changes, design rationale, and other pertinent information on decisions or clarifications made to system requirements." A functional baseline describes the system functional specifications as derived from system performance requirements during the concept definition phase. An allocated baseline is the allocation of functions to system components (or CIs) and is validated by analyses and tests. The result is a specification for each CI as well as the technical approach developed to specify the specified need or objective. The product baseline consists of product, process, and material specifications and engineering drawings.

Question 6	Which of the following best describes the system baseline?
A	A design of the system established at a beginning point in time that captures the configuration structure and details
B	The system functional specifications as derived from system performance requirements during the concept definition phase
C	A specification for each CI as well as the technical approach developed to specify the specified need or objective
D	A specification containing product, process, and material specifications and engineering drawings
Answer	A
Rationale	A functional baseline describes the system functional specifications as derived from system performance requirements during the concept definition phase. An allocated baseline is the allocation of functions to system components (or CIs) and is validated by analyses and tests. The result is a specification for each CI as well as the technical approach developed to specify the specified need or objective. The product baseline consists of product, process, and material specifications and engineering drawings.

Question 7	During the assembly and fabrication phase, what is used for guidance to complete the subsystem and component levels?

A	Acquisition strategy
B	Installation plan
C	Detailed system design
D	Transition plan
Answer	C
Rationale	The acquisition plan identifies any hardware, software, and communications equipment needed to install and operate the product at the customer site. The installation plan addresses the installation of any hardware, software, firmware, and communications equipment needed to operate the product at the customer site. The transition plan describes the detailed plans, procedures, and schedules that will guide the transition process.

Question 8	Which one of the following is NOT a task completed during the preliminary design activities?
A	Identify component and component interfaces
B	Assess component risks
C	Identify assemblies and assembly interfaces
D	Prepare integrated data package
Answer	D
Rationale	Preparing the integrated data package is part of the detailed design activities that follow the preliminary design.

Question 9	What does an information systems security engineer (ISSE) determine when conducting a reliability analysis?
A	Whether the preliminary subsystem specification and final subsystem specification are consistent with the preliminary and final system specifications
B	Whether a product will perform consistently over time within a given environment
C	Whether the human/system interfaces are meeting the predetermined performance measurements
D	Whether the build-to requirements reflect workforce, personnel, and training specification
Answer	B

Rationale	Reliability has to do with the quality of measurement and the extent to which those measures have consistency or repeatability over a specified time period, with performance over time being a key factor. The other answers are related to the preliminary and final design.

Question 10	Which of the following best describes a prototype?
A	An abstract and theoretical system design
B	An integration of hardware and software to verify the design concepts
C	An integration of hardware, software, and firmware according to the proper system configurations
D	An integration of hardware, software, and firmware to evaluate the complexity of repeating it throughout the system
Answer	C
Rationale	Prototyping is the iterative process of combining and integrating the system components, such as hardware, software, and logistic support, into the proper system configuration and evaluate whether it meets the system requirements.

Question 11	When should the systems engineer (SE) conduct the System Design Review (SDR)?
A	At the end of the architecture phase
B	At the end of the design phase
C	At the end of the implantation phase
D	At the end of the certification phase
Answer	B
Rationale	At the end of the design stage, the SE needs to conduct some type of formal review. The goal of the System Design Review (SDR) is to verify the conceptual design against activities conducted in the preliminary and detailed system design. The system specifications are reviewed against the system requirements and the system architecture.

Question 12	What is the goal of the System Design Review (SDR)?
A	To review the system specifications against the system requirements and the system architecture
B	To review the security architecture against the system requirements
C	To review the system design against the operational scenarios
D	To review the system functions against the system requirements and the system architecture
Answer	A
Rationale	The goal of the System Design Review (SDR) is to verify the conceptual design against activities conducted in the preliminary and detailed system design. The system specifications are reviewed against the system requirements and the system architecture.

Question 13	Where does the ISSE document the security synthesis?
A	System security specifications
B	Security CONOPS
C	Functional flow block diagram
D	Development baseline
Answer	A
Rationale	The security CONOPS defines the concept of operations for the security functions at a user level. The functional flow block diagram is a tool to structure the system requirements into functional terms. A development baseline is an approved build of the product and can be a single component or a combination of components.

Question 14	What does the ISSE conduct at the end of the detailed security design phase?
A	Timeline analysis
B	Critical Design Review

C	Service test analysis
D	High-level Design Review
Answer	B
Rationale	A timeline analysis is a technical management tool. A service test analysis and high-level design review are distracters. The objective of the detailed security design phase is to complete the design of the CIs requiring development. The conclusion of this phase is the system Critical Design Review (CDR).

Question 15	Which of the following would an ISSE complete during the detailed security design?
A	Build custom security products
B	Regression tests
C	Identify COTS/GOTS security products
D	Operation manuals
Answer	C
Rationale	The build of custom security products may begin in the design phase, but it would be completed during the implementation phase. Regression tests and operation manuals would also be completed during the implementation phase.

Question 16	What is the best method of choosing a COTS/GOTS security product?
A	Conduct a trade-off analysis based on performance and function.
B	Conduct a trade-off analysis based on cost, schedule, and risk.
C	If costs are too high, modify security requirements to meet budget limitations so product can be acquired.
D	Review security requirements against schedule and costs.
Answer	A
Rationale	When deciding on security products, the ISSE team must balance factors such as operational function and performance, cost, schedule, and risk. Operational function and performance should be the deciding factors.

Question 17	When should the initial test plan be developed?
A	Security organization phase
B	Security design phase
C	Security implementation phase
D	Security accreditation phase
Answer	B
Rationale	The documentation for security verification and validation usually begins in the design phase. However, in some instances, security test planning begins in the conceptual phase when security requirements are initially established. Essentially, if a security requirement is specified, there must be a method of evaluating and validating that the final system met the requirement. Thus, considerations for test and evaluation are an integral part of all phases, but should not be documented later than the design phase.

Question 18	What is the difference between a Test and Evaluation Master Plan (TEMP) and a Security Test and Evaluation Master Plan (STEMP)?
A	The TEMP includes hardware, software, and environmental conditions, while the STEMP also includes personnel responses.
B	The TEMP includes hardware and software, while the STEMP only includes software security components.
C	The TEMP is conducted on component items before they are integrated, while the STEMP is conducted on component items before and after they are integrated.
D	Security controls are evaluated.
Answer	D
Rationale	During the design phase, the role of the ISSEP is to ensure that security is included in the TEMP or, if necessary, develop a Security Test and Evaluation Master Plan (STEMP).

Question 19	What does the ISSE do in order to verify the security concepts and design configurations?
A	Review the Security Requirements Traceability Matrix (RTM)

B	Review the Information Protection Policies
C	Conduct reliability analysis
D	Develop prototypes
Answer	D
Rationale	The RTM matches security functions to requirements. The information protection policies would not validate the design configurations because they are defining what high-level security services are needed. A reliability analysis reviews the performance of the components over a specified time frame. The ISSE can verify documented security concepts and design configurations through the use of a physical working model or prototype.

Question 20	What monitors the changes to the initial security baseline?
A	Security Requirements Traceability Matrix (RTM)
B	Configuration Management
C	Test and Evaluation Management Plan (TEMP)
D	Systems Engineering Management Plan (SEMP)
Answer	B
Rationale	The RTM matches security functions to requirements. The TEMP is the initial test plan. The SEMP is the management plan for system development and integration. Configuration management explains how to monitor changes after creating an initial security baseline.

ISSEP Questions: Chapter 6

Question 1	When is a system ready for construction and production?
A	Following establishment of functional baseline
B	Before assembly and integration
C	After scheduled development
D	During integration and testing
Answer	B

Rationale	System engineering activities systems implementation is called construction and production. After the functional baseline is established, construction and production begin.

Question 2	Which of the following describes the plans, procedures, and schedule that will guide the system from the construction phase to full operation?
A	Acquisition plan
B	Installation plan
C	Transition plan
D	Maintenance plan
Answer	C
Rationale	The transition plan describes how to get from construction to full operation. This is done well in advance of the system being installed and maintained, but after acquisition.

Question 3	Which of the following is the process of making the new system available to the users?
A	Certification and accreditation (C&A)
B	System design
C	System implementation
D	System architecture
Answer	C
Rationale	C&A evaluates the security controls; system design is decomposing functions and components into a workable solution; and system architecture provides a blueprint for designing the system.

Question 4	What is the role of the information systems security engineer (ISSE) during the system security implementation phase?
A	Ensures that the security mechanisms in the security specifications are integrated into the functional operation of the system
B	Identifies one or more solution sets that can meet the information protection needs

C	Defines the requirements for the target system and also the interconnections to other external outside systems
D	Identifies and allocates functions to the security requirements documented in the system security requirements
Answer	A
Rationale	"b" and "c" are processes from Phase 2, Requirements, and "d" is a process in Phase 3, Architecture.

Question 5	Which of the following is NOT an issue that should be addressed during the system implementation phase?
A	Personnel resources
B	Schedule development
C	Material availability
D	System context
Answer	D
Rationale	The system context is the result of SEs and ISSEPs translating requirements into system parameters and possible measurement concepts that meet the defined requirements; it is part of the requirements phase.

Question 6	What document should be created to identify the hardware, software, or communications needed during the system implementation phase
A	Systems engineering management plan (SEMP)
B	Acquisition plan
C	Configuration management plan
D	Transition plan
Answer	B

Rationale	The SEMP provides an integration of documents from previous activities and any design-related tasks necessary to enhance the integration and implementation activities. The acquisition plan defines the acquisition and installation of the operating environment hardware and software. The configuration management plan ensures that significant changes during development are evaluated and that the security design has not been compromised. The transition plan describes the detailed plans, procedures, and schedules that will guide the transition process.

Question 7	Which of the following is considered a construction activity?
A	Conducting unit testing
B	Allocating security functionality
C	Conducting a reliability analysis
D	Initiating the requirements traceability matrix
Answer	A
Rationale	Allocating security functionality is considered a design activity, conducting a reliability analysis is also a design activity, and an RTM would be initiated during the architecture activity.

Question 8	Which of the following would NOT be included in an acquisition plan?
A	Description of currently used products to meet the products
B	Description of the methodology used to acquire the products
C	Identification of who must approve the acquisitions
D	Description of the training requirements for the products
Answer	D
Rationale	Answer D is incorrect because this would be an element of the transition plan.

Question 9	Which of the following is an acquisition consideration for a system that will process classified information?
A	Short-term leasing equipment

B	Asset management
C	Remote vendor maintenance
D	Can be returned for credit
Answer	B
Rationale	A, C, and D would not be suitable for a classified system because most classified equipment would be destroyed at the end of the life cycle and remote vendor maintenance would not be allowed. The ability to manage the assets is of key importance because one needs to know where classified equipment is and its status.

Question 10	What is a development baseline?
A	A representation of a current or necessary real-world configuration of resources, rules, and relationships
B	A description of the tasks and activities, operational elements, and information flows required to accomplish or support a military operation
C	An approved build of the product
D	An approved definition of the configuration items (CIs) that will work within the system
Answer	C
Rationale	Answer A is the definition of an architecture; B is the definition of an operational architecture; and D is the definition of the system design.

Question 11	Which of the following best defines a regression test on a system build?
A	Verifies that capabilities in earlier builds continue to work correctly in subsequent builds
B	Verifies that the build meets its data requirements and correctly generates each expected display and report
C	Identifies the performance thresholds of each build
D	Identifies the reliability thresholds of each build
Answer	A

Rationale	Regression tests are designed to verify that capabilities in earlier builds continue to work correctly in subsequent builds. Functional tests focus on verifying that the build meets its functional and data requirements and correctly generates each expected display and report. Performance tests are used to identify the performance thresholds of each build. Reliability tests are used to identify the reliability thresholds of each build.

Question **12**	Which of the following best defines a functional test on a system build?
A	Verifies that capabilities in earlier builds continue to work correctly in subsequent builds
B	Verifies that the build meets its data requirements and correctly generates each expected display and report
C	Identifies the performance thresholds of each build
D	Identifies the reliability thresholds of each build
Answer	B
Rationale	Regression tests are designed to verify that capabilities in earlier builds continue to work correctly in subsequent builds. Functional tests focus on verifying that the build meets its functional and data requirements and correctly generates each expected display and report. Performance tests are used to identify the performance thresholds of each build. Reliability tests are used to identify the reliability thresholds of each build.

Question **13**	During which phase is the systems operations user manual developed?
A	Analysis
B	Design
C	Development
D	Implementation
Answer	D
Rationale	Another activity in the construction phase is the development of the operating documentation, such as user manuals.

Question 14	During which phase is the training program developed?
A	Analysis
B	Design
C	Development
D	Implementation
Answer	D
Rationale	The final activity in the construction phase is to develop a training program that defines the training needed for users to implement and operate the system successfully.

Question 15	Which of the following best describes integration testing?
A	Combines one or more modules into a build, tests the build, and then integrates the build into the structure
B	Once the system is completely integrated, it validates that the system meets all requirements
C	Verifies that any corrections or changes to the system are included and controlled under the configuration management plan
D	Integrates and installs system, then verifies whether users can operate the system in a secure manner before final deployment
Answer	A
Rationale	Answer B is the definition for system testing, C is an element of system testing, and D would be part of the acceptance testing.

Question 16	Which of the following would be conducted during the system acceptance activity?
A	System documentation is given to the support staff.
B	Assess the integration of the physical architecture of the system.
C	Assess the internal and external interfaces and interoperability requirements.

D	Final comparison of implemented system with original capabilities.
Answer	A
Rationale	Answers B and C are architecture activities and D is a distracter.

Question 17	What role does the information systems security engineer (ISSE) perform during the implementation phase?
A	Determines whether there any system level requirements that have not been considered or fully satisfied by the individual component items
B	Confirms that the integrated system design meets the security functional baseline requirements and user requirements
C	Verifies that the system as implemented protects against the identified threats
D	Chooses communication security components that will enforce the security requirements for each interface
Answer	C
Rationale	Answers A and B are activities during the design phase; D is an architecture activity.

Question 18	Which of the following best identifies the factors involved in determining which security component to acquire?
A	Cost and availability
B	Cost, availability, and expected life cycle
C	Cost, availability, and how it will mitigate the risk of the overall system
D	Cost, availability, and future availability of the product
Answer	C
Rationale	All would be considered factors, but C includes whether it will mitigate the risk to the system; thus, it is the best answer.

Question 19	What was a requirement from NSTISSP No. 11, National Policy Governing the Acquisition of IA and IA-enabled IT Products?
A	Agencies must develop policies for the procurement and use of evaluated products.

B	After 2002, the acquisition of all COTS IA and IA-enabled IT products to be used on national security systems shall be limited only to those that have been evaluated and validated in accordance with the common criteria or FIPS schemes.
C	Agencies must be aware of how assurance in the acquired products supports security.
D	IA and IA-enabled IT products for use on national security systems must follow the NSA configuration guidelines.
Answer	B
Rationale	The other items are good practices, but the actual requirement form NSTISSP No. 11 is the requirement to have products evaluated by NIAP, Common Criteria, or FIPS cryptographic schemes.

Question 20	Which of the following is NOT a recommended guideline from NIST SP 800-23, Acquisition Guidelines for Security Components?
A	Agencies should understand the concepts of computer security assurance.
B	Agencies should be aware of how assurance in the acquired products supports security.
C	Agencies should be aware of where (in which country) the software code was developed.
D	Agencies should be knowledgeable of many approaches to obtaining security assurance in the products they procure.
Answer	C
Rationale	This is not a recommended guideline from NIST SP 800-23.

Question 21	What type of changes can be made to a security component after the information systems security engineer (ISSE) has verified that the security features of the security components are enabled and providing for the security services?
A	No changes can be made
B	Only changes that have been previously funded
C	Only changes that have been through a change control process
D	All changes can be made if they are funded
Answer	C

Rationale	Once the security configuration for the system has been established, any differences in settings must be recorded and approved following configuration management or waiver procedures.

Question 22	Which of the following tests is most likely conducted during the security test and evaluation (ST&E)?
A	Requirements traceability test
B	Penetration test
C	Integration test
D	Transition test
Answer	B
Rationale	The most common ST&E is functional testing that demonstrates whether a system behaves according to its specifications and produces specified outputs when inputs are introduced. Additional types of ST&E are penetration testing, cryptographic verification testing, security independent verification & validation (IV&V), security assurance analysis methods, and TEMPEST testing.

Question 23	What does NIST SP 800-42, Guideline on Network Security Testing, state as a goal of security test and evaluation (ST&E)?
A	The technical approach developed will meet the specified need or objective
B	To determine whether the implementation of a security component placed a constraint on the system
C	To assess the reliability of the security component under attack
D	To uncover design, implementation, and operational flaws that could allow the violation of security policy
Answer	D
Rationale	SP 800-42 outlines the objectives of the ST&E as: (i) uncover design, implementation, and operational flaws that could allow the violation of security policy, (ii) determine the adequacy of security mechanisms, assurances, and other properties to enforce the security policy, and (iii) assess the degree of consistency between the system documentation and its implementation.

Question 24	Which of the following would NOT be included in the scope of a security test and evaluation (ST&E)?
A	Communications security
B	Risk management
C	Emanations security
D	Personnel security
Answer	B
Rationale	According to SP 800-42, the scope of an ST&E plan typically addresses computer security, communications security, emanations security, physical security, personnel security, administrative security, and operations security.

Question 25	What does a verification and validation test provide to the information systems security engineer (ISSE)?
A	The security implementation satisfies the stated security requirements (verify) and the security requirements satisfy the real-world needs (validate).
B	The security requirements satisfy the real-world needs (verify) and the security implementation satisfies the stated security requirements (validate).
C	The security mechanisms, assurances, and other properties enforce the security policy.
D	The consistency between the security documentation and security implementation is equal to the security requirements and security objectives.
Answer	A
Rationale	Answers B, C, and D are distracters. Verification ensures that the integration and implementation of the system satisfies the requirements as stated and documented in the requirements. Validation can reveal problems in requirements analysis where the security meets all of its written specifications but, unfortunately, does not meet a key operational need or constraint.

Question 26	Which type of security testing answers the question of whether you built the right system?
A	Certification and accreditation
B	Verification

C	Validation
D	Security assurance analysis
Answer	C
Rationale	Validation answers the question: Did you build the right system?

Question **27**	Which type of security testing answers the question of whether you built the system right?
A	Certification and accreditation
B	Verification
C	Validation
D	Security assurance analysis
Answer	B
Rationale	Verification answers the question: Did you build the system right?

Question **28**	What is the final step of the ISSE implementation activities?
A	Certify and accredit the system
B	Train the users in how to use the security features of the security components
C	Transfer the responsibility for security of the system to the customer
D	Conduct the security test and evaluation (ST&E)
Answer	C
Rationale	The final step in the ISSE implementation activities is to transfer the responsibility for security of the system to the customer. At this point, the system will now be operated and maintained by the customer, including the secure operation of the system.

ISSEP Questions: Chapter 7

Question **1**	Which one of the following focuses on performance excellence for the entire organization in an overall management framework?
A	Six sigma

B	ISO 9001
C	Baldrige criteria
D	Benchmarking capabilities
Answer	D
Rationale	The Baldrige criterion for performance excellence of the organization is correct. The ISO is a conformity model while Six Sigma measures product quality. Benchmarking capabilities provide a reference for measurements.

Question 2	Which of the following best describes ISO 9001?
A	A model for fixing quality system defects
B	A base model for which measurements can be made
C	A model for evaluating personnel performance to quality
D	A model for matching requirements to processes
Answer	A
Rationale	Answer B describes benchmarking. Answers C and D are distracters.

Question 3	Which of the following best describes benchmarking?
A	Improving performance by learning from best practices and successful processes
B	Improving performance by measuring product quality
C	Establishing guidelines to evaluate quality processes
D	Improving products by ensuring objectives accommodate the customer needs and expectations
Answer	A
Rationale	All answers involve quality items, but answer A best describes the specific objective of benchmarking.

Question 4	Which quality award does the National Institute of Standards and Technology (NIST) manage?
A	ISO 9001

B	Six Sigma
C	Malcolm Baldrige
D	John Burns
Answer	C
Rationale	ISO 9001 is an international standard. Six Sigma was developed by Motorola and is now used by private-sector companies. John Burns (answer D) is a distracter. NIST manages the Malcolm Baldrige National Quality Award.

Question 5	Which of the following is a key task for achieving ISO 9001 certification?
A	Establishing a configuration management plan
B	Establishing and documenting a quality process
C	Establishing a task management plan
D	Establishing a semi-annual auditing of quality processes
Answer	B
Rationale	Establishing a configuration management plan is related to managing changes to a system. Answer C is a distracter. A semi-annual audit (answer D) is not a good answer because auditing of quality processes is a continuing task.

Question 6	Which of the following ISO 9001 principles states that effective decisions are based on the analysis of data and information?
A	Leadership
B	Involvement of people
C	Continual improvement
D	Factual approach to decision making
Answer	D
Rationale	Leadership states that leaders establish unity of purpose and direction for the organization. The involvement of people involves enabling people at all levels to use their abilities for the organization's benefit. Continual improvement states that performance should be a permanent objective of the organization.

Question 7	What quality management phrase captures the essence of continual improvement?
A	Plan, Do, Evaluate, Act
B	Plan, Do, Evaluate, Redo
C	Plan, Do, Check, Act
D	Do, Evaluate, Do, Evaluate
Answer	C
Rationale	Deming made this model popular in the 1950s. Plan: establish the objectives and processes necessary to deliver results in accordance with customer requirements and the organization's policies. Do: implement the processes. Check: monitor and measure processes and product against policies, objectives, and requirements for the product and report the results. Act: take actions to continually improve process performance.

Question 8	Which methodology uses the "Define, Measure, Analyze, Improve, Control" methodology?
A	ISO 9001
B	Six Sigma
C	ISSE
D	IEEE 1220
Answer	B
Rationale	In Six Sigma, the first improvement system, "Define, Measure, Analyze, Improve, Control (DMAIC)," is implemented to find incremental improvement when existing processes fall below specification.

Question 9	What quality process designates green belts and black belts?
A	Baldrige National Quality Process
B	ISO 9001
C	Six Sigma
D	CMMI
Answer	C

Rationale	In-house technical leaders are known as Six Sigma green belts, black belts, or master black belts. These "change agents" provide the key to successfully implementing Six Sigma processes in the organization.

Question 10	Which of the following is NOT a CMMI objective?
A	Provides guidance for improving an organization's processes
B	Provides guidance for improving the development, acquisition, and maintenance of products or services
C	Provides guidance for organization's to evaluate their organizational maturity
D	Provides guidance on establishing a base model for which measurements can be made
Answer	D
Rationale	A, B, and C are related to CMMI, while D is a benchmarking objective.

Question 11	Which of the following is the best definition for "level 3 defined" of the CCMI capability levels?
A	A performed process that satisfies the specific goals of the process area
B	A performed process that is planned and executed in accordance with policy
C	A performed process that is tailored from the organization's set of standard processes according to the organization's tailoring guidelines
D	A performed process that is changed and adapted to meet relevant current and projected business objectives
Answer	C
Rationale	A is level 1 (performed), B is level 2 (managed), and D is level 5 (optimizing).

Question 12	What method can be used mid-way through the system design phase to assess the security strengths and weaknesses of the design?
A	System security profiling

B	Security requirements traceability matrix (SRTM)
C	Security engineering management plan (SEMP)
D	Security test and evaluation management plan (STEMP)
Answer	A
Rationale	Identification of security capabilities and weaknesses is the essential element of a security profile. The SRTM matches functions to requirements. The SEMP is a management tool. The STEMP is used to test the security functions during the implementation phase.

Question 13	Which of the following best defines "processes" according to the information assurance category?
A	Assurance mechanisms that involve how a system or product is designed, developed, shipped, and maintained
B	Assurance mechanisms that involve the structure or characteristic that system or product components must have to convince the developers and evaluators that the system or product is implemented correctly
C	Assurance mechanisms examining a description of an aspect of the system or product and not the physical entity itself
D	Assurance mechanisms that involve exercising an actual implementation of a system or product to determine certain characteristics of its operation
Answer	A
Rationale	A is Processes, B is Properties, C is Analysis, and D is Testing. The other two assurance categories are Guidance and Fielded Systems Evaluation.

Question 14	Which of the following best defines "analysis" according to the information assurance category?
a	Assurance mechanisms that involve how a system or product is designed, developed, shipped, and maintained
b	Assurance mechanisms that involve the structure or characteristic that system or product components must have to convince the developers and evaluators that the system or product is implemented correctly

c	Assurance mechanisms examining a description of an aspect of the system or product and not the physical entity itself
d	Assurance mechanisms that involve exercising an actual implementation of a system or product to determine certain characteristics of its operation
Answer	c
Rationale	A is Processes, B is Properties, C is Analysis, and D is Testing. The other two assurance categories are Guidance and Fielded Systems Evaluation.

Question 15	Which of the following best defines "properties" according to the information assurance category?
A	Assurance mechanisms that involve how a system or product is designed, developed, shipped, and maintained
B	Assurance mechanisms that involve the structure or characteristic that system or product components must have to convince the developers and evaluators that the system or product is implemented correctly
C	Assurance mechanisms examining a description of an aspect of the system or product and not the physical entity itself
D	Assurance mechanisms that involve exercising an actual implementation of a system or product to determine certain characteristics of its operation
Answer	B
Rationale	A is Processes, B is Properties, C is Analysis, and D is Testing. The other two assurance categories are Guidance and Fielded Systems Evaluation.

Question 16	Which of the following mechanisms would be included in the "processes" assurance mechanism?
a	Configuration management
b	Penetration testing
c	Security operations manual
d	Evaluation of deployed system
Answer	A

Rationale	Penetration testing is considered a testing assurance mechanism, operations manual is considered a guidance assurance mechanism, and evaluation of deployed system is considered a fielded systems evaluation assurance mechanism.

Question 17	Which information assurance categories would program reviews (meetings conducted at milestones to gather info and make decisions) fit into?
A	Processes
B	Properties
C	Analysis
D	Guidance
Answer	A
Rationale	Program reviews are considered a process mechanism that involves how a system is designed, developed, operated, etc.

Question 18	If the ISSEP conducts a covert channel analysis, which information assurance categories would this fit into?
A	Processes
B	Properties
C	Analysis
D	Guidance
Answer	C
Rationale	Analysis assurance mechanisms examining a description of an aspect of the system or product and not the physical entity itself. Different aspects of system and products that should be considered include covert channels, cryptography, key and privilege management, system architecture, TEMPEST, etc.

Question 19	If the ISSEP conducts a traceability analysis, which information assurance categories would this fit into?
A	Processes
B	Properties
C	Analysis
D	Guidance

Answer	B
Rationale	Property mechanisms are those that involve the structure or characteristic that system or product components must have to convince the developers and evaluators that the system or product is implemented correctly. This includes items such as redundancy, modularity, traceability, mature technology, alarm
	philosophy/fail-safe design, physical integrity/tamper resident-evident, environment, distribution/installation, modularization, etc.

Question 20	Which of the following is NOT an end product of conducting security testing?
A	Confirms the presence of vulnerabilities
B	Demonstrates whether a system behaves according to its specifications
C	Demonstrates whether a system can be broken into
D	Shows the absences of vulnerabilities
Answer	D
Rationale	Testing cannot show the absences of vulnerabilities in a system; it can merely confirm the presence of some vulnerability. B is a result of functional testing and C is a result of penetration testing.

Question 21	Which law mandated that security control objectives and techniques for systems and programs must be reviewed and reported annually to the Office of Management and Budget (OMB)?
A	Computer Security Act
B	Clinger-Cohen Act
C	EGov Act
D	Federal Information Security Management Act
Answer	D
Rationale	FISMA requires federal agencies to demonstrate that they are meeting applicable security requirements, and agencies must document the actual level of performance based on the results of annual security program reviews.

Question 22	Which of the following is one of the six phases that organizations can use to design security metrics?
A	Identify corrective actions.
B	Confirm that the evolving system development and integration complies with the agreements between role players.
C	Produce an agreement (i.e., SSAA) on the method of implementing the security requirements.
D	Define the users' security clearances, their access rights to specific categories of information processed, and the actual information that the system is required to process.
Answer	A
Rationale	According to NIST SP 800-55, the six phases are Prepare for Data Collection, Collect Data and Analyze Results, Identify Corrective Actions, Develop Business Case, Obtain Resources, and Apply Corrective Actions. B, C, and D are DITSCAP activities for C&A.

Question 23	According to NIST SP 800-55, what occurs during the "develop business case and obtain resources" phase?
A	Implementation steps should be defined on how to collect, analyze, and report the metrics
B	Development of a plan that provides the roadmap of how to close the security gaps
C	Assessment of the budgeting cycle required for obtaining resources required for implementing remediation actions
D	Implementation of corrective actions in technical, management, and operational areas of security controls
Answer	C
Rationale	A occurs in Phase 1, Prepare for Data Collection; B occurs in Phase 2, Collect Data and Analyze Results; and D occurs in Phase 6, Apply Corrective Actions.

Question 24	Which NIST Special Publication provides guidelines for agencies to conduct self-assessments?
A	SP 800-18
B	SP 800-26

C	SP 800-50
D	SP 800-16
Answer	B
Rationale	SP 800-26 provides a method for agency officials to determine the current status of their information security programs and, where necessary, establish a target for improvement. SP 800-18 is a guideline for developing system security plans, SP 800-50 is a guideline for developing an awareness and training program, and SP 800-16 is a guideline for developing a role-based training program.

Question 25	According to the NIST SP 800-26 guidelines, what would achieving level 3 indicate?
A	Security controls are documented as procedures.
B	Procedures have been implemented.
C	Procedures and security controls are tested and reviewed.
D	Procedures and security controls are fully integrated into a comprehensive program.
Answer	B
Rationale	Level 1 – control objective documented in a security policy Level 2 – security controls documented as procedures Level 3 – procedures have been implemented Level 4 – procedures and security controls are tested and reviewed Level 5 – procedures and security controls are fully integrated into a comprehensive program

Question 26	According to the NIST SP 800-26 guidelines, what would achieving level 2 indicate?
A	Security controls are documented as procedures.
B	Procedures have been implemented.
C	Procedures and security controls are tested and reviewed.
D	Procedures and security controls are fully integrated into a comprehensive program.
Answer	A

Rationale	Level 1 – control objective documented in a security policy
	Level 2 – security controls documented as procedures
	Level 3 – procedures have been implemented
	Level 4 – procedures and security controls are tested and reviewed
	Level 5 – procedures and security controls are fully integrated into a comprehensive program.

Question 27	According to the NIST SP 800-26 guidelines, what would achieving level 5 indicate?
A	Security controls are documented as procedures.
B	Procedures have been implemented.
C	Procedures and security controls are tested and reviewed.
D	Procedures and security controls are fully integrated into a comprehensive program.
Answer	D
Rationale	Level 1 – control objective documented in a security policy
	Level 2 – security controls documented as procedures
	Level 3 – procedures have been implemented
	Level 4 – procedures and security controls are tested and reviewed
	Level 5 – procedures and security controls are fully integrated into a comprehensive program

Question 28	Which of the following tests scans hosts in a network and is considered a prelude to penetration testing?
A	Log analysis
B	Password cracking
C	Network scanning
D	File integrity checkers
Answer	C
Rationale	Log analysis scans log files, not network hosts. Password cracking identifies weak passwords in a password file. File integrity checkers review file checksums and this is not a prelude to penetration testing. Network scanning provides an overview of the network and can be helpful for those conducting penetration testing.

Question 29	Which of the following best detects unauthorized modems on a network?
A	War driving
B	War dialing
C	Integrity checkers
D	Virus detectors
Answer	B
Rationale	War driving looks for wireless access points. Integrity checkers are looking at file modification. Virus detectors are looking for malicious code.

Question 30	Which of the following best detects unauthorized file modifications?
A	War dialing
B	Virus detectors
C	Password cracking
D	Integrity checking
Answer	D
Rationale	War dialing detects modems. Virus detectors are looking for malicious code. Password crackers look for passwords that are easy to crack.

ISSEP Questions: Chapter 8

Question 1	According to the DITSCAP process, which level of effort requires the use of a "Requirements Traceability Matrix" (RTM)?
A	All certification efforts regardless of the level of effort
B	Only for components requiring evaluation assurance level 4
C	Only for certification of systems processing information classified as secret or above
D	Only for certification of systems at the first level of effort
Answer	A
Rationale	EAL 4 is a common criteria level; answers C and D are incorrect because all certification efforts must utilize an RTM.

Question 2	Penetration testing is recommended for systems with any criticality or complexity that requires a minimum certification level of _____.
A	CL 1
B	CL 2
C	CL 3
D	CL 4
Answer	C
Rationale	CL 3 and 4 both require penetration but the minimal level beginning at CL 3. CL 1 and 2 require basic and detailed evaluations. Penetration testing is reserved for those systems protecting sensitive information that could have a higher impact to the organization's mission or loss of life.

Question 3	Which one of the following best describes the pivotal roles in the DITSCAP/NIACAP process?
A	Designated approving authority, program manager, certifier, user community representative
B	Designated approving authority, program manager, network manager, and user community
C	Designated approving authority, certifier, network manager, and system staff
D	System owner, program manager, network manager, and user community representative
Answer	A
Rationale	Typically, the network manager is not a pivotal role in the C&A process. The network manager may be involved but would not be considered central to the process.

Question 4	Information systems that are being developed for deployment in multiple locations must first undergo which of the following types of security evaluations?
A	Security Test and Evaluation (ST&E)
B	Demonstration Test and Evaluation (DT&E)
C	Customer Test and Evaluation (CT&E)
D	Certification Test and Evaluation (CT&E)

Answer	D
Rationale	When the same or similar systems are deployed to multiple locations, "Type Accreditation" is typically the accreditation method. CT&E evaluates these systems in the lab environment so that as the systems are deployed, minimal additional evaluation will be required at the deployed sites. ST&E (A) is conducted during phase 3. DT&E (B) and Customer Test and Evaluation (C) are not security-related evaluations but fall under functional systems test.

Question 5	Which one of the following best describes the elements taken into account during the DITSCAP/NIACAP registration activity?
A	Integrity, confidentiality, availability, accountability, and non-repudiation
B	Integrity, confidentiality, availability, accountability, system life cycle, business function and documentation
C	Integrity, confidentiality, accountability, system life cycle, business function and documentation
D	Integrity, confidentiality, availability, non-repudiation, system life cycle, business function and documentation
Answer	B
Rationale	In answers A and D, non-repudiation is not part of the registration activities; answer C does not include availability. Thus, B is more inclusive of all registration activities.

Question 6	During the preparation activity of the DITSCAP/NIACAP process, which one of the following best describes good information sources?
A	Mission statement, system specifications, system access request forms, and password receipt forms
B	Phone interviews, face-to-face interviews, and observations of operations during site visits
C	Mission statement, system specifications, and physical and environmental inspections
D	Mission statement, system specifications, design document, user manuals, operating procedures, and configuration management documentation
Answer	D

Rationale	The preparation activity involves the collection of information and documentation about the system. System access request forms and password receipts would not be necessary for the preparation activity. Answer B does not include any documentation sources. Answer C is not a complete response, while D contains most of the sources that would be needed for gathering documentation during the preparation activity.

Question 7	What are the four DITSCAP /NIACAP phases?
A	Initiation and design, development, operation, and disposal
B	Initiation, design, verification and validation, and accreditation
C	Definition, verification, validation, and post-accreditation
D	Definition, design, validation, and accreditation
Answer	C
Rationale	Answer A includes phases of the SDLC; initiation and design are distracters.

Question 8	Why are DITSCAP/NIACAP processes considered scalable?
A	It is applicable to systems differing in security requirements, size, complexity, connectivity, and data policies.
B	It results in and maintains an accreditation for the target system.
C	It provides corresponding results when applied or reapplied to similar IS.
D	It minimizes personal opinion and subjectivity.
Answer	A
Rationale	Answer A defines scalability while B defines effective, C defines repeatable, and D provides predictability. All are considered characteristics of the DITSCAP/NIACAP process.

Question 9	Which one of the following is a true statement?
A	DITSCAP/NIACAP activities are designed to support only DoD and federal unclassified systems.

B	DITSCAP/NIACAP activities are designed for systems with multiple interfaces and clear distinctions of boundaries.
C	DITSCAP/NIACAP activities are designed to support only the accreditation of DoD systems processing classified information.
D	DITSCAP/NIACAP activities use an infrastructure-centric approach with a focus on the mission, environment, and architecture.
Answer	D
Rationale	The use of "only" in A limits the answer because NIACAP, by definition, is for accrediting classified systems. The clear distinctions in B would make it false, and C is too limiting of an answer.

Question *10*	Which system must implement and follow the DITSCAP phases?
A	All DoD systems, regardless of information sensitivity
B	Only DoD systems processing unclassified or sensitive information
C	Only DoD systems processing classified information
D	Only DoD systems processing intelligence information
Answer	A
Rationale	In accordance with (IAW) DoD 8500.1, the implementation of DITSCAP is mandatory for all systems that process both DoD classified and unclassified information.

Question *11*	What is the main purpose of DITSCAP/NIACAP?
A	Provide an enterprisewide view of information flows between interfaces.
B	Provide a standard set of activities to certify and accredit systems that will maintain the security posture throughout the system life cycle.
C	Provide a more consistent, comparable, and repeatable evaluation of security controls to reduce costs throughout the system life cycle.

D	Provide a process for evaluating the security design and architecture of new system designs before implementation and operation begins.
Answer	B
Rationale	Although information flows can be defined during the process, it is not the best answer. DITSCAP/NIACAP processes may provide an ability to reduce costs, but it is not the main purpose. DITSCAP/NIACAP can be used throughout the system life cycle, including implementation and operations.

Question 12	Which one of the following is not considered part of the Defense Information Infrastructure (DII)?
A	Information and data storage, manipulation, retrieval, and display
B	Unique user data, information, and user applications software
C	Computers, communications, security, people, and training
D	Information transfer and processing resources
Answer	B
Rationale	Unique user data, information, and user applications software are not considered part of the DII because these items are created by the users who processes, transmits, and stores their information on the DII.

Question 13	Which one of the following contains the four phases of the DoD Information Technology Security Certification and Accreditation Process (DITSCAP)?
A	Tier 1, Tier 2, Tier 3, and Tier 4
B	Definition, Validation, Verification, and Post Accreditation
C	Concept, Development, Verification, and Operations and Maintenance
D	Design and Development, Test and Evaluation I, Test and Evaluation II, and Operations and Maintenance
Answer	B
Rationale	A – are levels of maintenance activities; C – refers to the system development life-cycle development; D – is similar but documented in DCID 6/3. The DITSCAP discusses four phases (labeled definition, validation, verification, and post accreditation).

Question 14	During the DITSCAP Phase 1, which one of the following must be accomplished?
A	Registration and negotiation
B	Verification and validation
C	Test and development
D	Approval to operate
Answer	A
Rationale	Options B, C, and D are conducted in phases 2, 3,, and 4 not in phase 1. During phase 1, registration of the systems is performed to identify what is being accredited. The negotiations between the DAA and the system developer occur when trade-offs are made for which requirements must be satisfied and how they will be satisfied (i.e., whether a required technical capability cannot be implemented because the capability does not exist or has some kind of flaw and a procedure will be implemented instead). Another example would be deciding which software application among many will be used in lieu of another.

Question 15	Which one of the following accreditations evaluates the application and systems at a specified, self-contained location?
A	System accreditation
B	Site accreditation
C	Type accreditation
D	Fixed accreditation
Answer	B
Rationale	Site accreditation; B is defined in the question. The DITSCAP/NIACAP section in the book discusses three types of accreditation, A, B, and C. Option D is not an accreditation type.

Question 16	Which one of the following is primarily used to determine how critical the information is to the mission of an organization?
A	Confidentiality and non-repudiation
B	Authentication and identification (I&A)
C	Mission assurance category (MAC)
D	Availability and integrity

Answer	C
Rationale	MAC has three categories (I, II, and III) that determine information criticality. Options A and D are the elements of data protection provided by information security and B is a method of authenticating and identifying users who which to gain access to an IS.

Question **17**	What is the Certification Level (CL) that requires extensive analysis of an information system?
A	CL 1
B	CL 2
C	CL 3
D	CL 4
Answer	D
Rationale	Table 8.5, Certification Levels (8510-M, p. 53), defines the certification level starting with Basic, Minimum, and Detailed analysis (CL 1 to 3, respectively); extensive analysis is designated as CL 4.

Question **18**	The DITSCAP/NIACAP phase that includes registration, preparation, and negotiation is the _____.
A	Definition phase
B	Verification phase
C	Validation phase
D	Post-accreditation phase
Answer	A
Rationale	The general components of the definition phase (A) are registration, preparation, and negotiation. The verification phase (B) includes systems development and integration as well as certification analysis. The validation phase (C) consists of systems security testing, and the post accreditation phase (D) consists of operations, monitoring, and maintenance.

Question **19**	Which of the following is a key output from DITSCAP/NIACAP phase 2?
A	Configuration Management (CM) Plan

B	Security Requirements Traceability Matrix (SRTM)
C	Certification Test and Evaluation (CT&E) Plans and Procedures
D	Security Test and Evaluation (ST&E) Plans and Procedures
Answer	C
Rationale	The output of Phase 2 is the CT&E Plans and Procedures. The ST&E (D) and CM plan (A) are the output of phase 3, while the SRTM (B) is developed during phase 1.

Question 20	What is DITSCAP/NIACAP document is the cornerstone of C&A and serves as the tracking document for C&A activities?
A	System Security Plan (SSP)
B	Facility Security Plan (FSP)
C	Security System Authorization Agreement (SSAA)
D	Automated Information Systems Security Plan (AISSP)
Answer	C
Rationale	The SSAA is the document required and used to reference the question. The SSP is similar but governed under DCID 6/3. The FSP covers physical security accreditations of facilities, and the AISSP is an earlier version of the IS security plan before the adoption of DITSCAP.

Question 21	During phase 3 of the DITSCAP/NIACAP, which one of the following activities is the certifier's responsibility?
A	Report vulnerability and security incidents.
B	Determine if system is ready for certification.
C	Determine the level of certification effort.
D	Assess vulnerabilities and residual risk.
Answer	D
Rationale	Table 8.2, Management Responsibilities by C&A Phases (Based on NSTISSI No. 1000 and DoDI 8510.1-M, page 138) shows all phases and who is responsible for what activities. Assessing vulnerabilities and residual risk are two of the phase 3 activities the certifier performs. Option B is a phase 2 activity, while option C is a phase 1 activity for the certifier. Option A is a user responsibility during phase 4.

Question 22	Which one of the following determines whether TEMPEST countermeasures are needed and provides recommendations on how to control or suppress those signals?
A	CTTA
B	ISSO
C	ISSM
D	DAA
Answer	A
Rationale	The Certified TEMPEST Technical Authority (CTTA) (option A) is the only individual within the U.S. Government to recommend and/or approve TEMPEST countermeasures. The ISSO (option B) is responsible for the day-to-day security activities, while the ISSM (option C) usually conducts or assists with the risk assessment and preparation of C&A documentation and management of the IS. The DAA (option D) is the official with authority to formally assume responsibility for operating an IS or network at an acceptable level of risk.

Question 23	What defines the system security requirements?
A	The national, DoD, and data sensitivity requirements; government requisites; network connectivity rules; and configuration management requirements
B	Applicable instructions and directives, data security requirement, security concept of operation, network connection rules, configuration management plan, reaccreditations requirements, and requirement traceability matrix
C	Both A and B
D	None of the above
Answer	C
Rationale	

Question 24	Which one of the following includes the elements of the "system and functional description" conducted during the DITSCAP/NIACAP system identification task?
A	System mission, system capabilities, and concept of operations (CONOPS)

B	System identification, system description, functional description and capabilities, system capabilities, system criticality
C	System CONOPS, system capability, system design, and system life-cycle development
D	All of the above
Answer	B
Rationale	Item A is not the best description; however, item B is more complete. System design in item C would not be completed during this task.

Question 25	Which of the following best describes the items included in the Security System Authorization Agreement (SSAA)?
A	Organization's mission, security requirements, risk assessment, concept of operation, level of effort, schedule, system security architecture description, operating environment, and threats identification, documents C&A boundaries, documents C&A process, documents test plan, risk management, and certification results
B	Organization's mission, security requirements, risk assessment, system security plan, requirement traceability matrix, level of effort, schedule, system security architecture description, operating environment, and threats identification
C	Certification levels, basic security review, minimum analysis, detailed analysis, and extensive analysis
D	None of the above
Answer	A
Rationale	Answer A has more of a complete listing of all items that would be seen in the SSAA.

Question 26	What is the main purpose of the negotiation activity?
A	To ensure that the RTM drafted during the registration activity properly and clearly defines the approach and level of effort.
B	To ensure that C&A agreements are documented in the SSAA and eventually become the baseline security configuration document
C	To ensure the SSAA drafted during the registration activity properly and clearly defines the approach and level of effort

D	To ensure that the participants in the C&A activity feel they are part of the team
Answer	C
Rationale	Answer A is not correct because RTM is Requirement Tractability. Answer B is not correct because development of configuration management does not require negotiation. Answer D is not a correct answer because the team already has been selected and their role and responsibilities are identified.

Question 27	What does the verification activity accomplish during phase 2?
A	Verifies that the negotiation activity was completed and updated completely
B	Verifies that the final task will not be overlooked
C	Verifies that phase 1 activities are mapped to the RTM
D	Verifies that the evolution of the system complies with the risk management requirements as detailed in the SSAA
Answer	D
Rationale	Rule of reduction; A, B, and C are not correct and they are irrelevant.

Question 28	What constitutes the Task Analysis Summary Report?
A	Recording the findings, evaluating the vulnerabilities discovered during evaluations, summarizing the tools used and results obtained, and making recommendations
B	Recording the findings, evaluating the vulnerabilities discovered during evaluations, summarizing the analysis level of effort, summarizing the tools used and results obtained, and making recommendations
C	Recording the findings, evaluating the vulnerabilities discovered during evaluations, summarizing the analysis level of effort, and making recommendations
D	Recording the findings, evaluating the vulnerabilities discovered during evaluations, summarizing the tools used and results obtained, making recommendations, and distributing a memo indicating the start date of the next task

Answer	B
Rationale	Options A and C are not complete answers. Option D is an incorrect answer due to the last item (the memo).

ISSEP Questions: Chapter 9

Question 1	What C&A guidance document identifies common security controls applicable to federal information systems?
A	NIST SP 800-30
B	NIST SP 800-37
C	NIST SP 800-26
D	FIPS 199
Answer	B
Rationale	SP 800-30 (option A) is the risk management guide, SP 800-26 (option C) is the security self-assessment guide, and FIPS 199 (option D) is a standard for security categorization of federal information and information systems.

Question 2	What NIST document contains the recommended security controls for federal information systems?
A	NIST SP 800-30
B	NIST SP 800-37
C	NIST SP 800-53
D	NIST SP 800-26
Answer	C
Rationale	SP 800-30 is the risk management guide, SP 800-37 is the C&A guide, and SP 800-26 is the security self-assessment guide.

Question 3	What is the purpose of evaluating controls during the security certification phase of the NIST SP 800-37 model?
A	Compliance with FIPS 199
B	Determining the residual risk assessment
C	Determining non-repudiation
D	Determining the effectiveness

Answer	D
Rationale	FIPS 199 deals with security categorizations for information and information systems, residual risk assessment is not a real term, and non-repudiation is a term for assuring the sender and receiver of electronic transactions.

Question 4	NIST SP 800-37 C&A methodology is based on four well-defined phases. In which of the four phases does security categorization occur?
A	Initiation
B	Security certification
C	Requirements development
D	Security accreditation
Answer	A
Rationale	Security certification evaluates the controls and documentation, and the security accreditation phase examines the residual risk for acceptability and prepares the final security accreditation package. Requirements development is a distracter.

Question 5	According to NIST SP 800-30, what are common information systems deployed at multiple operational sites called?
A	Distributed systems
B	Duplicates
C	Clients
D	Types
Answer	D
Rationale	Option A is close, but if looking at it from a C&A perspective (SP 800-30), this is the definition for type certification.

Question 6	The plan of actions and milestones are part of which set of C&A documentation?
A	Security accreditation package
B	Development and acquisition package
C	Implementation package
D	Security assessment report package

Answer	A
Rationale	The plan of action and milestones results once the certification team has completed an assessment. Thus, it would occur after the development and acquisition, implementation, and security assessment phases.

Question 7	During which phase of the NIST SP 800-37 model would configuration management and control be most important?
A	Initiation
B	Security certification
C	Security accreditation
D	Continuous monitoring
Answer	D
Rationale	During the continuous monitoring phase, federal agencies must establish configuration management and control procedures that will document proposed or actual changes to the information system (including hardware, software, firmware, and surrounding environment).

Question 8	According to NIST SP 800-37, who is responsible for authorizing to approve operation of the information system?
A	Information system owner
B	Information systems security officer
C	Authorizing official
D	Information owner
Answer	C
Rationale	The "authorizing official" is the executive or senior manager authorized to approve the operation of the information system. The "system owner" notifies key officials within the agency of the need for a security C&A of the information system, makes resources available, and provides the relevant documents to support the process. The "information system security officer" is responsible to the authorizing official, information system owner, or the CISO for ensuring the appropriate operational security posture is maintained for an information system or program. The "information owner" is the agency official with statutory or operational authority for specified information and responsibility for establishing the controls for its generation, collection, processing, dissemination, and disposal.

Question 9	In NIST SP 800-37, which of the following occurs during the initiation phase?
A	Preparation, security plan analysis, plans of action and milestones
B	Preparation, notification and resource identification, security plan analysis and acceptance
C	Plans of action and milestones, security verification, security validation
D	Preparation, Notification, and Resource Identification; Plans of Action and milestones
Answer	B
Rationale	Except for option B, all other answers contain Plans of Action and Milestones, which is completed during the Security Certification phase.

Question 10	According to NIST SP 800-37, which of the following best defines the elements in a security accreditation package?
A	Information protection needs, system owner analysis, plan of action and milestones
B	Information protection needs, approved system security plan, plan of action and milestones
C	Approved system security plan, security assessment report, plan of action and milestones
D	Approved system security plan, system owner analysis, plan of action and milestones
Answer	C
Rationale	An accreditation package must include the security assessment report. The other answers may be included, but option C is the best answer because it contains the security assessment report..

Question 11	If the authorizing official allows the system to operate but limits the current configuration until additional controls can be implemented, what type of accreditation authorization has been granted?
A	Full authorization
B	Interim approval to operate
C	Partial-denial of authorization

D	Denial of authorization
Answer	B
Rationale	An IATO is granted to allow the system owner to operate the Information system under specific terms and conditions. A full authorization is without any specific conditions. A partial denial is a distracter and is not a standard C&A term. Denial would be no operation until additional controls had been added.

Question 12	NIST SP 800-37 applies primarily to which of the following types of information systems?
A	National security information systems (IS)
B	Non-national security information systems
C	Department of Defense information systems
D	Intelligence community information systems
Answer	B
Rationale	NIST SP 800-37 applies primarily to non-national security information systems under the Department of Commerce. The NIST SP 800-37 does not cover intelligence community IS (D), DoD IS (option C), or systems that process classified information (option A), also known as national security information systems.

Question 13	NIST SP 800-37 phase 3 activities, when mapped to the Systems Life-Cycle Development (SDLC) phases would map directly to which of the following SDLC phase(s)?
A	Initiation
B	Development
C	Implementation
D	Definition
Answer	C
Rationale	Under SP 800-37, option A would fall into phase 1, option B would be covered in phase 2, and option D is the first three of the four phases of DITSCAP.

Question 14	Which individual has the responsibility of rejecting or accepting the residual risk for a system?
A	The Designated Approving Authority (DAA)

B	The Chief Information Security Officer (CISO)
C	The Information Systems Security Officer (ISSO)
D	The system owner
Answer	A
Rationale	The CISO is responsible for carrying out the CIO's FISMA responsibilities and is required to administer the information security program functions. The ISSO is responsible to the authorizing official, information system owner, or the CISO for ensuring that the appropriate operational security posture is maintained for an information system or program. The system owner is responsible for notifying key officials within the agency of the need for a security C&A of the information system, makes resources available, and provide the relevant documents to support the process.

Question 15	What does the security certification phase evaluate?
A	The thoroughness of the System Security Plan (SSP) and the inclusion of appropriate controls
B	That the risks pointed out in the FIPS 199 categorization are appropriately scored
C	The effectiveness of the security controls in the particular environment and the vulnerability of the information
D	That the residual risk has the necessary controls applied for a given threat
Answer	C
Rationale	The SSP is input to the security certification phase. The risk evaluation occurs after the security certification phase. Option D is a distracter.

Question 16	Which document provides a predefined baseline of security controls for all federal information systems except national security systems?
A	NIST SP 800-53
B	NIST SP 800-30
C	NIST SP 800-37
D	OMB Circular A-130

Answer	A
Rationale	SP 800-53 provides the recommended security controls for federal information systems. SP 800-30 is the risk management guide, SP 800-37 is the C&A guide, and OMB Circular A-130 is a guidance document.

ISSEP Questions: Chapter 10

Question 1	Which of the following does NOT occur during the "planning the effort" phase of technical management?
A	Tracking the project resources
B	Defining the management structure
C	Developing schedules and dependencies
D	Determining the requisite resources
Answer	A
Rationale	Answer A is considered part of the "managing the effort" phase of technical management..

Question 2	According to the IATF, during which phase are the tasks for identifying project costs and identifying technical activities completed?
A	Planning the effort
B	Managing the effort
C	Operating the effort
D	Evaluating the effort
Answer	A
Rationale	These two tasks should be conducted during the initial planning, not after the effort has begun. Answers C and D are distracters.

Question 3	What is the scope level for a project estimated to take 18 months?
A	Small
B	Medium

C	Large
D	Very Large
Answer	B
Rationale	A small project is from 1 to 8 months, a medium project is from 9 to 24 months, and a large project is 25+ months. Very large (option D) is a distracter.

Question *4*	According to the IATF, during which phase are the tasks for tracking project resources and ensuring quality of deliverables completed?
A	Planning the effort
B	Managing the effort
C	Operating the effort
D	Evaluating the effort
Answer	B
Rationale	These are tasks after the effort begins; thus, it is not part of planning the effort. Options C and D are distracters.

Question *5*	Who is responsible for the daily planning and control of the project?
A	System owner
B	Quality assurance manager
C	Information systems security engineer
D	Project manager
Answer	D
Rationale	The system owner has overall responsibility and accountability for system and data. The quality assurance manager reviews and approves project deliverables from a QA perspective. The ISSE is responsible for reviewing the security aspects.

Question *6*	Who is responsible for administering funded contractor task assignments?
A	Federal program manager
B	Federal technical monitor
C	Contractor program manager

D	Contracting officer
Answer	B
Rationale	The federal program manager is generally assigned to a federal employee who is responsible for the oversight of a program that is supported by a team of people that may include, or be exclusively comprised of contractors. The federal technical monitor is typically the federal project manager who administers funded contractor task assignments. The contractor program manager administers the funding issues; this is something needed from a federal representative. The contracting officer typically does not deal with task assignments.

Question 7	Which document brings together many of the independent plans and is considered the master document?
A	Risk Management Plan (RMP)
B	Quality Management Plan QMP)
C	Systems Engineering Management Plan (SEMP)
D	Statement of Work (SOW)
Answer	C
Rationale	The SEMP is a master document that references and explains who, what, where, when, and how the project will be managed. The risk management plan defines how risk management is to be implemented in the context of a particular project. The quality management plan answers the performance of who, what, when, and how by specifying the procedures and resources to be used. The SOW details all of the deliverable products, services, and associated work required for a project..

Question 8	Which plan is created to ensure that a product is suitable for the customer's needs, is reasonable for its costs, and will meet the performance requirements?
A	Quality management plan (QMP)
B	Test and evaluation master plan (TEMP)
C	Configuration management (CM) plan
D	Risk management (RM) plan
Answer	A

Rationale	The TEMP and CM plan are not concerned with costs; and the risk management plan defines how risk management is to be implemented in the context of a particular project.

Question 9	Which plan is created to control changes throughout the system life cycle?
A	Quality management plan (QMP)
B	Test and evaluation master plan (TEMP)
C	Configuration Management (CM) plan
D	Risk management (RM) plan
Answer	C
Rationale	CM provides a methodical and logical approach to managing change to ensure that the correct version, which is typically the latest version, of the product or process is in use. The TEMP outlines a plan to evaluate the functionality of the components and system. The quality management plan would contain something about CM, but it is not the primary focus. The RM plan is concerned with assessing the risks to the system not only from internal changes, but also changes to the external environment, such as new threats.

Question 10	Which of the following is NOT a reason for change in a project?
A	New user requirements
B	Product is no longer available or supported by the manufacturer
C	Product no longer meets the defined requirements
D	The system owner prefers a different operating system
Answer	D
Rationale	Even if the system owner likes the Macintosh OS better than the Microsoft OS, change should derive from a business need.

Question 11	Which document would contain the reason for a change request and who initiated the change?
A	Configuration management plan
B	Information systems security engineering proposal

C	Change proposal
D	Independent verification proposal
Answer	C
Rationale	The document that initiates the change, generically called a change proposal, should include: • Who initiated the change request • CI tracking details (such as revision number, etc.) • Description of requested change • Reason for request (justification or need) • Impact of on configuration items or interfaces • Categorization of change (in terms of product complexity and impact to resources and scheduling)

Question 12	What is the final step in the change control process?
A	Approve the change.
B	Verify the change.
C	Announce the change to the user community.
D	Verify and document the change.
Answer	D
Rationale	D is the best answer. Answers A and B are elements of the process, while answer C may happen; all changes do not need to be announced to the entire user community.

Question 13	Which document details all the deliverable products, services, and associated work required for a project?
A	Information systems security engineering (ISSE) proposal
B	Work breakdown structure (WBS)
C	Statement of work (SOW)
D	Plan of action and milestones (POA&M)
Answer	C
Rationale	The ISSE proposal is a distracter. The WBS details only products and is considered a good starting point for the SOW. The POA&M is an outline of what needs to be done and a timeline and would not necessarily outline deliverables for a project.

Question 14	Which of the following would be included in a statement of work (SOW)?
A	Scope, applicable documents, requirements
B	Scope, requirements, required personnel
C	Scope, required personnel, evaluation factors
D	Scope, evaluation factors, design criteria
Answer	A
Rationale	Required personnel, evaluation factors, and design criteria (option D) would not be included as they may be deemed limiting and are better suited for inclusion in management plans and system specifications.

Question 15	What management document describes the primary products at the top level and the items that make up the primary products at the lower levels?
A	Statement of work (SOW)
B	Work breakdown structure (WBS)
C	PERT chart
D	GANTT chart
Answer	B
Rationale	A work breakdown structure (WBS) is a hierarchical product-oriented description of the items to be developed by a systems engineering effort. A tree diagram can visually represent the WBS, where the top block of the tree describes the primary product and the lower branches describe the items that make up the primary product in ever-increasing detail.

Question 16	Which of the following is NOT included in a work breakdown structure (WBS)?
A	The entire product of the engineering effort
B	Hardware platform
C	Software application
D	Processes of the engineering effort
Answer	D
Rationale	The WBS is strictly for identifying products and deliverables and would not define the processes of the engineering effort.

Question 17	Which document best defines significant events and reasonable deadlines?
A	Work breakdown structure (WBS)
B	Milestone plan
C	Statement of work (SOW)
D	Time management plan
Answer	A
Rationale	The WBS identifies products; the SOW details all the deliverable products, services, and associated work required for a project; and the time management plan is a distracter.

Question 18	Which agency has the mission to monitor contractor costs and perform contractor audits?
A	National Security Agency (NSA)
B	Office of Management and Budget (OMB)
C	Defense Contract Audit Agency (DCAA)
D	National Institutes of Standards and Technology (NIST)
Answer	C
Rationale	The DCAA is responsible for performing contract audits for the Department of Defense.

Question 19	Which document displays project tasks in a vertical column and time increments horizontally on a bar graph?
A	PERT chart
B	GANTT chart
C	Work breakdown structure (WBS)
D	SLANT chart
Answer	B
Rationale	Both the PERT and GANTT are scheduling tools; however, this description is for the GANTT chart. The WBS identifies products and would not include timelines. The SLANT chart is a distracter.

Question 20	Which chart is also known as the critical path method?
A	PERT chart
B	GANTT chart
C	Work analysis chart
D	Requirement to functions method
Answer	A
Rationale	The PERT chart is also known as the critical path method because it plots the logical flow of the tasks against their interdependencies.

Question 21	Which technical management tool plots the logical flow of tasks against their interdependencies?
A	GANTT chart
B	Work analysis
C	SLANT chart
D	PERT chart
Answer	D
Rationale	The GANTT chart does not plot tasks based on critical paths. The work analysis and SLANT charts are distracters.

Question 22	Which of the following best defines the PERT chart?
A	Defines work flow in terms of days or months
B	Defines work flow in terms of personnel needed to perform each event
C	Defines work flow in terms of time required to reach the next event
D	Defines work flow in terms of milestones requiring customer approval
Answer	C
Rationale	The GANTT chart shows workflow in days or months; answers B and D are distracters.

Question 23	If using a PERT chart, how is slack time determined?
A	Calculating the difference between the critical path times and the earliest estimated times
B	Calculating the difference between latest estimated time and earliest estimated time
C	Calculating the difference between the late finish times and the early finish times
D	Calculating the difference between the latest finish time and the latest estimated time
Answer	B
Rationale	Options A, C, and D are distracters.

ISSEP Questions: Chapter 11

Question 1	Which one of the following is a policy entitled "Protecting America's Critical Infrastructures," and outlines a national effort to assure the security of the United States interconnected infrastructures, such as telecommunications, banking and finance, energy, transportation, and essential government services?
A	Homeland Security Presidential Directives (HSPDs)
B	Computer Security Act of 1987 (P.L. 100-235)
C	Presidential Decision Directives (PDDs) 63
D	Executive Order (EO) 13231
Answer	C
Rationale	HSPDs (option A) record and communicate presidential decisions about the homeland security policies of the United States. The Computer Security Act of 1987 (option B) was enacted by Congress and declared that improving the security and privacy of sensitive information in federal computer systems is in the public interest, and hereby creates a means for establishing minimum acceptable security practices for such systems, without limiting the scope of security measures already planned or in use. EO 13231 (option D) authorizes a protection program to secure information systems for critical infrastructure, including emergency preparedness communications and the physical assets that support such systems.

Question 2	Which one of the following is charged with the responsibility to evaluate the effectiveness of agency programs, policies, and procedures; assesses competing funding demands among agencies; and sets funding priorities?
A	National Information Assurance Partnership (NIAP)
B	Committee on National Security Systems (CNSS)
C	NSA Information Assurance Directorate (IAD)
D	Office of Management and Budget (OMB
Answer	D
Rationale	The NIAP (option A) is a USG initiative designed to meet the security testing, evaluation, and assessment needs of both information technology (IT) producers and consumers. The IAD's (option C) mission is detecting, reporting, and responding to cyber threats. CNSS (option B) provides a forum for discussion of policy issues, sets national policy, and promulgates direction, operational procedures, and guidance.

Question 3	Which one of the following required federal agencies to tie their information security programs and practices with their overall information technology program management, capital planning, and budget?
A	Computer Security Act of 1987
B	Paperwork Reduction Act of 1995 (PRA)
C	Government Information Security Reform Act (GISRA)
D	Information Technology Reform Act of 1996 (Clinger-Cohen)
Answer	C
Rationale	The Computer Security Act of 1987 (option A) was enacted by the Congress and declared that improving the security and privacy of sensitive information in federal computer systems is in the public interest, and hereby creates a means for establishing minimum acceptable security practices for such systems, without limiting the scope of security measures already planned or in use.

Question 4	Which one of the following provides a comprehensive framework for ensuring the effectiveness of information security controls over information resources that support federal operations and assets?

A	U.S. Federal Privacy Act of 1974
B	Federal Information Security Management Act (FISMA)
C	Computer Fraud and Abuse Act
D	Director of Central Intelligence Directive DCID 6/3
Answer	B
Rationale	The Privacy Act of 1974 attempts to regulate the collection, maintenance, use, and dissemination of personal information by federal executive branch agencies. The Computer Fraud and Abuse Act defines illegal activities for government and financial systems. DCID 6/3 provides policy and procedures for handling classified intelligence information under the purview of the Director of Central Intelligence (DCI).

Question 5	What requires all agency information systems to provide a level of security commensurate with the sensitivity of the information, the risk of its unauthorized access, and the harm that could result from improper use?
A	U.S. Federal Privacy Act of 1974
B	Computer Fraud and Abuse Act
C	Office of Management and Budget (OMB) Circular A-130
D	Director of Central Intelligence Directive DCID 6/3
Answer	C
Rationale	The Privacy Act of 1974 attempts to regulate the collection, maintenance, use, and dissemination of personal information by federal executive branch agencies. The Computer Fraud and Abuse Act defines illegal activities for government and financial systems. DCID 6/3 (option D) provides policy and procedures for handling classified intelligence information under the purview of the Director of Central Intelligence (DCI).

Question 6	Which Appendix of OMB Circular A-130 defines "Adequate Security" to mean security commensurate with the risk and magnitude of the harm resulting from the loss, misuse, or unauthorized access to or modification of information?
A	Appendix I
B	Appendix II
C	Appendix III

D	Appendix IV
Answer	C
Rationale	Appendix I covers Federal Agency Responsibilities for Maintaining Records about Individuals. Appendix II discusses the implementation of the Government Paperwork Elimination Act, and Appendix IV discusses the analysis of Key Sections.

Question 7	Assuming there are no major changes to the information system (IS), how often should a formal management review of an information system occur?
A	Every year
B	Every two years
C	Every three years
D	Every four years
Answer	C
Rationale	Key policies and guidance require information to be reaccredited every **three** years unless significant changes to the IS have occurred during that period.

Question 8	Which memorandum reminds federal agencies that it is required by law and policy to establish clear privacy policies for its Web activities and to comply with those policies?
A	OMB M-99-18
B	OMB M-00-13
C	OMB M-00-07
D	OMB M-01-08
Answer	B
Rationale	OMB M-99-18 (option A) directed federal departments and agencies to post clear privacy policies on World Wide Web (WWW) sites and provided guidance on how to post privacy policies but option B took it a step further, as defined in the question. OMB M-00-07 (option C) discusses incorporating and funding security in information systems investments Key Sections and OMB M-01-08 (option D) provides guidance on implementing the Government Information Security Reform Act.

ISSEP Questions: Chapter 12

Question 1	Which one of the following consists of an interconnected, end-to-end set of information capabilities, associated processes, and personnel for collecting, processing, storing, disseminating, and managing information on demand to warfighters, defense policymakers, and support personnel?
A	Community of Interest (COI)
B	Global Information Grid (GIG)
C	Global Command and Control System (GCCS)
D	Department of Defense Architecture Framework (DoDAF)
Answer	C
Rationale	COI (option A) identifies specific organizations with common information protection needs. GCCS (option C) is a large command and control network. The DoDAF (option D) is a framework being developed as the standard architecture throughout the DoD.

Question 2	Which one of the following are the three key elements of the Net-Centricity data vision?
A	Community of interest, metadata and GIG enterprise services
B	Management, implementation, and evaluation
C	Verification, validation, and accreditation
D	Confidentiality, availability, and integrity
Answer	A
Rationale	Answer B represents the three basic components into which GIRSA divides security programs. Answer C represents elements of the DITSCAP phase. Answer D represents the three tenets of information security protection.

Question 3	Which one of the following is chartered to protect and defend DoD information, information systems, and information networks that are critical to the DoD and the armed forces during day-to-day operations and operations in times of crisis?
A	Information Assurance Support Environment (IASE)
B	Defense Technical Information Center (DTIC)

C	Defense Information Systems Agency (DISA)
D	Defense Information Assurance Program (DIAP)
Answer	D
Rationale	

Question 4	Which organization has the mission to detect, report, and respond to cyber-threats, make encryption codes to securely pass information between systems, and embed IA measures directly into the Global Information Grid?
A	The Defense Information Systems Agency (DISA)
B	The National Security Agency Information Assurance Directorate (NSA IAD)
C	The National Institute of Standards and Technology (NIST)
D	The Defense Technical Information Center
Answer	B
Rationale	DISA is responsible for planning, engineering, and supporting the GIG to serve the needs of the Executive branch of government and the Joint Chiefs of Staff. The National Institute of Standards and Technology does not make encryption codes, and the Defense Technical Information Center is responsible for the collection and dissemination of scientific and technical information for the DoD.

Question 5	What are the primary actions of the Information Assurance Support Environments Computer Network Defense?
A	To monitor and detect unauthorized activity of computer and information systems supporting the Office of the Secretary of Defense
B	To protect, monitor, analyze, detect, and respond to authorized activity within Department of Defense information systems
C	To protect, monitor, analyze, detect, and respond to unauthorized activity within Department of Defense information systems
D	To protect, monitor, analyze, detect, and respond to unauthorized activity within Intelligence Community computer and information systems only
Answer	C

Rationale	Option A only deals with protecting the Secretary of the Defense's office and not the Department of Defense. Option B is incorrect because it states that the CND protects authorized, not unauthorized, activity. Option D is a distracter because it only deals with the IC community, not the DoD.

Question 6	Which one of the following is one of the primary objectives of the net-centric data strategy?
A	To define data structures and relationships
B	To provide reliable identification and authorization services
C	To increase the data that is available to communities or the enterprise
D	To allow communities of interest to collaborate more effectively solely within their own communities
Answer	C
Rationale	Option A is defining data structures that involve metadata. The GES provides reliable I&A services. The two primary objectives of net-centric data increasing the data available to communities or the enterprise and ensuring that data is usable by both anticipated and unanticipated users and applications.

Question 7	Which of the following is NOT a goal of the net-centricity approach?
A	Support a substantially improved military situational awareness.
B	Increase decision cycles.
C	Empower users to better protect assess and more efficient exploit information.
D	Create extended collaborative communities to focus on the mission.
Answer	B
Rationale	Option B is not a goal because the net-centricity approach is intended to decrease the decision cycle.

Question 8	Which of the following OSD staff components is responsible for development, oversight, and integration of DoD policies and programs relating to the strategy of information superiority for the DOD?

A	Joint Chiefs of Staff (JC Component)
B	Assistant Secretary of Defense Networks and Information Integration (ASD NII)
C	Secretary of Defense
D	Defense Information Systems Agency (DISA)
Answer	B
Rationale	The JC component is an operation versus a policy component. The Defense Information Systems Agency (DISA) is a DoD agency that is responsible for planning, engineering, acquiring, fielding, and supporting global net-centric solutions and operating the GIG. The Secretary of Defense option is a distracter.

Question 9	What type of DoD issuance is DoD 8500.1?
A	DoD instruction
B	DoD publication
C	DoD directive type memorandum
D	DoD directive
Answer	D
Rationale	DoD 8500.1 establishes policy and assigns responsibilities to achieve DoD IA through a defense-in-depth approach that integrates the capabilities of personnel, operations, and technology, and supports the evolution to network-centric warfare. Thus, it is a directive.

Question 10	What is the defense technical information center?
A	The central facility for the collection and dissemination of scientific and technical information for DoD
B	Responsible center for planning, engineering, and supporting global net-centric solutions
C	Center to plan, monitor, and integrate information assurance activities

D	The primary policy branch for the DoD
Answer	A
Rationale	Answer B relates to DISA's mission, answer C relates to DIAP's mission, and answer D is a distracter.

Question 11	Which of the following establish or describes policy, programs, and organizations?
A	DoD Directives
B	DoD Instructions
C	DoD Administrative Instruction
D	DoD Publication
Answer	A
Rationale	DoD Directives establish or describe policy, programs, and organizations; define missions; provide authority; and assign responsibilities. DoD Instructions (DoDIs) are DoD issuances that implement the policy, or prescribe the manner or a specific plan or action for carrying out the policy, operating a program or activity, and assigning responsibilities. A DoD Administrative Instruction (DoD AI) is an instrument that supplements DoD Directives and DoD Instructions that apply to the OSD/WHS Components and the DoD Field Activities. A DoD Publication (DoDP) is a DoD issuance that implements or supplements a DoD Directive or a DoD Instruction by providing uniform procedures for management or operational systems and disseminating administrative information.

Question 12	Which of the following includes catalogs, directories, guides, handbooks, indexes, inventories, lists, and manuals?
A	DoD Directives
B	DoD Instructions
C	DoD Administrative Instructions
D	DoD Publications
Answer	D

| Rationale | DoD Directives establish or describe policy, programs, and organizations; define missions; provide authority; and assign responsibilities. DoD Instructions (DoDIs) are DoD issuances that implement the policy, or prescribe the manner or a specific plan or action for carrying out the policy, operating a program or activity, and assigning responsibilities. A DoD Administrative Instruction (DoD AI) is an instrument that supplements DoD Directives and DoD Instructions that apply to the OSD/WHS Components and the DoD Field Activities. A DoD Publication (DoDP) is a DoD issuance that implements or supplements a DoD Directive or a DoD Instruction by providing uniform procedures for management or operational systems and disseminating administrative information. |

Question 13	Which of the following prescribe the manner or action for carrying out a DoD policy or program?
A	DoD Directives
B	DoD Instructions
C	DoD Administrative Instructions
D	DoD Publication
Answer	B
Rationale	DoD Directives establish or describe policy, programs, and organizations; define missions; and provide authority; and assign responsibilities. DoD Instructions (DoDIs) are DoD issuances that implement the policy, or prescribe the manner or a specific plan or action for carrying out the policy, operating a program or activity, and assigning responsibilities. A DoD Administrative Instruction (DoD AI) is an instrument that supplements DoD Directives and DoD Instructions that apply to the OSD/WHS Components and the DoD Field Activities. A DoD Publication (DoDP) is a DoD issuance that implements or supplements a DoD Directive or a DoD Instruction by providing uniform procedures for management or operational systems and disseminating administrative information.

Question 14	When the ISSE is working in the DoD environment, which information categorization must be used?
A	FIPS 199
B	NIST SP 800-60

C	Mission Assurance Category
D	Protection Levels
Answer	C
Rationale	DoD 8500.1 Section 4.7 states: All DoD information systems shall be assigned a mission assurance category that is directly associated with the importance of the information they contain relative to the achievement of DoD goals and objectives, particularly the warfighters' combat mission.

Question **15**	According to DoD 8500.1, which of the following is true for government contractors?
A	Only those requiring access to the system need a background check.
B	Their affiliation must be displayed as part of their e-mail addresses.
C	They are never allowed remote access to networks.
D	The OSD NII must clear for release all classified information.
Answer	B
Rationale	DoD 8500.1 Section 4.10 states: Authorized users who are contractors, DoD direct or indirect hire foreign national employees, or foreign representatives as described in paragraph 4.9, shall always have their affiliation displayed as part of their e-mail addresses.

ISSEP Questions: Chapter 13

Question **1**	Which Committee of National Security Systems (CNSS) issuance assigns responsibilities and establishes criteria?
A	Policies
B	Directives
C	Advisory Memoranda
D	Instructions
Answer	A

Rationale	Policies assign responsibilities and establish criteria. Directives establish or describe policy, programs, provide authority, or assign responsibilities. Instructions describe how to implement the policy or prescribe the manner of a policy. Advisory Memoranda provide guidance on policy and may direct policy.

Question 2	Which Committee of National Security Systems (CNSS) issuance describes policy, programs, or assigns responsibilities?
A	Policies
B	Directives
C	Advisory Memoranda
D	Instructions
Answer	B
Rationale	Policies assign responsibilities and establish criteria. Directives establish or describe policy, programs, provide authority, or assign responsibilities. Instructions describe how to implement the policy or prescribe the manner of a policy. Advisory Memoranda provide guidance on policy and may direct policy.

Question 3	Which Committee of National Security Systems (CNSS) issuance describes how to implement policies?
A	Policies
B	Directives
C	Advisory Memoranda
D	Instructions
Answer	D
Rationale	Policies assign responsibilities and establish criteria. Directives establish or describe policy, programs, provide authority, or assign responsibilities. Instructions describe how to implement the policy or prescribe the manner of a policy. Advisory Memoranda provide guidance on policy and may direct policy.

Question 4	Which agency is responsible for chairing the Committee of National Security Systems (CNSS)?
A	Department of Defense
B	National Security Agency
C	Central Intelligence Agency
D	Department of Commerce
Answer	A
Rationale	The Department of Defense continues to chair the committee under the authorities established by NSD-42.

Question 5	Which organization provides a forum for the discussion of policy issues and sets national policy for the security of national security systems?
A	National Security Agency (NSA)
B	Committee of National Security Systems (CNSS)
C	Central Intelligence Agency (CIA)
D	National Institute of Standards and Technology (NIST)
Answer	B
Rationale	NSA and CIA have involvement in the CNSS, but the CNSS is responsible for setting policies and guidelines for securing national security systems. The NIST is responsible for setting standards and guidelines for sensitive and unclassified systems.

Question 6	Which of the following is NOT considered a national security system?
A	Contains information related intelligence activities
B	Contains classified information
C	Contains medical data for all direct-hire government employees
D	Contains data related to command and control activities of military forces
Answer	C

Rationale	Medical data would be considered sensitive data. Answers A, B, and D are considered information contained in a national security system.

Question 7	Which of the following is NOT a voting member of the Committee of National Security Systems (CNSS)?
A	Federal Emergency Management Agency
B	Department of Justice
C	Department of Defense
D	Department of Interior
Answer	D
Rationale	The Department of Interior is not currently listed as a CNSS voting member.

Question 8	What does the Committee of National Security Systems (CNSS) NSTISSP No. 11 require?
A	All federal agencies operating national security systems must establish and implement Certification and Accreditation (C&A) programs.
B	Electronic messaging services must yield a business-quality electronic mail service suitable for the conduct of official government business.
C	All IT and IA-enabled products must be evaluated according to the guidelines set forth by the Common Criteria evaluation levels.
D	All military voice radio systems must be secured.
Answer	C
Rationale	Answer A is from NSTISSP No. 6 the policy for C&A. Answer B is from NSTISSP No. 7 National Policy on Secure Electronic Messaging Service. Answer D is from NSTISSP No. 101 National Policy on Securing Voice Communications.

Question 9	Which of the following is a CNSS requirement for controlled access protection?
A	Maintenance of audit trails of security-related events

B	Civil government voice systems, which carry traffic of significant intelligence value must be secured
C	All personnel are denied remote access to national security systems
D	Only those personnel maintaining a Top Secret security clearance may access national security systems
Answer	A
Rationale	NSTISSP No. 200 states the major characteristics of controlled access protection are: "Individual accountability through identification and authentication of each individual automated information system user; maintenance of audit trails of security-relevant events; an ability to control a user's access to information according to the authorization the user has; and preventing one user from obtaining another user's residual data." Answer B is a voice system requirement. Answers C and D are distracters.

Question 10	Which statement below is from CNSS Policy No. 14 , which governs the release of information assurance products to persons not part of the federal government?
A	Individuals who are granted access to classified IA products must, at a minimum, be granted a Top Secret clearance.
B	Contractors who perform maintenance on national security systems must be visually monitored at all times.
C	Foreign nationals who perform maintenance on classified systems must be granted a Top Secret clearance and must still be visually monitored at all times.
D	A valid need must exist for the individual to install, maintain, or operate security network equipment for the U.S. Government.
Answer	D
Rationale	Clearance requirements are based on the sensitivity of the information. The stated requirement for maintenance is that they must receive formal NSA-approved training for the equipment — it does not list anything about contractors and visual monitoring. With very few exceptions, foreign nationals would not be granted the right to provide maintenance on classified equipment.

Question 11	Which directive establishes the requirements for federal agencies to develop and implement information system security training for national security systems?
A	NIST SP 800-16
B	NIST SP 800-50
C	NSTISSD-500
D	DoD 8500.1
Answer	C
Rationale	NIST SP 800-16 and SP 800-50 do not apply to national security systems. DoD 8500.1 is a Defense Department directive and would not apply to federal agencies.

Question 12	What activities must national security system information assurance training programs include?
A	Advanced education and training equal to duties and responsibilities
B	Systems administrators must receive operating system and applications certifications
C	Contractors must receive the same custom-designed training programs as direct-hire government employees
D	Certification and professional activities that further enhance the development of information assurance professionals in the government workforce
Answer	A
Rationale	CNSS -500 states that "every INFOSEC education, training, and awareness program will contain three types of activities: initial orientation, more advanced education and training commensurate with duties and responsibilities, and reinforcement activities.

Question 13	Which of the following is listed as a minimum training requirement for all information assurance professionals?
A	Ability to evaluate known vulnerabilities at the awareness level
B	Understanding of CNSS policies and procedures at the performance level
C	Ability to enforce the CNSS policies at the performance level

D	Ability to prepare the System Security Authorization Agreement
Answer	B
Rationale	Answers A and C are a specific requirements for ISSO and answer D is a specific requirement for certifiers conducting C&A activities.

Question 14	Which of the following best describes a protected distribution system (PDS)?
A	A virtual private network using IPSec to transmit unencrypted classified information
B	A fiber-optic distribution system connected between a contractor company and a U.S. Government controlled facility requiring Type 2 encryption
C	A wire-line distribution system used to transmit unencrypted classified through an area of lesser classification or control
D	A telecommunications channel used to transmit unencrypted classified information between a contractor company and a U.S. Government controlled facility that requires Type 1 encryption
Answer	C
Rationale	NSTISSI No. 7003 defines the a PDS as either a wire-line or fiber-optic distribution system that is used to transmit unencrypted classified National Security Information (NSI) through an area of lesser classification or control. Answers A, B, and D all include encryption requirements, while a PDS does not use encryption.

Question 15	Which type of environment can use a protection distribution system?
A	Only low threat environments inside the U.S. physical boundaries
B	Low threat environments inside and outside U.S. physical boundaries
C	Only medium and high threat within the U.S. physical boundaries
D	Only on a case-by-case basis

Answer	B
Rationale	NSTISSI No. 7003 provides instructions for PDS installations within low and medium threats, both within the United States and a location outside the United States if the threat is low. High threat environments, regardless of location, are on a case-by-case basis.

Question 16	Which of the following is a CNSS recommendation regarding guards?
A	Guards should be used to protect connections between classified systems and unclassified systems.
B	Guards should be used to protect classified systems from unwanted port scanning because they will drop the connection.
C	Guards should be used when it is necessary to drop the Internet Protocol address from outside users.
D	Guards should only be specified for use in security configurations bridging and protecting local networks with classified information from unclassified networks.
Answer	D
Rationale	According to NSTISSAM 1-98, answer A is wrong because guards should never be used to protect connections between classified and unclassified systems; answers B and C relate more to firewalls than to guards.

Question 17	Which evaluation system must be used for evaluation security products or system?
A	Trusted Computer System Evaluation Criteria
B	Common Criteria
C	Information Technology Security Evaluation Criteria (ITSEC)
D	Federal Systems Security Evaluation Criteria
Answer	B
Rationale	NSTISSAM 1-99 provides guidance regarding the transition from the TCSEC to the CC evaluation system. ITSEC is a legacy European criterion; answer D is a distracter.

Question 18	Which evaluation system must be used for evaluating cryptographic modules?
A	FIPS 140
B	Trusted Cryptographic Component Evaluation Criteria (TCCEC)
C	Trusted Computer System Evaluation Criteria (TCSEC)
D	Cryptographic Validation Criteria (CVC)
Answer	A
Rationale	NSTISSAM 1-00 requires the use of FIPS 140 or Common Criteria validation for all cryptographic modules. Answers B and D are distracters; and answer C is a legacy criterion.

Question 19	What is the best approach for architecting security into information systems?
A	A multi-layer and multi-vendor approach
B	Ensuring robustness is a built-in capability of IA or IA-enabling products
C	Verifying protection through formal documentation methods
D	Creating realistic operational scenarios
Answer	A
Rationale	CNSSAM 1-04 advises U.S. Government agencies to emphasize a multi-layered and multi-vendor approach to security when architecting information systems, such as a defense-in-depth solution.

ISSEP Questions: Chapter 14

Question 1	Which type of cryptographic algorithm should be used when designing a system that will process classified information?
A	Type I
B	Type II
C	Type A
D	Type B

Answer	A
Rationale	Type I is approved by the NSA for protecting classified information. Type II is approved by the NSA for protecting unclassified information. Type A and Type B are distracters.

Question 2	Which of the following best describes file security?
A	Enciphering data at the transmitting point and deciphering at the receiving point
B	Enciphering data when it is recorded on a storage medium and deciphering it when read back
C	Enciphering data at the transport level and deciphering at the application level
D	Enciphering and deciphering at the application level
Answer	B
Rationale	Answer A is the definition for communications security; answers C and D are distracters.

Question 3	Which cryptographic algorithm is only allowed for legacy systems?
A	Single DES
B	Double DES
C	Triple DES
D	Four DES
Answer	A
Rationale	FIPS 46-3 states that single DES will be permitted for legacy systems only.

Question 4	Which of the following is NOT an acceptable cryptographic mode for federal information systems?
A	Electronic codebook mode
B	Cipher block chaining mode
C	Cipher feedback mode
D	Electronic feedback mode
Answer	D

Rationale	Electronic feedback mode is not one of the modes listed in FIPS 46-3.

Question 5	What is the most Important element of cryptographic security?
A	Protecting the algorithm
B	Protecting the source code
C	Protecting the key
D	Protecting the certification authority
Answer	C
Rationale	Since the beginning of DES, the USG has openly shared algorithms; thus, it is not necessary to protect the algorithm. Protecting the source code (answer B) is a distracter. Protecting the certification authority (answer D) is important for public key, but answer C (protecting the key) pertains to all methods and is the best answer.

Question 6	Typically, what information categorization should FIPS 140.2 be used for?
A	Sensitive but unclassified information
B	Secret information
C	Top secret information
D	Special compartmentalized information (SCI)
Answer	A
Rationale	FIPS 140-2 specifies the security requirements that will be satisfied by a cryptographic module utilized within a security system protecting sensitive but unclassified information. Secret, top secret, and SCI would all be considered "classified "or higher and would follow CNSS or DCID requirements.

Question 7	According to FIPS 140 security levels, which level provides the basic security requirements for a cryptographic model?
A	Security Level 1
B	Security Level 2
C	Security Level 3

D	Security Level 4
Answer	A
Rationale	Security Level 1 provides the lowest level of security; it specifies basic security requirements for a cryptographic module. Security Level 2 improves the physical security of a Security Level 1 cryptographic module by adding the requirement for tamper evident coatings or seals, or for pick-resistant locks. Security Level 3 requires enhanced physical security, attempting to prevent the intruder from gaining access to critical security parameters held within the module. Security Level 4 provides the highest level of security. Level 4 physical security provides an envelope of protection around the cryptographic module to detect a penetration of the device from any direction.

Question 8	According to FIPS 140, which security level requires the physical security mechanism to detect and respond to all unauthorized attempts?
A	Security Level 1
B	Security Level 2
C	Security Level 3
D	Security Level 4
Answer	D
Rationale	Security Level 1 requires no physical security mechanisms. Security Level 2 requires tamper-evident seals placed on a crypto module so the seal must be broken to attain physical access. Security Level 3 is intended to have a high probability of detecting and responding to attempts at physical access.

Question 9	How often must the National Institute of Standards and Technology (NIST) reexamine and reaffirm FIPS 140?
A	Every year
B	Every three (3) years
C	Every four (4) years
D	Every five (5) years
Answer	D
Rationale	FIPS 140 states that the standard is reexamined and reaffirmed every five (5) years.

Question 10	If you were designing a system that will process Top Secret information, which AES key length must be used?
A	56
B	128
C	256
D	784
Answer	C
Rationale	CNSS Policy 15 states that the design and strength of all key lengths of the AES algorithm (i.e., 128, 192, and 256) are sufficient to protect classified information up to the SECRET level. TOP SECRET information will require the use of either the 192 or 256 key lengths. Answer D (784) is a distracter.

Question 11	Which of the following controls focus on those implemented and executed by people?
A	Management
B	Operational
C	Technical
D	Personnel
Answer	B
Rationale	Management controls focus on the management of the computer security program and the management of risk within the organization. Operational controls focus on controls that are implemented and executed by people (as opposed to systems). Technical controls are ones that the computer system executes. However, operational and management controls are necessary to make sure they are implemented correctly and managed appropriately. Personnel controls include requirements such as background checks or security clearances.

Question 12	Which of the following best describes management controls?
A	Controls that focus on the management of the computer security program
B	Controls that focus on the management of the data center and its environment

C	Controls that focus on the management of the auditing and identification and authentication
D	Controls that focus on the management of the security clearances for personnel and security labels for information
Answer	A
Rationale	Management controls focus on the management of the computer security program and the management of risk within the organization. Operational controls focus on controls that are implemented and executed by people (as opposed to systems). Technical controls are ones that the computer system executes. Personnel controls include requirements such as background checks or security clearances.

Question 13	Which of the following does SP 800-14 recommend for the three types of policies that organizations should have?
A	Program policies, issue-specific policies, system-specific policies
B	Program policies, information-specific policies, system-specific policies
C	Information-specific policies, system-specific policies, location-specific policies
D	Program policies, system-specific policies, location-specific policies
Answer	A
Rationale	The three different types of computer security policies to support the mission are: (1) program policies should (a) create and define a computer security program, (b) set organizational strategic directions, (c) assign responsibilities, and (d) address compliance issues; (2) issue-specific policies should (a) address specific areas, (b) be updated frequently, and (c) contain an issue statement.; (3) System-Specific policies should (a) focus on decisions, (b) be made by management officials, (c) vary from system to system, and (d) be expressed as rules.

Question 14	Which of the following does SP 800-14 state as an incident handling capability?
A	It must support an organization's goal of continued operations.
B	It must contain and repair damage.

C	It must differentiate between incidents based on the sensitivity of the information.
D	It must be tested on a periodic basis to ensure reliability
Answer	B
Rationale	Answer A is more appropriate for a contingency plan. Answers C and D are distracters.

Question 15	According to NIST SP 800-14, what does authentication provide?
A	The means by which a user provides a claimed identity to the system
B	The means by which a user is given permission to access a network resource
C	The means to establish the validity of a claimed identity
D	The means to record user activity on the system
Answer	C
Rationale	SP 800-14 states that identification is the means by which a user provides a claimed identity to the system. Authentication is the means of establishing the validity of this claim. Answer B is authorization and answer D is auditing.

Question 16	Which of the following best defines a System Security Plan?
A	Describes the practices for continued system operations
B	Describes the principles for conducting the risk assessment and the risk mitigation
C	Describes the practices for security personnel, such as staffing requirements and position sensitivities
D	Describes the controls in place or planned for meeting the defined security requirements
Answer	D
Rationale	A would be a contingency plan, answer B would be the risk management plan, and answer C would be an access control plan. All of these might be subsets of the SSP. SP 800-18 defines the SSP as providing an overview of the security requirements of the system and describes the controls in place or planned for meeting those requirements.

Question 17	Which of the following is necessary when designing a public key system for electronic transactions?
A	The transmitted info is not altered deliberately.
B	The sender's information is encrypted using Type 1 cryptographic algorithm.
C	The sender is not authorized access to the recipient's public key.
D	It is not permissible to send financial or medical data about USG employees.
Answer	A
Rationale	SP 800-25 defines this use (answer A) of public key systems for USG data. Type 1 typically refers to symmetric algorithms. The sender needs the public key to send the information. As of publishing date, there were no federal policies specifically restricting a public key algorithm for USG financial or medical data.

Question 18	Which of the following is a benefit of risk management?
A	Enables management to make risk-based decision when authorizing a system to operate
B	Enables management to review internal processes for configuration management
C	Enables management to assess the work division among the IT staff
D	Enables management to review the processes for designing a secure system
Answer	A
Rationale	SP 800-30 states that risk management assists management in authorizing (or accrediting) the IT systems on the basis of the supporting documentation resulting from the performance of risk management.

Question 19	What is the process that allows managers to balance the operational and economic costs of protective measures?
A	Configuration management
B	Quality management
C	Risk management

D	Technical management
Answer	C
Rationale	SP 800-30 defines risk management as the process that allows managers to balance the operational and economic costs of protective measures and achieve gains in mission capability by protecting the IT systems and data that support their organizations' missions.

Question 20	If a risk assessment was conducted because a major change had been made to the system, which phase of the life cycle would the system be in?
A	Initiation
B	Development
C	Implementation
D	Operation
Answer	D
Rationale	During the operation phase, risk management activities are performed for periodic system reauthorization (or reaccreditation) or whenever major changes are made to an IT system in its operational or production environment (e.g., new system interfaces).

Question 21	According to NIST SP 800-30, which of the following is a risk management activity?
A	Risk assessment
B	Certification testing
C	Operational validation
D	Verification and validation
Answer	A
Rationale	Answers B, C, and D are C&A activities.

Question 22	Which of the following should be done when determining the likelihood of a threat exercising?
A	Assess the motivation and capability of the threat source.
B	Assess the sensitivity of the information.

C	Assess the level of damage to operational effectiveness.
D	Assess the level of damage to technical controls.
Answer	A
Rationale	When determining the likelihood of a threat, one must consider threat-sources, potential vulnerabilities, and existing controls. Answer B would occur during the system characterization. Answers C and D would occur when determining the impact of the threat exercising.

Question 23	Which of the following is NOT a risk of implementing public key technology?
A	Failure of the system to fulfill its mission
B	Failure of the system to link to organizational goals
C	Failure of the system to create new vulnerabilities
D	Failure of the system to identify the sender
Answer	D
Rationale	Answer D would not be a risk; it would be a benefit.

Question 24	What is the likelihood level when a threat source is highly motivated and sufficiently capable and controls in place are ineffective?
A	None
B	Low
C	Medium
D	High
Answer	D
Rationale	High: the threat-source is highly motivated and sufficiently capable, and controls to prevent the vulnerability from being exercised are ineffective. Medium: the threat source is motivated and capable, but controls are in place that may impede successful exercise of the vulnerability. Low: the threat source lacks motivation or capability, or controls are in place to prevent, or at least significantly impede, the vulnerability from being exercised.

Question 25	What is the impact level if the result of the exercised threat resulted in the costly loss of tangible assets?
A	None
B	Low
C	Medium
D	High
Answer	C
Rationale	High: exercise of the vulnerability (1) may result in the highly costly loss of major tangible assets or resources; (2) may significantly violate, harm, or impede an organization's mission, reputation, or interest; or (3) may result in human death or serious injury. Medium: exercise of the vulnerability (1) may result in the costly loss of tangible assets or resources; (2) may violate, harm, or impede an organization's mission, reputation, or interest; or (3) may result in human injury. Low: exercise of the vulnerability (1) may result in the loss of some tangible assets or resources or (2) may noticeably affect an organization's mission, reputation, or interest.

Question 26	Which of the following is NOT a determination of risk?
A	The likelihood of a given threat-source's attempting to exercise a given vulnerability
B	The magnitude of the impact should a threat-source successfully exercise the vulnerability
C	The adequacy of planned or existing security controls for reducing or eliminating risk
D	The last certification and accreditation
Answer	D
Rationale	SP 800-30 states that the "determination of risk for a particular threat/vulnerability pair can be expressed as a function of (1) the likelihood of a given threat-source's attempting to exercise a given vulnerability, (2) the magnitude of the impact should a threat source successfully exercise the vulnerability, and (3) the adequacy of planned or existing security controls for reducing or eliminating risk.

Question 27	If the risk assessment shows a "high" risk level, what type of action must be taken?
A	A plan must be developed to incorporate these actions within a reasonable period of time.
B	An existing system may continue to operate, but a corrective action plan must be put in place as soon as possible.
C	An existing system must be taken off-line.
D	No actions must be taken.
Answer	B
Rationale	High: if an observation or finding is evaluated as a high risk, there is a strong need for corrective measures. An existing system may continue to operate but a corrective action plan must be put in place as soon as possible. Medium: if an observation is rated as medium risk, corrective actions are needed and a plan must be developed to incorporate these actions within a reasonable period of time. Low: if an observation is described as low risk, the system's DAA must determine whether corrective actions are still required or decide to accept the risk.

Question 28	If the risk assessment shows a "low" risk level, what type of action must be taken?
A	A plan must be developed to incorporate these actions within a reasonable period of time.
B	An existing system may continue to operate but a corrective action plan must be put in place as soon as possible.
C	The approving authority must determine whether correction actions are still required or decide to accept the risk.
D	No actions must be taken.
Answer	C
Rationale	High: if an observation or finding is evaluated as a high risk, there is a strong need for corrective measures. An existing system may continue to operate but a corrective action plan must be put in place as soon as possible. Medium: if an observation is rated as medium risk, corrective actions are needed and a plan must be developed to incorporate these actions within a reasonable period of time. Low: if an observation is described as low risk, the system's DAA must determine whether corrective actions are still required or decide to accept the risk.

Question 29	If the risk assessment shows a "medium" risk level, what type of action must be taken?
A	A plan must be developed to incorporate these actions within a reasonable period of time.
B	An existing system may continue to operate but a corrective action plan must be put in place as soon as possible.
C	The approving authority must determine whether correction actions are still required or decide to accept the risk.
D	No actions must be taken.
Answer	A
Rationale	High: if an observation or finding is evaluated as a high risk, there is a strong need for corrective measures. An existing system may continue to operate but a corrective action plan must be put in place as soon as possible. Medium: Ii an observation is rated as medium risk, corrective actions are needed and a plan must be developed to incorporate these actions within a reasonable period of time. Low: if an observation is described as low risk, the system's DAA must determine whether corrective actions are still required or decide to accept the risk.

Question 30	Which of the following is a true statement?
A	Elimination of all risk is possible.
B	Elimination of all risk is impractical.
C	Elimination of all risk is reasonable.
D	Elimination of all risk within an organization's resources is possible if senior management agrees to spend the resources.
Answer	B
Rationale	Because the elimination of all risk is usually impractical or close to impossible, the guidance provided in SP 800-30 is that senior management and functional and business managers should "use the least-cost approach and implement the most appropriate controls to decrease mission risk to an acceptable level, with minimal adverse impact on the organization's resources and mission."

Question 31	According to SP 800-47, what are the phases of the interconnection life cycle?
A	Planning, establishing, maintaining, and disconnecting
B	Planning, establishing, verifying, and validating
C	Establishing, maintaining, verifying, and disconnecting
D	Establishing, evaluating, operating, and disconnecting
Answer	A
Rationale	The four phases of the interconnection life cycle are planning, establishing, maintaining, and disconnecting. Verifying, validating, evaluation, and operating are all distracters.

Question 32	During which phase of the interconnection life cycle would organizations review each other's System Security Plans?
A	Planning
B	Establishing
C	Maintaining
D	Disconnecting
Answer	A
Rationale	According to SP 800-47, during the planning stage, the participating organizations perform preliminary activities; examine all relevant technical, security, and administrative issues; and form an agreement governing the management, operation, and use of the interconnection.

ISSEP Questions: Chapter 15

Question 1	Which of the following is NOT a method for evaluating products or systems?
A	Reviewing advertisements and documentation from the manufacturer or vendor
B	Performing system tests internally within the organization
C	Trusting an impartial independent assessment authority
D	Accepting software configurations out-of-the-box
Answer	D

Rationale	Answers A, B, and C are all methods for evaluating products. Answer D is an implementation characteristic and not an evaluation method.

Question 2	Which of the following best describes an evaluation of a product?
A	Evaluating a specific operating system that will be used in any number of applications
B	Evaluating a collection of components that meet the specific requirements
C	Evaluating a collection of products
D	Evaluating volume discounts and pricing alternatives for the components
Answer	A
Rationale	Answers B and C are related to evaluations of systems, while answer D is an evaluation characteristic.

Question 3	Which of the following would be a security consideration for selecting a product?
A	Length of company commitment to product
B	Ability to accommodate changes in user procedures
C	Ability to manage access control and privilege management
D	Maintenance costs associated with hardware or software updates
Answer	C
Rationale	Answers A, B, and D are all considerations for selecting a product, but C is a security consideration.

Question 4	What was the first evaluation standard to gain widespread acceptance in the United States?
A	Trusted Network Interpretation (TNI)
B	Trusted Computer System Evaluation Criteria (TCSEC)
C	Trusted Computer Product Evaluation Criteria (TCPEC)
D	Information Technology Security Evaluation Criteria (ITSEC)
Answer	B

Rationale	TNI was released after TCSEC, TCPEC is a Canadian standard, and ITSEC is a European standard. From a historical standpoint, TCSEC, released in 1985, was the first evaluation standard that addressed risks in products.

Question 5	What are the three principles the Trusted Computer System Evaluation Criteria (TCSEC) attempted to give assurance that a product was secure?
A	Robustness, effectiveness, assurance
B	Functionality, effectiveness, confidentiality
C	Confidentiality, integrity, assurance
D	Functionality, effectiveness, assurance
Answer	D
Rationale	According to TCSEC, an evaluation tried to give assurance that a product or system was secure based on three principles: (1) functionality — the security features of the system, such as authentication and auditing; (2) effectiveness – the mechanisms used are appropriate to the stated security requirements; (3) assurance — the completeness of the evaluation identifying to what level the functionality can be trusted to perform.

Question 6	Which of the following Trusted Computer System Evaluation Criteria (TCSEC) levels required mandatory access controls over named subjects and objects, but did not require the use of formal methods for documentation?
A	Verified Protection
B	Mandatory Protection
C	Discretionary Protection
D	Minimal Protection
Answer	B
Rationale	Verified protection required the formal methods. Discretionary and Minimal Protection did not require mandatory access controls.

Question 7	Which of the following are ratings of the Information Technology Security Evaluation Criteria (ITSEC)?
A	Function and Assurance

B	Effectiveness and Verifiable
C	Verifiable and Assurance
D	Verifiable and Correctness
Answer	A
Rationale	The ITSEC ratings are based on effectiveness (Function) and correctness (Assurance). Effectiveness describes how well a system is suited for countering the predicted threats. Correctness involves assurance aspects related to the development and operation of a system.

Question **8**	According to the Information Technology Security Evaluation Criteria (ITSEC), what is a Target of Evaluation?
A	A hardware or software package bought off-the-shelf
B	A system deployed in a specific real-world environment built for the needs of a specific user
C	Products and systems comprised of components, such as hardware and software
D	All of the above
Answer	D
Rationale	The ITSEC criterion makes a distinction between products and systems. A product can be a hardware or software package bought off-the-shelf and used in a variety of operational environments. A system is deployed in a specific real-world environment and designed and built for the needs of a specific user. Both products and systems are comprised of components. To cover both options, ITSEC uses the term "Target of Evaluation" (TOE).

Question **9**	Which U.S. Government agencies are partners in the National Information Assurance Partnership?
A	National Security Agency and Department of Defense
B	National Security Agency and National Institute of Standards and Technology
C	National Institute of Standards and Technology and Department of Defense
D	National Institute of Standards and Technology and Department of Commerce

Answer	B
Rationale	NIAP is a collaboration between NIST and NSA to fulfill their respective responsibilities under both the Computer Security Act of 1987 and, most recently, FISMA.

Question 10	Which organization is responsible for supporting Common Criteria in the United States?
A	National Information Assurance Partnership
B	Defense Information Assurance Program Office
C	National Security Institute
D	National Infrastructure Protection Center
Answer	A
Rationale	NIST and NSA formed NIAP to coordinate the CC issues in the United States. DIAP is a DoD program office, NSI is a commercial organization, and NIPC was set up as a center for reporting incidents.

Question 11	What are the two primary Common Criteria measures?
A	Function and Assurance
B	Effectiveness and Verifiable
C	Verifiable and Assurance
D	Verifiable and Correctness
Answer	A
Rationale	The CC supports understanding "what security does the product have" (security functionality) and "how sure you are of that security" (security assurance).

Question 12	Prior to the Common Criteria, what was the evaluation criterion that was accepted worldwide?
A	Trusted Computer System Evaluation Criteria (TCSEC)
B	Trusted Computer Product Evaluation Criteria (TCPEC)
C	Information Technology Security Evaluation Criteria (ITSEC)
D	None of the above

Answer	D
Rationale	There was not a worldwide accepted evaluation criterion prior to the Common Criteria. That was the goal of the Common Criteria.

Question 13	What is the purpose of the Common Criteria Mutual Agreement?
A	Member nations have agreed to accept the evaluation certificates produced by those nations that have evaluation programs.
B	Member nations have agreed to a standard set of protection profiles.
C	Member nations have agreed to support specific vendors regardless of country of origination.
D	Member nations have agreed to sponsor evaluation costs from small, underprivileged vendors and from member countries that are considered developing countries.
Answer	A
Rationale	Answers B, C, and D are distracters and not true statements.

Question 14	Which of the following best describes a protection profile?
A	A combination of the Target of Evaluation (TOE) security threats, objectives, requirements, and summary specifications of security functions and assurance measures used as the basis for evaluation
B	An IT product or system and its associated administrator and user guidance documentation that is the subject of an evaluation
C	An implementation-independent set of security requirements for a category of Target of Evaluations (TOEs) that meet specific consumer needs
D	Predefined assurance packages that are a baseline set of assurance requirements for evaluation
Answer	C
Rationale	Answer A is a security target, B is a target of evaluation, C is a protection profile, and D is an evaluation assurance level.

Question 15	Which of the following best describes a security target?
A	A combination of the Target of Evaluation (TOE) security threats, objectives, requirements, and summary specifications of security functions and assurance measures used as the basis for evaluation
B	An IT product or system and its associated administrator and user guidance documentation that is the subject of an evaluation
C	An implementation-independent set of security requirements for a category of Target of Evaluations (TOEs) that meet specific consumer needs
D	Predefined assurance packages that are a baseline set of assurance requirements for evaluation
Answer	A
Rationale	Answer A is a security target, B is a target of evaluation, C is a protection profile, and D is an evaluation assurance level.

Question 16	Which of the following best describes a target of evaluation?
A	A combination of the Target of Evaluation (TOE) security threats, objectives, requirements, and summary specifications of security functions and assurance measures used as the basis for evaluation
B	An IT product or system and its associated administrator and user guidance documentation that is the subject of an evaluation
C	An implementation-independent set of security requirements for a category of Target of Evaluations (TOEs) that meet specific consumer needs
D	Predefined assurance packages that are a baseline set of assurance requirements for evaluation
Answer	B
Rationale	Answer A is a security target, B is a target of evaluation, C is a protection profile, and D is an evaluation assurance level.

Question 17	Typically, who develops a protection profile?
A	Systems engineers

B	User communities
C	System certifiers
D	Approving authorities
Answer	B
Rationale	User communities (answer B) is the best answer. The remaining options may occasionally write a protection profile, but are not the best answer.

Question 18	Which Common Criteria document contains the rationale for security objectives and security requirements, including an evaluation assurance level?
A	Protection target
B	Protection profile
C	Security functionality
D	Security effectiveness
Answer	B
Rationale	Answers A, C, and D are distracters.

Question 19	Which Common Criteria document is the basis for agreement between all parties as to what security the target of evaluation offers?
A	Security target
B	Security profile
C	Protection profile
D	Protection target
Answer	A
Rationale	Answers B and D are distracters. A protection profile is not an agreement between all parties.

Question 20	Which of the following documents provides an expression of the security requirements for a specific target of evaluation, which will be shown by evaluation to be useful and effective in meeting the identified objectives?
A	Security target
B	Security profile

C	Protection profile
D	Certification target
Answer	A
Rationale	Answers B and D are distracters. A protection profile is an implementation-independent set of security requirements for a category of Target of Evaluations (TOEs), while the security target is for a specific TOE.

Question 21	Which of the following is needed for an evaluation?
A	Security requirements
B	Security functions needed to meet the security requirements
C	The IT product and related documentation
D	All of the above
Answer	D
Rationale	The inputs to the evaluation are the documented security requirements (PP), a documented definition of the security functions needed to meet the security requirements (ST), and the IT product and related documentation (the TOE).

Question 22	During an evaluation, why is the protection profiled reviewed?
A	To demonstrate that it is complete, consistent, and technically sound and hence suitable for use as the basis for the corresponding target of evaluations
B	To demonstrate that the TOE meets the security requirements contained in the security target
C	To demonstrate that the user guidance provided in the TOE is suitable for the protection profile
D	To demonstrate that it is complete, consistent, and technically sound and suitable for use as a TOE statement of requirements
Answer	D
Rationale	The key word in answer D is requirements; a protection profile has to do with the security requirement; thus, a review would verify the requirements. Answer A is why a security target is reviewed. Answer B is why a TOE is reviewed. Answer C is a distracter.

Question 23	What are the three distinct audiences of the Common Criteria (CC)?
A	Consumers, developers, and evaluators
B	Consumers, developers, and certifiers
C	Developers, evaluators, and nation members
D	Consumers, developers, and nation members
Answer	A
Rationale	The CC involves three distinct audiences: (1) consumers –– those who purchase the product and thus will create the security requirements; (2) developers – those who design and develop the product to meet the security requirements of the consumers; (3) evaluators – those who evaluate whether the developer's products meet the stated security requirements of the consumers.

Question 24	Which Common Criteria audience would use the security functional requirements for guidance on formulating statements of requirements for security functions?
A	Certifiers
B	Developers
C	Consumers
D	Evaluators
Answer	C
Rationale	Developers would use the security functional requirements as reference when interpreting statements of functional requirements and formulating functional specifications of TOEs. Evaluators would use the security functional requirements as a mandatory statement of evaluation criteria when determining whether a TOE effectively meets claimed security functions. Certifiers (answer A) are a distracter.

Question 25	Which Common Criteria audience would use the security assurance requirements as mandatory statements for determining the assurance of Target of Evaluations (TOEs)?
A	Certifiers
B	Developers
C	Consumers

D	Evaluators
Answer	D
Rationale	Consumers would use it as guidance when determining required levels of assurance. Developers would use it for reference when interpreting statements of assurance requirements and determining assurance approaches of TOEs. Certifiers are a distracter.

***Question* 26**	Which of the following defines what security requirements are wanted or needed from a product?
A	Functional requirements
B	Assurance requirements
C	Topical requirements
D	Organizational requirements
Answer	A
Rationale	Functional requirements define the desired security requirements. Assurance requirements define the basis for gaining confidence that the claimed security measures are effective and implemented correctly. Topical and organizational requirements are distracters.

***Question* 27**	Which of the following defines the basis for gaining confidence that the claimed security measures are effective and implemented correctly?
A	Functional requirements
B	Assurance requirements
C	Topical requirements
D	Organizational requirements
Answer	B
Rationale	Functional requirements define the desired security requirements. Assurance requirements define the basis for gaining confidence that the claimed security measures are effective and implemented correctly. Topical and organizational requirements are distracters.

***Question* 28**	In the Common Criteria hierarchy, which level defines the laws and organizational security policies?

A	Security objectives
B	Security requirement
C	Security environment
D	TOE implementation
Answer	C
Rationale	The security objectives are a statement of intent to counter the identified threats or satisfy intended organizational security policies. The security requirement is a refinement of the IT security objectives into a set of technical requirements for security functions and assurance, covering the TOE and its IT environment. The security environment defines the context in which the TOE is to be used, including any laws, organization security policies, etc. The TOE implementation is the realization of a TOE in accordance with its specifications.

Question 29	In the Common Criteria hierarchy, which level defines the IT security objectives into a set of technical requirements for security functions and assurance?
A	Security objectives
B	Security requirement
C	Security environment
D	TOE implementation
Answer	B
Rationale	The security objectives are a statement of intent to counter the identified threats or satisfy intended organizational security policies. The security requirement is a refinement of the IT security objectives into a set of technical requirements for security functions and assurance, covering the TOE and its IT environment. The security environment defines the context in which the TOE is to be used, including any laws, organization security policies, etc. The TOE implementation is the realization of a TOE in accordance with its specifications.

Question 30	In the Common Criteria hierarchy, which level defines the statements to counter the identified threats and satisfy organizational security policies?
A	Security objectives
B	Security requirement

C	Security environment
D	TOE implementation
Answer	A
Rationale	The security objectives are a statement of intent to counter the identified threats or satisfy intended organizational security policies. The security requirement is a refinement of the IT security objectives into a set of technical requirements for security functions and assurance, covering the TOE and its IT environment. The security environment defines the context in which the TOE is to be used, including any laws, organization security policies, etc. The TOE implementation is the realization of a TOE in accordance with its specifications.

Question 31	In the Common Criteria hierarchy, which level defines an actual or proposed implementation for the target of evaluation?
A	Security objectives
B	Security requirement
C	TOE summary specification
D	TOE implementation
Answer	C
Rationale	The security objectives are a statement of intent to counter the identified threats or satisfy intended organizational security policies. The security requirement is a refinement of the IT security objectives into a set of technical requirements for security functions and assurance, covering the TOE and its IT environment. The TOE implementation is the realization of a TOE in accordance with its specifications.

Question 32	What hierarchy organizes the Common Criteria security requirements?
A	Family, component, assurance
B	Class, family, component
C	Class, family, level
D	Family, level, package
Answer	B

Rationale	The CC security requirements are organized into a hierarchy of class – family – component. At the top level is a "class" of security requirements used for the most general grouping of security requirements. The members of a class are "families" that share security objectives but may differ in emphasis or rigor. The members of a family are termed "components." A component describes a specific set of security requirements and is the smallest selectable set of security requirements defined in the CC.

Question 33	Which document can make a claim that the Target of Evaluation conforms to the requirements of a protection profile?
A	TOE Summary Specification
B	Security Requirements
C	TOE Security Environment
D	Security Target
Answer	D
Rationale	The Security Target (ST) can, optionally, make a claim that the TOE conforms to the requirements of one (or possibly more than one) PP. The Toe Summary Specification defines the instantiation of the security requirements for the TOE. The Security Requirements defines the detailed security requirements that shall be satisfied by the TOE or its environment. The TOE Security Environment describes the security aspects of the intended TOE environment and the manner in which it is expected to be employed.

Question 34	Which requirement class contains configuration management?
A	Security Function Requirement
B	Assurance Requirement
C	System Function Requirement
D	System Management Requirement
Answer	B

Rationale	Security Function Requirements describe security properties that users can detect by direct interaction with the TOE, such as inputs or outputs, or by the product's response to stimulus. Assurance requirements are the grounds for confidence that an IT product or system meets its security objectives. Assurance can be derived from reference to sources such as unsubstantiated assertions, prior relevant experience, or specific experience. Answer C and D are distracters.

Question 35	Which requirement class contains auditing?
A	Security Function Requirement
B	Assurance Requirement
C	System Function Requirement
D	System Management Requirement
Answer	A
Rationale	Security Function Requirements describe security properties that users can detect by direct interaction with the TOE, such as inputs or outputs, or by the product's response to stimulus. Assurance Requirements are the grounds for confidence that an IT product or system meets its security objectives. Assurance can be derived from reference to sources such as unsubstantiated assertions, prior relevant experience, or specific experience. Answers C and D are distracters.

Question 36	Which requirement class contains guidance documents?
A	Security Function Requirement
B	Assurance Requirement
C	System Function Requirement
D	System Management Requirement
Answer	B

Rationale	Security Function Requirements describe security properties that users can detect by direct interaction with the TOE, such as inputs or outputs, or by the product's response to stimulus. Assurance Requirements are the grounds for confidence that an IT product or system meets its security objectives. Assurance can be derived from reference to sources such as unsubstantiated assertions, prior relevant experience, or specific experience. Answers C and D are distracters.

Question **37**	Which requirement class contains cryptographic support and security management?
A	Security Function Requirement
B	Assurance Requirement
C	System Function Requirement
D	System Management Requirement
Answer	A
Rationale	Security Function Requirements describe security properties that users can detect by direct interaction with the TOE, such as inputs or outputs, or by the product's response to stimulus. Assurance requirements are the grounds for confidence that an IT product or system meets its security objectives. Assurance can be derived from reference to sources such as unsubstantiated assertions, prior relevant experience, or specific experience. Answers C and D are distracters.

Question **38**	Which functional class ensures the unambiguous identification of authorized users and the correct association of security attributes with users and subjects?
A	Auditing (FAU)
B	User Data Protection (FDP)
C	Identification and Authentication (FIA)
D	Privacy (FPR)
Answer	C
Rationale	Security auditing involves recognizing, recording, storing, and analyzing information related to security activities. User data protection contains families specifying requirements relating to the protection of user data. Privacy requirements provide a user with protection against discovery and misuses of his identity by other users.

Question 39	Which functional class is concerned with communication paths between the users and the target of evaluation security functions?
A	User Data Protection (FDP)
B	Communications (FCO)
C	TOE Access (FTA)
D	Trusted Path/Channels (FTP)
Answer	D
Rationale	FDP contains families specifying requirements relating to the protection of user data. FCO provides two families concerned with assuring the identity of a party participating in data exchange. FTA specifies functional requirements, in addition to those specified for I&A, for controlling the establishment of a user's session.

Question 40	Which functional class details requirements for fault tolerance, priority of service, and resource allocation?
A	User Data Protection (FDP)
B	Resource Utilization (FRU)
C	Communications (FCO)
D	Security Management (FSM)
Answer	B
Rationale	FDP contains families specifying requirements relating to the protection of user data. FCO provides two families concerned with assuring the identity of a party participating in data exchange. FSM is used to specify the management of the product's security functions' attributes, data, and functions.

Question 41	Which assurance class provides requirements that are intended to be applied after a target of evaluation has been certified against the Common Criteria?
A	Evaluation Assurance Class (Axx)
B	Security Target Evaluation (STE)
C	Protection Profile Evaluation (APE)
D	Delivery and Operations (DO)

Answer	A
Rationale	The requirements for the STE are concerned with the TOE Description, Security Environment, Security Objectives, any PP claims, TOE Security Requirements, and the TOE Summary Specifications. The APE families are concerned with the TOE Description, Security Environment, Security Objectives, and TOE Security Requirements. The DO provides families concerned with the measures, procedures, and standards for secure delivery, installation, and operational use of the TOE.

Question 42	Which assurance class is concerned with identifying vulnerabilities through covert channel analysis?
A	Trusted Path/Channels (FTP)
B	Tests (ATE)
C	Communications (FCO)
D	Vulnerability Assessment (AVA)
Answer	D
Rationale	Both answers A and C are functional requirement classes. Tests are concerned with demonstrating that the TOE meets its functional requirements.

Question 43	Which assurance class is aimed at maintaining the level of assurance that the TOE will continue to meet its security target as changes are made to the TOE or its environment?
A	Evaluation Assurance Class (Axx)
B	Life Cycle Support (ALC)
C	Assurance Maintenance Class (AMA)
D	Configuration Management (ACM)
Answer	C
Rationale	The Evaluation Assurance Class provides requirements that are intended to be applied after a TOE has been certified against the CC. The Life Cycle Support Class is concerned with the life cycle of the TOE, including life-cycle definition, tools and techniques, security of the development environment, and the remediation of flaws found by TOE consumers. The configuration management class is concerned with the capabilities of the CM, its scope, and its automation.

Question 44	Which evaluation assurance level provides an evaluation of the TOE as it is made available to the customer?
A	EAL 1
B	EAL 2
C	EAL 3
D	EAL 4
Answer	A
Rationale	EAL 1 provides an evaluation of the TOE as it is made available to the customer. EAL 2 adds requirements for TOE configuration list, delivery and high-level design documentation, developer functional testing, vulnerability analysis, and more independent testing. EAL 3 adds requirements for development environment controls of TOE, Configuration Management, high-level design documentation, more complete developer functional testing, and analysis of guidance documents. EAL 4 has additional requirements for CM system automation, complete interface specs, low-level design documentation, analysis of a subset of the TSF implementation, life-cycle definition, and informal security policy model.

Question 45	Which evaluation assurance level is considered methodically designed, tested, and reviewed?
A	EAL 1
B	EAL 2
C	EAL 3
D	EAL 4
Answer	D
Rationale	EAL 1 is functional tested, EAL 2 is structurally tested, and EAL 3 is methodically tested and checked. EAL 4 is methodically designed, tested, and reviewed.

Question 46	Which evaluation assurance level is considered formally verified design and tested?
A	EAL 4
B	EAL 5
C	EAL 6

D	EAL 7
Answer	D
Rationale	EAL 4 is methodically designed, tested, and reviewed. EAL 5 is semi-formally designed and tested. EAL 6 is semi-formally verified design and tested. EAL 7 is formally verified design and tested.

Question 47	For implementation in a U.S. Department of Defense system, other than the United States, which country could conduct the evaluation for an EAL 4?
A	Britain
B	France
C	Australia
D	All of the above
Answer	D
Rationale	Up to EAL 4, the U.S. Government will accept the evaluations conducted by any of the member nations that have participating evaluation laboratories.

Question 48	For implementation in a U.S. Department of Defense system, other than the United States, which country could conduct the evaluation for an EAL 6?
A	Britain
B	France
C	Australia
D	None of the above
Answer	D
Rationale	Up to EAL 4, the U.S. Government will accept the evaluations conducted by any of the member nations that have participating evaluation laboratories. Anything above EAL 4 and the USG must be involved.

Question 49	What evaluation level is considered the highest level likely for retrofit of an existing product?
A	EAL 3
B	EAL 4

C	EAL 5
D	EAL 6
Answer	B
Rationale	According to the CC, EAL 4 is the highest level likely for retrofit.

Question 50	Which of the following is NOT a role of the Common Criteria Evaluation and Validation Scheme (CCEVS)?
A	Establishes a national program for the evaluation of IT products for conformance to the Common Criteria
B	Approves participation of security testing laboratories in the Common Criteria scheme
C	Serves as an interface to other member nations on the evaluations conducted by U.S. security testing laboratories
D	Serves as an international forum for all member nations and is staffed by representatives for all member nations
Answer	D
Rationale	CCEVS is staffed by NIST And NSA employees.

INDEX

Index

F

Fabrication, assembly, integration, and test (FAIT) stage, 221, 225
    IEEE 1220 perspective on, 285–287
Fail-safe design, 332
Fair information practices, 549–550
Fallback modes, 132
Fault detection, and integrity, 198
Fault injection, 395
Fault tolerance, 198
Federal agencies, 538
    Committee on National Security Systems (CNSS), 538, 543
    Director of Central Intelligence, 538, 540–541
    documentation guidelines, 303
    National Information Assurance Partnership (NIAP), 538, 543
    National Institute of Standards and Technology (NIST), 538, 542–543
    National Security Agency (NSA), 538, 541
    Office of Management and Budget, 538, 540
    privacy policy postings by, 560–561
    risk assessment process frequency, 348
    security component acquisition guidelines, 293–295
    software security feature settings for, 298
    U.S. Congress, 538, 539
    White House, 538, 539
Federal Bureau of Investigations (FBI), 552
Federal Chief Information Officer (CIO) Council, 338
Federal Computer Security Program managers' Forum, 640
Federal Enterprise Architecture Framework (FEAF), 150–152, 779, 831–832
Federal information, categorization of, 66
Federal Information Processing Standards (FIPS), 536, 542, 640, 641–642
    FIPS 81, DES Mode of Operation, 645–652
    FIPS 102, Guidelines for Computer Security Certification and Accreditation, 652
    FIPS 197, Advance Encryption Standard, 664, 665–666
    FIPS 46-3, Data Encryption Standard (DES), 642–645

FIPS 140-2, Security Requirement for Cryptographic modules, 652, 655–664
    mandatory nature of, 641
Federal Information Processing Standards Publication 102 (FIPS 102), 415
Federal Information Processing Standards Publication 199 (FIPS 199), 420, 428. *See also* FIPS 199
Federal Information Security Incident Center, 547–548
Federal Information Security Management Act (FISMA), 357, 417, 546–547, 869, 904
    annual independent evaluation, 547
    Federal Information Security Incident Center, 547–548
    FISMA metrics and OMB guidance reference, 782
    information technology security training program, 548
    OMB guidelines on implementing, 564–565
    responsibilities for federal information systems standards, 548
Federal Information Systems (IS), 355
    complexity of, 415
Federal Information Systems Security Educators' Association (FISSEA), 640
Federal IT Security Assessment Framework, 338
Federal laws, 535, 543
    10 USC 2315 Defense Program, 548–549
    Chapter 35 of Title 44, United States Code, 544–546
    fraud and related computer crimes, 550–551
    H.R. 2458-48, Chapter 35 of Title 44, Federal Information Security Management Act (FISMA), 546–547
    H.R. 145 Public Law 100-235, Computer Security Act of 1987, 544
    PL 93-579, U.S. Federal Privacy Act of 1974, 549–550
    PL 99-474, Computer Fraud and Abuse Act of 1984, 551–552
Federal Program Manager, 464
Federal Project Manager, 468
Federal Register, 539
Federal regulations, 51

O

T - #0206 - 101024 - C0 - 234/156/55 [57] - CB - 9780849323416 - Gloss Lamination